1000Events
That Shaped the World

1000Events
That Shaped the World
FOREWORD BY JARED DIAMOND

NATIONAL GEOGRAPHIC

WASHINGTON, D.C.

CONTENTS

PREVIOUS PAGES | *Backdropped against the blue and white Earth, astronaut Mark C. Lee tests an extravehicular rescue system.*
OPPOSITE | *Detail of a miniature shows one of the battles of Charlemagne's soldiers against the "Barbarians."*

FOREWORD

You have just opened an unusual history book. Within the limits of a small volume, it covers the history of the whole world on all continents. A mere two sentences in the first paragraph whisk us from the mastery of fire by primitive humans hundreds of thousands of years ago, to the development of writing around 3300 B.C.E. Thereafter, about 175,000 words of text carry the story from 3300 B.C.E. up to the present.

You can easily do the underlying math. You'll be racing along at one word per year of written history until the fall of the Roman Empire, slowing down to 100 words per year for the Middle Ages, and finally a generous 750 words per year for the 20th century. That calculation may make you wonder: What can I really learn about history when it is being covered at such a breakneck pace? Is this serious, or is it a humorous spoof, like Tom Stoppard's *15-Minute Hamlet,* which reduces Shakespeare's monumental tragedy to just one minute of fast talking?

This question about the usefulness of short summaries is one that I have encountered in my own historical writing. For several decades, I wrote technical articles on gallbladder physiology, meant to be read by the world's six other scientists interested in the gallbladder, and exploring the subject in leisurely detail appropriate to the fascination that gallbladder physiology held for me and its six other devotees. Naturally, I never got phoned by reporters requesting interviews and summaries.

Things changed when I eventually began writing books about geographic influences on world history, aimed at the general public. At that point, I suddenly found myself confronted by the occupational hazard facing any scholar who addresses the public: demands by reporters for understandable sound bites. In my case, the reporters' demand took the form: "Mr. Diamond, I know that you have devoted the last five years of your life to reading hundreds of books and articles, in order to describe the history of everybody on all continents for the last 13,000 years in your 518-page book. But you have to realize, Mr. Diamond, that my newspaper readers (or my TV viewers, or my radio listeners) are busy people. They don't have time to read a 518-page book. So, won't you please try to summarize everything that happened to everybody in one sentence?"

At first, I was outraged. What could be more ridiculous than summarizing in one sentence this important and fascinating subject to which I had devoted five years? Eventually, though, I did come up with a sentence to summarize world history. Granted, it was a longish sentence, with several clauses, but it was still just a single sentence. I also learned how to summarize the history of everybody in a lecture of any length, ranging from 20 seconds to a Fidel Castro–like three hours. I thereby came to realize that requests for short histories are legitimate, and not at all ridiculous. At any given moment in your life, you have other concerns besides immersing yourself in all of world history. Instead, you may just want to remind yourself quickly of what happened in the Middle Ages. A few well-chosen pages of explanation will suffice; you don't want a 700-page monograph on the Middle Ages that would take you a month to read—if it didn't put you to sleep after a few pages. A brief account, laying out a framework and readable in a short time, will actually let you grasp the big picture better than will that 700-page monograph. Even if you did choose to devote a month of your spare time to the monograph, at the end of that month you wouldn't have progressed beyond the end of the Middle Ages, whereas if you had instead opted to read the briefer account, you would have had ample time to read on about the Renaissance, the industrial revolution, the World Wars, and much else beyond the purview of the medieval scholar.

For readers who want the big picture and a tantalizing selection of details, this book offers an answer. Yes, it does try to summarize everything important about history in 175,000 words of text. That text has been enriched by tantalizing sidebars. You'll find excerpts from contemporary eyewitness accounts of great moments of history, by participants: Marco Polo's account of his visit to China, a survivor's account of the Black Death, Columbus's log on the day that he discovered the New World, Queen Elizabeth talking about the burdens of the throne, and Isaac Newton explaining mechanics. You'll find thumbnail biographies of figures such as Attila the Hun, Charlemagne, Genghis Khan, Ivan the Terrible, and Machiavelli. There are reflections on fundamental historical debates, such as: Is war ever justified? You'll read about the invention of coal mining, microscopes, newspapers, paper money, portable clocks, rudders, slide rules, and toilet paper. Still other sidebars offer tidbits of information that are harder to pigeonhole, except for being fascinating, such as the discovery of sun spots, the extinction of the dodo, the first map, and the invention of the first system for writing down music.

Just as different types of wines are meant to be drunk in different ways, different types of books are meant to be read in different ways. This book is not like a light wine cooler, intended to be gulped down without stopping until you have drained your glass. Instead, it's meant to be sipped, like a great sweet sauterne. Start anywhere, and read for as long as you like. This book is worth picking up, even if you have only a minute or two to spare for reading at this particular moment. Even one minute's reading will be enough for you to enliven tonight's cocktail party by explaining who invented toilet paper. By the time you have sipped your way through the whole book, you will have a good feel for the big picture of history. Perhaps most important, you will actually enjoy history, and you will want to read more.

—Jared Diamond

ABOUT THIS BOOK

WELCOME TO THE BROAD, EXPANSIVE, COLORFUL, QUIRKY LANDSCAPE OF HUMAN HISTORY, TOLD THROUGH a selected 1000 great events that shaped it.

You would think that, given such a number, the choice of history-shaping events would be a breeze. One thousand! Surely an abundance! But when you're starting with a good ten millennia, maybe more, you have a lot of events to choose from—ideas and accomplishments, developments and downfalls, triumphs and disasters, wars and treaties, arts and sciences. Once we got down to the challenge, the choice was difficult.

And yet what a fascinating task, for with every event one can see other events unraveling through time, causes and effects, influences and alternatives. Themes weave in and out of this volume, empires rise and fall.

You can, if you wish, start from the beginning and read right through to the end, with pauses here and there for embellishment. Or you can select the period of history that fascinates you the most and plunge in there, moving backward and forward to get a fuller sense of context and consequences.

Some events harmonize, some collide. Some of the juxtapositions are downright surprising. Each spread offers an array of events big and small, famous or forgotten. Every one has had some influence on the world in which we live today.

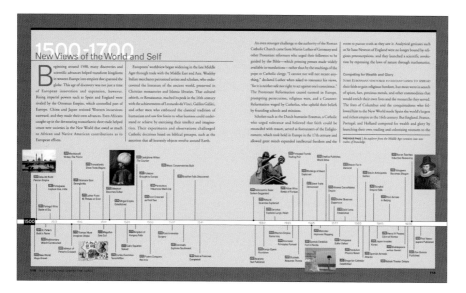

TIME LINE

Each chapter begins with an overview of the events represented in it, charted on a time line to illustrate graphically the intersections and interactions of events around the world during that period of history. Red number boxes indicate the primary events of the period, which are also highlighted in the coming pages of the chapter. An opening narrative paints the picture of the historical period in broad brushstrokes, connecting events and intellectual trends in the grand sweep of time.

Occasionally we offer the opportunity for more details and a closer look at an event and its period in history, focusing visually by using a spectacular work of art or a telling photograph. An event number in the upper left-hand corner connects this visual piece to the event it expands. If a picture is worth a thousand words, we manage to pack a lot on each of these pages.

PRIMARY EVENTS AND FIRST PERSON FEATURES

Throughout each chapter, we single out primary events—those with the greatest impact on the world and its future—and signal them with a red number box. We also highlight occasional "First Person" features: voices from the past, in passages from actual documents and works of literature; each gives a sense of what it was like to be alive at that moment in history.

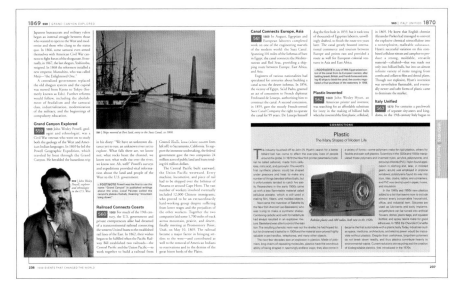

FOOTNOTES AND CONNECTIONS

Here and there, throughout the spreads, we sprinkle "Footnotes": additional bits of information that may amuse or enrich your understanding of the event that comes before it. Occasionally, too, we offer "Connections." These essays begin with one of the events on the spread and move forward and backward through time, showing how one moment in time affects future events.

Ancient World

Prehistory-400 C.E.

Civilization Dawns

Recorded history spans little more than 5,000 years—a brief chapter in the long and eventful saga of humanity. Before people learned to write and thus were able to record their memories and create a history, they mastered fire and crafted tools, domesticated plants and animals, developed pottery and the wheel, told myths and stories, produced astonishing works of art, buried their dead with apparent ceremony, built towering monuments, and founded kingdoms. Archaeological evidence allows us to retrace such prehistoric events and determine roughly when they occurred.

Writing first developed around 3300 B.C.E. in Mesopotamia, where a surge in agricultural productivity, made possible in part by irrigation projects, fostered the growth of cities and supported people with special skills such as artisans and scribes, who evolved a script called cuneiform. In powerful city-states such as Ur, strong rulers emerged who were buried in splendor by their survivors and, as we gather from the things buried with them, believed they could look forward to a glorious afterlife.

A similar process unfolded in Egypt a few centuries later as pharaohs extended their authority along the Nile River and commissioned monumental tombs for their remains—architectural splendors such as the Great Pyramid at Giza. By 2000 B.C.E., civilizations had developed along the Indus River in what is now Pakistan and the Yellow River in China,

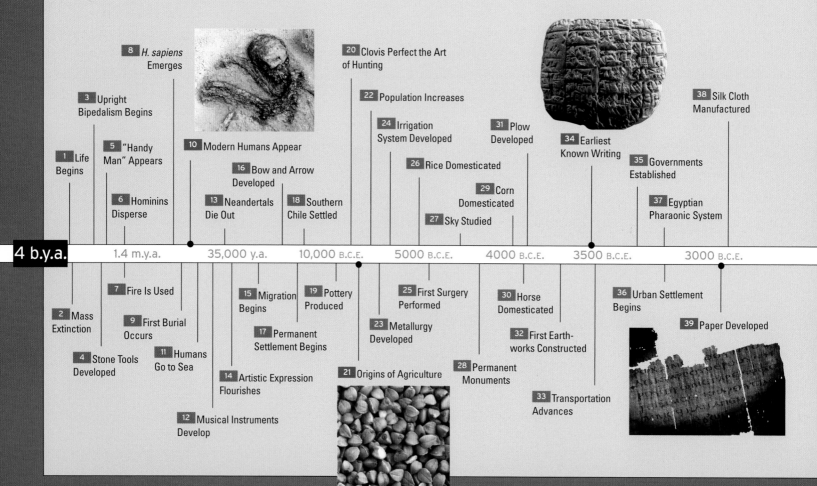

8 *H. sapiens* Emerges

20 Clovis Perfect the Art of Hunting

3 Upright Bipedalism Begins

22 Population Increases

38 Silk Cloth Manufactured

24 Irrigation System Developed

31 Plow Developed

34 Earliest Known Writing

5 "Handy Man" Appears

10 Modern Humans Appear

1 Life Begins

26 Rice Domesticated

35 Governments Established

16 Bow and Arrow Developed

29 Corn Domesticated

6 Hominins Disperse

13 Neandertals Die Out

18 Southern Chile Settled

37 Egyptian Pharaonic System

27 Sky Studied

| 4 b.y.a. | 1.4 m.y.a. | 35,000 y.a. | 10,000 B.C.E. | 5000 B.C.E. | 4000 B.C.E. | 3500 B.C.E. | 3000 B.C.E. |

7 Fire Is Used

15 Migration Begins

19 Pottery Produced

25 First Surgery Performed

30 Horse Domesticated

36 Urban Settlement Begins

2 Mass Extinction

9 First Burial Occurs

17 Permanent Settlement Begins

23 Metallurgy Developed

39 Paper Developed

32 First Earthworks Constructed

4 Stone Tools Developed

11 Humans Go to Sea

14 Artistic Expression Flourishes

21 Origins of Agriculture

28 Permanent Monuments

33 Transportation Advances

12 Musical Instruments Develop

and an advanced society was emerging on the island of Crete among people called Minoans. Elsewhere around this time, villagers came together to construct impressive monuments such as Stonehenge in Britain, but they did not record their history, laws, and beliefs for posterity as scribes did in Egypt and other great kingdoms.

Invaders and Innovators

DURING THE SECOND MILLENNIUM B.C.E., THE WORLD'S MOST advanced societies faced fierce challenges from outsiders, who were viewed as barbarians but were often better armed and organized for battle than their civilized opponents. Wave after wave of invaders descended from the Eurasian steppes with warhorses and chariots and occupied a vast area, shaping the development of such diverse Indo-European languages as Greek, Persian, and Sanskrit. One group called Mycenaeans overrode Greece and subjugated the Minoans

on Crete. Another known as Hittites swept into Mesopotamia and conquered Babylon. A third called Aryans settled in Iran before advancing through Afghanistan into India. Egypt too was invaded, by people called Hyksos, who waged war in chariots and dominated the land until the Egyptians adopted similar tactics and drove them out. In later centuries, chieftains in China acquired horses and chariots from nomads to their northwest and vied for power with rival warlords and with the country's rulers. Eventually, China fragmented into warring states, but it would later be reunited.

By 1000 B.C.E., technological and social changes were transforming the Middle East and the Mediterranean world, toppling old empires and raising up new ones. Iron replaced bronze in the production of tools and weapons, which became sturdier and more widely available because iron ore

PREVIOUS PAGE | *Modern-day tomb robber near Veio, Italy. The remains of ancient monuments shed light about how the cultures that built them lived.*

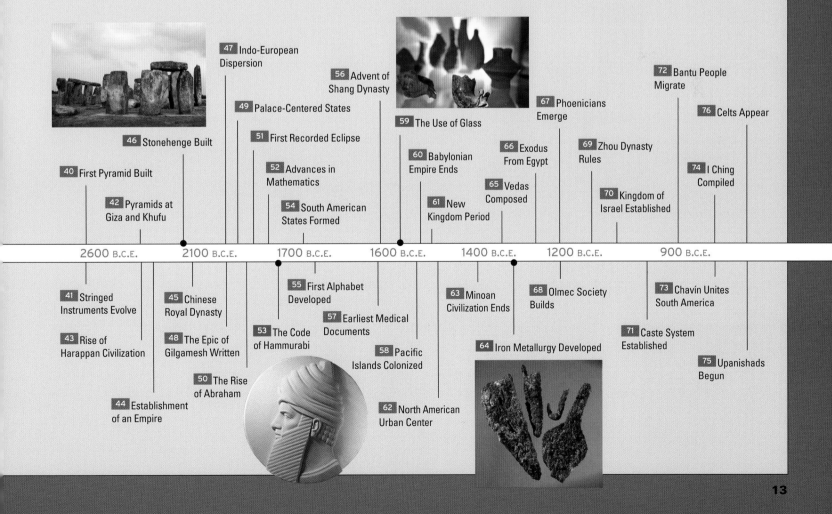

47 Indo-European Dispersion

56 Advent of Shang Dynasty

72 Bantu People Migrate

49 Palace-Centered States

67 Phoenicians Emerge

76 Celts Appear

46 Stonehenge Built

51 First Recorded Eclipse

59 The Use of Glass

66 Exodus From Egypt

69 Zhou Dynasty Rules

40 First Pyramid Built

52 Advances in Mathematics

60 Babylonian Empire Ends

65 Vedas Composed

74 I Ching Compiled

42 Pyramids at Giza and Khufu

54 South American States Formed

61 New Kingdom Period

70 Kingdom of Israel Established

| 2600 B.C.E. | 2100 B.C.E. | 1700 B.C.E. | 1600 B.C.E. | 1400 B.C.E. | 1200 B.C.E. | 900 B.C.E. |

41 Stringed Instruments Evolve

45 Chinese Royal Dynasty

55 First Alphabet Developed

63 Minoan Civilization Ends

68 Olmec Society Builds

73 Chavín Unites South America

43 Rise of Harappan Civilization

48 The Epic of Gilgamesh Written

53 The Code of Hammurabi

57 Earliest Medical Documents

71 Caste System Established

50 The Rise of Abraham

58 Pacific Islands Colonized

64 Iron Metallurgy Developed

75 Upanishads Begun

44 Establishment of an Empire

62 North American Urban Center

was more plentiful than tin and copper—the components of bronze—and emerged harder than bronze when forged.

Once that occurred, it was possible for warlike groups like the Assyrians to amass huge hoards of weapons and equip vast armies. After routing the Hittites, the Assyrians dominated the Middle East until the resurgence of the Babylonians, who in turn fell prey to the Persians in the sixth century B.C.E. Led by Cyrus the Great, Persian warriors forged the greatest empire yet witnessed, reaching from the Indus River to the Aegean Sea.

A Cultural Revolution

MEANWHILE, A CULTURAL REVOLUTION WAS TAKING PLACE around the Mediterranean as far-ranging Phoenicians and Greeks engaged in maritime trade, founded colonies, and introduced concise phonetic alphabets that made it far easier for people to learn to read and write. Unlike most writing systems in the ancient world—which contained hundreds or thousands of characters and were mastered by an elite group of officials, priests, and scribes—the Greek alphabet, adopted in modified form by the Romans, contained only two dozen letters and was accessible to large segments of the population. The ability to read and write empowered Greeks and Romans as citizens by making them more aware of their rights and responsibilities, spurring intellectual creativity and making Greek and Roman literature the foundation for European culture.

In the fifth century B.C.E., the Greeks rebelled against the Persians and gained power and glory, only to be vanquished in the fourth century by Macedonians, who descended from the north, assimilated Greek culture, and spread it across a wide area through the epic conquests of Alexander the Great. Alexander's empire fractured after his death, but his example inspired Roman conquerors.

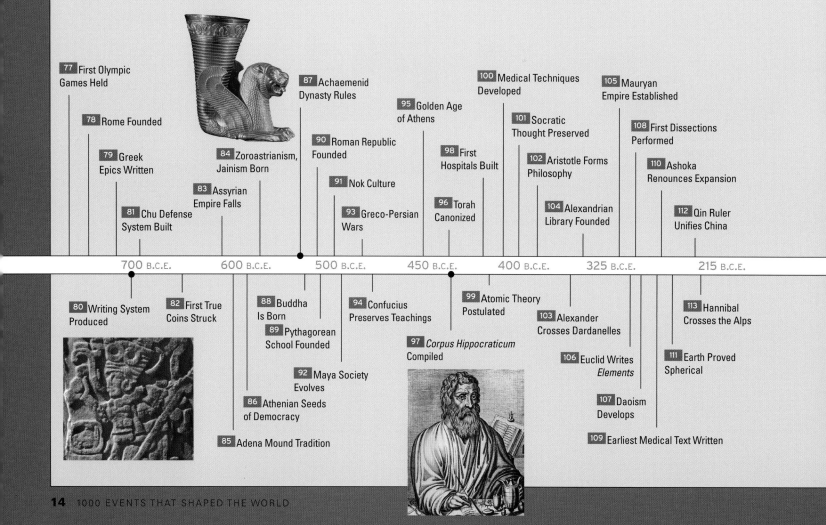

77 First Olympic Games Held

78 Rome Founded

79 Greek Epics Written

81 Chu Defense System Built

84 Zoroastrianism, Jainism Born

83 Assyrian Empire Falls

87 Achaemenid Dynasty Rules

90 Roman Republic Founded

91 Nok Culture

95 Golden Age of Athens

98 First Hospitals Built

96 Torah Canonized

100 Medical Techniques Developed

101 Socratic Thought Preserved

102 Aristotle Forms Philosophy

104 Alexandrian Library Founded

105 Mauryan Empire Established

108 First Dissections Performed

110 Ashoka Renounces Expansion

112 Qin Ruler Unifies China

700 B.C.E.   600 B.C.E.   500 B.C.E.   450 B.C.E.   400 B.C.E.   325 B.C.E.   215 B.C.E.

80 Writing System Produced

82 First True Coins Struck

88 Buddha Is Born

89 Pythagorean School Founded

92 Maya Society Evolves

86 Athenian Seeds of Democracy

85 Adena Mound Tradition

94 Confucius Preserves Teachings

97 *Corpus Hippocraticum* Compiled

99 Atomic Theory Postulated

103 Alexander Crosses Dardanelles

106 Euclid Writes *Elements*

107 Daoism Develops

109 Earliest Medical Text Written

113 Hannibal Crosses the Alps

111 Earth Proved Spherical

By the second century C.E., the Roman world encircled the Mediterranean and embraced much of Europe, with the exception of Germanic territories north of the Danube River and Celtic strongholds such as Ireland and Scotland, separated from Roman Britain by Hadrian's Wall. Aqueducts, baths, bridges, roads, and other products of Roman engineering enhanced this huge empire and enriched its capital. "From neighboring continents far and wide a ceaseless flow of goods pours into Rome," wrote one visitor there. "Anything that cannot be seen in Rome does not exist."

A World of Wonders

IMPERIAL ROME WAS THE GREATEST CITY OF ANCIENT TIMES, WITH a population exceeding one million, but there were other magnificent urban centers around the globe. Chang'an (modern-day Xi'an), the capital of China's Han dynasty, flourished as the eastern terminus of the silk roads, a network of trade routes linking Asia to Europe. In Mesoamerica, the stunning city of Teotihuacan, dominated by the massive Pyramid of the Sun, emerged in the Valley of Mexico and thrived through traffic with enterprising trading partners like the Maya, who lived in rival city-states around the Yucatán Peninsula and set down in writing the accomplishments of their rulers. In many parts of the world, including West Africa and Southeast Asia, well-organized societies were emerging that would develop into wealthy and accomplished kingdoms.

A number of historical forces brought distant societies in contact with one another during this era. Those forces included trade, imperial expansion, and the spread of religions such as Buddhism, which originated in India and slowly but surely won converts throughout much of Asia. By 400 C.E., Christianity—once a small, persecuted sect—was the official Roman religion and would continue to gain strength even as that once mighty empire declined and fell.

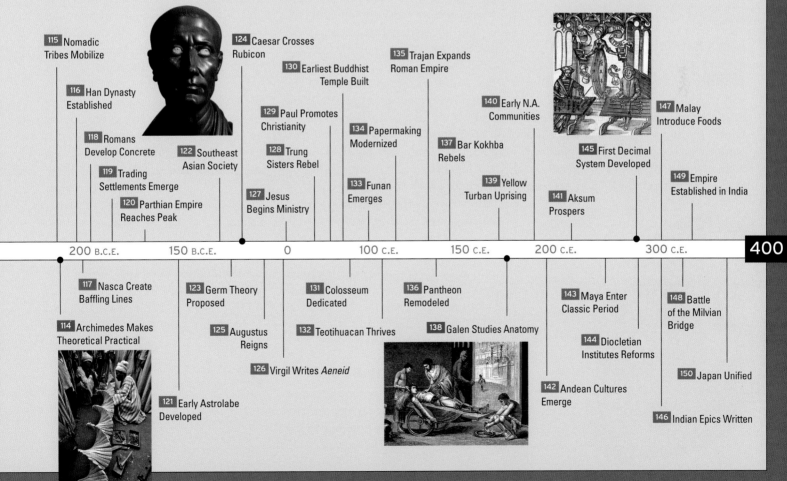

115 Nomadic Tribes Mobilize

116 Han Dynasty Established

118 Romans Develop Concrete

119 Trading Settlements Emerge

120 Parthian Empire Reaches Peak

124 Caesar Crosses Rubicon

130 Earliest Buddhist Temple Built

129 Paul Promotes Christianity

128 Trung Sisters Rebel

127 Jesus Begins Ministry

122 Southeast Asian Society

135 Trajan Expands Roman Empire

134 Papermaking Modernized

133 Funan Emerges

140 Early N.A. Communities

137 Bar Kokhba Rebels

139 Yellow Turban Uprising

145 First Decimal System Developed

141 Aksum Prospers

147 Malay Introduce Foods

149 Empire Established in India

200 B.C.E.　150 B.C.E.　0　100 C.E.　150 C.E.　200 C.E.　300 C.E.

400

117 Nasca Create Baffling Lines

114 Archimedes Makes Theoretical Practical

121 Early Astrolabe Developed

123 Germ Theory Proposed

125 Augustus Reigns

126 Virgil Writes *Aeneid*

131 Colosseum Dedicated

132 Teotihuacan Thrives

136 Pantheon Remodeled

138 Galen Studies Anatomy

143 Maya Enter Classic Period

144 Diocletian Institutes Reforms

142 Andean Cultures Emerge

148 Battle of the Milvian Bridge

150 Japan Unified

146 Indian Epics Written

Life Begins

1 **3.8 b.y.a.** Out of the primordial soup of Earth's early oceans arose the first simple chains of carbon-based chemical compounds that somehow catalyzed into unicellular organisms capable of metabolism and reproduction. Some 3.8 billion years ago, Earth was a very different place than it is today. Abundant volcanoes and hydrothermal vents spewed massive amounts of sulfur and methane into a thin atmosphere nearly devoid of oxygen. Meteorites, comets, and lightning strikes continually pounded the Earth, bringing additional elements with them from space. And it was hot, likely over 200°F. Out of these torrid conditions that would immediately paralyze almost all forms of life today, the first heat-loving, sulfur-eating, oxygen-loathing bacteria are theorized to have emerged, setting off a chain reaction of unprecedented proportions.

FOOTNOTE Evidence of the earliest life forms appears in the fossil record around 480 million years ago. Bacteria and possibly some algae moved from the oceans and fresh water to evolve into land plants; fungi branched into animals.

Mass Extinction

2 **65 m.y.a.** A cataclysmic mass extinction, which wiped out not only the dinosaurs but also countless other organisms on land, sea, and sky approximately 65 million years ago, effected a worldwide change in the landscape and biota of Earth. Most likely a number of factors contributed short- and long-term

2 | Caudipteryx zoui, *a 120-million-year-old dinosaur just three feet long, does a courtship dance.*

effects to the upheaval. A meteorite six miles wide struck the Yucatán Peninsula in Mexico, sending massive amounts of rock dust into the air, earthquakes across the land, and tsunamis through the oceans. Skies darkened with smoke and ash as volcanic eruptions belched sulfur into the atmosphere, producing rampant wildfires and acid rain. Temperatures and sea levels dropped worldwide. Thousands of species large and small could not survive the changing environment, and the food chain was drastically altered over the course of the next few million years. The K-T extinction event, as it is called, was neither the first nor the most devastating of its kind, but was perhaps the most pivotal to the world as we know it today. With reptiles knocked from their position at the top of the food chain, the opportunity was opened to mammals, and eventually humans, to claim that status.

Upright Bipedalism Begins

3 **3.56 m.y.a.** The emergence of upright bipedalism in the ancient members of the hominid family

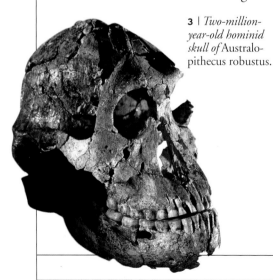

3 | *Two-million-year-old hominid skull of* Australopithecus robustus.

was a tremendous step forward in the evolutionary divergence of hominin from ape. Studies in comparative anatomy and paleoclimatology place this event as far back as six million years, though the earliest indisputable evidence dates to about 3.56 m.y.a. At that time, three members of the extinct hominin species *Australopithecus afarensis* walked across the ash near an East African volcano in Tanzania, where their footprints were buried, fossilized, and then rediscovered in 1978. With hands and arms no longer essential for locomotion, australopiths could cover greater distances while foraging and use their hands for grasping objects. Due to the absence of the thumblike opposable big toe found in other apes, australopith infants had to be carried, perhaps limiting the females' ability to forage and strengthening the social bonds of the family unit.

FOOTNOTE In 1999 paleoanthropologist Zeresenay Alemseged discovered a 3.3-million-year-old *Australopithecus afarensis* skeleton in Ethiopia. This ancient three-year-old walked upright but may also have spent time in trees.

Stone Tools Developed

4 | **2.6 m.y.a.** The development of stone tool technology by early hominins in East Africa is heralded by some scholars as the first extant manifestation of cultural behavior in the history of the world. The earliest known recognizable stone tools wrought by the hand of hominins date back to about 2.6 m.y.a. and were found near the Kada Gona River in Ethiopia. These tools belong to the Oldowan tradition, named after Olduvai Gorge in Tanzania. It is here that they were first found in association with the fossilized bones of extinct elephants and other animals. Some of these bones reveal the scrape marks of tool use superimposed on gnaw marks made by carnivorous animals, indicating that early hominins were more scavenger than hunter. Regardless, a threshold had been crossed; objects provided by nature could, and would, be manipulated for the many purposes of man and woman.

"Handy Man" Appears

5 | **1.9 m.y.a.** One of the earliest members of the genus *Homo*, the same genus to which modern humans belong, is an extinct species suitably named *Homo habilis,* or "handy man." Remains of *H. habilis* are dated to at least 1.9 m.y.a. and have been found in both East and South Africa. They are set apart from other contemporaneous hominins by an increased cranial capacity; the appearance of well-developed incisor and canine teeth alongside molars, indicating an omnivorous diet; and increased manual dexterity, evidenced by the stone tool debris they left behind. In addition to stone tools, these ancient "handy men and women" likely made tools of wood, bone, plant fiber, and other perishable materials that are no longer preserved. They also traveled considerable distances to known locations where they could procure the specific types of stone they needed to fashion tools, foreshadowing the enterprising migrations to come.

■ **FOOTNOTE** Researchers have long believed that *H. erectus* evolved from *H. habilis,* but recent fossil finds by a team led by Meave Leakey in Kenya indicate that they may have lived side by side for more than 500,000 years.

Hominins Disperse

6 | **1.4 m.y.a.** The earliest exodus of hominins out of Africa is an unresolved matter. The oldest tentative

---

CONNECTIONS

Born From the Water
Creation myths frequently take an aqueous turn

Billions of years passed between the evolution of early marine life-forms and early primates, yet humanity's collective imagination has often looked seaward to explain our origins. Creation myths from around the world describe life as emerging from the sea. These epic water births are rarely more fantastical than the biblical creation story or today's scientifically accepted truth: that Earth's earliest living things had just one cell each and thrived in violent, sulfuric hydrothermal ocean vents.

Two ancient Babylonian tablets, the Enuma Elish and the Astrahasis, tell of Marduk, most powerful of gods and creator of life. Both written between 1900 and 1500 B.C.E., the incomplete tablets complement each other to paint a full picture of Babylon's creation myth. In the story, before Earth's creation only a water power existed. Eventually this power divided into three distinct deities: the freshwater god Apsu, his consort the ocean-water goddess Tiamat, and the mist god Mummu. Apsu and Tiamat became great-great-grandparents to Marduk, god of thunder, who would eventually split Tiamat's body in two to make heaven and Earth. Marduk also commanded the Tigris and Euphrates Rivers to flow from the slain matriarch's eyes.

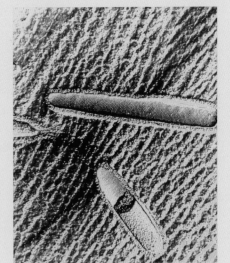

Heat-loving bacteria Thermoproteus tenax.

Hawaii's creation myths come from an oral poem called "The Kumulipo," a chant recounting the islands' origins and dynastic geneaologies. Inhabiting land that literally had erupted from the ocean, the islanders give an eerily accurate description of life's creation: "When the Earth first became hot and the heavens churned and the sun was dark, land emerged from the slime of the sea. The deepest darkness of caverns, a male, and the moonless darkness of night, a female, gave birth to the simple life-forms of the sea. The coral that builds islands was born, and the grub, the sea cucumber, the sea urchin, the barnacle, the mussel, the limpet, and cowry, and the conch and other shellfish." "The Kumulipo" describes the emergence of the first sea grasses, ocean fish, seabirds, legged marine creatures such as turtles, land animals, and—finally—humans.

Some inland cultures also saw water as the font of life. Native American Cherokee tradition holds that in the beginning Earth was only water and darkness. Animals existed, but dwelled above the sky in a realm called Galúnlati. Overcrowding on high inspired the animals to send water beetle to explore habitation on Earth, so the insect dove into the primordial waters. Water beetle dredged up mud on his return, creating the land. After the mud dried out, animals and plants moved down to inhabit Earth.

dates of the first dispersal into the Middle East go back approximately 1.9 million years, though more conservative dates place this event at about 1.4 m.y.a. The first intercontinental migrants have traditionally been assumed to belong to a new, more robust group of hominins called *Homo erectus,* or *H. ergaster* by some scholars, who were able to use their large size and technologically advanced tool kit to colonize much of Eurasia. This assumption, though, has been called into question by two sites discovered in the 1990s, Dmanisi in southern Georgia and Longgupo Cave in central China. These sites are characterized by crude stone tools and fossil remains resembling those of *H. habilis.* What is more, the earliest known remains of *H. erectus* in East Africa and Southeast Asia both date back to about 1.8 m.y.a., albeit with controversy. These finds have produced the theory that perhaps *H. erectus* first emerged in central Asia from earlier migrants, then spread from there both into East Asia and back into Africa. Only further research and discoveries will reveal the full story of the world's earliest long-distance migrants.

■ FOOTNOTE Evidence of human occupation over a million years ago of the southwestern Chinese provinces and hills of Burma, Thailand, Laos, and Vietnam suggests migration routes from northern Pakistan and dispersal east into Asia.

Fire Is Used

7 **1.4 m.y.a.** Fire served a number of functions for early men and women, such as warmth, illumination, defense, cooking, and social gathering. By at least a million years ago, early members of the human family were spread throughout much of the Eurasian landmass, including regions subject to seasonal cold and recurrent glaciation. In order for subtropical hominins to survive in such severe conditions, a number of technological advances had to occur, among them the controlled use of fire. The two earliest known, though disputed, examples of the deliberate use of fire come from Chesowanja, Kenya, and Swartkrans,

South Africa, and date respectively to 1.4 and 1.3 million years ago. The earliest known examples of hearths are found in cavelike hollows of China and southern Europe and date as far back as 460,000 years ago. Though these sites, too, are not without controversy, the undisputed presence of hominins in these areas says almost as much about their use of fire as would the undisputed presence of hearths.

H. sapiens Emerges

8 **500,000 y.a.** The emergence of *Homo sapiens sapiens,* or anatomically modern humans, is not so much a moment in time as a long evolutionary process. Genetic information reveals two lines of descent from a common ancestor some 500,000 years ago, eventually resulting in two distinct subspecies of *H. sapiens:* modern humans, who arose in Africa, and Neandertals, whose remains have been found in Europe and the Middle East. A possible common ancestor has been posited by some scholars as *H. heidelbergensis,* whose remains have been found in both Africa and Europe and date as far back as 600,000 y.a. Regardless of ancestry, around 200,000 y.a. anatomically modern humans, *Homo sapiens sapiens,* emerged in East Africa. Though not naturally imbued with great size or strength, they were armed with a large, well-developed brain that was capable of reflective thought, abstract expression, and spoken language.

First Burial Occurs

9 **300,000 y.a.** The first burial of a deceased human marks not only the beginning of a long tradition still upheld in most parts of the world today, but also the beginning of symbolic behavior not directly associated with the everyday means of survival, perhaps even the notion of an afterlife. The oldest known evidence for reverential handling of the dead is dated to about 300,000 y.a. and

Modern Humans Appear

10 **120,000 y.a.** Modern humans—*Homo erectus*—dispersed at a steady rate from their ancestral homeland in East Africa, spreading across all of Africa and reaching the continent's southern tip. Current theory holds that these early humans migrated

These H. sapiens sapiens *remains from Qafzeh, Israel, are considered to be anatomically modern.*

to the Middle East about 120,000 y.a.; that they continued on to East Asia by about 50,000 ya, to Europe around 40,000 ya, and onward to almost all unglaciated portions of the eastern hemisphere. These movements were likely driven on by opportunistic climatic conditions, increasing population density, and by the migrants' own ability to adapt to inhospitable environments. They developed more durable shelters, warmer sewn clothing, and composite tools, such as small stone blades that could be hafted onto handles of wood or bone. Along the way, they encountered Neandertals and perhaps remnant archaic members of the genus Homo. Though some scant amount of hybridization may have taken place, genetic information firmly attests that these other forms were displaced by, rather than subsumed into, the growing population of modern humans.

comes from the Atapuerca Hills of northern Spain, where the remains of at least 29 early hominins were dropped down a deep vertical fissure in the limestone. The first known inhumations date to about 200,000 years later and are located in the Skhul and Qafzeh Caves in Israel. Some form of ritual is suggested at these sites by the presence of a natural pigment called red ocher, carefully placed animal bones, and perforated snail shells that could be the earliest known example of jewelry.

■ **FOOTNOTE** The presence of artifacts in early burials without any apparent practical function is interpreted as an expression of symbolic behavior, suggesting that the mind of our early ancestors is closer to ours than previously thought.

Humans Go to Sea

11 **50,000 y.a.** The earliest inhabitants of Australia may well have been among the first humans to construct sea-going vessels and venture an open-water crossing some 50,000 years ago. With much of the world's water trapped in glaciers at the time, sea levels were upwards of 330 feet lower than they are today, linking Australia with New Guinea and Tasmania in a landmass known as Sahul. Early seafarers may have constructed rafts of bamboo and island-hopped to Sahul, which was still separated from Southeast Asia by a good 62 miles. Once there, they produced the first known rock art around 45,000 years ago and were practicing cremation by 26,000 years ago, evidence of ritual activity not yet known at that time in any other part of the world. Once sea levels rose again, this relatively small human population was left in isolation for tens of thousands of years.

Musical Instruments Develop

12 **36,800 y.a.** The development of musical instruments is an event that likely occurred independently in disparate parts of the world at different opportunistic moments. The voice was almost certainly the medium of humankind's first experimentations with melody, followed by the use of naturally occurring materials such

14 | *Ancient rock drawings made by Aborigines in Australia.*

as reeds, hollow branches, conch shells, and rocks struck together percussively, materials that either would not be preserved or would not reveal an early musical function. The earliest preserved undisputed musical instruments are bone flutes, whistles, and rasps found in Europe and dated back to 36,800 years ago, though some researchers are attempting to push that date even further back into strictly Neandertal contexts. One particular cave in the French Pyrenees known as Isturitz has produced a total of 17 bone flutes spanning thousands of years of occupation, perhaps evidence of one of the world's first concert halls.

Neandertals Die Out

13 **35,000 y.a.** The Neandertals of Europe and western Asia were a vanishing race by 35,000 years ago, with the last of their line falling from the evolutionary ladder about 28,000 years ago. With large nasal openings to warm inhaled air and short broad muscular bodies to maximize heat production, Neandertals were adapted to the extreme cold of glacial Europe. But like several other species of Ice Age mammals, Neandertals may nevertheless have fallen victim to the climate as they came into closer contact with modern humans who could have outcompeted them for their primary food resource, meat from hunted animals. Modern humans, with their ability to communicate complex ideas through sophisticated language and with an advanced tool kit that could produce permanent dwellings and woven clothing, may simply have been better able to survive in an increasingly harsh climate of advancing ice sheets.

Artistic Expression Flourishes

14 **35,000 y.a.** A flourishing of artistic expression between 35,000 and 10,000 y.a. is evidenced throughout widespread regions of the inhabitable world. More than 150 localities in Africa, Europe, and Australia from this time period have revealed polychrome cave paintings, many depicting large animals such as horses, mammoths, bison, or rhinoceroses, and signed with stencils of human hands. Paint was produced by ancient artisans by mixing water or saliva with natural pigments such as red ocher, charcoal, or chalk, and was then applied using fingers, branches, moss, or brushes of animal hair. The resulting depictions were sometimes remarkable in their figurative detail, as in the two well-known sites of Altamira, Spain, and Lascaux, France, where ancient fat-burning stone lamps have also been recovered from the dark cave interiors. Three-dimensional relief sculptures, hewn into cave walls, often accompany these early paintings. Portable figurines and engraved pieces of stone, bone, ivory, shell, and fired clay were also widespread and reveal a high propensity for abstract symbolic expression and perhaps ritual practices.

Migration Begins

15 **25,000 y.a.** The peopling of the Americas is a process that likely involved multiple stages of migration, probably along different routes, and maybe even by different means of transport. About 25,000 y.a., the most recent ice age was well into its coldest phase and enough water was trapped in the world's glaciers that a large landmass known as Beringia connected Siberia to Alaska. Persisting until about 14,000 y.a., this land bridge served as a migration route for several groups of people following herds of large animals such as caribou, bison, and musk oxen. As the North American glaciers retreated, a corridor between them opened up, allowing an overland passage to regions farther south after about 12,000 y.a. But a number of sites in North and South America predate this

---

CONNECTIONS

Prehistoric Painting
Priceless information sources, many works are also masterpieces of form

Across the globe, preliterate human societies learned to express themselves through art. Cave paintings, sculpture, sand drawings, and stone monoliths are all windows into ancient cultures that left no literature to directly record their lifeways. Regardless of when created, prehistoric art represents a culture's earliest foray into abstract thought.

Although the Paleolithic conjures images of cave paintings (see event 14), much prehistoric art was made outside cavern walls. The Gravettian culture (28,000-20,000 B.C.E.) produced one of the most famous examples of early abstraction: small voluptuous sculptures known as Venus figures. With exaggerated hips and breasts and no facial features, the figurines clearly represent the female form rather than a specific woman. Scholars believe the small stone women were used as fertility fetishes.

One example of more recent prehistoric art comes from the Nasca people of Peru, who flourished from 200 B.C.E. to 600 C.E. (see event 117). In addition to brilliantly colored pottery, the Nasca left a mystery that was not discovered until the advent of airplanes, when people flying overhead noticed enormous line drawings in the Peruvian desert sands. Among the approximately 70 "Nasca lines"

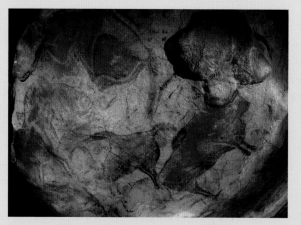

Prehistoric cave art in Altamira, Spain.

are detailed illustrations of a monkey, a killer whale, a hummingbird, a pelican, and other birds and plants—the largest almost 1,000 feet long. Some scholars have theorized that the lines, which also feature geometric designs, are a celestial calendar, although no correlation with the southern sky has been proved. Another theory is that the art was an outdoor temple.

On Rapa Nui (Easter Island), tribespeople excavated volcanic rock to sculpt enormous statues of deified ancestors. Early specimens from about 900 C.E. vary in form and size, but a few centuries later almost all featured the classic Easter Island look: elongated heads with sharp chins, deep-set eyes, little body. The tallest existing statue towers 37 feet over Rapa Nui's grassy soil. Many rest on *ahus,* enormous stone platforms that required great skill to cut and transport. The statues and ahus were made until about 1600 C.E., when, scholars believe,

escalating warfare ended the era of stone sculpture.

When Europeans first contacted Polynesian islanders, they encountered another art form, the tattoo, with nobles and warriors covered in intricate designs displaying their status. The geometric motifs of Polynesian tattoos clearly have resulted from generations of refinement.

event, some by thousands of years. This means that the Americas' first inhabitants may have arrived by boat, following the Pacific ice sheet south to a point where they could safely travel inland and then onward to inhabit widespread portions of the landmass within a few millennia.

■ **FOOTNOTE** Recent DNA studies show strong relations between Amerindian groups of the Arctic to Siberian people, whereas more southerly Amerindian groups share fewer genetic traits with the Siberians.

Bow and Arrow Developed

16 **15,000** B.C.E. The development of the bow and arrow was a momentous technological advance that allowed early hunters not only the safety of pursuing large prey from a greater distance, but also a far superior degree of accuracy and velocity than was previously possible. The exact date of its invention is elusive since the earliest examples may have been made completely of perishable materials, but it likely followed other technological advances such as the spear-thrower, the barbed harpoon, and the boomerang at around 15,000 B.C.E. or earlier. It was not long, though, before this early missile was adapted to warfare, for which it would be a prominent weapon for many thousands of years.

Permanent Settlement Begins

17 **13,000** B.C.E. The origins of permanent settlement were, as with many transitions in human prehistory, driven by changing climatic conditions. As glaciers continued to retreat and world temperatures continued to steadily rise, the range and abundance of wild grains such as wheat and barley continued to grow. By 17,000 B.C.E., evidence exists for the collecting of these grains by people wintering along the shore of Lake Galilee in modern-day Israel. By around 13,000 B.C.E., year-round settlements of communities, known collectively as Natufian, had emerged. Their way of life was at least partly based on the intensive harvesting and processing of wild grains by means of new tools such as the stone-bladed sickle and the mortar

15 | *Ice Age caribou hunters return to their encampment on the Bering Land Bridge.*

and pestle. They built stone-walled huts, buried their dead in cemeteries, and had likely domesticated wild dogs by around 11,000 B.C.E., further indications of an established sedentary lifestyle.

Southern Chile Settled

18 **10,500** B.C.E. The first inhabitants of South America traveled rapidly through their newfound land, reaching the glaciated southern portion of Patagonia by at least 10,500 B.C.E. At this time, early colonizers in southern Chile had already established a sophisticated community with a strong knowledge of the natural resources of their surroundings. At a site known as Monte Verde, clay-lined hearths provided warmth and a means of cooking, and tools such as spears, sling stones, mortars, and digging sticks provided for a varied diet that ranged from mastodon meat to mollusks, and from potatoes to seaweed. Inhabitants collected a number of medicinal plants from upwards of 40 miles away, some of which

are still used today for various skin and lung ailments. Just how the Monte Verdeans arrived in southern Chile is still in question, but a lack of contemporaneous sites farther to the north suggests that they could have been among the Americas' earliest long-distance coastal migrants.

■ **FOOTNOTE** Since discovery of the earliest settlement in Monte Verde, Chile, a number of possible sites in North America—Virginia, Pennsylvania—indicate origin before 14,000 y.a., but archaeologists remain cautious.

Pottery Produced

19 **10,500** B.C.E. The world's first known pottery was produced around 10,500 B.C.E. by a group of hunters and fishers, known as the Incipient Jomon, living on the islands of Japan. Made from coiled clay baked over an open fire, the earliest examples of Jomon pottery all exhibit rounded or pointed bases probably so they could be dug into the soil and ash in the center of a fire pit in order to cook food. Later examples have flat bottoms, indicating they were likely also used for storage. Decorative elements were minimal at first but later developed into complex patterns that were created by impressing twisted cords into the clay before firing. This appliqué technique gave the culture its name, Jomon, which means "cord marks." As their technical and artistic skill increased, the Jomon also produced stylized figurines of fired clay, known as *dogu,* many of which represent pregnant females and may have served a role in fertility rituals.

Clovis Perfect the Art of Hunting

20 **9500 B.C.E.** Inhabitants of North America, known as the Clovis, had by around 9500 B.C.E. devised a number of effective strategies for hunting the largest animals of their day, mammoths and bison. This type of hunt would have been a dangerous venture, perhaps lasting many days and relying not only on force of numbers but also on ambush strategies such as driving the animals into steep gullies where they could be corralled and more easily killed. The meat from such a kill could have lasted months, and many other parts of the animal would have been put to use as well: bones and horns for making tools and hides for making leather. Though changing climatic conditions were likely the main cause, by 8000 B.C.E. the Clovis hunters may even have helped to drive North America's large Ice Age mammals to their final extinction.

> ■ **FOOTNOTE** The people of the Clovis culture, named for the town of Clovis, New Mexico, hunted with spears equipped with the characteristic Clovis point, a fluted rock spear point that could be fastened to a wooden shaft.

Population Increases

22 **8000 B.C.E.** The population explosion that followed the transition to agriculture produced long-lasting and widespread developments, including the origins of urban life. By 8000 B.C.E., the site of Tell el Sultan, better known as Jericho, hosted a thriving agricultural community centered around a perennial natural spring in modern-day Israel. With 2,000 or more inhabitants, this incipient town was considerably larger than other early farming villages and dwarfed the size of contemporaneous hunter-gatherer groups. Jericho's inhabitants were the first to utilize mud bricks for building. They also constructed a stone wall 12 feet high around their town, likely to defend against floodwaters or other humans. Trappings of urban life, evident at Jericho and other early towns such as Çatal Hüyük in modern-day Turkey, include a barter economy, religious worship, division of labor, social hierarchy, and private ownership of land, all part of urban life today.

Metallurgy Developed

23 **6500 B.C.E.** The development of metallurgy, which began in the Middle East around 6500 B.C.E., introduced a strong, durable medium from which humans could fashion any number of usable objects. The process of firing molded clay into pottery by baking it within kilns came into use in the Middle East around 7000 B.C.E., and it was not long before these same kilns were employed in the first experiments with copper smelting. Early metallurgists in Çatal Hüyük and the towns of Mesopotamia mostly cast their copper into beads and other small decorative objects. Then, around 4000 B.C.E., it was discovered that copper alloyed with tin could produce an even stronger metal, bronze, which was soon being cast by those in power into an array of forms that functioned widely in utilitarian, agricultural, military, and artistic endeavors.

> ■ **FOOTNOTE** The breakthrough of alloying copper with tin came with trade. Deposits of tin from the British Isles and copper from the Middle East brought about the development of more durable bronze tools and weapons.

Irrigation System Developed

24 **6000 B.C.E.** Methods of irrigation, developed in Mesopotamia

Origins of Agriculture

21 **9000 B.C.E.** The origins of agriculture marked a tremendous transition in the history of humankind. Around 9000 B.C.E., a regional dry spell in the Middle East limited the amount of wild grain available for harvesting. With a lifestyle dependent on these grains for subsistence, settled communities of the area began to supplement wild crops with their own plantings and to store the excess year-round to ensure the food supply. Around 8000 B.C.E., these communities also began to domesticate and breed wild animals of the region. The practices of agriculture and animal domestication arose quickly in different parts of the world, appearing in the Americas by 8000 B.C.E., Africa and India by 7000 B.C.E., and in East Asia and Europe by 6000 B.C.E. Each area cultivated regional foods, though a number of crops were spread across geographic boundaries by traders and migrants. Widespread deforestation and proliferation of animal-borne diseases were side effects that also accompanied these innovations. Though hunter-gatherer societies continued to flourish in some areas, sedentary agricultural villages became the primary way of life for humankind for many thousands of years.

Buckwheat plants thrive in arid, cool, hilly land and yield triangular kernels.

21 | *Water shoots from the hose of a modern-day irrigation rig to quench an alfalfa crop in Greybull, Wyoming.*

around 6000 B.C.E., produced a pro-longed food surplus. Up until this time, nascent agriculturalists had depended solely upon rainfall to water their crops. Mesopotamia is a hot, dry region with lit-tle rainfall, though portions are flooded annually by the Tigris and Euphrates Rivers. New canals, reservoirs, dikes, dams, and embankments, farmers were able to channel the fresh water and silt deposits of these rivers directly into their fields, making their soil fertile and increasing agricultural yield. By 5000 B.C.E., as the irrigation system became more intricate, harvests became even more productive, creating a food surplus that not only supported the rapidly increasing resident population, but also attracted new migrants who provided the basis for what would become the world's first cities.

First Surgery Performed

25 **5100** B.C.E. The first known form of surgery to have been practiced on humans successfully is trepanation, or the intentional removal of a small portion of the skull. The earliest known case comes from the Ensisheim burial site in France and dates to about 5100 B.C.E., though the practice likely extended even further back into prehistory. The trepanned skull from Ensisheim shows evidence of healing around two separate incisions and belongs to a man of about 50 years, indicating a relatively healthy and long life following the surgery. This type of operation would have been conducted using sharp, stone microblades and would have required a high level of precision and skill, par-ticularly in preanesthetic times. Evidence of its practice has been found as distantly as Europe, Africa, Melanesia, and the

Americas. If the purpose of this surgery was to provide a route of exit for disease or affliction caused by demonic spirits, as sug-gested by some researchers, it reveals a very early correlation in the prehistoric mind between the brain and behavior, something even Aristotle did not recognize more than 4,500 years later.

FOOTNOTE In the earliest trepanations, sur-geons scraped the bone away with sharp stones. With the invention of primitive drilling tools, they bored small holes arranged in a cir-cle and removed the piece of bone inside.

25 | *Human craniums, part of skull removed.*

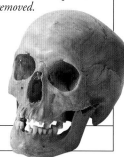

Rice Domesticated

26 **5000** B.C.E. The domestication of rice in southern China, which requires flooded fields and hence means of water control, brought about a large-scale organization of society in the construction of dams, dikes, and canals that was unprecedented in this region of the world. By at least 5000 B.C.E. and perhaps much earlier, these methods of irrigation were established by farmers who lived in timber dwellings raised above the marshes at sites such as Hemudu on the Yangtze River Delta. Tools of wood and bone aided these farmers in producing as many as three crops a year. Methods of cultivating rice were spread by migrants from southern China to India, Southeast Asia, and Taiwan, establishing it as a staple crop throughout these areas as well, a position that it still holds today.

Sky Studied

27 **ca 5000** B.C.E. Study of the sun, moon, and stars was likely undertaken by many early farming communities, who depended upon the seasonal wax and wane of floodwaters and sunlight to provide necessary conditions for a successful harvest. The earliest known physical manifestation of the monitoring of celestial bodies comes from a circular cluster of standing megaliths erected sometime after 5000 B.C.E. at the site of Nabta Playa in the Nubian Desert of southern Egypt. One of the lines of sight created by these megaliths would have matched up along the horizon with sunrise on the summer solstice, a time of year that was significant for the rainy season. Nabta Playa anticipated the later formation of the Egyptian solar calendar, the first of its kind, which was based on the reappearance in the eastern sky of Sirius, the Dog Star, coinciding with the annual flooding of the Nile River. The Egyptian calendar was divided into 365 days, 12 months, and three seasons named Inundation, Growth, and Drought for their inherent associations with phases of the harvest.

> ■ **FOOTNOTE** As they were observing the stars during summer nights, the ancient Egyptians divided time into 12 hours of darkness, 1 hour for each twilight period, and 10 hours of day between sunrise and sunset.

Permanent Monuments

28 **ca 4500** B.C.E. Megalithic builders of Africa, Europe, and Southeast Asia were among the world's first people to organize massive efforts of thousands of hours of labor in order to erect permanent monuments that would function not in

---

CONNECTIONS

The Horse Through History
Its usefulness and affectionate nature have made it a beloved companion

Horses hold a unique place in the animal kingdom. Modern breeds of *Equus caballus* are all the result of domestication—for 6,000 years, humans have honed the species into creatures specialized for farming, for speed, and for war. As the Koran says, "When God created the horse, he said to the magnificent creature:...'Thou shalt be favored above all other creatures, for to thee shall accrue the love of the master of the Earth. Thou shalt fly without wings and conquer without sword.' "

Every modern horse descends from the herds of the Asian steppe. In China, archaeologists have unearthed ceramics featuring harnessed horses dating to 3500 B.C.E., suggesting their use in agriculture by then, while a Persian bronze war chariot from 2800 B.C.E. shows that the animals were used for battle not long after. The Hittites left humanity the oldest extant manual for the care and breeding of the species, written in cuneiform about 1600 B.C.E. In Greek mythology Poseidon rose from the sea on magical horses and used the winged Pegasus to show man where to find fresh water sources. Centaurs were a literal manifestation of the closeness of man and beast. The hero Hercules was tutored by a centaur. Curiously, Chinese mythology also exalts a race of man-horses called the Ting-Ling, embuing them with great wisdom.

A Bedouin and his horse frame the Citadel of Palmyra.

As a tool of war, the horse gave ancient armies a formidable advantage over their enemies. In the fourth century B.C.E., Alexander the Great led his cavalry on his beloved horse Bucephalus, building his enormous empire from horseback. The Huns and other Central Asian nomads first developed the stirrup in the early centuries C.E. With two hands for their bow and the ability to stand astride their steeds, the Huns rained arrows and terror on fifth-century Europe.

Later, in medieval Europe, several innovations such as the horseshoe and horse-drawn plow led to an agricultural boom. This in turn resulted in food surpluses that inspired Europe's earliest money economies. In fact, horses became so important in European agriculture and warfare that the creatures sailed to the New World with 16th-century explorers and conquistadores.

These horses would soon transform the American wilderness and revolutionize Plains Indian culture. The cowboy-and-Indian culture of Hollywood Westerns evolved by the mid-18th century, when Indian tribes adapted the horse for use in buffalo hunts and warfare. In the mid-19th century, the young United States established its Pony Express mail service—borrowing an idea from ancient Persia, where correspondence had been carried by relays of mounted couriers.

the everyday means of survival but as ceremonial centers utilized at important times of the year. This tradition is most evident in western Europe, where farming communities from the island of Malta, off the southern coast of Sicily, to the Orkney Islands, off the northern coast of Scotland, were erecting freestanding megalithic structures of various forms beginning around 4500 B.C.E. The earliest of these were communal tombs, many engraved with ornate geometric motifs. Others were single standing stones, called menhirs, often arranged into long parallel alignments that may have served in ceremonial processions. These avenues of stone often terminated in circular arrangements of megaliths that likely served as ritual centers. The best known and most enigmatic of these stone circles, still standing after more than 4,000 years, is known as Stonehenge.

■ FOOTNOTE Many megalithic structures are interpreted as early calendars that accurately mark the summer or winter solstice. Most archaeologists agree that megaliths of western Europe were spread by a homogenous culture.

Corn Domesticated

29 **4000 B.C.E.** The independent development of agriculture in the Americas is testament that the global transition to farming did not stem from just one source, but rather occurred incrementally in different parts of the world at disparate times. Though crops such as chilies, squash, avocados, and potatoes had been cultivated on a small scale at seasonal campsites in Central and South America for thousands of years, village life did not begin in earnest in the Americas until after the domestication of corn by around 4000 B.C.E. Corn, also known as maize, was developed from types of wild grass indigenous to Mexico that produce only a scant amount of kernels. Early agriculturalists in Mesoamerica experimented with a number of hybrid strains in order to increase the yield on each cob. The production of corn would later provide an economic base to the empires of Mesoamerica and would become such an important aspect of everyday life that it

31 | *An Afghan boy carries a handmade plow in the hilly grasslands of Afghanistan.*

figured in a number of creation myths spanning North and South America.

Horse Domesticated

30 **4000 B.C.E.** Domestication of the horse is a difficult matter to date precisely, but the earliest evidence of its occurrence comes from middens in modern-day Ukraine, dated to about 4000 B.C.E. and associated with seminomadic pastoralists known as the Kurgan. Living in close contact with the native horses of the Russian steppes, the Kurgan were familiar with their natural patterns of behavior. Once domesticated, the horse was likely at first used for its meat, milk, and hide, but bit marks worn into the teeth of some of these early domesticates suggest they were also ridden. This facilitated the Kurgan's seminomadic lifestyle and allowed long-distance migrations.

Plow Developed

31 **4000 B.C.E.** Development of the ox-drawn plow freed much of the human workforce from the arduous labor of tilling and weeding fields by hand with

a simple fire-hardened digging stick or hoe. The plow's first appearance in the archaeological record, dating to about 4000 B.C.E., is etched into the soil of southern European fields in the form of long, narrow, shallow furrows, in which early farmers would plant seeds for crops. The plow made heavy soil more easily worked and so opened up new lands for agriculture. As the efficiency of the plow increased and spread throughout the world, the consequences were manifold, since it enabled populations to grow and workers to devote more energy to other pursuits, such as the production of larger stone buildings and more refined material goods. The plow was one of the technical innovations in agriculture that created such an abundant yield that it indirectly allowed for progressively more sophisticated developments in human civilization.

First Earthworks Constructed

32 **3700 B.C.E.** The earliest known earthworks built in the Americas date to 3700 B.C.E., their construction attributed to a group of hunter-gatherers living seasonally along the Ouachita River of northeastern Louisiana. The most substantial site of this period, known as Watson Brake, consists of at least 11 mounds, ranging from 3 to 25 feet tall and connected by ridges forming a rough oval about 850 feet wide. Though the exact purpose of these early mounds is yet unknown, the practice of constructing earthworks would take on a number of ceremonial and political functions at settlements throughout the eastern North American woodlands for upwards of 5,000 years.

Transportation Advances

33 | **3500 B.C.E.** The invention of the wheel and contemporaneous advances in shipbuilding brought neighboring lands together into a growing web of trade networks, which cropped up independently all around the globe. Though the earliest geographical origins of the wheel are still a matter of dispute, by around 3500 B.C.E. the wheel was being employed in Mesopotamia in two distinctly important ways. The first was as a turntable, or potter's wheel, which enabled craftsmen to produce highly refined vessels in large numbers. The second, as depicted in an early Sumerian pictograph from this time, was as a means of transport when equipped onto a sledge, which enabled merchants to portage large loads of bulk goods considerably long distances. Once spoked and coupled with the strength of the domesticated horse, the wheel also became a powerful tool of warfare in the form of the chariot. Use of the wheel spread rapidly throughout Eurasia and quickly became intimately tied to various forms of overland transportation, which it has remained to this day.

Earliest Known Writing

34 | **3500 B.C.E.** The world's earliest known writing, like a number of other firsts in human civilization, comes from Mesopotamia. Perhaps as early as 8000 B.C.E., merchants of the region used clay tokens, fashioned into various stylized shapes, as bills and receipts for stores of grain and animals, and as an early form of currency. By around 3500 B.C.E., these tokens were being enclosed within hollow clay balls, called *bullae*, which were impressed with the form or the number of the tokens within. In this way, people could "read" the label on a clay ball, or in a case of dispute, they could break open the "envelope" and recount the tokens. Now that the surface of the envelope could be read, the tokens themselves became obsolete. The balls were flattened into small tablets by around 3300 B.C.E., and the pictographs incised on them constituted the basis for the world's first known writing system. Over the centuries, the pictographs became ever more abstract and symbolic cuneiform scripts emerged throughout the Middle East, as hieroglyphic scripts emerged in Egypt. Business transactions, codes of law, and oral traditions could now be put down into a permanent form, easily referenced by the scribes of literate societies.

Clay tablet from Ebla inscribed with cuneiform characters roughly 4,500 years ago.

Governments Established

35 | **ca 3200 B.C.E.** The formation of city-states in Mesopotamia heralded a new transition in human history, the first institutional governments. One of these city-states, Uruk, located along the Euphrates River in modern-day Iraq, by 3200 B.C.E. had organized itself into residential, religious, and marketplace districts covering 1,000 acres, all enclosed by walls of brick spanning six miles. The White Temple and ziggurat of Uruk, built around this time by a force of perhaps 1,500 laborers, was one of the world's first examples of monumental architecture dedicated to a patron deity. Rising some 40 feet above the city streets, this mud-brick temple was adorned with mosaics and motifs of gold, silver, and copper. This display of wealth attracted the conquering zeal of groups of people coming from outside the city walls. With wealth came an increase in military forces, powerful kings who had distinguished themselves in battle, and eventually empire.

> ■ **FOOTNOTE** Sumer's numerous city-states each controlled areas of several hundred square miles. The names of these cities—Lagash, Eridu, Kish, Nippur, Uruk, Sippar, Akshak, and Ur—echo from a distant past.

Urban Settlement Begins

36 | **3100 B.C.E.** The origins of urban settlement and monumental architecture in Andean regions of South America date back to about 3100 B.C.E., roughly contemporaneous with that of Egypt and Mesopotamia. One of the earliest known examples, a site called Aspero, is located on the northern coast of Peru and is characterized by at least six pyramidal platform mounds and a number of other mud-and-stone structures. The largest of the platform mounds was about 35 feet tall, 130 feet long at its base, and supported what may have been one of the Americas' first religious structures. Oriented to face the open water, this temple-pyramid could have been associated with worship of the sea, from which the

33 | *A skilled potter in a village in Uttar Pradesh, India, crafts a clay cup on a spinning wheel.*

inhabitants of this complex received much of their sustenance. Other nearby urban complexes, such as Caral, show evidence of irrigation, trade, recordkeeping, cotton weaving, and musical instrumentation, trappings of a complex society nearly as advanced as those that formed the basis of Western civilization.

Egyptian Pharaonic System

37 ca 3100 B.C.E. The cultural and political unification of the kingdoms of Upper and Lower Egypt into one centralized nation-state, which occurred gradually sometime after 3100 B.C.E., brought into power one of the most iconic figures in ancient history, the Egyptian pharaoh. Though traditionally ascribed to a conquering king alternately named Menes or Narmer, the unification of Egypt probably occurred in stages that spanned centuries. Regardless of the exact circumstances, Egyptian culture started flourishing after 3100 B.C.E. Cities such as Memphis, Thebes, and Heliopolis emerged, writing spread, and art and architecture became characteristically stylized and, in the case of pharaonic art, lavishly opulent. Taking a cue from earlier Sudanic kings, pharaohs were viewed by their contemporaries as gods on Earth, serving as intermediary between human and divine. As such, they enjoyed absolute power in life and grand memorials in death. Under the leadership of 31 pharaonic dynasties, Egypt remained a powerful autonomous state for the bulk of the next 3,000 years.

Silk Cloth Manufactured

38 3000 B.C.E. The manufacture of silk cloth from the filaments of the silkworm caterpillar's cocoon, a process

38 | *A young man works a silk loom in a factory in India.*

Paper Developed

39 ca. 3000 B.C.E. The development of papyrus as a writing medium led to the first books that could be transported easily across wide geographic ranges. Papyrus was first produced in ancient Egypt around 3000 B.C.E. from the marsh reed of the same name. Egyptian papermakers cut the inner portions of the papyrus stem into long, narrow strips, then placed them side by side on a cloth in two perpendicular layers. They would dampen, pound, and press the strips until the sap of the reed adhered the layers into a single sheet. Papyrus sheets were glued together into long scrolls with a flour paste. Inks of various colors were applied with reed pens.

Fragment of papyrus from the Gnostic text of the Gospel of Judas, Geneva, Switzerland.

The use of scrolls led to a growing number of educated, literate scribes, who now could set down more easily their thoughts on science, medicine, history, architecture, and religion. Through the use of papyrus scrolls, the collective knowledge and cultural mores of the ancient Egyptians, Greeks, and Romans could be disseminated and preserved for future generations.

known as sericulture, produces the world's finest natural fabric, one so coveted in antiquity that it lent its name to a wide-ranging network of trade routes spanning Eurasia, the silk roads. The earliest known fragments of woven silk date to about 3000 B.C.E., though evidence suggests its roots lay centuries deeper with the Yangshao people, agricultural inhabitants of the Yellow River Basin in eastern China. Knowledge of silk production was slow to travel and was not known in most other parts of China until the second century B.C.E. For much of its history, China maintained a monopoly on silk production and was able to ship this highly prized luxury item along the silk roads to lands as distant as India, Persia, Mesopotamia, and even Rome.

First Pyramid Built

40 ca 2600 B.C.E. Imhotep is the first physician in recorded history, and as architect of Egypt's first pyramid, he is also the earliest artist and engineer whose name has been preserved. Born a commoner, Imhotep distinguished himself as a skilled and intelligent administrator during the reign of Pharaoh Djoser from 2630 to 2611 B.C.E. Although he was deified after death, Imhotep's many achievements in life may have been embellished by later generations. His esteemed position and reputation, though, add credence to his skill as a physician. It was as architect and designer of the step pyramid of Djoser that Imhotep's work was truly unprecedented. Rising about 200 feet, the step pyramid is the world's first building constructed completely of quarried stone and stands as the first imposingly grandiose royal tomb in ancient Egypt. It set off a flurry of pyramid construction over the following centuries that would result in the largest buildings the world had ever known.

Stringed Instruments Evolve

41 2600 B.C.E. The development of stringed instruments is indicative of the increasingly important role that music played in the daily and courtly life of the ancient world. The earliest stringed instrument was likely the musical bow, whose origins are obscured in prehistory. The oldest extant stringed instruments are nine lyres and three harps, unearthed from royal burial chambers in the Mesopotamian city of Ur and dating back to about 2600 B.C.E. These ornately engraved instruments were sacrificed along with their owners in order to accompany the nobility of Ur to the afterlife, evidence of their status as prized commodities. Wall paintings and figurines attest to the presence of almost identical instruments in Egypt and the Aegean Islands around the same time. The lyre seems to have functioned for poetic and religious purposes, while the harp, often represented as played by women, may have served a role in erotic entertainment. The lute, or oud, may originally have been the instrument of farmers and shepherds, but its successors, the guitar, fiddle, sitar, banjo, and others, are now played the world over.

■ **FOOTNOTE** Music exists in every culture. Scientists believe that it has been present in some form since the great migration of humans out of Africa. The sounds may have been influenced by birdsong or other sounds in nature.

Pyramids at Giza and Khufu

42 ca 2550 B.C.E. The Pyramids and Sphinx at Giza still stand as perhaps the most remarkable technical feats of construction, engineering, and sheer organization of labor in the ancient world. Harnessing the energies of tens of thousands of masons, craftsmen, laborers, and slaves, these massive monuments were constructed using relatively simple tools of copper, stone, wood, and rope. The largest of all the Egyptian pyramids, the Great Pyramid of Khufu at Giza, erected between 2551 and 2528 B.C.E., originally rose 481 feet above the desert sand and is composed of some 2,300,000 blocks of limestone, some weighing up to 15 tons. With perfectly sloped sides oriented to the cardinal points of a

42 | *An Egyptian leads his camels past the Pyramids at Giza, the architectural legacy of the kings of the 4th dynasty.*

compass, it is a marvel of precision, intended to stand for eternity. Weighing in at about 5,750,000 tons, the Great Pyramid of Khufu is arguably the largest structure ever made by humans, not surpassed in height until perhaps as late as the 19th century C.E.

Rise of Harappan Civilization

43 **2500** B.C.E. Harappan civilization, centered around the Indus River Valley in modern-day Pakistan, had by 2500 B.C.E. established two major urban centers as well as hundreds of smaller settlements that spanned an area of almost 500,000 square miles, stretching from the Persian Gulf to the foothills of the Himalaya. With such a far-flung cultural continuity, some form of administrative centralization can be inferred, though the exact nature of the Harappans' political

organization is still a matter of conjecture, owing to the facts that their script is not fully deciphered, they built no palaces or royal tombs, and they left behind few prestige objects. What is known through the excavation of the large, grid-patterned cities of Harappa and Mohenjo-daro are aspects of daily life, such as the importance of personal hygiene. Each residence in these cities was fitted with a private bathroom equipped with a toilet that fed into a central citywide drainage, one of the most sophisticated public sewage systems of the ancient world.

Establishment of an Empire

44 **2334** B.C.E. Sargon, semilegendary king of the Mesopotamian city of Akkad, was among the first rulers in history to extend his authority beyond the borders of his own society—in other words,

to establish an empire. The precedent had likely been set on a smaller scale by earlier Mesopotamian kings, such as Lugalzagesi, whom Sargon is purported to have overthrown in a coup around 2334 B.C.E. During the course of his 56-year reign, Sargon asserted his influence, if not direct rule, by conquest and other means from the Persian Gulf to the Mediterranean Sea. Through control and taxation of previously existing trade routes, he was able to finance his military operations

44 | *Bronze head of Sargon, Mesopotamian conqueror.*

and enhance the prestige of his capital city. Since few contemporary sources remain, the full extent of Sargon's exploits is questionable; regardless, later Mesopotamians ascribed to him the model of a dynastic military tradition that would characterize the ensuing Babylonian, Assyrian, and New Babylonian empires of Mesopotamia for more than 1,500 years.

Chinese Royal Dynasty

45 **2200 B.C.E.** The earliest recorded royal dynasty in China, the semi-legendary Xia dynasty of the Yellow River Valley, was founded around 2200 B.C.E. at a time when urban centers surrounded by walls of pounded earthen ramparts were being established throughout northeastern China. These incipient urban centers, belonging to the Longshan culture, produced China's first bronze tools and vessels and the earliest known Chinese script, as well as carved pieces of jade and wheel-thrown pottery only half an inch thick. The region's first known full-blown city, Erlitou, was founded on the Yellow River around 1900 B.C.E. and may have served as a capital of the Xia dynasty, owing to its palacelike structure encompassing more than 300 square feet. Though little information is preserved about its political organization, the Xia dynasty is known to have precipitated China on a course of large-scale urbanization that continues to this day.

Indo-European Dispersion

47 **ca 2000 B.C.E.** The migration of Indo-European groups from grasslands north of the Black Sea in the centuries before and after 2000 B.C.E. left its linguistic and cultural marks on lands as distant as Scandinavia and Sri Lanka. With a seminomadic lifestyle that lent itself to annual travels on horseback of as many as 500 miles, the Indo-Europeans were well equipped to expand once population pressures demanded it. On wheeled vehicles, they gradually and in most cases peacefully migrated into central Europe by 2300 B.C.E., Anatolia by 2000 B.C.E., and northern India by 1500 B.C.E. One isolated group even ventured into northwestern China. Along the way, they established settlements that spread their culture, which assimilated into such ethnicities as Celtic, Hittite, Persian, and Aryan, and their language, which developed regionally into modern English, Spanish, Russian, Farsi, and Hindi, among others. Waves of Indo-European migration continued for thousands of years, the effects of which are an integral aspect of human history throughout the world.

The Epic of Gilgamesh Written

48 **ca 2000 B.C.E.** The Epic of Gilgamesh is one of the earliest works of literature to reflect on moral issues and establish archetypal narrative motifs that resound through the poetry of societies to follow. Gilgamesh was a historical king who ruled the Mesopotamian city of Uruk around 2700 B.C.E. Upon his death, his exploits were embellished in legend by a cycle of Sumerian poems. These poems formed the basis of an Akkadian version, written around 2000 B.C.E. in a style that combined history, myth, and poetry into a new form, the heroic epic. This and other Akkadian epics employed motifs such as the great flood, the evil serpent, the alluring goddess, and the quest for immortality, later echoed in the narratives of the Old Testament and in the epics of the Hittites, Greeks, Romans, and others. In Gilgamesh, the reader finds a hero struggling with the meaning of life and the

Stonehenge Built

46 **2100 B.C.E.** Stonehenge, the monumental circle of megaliths located on the Salisbury Plain of southern England, is a feat of engineering 1,600 years in the making. The main phases of construction commenced around 2100 B.C.E., though inhabitants of the area had earmarked the site as many as 1,000 years earlier by digging a circular ditch and embankment 320 feet across. Generations later, the builders of Stonehenge quarried some 80 blocks of igneous bluestone from the Preseli Mountains of Wales 240 miles away. Exactly how these four-ton stones were transported such a distance is still unknown. Once on-site, they were erected in two concentric circles with an entranceway aligned to sunrise on the summer solstice, an arrangement that suggests Stonehenge may have hosted ritual seasonal

The massive rocks of Stonehenge, transported and erected by ancient peoples, stand against a cloudy sky.

gatherings. About 2000 B.C.E., dozens of enormous sandstone blocks, averaging 26 tons apiece, were quarried from 20 miles away and erected in a post-and-lintel formation that is found nowhere else on the British Isles. The massive effort required in the construction of Stonehenge is evidence of the remarkable technical skill of a people about whom little else is known.

BRONZE AGE DYNASTIES OF CHINA

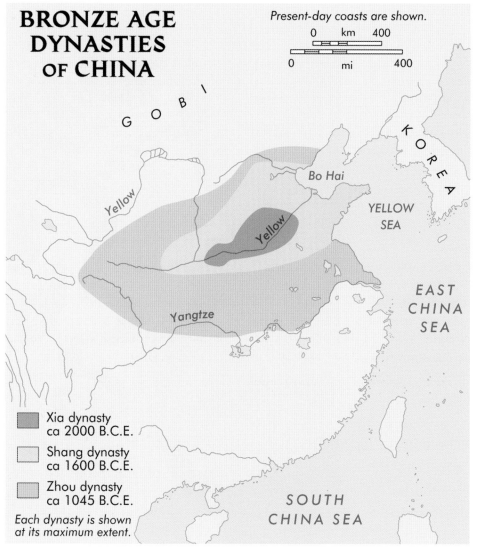

Present-day coasts are shown.

0 km 400

0 mi 400

Xia dynasty ca 2000 B.C.E.

Shang dynasty ca 1600 B.C.E.

Zhou dynasty ca 1045 B.C.E.

Each dynasty is shown at its maximum extent.

45 | *The Yellow River Valley spawned the Bronze Age dynasties: the Xia, the Shang, and the Zhou.*

inevitability of death, notions to which humans through the ages can relate.

Palace-Centered States

49 ca 2000 B.C.E. The Minoans of Crete established the first palace-centered states and, arguably, the first materially advanced civilization of the Western world. Beginning around 2000 B.C.E., they constructed elaborate, labyrinthine palace complexes, decorated with ornate frescoes, delicate sculptures, polychrome pottery, and other objects of gold and ivory. The earliest and largest of the palaces, Knossos, was even the inspiration for the mythological tale of King Minos and the Minotaur, which in turn lent the society its name. The

Minoans were extensive maritime traders, exchanging wine, olive oil, and wool for wares from Egypt, the Levant, Anatolia, and Greece. Their geographic locale had disadvantages, though. Located in a region of geologic instability, the Minoans had to deal with a number of natural catastrophes, such as earthquakes, tidal waves, and volcanic eruptions. One such eruption on the nearby island of Thíra in 1628 B.C.E. was so devastating that it may even have spawned the enigmatic legend of the lost city of Atlantis.

The Rise of Abraham

50 ca 2000 B.C.E. The Hebrew patriarch Abraham is a sacred prophet

of three of the world's most widely practiced monotheistic religions, Judaism, Christianity, and Islam. According to Scripture, Abraham was born in Ur, a Mesopotamian city whose religion was vigorously polytheistic. He migrated with his tribe sometime after 2000 B.C.E. to the Semitic village of Haran, a pilgrimage site for the worship of Sin, a moon god associated with the well-being of cattle herds, upon which Abraham and his people depended for their livelihood. After his father's death, Abraham moved on to Canaan, modern-day Israel and Palestine, where the god among gods was known as El, an epithet later used in the Old Testament as a synonym for Yahweh. Abraham and his people remained in Canaan for a time, blending Mesopotamian, Semitic, and Canaanite traditions with their own, before migrating south into Egypt. Though Abraham's exact beliefs and teachings are lost, they were surely the singular product of crosscurrents of thought encountered through the course of a semi-nomadic existence.

FOOTNOTE Abraham is said to be the father of nations. Christians and Jews consider him the father of the people of Israel through his son Isaac. To Muslims, he is a prophet of Islam through his son Ishmael.

First Recorded Eclipse

51 1876 B.C.E. The first recorded eclipse, which was set down in writing by Chinese astronomers, took place in 1876 B.C.E. The records kept are so accurate that the occurrence of this eclipse can be calculated back to a specific date, October 16. Early Chinese astronomers of the Xia dynasty and in the millennia that followed used astronomical events such as eclipses to record the reigns of kings and other important events, allowing ancient Chinese history to be dated precisely. What is more, the early growth of astronomy in China stimulated the study of other sciences, such as mathematics, chemistry, geology, and medicine, as well as the development of an accurate calendar based on the movement of celestial bodies. With a

49 More Details on the Minoans of Crete

Among the many illustrious civilizations of the ancient world, the Minoans stand out as a people concerned not with military power but with culture, the arts, and the establishment of a successful bureaucratic state. With virtually none of their economic resources allotted for defense or for the upkeep of a standing army, the Minoans were free to develop culture and commerce. Their sophisticated naval fleet was employed not for exploration or conquest but for maritime trade. In exchange for goods such as wine, oil, and crafts, the Minoans imported the raw materials that their island lacked and easily enjoyed a comfortable standard of living.

Even more remarkable than this advanced mercantile trade system are the detailed trade records kept by the state. Although today we cannot decipher the Minoan script, it is clear that the records are accurate and plentiful and that the civilization had developed what was probably the most highly evolved bureaucratic system of its time.

These records speak to the Minoans' social sophistication, but what we know of the Minoan people comes mostly from the remains of their elaborate palaces, around which their culture was founded and expanded. Within and on the walls of these palaces is Minoan art—the single most important and mesmerizing legacy of this people.

> People appear to be caught in the midst of movement or emotion rather than being artificially posed.

Often joyous and in celebration of life and the natural world, the Minoan frescoes borrow their form from Egyptian art, with boldly outlined profiles that show a single, forward-facing eye. They are distinct from other Mediterranean art, however, in their bright and often contrasting colors and in the spontaneity of the scenes that they depict. People appear to be caught in the midst of movement or emotion rather than being artificially posed, and scenes of the natural world are almost alive with freshness and depth—fitting expression for a seafaring culture that enjoyed an unusual amount of wealth and security.

Fresco depicts elegantly adorned Minoan women gesturing animatedly.

cosmology based on the inherent order of the heavens, rather than the chaotic actions of supernatural gods, ancient Chinese society attained a high level of practical technology, in certain respects unsurpassed anywhere else in the world.

Advances in Mathematics

52 ca 1800 B.C.E. Advances in mathematics had been achieved by ancient Babylonians by around 1800 B.C.E., in large part due to the earliest known development of place-value notation. In the Babylonian system, like the modern one, the same symbol can stand for different powers of a base number dependent on its relation to other symbols. Unlike the modern system, which uses 10 as its base number, the Babylonians used 60, a value that still persists to this day through the designation of 60 seconds in a minute, 60 minutes in an hour, and 360 degrees in a circle. With place-value notation, Babylonian mathematicians solved simple arithmetic problems but also made the first stirrings in the fields of geometry, algebra, and number

52 | *The solution to a mathematical problem in cuneiform on a Babylonian clay tablet.*

The Code of Hammurabi

53 ca 1792 B.C.E. The Code of Hammurabi was one aspect of a series of administrative and moral reforms enacted by Hammurabi after ascending to the Babylonian throne about 1792 B.C.E. Though not actually the earliest code of law that survives from ancient Mesopotamia, it is the most extensive and one of the best preserved, inscribed in more than 3,500 lines on a slab of basalt stone standing almost seven and a half feet tall. Over the course of 282 judgments on a case-by-case basis, the code covers criminal and civil matters ranging from murder to marriage, and from trade deals to slavery disputes. Hammurabi's well-known law of retaliation, "an eye

Hammurabi medallion that hangs over a doorway in the U.S. Capitol.

for an eye," later echoed in the Old Testament, is actually one of the exceptions in a code of law that is mostly devoid of primitive retributive customs. Whether treated as absolute edict or as royal advice, the Code of Hammurabi was one of the first written works to promulgate standard behavioral mores for an entire empire. The code, however, empowered men, allowing them to sell their wives and children in case of insolvency. Men could engage in sexual relations with concubines, slaves, or prostitutes, whereas wives would be condemned for adultery by drowning.

theory, employing the Pythagorean theorem more than 1,000 years before the man after whom it is named. Unlike the contemporaneous Egyptians, the Babylonians used mathematics beyond its immediate application in accounting, perhaps deeming this knowledge worthy for the sake of knowledge itself.

■ **FOOTNOTE** Some Babylonian clay tablets showed quadratic equations in planning irrigation canals or land measurements; others solved cubic equations to find the volume of a rectangular excavation, as for a cellar.

South American States Formed

54 ca 1700 B.C.E. The formation of states in Andean regions of South America was under way by around 1700 B.C.E. as evidenced by the scale of the ceremonial center known as Huaca La Florida in the Rimac Valley of central Peru. In its day, Huaca La Florida was the largest building in South America, almost 100 feet tall, 200 feet deep, and 820 feet

wide, with a central plaza that could accommodate 100,000 people. The construction of La Florida was an undertaking of engineering and organization that could only have been accomplished through the combined resources of several communities: in other words, a state.

First Alphabet Developed

55 ca 1700 B.C.E. The development of the first alphabet, or system of writing based on letters representing individual sounds rather than symbols representing ideas or things, began on the eastern shores of the Mediterranean around 1700 B.C.E. At this time, the earliest known alphabetic inscriptions were carved onto bowls and other wares at various sites in the territory of the ancient Canaanites, though similar efforts were likely taking place throughout Syria, Palestine, Phoenicia, and Sinai. This early alphabetic script, incomplete and still undeciphered, is a precursor to the North Semitic script of

Phoenicia, consisting of 22 consonantal letters written right to left. The memorization of 22 letters as opposed to hundreds or thousands of cuneiform or hieroglyphic symbols made reading and writing far more accessible to larger groups of people. The North Semitic script was in turn adopted and adapted by the Hebrews, Greeks, Romans, Arabians, Indians, and all their modern cultural successors, making it the probable ancestor of almost all alphabetic scripts used today across the globe.

> ■ **FOOTNOTE** The word "alphabet" comes from the Greek, the first two letters of which—alpha and beta—are in turn derived from the first two letters of the Hebrew alphabet, a testament to the complex evolution of writing.

Advent of Shang Dynasty

56 ca 1600 B.C.E. The advent of the Shang dynasty in northeastern China marked advances in material culture not just in the Yellow River Valley, but throughout China. Coming into power by at least 1600 B.C.E., the Shang dynasty may have overrun the preceding Xia by controlling copper and tin resources of the region, thereby monopolizing the production of superior bronze weapons. Shang kings thereafter banned any unsanctioned bronze production by regional governors, keeping would-be rebels at bay for more than 500 years. Shang rulers did, however, employ craftsmen in the mass production of remarkably exquisite bronze vessels, cast from clay molds, as well as finely carved pieces of jade and ivory, not to mention elaborate timber palaces. Scribes were also encouraged to record important events on strips of bamboo or silk, furthering the art of Chinese calligraphy. These advances applied only to the ruling elite, though; peasant farmers and slaves, from whom the nobility claimed a large portion of each harvest, continued tilling the fields with simple tools of wood, bone, and stone.

Earliest Medical Documents

57 ca 1600 B.C.E. The earliest comprehensive medical documents yet discovered are two scrolls of papyrus written in ancient Egypt around 1600 and 1550 B.C.E., though they may actually be transcriptions of texts dating as far back as 3000 B.C.E. The first, known as the Edwin Smith Papyrus for the Egyptologist who purchased it in Luxor in C.E. 1862, is primarily an inventory of surgical procedures that range from setting a broken bone to circumcision. The second, the Ebers Papyrus, is more extensive, dealing with dozens of conditions and diseases and listing hundreds of natural remedies. Some of

57 | *This painting depicts a head pharmacist dictating the Ebers Papyrus while he directs the preparation of drugs.*

these concoctions are fantastical potions, but others are medicinal compounds that seem to be the product of experiential observations. One striking aspect of the Ebers Papyrus is its accurate description of the circulatory system as a fluid-transporting network of vessels with the heart at its center. Both texts reveal a knowledge of human physiology that was highly respected in the ancient world and unparalleled in its day.

Pacific Islands Colonized

58 1600 B.C.E. The Pacific Islands of Oceania were among the last habitable places on Earth to be settled. The story of their earliest colonization is still a matter of speculation, but by around 1600 B.C.E. a group of adept seafarers and fishers known as the Lapita struck out into open waters of the Pacific from islands off the coast of New Guinea. They traveled in double-hulled outrigger canoes, bringing a distinctive brand of pottery, as well as livestock and crops. Island-hopping, they traveled to Fiji by 1300 B.C.E. and to Tonga and Samoa by 1000 B.C.E., where they established the hallmarks of Polynesian culture. As new islands were discovered, knowledge of the winds, stars, and currents as navigational beacons increased, facilitating a trade network that spanned vast stretches of ocean. Explorations continued, perhaps spurred on by population pressures, until even the most remote of the Pacific Islands hosted unique and vibrant settlements.

Babylonian Empire Ends

60 1595 B.C.E. The Old Babylonian Empire in Mesopotamia came to an end in 1595 B.C.E. at the expense of a new regional power in the Middle East, the Hittite Empire of Anatolia. The Hittite king, Mursilis I, led his army—equipped with such military innovations as the lightweight horse-drawn chariot and the battering ram—on campaigns in northern Syria and the Levant. He then trekked nearly 500 miles down the Euphrates River and sacked the city of Babylon, unseating the king there and establishing the Hittites as a military power. Cultural interchanges followed, resulting in the admixture of Anatolian, Mesopotamian, and Egyptian art, religion, literature, technology, and even brides. Despite several power struggles with Egypt, the Hittites remained a dominant regional empire for 400 years.

FOOTNOTE Hattusa, capital of the Hittite Empire, was located near the modern-day town of Bogaskale, Turkey. At its peak the city covered more than 0.7 square mile of stately houses, palaces, and temples, surrounded by massive walls.

New Kingdom Period

61 ca 1540 B.C.E. The height of Egyptian civilization is widely considered the New Kingdom period, commencing around 1540 B.C.E. following an era of political turmoil. In the 17th century, a group of invaders known as the Hyksos overran northern Egypt through the use of bronze weaponry and horse-drawn chariots, innovations not yet known there. Once native Egyptian rulers regained power, they used these new military technologies to go on the offensive, seizing land to the north in the Levant and to the south in Nubia. Tribute, trade, and agricultural surplus fueled economic wealth in Egypt itself, resulting in the construction of massive temple complexes such as those at

The Use of Glass

59 ca 1600 B.C.E. The earliest use of glass as a glaze for stone beads and ceramic vessels is obscured in the prehistory of Egypt and Mesopotamia, but around 1600 B.C.E. workshops throughout the Middle East began to cast this translucent substance into new forms such as decorative vessels and molded figurines. The earliest vessels were core-formed by heating a mixture of potash and either sand or crushed quartz to its liquid form and winding the molten glass around a clay core attached to a metal rod. The artisans shaped the surface with tools and decorated it with lighter colored strands of molten glass. Finally they rolled the vessel on a smooth surface to produce an even finish. After cooling, they scraped the core out of the hardened vessel. From potters and metalworkers the artisans learned and adapted the process of pouring molten glass into ceramic molds called crucibles. By mixing in copper or other minerals they produced colored and iridescent objects that were as prized as semiprecious stones, or sometimes in imitation of semiprecious stones such as lapis lazuli and turquoise. This luxury commodity was coveted even by the pharaohs of Egypt, who went on to set up factories for its production from raw materials. The Egyptians produced amulets, perfume flasks, and other prized objects, one famous example of which is the blue glass inlay of Tutankhamun's gold mask. Glass vessels and figurines would remain prestige objects until the advent of glassblowing, developed in Syria in the first century B.C.E., which greatly increased the variety of shapes possible and the quantity of vessels that could be produced. The new technology allowed for mass production, without the use of cores, molds, or kilns. Glass objects rapidly made their way throughout the region, shaped as tableware, vases and bottles, funerary goods, and precious keepsakes.

Remnants of glass vessels found by an amateur archaeologist in Israel.

61 | *A tomb painting shows New Kingdom pharaoh Horemheb being received by Osiris to the underworld.*

Karnak, Luxor, and Abu Simbel. Pharaohs and queens presided over an elaborate bureaucracy that divided the administration of the growing empire into various departments. So great was their wealth and prestige that even minor rulers, such as Tutankhamun, were immortalized at death in the many inscriptions and lavishly opulent art that accompanied their mummified bodies to the grave.

> ■ **FOOTNOTE** Queen Hatshepsut reigned for 22 years as pharaoh of the 18th dynasty of ancient Egypt. She oversaw mammoth building projects of temples and expanded Egypt's trade networks to foreign lands, bringing back new luxuries.

North American Urban Center

62 ca **1500** B.C.E. The first known urban center in North America, known as Poverty Point, was located along the Mississippi River in modern-day Louisiana. It was occupied beginning around 1500 B.C.E. by hunter-gatherers who constructed a complex of earthworks organized into six concentric semicircles surrounding a broad, flat plaza. Each semicircle consisted of four ridges, rising more than 20 feet high and capped by some 600 houses altogether. A 70-foot mound on the outer edge of the complex is perhaps evidence of Poverty Point's importance as the major ceremonial center of the area, though the mound's exact function is still speculative. The precedent established by Poverty Point of urban centers and ceremonial monuments built of earthen mounds would be continued in eastern North America over the next 2,000 years.

Minoan Civilization Ends

63 ca **1450** B.C.E. The demise of Minoan civilization on Crete came at the hands of the Mycenaeans of mainland Greece, a group of people that became in many respects the Minoans' cultural successors. Though they had been trading partners for as many as 150 years, a group of Mycenaeans invaded Minoan Crete around 1450 B.C.E., burning their towns to the ground, ransacking their palaces, and possibly even enslaving their artisans and engineers. Soon afterward, rough-hewn stone fortresses employing Minoan building techniques began to appear on the Greek mainland, complete with wall paintings of a Minoan style. Back on Crete, the Minoans' script was commandeered to produce what may be the first written form of ancient Greek, a language known as Linear B. The Mycenaeans also took over the Minoans' trade routes, establishing outposts on a number of Aegean Islands and in western Anatolia.

Iron Metallurgy Developed

64 **1400 B.C.E.** The development of iron metallurgy is a watershed event that effected widespread changes in farming, warfare, migratory trends, and daily life. Though cast iron had been produced in Asia Minor as far back as 2000 B.C.E., it

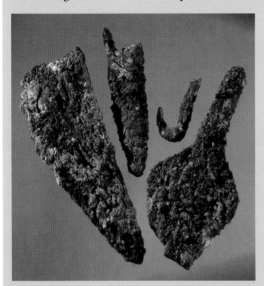

Four iron fishing implements (one hook and three spearheads) found at a dig site in Djenné, Mali.

was not until around 1400 B.C.E. that the Hittites refined the process that created wrought iron, a strong, durable material that could be made on a large scale for a number of uses.

When the Hittite Empire collapsed in the 12th century B.C.E., Hittite craftsmen dispersed, spreading iron metallurgy throughout the Middle East and inaugurating what is known as the Iron Age. The technology radiated to Europe and India by 1000 B.C.E., arose independently in Africa by 900 B.C.E., and diffused to China around 700 B.C.E.

Naturally abundant and readily available, iron brought about tremendous transitions wherever it traveled. It made the war chariot obsolete in the Middle East by equipping infantry forces with stronger weapons; not until the invention of gunpowder did weaponry change in significant ways. It also allowed migratory groups to expand in Europe, Africa, and India since new land could be cleared for agriculture far more rapidly, producing a surplus that stimulated population growth, and it revolutionized farming along with the entire social order in China, where previously the masses of agriculturalists had toiled with stone, wood, and bone tools. The widespread effects of this technological breakthrough reverberate throughout the world to this day.

With the onset of this period, called Iron Age, begins the final technical and cultural stage in the Stone-Bronze-Iron Age sequence of historical dating.

Later Greek writers would preserve the legends of the warfaring Mycenaeans in some of the world's best-known epic poetry, *The Iliad* and *The Odyssey*.

The explanation of the Minoans' demise is still controversial. Many archaeologists maintain that a cataclysmic volcanic eruption in about that same period, which destroyed the Minoan island of Thíra, may have led to the civilization's collapse. The eruption rained ash and debris in a wide swath to Crete and surrounding shores. Merchant vessels of this seafaring power would have been destroyed by tsunami-like

waves, crippling a key economy. Ensuing climate change—a volcanic winter caused by particles ejected into the atmosphere—would have affected crops severely.

No palace complexes have been found, as on Crete, but excavations on Thíra show remnants of a major Minoan settlement at Akrotiri, with three-story-high structures, wide streets and squares, and a drainage system. Noted for its colorful frescoes and pottery, Akrotiri shows all the signs of a sophisticated culture. Script called Linear A—the forerunner of Linear B—is incised on pottery and clay tablets. It has not yet

been fully translated, but it shares many symbols with Linear B.

■ FOOTNOTE The Bronze Age town of Akrotiri was buried in ash from the volcano, causing its preservation and making it one of the most important archaeological sites in the Aegean. Of particular interest are its frescoes.

Vedas Composed

65 **ca 1400 B.C.E.** The Vedas, ancient Indian compilations of hymns, prayers, and rituals, are among the world's earliest sacred scriptures and possess such historical import that they lend their name to the time period, the Vedic Age of India. Composed in archaic Sanskrit beginning around 1400 B.C.E., they are the product of the migratory Indo-European Aryans, who entered India only about 100 years earlier. The Vedas were orally transmitted and expanded upon for almost a thousand years before taking their final form in writing. The oldest is the Rig Veda, which means "wisdom of the verses" and consists of 1,028 hymns addressed to various deities of the Aryan canon. Thousands of these deities personify natural and cosmic forces, such as Indra, associated with war, rain, and creation; Agni, associated with fire; Vishnu, associated with the sun; and Soma, associated with a hallucinogenic substance of unknown origin. Vedic religion gradually evolved into Hinduism, which still reveres the Vedas as sacred texts, parts of which are memorized and recited to this day.

Exodus From Egypt

66 **ca 1300 B.C.E.** The exodus of the Hebrews out of Egypt around 1300 B.C.E., led by the legendary political and military leader, Moses, has become one of the most storied allegories of the western world, preserved in the Book of Exodus in the Old Testament. Following oppressive measures and probable enslavement under the pharaoh Ramses II, Moses led the Hebrews across the Sea of Reeds and into the Sinai Peninsula, where he is said to have issued a moral code of law known as the Ten Commandments. With an early form of monotheism as its foremost edict,

67 | *A sailor tugs at a sail on a replica of a Phoenician boat in the harbor at Tyre, Lebanon.*

Moses' commandments set the framework of the religion that would be known as Judaism. Moses then led the Hebrews north through conquest and, following his death, the Hebrews continued into Canaan, where they carved out a territory by overpowering established settlements. Though certainly not the first monotheist, Moses was one of the single most influential, revered as a prophet by three of the most widespread religions in the world, Judaism, Christianity, and Islam.

Phoenicians Emerge

67 **ca 1200 B.C.E.** The Phoenicians emerged as a colonial and commercial power in the Mediterranean beginning around 1200 B.C.E. Though they had been settled in modern-day Lebanon and actively trading for almost 2,000 years, they had intermittently been subjected to imperial rule by Mesopotamians, Egyptians, and Hittites. As the sway of these empires decayed and Cretan shipping routes collapsed, sturdily built Phoenician cargo ships became the preeminent vessels of commerce and trade throughout the Mediterranean and beyond. Phoenician merchants exported cedar and pine wood, dyed cloth, glass, metalwork, wine, and

fish for any number of raw goods. With an advanced and carefully guarded knowledge of the stars, winds, and currents, Phoenician seafarers established commercial colonies in Cyprus, Greece, Italy, Spain, and North Africa. Beyond the Mediterranean, Phoenician merchants visited ports in Portugal, France, and even the British Isles. They also ventured south along the coast of Africa, rounding the whole of West Africa and perhaps farther more than 2,000 years before later European explorers.

■ **FOOTNOTE** Called Phoenicians by the Greeks, from the word "phoenix" for purple, because of their purple cloaks, the seafaring traders benefited from a rare dye, obtained from Murex snails, that became a sought-after commodity.

Olmec Society Builds

68 **ca 1200 B.C.E.** The Olmec society of Mesoamerica, evident by around 1200 B.C.E. in the humid lowlands along the Gulf Coast of southern Mexico, marks the first civilization in Central America characterized by extensive material and architectural remains through which scholars can piece together a relatively clear picture of their cultural traditions and political structure. Within a stratified, nonegalitarian social order, Olmec elites

Moses

EXODUS 24:12

The Lord said to Moses, "Cut two tablets of stone like the former ones, and I will write on the tablets the words that were on the former tablets, which you broke. Be ready in the morning, and come up to Mount Sinai and present yourself there to me, on the top of the mountain. No one shall come up with you, and do not let anyone be seen throughout all the mountain; and do not let flocks or herds graze in front of that mountain."

So Moses cut two tablets of stone like the former ones; and he rose early in the morning and went up on Mount Sinai, as the Lord had commanded him, and took in his hand the two tablets of stone. The Lord descended in the cloud and stood with him there, and proclaimed the name, "The Lord." The Lord passed before him, and proclaimed, "The Lord, the Lord, a God merciful and gracious, slow to anger, and abounding in steadfast love and faithfulness, keeping steadfast love for the thousandth generation, forgiving iniquity and transgression and sin, yet by no means clearing the guilty, but visiting the iniquity of the parents upon the children and the children's children, to the third and the fourth generation."

And Moses quickly bowed his head toward the earth, and worshipped. He said, "If now I have found favor in your sight, O Lord, I pray, let the Lord go with us. Although this is a stiff-necked people, pardon our iniquity and our sin, and take us for your inheritance."

He said: I hereby make a covenant...

66 | *Fragments of spinning pots used to turn flax fiber into thread in ancient Israel.*

commissioned thousands of laborers to construct elaborate monumental temples, pyramids, and altars dedicated to a pantheon of animalistic gods. Ceremonial centers were built up and flanked by large-scale drainage ravines. Giant basalt boulders were quarried, transported, and hewn into imposing ten-ton busts, artistry that was re-created on a smaller scale with stone, wood, and ceramic figurines. A calendar and the Americas' first known glyphs were developed. Knowledge of these technical and intellectual achievements were exported along with manufactured goods through an extensive trade network that influenced groups of people throughout Mesoamerica at that time and for millennia to come.

Zhou Dynasty Rules

69 ca 1027 B.C.E. The Zhou dynasty of China rose to power around 1027 B.C.E. and presided over dramatic transitions in Chinese culture for 250 years. Foremost among them was a reexamined relationship between gods and humans that, for example, depended less on entreaties for rain and more on large-scale methods of irrigation. The Zhou dynasty established a theory of imperial succession that was based not on divine right, but on divine mandate. This "Mandate of Heaven" was retained if the virtuous performance of a ruler, the "Son of Heaven," effected stability within the land and harmony in the cosmos, but could be revoked if a ruler's actions led to social or political disunity and cosmic imbalance. The Mandate of Heaven was continually invoked by Chinese kings and emperors all the way up until the dissolution of China's final ruling line, the Qing dynasty, in 1912.

■ **FOOTNOTE** During the rule of the Zhou dynasty, the philosophers Confucius, founder of Confucianism, and Laozi, founder of Daoism, developed their views, influencing future generations to this day.

Kingdom of Israel Established

70 1021 B.C.E. The kingdom of Israel was established around 1021

72 | *A Bantu woman burns brush to clear a garden in the Democratic Republic of the Congo.*

B.C.E. with Saul as its first king. Defeated and slain in battle, Saul was succeeded by David, who set up his capital at Jerusalem, a newly conquered Canaanite city, and then by Solomon, who erected the first temple in Jerusalem, among a number of other building projects. Solomon transformed Israel's economy, setting up networks of trade and commerce throughout North Africa and the Middle East. Around this time, a Hebrew alphabet was derived from Phoenician neighbors to the north and the earliest writings of the Torah were set down by Israel's scribes, codifying the growing canon of Jewish law and elaborating on moral teachings that had been passed down orally for centuries. A unified kingdom of Israel was short-lived though and was ultimately dissolved by repeated Mesopotamian conquests.

Caste System Established

71 ca 1000 B.C.E. The origins of the caste system in India are rooted in the social developments and interactions that occurred following the entry of Indo-European Aryans into an area already inhabited by an ethnic group known as Dravidians, to which the previous Harappan society had belonged. The Aryans did not organize themselves into states or empires, but rather ordered their society by hereditary distinctions based on occupation. By about 1000 B.C.E., various occupations were grouped into four main *varnas,* Sanskrit for both "class" and "color," suggesting that early class distinctions were based on the lighter-skinned complexion of the Aryans compared to the Dravidians. These four varnas, in order of perceived religious purity, were priests; warriors and nobility; farmers, artisans, and merchants; and peasants, serfs, and slaves; followed some centuries later by untouchables, who performed such tasks as cleaning sewage and handling dead bodies. Within the caste system, strict guidelines applied to matters of daily life. One could only marry, care for, work with, and even eat with members of one's own varna. Interaction between varnas was dictated by meticulous rules that, if broken, could result in expulsion from society at large. The system was further complicated by the development around 600 B.C.E. of subcastes, known as *jatis,* or "births." Today nearly 3,000 jatis exist in Hindu society, and though they are now largely divorced from matters of economic or political status, they continue to influence the daily lives of millions of people throughout southern Asia.

Bantu People Migrate

72 **ca 900 B.C.E.** The migrations of Bantu-speaking people of eastern West Africa profoundly altered the ways of life of countless millions of inhabitants of sub-Saharan Africa, as well as the landscape of all the lands in which they lived. Though pockets of Bantu people had been slowly spreading out on a small scale as early as 3000 B.C.E., the pace and extent of these migrations increased exponentially following the development of iron metallurgy in Africa around 900 B.C.E. With the Bantu went their language, their iron technology, and their means of subsistence, namely agriculture and herding. Two major waves of Bantu migration after 500 B.C.E. traveled southward roughly along either coast of the continent, encountering hunter-gatherer groups as they went. Though some of these groups maintained their traditional ways of life, some began peaceably trading with the new immigrants, some had their land claimed by force of superior weapons, and many were absorbed into growing agricultural societies. Even genetic factors, such as the ability to digest milk, were spread by intermarriage with the Bantu. By 1000 C.E., Bantu chiefdoms could be found throughout southern Africa, where agriculture and herding were practiced in all but the densest forests and driest deserts.

Chavín Unites South America

73 **850 B.C.E.** The Chavín cult and its ceremonial complex of Chavín de Huántar, constructed in the Andean highlands of modern-day Peru beginning around 850 B.C.E., served as one of the first culturally unifying forces in South American history. Though never the center of any political import, Chavín de Huántar was a pilgrimage site to which farmers would travel great distances to leave offerings for a successful harvest. Built up over the course of 500 years, its attendant community spanned 105 acres at its peak. The artistic style employed at Chavín de Huántar,

---

CONNECTIONS

Social Stratification
The historical precedents for knowing one's place

Even in a small unit like the nuclear family, humans assign labels to group members. Such titles are a uniquely human way of organizing social relationships and denoting an individual's position within a group. In many civilizations throughout history, rank has been the determining factor in a person's professional, geographical, and marital opportunities—or lack thereof.

During the Old World's Neolithic period, as nomadic bands settled into permanent farming communities about 9000 B.C.E., social stratification increased in complexity. Early agrarian economies naturally featured a majority of farmers, with a few leaders who oversaw land distribution and settled disputes. By the time of ancient Egypt's Old and Middle Kingdoms (2575-1630 B.C.E.), kings were the primary landowners. The bulk of the people worked royal lands, not slaves but also not free to leave their plots. Efficient irrigation practices provided food surpluses, freeing peasants to be claimed for the king's huge pyramid-building labor forces. Women claimed relatively equal social status, with the rights to own property and initiate divorce. Small artisan classes, scribes, and priests had specialized duties.

Egypt's agrarian social system has had many corollaries throughout history, including in the Roman Empire, feudal Europe, ancient China, the Maya civilization, and the Inca Empire. Urban areas naturally developed their own social classes ranked by professions, which were often inherited. In addition, large religious institutions such as the Roman Catholic Church developed complex rankings for clergy, from the novice monk to the pope, who sits just under Jesus and God in his authority.

Humans have developed elaborate rituals to publicly solidify changes in social rank. Among indigenous tribes of America's Pacific Northwest, a person whose rank increased invited people to a potlatch, in which the host gave his own possessions and property to his guests, thus confirming his new social position outwardly. The southern Kwakiutl people developed the most elaborate potlatch rituals in the 19th century, including ceremonial dances and songs that became transferable gifts.

The world's rapidly globalizing economy is offering opportunities to lower classes, especially in India, where the caste system has defined lives for 3,000 years. International companies have been recruiting Dalits and others, offering them a path out of demeaning careers. India's government has long followed an affirmative-action program for oppressed castes, but with the private sector getting involved too, today many families are rising from poverty for the first time in millennia.

Indian Dalits clean laundry in a river near Delhi.

featuring feathered serpents and other mythological creatures seen in stone carvings, textiles, pottery, and goldwork, appeared contemporaneously at sites from the northern highlands to the southern coast of Peru. The craftsmen and architects that poured their skills into elaborating this unprecedented ceremonial complex ushered in a new age of artistic expression that was uniquely South American.

I Ching Compiled

74 ca 800 B.C.E. The I Ching, or Book of Changes, is the oldest classic of Chinese literature and one of the world's earliest intact books. Compiled sometime before 800 B.C.E. as a manual of divination, it serves as a philosophical treatise on the interaction between what can and cannot be controlled. The book consists of the presentation and interpretation of 64 sets of hexagrams, stacked arrangements of six solid or bisected lines. Each hexagram is divided into two trigrams, which individually represent various

77 | *Discus thrower in ancient Greece.*

natural, cosmic, and elemental forces. Themes that continually occur in the interpretations of the hexagrams include the immutable nature of change and the dynamic balance of opposites, drawing on the ancient principles of the yin and the yang. Influencing both Confucianist and Taoist thought, the I Ching figures prominently in the history of Chinese philosophy and, once translated in the 19th century, has influenced thinkers as varied as Carl Jung and Allen Ginsberg.

■ FOOTNOTE The I Ching, composed during the Zhou dynasty, was written using tens of thousands of Chinese characters to form symbols called logographs. The modern language requires a basic knowledge of 2,000 characters.

Upanishads Begun

75 ca 800 B.C.E. The Upanishads constitute a seminal body of work in the development of Vedic religion as it incorporated aspects of Dravidian beliefs and gradually gave way to Hinduism. The Upanishads were begun in earnest around 800 B.C.E. and represent the philosophical musings of a succession of Indian sages. Translated literally as "sitting in front of," the Upanishads often took the form of dialogues that reflected and speculated on the teachings of the Vedas. A number of ideas that would become integral to Hindu theology and mysticism were expounded in the Upanishads. These include concepts such as reincarnation, karma, meditative yoga, asceticism, vegetarianism, and the one universal soul, known as Brahman. Composed at a time of considerable social upheaval, the Upanishads preached a denouncement of wealth and material preoccupations when trade and economic prosperity were bringing just those things into the Ganges River Valley. Over the course of thousands of years of interpretation and elaboration, the Upanishads' impact on Indian moral and ethical values has been immensely profound.

Celts Appear

76 ca 800 B.C.E. The Celts—tribal agricultural communities that

78 | *Trajan's army battles the Dacian people in a frieze on Trajan's Column in Rome, Italy.*

shared a common religion, artistic style, and language—first appeared around 800 B.C.E. in modern-day Austria. The early group, known as the Hallstatt culture, excelled in the manufacture of ornate metalwork of bronze, gold, silver, and iron, decorated with abstract curvilinear motifs. The Celts were some of the first Europeans to develop iron metallurgy, and so were able to expand across the continent through the use of superior weapons and reliable transportation. Their settlements eventually spread from the British Isles to Asia Minor and formed the ethnicities known as the Gauls, Gaels, Galatians, and Britons. Their religion spread with them, a polytheistic naturalism administered by the druids, a word which means "knowing the oak tree." Though the incursions of the Roman Empire in the first century B.C.E. forced Celtic culture into isolated pockets of western Europe, the legacy of its traditions remains intact to this day.

First Olympic Games Held

77 **776 B.C.E.** The world's first Olympic Games, held in Olympia, Greece, in 776 B.C.E., heralded not only the beginning of an athletic tradition still enjoyed to this day, but also the reemergence of Greece in Mediterranean affairs, since it had remained mostly isolated following the mysterious demise of Mycenaean society 300 years previous. The first Olympic Games were held between city-states, or poleis, institutions that were only just becoming urban centers of commerce and politics within Greek society. The Greeks did not stay confined to city-states for long though, as population pressures and advances in shipbuilding urged them seaward to found colonies throughout the Mediterranean and the Black Sea. Greek colonists spread their language, culture, art, architecture, religion, and even diet to all the port cities they founded. Through increased communication and trade, the Greek colonies also quickened the pace of

life in many areas that had previously hosted only small agricultural communities, making the Mediterranean world better connected than ever before.

Rome Founded

78 **753 B.C.E.** The founding of Rome on the Tiber River is traditionally ascribed to 753 B.C.E., a date that owes more to legend than history. Around this time, the main sphere of influence on the Italian peninsula belonged to the Etruscans to the north. Aided by the mineral resources of iron, tin, copper, and silver that abounded in their land, the Etruscans were the first materially advanced culture in Italy. They built cities that engaged in long-distance trade, art, and festivals when Rome was little more than a farm village. In fact, from 616 to 509 B.C.E. Rome was ruled by a dynasty of Etruscan kings, who introduced such public works as improved streets, sewers, defensive walls, large-scale temples, and a stadium. Subsequent Roman culture owed a great deal to the Etruscans, from whom they borrowed such classically Roman traditions as gladiatorial matches, triumphal processions, the toga, and even the fasces, Rome's insignia of political authority.

> **FOOTNOTE** Legend has it that twins Romulus and Remus, royal descendants of a Trojan War hero, were abandoned on the banks of the Tiber River and suckled by a wolf. As young men they founded the city of Rome on those shores.

Greek Epics Written

79 **ca 750 B.C.E.** *The Iliad* and *The Odyssey,* the two great epics of ancient Greek literature and the earliest known examples of European poetry, are traditionally credited to the blind poet, Homer, who may have lived sometime around 750 B.C.E. Though Homer could have been a historical figure who played a prominent part in the final codification of these two works, they originally belong to a tradition of oral poetry and were likely passed down, developed, and elaborated upon by a score of Greek bards stretching back into Mycenaean times. In Homer's

FIRST PERSON

Homer

THE ODYSSEY, CA 750 B.C.E.

I am Odysseus, son of Laertes, who am known among men for all manner of wiles, and my fame reaches unto heaven. But I dwell in clear-seen Ithaca, wherein is a mountain, Neriton, covered with waving forests, conspicuous from afar; and round it lie many isles hard by one another, Dulichium, and Same, and wooded Zacynthus. Ithaca itself lies close in to the mainland the furthest toward the gloom, but the others lie apart toward the Dawn and the sun—a rugged isle, but a good nurse of young men; and for myself no other thing can I see sweeter than one's own land.... So true is it that naught is sweeter than a man's own land and his parents, even though it be in a rich house that he dwells afar in a foreign land away from his parents....

Let me tell thee also of my woeful homecoming, which Zeus laid upon me as I came from Troy. From Ilios the wind bore me and brought me to the Cicones, to Ismarus. There I sacked the city and slew the men; and from the city we took their wives and great store of treasure, and divided them among us, that so far as lay in me no man might go defrauded of an equal share. Then verily I gave command that we should flee with swift foot, ... but against our ships Zeus, the cloud-gatherer, roused the north wind with a wondrous tempest, and hid with clouds the land and the sea alike, and night rushed down from heaven.

79 | *Roman mosaic of Odysseus lashed to a ship's mast.*

Writing System Produced

80 **700 B.C.E.** The earliest known, fully attestable example of a complex writing system in the Americas was produced in the Zapotec capital of Monte Albán, founded in the Oaxaca region of Mexico around 700 B.C.E. Carved onto a public monolithic stele and other monuments, in an extended glyphic script, the texts seem to record the names of rulers and their deeds, indicating the state-sponsored origins of writing in Mesoamerica. The writing is considered the basis of other Mesoamerican scripts developed by the Maya, Mixtec, and Aztec. This system developed wholly independently, but the script has not yet been deciphered. Zapotec is a language of a large subfamily, including possibly some 40 variants still spoken in the states of Oaxaca and Veracruz.

Stelae containing glyphs in the ruins of Monte Albán, center of the Zapotec civilization.

Monte Albán was the first major city in the Western Hemisphere with monumental structures along its central axis and around its periphery, interspersed with great plazas and ball courts. About 170 tombs, the most elaborate uncovered in the Americas, appear to be single burials for the elite, decorated with stone carvings and frescoes.

The Zapotec were technically advanced in more ways than one: An astronomical observatory aided in the formation of a well-developed calendrical system, ornate ceramic urns were produced from molds in assembly-line fashion, and wares were traded in a large regional marketplace. Due to these and other innovations, Monte Albán was a bustling center of Mesoamerican culture and commerce for more than a thousand years.

day, the Greek world had just recently adopted a written alphabet from the Phoenicians, and it was no coincidence that *The Iliad* and *The Odyssey* were among the first Greek works to be committed to writing. In their pages, these epics recount heroic deeds and tragic events, but they also explore moral, ethical, and psychological themes with remarkable subtlety and finesse. Based on quasi-historical events, they also record a way of life that was not far removed from that of Greek society in the eighth century B.C.E. Forming the basis of much of Greek culture, literature, and education, these two epics have continually been mined for inspiration by Greek, Roman, Byzantine, Renaissance, and modern writers. Their impact on western literature on a whole can hardly be underestimated.

FOOTNOTE The Homeric poems, although set in mythical times, infer real historical events as background. In modern times, archaeologists have searched for and excavated likely sites pointing to Troy, Knossos, and Mycenae.

Chu Defense System Built

81 **656 B.C.E.** The Chu state, one of several regional states that emerged in China following the dissolution of the Zhou dynasty's central authority, began to construct a permanent, contiguous defensive system known as the Square Wall around 656 B.C.E. This first earth-and-stone fortification was followed by several more, built by various states throughout China over the next few centuries. This flurry of wall-building was the product of attempts by rulers to defend their territories from neighboring states as well as from nomadic horsemen from the northern steppes of Asia. With few horses and unreliable armies, regional Chinese states depended primarily on these walls to combat tribes of swift, fierce nomads who did not recognize political boundaries. Though most have long since tumbled, remnants of some of these early Chinese walls still stand, having been incorporated into the longest and youngest of their kind, the Great Wall of China.

First True Coins Struck

82 **ca 650 B.C.E.** The first true coinage was struck by the kingdom of Lydia, located in western Anatolia along the gold-bearing Pactolus River, around 650 B.C.E. Previous metal currencies in the form of gold bars, copper ingots, lumps of bronze, or even small farming implements had existed in various reaches of the globe for millennia, but the Lydians were the first to stamp their small, bean-shaped pieces of a gold-and-silver alloy, known as electrum, with a visible insignia of the issuing authority, guaranteeing them an established value and making them the world's first true coins. The Lydians' trading partners, the Greeks, quickly recognized the advantages of this practice and were minting silver coins at colonies throughout the Mediterranean by the close of the sixth century. Persia, India, and China soon followed suit as well, establishing precious metals as the accepted measure of value across Eurasia and inaugurating a new era in trade relations.

Assyrian Empire Falls

83 **612 B.C.E.** The Assyrian Empire of Mesopotamia toppled in 612 B.C.E. in large part due to the sacking of their capital city, Nineveh, by a coalition of nomadic tribal horsemen, collectively known as the Scythians. The vacuum of power created by their immediate withdrawal would be filled by Nebuchadrezzar and the Babylonians, but this was of little concern to the Scythians, who had taken their fill of war booty and returned to their kingdoms on the western steppes in modern-day Ukraine and Russia. They had been loosely settled there for upwards of a century, but as seminomadic herders, built few urban centers or permanent structures except for kurgans, the burial mounds of their elite. The Scythians were expert metallurgists, and their kurgans were filled with elaborately worked jewelry and ornaments of gold and other precious materials. Highly skilled in combat, the Scythians remained a constant threat to established Asian empires for nearly 500 years.

■ **FOOTNOTE** Greek historian Herodotus distinguished between the Scythians from Scythia Minor in modern-day Romania and Bulgaria and the Greater Scythians from the area of a 21-day ride east from the Danube to the Don River.

Zoroastrianism, Jainism Born

84 ca 600 B.C.E. Numerous religious and philosophical sects were born out of the reflections of charismatic figures who lived in the increasingly cosmopolitan societies of the centuries before and after 600 B.C.E. Among those that influenced more widely practiced later religions were Zoroastrianism in Persia and Jainism in India. Zoroastrianism embraced the trappings and pleasures of the material world, enjoyed in moderation; Jainism sharply rejected earthly concerns, favoring instead a doctrine of rigorous asceticism. Though many of their basic tenets were distinctly opposed, Zoroastrianism and Jainism both represent a turning away from the anachronistic rituals of their ancestor religions. Both are also said to have been proclaimed by men born into wealthy families, only to renounce their upbringing and embark on years of reflective wandering. The respective faiths of Zarathustra and Vardhamana Mahavira are today observed only by pockets of adherents in Iran and India, though aspects of their moralistic teachings resound through all five of the world's major religions.

Adena Mound Tradition

85 ca 600 B.C.E. The Adena culture, centered around the Ohio River Valley of eastern North America, began to construct conical burial mounds in which to inter their elite by around 600 B.C.E. Many of these complex burial sites were adorned with elaborate grave goods such as carved pipestone from modern-day Ohio, copper ornaments from the Great Lakes region, mica effigies from the southern Appalachians, and marine shells from coastal areas, evidence of the Adena's extensive network of trade. The Adena eventually gave way to the Hopewell, who extended their trade network from the Rocky Mountains to the Atlantic and from Canada to the Gulf Coast. They also elaborated the mound tradition into ceremonial complexes replete with geometrically precise enclosures spanning more than 1,000 acres and avenues stretching perhaps as many as 60 miles. Within centuries of their emergence, the enigmatic mounds of the Adena and Hopewell dotted the landscape over much of North America's eastern woodlands.

Athenian Seeds of Democracy

86 500s B.C.E. The roots of modern democracy are attributed to fifth-century-B.C.E. Athens, due largely to the legislation of two sixth-century-B.C.E. reformers, Solon and Cleisthenes. In an age characterized by tyrants and powerful landowners whose fields were worked by farmers pushed into serfdom by debt, the Athenian statesman Solon sought to avoid civil war by issuing a code of laws that absolved debt, prohibited enslavement for debt, and returned forfeited lands. He set up a sovereign body called the Council of 400, which ran weekly governing assemblies that any Athenian man could attend. Cleisthenes went even further by denoting a man 'Athenian' based on place of birth rather than hereditary tribe and establishing the Council as a representative body. Though Athens was still not a true democracy—the Council only represented about 15 percent of the Athenian populace, with women, immigrants, and slaves given no voice—it was certainly a step closer than tyrannical rule by a small group of aristocrats.

84 | *Visitors explore the Ellora caves in western India, which house five Jain temples.*

Achaemenid Dynasty Rules

87   **539 B.C.E.** When Cyrus the Great of Persia and his Achaemenid army overthrew Babylon in the summer of 539 B.C.E., the Persians became heirs to an empire that at its height would extend across three continents and stretch 2,600 miles end to end. It was the largest empire the world had yet seen. Cyrus was known as a respected and tolerant ruler, who did not impose Persian mores on his subjects, but acknowledged eclectic cultural traditions and religious freedom, even liberating the Jews held captive in Babylon. He divided the empire into 20 provinces called satrapies and put natives in command. His successors improved roads, including the 1,600-mile Royal Road between Lydia in western Turkey to the capitals of Susa and Persepolis in Persia that held 111 courier stations, constituting an early governmental postal system. The Achaemenids also expanded a system of underground canals, called qanats, for irrigation; issued coinage; and standardized laws and taxes; but also ruled over an empire with an extreme gap between rich and poor. In the quest for further conquest, Persia attempted to invade Greece twice in the fifth century B.C.E. Under Xerxes, Persia began to threaten Greece again, but was defeated by the army of Alexander the Great in 330 B.C.E. The Achaemenids were succeeded by the Seleucids—generals of Alexander. And Persia continued to expand and occupy much of western Asia for most of the next millennium, overseeing a multicultural economy that connected the worlds of Europe, Africa, India, and China.

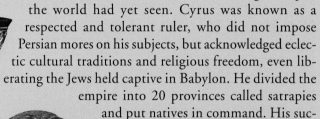

Gold rhyton, or drinking cup, in the shape of a winged lion, a hallmark of Achaemenid rule.

Buddha Is Born

88   **528 B.C.E.** Siddhartha Gautama began his public ministry in northern India in 528 B.C.E. with a sermon dubbed the "Turning of the Wheel of the Law." Like Zarathustra and Mahavira, Gautama is said to have been born into a prominent family, which he renounced to live as a mendicant and an ascetic in his search for an explanation of suffering. After six years of wandering, Gautama, unsatisfied with what he had learned from others, sat alone for 49 days under a bo tree, where he became the Buddha, or "enlightened one." He immediately set out to share his insights: the Four Noble Truths and the Noble Eightfold Path. These doctrines, or dharma, promulgated the middle way, that a moderate, reflective, disciplined lifestyle would eventually lead to detachment from material desires, liberation from the cycle of rebirth, and attainment of spiritual enlightenment, or nirvana. Though the Buddha never traveled more than 150 miles from his birthplace, later adherents, kings and emperors among them, would spread his teachings throughout the world.

Pythagorean School Founded

89   **525 B.C.E.** Pythagoras of Samos, Greek philosopher and pseudo-mathematician, migrated sometime around 525 B.C.E. to Croton in southern Italy, where he founded an academy that espoused the principles of rationalism, which in Pythagoras's case held that all natural phenomena, including the essence of reality, could be explained through the metaphysics of numbers. Though the many innovations attributed to Pythagoras are likely embellishments of later Pythagoreans, the philosophical school of thought that he founded did produce a number of thinkers who contributed to the burgeoning fields of arithmetic, geometry, music theory, and astronomy. Certain Pythagoreans even challenged long-held notions by claiming that the Earth is a sphere and is not the center of the universe over a millennium before Copernicus and Galileo made the same assertions. The Pythagorean worldview pervaded much of Greek intellectual culture and influenced several non-Pythagorean scholars such as Hippocrates, Plato, and Aristotle. Modern rationalist philosophies continued to draw on these sources well into the 20th century.

> ■ **FOOTNOTE** Pythagoras is best known for the theorem named after him, although it was already known to the Babylonians: "The square of the length of the hypotenuse of a right triangle is equal to the sum of the squares of the legs."

Roman Republic Founded

90   **509 B.C.E.** The Roman Republic was founded in 509 B.C.E. following the overthrow of the last Etruscan king of Rome. In the wake of the deposed monarchy, Roman aristocrats, known as patricians, instituted a system of government divided between two annually appointed consuls, who wielded civil and military authority, and a senate, which oversaw and ratified the decisions of the consuls. Since the consuls and senate only represented the interests of Rome's upper classes, there was almost immediate tension between the patricians and Rome's working classes, known collectively as plebeians. This tension came to a head following a grain shortage that resulted in the establishment of a tribunate to protect the

90 | *Corinthian columns continue to support remains of the Roman Forum.*

throughout the Yucatán Peninsula and its hinterlands, initiating cultural traditions that persist in the area to this day.

■ **FOOTNOTE** The Maya refined a rudimentary script into a complex arrangement of 800 pictorial and phonetic hieroglyphs and developed a numerical system of dots and bars. They recorded their history, and a calendar, in stone.

Greco-Persian Wars

93 | **492 B.C.E.** The Greco-Persian Wars, which raged intermittently for over 150 years beginning in 492 B.C.E., were a turning point in European-Asian relations that contributed to the downfall of the Achaemenid Empire. Years of sparring ended in August 480 B.C.E., when a massive Persian force met with the greatly outnumbered Greeks at the battles of Thermopylae and Artemisium. At the narrow pass of Thermopylae, about 7,000 Greeks under the command of the Spartan Leonidas held off the Persians for two days while a Greek fleet of 350 vessels wrestled with a Persian navy three times its size. Sabotaged by a Greek traitor on the second night of their stand, Leonidas dispatched most of his men to safety. About 1,500 troops all fought to the death the next day. Though the Persians were victorious, they suffered enough casualties that they were defeated multiple times by outnumbered forces of

interests of the plebeians and the codification of Rome's first written set of laws, the Law of the Twelve Tables. Rome then went on the offensive, carving out a large state that would eventually encompass much of the Mediterranean coast. Class disputes at home though would continue to plague the overcrowded city for the duration of the Roman Republic.

Nok Culture

91 | **ca 500 B.C.E.** The Nok culture of modern-day Nigeria was seminal in two distinct, but not altogether unrelated, material advances in sub-Saharan Africa, iron metallurgy and terra-cotta sculpture. By at least 500 B.C.E., ironworking had followed trade routes into the Niger River Valley of West Africa, where the Nok were smelting iron ore in shallow pit-furnaces with cylindrical clay walls. Within these furnaces the Nok manufactured knives, axes, and hoes, which enabled them to clear the tropical forest more efficiently, expanding the amount of land available for agriculture and leading to large-scale population growth. By firing clay in their furnaces, the Nok created

sub-Saharan Africa's earliest known terra-cotta sculptures, stylized human effigies with exaggerated features, elaborate hairstyles, and abstract geometrical treatments. The Nok's unique style of art is exceptionally preserved and provides testimony to the independent mastery of ceramic manufacture in sub-Saharan Africa.

Maya Society Evolves

92 | **ca 500 B.C.E.** Maya communities of the highlands and Petén region of modern-day Guatemala, such as Kaminaljuyú and Nakbe, having been settled into simple agricultural villages for centuries, began around 500 B.C.E. to radically transform their settlements with the construction of large limestone temple-pyramids, ceremonial plazas, and royal tombs. This shift in architecture brought with it a shift in social organization, moving from the more or less egalitarian quality of farming life to the hierarchical quality of autocratic city-state life. What exactly triggered this transition is still speculative, but it was certainly not isolated. Distinctively Maya art, architecture, and technology soon appeared in growing settlements

92 | *Maya god of maize.*

Greeks in the months to follow. The Delian league, a coalition of Greek city-states with Athens at its head, was founded in 478 B.C.E. to combat the Persians on their own soil, an endeavor soon to be soundly realized by Alexander the Great.

Confucius Preserves Teachings

94 *ca 479* B.C.E. Chinese statesman and philosopher Confucius died in 479 B.C.E. following an uneventful and disappointing political career. Confucius's philosophy, which exhorted rulers to lead through moral authority rather than force of arms, fell mostly on deaf ears in a political climate of turmoil and confusion, soon to devolve into the Period of the Warring States. Confucius did however succeed in amassing a number of disciples who would go on to preserve his

94 | *Statesman and philosopher Confucius's teachings were more influential after his death than in his life.*

FIRST PERSON

Confucius

THE ANALECTS, ca 500 B.C.E.

The Master said, "He who exercises government by means of his virtue may be compared to the north polar star, which keeps its place and all the stars turn towards it."

The Master said, "In the Book of Poetry are three hundred pieces, but the design of them all may be embraced in one sentence: "Having no depraved thoughts.""

The Master said, "If the people be led by laws, and uniformity sought to be given them by punishments, they will try to avoid the punishment, but have no sense of shame. If they be led by virtue, and uniformity sought to be given them by the rules of propriety, they will have the sense of shame, and moreover will become good."

The Master said, "At fifteen, I had my mind bent on learning. At thirty, I stood firm. At forty, I had no doubts. At fifty, I knew the decrees of Heaven. At sixty, my ear was an obedient organ for the reception of truth. At seventy, I could follow what my heart desired, without transgressing what was right."

---

sayings and teachings in a book known as *The Analects. The Analects* held that social cohesion could be achieved through reciprocal relationships of respect, propriety, and filial devotion. Confucius also stressed the importance of formal education in order to better oneself and one's society. Confucius established a course of studies for his disciples that formed the intellectual foundation of the classical Chinese world. Confucius's teachings and social philosophy would hold sway over much of Chinese politics, education, and daily life for more than 2,000 years.

Golden Age of Athens

95 *447* B.C.E. The height of artistic expression in the ancient world arguably belongs to the so-called golden age of Athens, the crowning achievement

96 | *The Torah holds Israel's laws and history.*

of which may be the Parthenon and adjacent buildings of the Acropolis, begun in 447 B.C.E. Athens at the time was under the leadership of Pericles, who directed funds from the Delian League to finance his massive building projects. The Parthenon, designed by the architects Ictinus and Callicrates, was a 228-foot-long marvel of perfect proportions. Slight adjustments in the lines and angles of the building, likely to compensate for natural optical illusions, mean that every block of marble used had to be hewn according to exact specifications dependent on its position in the structure. The interior of the Parthenon housed a dedicatory statue of Athen's patron goddess, Athena. This 38-foot-tall, gold-and-ivory figure was sculpted by the artist Phidias, using bone chisels and clay molds. Phidias also directed the sculpting of the Parthenon's 92 windowlike metopes, its interior processional frieze, and its pedimental statuary, all of which were painted, adorned in bronze, and executed in classic contrapposto style. Completed in 432 B.C.E., the Parthenon has endured almost 2,500 years of alteration, corrosion, and even bombing, yet still stands atop the Acropolis as a testament to the sophistication of Greek artistry.

> ■ **FOOTNOTE** Several hundred city-states gained renown during Greece's golden age, including Athens, Sparta, Thebes, and Corinth. Sparta devoted itself to excellence in warfare; rival Athens became a center of culture and learning.

Torah Canonized

96 | **444 B.C.E.** The final canonization of the Torah, Judaism's most sacred scripture, is said to have come in 444 B.C.E., following nearly six centuries of written compilation and several more of oral tradition. In these centuries, the Israelites suffered numerous military defeats, forced diasporas, and even enslavement. Throughout these trials, many Israelites maintained a sense of faith and community in large part due to a series of prophets whose teachings and reassurances formed the basis of much of Judaism's later scriptures. In 444, a temple scribe named Ezra was granted the authority to proclaim the Torah as the official law of the district of Judah, at that time a vassal state of the Achaemenid Empire. Thus began centuries more of interpretation and reinterpretation. The Torah would go on to profoundly influence the morals and values of countless scores of Jews, Christians, and Muslims alike.

First Hospitals Built

98 | **431 B.C.E.** The world's earliest known hospitals, buildings committed strictly to the purpose of caring for the infirm, were founded as early as 431 B.C.E. on the island of Sri Lanka off the southeast coast of India. According to the Mahavamsa, a dynastic chronology of the ancient Sinhalese of Sri Lanka, King Pandukabhaya had these hospitals constructed in an effort to control sanitation within his newly fortified capital city of Anuradhapura. At these hospitals, any number of herbal and magical remedies were presumably administered to those suffering from

Corpus Hippocraticum Compiled

97 | **440 B.C.E.** Compilation of the *Corpus Hippocraticum* was begun as early as 440 B.C.E., likely by several physicians working at the time in ancient Greece. Little is known about the life of Hippocrates, except that he was a full-time professional physician who made a livelihood of teaching students for pay. Of the 60 or so works that make up the *Corpus,* most if not all were written by later physicians.

Regardless, Hippocrates is considered to mark the transition in Western medicine when reason overtook superstition and disease began being looked upon as a natural phenomenon, devoid of supernatural interference. Hippocratic medicine stressed the importance of clinical observation by frequent patient visits, relying more on the "healing power of nature" than on medicinal drugs or surgery. The guidelines set out in the Hippocratic Oath, which was

Hippocrates is credited with the transition to clinical observation to treat illness.

probably not written by Hippocrates himself, established a standard code of humane, ethical behavior for physicians that has persisted in one form or another to this day.

93 More Details on the Greco-Persian Wars

The Persian armies greatly outnumbered their opposition when they landed on the Greek mainland at Marathon, just north of Athens, in 490 B.C.E. Herodotus, the Greek historian, numbered their fleet at 600 ships. With the cavalry as its centerpiece, the Persian army was reinforced by highly skilled chariot drivers and archers. The bow was, in fact, that most important Persian weapon and lay at the heart of its military successes. Ground troops wore light armor to enable quick movement and realignment; combined with the cavalry, the army was characterized by its ability to engage its enemy in a swift and decisive manner.

The Greek style of fighting, in contrast, consisted of troops of heavily armored men wielding spears and a heavy shield known as the *hoplon;* the warriors, as a result, were known as hoplites. They typically met their opposition at a steady charge and in a solid, wall-like formation—known as a phalanx—that was almost impenetrable. The benefit of this formation was not only its impenetrability but also the protection it afforded the hoplites, for each fighter was partially protected by the shield of the man to his right. The ensuing battle was a clash of spears and shields, wherein individual fighters attempted to penetrate the armor of their enemy.

> When the Greeks and the Persians met on the plains of Marathon, the advantage clearly belonged to the Persians.

When the Greeks and the Persians met on the plains of Marathon, then, the advantage clearly belonged to the Persians, both for their superior numbers and for the edge that the wide, open plain afforded their cavalry. But the Greek hoplites, fighting to protect their home territory, charged the Persians first, preventing the cavalry from exercising its full potential on the battlefield. In his *History* Herodotus describes the casualty count on the side of the "barbarians" as about 6,400 men. The Athenians, on the other hand, lost only 192 men.

This daring move by the Greeks and their resulting victory marked a turning point in the Greco-Persian conflict.

Life-size archers like those fighting in the Battle of Marathon adorn the enameled tile frieze from the palace of Darius the Great.

ailments such as tuberculosis, smallpox, leprosy, and other less severe conditions. Within centuries, a hospital system appeared in mainland India, and later within the Roman and Persian Empires, eventually becoming the nearly worldwide phenomenon it is today.

Atomic Theory Postulated

99 **430 B.C.E.** The earliest known postulation of atomic theory

Socrates on Death

PLATO, *EUTHYPHRO* (CA 450 B.C.E.)

For the body is a source of endless trouble to us by reason of the mere requirement of food; and also is liable to diseases which overtake and impede us in the search after truth: and by filling us as full of loves, and lusts, and fears, and fancies, and idols, and every sort of folly, prevents our ever having, as people say, so much as a thought.

For whence come wars, and fightings, and factions? whence but from the body and the lusts of the body? For wars are occasioned by the love of money, and money has to be acquired for the sake and in the service of the body; and in consequence ... the time which ought to be given to philosophy is lost.

All experience shows that if we would have pure knowledge of anything we must be quit of the body, and the soul in herself must behold all things in themselves: then, I suppose, that we shall attain that which we desire, and of which we say that we are lovers, and that is wisdom; not while we live, but after death ...; for if while in company with the body, the soul can not have pure knowledge...either knowledge is not to be attained at all, or, if at all, after death. For then, and not till then, the soul will be in herself alone and without the body.... And then ... we shall be pure and hold converse with other pure souls, and know of ourselves the clear light everywhere; and this is surely the light of truth.... These are the sort of words, Simmias, which the true lovers of wisdom can not help saying to one another, and thinking. You will agree with me in that?

—Certainly, Socrates.

came from the hand of the Greek philosopher Leucippus of Miletus, whose better-known pupil Democritus of Abdera first coined the term atomon, literally "indivisible," around 430 B.C.E. This first version of atomic theory was based solely on reason as opposed to experimental observation, but nevertheless produced a number of conclusions that were remarkably prescient. Among them was that all matter, physical, metaphysical, and otherwise, is composed of eternal, indestructible, perpetually moving particles called atoms, so small that the human eye cannot see them. Perceived differences in reality, such as hot versus cold, sweet versus bitter, or hard versus soft, were said to be the product of different arrangements and combinations of atoms. Atomic theory had its adherents in the ancient Greek and Roman worlds, such as Empedocles who posited the notion of basic elements, but lost steam in the face of the Platonic view that rejected "mechanical manifestations of material atoms." Not until the 18th century was atomic theory scientifically verified.

FOOTNOTE During the enlightened times of ancient Greece, various schools of philosophy and science discussed new ideas. Leucippus and his disciples met with like-minded seekers in a group called the Ionian school of philosophy.

Medical Techniques Developed

100 **ca 400 B.C.E.** The Indian surgeon Susruta, practicing in towns along the Ganges River as early as 400 B.C.E., developed methods of repairing cataracts, removing gallstones, and reconstructing the nose, long before these operations were known elsewhere. The collective teachings of Susruta and his successors on surgical techniques, various maladies and their suggested medicinal remedies, and general hygiene and diet, as well as magical potions, were compiled over many centuries into the *Susruta Samhita,* or *Compendium of Susruta.* Though application of Susruta's techniques appears to have waned with time in India, perhaps due to rigid taboos associated with the caste system, his method of rhinoplasty by

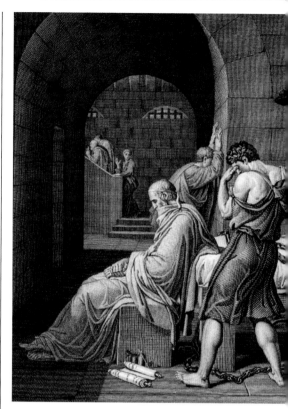

101 | *Supporters despair as Greek philosopher Socrates is served poison hemlock in prison.*

grafting a piece of skin from the forehead or cheek was revived as the "Hindu method" in 19th-century Europe. Susruta's precedent and renown have earned him the epithet, the "Father of Surgery."

Socratic Thought Preserved

101 **399 B.C.E.** When the Greek philosopher Socrates committed suicide in 399 B.C.E. by drinking a mixture of hemlock sap, having been condemned to death by a jury of Athenian peers on unfounded charges of impiety and corruption, his philosophy may have died with him if not for the efforts of his most prominent disciple, Plato. Socrates valued striving for self-knowledge above all, but asserted that he himself knew nothing. He esteemed personal integrity far higher than wealth, fame, or accolades, and in a manner that outraged many, he often engaged in questioning that revealed discrepancies in the opinions and actions of his fellow Athenians. Since Socrates himself wrote nothing, Plato systematized many of his

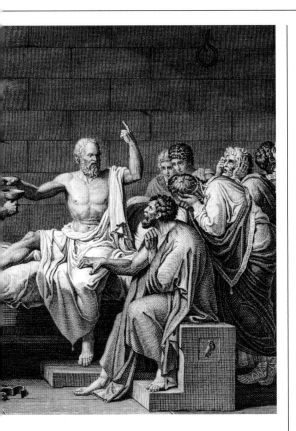

views in a series of dialogues, Socrates' preferred method of inquiry and reflection. In other writings, Plato would go on to expound his own philosophy, an abstruse extension of Socratic thought which viewed reality as an imperfect reflection of a world of eternal, transcendent forms that was imperceptible to earthly senses but through the pursuit of self-knowledge. In 380 B.C.E., Plato founded the Academy, the products of which dominated ancient Greek and Roman philosophy, profoundly influenced later Islamic philosophy, and provided the foundations of subsequent European philosophy.

Aristotle Forms Philosophy

102 367 B.C.E. Aristotle entered Plato's Academy in 367 B.C.E. at the age of 17, and was soon espousing a philosophy of his own, quite apart from those of his predecessors. Unlike Socrates and Plato, who eschewed sense experience and studies of the natural world, Aristotle felt that to know the processes and purposes of nature was to better understand human beings' place among them. As much

scientist as philosopher, Aristotle launched a program of investigations into fields as varied as physics, metaphysics, chemistry, astronomy, biology, zoology, botany, human anatomy and embryology, psychology, teleology, politics, and ethics, establishing a rigorous methodology for empirical scientific observation that in many ways was unsurpassed for more than 2,000 years. He also founded the discipline of logic in such a way that almost nothing was added to it for many centuries. Filtered through the Islamic and Byzantine worlds, Aristotle's works formed the intellectual basis for western Europe's first universities, where they continue to be studied to this day.

> ■ **FOOTNOTE** "If liberty and equality, as is thought by some, are chiefly to be found in democracy, they will be best attained, when all persons alike share in the government to the utmost." —Aristotle in *Politics*, Book III

Alexander Crosses Dardanelles

103 334 B.C.E. Alexander the Great, pupil of Aristotle and ruler of most of the Greek mainland that had already been annexed by his father, crossed the Dardanelles into Asia Minor in 334 B.C.E. with an army of about 37,000 men. His conquests systematically claimed the lands of the Achaemenid Empire of Persia and extended Greek rule from modern-day Libya to the Punjab region of India. Along the way he adopted many customs of the lands he took, allowing local governors to continue their administrations. He founded more than 70 cities throughout his conquered lands, effecting a flow of migrants that extended Greek language, art, culture, and religion throughout western Asia and ushered in what would become known as the Hellenistic Age. In June of 323 B.C.E., the ruler of the largest empire the world had yet known, Alexander the Great fell ill and died following a lavish banquet in Babylon. He was just 33 years of age.

Alexandrian Library Founded

104 323 B.C.E. The Library and Museum of Alexandria, the most

renowned research center in the ancient world, was founded by Ptolemy I Soter after he came to power in Egypt in 323 B.C.E. Alexandria had been founded by Alexander the Great, and Ptolemy made it his capital as the first ruler of the Ptolemaic dynasty, which gained control there following Alexander's death. Ptolemy's library was a storehouse of classical literature, and his museum, a state-sponsored institute of higher learning, drew scholars from all over the Hellenistic world. Among the prominent figures who studied at the museum are Euclid, Herophilus, Erasistratus, Eratosthenes, Archimedes, and Galen. At the library, Aristarchus of Samothrace collated the various texts associated with Homer, Jewish scholars translated much of the Old Testament from Hebrew to Greek, and punctuation and accentuation were added to many of the ancient classical texts. In the Roman period, an estimated 700,000 scrolls were housed at the library, the largest collection of its kind anywhere in the world.

Mauryan Empire Established

105 321 B.C.E. Chandragupta Maurya, an ambitious and opportunistic king of the Magadha region of northern India, capitalized on the vacuum of power left by the departure

103 | *Alexander the Great leads his fleet ashore in Asia.*

of Alexander the Great's forces from the Indus River Valley and established India's first large, centralized state, the Mauryan Empire, in 321 B.C.E. From his capital at Pataliputra, he oversaw the commerce and trade that flowed along the Ganges River and administered his lands using the former Achaemenid Empire as a model. By the end of his reign, Chandragupta's realm extended from the Kabul Valley of modern-day Afghanistan to the southern portion of the Indian subcontinent. Chandragupta is said to have spent his last days as a Jaina monk, dying in the traditional ascetic manner, deliberate self-starvation.

Euclid Writes *Elements*

106 ca 300 B.C.E. Euclid, a prominent mathematician teaching in Alexandria, Egypt, sometime around 300 B.C.E., attempted in the 13 books of his *Elements* to consolidate all the known advances in mathematics, particularly geometry, that he and his predecessors had deduced since the emergence of this field

106 | *Greek mathematician Euclid, world's greatest geometry teacher.*

of study. Book I begins with 23 definitions and 10 axioms from which several hundred theorems could be derived through deductive logic. Though it did not necessarily overturn any long-standing erroneous notions, the *Elements* was certainly considered by Euclid's contemporaries as an authoritative treatise to be studied in lieu of all previous similar efforts. Translated widely into Arabic, Latin, and English, the *Elements* maintained its position of prominence for more than 2,000 years until the development of so-called non-Euclidean geometry in the 19th century.

Daoism Develops

107 ca 300 B.C.E. The doctrines of Daoism were synthesized into a powerful cultural force in China around 300 B.C.E. At this time, the proverbs and aphorisms handed down since the days of the sixth-century sage Laozi were compiled into the Daodejing, Daoism's fundamental text. The widely influential Daoist philosopher Zhuangzi was also active at this time, extolling the virtues of a life lived simply and in harmony with nature. In contrast to the reform-minded activism of Confucianism, Daoism encouraged disengagement from self-righteous measures that despite their intended benevolence, nevertheless engender conflict. Daoism viewed an ideal society as one composed of small, self-governed, self-sufficient communities, so content that they would seek neither to overrun, trade, nor even visit with their neighbors. At a time in Chinese history when politics was devolving into warmongering, Daoism offered the means of a tranquil, introspective way of life that appealed to many.

First Dissections Performed

108 ca 300 B.C.E. The earliest known public dissections of deceased, and perhaps living, humans were conducted in Alexandria, Egypt, around 300 B.C.E. by the seminal anatomists, Herophilus of Chalcedon and Erasistratus of Chios. Banned elsewhere in the world due to taboos or limiting preconceptions about

cutting the body with a knife, the practice of human dissection allowed Herophilus and Erasistratus to make many new findings in the fields of human anatomy and physiology. In contrast to the views of Aristotle, both recognized the brain as the seat of intelligence by delineating the nervous system and distinguishing the cerebrum and cerebellum. In studying the circulatory system, Herophilus observed that arteries were filled not with air, but with blood, and Erasistratus correctly theorized the existence of capillaries. This window in medical history was brief, though. A ban on human dissection was soon reimposed and the works of Herophilus and Erasistratus were destroyed in the wake of civil wars and Christian ideology.

> ■ **FOOTNOTE** Herophilus and Erasistratus founded the medical school of Alexandria in about 330 B.C.E. Their courageous dissections also led to the understanding of nerves of the sensory and of the motor nervous system.

Earliest Medical Text Written

109 ca 300 B.C.E. The earliest known book of medicine in the Chinese tradition is the Nei Ching, or Inner Canon, compiled sometime after 300 B.C.E. Part Daoist philosophical treatise, part holistic physiological theoretics, the Nei Ching presents health as the harmonious distribution of qi by proper proportions of yin and yang. This distibution is said to be dictated not only by the internal workings of the body, but also by the external workings of the environment and society at large. Moderation is stressed above all, with curative measures relating to regulation of diet, exercise, meditation, sex, and acupuncture. A uniquely Chinese tradition, the practice of acupuncture predates the Nei Ching by thousands of years. It is so effective in relieving pain that it is used to this day in China as a local anesthetic during certain surgical procedures.

Ashoka Renounces Expansion

110 268 B.C.E. Ashoka Maurya, grandson of Chandragupta, began his reign as Mauryan emperor in 268 B.C.E. and

Anatomy of a Procedure
Dissection's earliest pioneers set the stage for surgery's evolution

Simple surgical procedures had been performed for millennia, but deeper knowledge of the human body was necessary before surgery could take its place as the lifesaving practice it is today.

Galen (129-216 C.E.), Rome's "emperor" of medicine, was an excellent clinician, but he gathered anatomical information by dissecting animals and assuming their structures to be identical to humans'. Galen erroneously deduced that humans had hearts with three ventricles and livers with five lobes. These and other misconceptions survived for more than a millennium.

In the Middle Ages, medicine remained primarily a discipline of prayer and folk remedy. Islamic physicians practiced surgery, especially for cauterizing wounds. As human dissection gained greater acceptance in Europe in the 14th to 16th centuries, surgical procedures advanced in their accuracy and effectiveness. In addition, the rise of gunpowder led to new and particularly gruesome battle wounds, requiring more sophisticated care.

Surgical procedures throughout the Renaissance remained fairly basic: tooth extractions, boil lancings, syphilitic chancre care. One famous

This 1899 painting shows a vivisection experiment.

panacea was bloodletting, with the theory that "humors" causing illness would leave the body with the blood. In difficult childbirths, caesarian sections occasionally saved a baby's life but almost never the mother's.

Surgeons held rather low social status—in some regions also working as barbers (needing only one set of tools)—and were seen as manual practitioners.

Two developments would greatly improve the surgeon's place in society—and people's chances of surviving illness. The development of anesthesia in the late 18th century allowed surgeons to cut deeper, excising tumors, stanching internal bleeding, and developing ever more sophisticated techniques for healing problems in the body cavity. Germ theory led to the sanitization of medical facilities and care. When the telescope revealed the existence of microscopic life and scientists discovered that these "germs" are agents of infection, practices such as instrument sterilization, hand washing, and wound cleansing were introduced that greatly reduced death rates from postsurgical sepsis. In the 20th century, development of antibiotics saved an even greater number of healing surgical patients.

---

soon thereafter dealt the independent Indian kingdom of Kalinga a bloody campaign of expansion, during which an estimated 100,000 Kalingans died and even more were made homeless and destitute. Profoundly affected by the scenes of violence and suffering, Ashoka adopted Buddhism around 260 and thereafter devoted his efforts at promoting the virtues of religion, rather than the commercial interests of expansion. Ashoka had edicts incribed on stone pillars and natural rock formations throughout his realm, all of which extolled the principles of dharma, encouraged observance of Buddhist values, and gave sincere expressions of his own thoughts and actions. In light of the Jaina doctrine of nonviolence to all living things, Ashoka banned animal sacrifices, gave up hunting, eliminated most meat from his own diet,

and established a number of hospitals for humans and animals alike. He also sent missionaries throughout India and beyond to modern-day Sri Lanka, Afghanistan, Myanmar, Thailand, and perhaps even as far as Egypt, elevating the status of Buddhism from that of a small localized cult to that of a major state religion.

> ■ **FOOTNOTE** Ashoka's pillars, erected throughout northern India during his reign and adorned with Buddhist symbols, were reminders to the Indian people to practice truth, compassion, and tolerance.

Earth Proved Spherical

111 255 B.C.E. The idea that Earth is a sphere may go as far back as the time of Pythagoras, though its proof may date to Eratosthenes of Cyrene, living and working in Alexandria, Egypt, by 255

B.C.E., and using Euclidean geometric principles. Eratosthenes noted that at noon on the summer solstice the sun's rays struck vertically into a well in the town of Syene. At the same time and date in Alexandria, about 500 miles to the northwest, the sun's rays struck at an angle of about seven degrees from vertical. On the assumption that the sun's rays are practically parallel at these two spots owing to the immense distance they travel, Eratosthenes estimated the circumference of the sphere of the Earth to be roughly 151,739,000 feet, just 15 percent larger than the currently accepted value. His other contributions included a star catalog of 675 stars, the measurements of the distance to the sun and the moon, and maps of the known world from the British Isles to Sri Lanka.

Qin Ruler Unifies China

112 **221 B.C.E.** The Period of the Warring States in China came to an abrupt end in 221 B.C.E. when the expansionist ruler of the Qin state, having systematically overpowered every last rival by means of a powerful, well-armed, terror-inspiring army, unified all of China into one centralized empire and adopted the title known to posterity, Qin Shihuangdi, the "First Sovereign Emperor of Qin." Neither Confucianist nor Daoist, Shihuangdi organized his empire according to Legalist principles, which valued the state above all. During his 11-year imperial reign, Shihuangdi ordered the burning of books and the execution of his critics; but he also codified the law; established standards for weights, measures, taxes, currency, writing, and even axle lengths; built new roads, canals, and irrigation systems; and consolidated existing defensive walls into a single massive structure, a forerunner to the 15th-century Great Wall. Despite his ruthlessness, or perhaps because of it, Qin (pronounced Chin) Shihuangdi established a legacy of strong, centralized bureaucratic rule that persists to this day in the country that still bears his name.

■ **FOOTNOTE** Qin Shihuangdi is known better today for his sumptuous tomb, buried with a terracotta army of 10,000 life-size soldiers, horses, and other treasures. Some 700,000 workers are said to have worked for 38 years to complete the site.

Hannibal Crosses the Alps

113 **218 B.C.E.** Carthaginian general Hannibal, having lost nearly half of his forces and all but one of his war elephants in a five-month forced march from Spain, descended from the icy heights of the Alps in 218 B.C.E. into the Po River Valley of northern Italy. For 15 years, Hannibal's army remained on the Italian peninsula, battling Roman forces and nearly cutting short the Republic's growing power. After the death of his brother and a failed alliance with the Macedonians, Hannibal returned to Africa in 203, where Roman forces under Scipio Africanus were threatening his native city. Hannibal's army was routed at the

Archimedes Makes Theoretical Practical

114 **213 B.C.E.** Greek mathematician and inventor Archimedes of Syracuse was groundbreaking in the practical mechanical applications he developed of theoretical mathematical principles. The Archimedes screw, traditionally attributed to him, raises water from a low level to a higher one and is still used in irrigation systems today. In 213 B.C.E., during a Roman siege of Syracuse, the principal Greek city-state in Sicily of the time, he proved instrumental in the defense of the city by creating all manner of military machinery employing levers and compound pulleys, concepts that he had helped to advance earlier in his career.

Egyptian carpenter works on part of an Archimedes screw, a device used to irrigate crops.

On the theoretical side, Archimedes' approximation of the value of pi became widely used both in antiquity and throughout the Middle Ages, and his determination of areas, surface areas of many bodies, and the volumes of solids laid the groundwork for integral calculus more than 1,500 years before its development. His most famous theorem, known as Archimedes' principle, states that any body completely or partially submerged in a fluid is acted upon by an upward force, which is equal to the weight of the fluid displaced by the body. In the end, Archimedes was killed in 212 B.C.E. in the aftermath of the same Roman siege during the second Punic War that he had helped to delay. His inventions and calculations were so fundamental that in the 19th century he was still being hailed as one of the three epoch-making mathematicians in the world along with Isaac Newton and Carl Friedrich Gauss.

Battle of Zama in 202, Carthage was taken and its navy dismantled, and Rome's political and economic hegemony in the Mediterranean was soon to be firmly established for the next 500 years.

Nomadic Tribes Mobilize

115 **210 B.C.E.** The nomadic horsemen of the Central Asian steppe initially built no cities or permanent fortifications; rather they herded animals across the vast grasslands, living off the byproducts and trading or raiding when convenient. With no written literature and scant archaeological remains except for burials, few details of their early history are known but from outside sources, such as those kept by Chinese scribes regarding the Xiongnu confederation of Maodun. Around 210 B.C.E., using the Chinese dynasties as a model, Maodun organized an unprecedented league of the nomadic tribes that encompassed much of modern-day Siberia and Mongolia. Able to mobilize as many as 300,000 horsemen, the Xiongnu were a formidable rival to their Chinese and nomadic neighbors alike, forcing a wave of migration that upset settled communities as distant as India, Persia, and Europe. Though Maodun's confederation was short-lived, the Xiongnu remained an almost constant threat to China's walled northern border for more than 500 years.

Han Dynasty Established

116 **206 B.C.E.** The Qin dynasty degenerated into violent revolt soon after Shihuangdi's death and could have been the only short-lived imperial power in ancient China if not for the efforts of the determined general Liu Bang, who established the Han dynasty in 206 B.C.E. For the most part ruling from Confucianist, rather than Legalist, principles, Han dynasty emperors maintained the central bureaucratic administration of Shihuangdi, but also oversaw a flourishing of literature, art, technology, and culture. Populous cities were linked by roads, canals, and a state ideology fostered at China's first imperial university. The expansionist emperor Han Wudi imposed Chinese government and values on the Korean peninsula, in northern Vietnam, and in a long strip of land through Central Asia extending to the borders of Bactria, a corridor that constituted the first of the silk roads. For more than 400 years, this dynasty, despite its shortcomings, maintained almost uninterrupted centralized rule in China, where the ethnic majority to this day is still referred to as Han.

Nasca Create Baffling Lines

117 **ca 200 B.C.E.** The Nasca people were farmers who settled around 200 B.C.E. in adjacent river valleys cutting through the arid bottomlands of the southern coast of Peru. Carving their living out of a harsh environment, they constructed irrigation canals and long, underground aqueducts that delivered groundwater into reservoirs. In the marked absence of many other masonry structures, their most enigmatic creations were etched directly into the earth, the Nasca lines. A monkey, a spider, a killer whale, birds, trees, and flowers, most of them hundreds of feet long, are crisscrossed and surrounded by lines, triangles, trapezoids, and spirals in a convoluted earthen tapestry hundreds of years in the making. Just why these lines were created is still largely unknown, though they may have served manifold functions in rituals associated with water and planting. Despite incursions by highways and illegal gold mines in recent decades, the enduring significance of the Nasca lines can still be felt in the deserts of southern Peru.

FOOTNOTE The Nasca lines are geoglyphs, a design produced on the ground by removing iron oxide-coated pebbles to expose the lighter-colored earth beneath. Once exposed, the lines were preserved in the constant desert climate.

Romans Develop Concrete

118 **200 B.C.E.** The Roman development of concrete around 200 B.C.E., an admixture of volcanic ash, lime, rubble, and water, revolutionized civil engineering by lowering costs of construction as well as allowing forms that were not strictly dependent on the limitations of quarried stone. The plastic nature of concrete allowed curved architectural forms, such as the vault and dome, that were so characteristic of Roman temples, monuments, basilicas, stadiums, and theaters. Concrete's waterproof quality made it essential in other feats of engineering, such as the aqueducts, bridges, harbors, and bath houses of the Roman world. Concrete was also employed in the paved roads that would eventually span 50,000 miles around the Mediterranean. With concrete, the Romans not only utilized natural landforms in their architecture as the Greeks had done before them, but were able to transform natural landforms into architecture.

Trading Settlements Emerge

119 **ca 200 B.C.E.** The benefits of widespread trade between far-flung lands, promoted by the administrative policies of large centralized states, were not lost on communities of sub-Saharan Africa. Sometime after 200 B.C.E., at least two sizable trading settlements emerged on opposite sides of the African continent, Rhapta on the East African coast, likely in modern-day Tanzania, and Djenné-Jeno on the inland Niger Delta, in modern-day Mali. Rhapta was served by networks of maritime trade linking India, Arabia, and Ptolemaic Egypt. African merchants exchanged ivory, rhinoceros horn, and coconut oil mostly for metal tools and weapons, suggesting that iron-smelting had not yet been developed there. Djenné-Jeno, where ironworking was present but natural resources were not, arose independently of intercontinental influence and exchanged fish, grain, and craftwork for the raw materials needed by specialized artisans. Though separated by thousands of miles, both settlements contemporaneously started Africa on a gradual course of urbanization within an increasingly smaller world.

Parthian Empire Reaches Peak

120 **171 B.C.E.** The Parthian Empire of Persia, which had wrested autonomous control from the Greek Seleucids in the aftermath of Alexander the Great's death, reached its greatest extent of power under the imperial command of Mithridates I, who came to the throne around 171 B.C.E. Formerly a group of seminomadic herders of the Iranian steppe, the Parthians were accustomed to fierce tribal warfare on horseback. What is more, the Parthians grazed their horses on alfalfa instead of strictly grass, making them bigger, stronger, and capable of supporting warriors equipped with full metal armor.

116 | *Clay heads from Han dynasty burial site.*

The first of their kind, these well-trained, metal-clad cavalrymen were a formidable match to any rival, particularly the archers of nomadic raiding parties, and were integral in the establishment of an empire spanning Parthia, Persia, and Mesopotamia.

Early Astrolabe Developed

121 **150 B.C.E.** An early form of the astrolabe is reasoned to have been developed in the Hellenistic world sometime around 150 B.C.E. Within an astrolabe, light from the stars and planets is reflected through a small aperture by both a prism and a pool of mercury. When the two reflections coincide, the celestial body's altitude relative to the horizon and position relative to other stars can be derived. Probably one of the first to use, and perhaps to invent, this instrument was Greek astronomer Hipparchus of Bithynia, who plotted a map of as many as 850 stars at his observatory on the island of Rhodes. The Egyptian astronomer Ptolemy pushed that number to 1,022 some 300 years later. Equipped with accurate maps of the sky, subsequent Islamic scholars refined the astrolabe into a pocket-size device capable of determining direction and time of day, useful in daily prayers, and of computing latitude and longitude, indispensable in maritime navigation.

■ FOOTNOTE Hipparchus's early contributions to astronomy are still being honored: The European Space Agency named the High Precision Parallax Collecting Satellite (HiPPaCS) after him, as well as a crater on the moon and an asteroid.

Southeast Asian Society

122 **ca 100 B.C.E.** Southeast Asian society was already characterized by local trading networks, organized by indigenous polities, when an increased amount of Indian and Chinese influences began to filter in through merchants, missionaries, and military by around 100 B.C.E. In northern Vietnam, this meant a check to the power of local rulers as the Han Empire imposed a Chinese-style government by force of arms. In other parts of Southeast Asia where no military

incursion occurred, this meant an increase in the power of local rulers, as regional governors adapted an Indian-style political organization and henceforth became known as kings. These kings expanded their trading networks to incorporate Indian goods, and they also absorbed Indian traditions of literature, art, architecture, and religion into their own courts. The gradual processes of Indianization and Sinicization would in their distinct ways profoundly influence the course of Southeast Asian society for over a millennium.

Germ Theory Proposed

123 **ca 90 B.C.E.** The first known postulation of germ theory was given by Roman scholar Marcus Terentius Varro around 90 B.C.E. Varro proposed the idea that imperceptibly small animals, too small to be seen by the human eye, could enter the body through the nose and mouth and cause illness and disease. Seventeen hundred years before the invention of the microscope, Varro was ill equipped to verify his theory scientifically. That would be left to 19th-century French chemist Louis Pasteur, who was completely unaware of the nearly two-millennia-old writings of Varro.

Augustus Reigns

125 **27 B.C.E.** Gaius Octavius was the great-nephew of Julius Caesar and, by virtue of Caesar's will, his adopted son and personal heir. To fully claim his inheritance was a 13-year ordeal involving civil wars and sticky alliances, but in 27 B.C.E. Octavius received the title of Augustus, or "consecrated," becoming for all intents and purposes the first in a long line of Roman emperors. During his 45 years of unopposed rule, Augustus overhauled the workings of Roman government, reorganized the military, installed a fire brigade and a police force in the city of Rome, and expanded the boundaries of the Roman Empire to include much of Europe, North Africa, and the eastern Mediterranean.

Caesar Crosses Rubicon

124 **49 B.C.E.** Gaius Julius Caesar led his army across the Rubicon River into Italian territory in 49 B.C.E., deliberately violating the law of the Roman Republic and initiating a bloody three-year civil war that would drastically change the face of the Greco-Roman world. The same army was fresh off their provincial conquests, which had subjugated some 300 Gallic tribes, caused the death of more than a million Gauls, enslaved a million more, and in one of the largest naval invasions in history brought much of Britain into the growing dominion of Rome. With this powerful force of loyal veterans behind him, Caesar had by early 46 B.C.E. proclaimed himself dictator-for-life, brought the Roman military and political bodies under his sole control, and enacted a number of large-scale building projects. So much power in the hands of one man was not yet tolerable to a

Detail of sculpture of Julius Caesar, who had a short but powerful reign.

number of Roman patricians, who plotted Caesar's assassination on the Ides of March, 44 B.C.E. As short as Caesar's reign was, it nevertheless laid the foundations of the ensuing Roman Empire.

In these lands, Augustus ushered in his so-called Pax Romana, or "Roman Peace," an era characterized by increased law, trade, communication, and relative prosperity. With the wealth of Egypt at his disposal, Augustus commissioned monuments, temples, public buildings, and roads that spanned his empire. Augustus's enduring legacy contends that he found Rome a city of brick and left it a city of marble.

■ **FOOTNOTE** The month of August is named after Augustus—matching July for Julius Caesar—because August was said to be the month in which the most important events in his rise to power occurred.

Virgil Writes *Aeneid*

126 | **29-19 B.C.E.** Roman poet Publius Vergilius Maro, better known simply as Virgil, died on September 21, 19 B.C.E., leaving his magnum opus, *The Aeneid,* yet unfinished. This national epic was 11 years in the making and not only recounts the legendary founding of Rome but also reveals a faith in the supposedly divine mission of that city. *The Aeneid* was written in some respects to embody the ideals and glorify the reforms of Augustus, qualities also found in the contemporaneous works of Horace and Livy, but also betrays a sensitivity to the price paid in individual suffering. In either respect, Virgil's mastery of the form and meter of epic poetry is unparalleled. Used as a textbook almost immediately after Virgil's death, *The Aeneid*'s influence in the schools and literature of the ancient, medieval, and modern worlds is inestimably profound.

Jesus Begins Ministry

127 | **29 C.E.** Jewish preacher Jesus of Nazareth began his public ministry in the Roman province of Palestine around 29 C.E. Palestine at the time was a land rife with political and social tensions between gentiles and Jews, between Roman overlords and subjects, and among various sects of Judaism itself. Though himself a man of peace, Jesus gathered large crowds with his preaching and any man capable of attracting such crowds was

127 | *A Currier & Ives depiction of Jesus speaking to a Samarian woman at Jacob's Well.*

viewed as politically dangerous by Roman governors and Jewish priests alike, as there was no dearth of Jews willing to mount rebellion against Rome. Jesus was never charged in his native region of Galilee with any serious legal offense, but when he entered Jerusalem to observe the Passover and was greeted by a mass of admirers, even his message of compassion became a portent of conflict. He was crucified as an agitator by Roman authorities around 30 C.E., but his teachings, preserved in the New Testament, have survived as some of the most powerful cultural and political forces in history.

Trung Sisters Rebel

128 | **39 C.E.** The rebellion of the Trung sisters in 39 C.E. marked the first of many vies for Vietnamese independence during more than 1,000 years of Chinese occupation. Following the assassination of her husband, Trung Trac, along with her sister Trung Nhi and other local aristocrats, amassed an impromptu army to march on the Chinese stronghold of Lien Lau, where they put Chinese forces to flight. Within a year, this untrained and undersupplied group of rebels had wrested dozens of citadels in northern Vietnam from Chinese rule and the sisters had proclaimed themselves joint queens of an autonomous Vietnamese state. Three years later, they were no match for a powerful Han army dispatched to depose them; facing sure defeat, they threw themselves into the confluence of the Day and Red Rivers. The Vietnamese people were once again under the dominion of Han China, but the Trung sisters' rebellion was not to be the last.

Paul Promotes Christianity

129 **40 C.E.** Christian convert turned missionary Paul of Tarsus is considered by many to be the second most significant figure in the history of Christianity. Against the wishes of some early traditionalist Christians who emphasized the prerequisite strictures of Jewish law, Paul by 40 C.E. sought to convert non-Jewish gentiles as well. Utilizing the same routes that spread commerce and trade across the Roman Empire, Paul spread Christianity. He traveled throughout Greece and the Middle East, leaving in his wake fledgling churches, with which he corresponded by letter on matters of faith. Paul's letters, the Epistles, contain theological insights and moral instructions that, preserved in the New Testament, are still taught to this day. In the end, Paul's tireless efforts helped to elevate Christianity from an isolated Jewish sect to a full-scale religious movement.

Earliest Buddhist Temple Built

130 **68 C.E.** The earliest Buddhist temple in China, the White Horse Temple, was constructed in 68 C.E. nine miles east of the city of Louyang. Though said to have been erected by Han emperor Mingdi, an early Buddhist convert, the temple was likely only used by foreign merchants and missionaries at first. Han China, where Confucianism was the primary mode of thought, did not take immediately to the introduction of Buddhism, but since these foreign merchants and missionaries were permitted to inhabit and preach from enclaves in several major cities, the number of converts gradually continued to grow. Once the Han Empire fell and nomadic horsemen from the Central Asian steppes flowed in from the north, the seeds of Buddhism sprouted into a cultural phenomenon.

Colosseum Dedicated

131 **80 C.E.** The Flavian Amphitheater, better known as the Colosseum, was dedicated by Emperor Titus in

---

CONNECTIONS

Christianity's Foundations
From modest beginnings grew one of the world's most powerful religious movements

Upon Jesus of Nazareth's Crucifixion, his Apostles went forth to spread the "Good News": that Jesus was the Messiah who had lived, died, and risen again for humanity's salvation, and the mending of creation. Those who followed this Christ would be blessed with everlasting life. The first Christians were Hebrews who believed Jesus' words that the Kingdom of God was at hand, that the baptized would be saved and the world as they knew it would come to an end.

The majority of Roman citizens appealed to a pantheon of Classical gods for physical success. Yet the Hebrew God offered spiritual immortality. The Apostles often disagreed, though, on how to spread the word. Peter, named by Jesus as the "rock" on whom he would build his church, believed that salvation would come only to born or converted Hebrews. Paul of Tarsus, a former Hebrew pharisee as well as a Roman citizen, believed the church should be universal. Paul traveled thousands of miles throughout the empire baptizing gentiles into Christianity without prerequisite conversion to Judaism. Jesus' brother James became head of the ministry in Jerusalem.

As decades passed, the Apostles developed rules and rituals for the nascent church. "Church" in its earliest sense simply meant a congregation—a gathering of followers who met in private homes to pray, study scripture, and share the ritual meal of communion.

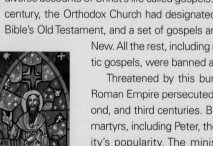
Jesus and Paul, stained glass.

Scripture varied from church to church, including the Jewish Torah and diverse accounts of Christ's life called gospels. By the middle of the fourth century, the Orthodox Church had designated the Torah as the Christian Bible's Old Testament, and a set of gospels and apostolic writings as the New. All the rest, including many of the so-called Gnostic gospels, were banned as heresies.

Threatened by this burgeoning monotheism, the Roman Empire persecuted Christians in the first, second, and third centuries. But by executing many early martyrs, including Peter, the empire only fed Christianity's popularity. The ministries steadily grew, until Emperor Constantine himself converted in 312 and subsequently decreed Christianity the official state religion of the Roman Empire. Local churches organized around urban centers, worshipping under a variety of leaders including presbysters (local priests), deacons, and bishops. Alexandria, Rome, Constantinople, Jerusalem, and Antioch emerged as the five powerful patriarchates of the first two centuries. Their bishops met regularly to grapple with power dynamics and evolving church doctrine. Early on, Rome claimed a position of authority for itself, exerting influence over the other Sees. This led to tensions that eventually split Christendom, with Constantinople as the seat of the Eastern Orthodox Church, Alexandria the seat of the Coptic Church, and Rome the center of the Roman Catholic Church.

80 C.E. with 100 straight days of gladiatorial combat, wild beast hunts, Christian executions, and even mock naval battles in its flooded interior. It was not the first time an artificial lake had flooded the site; ten years earlier, Emperor Vespasian had chosen to build the great arena atop the remains of the vast pleasure garden of the recently deposed Emperor Nero. Once Nero had been forced to commit suicide, Vespasian reclaimed the property for the Roman public with one of the most awe-inspiring constructions of the ancient world. An ellipse of concrete, brick, and stone 620 by 513 feet around, the Colosseum could accommodate some 50,000 people. What stands today is only two-thirds of the original structure, having been looted and quarried for hundreds of years for its lavish marble and limestone exterior. The Colosseum's grandiose, yet practical, design is reflected today in the many sporting arenas of the modern world.

■**FOOTNOTE** Titus's brief reign was troubled in 79 C.E. by the eruption of Mount Vesuvius, which destroyed the cities of Pompeii and Herculaneum, killing thousands of citizens. Titus personally gave financial aid in the disaster.

Teotihuacan Thrives

132 100 C.E. Teotihuacan, the Americas' first major metropolitan center and one of the largest cities in the world at its peak, boasting a dense international population of 150,000 or more, was located in the fertile Valley of Mexico near present-day Mexico City. Though settled by 400 B.C.E., the city may not have taken on its grandiose proportions until around 100 C.E., by which time its main avenue, the Street of the Dead, was flanked by its two largest structures, the Pyramids of the Sun and the Moon, each on par with the pyramids of Egypt in terms of cubic volume. Apart from its many temple-pyramids, Teotihuacan was filled with palatial residences, hundreds of workshops and marketplaces, and more than 2,000 apartment complexes that housed the masses of laborers, merchants,

131 | *A great deal of the massive Roman Colosseum still stands today.*

and artisans. With such a workforce, Teotihuacan was a hub of manufacturing, anchoring a trade network that extended throughout Mesoamerica. Hundreds of years after its demise, Teotihuacan's ruins were still visited annually by Aztec elites, who gave the city the name used today, Nahuatl for "where men became gods."

Funan Emerges

133 100 C.E. The first known large centralized trading empire of Southeast Asia was that of Funan, which emerged sometime after 100 C.E. Heavily influenced by the Indian style of government, the Funan elite ruled as rajas over an area that encompassed portions of modern-day Cambodia, Thailand, Vietnam, and Myanmar. Situated at an important crossroads of trade between India and China, Funan rulers became very wealthy by controlling portage at the Isthmus of Kra. They used this wealth to build gilded palaces and temples, freestanding stone sculptures of Hindu deities, and an extensive irrigation system that produced agricultural surpluses

and hence more wealth. As powerful as it was, the Funan state hastened the process of Indianization by blending indigenous and Indian traditions into a new composite Southeast Asian civilization.

Papermaking Modernized

134 105 C.E. The invention of paper revolutionized the dissemination of information by reducing its cost and ease of transmission to the extent that it eventually became accessible to the masses. A method of creating modern paper was described by Chinese court official Tsai Lun in 105 C.E., though the origins of the process may extend back centuries earlier. Tsai Lun made his paper by shredding and wetting hemp waste, old rags, fishnets, and the bark of mulberry trees, then pressing this pulp into a sheet that, once dried, was applied with ink. The use of paper spread quickly within China, but did not travel west along the silk roads until the eighth century. From Central Asia, it infiltrated the Islamic world and Europe, where it has remained the primary medium of writing to this day.

Trajan Expands Roman Empire

135 **117 C.E.** The greatest geographical extent of the Roman Empire came in 117 C.E. before the death of the Roman emperor Trajan. The first Roman emperor not born in Italy, Trajan pursued an expansionist policy throughout his reign. He subdued the Sarmatian tribes north of the Danube River, annexed the Nabataean kingdom of Arabia, incorporated the kingdom of Armenia, and invaded Parthia, for a short time pushing the boundaries of his empire through Mesopotamia to the Persian Gulf. Though the Middle East had long hosted centers of urban commerce, other frontier regions of the Roman Empire were drastically altered due to the occupation. The influx of resettled Romans stimulated local economies in modern-day France, Germany, Britain, and Spain as local goods were transformed into regional commodities, traded along newly constructed Roman roads. A number of European cities trace their origins back to this process, London and Paris among them.

FOOTNOTE Emperor Trajan's eastern conquest of Dacia—modern-day Romania—left a permanent impact in the country's language; it is the only land in Eastern Europe to speak a Romance language.

Pantheon Remodeled

136 **125 C.E.** The Pantheon, a temple literally dedicated to "all gods," standing in Rome since 27 B.C.E., was completely remodeled by Emperor Hadrian around 125 C.E. Entered through a conventional portico facade and huge bronze double doors, it is the spacious interior of the remodeled Pantheon that was truly innovative. Through the use of a domed roof, a maze of pillars was no longer necessary to support the structure. This afforded a full view of the ornate marble-veneered walls and gilded-bronze rosettes. To create the dome, an unknown architect utilized a succession of load-reducing concrete. Heavy basalt is a primary constituent of the concrete of the dome's foundation, yielding to lighter brick fragments in the next tier, then volcanic tufa, airy pumice, and finally air itself in the form of a 27-foot opening, or oculus, that lights the interior. Measuring 142 feet across, the span of the Pantheon's dome stood unsurpassed until the 20th century.

Bar Kokhba Rebels

137 **132 C.E.** Tensions between Jewish subjects and Roman overlords came to a decisive finality in 132 C.E. when Jewish reactionary Simeon bar Kokhba led a bitter revolt against the policies of the Roman emperor Hadrian. Among other measures, Hadrian had erected a Roman temple overtop the ruins of the Second Temple of Solomon, which had already been destroyed following the first Jewish revolt of 66. An enraged bar Kokhba and his followers drove Roman forces out of Jerusalem for a short time, but the rebellion was soon crushed following bar Kokhba's death in 135. Jews, thereafter banned from the city of Jerusalem, dispersed to form new communities throughout the Roman Empire. With no temple and few priests remaining, the role of the rabbi, or interpreter of Jewish law, was greatly enhanced. Foreseeing no end to persecution and upheaval, rabbis began to compile and codify the canon of oral law into what became known as the Mishnah,

Galen Studies Anatomy

138 **168 C.E.** Renowned Greek physician Galen was called to Rome around 168 C.E. to become personal physician to the Emperor Marcus Aurelius, having completed studies at the prominent medical centers of Alexandria, Smyrna, and Corinth. Born in Pergamum, modern-day Turkey, then a part of the Roman

Greek physician Galen treats gladiator in arena at Pergamum, developing early knowledge of anatomy and physiology.

Empire, Galen was eventually appointed to five Roman emperors. For several years he had worked as a physician at a gladiator school and gained great experience regarding trauma and open wounds. He demonstrated that arteries carry blood instead of air and identified seven of the 12 cranial nerves. He also put forward the long disproved theory of the four humors—blood, phlegm, cholery/yellow bile, and melancholy/black bile. He performed many courageous operations, including brain and successful cataract surgery. In his long career, Galen stressed anatomical studies and Hippocratic notions as the keys to proper medicine. In the absence of human dissection, which was against Roman law, he infused his understanding of the human body with animal attributes and philosophical and theoretical aspects. All in all, Galen was an erudite, logical, and self-congratulatory physician, who wrote prolifically and with conviction, penning more than 300 titles, which summed up medical knowledge up to his day. To some extent, this explains his subsequent massive influence. Galen's works were highly influential to classical, Byzantine, Islamic, and European physicians alike, until largely discredited by Renaissance thinkers of the 16th and 17th centuries.

140 | *About 100 Anasazi lived in Cliff Palace, built into a rock in Mesa Verde, Colorado, using sandstone, wooden beams and mortar.*

which would in turn constitute a large portion of the Talmud, one of Judaism's most important texts. Rabbis would not preach within the walls of their holy city of Jerusalem though until the creation of the modern state of Israel in 1948.

Yellow Turban Uprising

139 **184 C.E.** The Yellow Turban uprising broke out in eastern China in 184 C.E. against the imperial Han rule that was unable to regulate an equitable distribution of land ownership and government involvement. The peasant insurrectionists, discontented by economic disparities and epidemics that were raging through the countryside, wore yellow headdresses representing the color of the Chinese earth. Led by the Daoist mystic Chang Chueh, this first rebellion was put down at great cost to a government already weakened by

corruption and usurpers. Similar rebellions occurred periodically for the next 20 years, as China devolved into a military state. Finally in 220, the Han dynasty was split into three rival kingdoms, the Wei, Wu, and Shu. With the dissolution of the Han dynasty came a loss of interest in its state ideology, Confucianism. In the ensuing era of political turbulence, the speculative personal philosophies of Daoism and Buddhism began to attract many new adherents. The rival kingdoms of China would not be unified again for almost four centuries.

Early N.A. Communities

140 **200 C.E.** The arid deserts of the Southwest are an unlikely environment for the development of some of North America's earliest settled agricultural communities, but that is precisely where the

Hohokam, Mogollon, and Anasazi cultures began to cultivate corn by around 200 C.E. Perhaps due to Mesoamerican influences from the south, the Hohokam dug hundreds of miles of irrigation canals through the desert using just wood and stone tools. The Mogollon practiced irrigation on a much smaller scale, but developed the art of pottery-making, likely also a cultural borrowing from Mesoamerican peoples farther to the south. The Anasazi, expert weavers and basketmakers, stored their gathered and cultivated food in large underground pits, called kivas, the use of which would spread throughout the area. Communication and trade with Mesoamerica continued to stimulate these cultures into increasingly urbanized settlements for more than 1,000 years. Today though, they are truly the Hohokam, a Pima Indian word meaning "those who have vanished."

Aksum Prospers

141 **200 C.E.** The Ethiopian kingdom of Aksum had by 200 C.E. developed into the most prosperous power of sub-Saharan Africa. Dominating the trade routes through the Red Sea between Egypt, Arabia, and eastern Africa, Aksum's major port city, Adulis, housed a bustling market that received textiles, glass, jewelry, and metal tools in exchange for ivory, shell, horn, aromatic spices, gold, silver, and slaves. The rulers of Aksum minted bronze coins, commissioned carved stone thrones to sit within spacious palaces, and erected more than a hundred monolithic granite obelisks, one of which measured 110 feet, the tallest obelisk ever created. The kings of Aksum would eventually import Christianity into sub-Saharan Africa as well, extending their realm and new religion across neighboring lands for over 500 years.

■ **FOOTNOTE** At its greatest extent, the kingdom of Aksum controlled northern Ethiopia, Eritrea, northern Sudan, southern Egypt, Djibouti, western Somaliland, in Africa, and Yemen and southern Saudi Arabia on the Arabian Peninsula.

Andean Cultures Emerge

142 **200 C.E.** Societies in South America's Andean regions grew increasingly complex through the efforts of numerous small states that inhabited distinct ecological niches. Many of these states were in continuous contact through a network of trade that supplied regional products to the larger economy, producing hierarchical communities that supported accomplished metallurgists, potters, and architects. Two such prominent states that had emerged by around 200 C.E. were the Moche, situated along the northern lowland coast of modern-day Peru, and the Tiahuanaco, based around Lake Titicaca in the southern highlands of modern-day Bolivia. The Moche built hundreds of adobe-brick pyramids that often served as tombs for their elite, who were interred with sumptuous grave goods of gold, silver, and turquoise. The Tiahuanaco employed cut stone in the public buildings of their

143 | *Maya Indians used a wide variety of tools to make paper and write books.*

capital city that hosted a population of some 40,000. Though dominant within their respective regions, neither of these states reached the level of empire in a land where harsh environments and rugged geographical barriers did as much for societal organization as any other factors.

> ■ **FOOTNOTE** The Moche culture preserved noble dead in elaborate tombs, the mummified body shrouded in cotton fabric, including precious symbols of power. Some burials indicate that women may have been revered as leaders.

Maya Enters Classic Period

143 **250 C.E.** The Maya civilization of Mesoamerica entered its Classic period around 250 C.E., characterized by divine kings ruling over as many as 50 powerful, independent, hierarchically organized city-states. Beneath the warfaring monarchs was a large class of priests, who wrote on bark paper in an elaborate system of glyphs and maintained the world's most accurate calendar through the observation of the heavens and the application of mathematics. From the hereditary nobility came the merchants, who traded exotic goods and the work of local artisans throughout Mesoamerica. These artisans were expert in the production of polychrome pottery, fine stone tools, woven cotton textiles, and painted murals. A specialized class of professional architects and sculptors produced the most enduring symbols of Maya civilization, their ornately carved limestone pyramids, vaulted temples, palaces, plazas, ball courts, observatories, altars, and other large monuments. As integral to the construction of these massive buildings as the architects were the peasants and slaves that provided the intensive physical labor necessary to erect 230-foot pyramids. These peasants and slaves also worked the outlying farm fields, terraced and channeled to produce a higher agricultural yield. In all, the Maya of the Classic period produced one of the most technologically advanced, artistically sophisticated, and functionally specialized cultures of the Americas.

First Decimal System Developed

145 **300 C.E.** The first decimal number system, one requiring only ten symbols to represent an infinity of mathematical values, was developed in India sometime before 300 C.E. The direct ancestor of the ten Hindu numerals were the Brahmi numerals, which had been in use for at least 500 years but included different symbols for powers of ten as opposed to a single graphic symbol for zero. The earliest evidence of true decimal place-value notation comes from a Sanskrit adaptation of a Greek astrological text from the third century. The advantages of this system for large computational problems were manifold, allowing not only advances in mathematics, but also ease of accounting in business and commerce. This innovation had been passed on to the Muslim world by the end of the 8th century and to Christian Europe by the 12th, where the symbols became known as Arabic numerals. Today it is for the most part a universal mathematical language that has been adopted across the globe.

Artwork from 1508 shows Arabic numerals (left) replacing abacus calculations (right).

Some systems, however, were slow to adapt to the decimal system: In British coinage, for example, 20 shillings made a pound and 12 pence made a shilling. It was not until 1971 that Great Britain changed to the decimal system of coinage. In contrast, the United States did so in 1786.

Diocletian Institutes Reforms

144 **284 C.E.** Diocletian was proclaimed Roman emperor by his troops in 284 C.E., following almost 50 years of instability under 26 ineffective, short-lived, and easily overthrown rulers. Inheriting an empire wracked by civil and military insurrection, Germanic incursions, epidemics, and overstretched resources, Diocletian embarked on a series of reforms that split the Roman Empire into two distinct administrative units, an eastern and a western half, ruled by two co-emperors, each with an appointed second-in-command and heir. The tetrarchy, Greek for "rule by four," was supported by an increased number of specialized bureaucrats and a restored army. This massive reorganization made effective government less dependent on individuals and more so on an established legal system. Though the tetrarchy dissolved into power struggles and civil war after Diocletian himself retired from office in 305, Diocletian's reforms nevertheless laid the political and geographical foundations of the Byzantine Empire and much of medieval Europe.

> ■ **FOOTNOTE** Diocletian's reforms in 293 allowed the western Roman Empire to last for nearly another 200 years; the Byzantine Empire would continue in various forms for more than a thousand years.

Indian Epics Written

146 **300 C.E.** The two great Indian epics, the *Mahabharata* and the *Ramayana,* took on their final written forms around 300 C.E., following many centuries of oral transmission. Originally secular folk tales, by 300 these epics had taken on strong moral and ethical connotations of Hindu philosophy. One an account of an ancient war, the other a love story, both the *Mahabharata* and the

The Cosmic Form

BHAGAVADGITA, 300 B.C.E.-300 C.E.

Arjuna saw the Universal Form of the Lord with many mouths and eyes, and many visions of marvel, with numerous divine ornaments, and holding many divine weapons. Wearing divine garlands and apparel, anointed with celestial perfumes and ointments, full of all wonders, the limitless God with faces on all sides. If the splendor of thousands of suns were to blaze forth all at once in the sky, even that would not resemble the splendor of that exalted being.

Arjuna saw the entire universe, divided in many ways, but standing as all in One, and One in all in the transcendental body of Krishna, the Lord of celestial rulers.

Having seen the cosmic form of the Lord, Arjuna was filled with wonder; and his hairs standing on end, bowed his head to the Lord and prayed with folded hands.

Arjuna said: O Lord, I see in Your body all supernatural controllers, and multitude of beings, sages, and celestials. O Lord of the universe, I see You everywhere with infinite form, with many arms, stomachs, faces, and eyes. O Universal Form, I see neither your beginning nor the middle nor the end.

I see You with Your crown, club, discus; and a mass of radiance, difficult to behold, shining all around like the immeasurable brilliance of the sun and the blazing fire. I believe You are the Supreme Being to be realized. You are the ultimate resort of the universe. You are the Spirit, and protector of the eternal order (Dharma).

146 | *A 14th-century miniature shows Krishna battling the poisonous serpent Kaliya.*

Ramayana are populated by personifications of mythological Hindu gods and goddesses, who expound their views on dharma, or the proper Hindu code of conduct. In this way, both works reinforce the divisions of the caste system and the patriarchal nature of Indian society. In contrast to the material detachment espoused in the Upanishads, these epics made Hinduism accessible to more people by offering salvation to those who actively participated in social, economic, and physical activities, so long as these activities were pursued within the confines of the caste system. The *Bhagavadgita,* a self-contained portion of the *Mahabharata,* with its musings on the nature and purpose of existence, is widely considered the single most important sacred text of Hinduism.

> **■ FOOTNOTE** Among the Vedic schools of philosophy within Hinduism dealing with the nature of reality, the *Bhagavadgita,* the Upanishads, and the Brahma Sutras are considered to be the foundation texts.

Malay Introduce Foods

147 **300** C.E. The banana, originally native to the tropics of Southeast Asia, was introduced into sub-Saharan Africa sometime after 300 C.E. via the Malay settlers of Madagascar. Having traversed the entire Indian Ocean, these Indonesian seafarers brought with them bananas, yams, taro, and chickens, all of which they traded with peoples of the East African coast. Banana cultivation spread from there throughout most of the continent, boosting the nutritious content of the average diet and effecting an immense population increase. Able to grow in heavily forested areas where other crops could not, banana cultivation allowed migratory groups to expand as well as new towns to emerge, pushing Africa along its path of urbanization. Today there are still more varieties of banana grown in sub-Saharan Africa than anywhere else in the world. In East Africa alone, bananas and plantains, eaten as fruit or as vegetables, represent the main staple food for about 50 percent of the population.

Battle of the Milvian Bridge

148 **312** C.E. Roman co-emperor Constantine the Great met his rebellious brother-in-law Maxentius in combat at the Battle of the Milvian Bridge near Rome in 312 C.E. With Constantine's victory, Maxentius became not only one of the last pagan Roman emperors, but also the last emperor to rule from Rome itself. Constantine, who credited his military success to the one God of Christianity, issued the Edict of Milan in 313, confirming official toleration to Christianity and all other religions throughout the empire. He immediately set out to aggrandize the city of Rome with ornate Christian basilicas, though he ruled from Milan in northern Italy. Constantine became sole emperor in 324 and established Constantinople, modern-day Istanbul, as his capital, fashioning it a "New Rome." By the time Constantine himself was baptized a Christian on his deathbed in 337, the religion had developed into an intellectually mature and canonically standardized entity. Constantine's capital city, also the seat of one of the newly formed patriarchates of Christianity, would serve as the capital of the ensuing Byzantine Empire for more than a thousand years.

> **■ FOOTNOTE** As the first Roman emperor to be baptized as a Christian and forbidding persecution of Christians, Constantine, as well as his mother, Helena, are revered by the Eastern Orthodox Church as saints.

Empire Established in India

149 **320** C.E. The Gupta dynasty, prominent by around 320 C.E., established the first centrally administered empire in India since the dissolution of the Mauryan Empire almost 500 years previous. Through marriage alliances and military force, Chandra Gupta II and his successors extended their influence throughout much of the subcontinent, initiating a period of Indian history characterized by a flourishing of the arts and sciences, considered by some India's classical age.

149 | *Wall mural of Buddha dated to the Gupta dynasty, in which the arts and sciences flourished.*

Painting and sculpture under the Guptas achieved a new level of elegant and evocative refinement. Some of India's first free-standing stone temples were constructed. Poetry was imperially patronized and provided with a newly redeveloped alphabetic script. Advances were made in astronomy and mathematics in large part due to the decimal number system. With free rest houses and hospitals established throughout the countryside, the Gupta era in India, once established, created an atmosphere conducive to widespread peace, stability, and learning.

■**FOOTNOTE** Although Gupta emperors promoted religious tolerance and patronage of all religions, Hinduism gradually replaced Buddhism as the dominant religious and cultural tradition of India during their rule.

Japan Unified

150 **350 C.E.** The unification of Japan into a single large polity occurred around 350 C.E. under the Yamato court. Influenced by the centralized imperial government of China to the west, the simple fishermen and farmers of Japan's islands, who had developed iron-working technology, advanced agricultural techniques in rice growing, and horse domestication, had begun earlier in the third century to expand their base of power and evolved into a more warlike group of people.

Leading warriors divided into clans, called *uji,* and became the hereditary elite of a strongly aristocratic society. One clan, the Yamato, soon became preeminent and ruled the fertile Yamato plain of Honshu, Japan's main island, with their capital at Naniwa— modern-day Osaka. They claimed descent from the sun goddess and made her the highest of the nature gods, whose collective worship the Japanese came to call Shinto.

Soon this dominant clan had elevated their leader to the role of hereditary high priest of the realm, and later to emperor. By around 350, Japanese military forces were powerful enough to launch the first of a number of invasions into the Korean peninsula, which resulted in transmission of technology and culture. Soon the Yamato rulers spread these technological advances across the Japanese archipelago. They further imported the first script from mainland China and adapted it to their language. Along with Chinese books, they introduced Chinese philosophy. From Korean monks came the first instruction of Buddhism. The Yamato court also conscripted large numbers of forced laborers to construct monumental keyhole-shaped tombs in burial mounds, known as *kofun,* which were surrounded by moats and adorned with clay statues and occasioned rich funerary rituals.

The Yamato maintained political hegemony throughout Japan for roughly 200 years, during which time they molded a technologically sophisticated culture that was yet able to retain its long-held traditional values.

400-1500

Kings, Saints, and Imams

The era that dawned with the collapse of the Roman Empire in the fifth century C.E. was an age of faith that saw the rise of Islam and the expansion of established religions such as Christianity. Faith alone, however, cannot explain upheavals like the Crusades that set Christians against Muslims in the Holy Land. Now as in earlier times, the pursuit of wealth and power preoccupied rulers of various faiths, who drew inspiration not only from prayers and scriptures but also from the feats of fabled conquerors like Julius Caesar and Alexander the Great. The majesty of Rome lived on in the Roman Catholic Church and the Holy Roman Empire, and emperors in Constantinople, Baghdad, and Chang'an drew on the legacies of ancient Greece, Persia, and China. Seeds of the past were preserved during the Middle Ages and developed into something new, giving rise through reformation and revolutions to the world we know today.

By 400 C.E., the Roman Empire had divided into two parts. The western half, based in Rome, collapsed under pressure from Goths and other Germanic invaders displaced by Huns advancing across Central Europe. The eastern half, which was based in Constantinople, or Byzantium, withstood incursions by tribes descending from the north and emerged as the Byzantine Empire, which reached its peak in the sixth century under Emperor Justinian, whose realm encompassed much of the Mediterranean. Greek served as

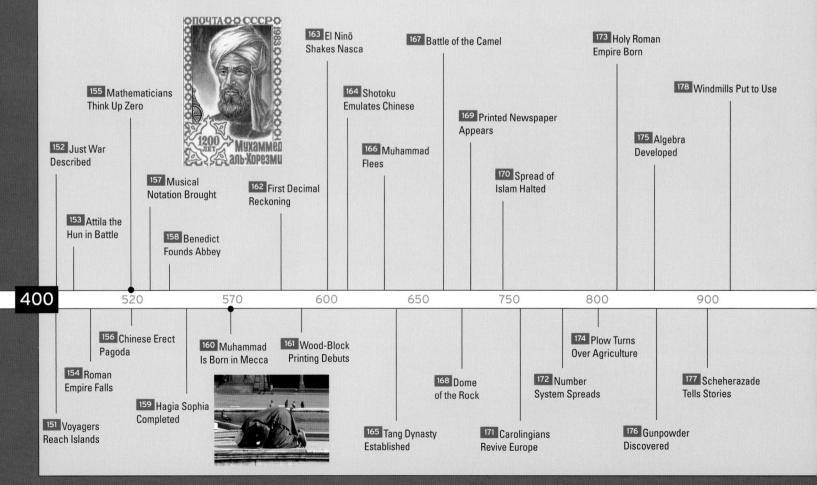

163 El Niñõ Shakes Nasca

167 Battle of the Camel

173 Holy Roman Empire Born

155 Mathematicians Think Up Zero

164 Shotoku Emulates Chinese

178 Windmills Put to Use

169 Printed Newspaper Appears

152 Just War Described

166 Muhammad Flees

175 Algebra Developed

157 Musical Notation Brought

162 First Decimal Reckoning

170 Spread of Islam Halted

153 Attila the Hun in Battle

158 Benedict Founds Abbey

400   520   570   600   650   750   800   900

156 Chinese Erect Pagoda

160 Muhammad Is Born in Mecca

161 Wood-Block Printing Debuts

174 Plow Turns Over Agriculture

154 Roman Empire Falls

168 Dome of the Rock

172 Number System Spreads

177 Scheherazade Tells Stories

159 Hagia Sophia Completed

151 Voyagers Reach Islands

165 Tang Dynasty Established

171 Carolingians Revive Europe

176 Gunpowder Discovered

the official language of this empire, and the Greek Orthodox Church later separated from the Roman Catholic Church, which preserved Latin in its liturgy and greatly influenced the development of Western Europe. Expansion of the Islamic world in the seventh century diminished the Byzantine Empire, but rulers in Constantinople retained control of the Balkan peninsula and Anatolia (modern-day Turkey) for hundreds of years to come.

Caliphs and Crusades

INSPIRED BY THE ARAB PROPHET MUHAMMAD, ISLAM SPREAD rapidly beyond the Arabian Peninsula through conquest and conversion, reaching Egypt not long after Muhammad's death in 632 and sweeping across North Africa to Spain by the early eighth century. This fast-expanding empire was ruled from Damascus by caliphs of the Umayyad dynasty until they were overthrown in 750 by the Abbasid

dynasty, whose new capital at Baghdad became a great center of learning. Enriched by trade with Asia and graced with splendid mosques, palaces, and libraries, the Islamic world of the early Middle Ages was more cultivated and coherent than Catholic Europe, which was divided into many feudal estates and had few rulers worthy of being called kings. One exception was Charlemagne, King of the Franks, crowned Holy Roman Emperor by Pope Leo III in 800. That empire fractured after Charlemagne's death and did not revive until the late tenth century under King Otto I of Germany. Meanwhile, many parts of Europe came under assault by Vikings, who sacked monasteries, laid siege to Paris and other towns, and occupied coastal areas such as Normandy, named for the Norsemen who settled there, adopted Christianity, and later conquered England.

PREVIOUS PAGE | *A scene from the Bayeux tapestry depicting the Norman conquest of Britain in 1066.*

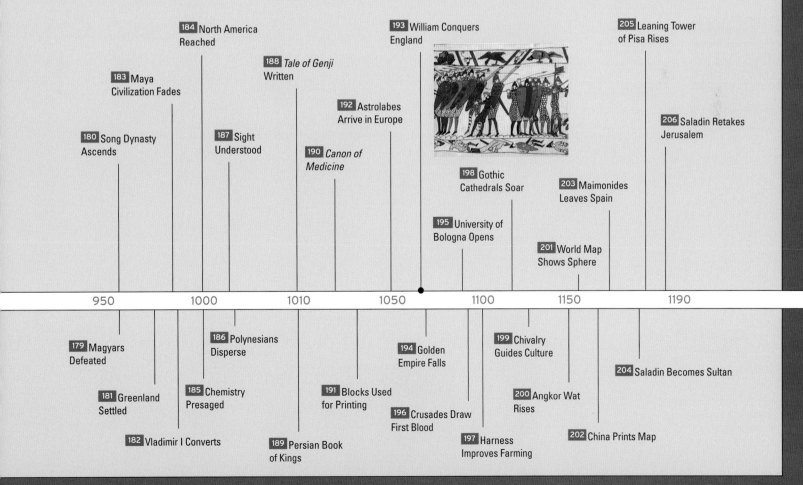

184 North America Reached

183 Maya Civilization Fades

180 Song Dynasty Ascends

179 Magyars Defeated

181 Greenland Settled

182 Vladimir I Converts

185 Chemistry Presaged

186 Polynesians Disperse

187 Sight Understood

188 *Tale of Genji* Written

189 Persian Book of Kings

190 *Canon of Medicine*

191 Blocks Used for Printing

192 Astrolabes Arrive in Europe

193 William Conquers England

194 Golden Empire Falls

195 University of Bologna Opens

196 Crusades Draw First Blood

197 Harness Improves Farming

198 Gothic Cathedrals Soar

199 Chivalry Guides Culture

200 Angkor Wat Rises

201 World Map Shows Sphere

202 China Prints Map

203 Maimonides Leaves Spain

204 Saladin Becomes Sultan

205 Leaning Tower of Pisa Rises

206 Saladin Retakes Jerusalem

950   1000   1010   1050   1100   1150   1190

Venturesome Lords and Knights

IN THE LATE 11TH CENTURY, VENTURESOME LORDS AND KNIGHTS in Europe turned their attention to the Middle East and the holy city of Jerusalem, which was sacred to Muslims as well as to Christians and Jews. The First Crusade, launched in 1095, came in response to advances by Seljuk Turks, Muslims from Central Asia who had recently taken power in Baghdad and defeated Byzantine forces in Turkey. When the Byzantine emperor appealed for help, Pope Urban II in Rome called for a crusade to be waged by faithful Catholics in an effort to repel the Turks and secure the Holy Land for Christianity.

Tens of thousands of crusaders answered the papal call, volunteering their time and services while seeking salvation, adventure, and plunder. The Turks were badly divided following the death of their sultan in 1092 but managed to beat back the first wave of crusaders—an unruly horde led by Peter the Hermit—before losing Jerusalem in 1099 to a stronger Christian army, whose chiefs carved out states along the eastern Mediterranean. That shocked the Islamic world, and new leaders emerged to deal with the crisis, notably the sultan Saladin, who took power in Egypt and went on to reclaim Jerusalem in 1187.

Later expeditions to the Holy Land by Catholic forces failed to end Muslim rule there but demonstrated the growing power of crusading monarchs like Richard I of England and spurred European trade with Asia as crusaders discovered the allure of Eastern goods and spices.

Merchants as Missionaries

TRADE ROUTES DURING THIS ERA SERVED TO CONVEY IDEAS AND beliefs as well as merchandise. Caravans and merchant ships brought Islam to West African kingdoms like Ghana and East African city-states like Mogadishu. Traders from India, meanwhile, were exporting Hinduism and Buddhism to

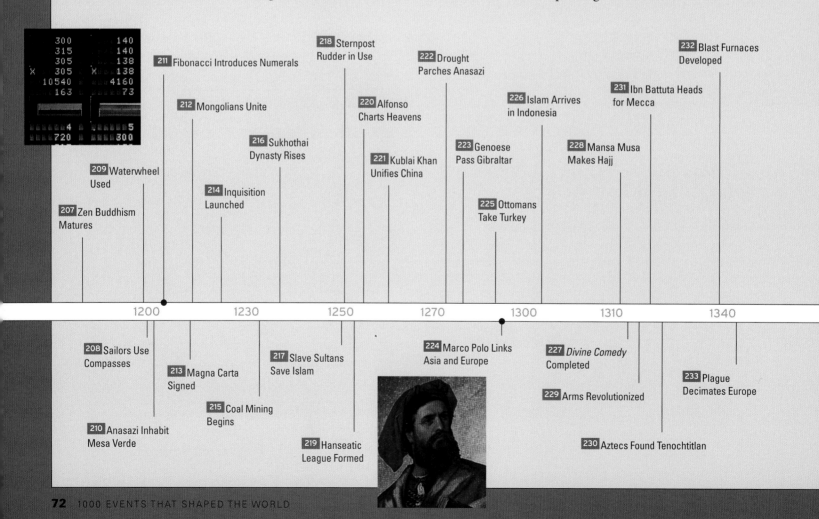

211 Fibonacci Introduces Numerals

218 Sternpost Rudder in Use

232 Blast Furnaces Developed

222 Drought Parches Anasazi

212 Mongolians Unite

220 Alfonso Charts Heavens

226 Islam Arrives in Indonesia

231 Ibn Battuta Heads for Mecca

216 Sukhothai Dynasty Rises

223 Genoese Pass Gibraltar

228 Mansa Musa Makes Hajj

209 Waterwheel Used

221 Kublai Khan Unifies China

214 Inquisition Launched

225 Ottomans Take Turkey

207 Zen Buddhism Matures

1200   1230   1250   1270   1300   1310   1340

208 Sailors Use Compasses

224 Marco Polo Links Asia and Europe

227 *Divine Comedy* Completed

213 Magna Carta Signed

217 Slave Sultans Save Islam

229 Arms Revolutionized

233 Plague Decimates Europe

215 Coal Mining Begins

210 Anasazi Inhabit Mesa Verde

219 Hanseatic League Formed

230 Aztecs Found Tenochtitlan

Southeast Asia, inspiring stunning monuments like the temple complexes at Angkor Wat, capital of the Khmer kingdom in Cambodia.

Although Confucianism remained the guiding philosophy of China's rulers, some of them also supported Buddhist monasteries, demonstrating a religious tolerance and flexibility seldom found among kings in Europe. Under the Song dynasty, which came to power in the tenth century, China reached new heights of prosperity and inventiveness, bequeathing to the world gunpowder and printing presses with movable type.

China's wealth proved an irresistible target for Mongol invaders, who defeated Song rulers in the 13th century but failed to take Japan when gales called kamikaze ("divine winds") wrecked the Mongol invasion fleet. By 1300, the vast Mongol empire extended from the Pacific Ocean to the eastern Mediterranean.

Disease and Conquerors

WESTERN EUROPE, WHICH HAD DEVELOPED RAPIDLY IN RECENT centuries and now boasted thriving cities with soaring cathedrals, escaped invasion by Mongol hordes but fell prey in the 14th century to a scourge that Mongols helped spread—bubonic plague, or Black Death. Despite losing roughly one-fourth of its population, Europe fared better than other regions that were afflicted by this terrible plague but recovered slowly.

When Ottoman Turks seized Constantinople in 1453, Western European traders sought alternatives to overland routes to Asia, which the Turks controlled. Maritime exploration in the late 1400s led Europeans around the Horn of Africa and across the Atlantic to the New World, where the flourishing Aztec and Inca Empires would be devastated by contact with those well-armed conquerors and diseases they brought with them.

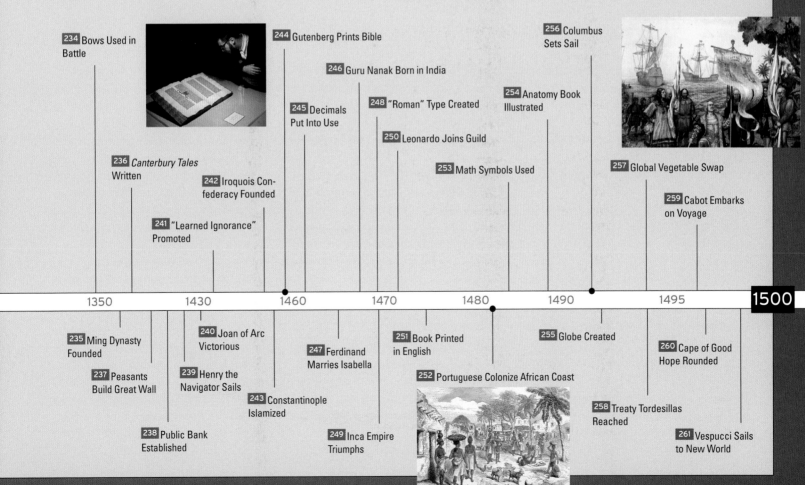

234 Bows Used in Battle

244 Gutenberg Prints Bible

246 Guru Nanak Born in India

256 Columbus Sets Sail

245 Decimals Put Into Use

248 "Roman" Type Created

254 Anatomy Book Illustrated

250 Leonardo Joins Guild

236 Canterbury Tales Written

253 Math Symbols Used

257 Global Vegetable Swap

242 Iroquois Confederacy Founded

259 Cabot Embarks on Voyage

241 "Learned Ignorance" Promoted

1350   1430   1460   1470   1480   1490   1495   **1500**

235 Ming Dynasty Founded

240 Joan of Arc Victorious

251 Book Printed in English

255 Globe Created

260 Cape of Good Hope Rounded

237 Peasants Build Great Wall

239 Henry the Navigator Sails

247 Ferdinand Marries Isabella

252 Portuguese Colonize African Coast

258 Treaty Tordesillas Reached

243 Constantinople Islamized

238 Public Bank Established

249 Inca Empire Triumphs

261 Vespucci Sails to New World

151 | *Native Hawaiian pushes his outrigger canoe up onto the beach in Honolulu.*

Voyagers Reach Islands

151 **400** Guided only by the stars, seafarers traversed vast distances in outrigger canoes to settle the Polynesian islands like a dot-to-dot puzzle. Arriving in Hawaii around the turn of the fifth century, settlers terraced the hillsides to plant taro and other crops. They developed a rich religion honoring a pantheon of gods, including the famous Pele, goddess of the volcano.

For more than a thousand years, the islands' culture was passed down through the art of hula—dancing and chanting that honored the gods and retold Hawaiian history. Hawaiians also developed *he'enalu*, a sport using a flat board to ride ocean waves while standing. Today, surfing is one of the world's most popular water sports.

Just as the stars led humankind to Hawaii, Hawaii has led us to the stars: Mauna Kea Observatory on the Big Island is the world's largest, with 13 telescopes operated by astronomers from 11 countries. Mauna Kea's peak is unparalleled as an observatory site. It sits above 40 percent of Earth's atmosphere in clear skies free from atmospheric and light pollution. Through the mountain's telescopic eyes, astronomers have discovered everything from moons in our own solar system to galaxies at the far reaches of space.

Just War Described

152 **400** Under what circumstances is violence an acceptable means to an end? And what limits should be placed on how war is waged? These are questions that have troubled the conscience of humanity for millennia. As early as the first century B.C.E., Rome's Marcus Tullius Cicero theorized on the justified use of armed force *(jus ad bellum)*, and today's scholars still debate the concept. Indeed, although the theory's intent is to avoid unnecessary violence, "just war" has been invoked as a battle cry for conflicts from the Crusades to the U.S.'s 2003 Iraq invasion.

Modern just war theory coalesced in the fifth century with the teachings of St. Augustine of Hippo (354-430). His late fourth-century work "The City of God" explored the inherent conflict between Christianity and violence. Augustine concluded that, although wars of aggression were never acceptable, sometimes war was a necessity for self-defense or protection of the innocent. Another of his lasting concepts is that, in order to be considered just, warring parties must not target neutral parties—so-called noncombatant immunity, most famously invoked by Switzerland in World War II.

Four primary standards must be met for a military campaign to be considered "just" today: The war must be openly declared by an appropriate authority; it must be motivated by just intentions; it must have a just cause; and the ultimate goal must be to establish a just peace.

■ FOOTNOTE Born in Algeria of Berber descent, St. Augustine is hailed as a founder of Western theology. His influence on Christianity is said to be second only to St. Paul's.

Attila the Hun in Battle

153 **ca 404-53** The "Scourge of God," Attila has been portrayed as a bloodthirsty conqueror by everyone from Latin scholars to Hollywood producers. If the Huns had had a literature of their own, Attila's reputation might have fared better. Unfortunately, only his enemies the Romans left written records of the man and of the years he terrorized Europe. Today, his name is synonymous with barbaric violence.

Attila was the most famous king of the Huns, nomadic horsemen who rode out of Central Asia in the late fourth century, conquering European cities as they moved west. One small technological development gave their cavalry a huge advantage: the stirrup. Able to stand securely astride their horses, Huns could fight with both hands, shooting arrows and hurling spears with deadly accuracy. These "half-horse, half-human" warriors earned a fearsome reputation throughout the Roman Empire.

Attila the Hun met his definitive defeat—and the western Roman Empire its final victory—on the flatlands outside Châlons in Gaul. On a raging campaign west, the Scourge of God and his 100,000 troops had laid waste to a trajectory of cities across today's France, Switzerland, and Belgium.

Attila could be only stopped by a mighty force. The Visigoths and the Romans joined their armies in a historic alliance. They advanced north in the spring of 451 to stop the Huns. The armies clashed on the Catalaunian Plains, where the joint forces defeated Attila. Although he invaded Italy next, Châlons is where Attila stopped being a true threat to the empire.

However, the damage was done. For eight decades the Huns had continually pushed the Germanic tribes deeper into Latin Europe, forcing attacks and weakening the empire's military strength. Attila left the western Roman Empire hanging on by a thread.

■ **FOOTNOTE** The islands in the Venetian Lagoon became a refuge for Roman residents from the mainland trying to escape the Huns. In time they founded a city there known as Venice today.

Roman Empire Falls

154 **476** Barbarian invasions had plagued the West for decades. Rome was in decay—sacked once in 410 by the Visigoths and again in 455 by the Vandals, the once great city had been abandoned for Ravenna, new seat of the western Roman Empire.

The fifth-century emperors were a weak lot; many of them were the puppets of various Germanic generals and chieftains. Tensions mounted with Constantinople as the eastern Roman Empire gained strength. Finally, in the year 476 a Germanic prince named Odoacer conquered Ravenna, dethroned Emperor Romulus Augustus, and named himself king of the Germans in Italy. Officially he served as the viceroy of the eastern emperor—the world's only remaining Roman emperor.

The mighty Roman Empire's legendary roadways, architecture, agricultural systems, and public education system died with it, leading modern scholars to dub the following centuries the Dark Ages. Europe's social cohesion was gone, to be replaced by small tribal

---

CONNECTIONS

Philosophy
St. Augustine sets the Christian Church on its path

Perhaps no thinker shaped medieval Europe more than Aurelius Augustinus (d. 430). This North African Berber forged a solid bridge between the classical scholarship and Christian scripture. Augustine's highly influential writings are known both for their volume—more than five million of his words survive today—and their compelling nature.

Augustine's most influential concept was that of original sin: He rejected the Platonic view that people are basically good, using scripture to argue that people are born sinful and can only be "saved" by God's grace. However, his love for humanity showed in his argument that the church should be universal—welcoming all—and that religious men should work among the people, including the destitute. Christian churches today still quote his maxim: "Love the sinner and hate the sins."

Thanks to his writings, the church made the decision to branch out to German tribes beyond the dying empire. Thus his viewpoints spurred Europe's next 500 years of conversion to Latin Christianity. Cloistered monks may have saved classical literature, but monks who worked in the world saved Christianity as a religion.

Augustine also gave the Western world Progress with a capital P. Greek and Roman philosophers believed history was cyclical, bound to repetitive cycles of prosperity and decline. Augustine instead believed in Judaism's linear concept of time, writing that humanity was

St. Augustine, circa 430

on a path to great glory. This influence shaped the very core of Western society: We strive to be on a continuous path of improvement, believing that progress can be permanent.

The title of Augustine's most famous work, the *Confessions,* conjures images of a reformed libertine. Some modern psychoanalysts have dissected the writings for hints of orgies and homosexual relations. In actuality, "confession" as the bishop wrote it meant proclaiming one's belief in God. There is no substance to the rumors of promiscuity, although he does discuss being sexually active at 16 (years before his conversion to Catholicism). Augustine had a faithful 15-year relationship with a woman he loved deeply. His concubine gave him a son, whom they raised together.

Today, some fault the bishop for being limited in his views on women and for spurring anti-Semitism. He strengthened the church's rule that women, "tainted" by original sin, should not hold positions of power. And although not anti-Semitic himself, Augustine wrote that salvation could come only through the church, which he said should use its power to convert all pagans. Only those who accepted Christ as the Messiah—plus a few deserving rabbis, he said—would have seats near the Lord in the City of God. In later centuries these writings were used to justify the Inquisition, forced displacement of Jews, and other Church atrocities.

Mathematicians Think Up Zero

155 | **520** When counting livestock or pieces of gold, the lowest quantity necessary for computation is one. Ancient numbering systems started there—at one—for thousands of years. Although Babylonian and Greek mathematicians used a symbol like zero as a placeholder to indicate an empty spot in a sequence of numbers, such as 907, the concept of nothingness in math remained just that—nothing.

Al-Khwarizmi brought knowledge of the Indian numeral system to Baghdad.

And then northern India's Gupta dynasty reached its golden age. In this prosperous time emperors patronized the arts and sciences, and great mathematicians such as Aryabhata made great strides in abstract mathematics. Around 500, Aryabhata described "zero" as a quantity, and in the next few centuries, mathematicians worked out laws for adding, subtracting, and multiplying by nothing. By the eighth century, Indian works were translated into Arabic and greatly influenced the developments of the Islamic world's famous mathematicians.

After the Islamic conquest of the Middle East, Baghdad became the center of liberal and scientific studies at the House of Wisdom, founded by Caliph al-Mamoun. Among the scholars gathered there, the mathematician al-Khwarizmi, from Khorason province in Persia, brought along knowledge of the Indian numeral system. He further refined and added to the understanding of numbers and published widely on mathematics, astronomy, geography, and cartography. Translations of his works brought the concept of zero to the West. To this day, his name is synonymous with the words algorithm and algebra.

territories across which the only constant was the Roman Catholic Church. This set the stage for feudalism, which would become the defining social system of medieval Europe.

Chinese Erect Pagoda

156 | **520** During China's Six Dynasties era, a time known for small kingdoms and fragmented culture, one of the great symbols of Asian architecture developed: the pagoda. Adapted from the stupa of ancient India, the pagoda took on its familiar characteristics in Asia—multi-sided and open, with concentric storeys of diminishing size stacking toward the sky.

Most were built as Buddhist temples, including the 12-sided brick one at Songyue Temple in Hunan Province, which is the world's oldest extant pagoda. The Songyue pagoda is a paragon of Chinese architecture: Decorative carvings and curved rooflines change over the centuries, but all were built on the foundations exemplified by Songyue Temple.

Musical Notation Brought

157 | **521** In his treatise *De Institutione Musica*, Roman scholar Boëthius brought ancient Greek music to medieval Europe, and, eventually, to today: He assigned letters to pitch levels, which led to the modern A to G scale; he discussed consonance, scales, and the intervals between pitches; he described the nature of music as a holy creation. Although better known for his philosophical works, Boëthius adhered to the Classical notion that music was intertwined with all disciplines. Medieval scholars considered him the authority on music theory for 1,000 years, and Europe's cathedrals still echo with his harmonies today.

■ **FOOTNOTE** Boëthius wrote his most famous work, the *Consolation of Philosophy*, while languishing in prison. He was arrested by order of Theodoric the Great, ruler of Italy, on charges of treason and was executed in 524.

Benedict Founds Abbey

158 | **529** Today's collections of Cicero, Plato, and Aristotle can be credited to Europe's patron saint. A Christian monk with a utopian vision, Benedict of Nursia established Monte Cassino in Naples to provide a self-contained society for men to walk a path to God. His community flourished, and soon other monasteries adopted the Benedictine Rule—a life devoted to work and prayer—as a model.

158 | *St. Benedict gives follower monastic rules.*

159 | *Istanbul's Hagia Sophia, with its marble columns and rich mosaics, later to become a mosque, is a masterpiece of Byzantine architecture.*

What the saint could not have foreseen was that Benedictine monasteries were to become an asylum for literature as well as for souls. When Rome fell, so had its schools and libraries. But as the monasteries grew into powerful institutions all over Europe, scribes in their scriptoria quietly copied ancient texts and the early Christian gospels, illuminating them with gorgeous jewel-toned inks. These texts were virtually the only examples of Classical literature to survive to the European Renaissance, when scholars assembled surviving fragments to rebuild the masterpieces of ancient Greece and Rome.

■ FOOTNOTE St. Benedict's twin sister, Scholastica, adapted the Benedictine Rule, which can be summed up as "peace, prayer, and work," and established a monastic community for women near Monte Cassino. Adjoining monasteries of monks and nuns were not uncommon.

Hagia Sophia Completed

159 **537** Justinian's nascent reign was in ashes. His court at Constantinople, seat of the Byzantine Empire, had just squelched a rebellion in which 30,000 died and half the city burned. The people were enraged over food shortages and high taxes after several natural disasters had weakened the empire.

But instead of tightening his treasury's belt, Justinian dared a phoenix's rise. He wanted to stamp out challenges to Constantinople's legitimacy as the empire's holy seat. So he commissioned a magnificent cathedral, "the like of which has not been seen since Adam, nor will it be seen in the future."

Legend surrounds the Hagia Sophia's incredibly fast creation, a fitting mystery for this church of "Holy Wisdom." Some say its two architects designed the Roman masterpiece in one month. During construction, priests chanted hymns while builders incorporated salvaged marbles and columns from ruins throughout the empire. At the church's Christmas consecration, Justinian declared it a feat of God, while managing to take a little credit for himself too: "Glory and honor to the Highest, who found me worthy to complete such a work."

What we do know is that Hagia Sophia's 107-foot dome, raining rays of sun on worshippers below, was a feat unmatched in the world for 1,000 years. The basilica became both the center of Eastern Orthodox religious life and the city church of Constantinople, where emperors were crowned and heathens baptized. Its architecture inspired designers all over Christendom, who could mimic but never match the great church's magnificence.

Muhammad Is Born in Mecca

160 **570** The Kaaba, a pagan shrine of the Hubal cult, had attracted Arab pilgrims to the dusty city of Mecca for centuries. And then, in 570, a baby boy was born to the Bedouin tribe that guarded the shrine and its mysterious "Black Rock." This boy would change the Kaaba forever.

The orphaned Muhammad grew up with extended family in Mecca and participated in cultic rituals at the Kaaba. As a young man, he married into a wealthy family that operated camel caravans. Yet Muhammad was not at rest: He suffered visions in which a divine voice would speak to him.

Christians and Jews—both followers of the one God, Allah—were prospering on the Arabian Peninsula at this time. Their stability contrasted sharply with the rough-and-tumble, polytheistic Arab tribes. Muhammad recognized the value of a coherent doctrine for life and worship. He began to teach his message from Allah: "There is no god but Allah, and Muhammad is his prophet."

An adept organizer, Muhammad soon had thousands of followers. When the Prophet's forces conquered Mecca in 630, he ordered all pagan idols destroyed at the Kaaba and dubbed it Islam's holiest place. Today millions of pilgrims still flock to Mecca to pray at the shrine, making the hajj that is a central pillar of their faith.

A Muslim man prostrates himself in prayer in Delhi, India.

When Muslims conquered Constantinople in 1453, the new rulers simply added four minarets and converted the Ayasofya into a mosque. Workers whitewashed over mosaics of Christ, and worshippers prayed toward Mecca in its holy walls for centuries. Despite its Christian origins, the church's architectural influence can be seen in mosques all over the Islamic world.

In 1938, Ataturk declared the Ayasofya would become a museum. Today, visitors of all faiths can lose themselves in the splendor of this piece of heaven on Earth.

Wood-Block Printing Debuts

161 **593** In sixth-century China, a Buddhist craftsman developed a way to reproduce sacred scriptures cheaply and quickly: wood-block printing. The method's earliest recorded fan is Sui emperor Wen-ti, who ordered the production of Buddhist images and texts in a decree in 593.

Printing was simple, yet utterly revolutionary. A sheet of rice paper with original text and images was pasted, face down, onto a smooth wooden block. The block's print was then carved in a raised relief to make a full-page wooden stamp. An inked stamp could print up to 2,000 pages of rice paper on a good day. Today printing is honored as one of ancient China's "Four Great Inventions," along with the compass, paper, and gunpowder.

First Decimal Reckoning

162 **595** India's mathematicians were in love—with numbers. Hindu scholars dallied with unimaginably large numbers, flirted with equations, and created verse about the object of their affections.

In the late sixth century, intellects such as Aryabhata (see event 155) gave the medieval world a gift for modern life: the numeric decimal system. The system worked on a base of 10, with the numerals 0 through 9 representing specific values. Adapted from more primitive systems, decimal reckoning's oldest written record is on a tablet called the Gurjara Inscription, dated 595 C.E.

In flowing lyrics, Indian mathematicians launched into complex calculations using decimal reckoning. Their passion for numbers ushered in many centuries of mathematical discoveries, including advanced geometry and the development of trigonometry.

FOOTNOTE Indian mathematician Brahmagupta is credited with passing along modern concepts of arithmetic, algebra, and numerical analysis to the rest of the world. The Indian number system replaced Roman numerals.

El Niño Shakes Nasca

163 **600** Along Peru's coastline, two great civilizations flourished. The Moche along the northern coast maintained a complex canal system that irrigated maize, beans, and other crops to feed large urban centers. Their priests led ceremonies in grand pyramid temples; their rulers adorned themselves with precious jewelry.

To the south, the Nasca culture produced stunning four-color painted vessels

163 | *Piece of Nasca pottery, found in Peru*

depicting humans and wildlife in stylized scenes. Their most fascinating creations remain the enormous mazelike geoglyphs, called Nasca lines, that still decorate the arid deserts of southern Peru.

Yet both cultures collapsed abruptly around the year 600. Today, climatologists and geologists believe that the weather phenomenon El Niño destabilized the region, leading to catastrophic flooding that, essentially, starved both civilizations.

Shotoku Emulates Chinese

164 **600** The seeds of today's Japan were planted when a young prince named Taishi Shotoku came to power in the late sixth century. A Buddhist in a land still devoted to the ancient Shinto religion, Shotoku had great admiration for all things Chinese.

The prince admired China's unity under its strong emperors. He solidified Japanese emperors' power over its feudal lords under a government devoted to Confucian ideals of cooperation and human rights, codified in his famous Seventeen Article Constitution. He stratified the court system and gathered the first official Japanese history, both emulating the Chinese models of justice and historiography.

Japanese culture blossomed as Shotoku imported Chinese artists, craftsmen, and scholars in droves. He adopted the Chinese calendar and encouraged Buddhism among his people—the gorgeous temple complex at Horyuji, home to the world's oldest extant wooden structures, began at this time.

Tang Dynasty Established

165 **618** In a land ruled by great dynasties, China's Tang (618–907) towers over the others as a golden age of civil government and the arts. Its founder, Li Yuan, had been a high-ranking official in the short-lived Sui dynasty, which had successfully reunited China for the first time since the collapse of the celebrated Han dynasty (220 C.E.).

Under the Sui, Li was known for squelching rebellion—but in 617, with

164 | *Yumedono (Hall of Dreams) in Horyuji Temple in Japan has eight sides and a curving roof.*

his ambitious son, named Li Shimin, he launched a successful coup himself and announced the start of the Tang dynasty. Li Yuan was to rule for just six years before Li Shimin took the throne by murdering his older brother and forcing his father to abdicate.

Despite his bloody hands, Li Shimin, known by his imperial name Tang Taizong (Great Ancestor), became one of China's greatest emperors. He surrounded himself with able advisers who developed a model national system, complete with districts and prefectures, new currency, and public schools. His centralized government was strong and efficient, leading to an era of Chinese expansion west. Fine arts also flourished during this time, especially music and poetry.

■ FOOTNOTE During the Tang dynasty, China reached a high point of civilization. From its capital at Chang'an (now Xi'an) rulers reopened trade with the West along the Silk Road and shipped goods across the empire via the Grand Canal, allowing for expansion of settlements along its route. A new civil service system let young men without connections advance via official exams.

Muhammad Flees

166 **622** The Prophet's message was clear: Polytheism was fundamentally sinful, and those who did not join the path of humility and service to Allah would be damned for all eternity. Preaching in Mecca, Muhammad attracted a band of Believers drawn from Arab tribes and freed slaves. However his own Qurayshi kinsmen, and other prominent tribesmen, did not take Muhammad's perceived insults lightly. They were outraged by this upstart's condemnation of their ancient religion, which highly revered ancestors as well as a pantheon of gods.

Oppression and persecution of the Believers worsened as Muhammad's popularity grew. Yet a seed had been planted in a nearby town, Yathrib. There, Islam had quickly become the predominant religion. A large Yathrib delegation journeyed to Mecca, inviting Muhammad to move and become their de facto leader. His 622 *hijra,* or emigration, to the city that would become known as Medina, "the Prophet's city," marks the first year of the Islamic calendar.

In Medina, the Believers found legitimacy and political power they had never known as a minority band in Mecca. The Prophet established a set of governing rules based on religious principles, of which he was the high judge and ruler. Many Muslims today still look to his Constitution of Medina for guidance, as this first Islamic society is still revered as the ideal one.

> ■ **FOOTNOTE** Yathrib, about 200 miles north of Mecca, was renamed Medinat un-Nabi, the city of the Prophet, known as Medina in English. It is the second holiest city in Islam—after Mecca—and the town where Muhammad is buried.

Battle of the Camel

167 **656** Islam initially spread faster as an empire than as a religion. Muhammad and his first two successors harnessed the military potential of Arabia's populous tribes and turned their minds to conquest. They were gloriously successful, soon establishing a righteous religious government over an empire stretching to the borders of Egypt and Persia.

But the third ruler, or caliph, after Muhammad's death did not have unified support among the Believers. During this time, arguments erupted over who had the right to rule the Prophet's people: Should the caliphate pass down Muhammad's bloodline, or should caliphs be chosen for their leadership instead of their heritage?

Muhammad's favorite wife, A'ishah, led the second group. She opposed the selection of her son-in-law (and therefore the Prophet's as well) Ali as the new caliph. Gathering forces, she and her followers met Ali's along the Euphrates River, near Syria and Iraq. Legend says that A'ishah sat tall on her camel while fighting ensued around her, leading to this battle's name.

Although both sides agreed to a peaceful settlement and arbitration, the Battle of the Camel marks the first in a series of skirmishes known as the First Civil War (656-661). During this time Islam was rocked by its fundamental schism: A'ishah's followers became known as Sunni Muslims, and the party of Ali would become the Shiites.

Dome of the Rock

168 **692** It is a site revered by three of the major world religions. Jewish tradition holds that on this spot in Jerusalem, the patriarch Abraham prepared to sacrifice his son Isaac to the Lord. Nine hundred years later, Jewish king

---

CONNECTIONS

Two Islams
Sunnis and Shiites through history

The roots of Islam's largest schism lie in a political argument over who would succeed Muhammad as the Believers' caliph, or leader (see event 167). Arabic tribal custom decreed that the new leader should be a respected senior, chosen by a council of elders. The majority of Believers followed a line of caliphs chosen by community consensus. Today these "Sunni" Muslims compose approximately 90 percent of the world's 1.3-billion Muslim population. A small but vocal minority held that only the Prophet's relatives could become Islam's rightful leaders—this was the group that championed Muhammad's cousin and son-in-law, Ali, at the Battle of the Camel. Today these Shiites ("followers of Ali") make up roughly 10 percent of the Muslim population.

Sunnis and Shiites have different interpretations of the events that defined their groups. Ali's reign as the fourth caliph was marked by rebellion, ending in his assassination and the founding of the Umayyad Caliphate. In 680, his son Husayn was martyred in resistance to the Umayyads. The killings fueled Shiite loyalty to Ali's line.

From here on, politics and theology reinforced each other within each group. Shiites believed that Muhammad's spiritual attributes were passed through his bloodline in imams, descendants who alone were capable of fully interpreting the Koran and heading a righteous Islamic society. Imams were the highest authority for Shiites, who lived quietly under Sunni rule but did not recognize its

Mosque of the Prophet, Medina

legitimacy. A succession of 12 imams guarded Shiite faith until 939, when Shiites believe that Allah miraculously drew the Twelfth Imam into a state of occultation (hiddenness). Mainstream Shiite doctrine holds that the Twelfth Imam will return at the end of the world, to preside over a righteous Islamic kingdom.

Sunnis have historically revered the Koran over any specific spiritual leader and disapproved of Shiites' passion for their imams, seeing it as a form of idol worship. Their political loyalties went to powerful men who could maintain social order while upholding the Koran's basic doctrines. Eventually, the very fact of power became proof of a caliph's divine right to rule. Thus the two groups' paradigms of leadership led to the dynamic of a Sunni majority and Shiite minority throughout the Islamic world, with Sunnis often marginalizing and discriminating against their neighbors. One notable exception to this is Persia's 16th-century Shiite Safavid dynasty, which established Iran as a world center for Shiite culture.

Modern Sunnism and Shiism cut across many social lines, featuring beggars and kings; moderates and extremists; Arabs, Persians, and Southeast Asians. Many regions have a history of intermarriage and shared prayer. And today the Sunni revere Ali almost as deeply as the Shiites, a result of their neighbors' influence. In regions such as today's Iraq, though, centuries-old resentments have resulted in escalating violence and civil war.

Solomon would build his temple here to house his people's holiest object, the Ark of the Covenant.

Centuries of looting and rebuilding followed. In a new temple on the same spot, a prophet named Jesus would destroy merchants' tables over their blasphemous greed at trading in God's house. And in 632, Islam's Prophet, Muhammad, would ascend to heaven from here, the Temple Mount.

This final event inspired Caliph 'Abd al-Malik ibn Marwan to erect a shrine here, a place for Muslim pilgrims to honor Muhammad. Construction began in 685. The Dome of the Rock was designed with its 60-foot namesake balanced on a series of columns, reflecting Byzantine architectural influence while forever claiming domed architecture for Islam. Gorgeous mosaics and marble were added as the years passed. It was—and remains—the first great building of Islam.

■ **FOOTNOTE** The architecture of the magnificent Dome of the Rock, built in the shape of an octagon with a central dome and adorned with colored and gold mosaics, is a synthesis of the region's Romano-Byzantine-Islamic history.

Printed Newspaper Appears

169 **700** The expanding Tang Empire needed to keep its leaders in the know. Looking for a controlled means to do this, Tang officials harked back to an old Han dynasty tradition. They circulated news sheets known as *tipao* to officials and civil servants, ensuring that leaders could read about court affairs from an "official" source. Soon the tipao was produced using another recent innovation—wood-block type—and the printed word was born.

Spread of Islam Halted

170 **732** Western Europe teetered on the precipice of the Islamic world. To the west, the Iberian Peninsula was now Muslim, and Berbers from North Africa were adding numbers to the already great Arabic armies.

Frankish military leader Charles Martel intended to stop the Muslims. Aquitaine

170 | *Charles Martel delivers a blow to an enemy on his way to defeating the Moors at Tours, France, in 732.*

had just fallen to Cordoba's governor, 'Abd-ar-Rahman. Martel gathered his infantry to face the Islamic army, who advanced on horseback into today's southwestern France. Few details of the battle are known, and some scholars believe that the Arabs' resources for conquest were simply tapped out by this time. But at the Battle of Tours, Martel succeeded in turning away the Arabs—and Islam rule—from Europe once and for all.

As the dust settled, Martel received allegiance from Aquitane and established himself as king over southwestern France. The stage was set for a new dynasty, this time European. Martel began a line that led to one of Europe's most celebrated kings—his own grandson—who would come to be known as Charlemagne.

■ **FOOTNOTE** Whether a Muslim victory at Tours would have meant the further spread of Islam into Europe, remains a hot debate among historians to this day; but the Franks' victory ensured their control over unruly, ancient Gaul.

Carolingians Revive Europe

171 **751** Wresting power from inept Merovingian kings, the Frankish Carolingian family ushered in a European revival in the mid-eighth century with the coronation of Pepin III, Charles Martel's son. Carolingian kings leaned on Anglo-Saxon intellectuals—English and Irish monks—for advice, notably St. Boniface. They established theocratic kingships and worked to gain the loyalty of the papacy, which still looked to Byzantium for political leadership.

Carolingians' effective military leadership and mission of Christian conversion throughout Germanic lands led to the first unified Europe, eventually bringing France, the low countries, Germany, Austria, Switzerland, and Italy into its empire. During this time Europe's signature cultural attributes were

173 | *Reliquary containing part of Emperor Charlemagne's skull*

born. After its fall, the empire's core was divided into east and west—today's France and Germany.

■ **FOOTNOTE** The Carolingians rose from the office of mayor of the palace to the Merovingian kings to becoming virtual rulers of the Frankish kingdom. With consent of the pope, Pepin, the first Carolingian, became actual king.

Number System Spreads

172 **771** Hand in hand with the decimal place-value system in mathematics (see event 162) came the numeral system: the use of unique symbols to represent quantities, rather than using letters or pictures of fingers and toes. The oldest known record of Hindu numerals 0 through 9, which almost all societies use today, are from a 771 tablet of Caliph al-Mansur's court in Baghdad. It was a treatise on astronomy brought by a scholar from India.

The numeral-decimal team was a huge catalyst for mathematical advances in India and, soon, Arabia.

Holy Roman Empire Born

173 **800** The charismatic and ambitious King Charlemagne (Charles the Great) brought the Carolingian dynasty to its height of glory. Coming to power in 768, the Frank loved military life and ruled from the saddle, spreading his kingdom over Europe. At the same time, he supported the arts and funded great libraries in the monasteries of his land. During his reign, the ancient term "Europe" was revived to describe the realm.

Certainly the most famous moment of Charlemagne's reign, however, occurred at Christmas services in St. Peter's Basilica, Rome, in 800. As the king rose from prayer at the tomb of St. Peter, Pope Leo placed a

crown on his head and proclaimed him Charles Augustus, Holy Roman Emperor. From then on, the papacy was loyal to Europe rather than Byzantium.

Plow Turns Over Agriculture

174 **800** Since Roman times, Europe's farmers had used light, oxen-drawn plows to till their soil. This allowed for planting in the sunny climes of the Mediterranean, but such plows were of no use to the heavy soils of northwestern Europe. Sometime around 800, though, the heavy-wheeled plow was adopted from Asia, where it had been in use for centuries.

This muscular machine turned over the dense fields of Europe, leading to a revolution in agriculture and, for the first time, food surpluses there. Soon Europe's nobles began to grow rich, and the agrarian feudal system developed as the organizing factor for European society.

Algebra Developed

175 **825** Number play is an art, a dance with the power to solve mysteries lying at the very core of existence. In the ninth century, one of the world's greatest mathematicians danced with the unknowns and developed a set of rules for solving them.

Musa al-Khwarizmi was a scholar at the House of Wisdom, a scientific research center established by the caliph in Baghdad. During a time when the caliphs wanted to accumulate—and translate into Arabic—all world knowledge, al-Khwarizmi studied ancient mathematicians. One such ancient was the Greek Diophantus (third century C.E.), who had written about solving unknown quantities using a given set of known conditions. Al-Khwarizmi would expand on Diophantus's work greatly, developing descriptions of six types of equations and how to solve them.

Why? Al-Khwarizmi's stated aim was to aid mind-boggling matters of inheritance division (which followed intricate Islamic rules based on kinship in large families),

---

CONNECTIONS

Agricultural Changes
Innovations increase yield, define economy

Europe's first crop, wheat, arrived from Mesopotamia in ancient times. Neolithic Europeans cultivated the many varieties of the genus *Triticum*, enjoying the spring-and-fall labor seasons, free to follow other pursuits in summers and winters. Wheat sucks nutrients from the soil, so farmers developed a two-field crop rotation system, planting half the land while letting the other lie fallow. Thus Europe's arable land was limited in its production volume, reaching a level that remained relatively stagnant throughout the early medieval centuries.

Working within these limits, the feudal farm was an efficient, communal enterprise. From the top a king would grant lands to a lesser noble, who then managed the residents, villages, and farms on them. Both free and enslaved peasants worked and kept the harvest from individual strips of land (in an equitable split between productive and fallow field). They made porridge and rough breads from their wheat, supplementing their diets with kitchen-garden vegetables and free-range meat, especially pork and fowl. In addition to farming their own plots, peasants spent a day or two each week working the lord's land.

Five primary innovations would change this situation, to the extent that many scholars have dubbed the centuries around 1000 C.E. the

Oliena peasants in Sardinia sit on their plow.

Agricultural Revolution. The first three involved horses: the breeding of sturdier animals that were fit for heavy labor; the adoption of the horse-shoe; and the invention of the horse-collar, which evenly distributed weight across an animal's shoulders and thus increased its hauling capability. Oat cultivation—the horses' food staple—was the fourth change. Combined, these innovations enabled the heavy-wheeled plow to work Europe's soils (see event 174).

Finally, farmers transitioned to a three-field crop rotation system, adding a field of leguminous crops such as peas or alfalfa. This reduced the unused soil at any given time to one-third of the region's arable land. Food production exploded then, leading to surpluses that could be traded for commodities and sold to hungry cities. As the Renaissance neared, a market economy began to develop across Europe.

In the later Middle Ages, regional variation began to flavor Europe's products. For example, Muslim countries introduced crops such as eggplant and watermelon to southern areas like France and Spain. Both southern and eastern Europe increased their wine production, devoting more lands to the vines. But Britain was too far north for grapevines. There, much farmland eventually gave way to pasture for its prized sheep and increasingly profitable wool trade.

---

trade, and land use. He described his problems in two ways, first with verbal descriptions, and also with geometric diagrams. Publishing his work in his seminal treatise *A Brief Account of the Methods of al-Jabr and of al-Muqabala,* al-Khwarizmi gave his fellow scholars the bedrock on which to build their work on geometry, trigonometry, and astronomy. The word "al-Jabr" in the title also gave the world a name for this new discipline: algebra.

Gunpowder Discovered

176 **ca 850** What do you get when you combine sulfur, saltpeter, and charcoal? Immortality, Tang dynasty alchemists hoped. Disappointingly, though, the results exploded in their faces. But the alchemists' discovery of

gunpowder has had an eternal effect on world history.

At first used only in fireworks, by 1100 gunpowder was also used as a military tool. Song soldiers invented flame throwers—bamboo tubes filled with gunpowder and oil—which were very effective at repelling advancing enemies. Soon bombs were invented, and military leaders had a favorite new weapon in their arsenal.

Scheherazade Tells Stories

177 **ca 900** A papyrus from the late-ninth century mentions a story in which a girl named Dinazad asks another, Scheherazade, to tell her a story. The modest document betrays no other clues that it is the ancestor of the great Middle Eastern epic, *The Thousand and One Arabian Nights.*

A story within a story, the *Nights* tells of the cuckolded King Shahryar, who in a fury over his wife's infidelity weds—and then murders—a new woman each night. On her own wedding night, clever young Scheherazade saves herself and her kinswomen. She spins a tale for Shahryar and leaves it unfinished, promising to conclude it the next evening. The mesmerized king spares her to hear the end of the story, and each successive night she enchants him in the same way until he is in love.

In truth, there are almost as many versions of the *Nights* as there are evenings in the tale. The epic's historical importance lies in its variations—drawn from India, Persia, Iraq, Turkey, and Egypt, the stories are a mirror of the cultures newly unified under Islam. They offer insight into the customs and social mores of the maturing Islamic

168 More Details on the Dome of the Rock

From almost any street in Jerusalem, and even from many roads that lead to it, one can see the glittering gold cupola of the Dome of the Rock rising above the pale stone city. Resting in the center of the Temple Mount, this Muslim shrine marks the place where the prophet Muhammad began his nightlong journey to heaven with the angel Gabriel. The stone upon which it was built is also significant to Judaism and Christianity. Upon this rock Abraham prepared to sacrifice his son, Isaac, and later, Solomon's Temple was built here to house the Ark of the Covenant. For Christians, the rock holds special significance as the place where Jesus overturned the merchants' tables to chastise them for trading in the house of God. The Dome of the Rock is the oldest surviving Islamic monument in the world and possesses the world's oldest surviving mihrab (niche indicating the direction of Mecca).

Built by 'Abd al-Malik ibn Marwan from 685 to 692 C.E., the shrine was intended to be an important site of pilgrimage as well as a grand testament to the strength of the Islamic faith amid the more dominant Christian and Jewish religions. Said Mukaddasi, a tenth-century writer: "At dawn, when the light of the sun first strikes the dome and the drum catches the rays, then is this edifice a marvellous sight to behold, and one such than in all of Islam I have not seen the equal."

> "When the light of the sun first strikes the dome ..., then is this edifice a marvellous sight to behold."
> —**Mukaddasi**

And the Dome is, indeed, an impressive work of architecture. True to Byzantine style, the Dome's portions are mathematically perfect. The length of the outer walls is equal to the dome's diameter—which is in turn equal to the dome's height from the base of its drum.

The dome itself, now constructed of aluminum metal covered with gold leaf, is topped with a full moon reminiscent of the Islamic crescent. The shrine's exterior is covered in bright mosaic tiles, and verses of the Koran are etched in Arabic around the octagonal walls. The interior, which curves in a great circle around the holy rock, is decorated with ornate mosaics and lavish columns and archways.

The Dome of the Rock, also known as Haram esh Sharif, gleams above the Muslim Quarter of Jerusalem's Old City.

Middle East. And the *Nights* is vastly entertaining, giving the world such folk heroes as Aladdin, Sinbad, and Ali Baba. These tales later inspired musicians like Tchaikovsky and Rimsky-Korsakov to compose music on an oriental theme.

177 | *Poster advertising Imperial Burlesque Company's production of* The Arabian Nights

Windmills Put to Use

178 | **915** Harnessing the wind to do the work of human muscles revolutionizes agriculture wherever it is introduced. Although evidence shows windmills may have been invented earlier, a surviving inscription from 915 proves that Persian farmers already reaped the benefits of wind power for grinding their grain and irrigating their fields. Later, Genghis Khan's forces would capture Persian millwrights and send them to China to introduce the technology there, while Christian Crusaders would carry the technology back to Europe.

Magyars Defeated

179 | **955** Like wasps, Magyar invaders from the south repeatedly stung Europe's Carolingian and Saxon kingdoms in the late first millennium. The fierce warriors posed a serious threat to the adolescent states. But a strong German prince stopped them in their last invasion of Bavaria: Otto I of Saxony crushed the Magyars decisively at the Battle of Lechfeld. After the battle, all other regional princes and nobles declared their fealty to the Saxon, leading to the first unified Germany. And the Magyars? They settled throughout today's Hungary and neighboring lands, transforming into perfectly respectable farmers.

Song Dynasty Ascends

180 | **960** A well-fed, well-educated China flourished during the celebrated Song dynasty (960-1279). Founded by Chao K'yuang-yin, the dynasty benefited from his wise administrative policy, strong civil leadership, and modest adherence to Confucian ideals.

Agricultural advancements filled bellies all over Asia. A faster-ripening rice grain was cultivated, leading to twice-yearly harvests. This surplus not only fed the people, it led to a money economy and new avenues of commerce.

To become an official for the emperor, young men had to pass ever more rigorous civil service exams. Boys as young as five spent their daylight hours memorizing and copying Confucian classics, in order to one day pass the exams. In contrast, the Song era saw a decrease in women's education and freedom—in fact, footbinding began around the advent of the dynasty.

The Song dynasty is perhaps best remembered for the class of artists it supported. Their delicate painting, poetry, music, and ceramics exalted China's peaceful pastoral aura. In addition, the first encyclopedia was created during this time, with about 1,000 volumes of historical and practical information compiled into one work.

> ■**FOOTNOTE** Building on the invention of gunpowder during the Tang dynasty, the Song dynasty is marked by the development of firearms. Weapons included rifles, rockets, and a precursor of the cannon, not to mention a flame thrower.

Greenland Settled

181 | **ca 986** Like his father before him, Viking Erik Thorvaldsson was exiled from Iceland for manslaughter. So he packed up his household and embarked on a three-year tour abroad, with his sights set on an island almost 200 miles away. Erik the Red settled on this icy island, which had some arable land on the southern coast and—unbeknownst to him—indigenous Inuit settlements farther north.

After his exile, Erik returned to Iceland and touted the attractions of the island, which he dubbed Greenland in a clever marketing ploy. He led 25 ships back to Greenland in 986 and established Europe's first colony there. Norse settlements dotted the island for 500 years, until descending glaciers and accompanying Inuit drove the Vikings out.

Vladimir I Converts

182 | **987** Kiev Rus was a Viking society rich in culture and northern commodities—furs and beeswax topped its list—and on the rise. In 980, a pagan prince named Vladimir came to power and soon began enquiries into the religions of the south, probably motivated by reasons diplomatic as much as spiritual.

FIRST PERSON

Nestor

PRIMARY CHRONICLE, 1113

After the destruction of the tower and the division of the nations, the sons of Shem occupied the eastern regions, the sons of Ham those of the south, and the sons of Japheth the western and the northern lands. Among these seventy-two nations, the Slavic race is derived from the line of Japheth, since they are the Noricians, who are identical with the Slavs.

For many years the Slavs lived beside the Danube, where the Hungarian and Bulgarian lands now lie. From among these Slavs, parties scattered throughout the country and were known by appropriate names, according to the places where they settled. Thus some came and settled by the river Morava, and were named Moravians, while others were called Czechs.... The Slavs also dwelt about Lake Ilmen, and were known there by their own original name. They built a city which they called Novgorod. Still others had their homes along the Desna, the Sem, and the Sula, and were called Severians. Thus the Slavic race was divided, and its language was known as Slavic.

179 | *Holy Roman Emperor Otto I's troops defeat Magyars at the Battle of Lechfeld in 955.*

Russia's defining cultural moment arrived in 987, when Vladimir's scouting expeditions returned to Kiev with poor reviews of the other regional religions (folklore holds that he rejected Islam for its ban on alcohol). Already enjoying ties with Byzantium, where he had proffered military aid, Russia's prince chose Constantinople as his spiritual beacon. He converted, married a Byzantine princess, and declared Russia Christian. Today Russians revere St. Vladimir and honor him on his feast day, July 15.

Maya Civilization Fades

183 **987** Of all pre-Columbian civilizations in the Americas, the most is known about the Maya for one reason: They were literate. Their intricate hieroglyphic writing system is inscribed on temples, tablets, and pottery scattered throughout the jungles of the Yucatán Peninsula. Slowly scholars have deciphered the glyphs, learning that these majestic people kept an accurate calendar and were careful astronomers and brilliant mathematicians, although they also let a little blood from time to time to appease the gods.

Flourishing from the third through ninth centuries, the Classical Maya built great complexes around ceremonial temples and dizzying pyramids—without the wheel or the arch—and traded for precious items like jade with their neighbors. Temple centers such as Chichén Itzá and Tikal were also cities supporting hundreds of thousands, including slaves gleaned from neighboring tribes.

But this empire, built on intensive construction and agrarian labor, was unsustainable. One record states that a person's daily ration of maize was 1.5 pounds—too much for the tropical rain forest to support. Around the mid-ninth century the great Maya centers began to be abandoned in favor of smaller jungle settlements.

Toward the north in today's Mexico, another people was on the rise. The Toltec was a warrior tribe pushing south into the Yucatán Peninsula. In 987 C.E., they overran the great Maya center Chichén Itzá, and settled in Maya lands. Over the next generations, the Maya and Toltec peoples merged bloodlines and traditions. Although Maya civilization persevered, the post-Classical era never again reached the heights it had before 987.

Today, Maya people and language live on in Mexico and Guatemala. Their ceremonies still whisper from hidden caves. Stone ruins remain tucked under vines and trees, awaiting rediscovery by a new generation of intrepid jungle explorers.

> ■ **FOOTNOTE** The Toltec capital, located at Tula in the Valley of Mexico, had a large ceremonial center, surrounded by pyramids that were guarded by large stone warriors. At its height, the city housed up to 60,000 people.

North America Reached

184 **ca 1000** With one foot in legend and the other in archaeology, Leif Eriksson's journeys are shrouded in the mists of the past. Historians can agree on just one thing about the celebrated Viking discoverer of North America: He landed here.

Archaeological evidence supports the theory that Vikings landed on the western coast of Canada around 1000. The Icelandic sagas corroborate this, celebrating Erik the Red's second son, Leif, as leader of an expedition that discovers a land rich with grape vines—Vinland. Although the Vikings left no permanent settlements, Leif's one giant step for Vikingkind was the first imprint of change on native North America.

Chemistry Presaged

185 **ca 1000** In China and the Middle East, the study of alchemy

CONNECTIONS

Maya Survival
Jungle growth and missionaries' fires fail to eradicate heritage

After Hernán Cortés conquered the Aztec in the early 16th century, he sent troops south to claim the rain forest's riches. Conquistador Pedro de Alvarado marched into the jungle, discovering the descendants of the Classical Maya. He and Catholic missionaries launched a systematic campaign to destroy native religions and tongues and convert indigenous tribes to Christianity.

For although the majestic pyramids had been swallowed by jungle centuries earlier, the Maya hieroglyphic writing system and rich religious heritage still flourished among local tribes. Elders of the Quiché Maya in modern-day Guatemala followed their ancestors' guidance through one of the world's greatest holy texts, the *Popol Vuh*, which combined Maya creation myth, cosmology, and calendar. By consulting their folding-screen, bark-paper manuscripts, the elders knew when to plant, when to fight, when to prepare for drought. Upon contact with the Quiché, Spanish missionaries burned copies of the *Popol Vuh* as they had thousands of other sacred texts in their quest to cleanse the land of "satanic" influence.

Luckily, one copy survived. During this time, the missionaries taught their new "converts" to write Quiché in the Roman alphabet rather than hieroglyphics. In the 1550s, a scribe lost to time secretly transliterated

The Kukulcán Pyramid at Chichén Itzá

the original *Popol Vuh* into the alphabet. That copy somehow survived until 1702, when a Dominican friar translated it into Spanish. Thanks to their work, the world today can read about the Hero Twins, Hunahpu and Xbalanque, who bested the underworld gods of death and ascended into the heavens as Sun and Moon.

The surviving tales of Quiché Maya creation are just a hint of the rich literature that was lost in the missionaries' fires. Other than the *Popol Vuh*, only four Maya fragments survive—the Paris, Dresden, Madrid, and Grolier Codices—which provide priceless, if tragically scant, insight into Maya history.

And were the Catholics successful in their mission? Yes and no. Today, the seven million Maya of southern Mexico, Guatemala, and Belize pray both to the Catholic god and their ancestral gods. In addition to attending church, the tribes practice shamanistic rituals led by elders schooled in secret Maya knowledge. Despite government laws forcing public schools to teach in Spanish, more than 30 Mayan tongues are spoken today. Most Maya live at the subsistence level, raising corn, beans, and squash as their forebears did. In some regions, such as Belize and the Chiapas in Mexico, conflicts with the Spanish conquerors continue, as tribes struggle for land and the autonomy to preserve their ancient heritage.

---

flourished in the latter half of the first millennium. Whether searching for the secret to making gold or a path to eternal youth, alchemists were consistently rewarded with smaller discoveries. Along the way, they unconsciously laid the foundation for one of today's most important sciences: chemistry.

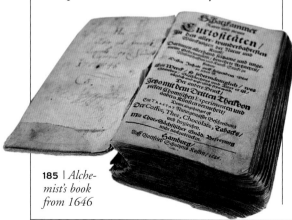

185 | Alchemist's book from 1646

By the turn of the millennium, Arab alchemists had developed practical tools for laboratory work. With extensive knowledge of the earth's metals, they could manipulate them by adding heat, water, or other compounds. Many chemical names are from Arabic—alcohol and elixir, to name just two—and illustrate how important this time was to the birth of chemistry. A thousand years later, chemists would build on alchemy and, with tools like the microscope, lead us into the atomic age.

Polynesians Disperse

186 **ca 1000** Sailing vast distances to discover new islands, the Polynesian people became the most geographically widespread on Earth when they settled New Zealand. Indigenous Maori myth holds that their ancestors came from

"Hawaiki" (thought to be Tahiti) around 1150, bringing their tribal social structure and ancestral religion with them. But archaeologists date their arrival farther back, to 800 C.E. The Maori prospered and maintained their Polynesian culture until the arrival of European explorer James Cook in the 18th century (see event 422).

Sight Understood

187 **1006** In Islam's great learning centers, scholars played with optics: refraction and reflection, rainbows and mirrors, lenses and eyeballs. Translations of great Greek thinkers such as Euclid and Ptolemy gave Muslim scientists a solid foundation on which to make new discoveries about light. Physiologists dissected eyes to map the structures of this remarkable organ.

One Arabic scientist, Ibn al-Haytham, forever changed the way we see sight. He rejected old theories, such as the notion that vision was the result of an eye emitting a ray to an object, or that the object transmitted an actual form of itself to the eye. Instead, al-Haytham wrote that light itself enters the eye, and all that we see is simply the image of physical objects reflecting that light.

Al-Haytham published his theories in Islam's greatest work on optics, *Kitab al-Manazir*. His work would greatly influence later innovators such as Roger Bacon and Johannes Kepler.

Tale of Genji Written

188 **1010** Unparalleled in Japanese literature, Murasaki Shikibu's *Tale of Genji* is a case where scholars agree that the first is truly the best. The world's first full novel, written in prose, is also the crown jewel of Japanese literature.

The *Tale of Genji* is also the world's first juicy tell-all: Murasaki Shikibu was a lady-in-waiting and companion to the empress at the Japanese court. Her hero, Genji, is thought to be modeled after Heian emperor Fujiwara Michinaga. The gorgeous prose masterfully follows his court and his romances, providing details about Heian royal life and about female characters of the time.

■ **FOOTNOTE** Until publication of the *Tale of Genji*, Japanese writing consisted largely of poetry, mythology, and legendary history. During the Heian era, ladies of the court played a central role in developing literature.

Persian Book of Kings

189 **1010** Thousands of miles from Japan, another national masterpiece was completed in the year 1010. Instead of focusing on just one king like the *Tale of Genji*, however, Persia's *Shahnameh* aimed to chronicle all the kings of the land, from mythical times through the seventh century.

Almost 60,000 couplets exalting Persia's kings were written by the poet Ferdowsi, from stories based on an older text.

Yet Ferdowsi's epic was to stick: the *Shahnameh* represents the height of Persian poetry and remains Iran's most celebrated work of literature. In the 16th century, when the Safavid shahs patronized the arts, artists added exquisite illustrations to the book, bringing both its mythical and pastoral scenes to life.

Canon of Medicine

190 **1020** The great Persian physician Ibn Sina (Avicenna, as he's known in the West) left no medical avenue unexplored. His exhaustive studies of anatomy, physiology, pathology, and therapy are compiled in the most influential medical book in history: his *Canon of Medicine*.

Avicenna's medical achievements are too numerous to list in full. Here are a few: He was the first physician to describe the pain-nerve connection, to discover that tuberculosis is contagious, and to acknowledge that emotional health has a profound effect on the body. Encyclopedic in size and scope, the *Canon* quickly

188 | *The left panel of a triptych depicting a scene from the* Tale of Genji

became the primary guide for medicine in all of Islam and Christendom. It remained the highest authority on health for 600 years.

Blocks Used for Printing

191 **1041** The first few hundred years of printing involved slow, painstaking work. Artisans slaved to create each template of type which, after the job, would be tossed in the ancient recycle bin. To produce their next page, artisans had to start from scratch—literally.

The Chinese alchemist Pi Sheng sought an answer to this problem by inventing individual clay blocks of type, which could be assembled to form a page and then later reused. Unfortunately Pi's movable type, which could have revolutionized printing were it for a different alphabet, proved too cumbersome for Chinese script and its hundreds of characters. Handcut woodblocks were to remain the primary printing tools in Asia, although his technology was never completely lost.

> ■ **FOOTNOTE** Many forms of printing existed before the invention of Pi Sheng's clay characters—printed patterns on cloth are the earliest examples from China, dating to before 220 C.E.—but none were durable enough for mass printing until the invention of movable wooden type. With the new printing method, tens of thousands of books were produced for China's libraries. Craftsmen stopped experiments with tin as the first metal type because ink did not adhere well.

Astrolabes Arrive in Europe

192 **1050** For pious Muslims in the late first millennium, necessity truly was the mother of invention. Required to pray toward Mecca five times a day, thousands throughout the vast new empire faced the same questions: Where is Mecca? And does anyone have the time?

Arab astronomers responded, inventing navigational and timekeeping tools to ensure that prayers could be performed properly throughout the realm. Great strides in cartography and astronomy were made, as well as ingenious tools such as the astrolabe. This primitive handheld computer, a version of which had appeared more than 1,000 years previously, could give the time and point its owner toward Mecca, regardless of location.

Arab traders soon packed their new tools and took their cartographic knowledge to sea. By 1050, European sailors had adopted the use of the astrolabe for navigating their own ships. Although it could not provide true longitudinal coordinates, the astrolabe was a strong catalyst for the increase in sea trading in the new millennium.

Golden Empire Falls

194 **1076** South of the brutal Saharan sands—newly navigable on Arabian camels—lay African kingdoms of gold. The earliest of these was ancient Ghana, nestled in the fertile lands of West Africa. Using gold simply for decoration, Ghanians harvested the metal from their rivers and traded with Arabs and Berbers for salt and

William Conquers England

193 **1066** The custom blend of Germanic English and Romance French you are reading on this page would never have existed had William of Normandy not invaded England. But, in 1066, Saxon England was suffering a succession crisis combined with a crippled military. To the east and south, the kings of Scandinavia and French Normandy licked their chops in anticipation. Invasion was imminent.

Although English Harold succeeded in beating back the Norsemen, his infantry was not so lucky against William of Normandy's cavalry. Meeting Harold at the Battle of Hastings, William's strength was further bolstered by his own family claim to the throne. Moreover, he enjoyed the support of the pope in Rome. On the battlefield, Harold took a fatal arrow in the eye, and then William the Conqueror took the throne. His coronation took place at Westminster Abbey, Christmas, 1066.

England's conqueror skimmed off the top of his new society, replacing the English nobility and clergy with imports from France. Although he kept some English institutions, such

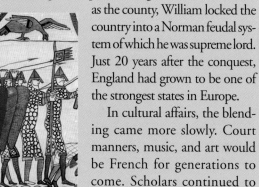

as the county, William locked the country into a Norman feudal system of which he was supreme lord. Just 20 years after the conquest, England had grown to be one of the strongest states in Europe.

In cultural affairs, the blending came more slowly. Court manners, music, and art would be French for generations to come. Scholars continued to write in Latin. And, interestingly, the Saxon peasant's life did not change much after 1066. While French became the language at the manor table, the Germanic

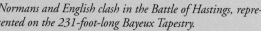

Normans and English clash in the Battle of Hastings, represented on the 231-foot-long Bayeux Tapestry.

sounds of Old English still rang in the stables. Servants cared for cattle, but served their lords *boeuf*.

England prospered under William the Conqueror's rule. As the generations passed, intermarriage led to a mixing of cultures and, eventually, language. Just a few centuries later, Geoffrey Chaucer would take his pen to write *The Canterbury Tales* (see event 236) and record the popular language of Middle English, a Germanic tongue with unmistakable Romance overtones.

other commodities. Growing rich on the trade, Ghana flourished from the seventh through the eleventh centuries.

Eventually the militant Almoravids invaded from the north, bent on jihad. In 1076, they sacked the capital of Kumbi and overtook Ghana in the name of Islam. The kingdom survived in name a bit longer, but as an Islamic settlement—ruins of a mosque have been found from this era.

Some scholars believe that the civilization declined due to overpopulation and stress on the region's natural resources. In the 13th century, the even wealthier kingdom of Mali would encompass the lands of Ghana, sub-Saharan Africa's first great empire.

University of Bologna Opens

195 **1088** As the 12th century approached, European states were growing away from papal Rome and toward secular government systems. The new systems were effective, yet they needed able officials—learned men—whose educations had not come from monasteries. Universities first arose in Europe as a place for youth to study civil law and to prepare themselves for positions of leadership in their king's secular governments.

The University of Bologna in Italy was founded in 1088 and is the oldest of such schools. Soon other professional and scientific "colleges" attached themselves to universities—some religious, some secular—and the institutions blossomed as centers of learning.

■ **FOOTNOTE** Famous alumni of the University of Bologna include: poet Dante Alighieri, humanist Francesco Petrarch, Polish astronomer Nicolaus Copernicus, Swiss alchemist Paracelsus, and German artist Albrecht Dürer.

Crusades Draw First Blood

196 **1095** Pope Urban II faced crises both at home and abroad: First, his prosperous French countrymen were growing crowded and starting to bicker among themselves. On top of that, Constantinople was appealing to him for aid in its struggles against the Muslim Seljuk Turks. Muslims controlled the Holy Land and, it was said, were harassing

196 | *Peter the Hermit, a priest in Amiens, France, and a leader of the First Crusade, rallies listeners.*

Christian pilgrims who came to pray at Christianity's sacred sites.

Here the pope saw an opportunity. In 1095 at the Synod of Clermont, he rallied Europe's Christians to war, urging them to travel to the Holy Land and free Jerusalem from its Saracen rulers. Warriors in the service of Christ, it was said, would be absolved of sin and glorified in the hereafter. Thousands answered the call, looking for adventure, salvation, or both.

The First Crusade (1095-1099) was a success for the Christians, who conquered many lands and established so-called crusader states throughout the Near East. In 1099, they took Jerusalem in a bloody massacre that has been memorialized in both European and Islamic art. A Christian Jerusalem, however, was not to last.

Grasping the full effect of the Crusades on Europe is an elusive task. Among the most prominent results: When Crusaders returned home, they brought with them Eastern culture and tastes; the Christian Crusader States opened trade routes previously closed; Islamic leaders halted offensive attacks on the West; and the Crusaders' stories are immortalized as a central theme in medieval literature.

■FOOTNOTE Following the First Crusade, several short-lived crusader states were established along the Mediterranean: the county of Edessa, the principality of Antioch, the county of Tripoli in Lebanon, and the kingdom of Jerusalem.

Harness Improves Farming

197 **1100** Heavily yoked oxen were Europe's primary draft animals until two inventions, the whiffletree and the horse-collar harness, enabled farmers to plow using the more graceful horse instead. Horsepower led to increased yields (and increased livestock to feed), which, in turn, led to more agricultural innovation—a good thing for the fragile agrarian economies of Europe, where famine was never more than one failed crop away. The inventions also inspired advancements in transportation, increasing the ability to haul loads for trade.

200 | *Roots of a giant fig strangle Angkor Wat in Cambodia.*

Gothic Cathedrals Soar

198 **1120** Perhaps the most famous era in Western architecture, the Gothic period began with a few small masonry innovations that were developed around 1120 in France. The ribbed vault and flying buttress both enabled cathedral towers to soar higher, with more interior open space for humble worshippers to pray in divine light. Intricate stained-glass windows and sculpted stone were the primary Gothic decorative devices. Architects and masons of the era gave the world some of Europe's greatest cathedrals, including Notre Dame, Chartres, and Westminster Abbey.

Chivalry Guides Culture

199 **1130** With the Crusades in full swing, the rough-hewn Christian soldier needed some refinement. And so, with a little help, he became a knight. Around 1130, St. Bernard of Clairvaux set out rules of behavior for these mounted, armed gentlemen: Above all, a knight must be devout to his God, loyal to his king, and chaste.

St. Bernard's rules first applied to history's famed warrior monks—The Knights Templar—but the ideals of chivalry soon spread to all knighthood. Romantic chivalry became one of the central themes of medieval literature, espoused in Edmund Spenser's *Faerie Queene* and Geoffrey Chaucer's *Canterbury Tales*.

Angkor Wat Rises

200 **1150** Flying proudly on the country's modern flag, Cambodia's iconic temples of Angkor Wat are both forbidding and utterly irresistible to modern travelers. The largest religious monu-

on Earth, Angkor Wat covers more than half a mile, including a 600-foot-wide moat surrounding the entire complex.

Monarch Suryavarman II built the temples in 1050 as both his tomb and a shrine to the Hindu god Vishnu, no doubt to emphasize the connection between the deity and himself as divine ruler. The breathtaking towers, built of intricately carved stone, and the moat each represent specific parts of the Hindu cosmos. The temples were a home as well: Scholars believe 20,000 people lived there at its height.

After the fall of the Hindu Khmer empire in the 14th century, the city of Angkor fell to ruin. The buildings, however, overgrown by jungle, were cared for by Theravada Buddhist monks and for centuries the complex was an important Buddhist pilgrimage site.

Angkor Wat is all the more remarkable for having been constructed without mortar. Weight and friction hold the temple stones together. Today the complex is protected as a UNESCO World Heritage site.

■ **FOOTNOTE** After the Angkor capital was sacked by the Cham in 1177, Khmer prince Jaya-varman VII built a new capital and temple. Angkor Wat, originally a Hindu temple, was rededicated to Theravada Buddhism in the 14th century.

World Map Shows Sphere

201 **1154** Roger II of Sicily wanted a scientifically accurate map of the entire world. At this time, maps were either mariners' charts of sea routes, or politically motivated illustrations showing the sponsor at the center of the world.

The king's esteemed court cartographer, ash-Sharif al-Idrisi, compiled geographical information from ancient sources—Greek and Arabic—while sending explorers into the field to survey new lands. The collective results indicated a spherical Earth, so al-Idrisi recorded his map of the seven continents and the seas on a silver sphere weighing almost 900 pounds.

China Prints Map

202 **1155** Mapmaking and printing tiptoed slowly toward each other in the centuries preceding Gutenberg. The oldest known map produced on a press dates to 1155 in China. Soon new tools such as the compass and charts would lead to a boom in seafaring, which in turn led to advances in cartography.

CONNECTIONS

Global Navigation: Pirates and Privateers
Prowling the seas for plunder through history

As maps, navigational instruments, and shipbuilding techniques increased in complexity, Earth's waters transformed into lands of opportunity. States and merchants grew wealthy through sea trading, from furs and honey in the north to pepper and gold in the south. The 10th to 18th centuries were full of sailors who continually stretched the known world's boundaries.

Enter the pirate. This beloved antihero, romanticized in his 18th-century form, had been prowling the seas for plunder since ancient times. Greeks, Romans, and Phoenicians all practiced piracy in the Mediterranean. In those times, there was little distinction between privateers—who stole in the name of a ruler—and pirates, who worked alone.

The Mediterranean was literally a fluid border between Christendom and Islam in the ninth century, during the era of Muslim expansion. Along the eastern and western coasts, Muslim pirates raided ships, villages, and monasteries. Europeans finally abandoned their ports along the western Mediterranean, heading to safer ground inland.

To the north, the Baltic and North Sea coasts were repeatedly terrorized by Vikings, a name that meant "pirate" in the early Scandinavian languages. Although today we apply "Viking" to all Norsemen, including farmers, in its day the term specifically applied to their own brand of seagoing warrior. Their colonies, from Iceland to Russia, greatly influenced northern Europe's cultural and genetic makeup.

Twelfth-century map of the world

In the early 16th century, Ottoman admiral Khayr ad-Din—known to his Christian targets as Barbarossa, or Redbeard—came to power through relentless piracy along the North African coast. He brought the eastern Mediterranean firmly under Ottoman control, encouraging the plunder of trade vessels and coastal towns. Three centuries of Barbary piracy ensued. Funded by rich patrons, pirates terrorized the coast with impunity. Patrons, from countries such as Tunisia, Morocco, Algeria, and Tunis, claimed 10 percent of booty for themselves.

Piracy's golden age of the 18th century was fueled when nations such as England and Spain cut ties to their privateers when not needed for war. Many of these unemployed ships simply began plundering on their own, especially along the trade route between Mexico and Spain. The Caribbean became home to a glut of outlaw fleets. Many pirate ships were captured slave-traders, whose new captains had offered the captive Africans a choice between piracy and slavery. The slave galley *Whydah,* which sank off Cape Cod in 1717, has yielded many clues to the age of Blackbeard. In addition to Spanish doubloons and African jewelry, divers have recovered a Scottish flintlock pistol and a plate engraved with the Freemasons' symbol from the wreck.

Despite international cooperation to eradicate piracy, it remains a problem today, especially in Southeast Asia. The word itself has entered our lexicon as a verb meaning "to steal."

Maimonides

ON TEMPERAMENTS

There are many temperaments, all of which are different and each of which is distinct, and which are possessed by different people. There are people of angry disposition who are always annoyed, and there are those who are even-tempered and are never angry, and if they do get angry, it is only slightly and rarely. There are people who are excessively haughty, and there are people who are excessively meek. There are those with many desires who are never satisfied with what they receive, and there are those with a very pure heart and do not desire even the simplest things that the body needs. There are those with an open heart who would not be satisfied with even all the money in the world, as it is written, "He who loves silver shall not be satisfied with silver," and there are those with a short heart for whom small amounts are enough and sufficient, and will not persevere to fulfil all their needs. Then there are those who mortify themselves with hunger and collect by hand, and will not even eat from a perutah of their own except with great suffering, and there are those who waste all their money without thinking....

Between the extremes of each temperament are the intermediate temperaments, each of which is also distinct. Of the temperaments, there are those which one has from the moment of one's creation [and] according to the one's nature, and there are those temperaments which direct one's nature and which one will quickly acquire in magnitudes greater than that of the other temperaments. Then there are those temperaments which one does not have from the moment of one's creation but which one learns from others, or which release themselves upon one depending upon one's thoughts, or which one heard is a good temperament to have and which is fitting to follow and accustom oneself to until it becomes fixed in one's behavior....

The way of the upright is [to adopt] the intermediate characteristic of each and every temperament that people have. This is the characteristic that is equidistant from the two extremes of the temperament of which it is a characteristic, and is not closer to either.

Maimonides Leaves Spain

203 **1159** Moses Maimonides figures large in history, both as the leading Jewish thinker of his age and the all-time authority on Jewish law (the Talmud). His life also highlights the various privileges and persecutions his people experienced at the turn of the millennium, making him a symbol for medieval Jewry in general.

Born into an elite family of Córdoba around 1135, Maimonides spent a comfortable childhood studying the Talmud under his father, a rabbi. Jews in Islam had held high status in the golden centuries of Arabic intellectualism and religious tolerance. However, twilight had set upon the great caliphates. Fundamentalist rulers such as the Almohads were coming on the scene, abolishing those medieval oases of scientific and classical knowledge, the Arabic learning centers.

When the Almohads took power in Spain, Judaism became punishable by death. Like thousands of others, young Maimonides and his family first went through the pretense of conversion to Islam. The family continued in Córdoba for a time, practicing their faith in secret.

When Maimonides was a teenager, the family left Spain and spent years migrating—first to Morocco, eventually to Egypt. He began penning his great treatises on philosophy and Talmudic law as a young adult. A product of Judaism and Islam, Maimonides wrote in both Hebrew and Arabic. In his lifetime, his works would be translated into Latin and several other languages. A true "Renaissance" man centuries early, Maimonides was also a practicing physician—notably for the sultan Saladin (see event 204).

The Jews of both Islamic Spain (Sephardim) and Christian Europe (Ashkenazim) suffered increasing anti-Semitism in the 12th and 13th centuries. Laws restricting their economic activity led to poverty and ghettoization. Crusaders unleashed vicious pogroms on their communities. In some areas, Jews were forced to wear yellow patches on their arms, a

206 | *Jerusalem's Dome of the Rock, an important pilgrimage site in Islam, with Mecca and Medina*

chilling label that would be seen again in Nazi Germany (see event 811).

In the face of expulsion from countries such as England (in 1290) and France (1306), many Jews converted to Christianity. Others, like Maimonides' family had done in Spain, outwardly converted while continuing to follow Judaism in secret. This hostile environment set the stage for the Spanish Inquisition and, a millennium later, the horrors of Hitler.

> **FOOTNOTE** Maimonides composed the Mishnah Torah, a crystallization of Jewish law and expressed Jewish theory in the 13 Principles of Faith. His philosophical work *The Guide for the Perplexed* influenced thinkers the world over.

Saladin Becomes Sultan

204 **1171** It was 80 years into the Crusades, Jerusalem had long been under Christian rule, and upstart crusader states were threatening Islamic

grand cathedral to celebrate its 1063 defeat of Muslim rule.

Yet the engineers were not expecting Pisa's soft, sandy soil to sink under the weight of so much marble. Construction on the cathedral went well until its final touch—the bell tower—began to list early on. Bonanno Pisano, the head engineer, tried to correct the tower's lean but gave up in frustration after building the third gallery. It would be 200 years before the tower was complete, bell and all.

Modern engineers, recognizing that the building faced imminent collapse, completed the huge undertaking of correcting the tower's angle in 2001. The adjustment was slight—it now leans 13.5 feet off the perpendicular, as opposed to 15 feet—but has stabilized the building for the next 200 to 300 years.

■ **FOOTNOTE** Galileo is said to have dropped two balls of different weight from the Leaning Tower to show that objects of different masses fall at the same speed, proving wrong Aristotle, who thought heavy objects fall faster.

Saladin Retakes Jerusalem

206 | **1187** On the fields of Hattin during the Second Crusade, Saladin's well-prepared military stomped a large army of Christian forces, crushing them so thoroughly that the crusaders would never recover. Saladin freed the rest of the Holy Land from crusader rule throughout the next three months, ending with the crown jewel, Jerusalem.

Saladin's gallantry upon Jerusalem's capture is legendary. Rather than avenging the 1099 massacre of his people by repeating the slaughter (see event 196), he showed mercy and spared Christian lives.

Europeans were surprised by such chivalry in a man whose culture they did not understand. They lionized Saladin as a worthy adversary of their leader in the Third Crusade, Richard the Lionheart of England. Both men are heroes of many romantic song cycles about the Crusades.

Zen Buddhism Matures

207 | **1200** Differing strains of Buddhism blossomed in Japan in the 12th and 13th centuries. The most lasting and influential of these was Zen, which had developed 600 years earlier in China, and was now becoming popular among Japan's military aristocrats. Zen teachings focus on meditation and self-discipline as a path to enlightenment. Samurai, especially, used Zen practice to clear their minds before battle—a central tenet of Bushido, the code of the warrior. Today, almost ten million Japanese follow the Zen path.

Sailors Use Compasses

208 | **ca 1200** A small rock with special properties became a favorite of seafarers in the second millennium. From Asia to Scandinavia, sailors were using the new discovery that lodestone—and iron, when magnetized by lodestone—consistently pointed to the polestar. With a sliver of metal on a spinner, ships could now find north on the stormiest of days.

Instead of having to hop from port to port for fear of getting lost, sea captains began to strike out across the ocean. A huge boom in trade and exploration followed, culminating in the discovery of the Americas.

208 | *A compass like this one would have helped early sailors navigate uncharted open seas.*

holdings throughout the Middle East. In this crisis, a desperate Muslim ruler beseeched a young Kurdish military commander for aid. Yet the vizier got more than he bargained for: Salah al-Din ibn Ayyub, or Saladin, as we know him, would soon wrest control from the ruler and name himself sultan of Cairo.

It was the best thing to happen to the struggling region. Saladin soon earned respect as a wise, generous ruler. He spent his first 15 years in power reining in neighboring factions, becoming sultan also of Syria, Palestine, and Yemen. Under one umbrella, the Muslim states finally had the military strength to face the crusaders (see event 196), which was Saladin's ultimate aim.

Leaning Tower of Pisa Rises

205 | **1173** Beloved by tourists and joke-tellers, Pisa's world-famous tower has tilted from the start. The city was a thriving, independent port in the late 12th century, with plans to build a

Waterwheel Used

209 **1200** Like windmills, waterwheels were one of the earliest innovations to replace muscle power with machine. Constructed of paddles around a wheel, the simple devices utilized the force of flowing water—downhill streams, ocean tides—to rotate. The wheel's rotation, in turn, powered grain mills, textile machines, and wells. Today's hydroelectric dams, which also harness the power of water, are modern descendants of early waterwheels.

■ **FOOTNOTE** One famous example of a medieval waterwheel survives in the Cistercian monastery in Aragon, Spain, used by the monks to divert river water to an aqueduct and power a circulation system for central heating.

Anasazi Inhabit Mesa Verde

210 **ca 1200** The Anasazi had thrived on the mesas of today's southern Colorado since about 600 C.E., cultivating maize, beans, and squash. They were accomplished weavers and potters, with a rich religious life centered on ceremonies in round pit rooms called kivas.

Around 1200, perhaps due to a drying climate up top, or perhaps under threat of raids by the Navajo and Apache, the Anasazi got the urge to climb—down. They built sandstone dwellings beneath cliff overhangs, multistoried complexes where up to 100 people could live in the shade of the rock.

Although the Anasazi dwelled in the cliffs for only a century or so, their homes, such as Cliff Palace and Balcony House, survive as some of the most fascinating artifacts of Native American history. Today, thousands of people a year visit Mesa Verde National Park, touring the ancient dwellings and sensing how it feels to live on the edge of a cliff.

211 | *Fibonacci spiral, based on mathematical sequence*

Fibonacci Introduces Numerals

211 **1202** "These are the nine figures of the Indians: 9 8 7 6 5 4 3 2 1. With these nine figures, and with this sign 0 which in Arabic is called zephirum, any number can be written, as will be demonstrated."

So opens *Liber Abaci, The Book of Calculation,* which Pisan merchant Leonardo

Fibonacci promoted the Hindu-Arabic numerical system in Europe.

Pisano published in 1202. Pisano (better known as Fibonacci) had picked up the numeral and decimal-place systems from Arabic traders. He immediately recognized their superiority to cumbersome Roman numerals, so he decided it was time to give Europe a little math lesson.

The numbers, of course, caught on. And another link was forged in the chain connecting ancient Indian mathematicians to the classrooms and banks of the modern world.

Fibonacci was the son of an Italian customs official doing business in Algeria. As a young man, Fibonacci traveled there with his father and learned of the Hindu-Arabic number system. He realized that these numbers simplified accounting and began to study with Arab mathematicians all around the Mediterranean. He returned to Italy in 1200 and soon published his *Liber Abaci.* Beyond the new number system, Fibonacci is best remembered for the Fibonacci sequence, in which each number is the sum of the two preceding numbers, as in 1, 1, 2, 3, 5, 8, 13, 21, 34, 55, and so on.

Mongolians Unite

212 **1206** A cunning young tribal leader with the charisma and ruthlessness necessary to command loyalty from his people, Genghis Khan began his reign in 1206. It was then that several Mongolian tribes united to elect him khan, and then that he turned his fellow herdsmen to conquest.

Riding east, south, and west in successive campaigns, Genghis and his 100,000-man horde took the world by storm. They were a disciplined army, riding quick Mongolian ponies and shooting whistling arrows, whose sound was designed to instill terror in their targets. Vicious war tactics ensured that their fearsome reputation preceded them wherever they rode. Ahead of them the Mongols pushed a human shield of thousands of prisoners; behind them trailed their families and herds.

Over the next decades, Genghis's horde conquered the Middle East and much of Europe and China. Mongol arrows wiped out entire cities—slaughtering thousands, but also enslaving many women and sending skilled men back to Mongolia as scholars, builders, and statesmen. Where he spared lives, he also spared lifestyles: Genghis did not try to subjugate his victims, preferring their taxes to their cultural assimilation. If you survived Genghis Khan's invasion, chances were you would be able to practice your religion in peace. Mongolian tribes included Christians and Buddhists for generations before Genghis (who was an animist himself).

By the time of his death in 1227, Genghis's lands stretched from the Adriatic to China's Pacific coast. His four sons would push farther, folding Baghdad and other great cities into the largest land empire the world has ever known. But the Great Mongol Empire would be as short-lived as it was vast, breaking up within the next few generations of khans (see event 235).

> ■ **FOOTNOTE** With the destruction of Baghdad, the Mongols wiped out for 500 years the intellectual center of the Islamic world, which had produced the best mathematicians, astronomers, pharmacists, physicians, and philosophers.

Magna Carta Signed

213 **1215** Thrust upon King John as rebels held London in 1215, the original "Articles of the Barons" was a document designed to limit the monarchy's power. To end the revolt, John signed it—and promptly cast it aside. The regent simply hoped to appease England's mutinous nobility and did not take these new limits on his power seriously.

But what came to be known as the Magna Carta, with its nine subject matters devoted to issues such as human rights, land ownership, law reform, and kingly duties, had sticking power. Future kings revised and reaffirmed its tenets, planting the seeds for parliamentary government. Indeed, the Magna Carta's influence can be seen in the U.S. Constitution and the constitutions of many modern democracies.

Inquisition Launched

214 **1231** Heretical groups—that is, Christians and mystics who did not look to Rome for guidance—were on the rise around 1200. Pope Innocent III sought to stamp these flames of independent thought by establishing an investigative arm of the Church. His

successor, Gregory, would do so by issuing the constitution Excommunicamus in 1231, officially establishing a permanent tribunal to try suspected heretics. The Inquisition led to the deaths of perhaps 10,000 scholars and independent thinkers in medieval Europe.

Inquisitors were given the power to accuse suspected heretics, who were then pressured to renounce their sins in the face of torture and, sometimes, death. Jews and scholars were also the subjects of investigations. Inquisitors focused their efforts on coercing their subjects to accept the Church, rejoicing when the accused embraced Catholicism instead of punishment.

It was an oppressive court, but not the bloodthirsty kangaroo court of Hollywood depictions. Most Inquisitors were educated lawyers and monks who avoided

400–1500 | Middle Ages

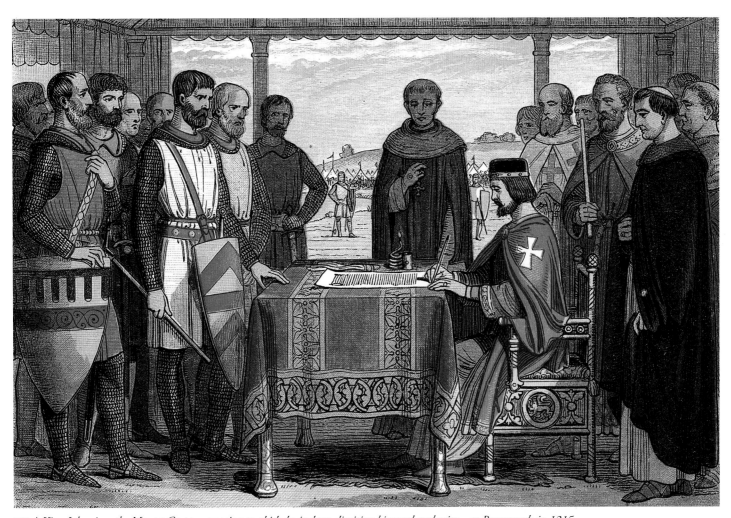

213 | *King John signs the Magna Carta—agreeing to abide by its laws, limiting his royal authority—at Runnymede in 1215.*

hysterical accusations. However, the papal Inquisition paved the way for the cruel Spanish Inquisition and the witch-hunt craze of Renaissance times.

Coal Mining Begins

215 **1233** *Homo sapiens* have used coal since the Bronze Age—loose coal, that is. To dig for it was a different story. But in the early 13th century, monks in Newcastle-upon-Tyne, England, established the earliest known mine for harvesting the most abundant fossil fuel on Earth. Bell mines, with narrow openings and wider bottoms, were the earliest style and soon dotted the northern England countryside. Early records indicate that coal miners provided coal to fuel ironworks for the forging of plows.

Sukhothai Dynasty Rises

216 **1238** Thailand traces its origins to 1238, the founding of the Sukhothai dynasty in what had been part of the Khmer kingdom. Naming themselves Thai, meaning "free," the people of Sukhothai emerged with a distinct language, an art style, and a profitable ceramics industry. King Ramkhamhaeng brought many neighboring states, such as Laos and Burma, into his empire, adding to its wealth.

But perhaps Ramkhamhaeng's greatest contribution to his people was the Thai alphabet, which he commissioned to be adapted from the Indian Devanagari script. Archaeologists know most information about the Sukhothai from a 1292 stone inscription that is the earliest example of the new Thai script. The tablet exults the great kingdom, describing it as a prosperous, peaceful society with a benevolent ruler.

■FOOTNOTE During the Sukhothai kingdom, Thailand reached its greatest extent, stretching from Burma and Laos into the Malay Peninsula. Buddhist monks from Ceylon introduced the Indian script.

Slave Sultans Save Islam

217 **1250** Saladin's Ayyubid dynasty was supplanted by a force within: Its own palace guards, Turkish military slaves called Mamluks. Around 1250 the slaves took over, naming an Abbasid as caliph but keeping the power with themselves as sultans. This marks the movement of Islam's focus from Baghdad (now overrun by Mongols) to Cairo.

CONNECTIONS

Coal Mining
The promise and problems of an energy source

Coal is primeval energy just waiting for release. And humans have done just that for millennia, prizing the abundant fuel for its slow burn and high heat. North American Hopi collected loose chunks for the kilns that fired their exquisite pottery. In Roman Britain, the nobility sported "jet" jewelry; blacksmiths fired their pits with coal; priests used it for their eternal flames at holy shrines. On his 13th-century travels to China, Marco Polo noted the interesting black rocks with which the locals heated their homes.

But it was in medieval Britain that coal was first mined on a grand scale. Deforestation had rendered wood scarce, and the British needed a new fuel to sustain them through frigid winters. Coal, efficient and available, seemed the ideal substance. The fuel became so popular that its noxious smoke was erroneously considered healthful, keeping away "miasmas" of bad air, which might carry diseases like the plague.

For centuries, England's coal mines operated on a steady, small scale, with miners lowered down to active veins and stone manually hauled to light. The dangers of mining were—and remain—many. In addition to the expected cave-ins and floods, mines occasionally filled with poisonous gases that killed without warning. This led to the practice of carrying rats and canaries into the mines, with the thought that their deaths would

indicate rising gas levels (the canary being preferable due to its audible *thunk* upon falling off its perch).

The need for strong water-pumping systems, which kept mines dry, led to the invention of the steam engine. This enabled mining on an increased scale—the industrial revolution of 1780 to 1830 was truly a coal-powered movement. Huge operations, employing thousands, required ever more sophisticated machinery.

With mass labor came mass health problems. Perhaps the gravest consequence was a rise in child labor, with children as young as six spending their waking hours in the dark—crouched, hungry, hauling loads. The smoggy air of industrial cities blocked out sunlight and led to a rickets epidemic. German revolutionary Friedrich Engels came to Manchester in 1842, where the miners' wretched lives spurred his socialist beliefs. Six years later Engels with Karl Marx would publish *The Communist Manifesto*.

Today, coal mining and its uses have a global impact: The substance and its by-products are primary contributors to the greenhouse effect. Yet millions of people still use coal, especially in developing countries, and millions more use electricity generated by coal. Modern technologies allow for cleaner coal processing, but the subject remains controversial.

A flanged-wheeled coal wagon navigates a railway line.

Two great legacies are attached to the Egyptian Mamluks: First, they destroyed the last of the straggling crusader states, ending Christian power in the Levant. Second, they held the Mongolians at bay, saving Egypt—including its charges, Mecca and Medina—from the stinging horde.

Sternpost Rudder in Use

218 **1252** Advances in shipbuilding went hand-in-hand with innovations such as the compass (see event 208) and maritime charts. In Europe, oar usage fell by the wayside as rudders—basically, an oar attached to a ship's hull—took over steering duty. The earliest versions were on boats' sides, but it was on the stern that post rudders were really effective, and where they remain today. Shipping logs in Flanders show that, by 1252, sailors distinguished between boats with side rudders and those with sternpost rudders.

Other advances that boosted the maritime economies of the late Middle Ages included triangular lateen sails, which allowed for sailing before or behind the wind, and rigid keels and sturdier hull construction techniques, which both enabled ships to navigate rough seas. This revolution in sailing capability spurred the great booms in trade, exploration, and cartography that would characterize the next four centuries.

Hanseatic League Formed

219 **1252** It was time for trade negotiations with Countess Margaretha, and this time the German towns of Lübeck and Hamburg banded together. They engaged in the same talks yet emerged with two different trade agreements with Flanders, the most powerful trading center in northern Europe.

These negotiations are the earliest actions of what would come to be called the Hanseatic League, a loose confederation of German towns that worked together to protect each other's trade interests at home and abroad. With feudalism in decline and a money economy on the rise, the league quickly grew into

221 | *Kublai Khan is shown hunting in this detail from a Yuan dynasty ink and color on silk painting.*

a trading power, establishing merchant towns in places like England and Russia. Hanseatic cities fought off pirates (and, in one instance, Denmark) for control of the Baltic, trading timber, furs, and honey.

Although not a political entity, the league was an economic force as Europe transitioned from a land of independent cities to a land of nation states. It would remain powerful for almost three centuries.

FOOTNOTE Hanseatic trade around the Baltic Sea began with timber, wax, amber, resins, furs, and grain; as business grew, new towns developed such as Danzig (Gdansk) in Poland, Riga in Latvia, and Reval (Talinn) in Estonia.

Alfonso Charts Heavens

220 **1252** Alfonso X of Castile and Leon earned his moniker, "the Wise"—he was an intellectual who had many Arabic and Classical scientific works translated into Latin. At the king's request, his court astronomers studied the ancient works and drew up planetary

charts that could pinpoint celestial bodies for any given time or place. Curiously, they were based on the Ptolemaic view of the cosmos, placing Earth at the center of creation. Dated from May 31, 1252, which had been the night before Alfonso's coronation, the charts had an illustrious centuries-long career as Europe's primary astronomical tables.

Kublai Khan Unifies China

221 **1260** Grandson of Genghis, Kublai came to power in 1260 in Mongolia proper, one of the four khanates that now made up the great empire. Although sovereign over the other three—in the regions of today's Russia, Afghanistan, and Iran—Kublai focused his energies at home, with the intention of building a Chinese dynasty of Mongolian origin.

Styling himself in the vein of China's great emperors, he founded the Yuan dynasty and built two majestic capitals (for summer and winter).

209 More Details on the Waterwheel

Waterwheels played a significant role in civilizations from ancient China to Rome and appeared on record as early as the second century B.C.E. Though slave labor was plentiful in early Western societies, making the waterwheel somewhat unnecessary, this engineering marvel was a prime example of invention and advancement. Several flour mills that relied on water power were at work in the outskirts of the Roman Empire in the first centuries C.E., including one large-scale mill in the south of France that likely produced enough flour to feed a neighboring city with a population of about 12,500. The ruins of this factory are studied today as an example of the kind of far-reaching industrial advancement that the Romans, with their abundance of manpower, otherwise lacked.

In the East, a lack of slave labor meant that technological advancement was more crucial, and the Chinese used the waterwheel, employing even greater innovation than their Western counterparts. A text from the first century C.E. reports that water power was harnessed to cast iron for agricultural tools, and advanced grinding systems were developed that would not be seen in the West until several centuries later. Some historians even believe that the Chinese waterwheel technology was exported to Europe via the Silk Road. The waterwheel was a staple of early Chinese society, and the remains of many of these early creations can be found alongside rivers throughout the countryside.

> Some historians believe Chinese waterwheel technology was exported to Europe via the Silk Road.

At their most basic, waterwheels come in two designs: horizontal or vertical. The horizontal is the simpler and relies on a direct jet of water, which turns the millstone directly. The vertical wheels are often constructed on riverbanks or bridges and rely on strong current. Attached gears then drive the millstone. The wheels can be constructed so that current flows either under or over the wheel; the latter is more powerful due to the added force of gravity.

A waterwheel near Jishou, China, is attached to a grindstone. The Chinese developed such technology centuries before Westerners.

Kublai was the first Khan interested in administering his empire, surrounding himself with advisers and establishing an efficient government. He issued a paper currency and commissioned a new script for use throughout the lands. Southern China and Korea became parts of the empire, although Kublai's men suffered great losses when he attempted to invade Japan in 1281.

Kublai became famous as a man who honored foreign knowledge (see event 224), often to the detriment of ethnic Chinese, who shared a mutual strong distrust with the Mongolians. Astronomers, sages, and mathematicians from distant lands gathered at the khan's court. He encouraged religious diversity and debate. Under Kublai's rule, the most populous empire in the world prospered, and his dream of a unified Asia became a reality.

■ **FOOTNOTE** Xanadu, Kublai Khan's opulent summer capital in Inner Mongolia, inspired Samuel Taylor Coleridge's lines "In Xanadu did Kubla Khan a stately pleasure-dome decree."

Drought Parches Anasazi

222 **1276** Thriving in the protection of Chaco Canyon and the cliff dwellings of Mesa Verde (see event 210), the Anasazi culture suffered a severe blow when drought hit in 1276. Massive crop failure brought the threat of famine. Climate change also spurred other tribes, such as the Navajo and Apache, to edge in on Anasazi land.

Soon, the ancestors of today's Pueblo tribes migrated south and east into today's Arizona, where they irrigated the land and resumed their basketweaving and pottery making. The Pueblo Indians today honor these ancestors as Hisatsinom, which means "ancient ones."

Genoese Pass Gibraltar

223 **1277** Europe and North Africa kiss at the Strait of Gibraltar, where they guard the Mediterranean Sea's only outlet to the Atlantic. This far edge of the Classical world remained an outer limit for millennia, until the 13th century C.E. By then, Europe's maritime boom

Marco Polo Links Asia and Europe

224 **1295** After years spent traversing Asia, Marco Polo returned to his native Venice with a few yarns to spin. About *il milione*, in fact, which is the title Polo gave to his classic travelogue about the unknown East. Too fantastic to be all true, many of the tales describe lands of monsters, such as dog-headed and headless peoples.

Mosaic of intrepid explorer Marco Polo in Genoa, Italy

But much of Polo's detail about regions such as Afghanistan and Mongol China is accurate. He, his father, and his uncle spent years at the court of the great Kublai Khan (see event 221), serving as officers in his government. The knowledge they brought home was priceless to Europe's increasing sophistication: Merchants began to seek out Asian spices, and Christopher Columbus used *Il Milione*'s description of Japan to pinpoint a target on his 1492 voyage.

They had started on their journey in 1271 when Marco was only 17 years old. On their return 24 years later, the family settled in Venice and continued their trade with the Far East. The story of their adventures might never have been written if chance had not brought Polo in touch with a writer. In 1298 during a war between Venice and Genoa, Polo was imprisoned by the Genoese. His cellmate, Rustichello da Pisa, a writer of romances, prompted Polo to dictate his story and, no doubt, embellished the accounts.

Although the Polos were not the first Europeans to travel as far as China, the description of their adventures through the steppes of Central Asia, the splendor of the court of Kublai Khan, and the unusual customs of using paper as currency or coal to fuel fires immediately caught on with readers. The book was soon translated into several European languages.

was in full sail. Armed with compass and ambition, a Genoese envoy of traders pushed through the Muslim-held strait in 1277 and journeyed onto the open Atlantic for the first time. The North Sea was their immediate destination, but opening the gates started a flood of sea trading and exploration that would define the next 500 years. It also set Gibraltar up to be the victim of repeated sieges, as powers vied for control of the strategic rock.

Ottomans Take Turkey

225 **1299** Rolling into Anatolia in the late 13th century, a Turkish tribal leader named Osman took power with the aim of jihad against Christian Byzantium.

He established the dynasty that would take his name—Ottoman—and rule until 1922, one of the last large world empires.

Successive sultans pushed steadily westward. More than 100 years after Osman, in fact, the sultan Memed II would take Constantinople, the most famous of the many conquests of the Ottomans. At their zenith, the Ottomans ruled most of southeastern Europe, much of North Africa, and the Middle East.

Islam Arrives in Indonesia

226 **1300** Home to the world's largest Muslim population, Indonesia is a primary figure in Islam today. Yet it took almost 600 years for Muhammad's message to reach this island cluster in Southeast Asia.

The first Muslim Indonesians were Arab merchants who settled on the northern coast of Sumatra to control the sea trade between Arabia, India, and China. Both Marco Polo (see event 224) and Ibn Battuta (event 231) mentioned Muslim kingdoms on Sumatra in their travelogues.

Scholars believe the religion slowly merged with older Hindu, Buddhist, and animist beliefs as it spread west. Indeed, today most Indonesians are moderate Muslims, who blend indigenous traditions with Islamic ones. Notable exceptions, however, are fundamentalist separatist groups such as those in Aceh and the Moluccas, which have violently clashed with the Indonesian government in recent years.

Divine Comedy Completed

227 **1321** Just before crossing to the hereafter himself, Italian literary master Dante Alghieri completed an epic first-person poem about his journey through hell and purgatory to reach heaven. His *Commedia*—later to be dubbed *Divine*—introduces the readers to

many historical figures (including seven Catholic popes in hell), giving a rich gloss to world history and social mores as they were in the 14th century. Purposely writing in his native Tuscan dialect rather than in Latin, Dante was central to the birth of Italian as a language. *La Commedia* quickly found its place in university studies next to the Classical authors of the ancient world, and today is considered the foundation of Western literature.

Mansa Musa Makes Hajj

228 **1324** Even brighter than Ghana (see event 194), the African kingdom of Mali was rich with gold. That precious metal, plus ivory and human slaves, were such hot commodities that the Mali kings were the wealthiest men in all of Africa. The kings converted to Islam, which further strengthened their relationships with the Arabs who traversed the Sahara, laden with salt and other luxuries.

One of those rulers, Mansa Musa, added to Mali's fame with his brilliant mind for public relations. In 1324 the flamboyant emperor made a legendary pilgrimage to Mecca, traveling with a

227 | *A crowd of Muslim pilgrims surrounds the Kaaba in the Haram Mosque in Mecca.*

FIRST PERSON

Marco Polo
TRAVELS, 1298-1299

Lop is a large town at the edge of the Desert, which is called the Desert of Lop, and is situated between east and north-east. It belongs to the Great Kaan, and the people worship Mahommet.... The length of this Desert is so great that 'tis said it would take a year and more to ride from one end of it to the other. And here, where its breadth is least, it takes a month to cross it. 'Tis all composed of hills and valleys of sand, and not a thing to eat is to be found on it.

But after riding for a day and a night you find fresh water, enough mayhap for some 50 or 100 persons with their beasts, but not for more. And all across the Desert you will find water in like manner, that is to say, in some 28 places altogether you will find good water, but in no great quantity; and in four places also you find brackish water. Beasts there are none; for there is nought for them to eat. But there is a marvellous thing related of this Desert, which is that when travellers are on the move by night, and one of them chances to lag behind or to fall asleep or the like, when he tries to gain his company again he will hear spirits talking, and will suppose them to be his comrades. Sometimes the spirits will call him by name; and thus shall a traveller ofttimes be led astray so that he never finds his party. And in this way many have perished. Sometimes the stray travellers will hear as it were the tramp and hum of a great cavalcade of people away from the real line of road, and taking this to be their own company they will follow the sound; and when day breaks they find that a cheat has been put on them and that they are in an ill plight. Even in the day-time one hears those spirits talking. And sometimes you shall hear the sound of a variety of musical instruments, and still more commonly the sound of drums.

Hence in making this journey 'tis customary for travellers to keep close together. All the animals too have bells at their necks, so that they cannot easily get astray. And at sleeping-time a signal is put up to show the direction of the next march.

So thus it is that the Desert is crossed.

humble entourage of 60,000 men, including 500 slaves holding golden staffs, and 80 camels, each carrying 300 pounds of gold. All of his party was clothed in Persian fabrics and silk—their finery combined with their generosity made them famous as they traveled through Egypt on their way to Mecca.

Although northern Muslims were impressed with the devout Malians, they were also shocked by African cultural traditions forbidden by Islam, such as the scanty attire of Malian women. On his hajj, in fact, Mansa Musa was taught a lesson about respecting the opposite sex: An Egyptian official informed him that usage of free women as if they were slave concubines was not allowed to Islamic men. "Not even to kings?" Musa is reported as asking. "Not even to kings," came the reply.

Musa returned from his pilgrimage with plans to make Mali an intellectual center. His capital, Timbuktu, included a palace, great mosque, and a library for his Arabic collections. All this became a university as well, attracting Arab scholars and adding literacy to Mali's long list of achievements.

Encompassing all the territory from the Atlantic coast to the borders of today's Nigeria, and from the edge of the tropical rain forest up to the Saharan sands, Mali was an empire on a par with Mongolia and Ottoman Turkey. Its lands were peaceful and its people prosperous. The great Arab traveler Ibn Battuta (see event 231) wrote of the kingdom: "Neither the man who travels nor he who stays at home has anything to fear from robbers or men of violence."

Arms Revolutionized

229 **1324** For centuries the Chinese had used gunpowder in fireworks and simple bombs (see event 176). But it was not used in Europe until around 1300, when knights did battle with it. Cannon were used at the Siege of Metz in France in 1324—from then on, medieval records are dotted with mentions of cannon and firearms.

In an astonishingly short time, inventors had realized that they could control an explosive to propel a metal sphere out of a cylinder. This harnessing of a chemical reaction to do the work of human muscles represents a huge leap forward for technology. Of all military developments, it is this deadliest of inventions that has had the most profound effect on warfare, the face of the planet, and the human family tree.

CONNECTIONS

Book Bans and Bonfires
Censorship through history

Words and power have been linked since the dawn of language. When the spoken word became the written word around 3000 B.C.E., freethinkers suddenly had a potent weapon: staying power. Recorded ideas can be preserved and disseminated, their impact magnified. Book bans and burnings can be perpetrated by a government, a church, or a small social group. Censors uniformly claim a higher authority than the writers, decrying "objectionable" books on the basis of political, religious, moral, or social (such as racist) grounds. In addition to controlling ideas, censorship—especially mass burnings such as those in Nazi Germany before World War II—can violently smash the cultural identity of entire populations.

One of the earliest recorded instances of a government ban comes from China's first great empire, the Qin dynasty. In 213 B.C.E., the emperor ordered a mass burning of almost all books, especially Confucian texts. Only practical treatises on topics such as agriculture and medicine survived.

An example of individual censorship took place in Florence, Italy, in 1497, when priest Girolamo Savonarola spoke against the Roman Catholic Church's excesses. Florentines were inspired to repent. At Carnival that spring, hundreds threw their worldly goods—clothing, jewelry, art, and books—onto fires, today remembered as the "Bonfire of the Vanities."

Censorship has existed almost as long as writing.

Usually, however, the church itself was the censor. It is no accident that, in the century after Gutenberg's press debuted, an increasing number of texts challenged Rome's position as God's authority on Earth. From 1559 to 1966, the church cultivated history's longest-lived list of banned texts, the *Index Librorum Prohibitorum*. The list included hundreds of "heretical" versions of the Bible. Church inquisitors used the ban to persecute outspoken thinkers, who, like Protestant martyr William Tyndale, were occasionally burned on the same pyre as their books. Luminaries such as Martin Luther and Galileo rubbed elbows with philosophers such as Kant and Locke on the *Index*. In its final edition, compiled in 1948, a total of 4,126 titles were forbidden to Catholics.

In the 20th century, book burnings peaked. In 1933, Nazi propagandists proudly publicized their upcoming burning of "un-German" books, an event that destroyed more than 25,000 texts. Pol Pot's regime in Cambodia destroyed books and murdered readers. In the 1990s, Serbia and Bosnia burned each other's libraries. Iran shocked the West in 1989 when it issued a fatwa against Salman Rushdie for writing *The Satanic Verses*. In U.S. school districts, parents today lobby to ban many titles, notably Mark Twain's *Huckleberry Finn* on the grounds that it is racist. As recently as 2003, conservative Christian churches held burnings of Harry Potter books, labeling the stories the work of Satan.

Aztec Found Tenochtitlan

230 **1325** The Aztec's chief deity, a god with the deceptively delicate name "Hummingbird to the left" (Huitzilopochtli in the Aztec tongue), played a major role in the founding of their capital. Despite a pacific name, Huitzilopochtli had sacrificed his own blood to the sun and required his human subjects to sacrifice to him—those who died in his name would become part of the god himself.

Huitzilopochtli gave the wandering Aztec sustenance and guidance as they searched for a permanent home in the deserts of northern Mexico. The god said their home would be marked by an eagle sitting atop a cactus. When the tribe reached Lake Texcoco in 1325, the great raptor was awaiting them on an island in the water. That day the Aztec founded what would become Mesoamerica's greatest city, Tenochtitlan.

Starting with small wooden huts, the tribe settled on the island and learned how to farm. They borrowed know-how from neighbors, reclaiming swampland and building elaborate irrigation systems. The crops flourished; the Aztec multiplied. Within a few generations, Tenochtitlan grew into a 300,000-person city of palaces and temples, the center of a great empire whose subjects paid tribute—and gave their lives in sacrifice—by the thousands.

Another prophecy of the gods said that the great deity Quetzalcoatl would come to the Aztec from the east in the form of a man with white hair and beard. In a disastrous coincidence, the Spanish conquistador Hernán Cortés arrived in 1519 and chief Moctezuma welcomed him as the god incarnate—to the ruin of himself and his great civilization.

■ **FOOTNOTE** Revolutionary artist Diego Rivera immortalized the capital city in his painting "The Great City of Tenochtitlan" on the walls of the National Palace.

Ibn Battuta Heads for Mecca

231 **1325** Perhaps the world's first professional traveler, Ibn Battuta

233 | *Victims of the bubonic plague, depicted in the Toggenberg Bible, suffered apple-size tumors.*

simply loved the road. The Tangier scholar traversed approximately 75,000 miles of it, beginning with a hajj at the age of 21. His path circumnavigated the Islamic sphere, stopping at courts as distant as Delhi and Mali to entertain, share news, and add to his harem. Dictating his travels upon his retirement, Battutah collected many cultures and histories into one remarkably accurate book, which remains a treasured source of information about the 14th-century Muslim world.

Blast Furnaces Developed

232 **1340** Before the 14th century, European iron "bloomeries" yielded wrought iron, which blacksmiths manually pounded into their desired forms. But innovators continually tinkered with oven designs to increase the quality and quantity of output. Blast furnaces developed, utilizing large oven chambers and water-powered air blasts to raise temperatures until iron ore produced a liquid runoff. The earliest recorded use of this transformative technology is a mention of a Flemish *flüssoven* in 1340.

Liquid iron could be poured into casts of different shapes—such as superlative one-piece gun barrels—and greatly increased the output capability of ironworks in general. Demand for cast-iron objects skyrocketed, especially weaponry, and set Europe on a path that would lead to the invention of the steam engine in the 19th century (see event 393).

■ **FOOTNOTE** Blast furnaces used charcoal, from burning wood, until the 18th century, when English ironworkers began to fuel furnaces with coke instead, producing a higher quality of iron.

Plague Decimates Europe

233 **1347** Modern scholars believe two diseases concurrently hit Europe to kill between 25 and 40 percent of its population between 1347 and 1351. Famous in history is the plague (both bubonic and pneumonic), transmitted by bites from infested fleas. The plague originated in Asia—where it also devastated the people in several epidemics—and came to Europe on merchant ships, thanks to that age-old stowaway, the rat.

According to historian Norman F. Cantor, however, recent excavations prove the presence of anthrax in Black Death corpses,

Giovanni Boccaccio
THE DECAMERON, 1350-1353

The symptoms were not the same as in the East, where a gush of blood from the nose was the plain sign of inevitable death; but it began both in men and women with certain swellings in the groin or under the armpit. They grew to the size of a small apple or an egg, more or less, and were vulgarly called tumours. In a short space of time these tumours spread from the two parts named all over the body. Soon after this the symptoms changed and black or purple spots appeared on the arms or thighs or any other part of the body, sometimes a few large ones, sometimes many little ones. These spots were a certain sign of death, just as the original tumour had been and still remained....

One citizen avoided another, hardly any neighbour troubled about others, relatives never or hardly ever visited each other. Moreover, such terror was struck into the hearts of men and women by this calamity, that brother abandoned brother, and the uncle his nephew, and the sister her brother, and very often the wife her husband. What is even worse and nearly incredible is that fathers and mothers refused to see and tend their children, as if they had not been theirs....

The plight of the lower and most of the middle classes was even more pitiful to behold. Most of them remained in their houses, either through poverty or in hopes of safety, and fell sick by thousands. Since they received no care and attention, almost all of them died. Many ended their lives in the streets both at night and during the day; and many others who died in their houses were only known to be dead because the neighbours smelled their decaying bodies. Dead bodies filled every corner. Most of them were treated in the same manner by the survivors, who were more concerned to get rid of their rotting bodies than moved by charity towards the dead. With the aid of porters, if they could get them, they carried the bodies out of the houses and laid them at the door; where every morning quantities of the dead might be seen. They then were laid on biers or, as these were often lacking, on tables.

leading to theories that the cattle-born murrain (anthrax) was also responsible for the pandemic of 1347-1351. The diseases run identical courses for the first five days, so it would be difficult to distinguish the two. Interestingly, some medieval physicians noted puzzlement over victims who lacked bubonic plague's telltale buboes—hard black bumps—in their armpits and groin.

Regardless of the germ, the Black Death was an indiscriminate killer, condemning its victims to a gruesome, excruciating death. Princess Joan of England succumbed on the way to her wedding with Prince Pedro of Castile. Clergy were especially hard hit, as they tended to their flocks in rat-infested homes. And millions of anonymous citizens fell unmemorialized, as proved by the mass graves that still dot Europe today.

Devastating Islam and Asia in roughly the same years, the Old World searched for answers. Many believed it was divine punishment for sins. Some physicians searched (unsuccessfully) for the underlying cause and transmission mode of the disease. Art from the period shows a preoccupation with the macabre, fitting for a society subjected to seemingly random cycles of doom.

But the hunt for blame was most heinous by far in the hysterical murder of thousands of European Jews, who were blamed for poisoning wells in an effort to eradicate Christianity. Jewish families who survived fled east, to the hinterlands of today's Poland and Russia, where they reestablished prosperous communities. Indeed, the rich culture of eastern European Jewry is a direct result of the Black Death.

Previous European plagues had been followed by baby booms that restored the population within a decade or two. The Black Death was different—such a devastating loss of life spiraled into an economic depression and a severe labor shortage. This led to an escalation of already increasing worker's rights and a money economy. And so the Black Death

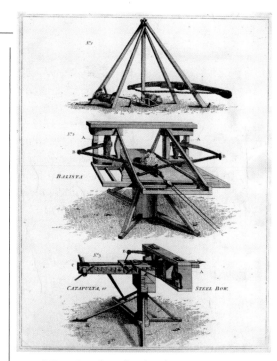

234 | *Drawing of wood and steel weapons, 14th century*

also killed an institution, dealing medieval feudalism a fatal blow.

FOOTNOTE The concept of quarantine arose in 1377 during an outbreak of the plague, when an official in Ragusa, Italy, ordered a 40-day isolation period for travelers and 30 days for ships.

Bows Used in Battle

234 ca 1350 European battles of the 14th century hinged on one of two archery weapons. First came the steel crossbow, much stronger than wooden bows and the first weapon capable of piercing armor. Despite its cumbersome loading process, short range, and unwieldiness, its piercing ability made it the dominant battle weapon until guns took over in the 15th century.

Dominant everywhere but England, that is. The British borrowed a Welsh invention and turned it into the English longbow, a famously graceful and powerful weapon. Shaped of strong, supple yew wood, longbows could also pierce armor and were more accurate in the hands of skilled yeomen. Scholars credit the longbow for England's victories against France in the Hundred Years' War, from Crécy (1346) to Agincourt (1415).

Ming Dynasty Founded

235 **1368** The man who would overthrow the khans didn't seem born under a lucky star. Orphaned by the bubonic plague at 16, young Zhu Yuanzhang buried his parents and older brother himself, then joined other orphans at a Buddhist monastery in central China. From there he would join a militant Buddhist sect fighting to "purify" China before the return of the Buddha—in other words, to end Mongolian rule.

In 1368, Zhu Yuanzhang did just that. He had spent a decade gathering military prowess and troops, and named himself emperor of a new dynasty just before attacking the Mongolian capital. There, he easily ousted the last khan—who fled north into the steppes—and pronounced that the Ming dynasty's new capital would be on the Yangzi River, today's Nanjing.

Zhu never forgot his humble beginnings: He was always conscious of the needy, and passed laws to protect debtors, small business owners, and women. He established an efficient government system that would last until the 19th century. Paradoxically, Zhu also was quick to torture and execute his critics. He is remembered for both his civic mind and his autocratic hand.

■ **FOOTNOTE** Ming rulers sent out four-masted ships carrying up to 500 men exploring sea routes to Japan and Africa. They traded goods like silks and porcelains for tropical woods and spices.

Canterbury Tales Written

236 **1386** Who can forget the lusty Wife of Bath, the pustule-plagued Cook, the pompous Friar? Just three of the pilgrims on their way to Canterbury in Geoffrey Chaucer's unfinished masterpiece, these icons remain some of the most vivid characters in English literature. Chaucer, a man at home with both peasants and kings, drew upon his varied experiences and vast literary knowledge to portray British society in all its strata: A group of pilgrims engage in a storytelling contest as they walk to Canterbury, allowing voices high and low to narrate. In courtly romances, fables, and other literary styles, the characters wax lyrical on themes from cuckoldry to divine grace. The result is an affectionately satirical, often bawdy, forever unparalleled view of 14th-century England.

Peasants Build Great Wall

237 **1400** The khans had been ousted, but Mongolian tribes still rode on the northern steppes, threatening the young Ming dynasty. It was time for drastic defensive action. To this end, Ming rulers conscripted farmers and laborers to

236 | *Chaucer's pilgrims, en route to Canterbury, congregate at the Tabard Inn in Southwark, London.*

230 More Details on Aztec Civilization

What began as a few modest wooden huts on an island in Lake Texcoco eventually grew to become Mesoamerica's greatest city, Tenochtitlan—a sprawling metropolis with 300,000-some inhabitants, grand boulevards, carefully planned districts, and a commerce system to rival the great urban centers of Europe. The city was, in fact, so impressive and modern that the Spanish conquistadores were in awe of its beauty and its likeness to great cities in their native Spain. "With such wonderful sights to gaze on we did not know what to say, or if this was real that we saw before our eyes," wrote Bernal Diaz del Castillo in his eyewitness account, *The Conquest of New Spain.* "On the land side there were great cities, and on the lake many more.... At intervals along the causeway there were many bridges, and before us was the great city of Mexico."

In its time, the central marketplace in Tenochtitlan was likely one of the largest in the Americas, with tens of thousands of the city's inhabitants trading foods and crafts there daily. Goods came from as far away as the Gulf of Mexico and the Pacific coast, and some historians have even supposed that trade routes existed between Tenochtitlan and the Inca Empire. As the nexus of Aztec commerce, the marketplace was situated in the heart of the city amid temples, schools, and other public buildings. Smaller marketplaces also existed in individual districts throughout the city and often reflected each district's artistic specialties.

> "With such ... sights ... we did not know what to say, or if this was real that we saw before our eyes."
> —Bernal Diaz del Castillo

These public spaces were the pride of the city planners, who enlisted hundreds of men to clean the streets and collect garbage. Public latrines also helped to keep the streets free of waste. Trade and travel were enabled by an elaborate waterway system that divided one district from the next; conquistadores marveled at the skillfully designed channels and at the number of canoes floating in and around the city. Still, Cortés and his men would bring the remarkable Tenochtitlan to ruin during their months-long siege of the empire.

Aztec Indians barter for goods at an open-air market at the base of pyramids in the Aztec capital of Tenochtitlan.

fortify China's ancient wall system. Most of today's 4,000-mile Great Wall of China was built during this time. It served not only as a fortress (soldiers were garrisoned at watchtowers and passes) but as a trader's road, connecting distant regions of the vast nation. Today the wall is China's most recognizable feature—and certainly its most popular tourist attraction.

Public Bank Established

238 **1407** Weary of the mandatory loans that the Republic of Genoa demanded from its wealthy, a group of nobles combined forces in 1407 to found Casa di San Giorgio, the world's first public bank. Investors could buy shares—anticipating future stock-market trading—and the bank, in turn, became the sole creditor to the republic. San Giorgio protected the rights of its investors; distinguished between forgivable ("acts of God") loan defaults and unforgivable; specialized in credit checks and tax collection; and offered public accounts.

■ **FOOTNOTE** Medieval moneychangers and bankers risked the most by granting loans to European monarchs to finance war. If the royals did not repay the debts, the business was likely to fail.

Henry the Navigator Sails

239 **1419** Although he never sailed to new lands himself, Henry the Navigator of Portugal earned his moniker by steering Europe into the age of exploration. Enamored with the far frontier, the prince methodically pushed Portuguese discoverers down the coast of Africa. Henry established a court at Sagres, the southwestern tip of Europe, where he drew together a veritable research lab: Astronomers, cartographers, shipbuilders, and tradesmen gathered to add to Henry's catalog of the known world.

Under his sponsorship, the discovery vessel caravel was invented, new navigational instruments developed, and all of history's cumulative geographical knowledge was cataloged in one place. His ships pushed steadily south, learning that the Southern Hemisphere was not a hell on Earth as previously thought; establishing trading relationships with West Africa; and bringing home the first black slaves. Indeed, Portugal's prowess at sea was to become a curse on the southern continent (see event 258).

Joan of Arc Victorious

240 **1429** When angels told a young peasant girl to fight as a knight for her beloved France, they gave the nation its greatest heroine. Young Joan of Arc cut off her tresses, donned armor, and rode to her people's defense against England. She was key in persuading the heir, Charles, to claim the throne for himself, and oust the upstart, the imposter British regent Henry VI. Leading her people to

240 | *Joan of Arc led an army to war and earned sainthood, and a French national holiday ensued.*

victory against the English at Orléans, Joan's fervor was later considered the source of French national identity. The English eventually got their hands on her and burned her at the stake as a heretic, only flaming the fire for her canonization. Today the French celebrate Ste. Jeanne d'Arc with a national holiday, the second Sunday in May.

"Learned Ignorance" Promoted

241 **1440** The last great medieval philosopher and the first true Renaissance man, Nicholas of Cusa made advances in many disciplines: The Catholic cardinal conducted the first botany experiments, concluding that air has weight and that plants derive nourishment from it; he invented an early instrument to measure humidity and the concave lens to correct nearsightedness; he theorized that the sun is only a star among stars, that we are not at the center of the universe, and that space is infinitely moving. Cusanus's astronomical observations were later confirmed by the Hubble telescope in the early 1990s.

But from this man who knew so much, his greatest lesson was what he called "learned ignorance." In his most famous work, *de Docta Ignorantia*, Cusanus philosophized that the only learned men are those who acknowledge their own ignorance, and that this path can lead one to direct communion with the divine.

■ **FOOTNOTE** Nicholas of Cusa is often referred to as the "first modern thinker," influencing the likes of such later philosophers as Locke, Hume, Kant, and Hegel.

Iroquois Confederacy Founded

242 **1451** During a full solar eclipse in the lands that would become New York, five American tribes founded a confederacy in the name of peace. The common-era year was 1451—or 1142, depending on which solar eclipse you choose. Although scholars differ on the date, one thing is certain: By the mid-15th century, the Iroquois Nation of Mohawk, Oneida, Onandaga, Cayuga,

and Seneca tribes was a powerful force. Women in the matrilineal society chose male kin to represent each family at the Great Council Fire, annual gatherings around an eternal flame, where the tribes legislated with the overriding values of peace and humane behavior.

The Iroquois did not war among themselves, but all bets were off outside the confederacy. Neighboring tribes such as the Huron and Mahican people regularly waged territory wars, and in the 17th century would almost conquer the Iroquois with firearms obtained from the Dutch. During the 18th century the confederacy (which had folded in a sixth tribe, the Tuscarora) remained autonomous among the French and British. Iroquois leaders taught the Europeans their elaborate rituals for negotiating treaties, which became the standard protocol for northeastern diplomacy. Several of the Indian tribes even fought beside the redcoats in the

American Revolution, preferring the king's rule to the unknown.

Indeed, the confederacy dispersed around the same time the United States was founded. The Oneida moved to a reservation in Ohio; the Mohawk and Cayuga journeyed north to Canada. The final three tribes remain in New York.

Constantinople Islamized

243 **1453** Revered by eastern Christendom, coveted by Islam, Constantinople had stood as a symbol for the power balance between the religions for centuries. Ottoman sultan Mehmed II would be the hero to win this prize for Islam: In April 1453 he launched a siege of the declining city, and after two months succeeded in conquering it. Crowning the jewel Istanbul, Mehmed converted churches such as the Hagia Sophia (see event 159) to mosques and established a palace for the sultans. Byzantium would never rise again.

Gutenberg Prints Bible

244 **1455** Literacy's watershed moment came to humanity when the German inventor Johannes Gutenberg altered a wine press to create the first modern printing press. Using the machine's heavy screw to press a printing block on a sheet of paper, Gutenberg pioneered a method that would remain largely unchanged until the 20th century. To produce enough of each letter for his type, he devised a punch-stamp mold that could cut precise letters en masse. A new metal alloy for the type and an oil-based ink completed his system.

Bringing forth his 42-line Bible in 1455, Gutenberg changed the course of history. Suddenly books could be had relatively cheaply, inspiring many middle-class people to learn to read. Writers published in the vernacular rather than Latin, strengthening the diverse Romance languages in Europe today. The great world of modern communications was taking off. Despite the importance of this event in retrospect, Gutenberg's financier sued him for the rights to his printing enterprise and grew rich while the inventor died in relative obscurity.

A carefully preserved Gutenberg Bible at the Gutenberg Museum in Mainz, Germany

Gutenberg's printing press, capable of producing about 240 pages per hour, endured for some 300 years until the industrial revolution superseded the equipment with a steam-powered press that could print more than 1,000 pages per hour.

246 | *A ceremonial Sikh guard stands watch over the Golden Temple, Sikhs' holiest site, in Amritsar, India.*

Decimals Put Into Use

245 **1460** Until about 1460, values between zero and one were always expressed as traditional fractions. Earlier experiments in decimal fraction calculations had not caught on, but the German mathematician Regiomantus (Johannes Müller) was able to make the point stick.

Using the same theory for numbers to the right of the decimal point as for numbers to the left, Müller devised a system based on 10 for the numbers to the right. He used these newly supple figures for his work in trigonometry.

Guru Nanak Born in India

246 **1469** With 20 million adherents worldwide today, Sikhism launched from the foundations of Islam and Hinduism, yet rejects the rituals of both. Founder Guru Nanak, born in 1469, preached that all cultural gods are one Supreme Being, with whom individuals can merge through repeated cycles of death and rebirth. Meditation with the divine is Sikhism's only ritual: All others are considered human constructs that lead nowhere. Sikhs preach the equality of all humans and seek balance between their secular and spiritual lives.

■ **FOOTNOTE** The Three Pillars of Sikhism are chanting God's name and remembering God at all times through meditation, earning an honest living, and sharing with others. These guidelines should be part of a Sikh's everyday routine.

Ferdinand Marries Isabella

247 **1469** All royal marriages make the headlines, but many don't make the history books. But when Isabella, heiress of Castile, chose King Ferdinand of Aragon behind her father the king's back, the political princess consciously united Spain. Despite an ensuing tussle over secession, the couple became King and Queen of Spain in 1479. The monarchs reclaimed Granada from Muslim rule, consolidated power over three disparate military orders, and together realized their dream of a strong nation. But history will always remember Isabella for being Christopher Columbus's 11th-hour champion, financing his Atlantic voyage to India (see event 256).

"Roman" Type Created

248 **1470** Under the tutelage of Johannes Gutenberg (see event 244), coin engraver Nicolas Jenson absorbed the genius of a printing pioneer. But his perfection of a readable typeface was entirely his own creation. Jenson developed the first "Roman" type, shaping lowercase letters into legible forms that did not imitate handwriting. Jenson's font came to be known as Old Venetian, and he is immortalized today in Adobe's Jenson typeface.

Inca Empire Triumphs

249 **1470** Upon conquering the Chimu people of the Peruvian coast in 1470, the Inca civilization stretched from Ecuador in the north to central Chile in the south. Ten thousand miles of road connected 12 million subjects, who all followed the totalitarian rule of the *Sapa Inca*—"only Inca." The preliterate society corresponded with a complex system of knotted ropes, which were used to send messages to distant officials. Glorious mountain temple complexes, such as at Machu Picchu, were centers to worship the Inca sun god.

The vast Inca Empire was ruled as a collective, without commerce or money. People gave their produce to the government, which redistributed goods as needed: llama meat and milk, textiles, vegetables. Gold, silver, and copper from the Peruvian soil sparkled throughout Cuzco, dazzling Francisco Pizarro and his men (see 282) in 1532. Indeed, the conquerors were a bit too dazzled: They would use subterfuge to divide the Inca royalty and decimate the great civilization, greedy for its land and riches.

■ **FOOTNOTE** Potatoes, an Inca staple of some 200 varieties, have become a world food. Introduced to Europe by the Spanish conquistadores in 1536, the potato is now grown in 130 countries and is the fourth largest food crop in the world.

Leonardo Joins Guild

250 **1472** Italy's consummate *uomo universale*—complete man—Leonardo da Vinci symbolizes the Renaissance like no other human being. Master of all trades and jack of none, Leonardo's boundless curiosity was fueled by the Renaissance mindset that humans could master their universe.

Through Classical studies, experimentation, and especially visual observation, the genius consistently expanded the breadth of human knowledge. His famously copious notebooks display sketches for inventions such as flying mechanisms, parachutes, and machine guns, most hundreds of years ahead of their time.

Painting and sculpture were Leonardo's livelihood. Art, Leonardo believed, was a pathway to divine knowledge. And his "divine knowledge" has given the art world some of its most divine works, including "The Last Supper" (1498) and "The Mona Lisa" (1506).

■ **FOOTNOTE** Leonardo's study of anatomy included dissection of corpses in collaboration with physician Marcantonio della Torre and resulted in detailed drawings of the human skeleton, the vascular system, and internal organs.

Book Printed in English

251 **1475** Britain's cocktail of mutually unintelligible common dialects began to mix in the 14th and 15th centuries. By the late 14th, documents written in English show that it was becoming the language of government as well as the people. But it was William Caxton, the printer of Westminster, who is credited with cementing the language into a uniform tongue with a distinct literature. Caxton printed the first English book (from abroad) in 1475, then set up shop at home, where he translated and published copious works for both royalty and common folk. In his opinion, all would be able to read books in "English not over rude, nor curious, but in such terms as shall be understood by God's grace."

Caxton's publication of Sir Thomas Malory's *Le Morte d'Arthur* kicked off England's passion with all things Camelot. This was as he wished, writing in his preface: "I direct (this book) unto all noble princes, lords and ladies, gentlemen or gentlewomen, that desire to read or hear read of the noble and joyous history of the great conqueror and excellent king, King Arthur."

Math Symbols Used

253 **1489** German math professor Johann Widman became the

Portuguese Colonize African Coast

252 **1482** With Portugal's coronation of King John II came its age of discovery in Africa. Henry the Navigator had already established the lucrative nature of this enterprise, and Portugal dominated the seas along the African coast. In fact, as Daniel Boorstin notes in his classic *The Discoverers,* "Cargoes of pepper, ivory, gold, and slaves had already become so substantial that they gave their names to the parts of the continent that faced the Gulf of Guinea. For centuries these would be called the Grain Coast (Guinea pepper was known as "Grains of Paradise"), the Ivory Coast, the Gold Coast, and the Slave Coast."

The king financed journeys that pushed incrementally farther south, establishing trade relationships and searching for the mythical Christian priest-king of Africa, Prester John, in hopes of finding an ally on the continent. All the while he looked toward the Cape of

Women at work at Cape Coast Castle, Ghana, on Africa's Gold Coast

Good Hope, with good hopes of finding a sea route to India. In 1488 Bartholomeu Dias would return home triumphant from reaching the cape. However, it would be another Portuguese explorer, Vasco da Gama, who opened the sea gates of Asia to European trade and colonization.

first person to publish plus and minus signs when he penned an early arithmetic book. The algebra expert used the symbols to indicate "more than" or "less than," not for mathematical functions or positive and negative integers. Although his book of mathematics was the first to print them, scholars believe plus and minus signs came into use in Germany around 1450—along with x for an unknown, and the symbol indicating a square root.

Anatomy Book Illustrated

254 **1491** Detailed pointers to muscles, organs, genitalia, and other bodily regions dominate the West's first illustrated anatomy book. Possibly compiled by the German physician Joannes de Ketham, *Fasciculus Medicinae* is a compendium of six medical treatises that offer us an accurate view of the human body—and of medieval medicine. Topics covered in the *Fasciculus* include anatomy, physiology, surgery, gynecology and obstetrics, urine, phlebotomy, and the plague. The gorgeous illustrations are preserved in the rare-books sections of several world-class libraries.

Globe Created

255 **1492** The world's oldest extant globe was made by one Martin Behaim in Nuremberg, Germany, where it still resides in a museum. The geographer created a 21-inch-diameter sphere, on which he marked the equator, the tropics, one meridian, and nearby celestial objects. No latitude or longitude lines are to be seen, and his outlines of the known continents were surprisingly inaccurate. Still, the Behaim globe proves, among

255 | *Martin Behaim rests elbow on his globe.*

other things, that educated Europeans knew that the Earth was a sphere well before Columbus set sail (see event 256).

■ **FOOTNOTE** Columbus and Behaim may have been acquainted, but it is not likely that the globe's construction had any influence on Columbus's voyage. Magellan, though, may have used it as reference for his global circumnavigation.

Columbus Sets Sail

256 **1492** Of all world adventures, the exploits of Christopher Columbus hardly need retelling. The Genoese sailor is one of the most recognized—and controversial—figures in history, who either discovered or destroyed the Americas, depending on whom you talk to.

The facts of Columbus's voyage are indisputable, however. In 1492, Queen Isabella of Castile championed Columbus's quest to chart a westward sea route to India. Promising the queen riches and an Asian trade monopoly, Columbus enthusiastically set sail. After a two-month journey he struck land at a place he named San Salvador, in the Bahamas. He spent the next three months collecting specimens of "Asian" flora and searching for people who could lead him to the Great Khan, China's ruler.

Perhaps Columbus's greatest unsung accomplishments were the routes he pioneered. On his very first transatlantic voyage, the captain mastered the winds and found the best to and fro paths between continents. Three successive voyages followed similar routes.

Columbus, with his ships, claims San Salvador (now Watling Island, Bahamas) for Spain.

Unfortunately, Native Americans never produced sufficient "Oriental" riches to convince the Spaniards that he had found Asia. Columbus himself began to face ridicule at home. Ever the zealot, he responded by collecting more evidence that he had discovered Asia—and died believing in that discovery, despite Europe's quick acceptance that the sailor had actually brought the Old World in touch with a previously unknown continent.

Global Vegetable Swap

257 **1492** Imagine: Marco Polo never tasted tomato sauce. The first Floridians never sucked the juice of an orange. No potatoes for Celtic Irish monks. And the medieval French did not smoke.

When Columbus returned to Spain with a ship of samples from the "Indies," he began a global food migration that has been called "arguably the most important event in the history of life since the death of the dinosaurs." A favorite anecdote from the voyage reports that, upon landing, the Europeans received gifts from the Native Americans, including a bundle of dried, fragrant leaves. Columbus, not recognizing fine Caribbean tobacco, tossed it.

But it would not be long before tobacco use spread like wildfire throughout the Old World. Many other ingestibles—chocolate, corn, and peppers among them—made slower world tours, eventually covering all corners of civilization. The international cuisines we recognize today, from spicy Thai curry to cheesy Mexican enchiladas, can all be traced to what historian Alfred Crosby has dubbed the Columbian Exchange.

Treaty Tordesillas Reached

258 **1494** Brazilians have the Treaty Tordesillas to thank for their language and culture. This agreement between the two squabbling Atlantic sea powers, Spain and Portugal, designated a line of longitude for splitting the spoils of exploration: All lands discovered to the east of the line (which ran 370 leagues to the west of Cape Verde)—and which did not already have a Christian regent—would belong to Portugal; all those to the west, Spain.

Tordesillas was a watershed treaty in its own right, despite maritime technology's inability to identify the precise boundary at the time. But imagine Portugal's surprise when a windblown ship accidentally landed on the east coast of South America and discovered a New World land on its side of the dividing line. Now Portugal split its colonial efforts among three continents: Asia, Africa, and the New World.

FOOTNOTE Pedro Alvares Cabral discovered the coast of Brazil in 1500 by sailing from the Cape Verde Islands southwesterly. Assuming that the new country lay east of the treaty's line of demarcation, he notified the king of Portugal.

Cabot Embarks on Voyage

259 **1497** Like Columbus, John Cabot—or Giovanni Caboto, as he was born—was a Genoese navigator sailing under a foreign flag. Inspired by his countryman's success for Spain, Cabot succeeded in obtaining orders from Britain's Henry VII to sail to unknown lands west. His 1497 expedition landed on the western coast of Canada, which he claimed for the English king, an act that later helped establish England's provenance over the region. Sailing down what is today called Cabot Strait, the Genoese explored Canada's capes and islands. He returned home with glowing reports about the northern "Indies," believing, like Columbus, that he had reached Asia.

Cape of Good Hope Rounded

260 **1497-98** When Portuguese admiral Vasco da Gama returned from his successful voyage to establish a sea route to India, King John II hailed him a hero. Here was a detour around Arabia's great blockage between Europe and Asia. Here was a way to break Genoa and Venice's monopoly of the spice and silk trade.

Charting a daring path around the Cape of Good Hope and using ruthless intimidation tactics in India, da Gama and his bravado can be credited for Portugal's success. Despite—or perhaps because of—his massacre of a Muslim ship and about 30 Indian fishermen, da Gama successfully established a trading colony on the Indian coast. The king appointed him admiral of an ensuing expedition and, eventually, viceroy of Portuguese India.

Asian luxuries now came directly to western Europe via the Atlantic. Italy and the Levant's monopolies were crushed. And Portugal grew richer, strengthening its claim as the world's premier maritime power.

Vespucci Sails to New World

261 **1499** The Italian Amerigo Vespucci sailed alternately under the Spanish and Portuguese flags in the late 15th century. But it was on a journey for the Portuguese king that Vespucci became the first European to reach South America. Through painstaking astronomical and geographical observations, Vespucci soon suspected he had found an entirely new continent—something Columbus died denying.

The christening of the Americas occurred when a German clergyman read a publication by Vespucci, detailing the explorer's evidence for the existence of a previously unknown continent. In the process of publishing a world atlas himself, the clergyman included a proposal that the new lands be named "America" after Vespucci. The atlas was a hit, and the clergyman's attempts at retraction met with futility: All of Europe was by then calling the New World "America."

Christopher Columbus

JOURNAL, 1492

Thursday, 9 August. The Admiral did not succeed in reaching the island of Gomera till Sunday night. Martin Alonzo remained at Grand Canary by command of the Admiral, he being unable to keep the other vessels company. The Admiral afterwards returned to Grand Canary, and there with much labor repaired the Pinta, being assisted by Martin Alonzo and the others; finally they sailed to Gomera. They saw a great eruption of names from the Peak of Teneriffe, a lofty mountain. The Pinta, which before had carried latine sails, they altered and made her square-rigged. Returned to Gomera, Sunday, 2 September, with the Pinta repaired.

The Admiral says that he was assured by many respectable Spaniards, inhabitants of the island of Ferro, who were at Gomera with Dona Inez Peraza, mother of Guillen Peraza, afterwards first Count of Gomera, that every year they saw land to the west of the Canaries; and others of Gomera affirmed the same with the like assurances. The Admiral here says that he remembers, while he was in Portugal, in 1484, there came a person to the King from the island of Madeira, soliciting for a vessel to go in quest of land, which he affirmed he saw every year, and always of the same appearance. He also says that he remembers the same was said by the inhabitants of the Azores and described as in a similar direction, and of the same shape and size. Having taken in food, water, meat and other provisions, which had been provided by the men which he left ashore on departing for Grand Canary to repair the Pinta, the Admiral took his final departure from Gomera with the three vessels on Thursday, 6 September....

Friday, 14 September. Steered this day and night west twenty leagues; reckoned somewhat less. The crew of the Nina stated that they had seen a grajao, and a tropic bird, or water-wagtail, which birds never go farther than twenty-five leagues from the land.

Age of Discovery

1500-1700

1500-1700

New Views of the World and Self

Beginning around 1500, many discoveries and scientific advances helped transform kingdoms in western Europe into empires that spanned the globe. This age of discovery was not just a time of European innovation and expansion, however. Rising imperial powers such as Spain and England were rivaled by the Ottoman Empire, which controlled part of Europe. China and Japan resisted Western incursions eastward, and they made their own advances. Even Africans caught up in the devastating transatlantic slave trade helped create new societies in the New World that owed as much to African and Native American contributions as to European efforts.

Europeans' worldview began widening in the late Middle Ages through trade with the Middle East and Asia. Wealthy Italian merchants patronized artists and scholars, who rediscovered the literature of the ancient world, preserved in Christian monasteries and Islamic libraries. That cultural rebirth, or Renaissance, reached its peak in the 16th century with the achievements of Leonardo da Vinci, Galileo Galilei, and other men who embraced the classical tradition of humanism and saw few limits to what humans could understand or achieve by exercising their intellect and imagination. Their experiments and observations challenged Catholic doctrines based on biblical precepts, such as the assertion that all heavenly objects revolve around Earth.

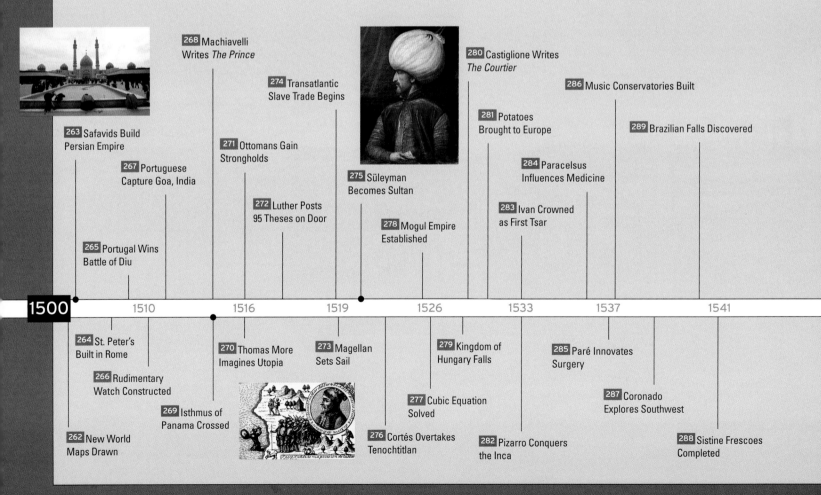

268 Machiavelli Writes *The Prince*

280 Castiglione Writes *The Courtier*

286 Music Conservatories Built

274 Transatlantic Slave Trade Begins

263 Safavids Build Persian Empire

281 Potatoes Brought to Europe

289 Brazilian Falls Discovered

271 Ottomans Gain Strongholds

267 Portuguese Capture Goa, India

284 Paracelsus Influences Medicine

275 Süleyman Becomes Sultan

272 Luther Posts 95 Theses on Door

283 Ivan Crowned as First Tsar

265 Portugal Wins Battle of Diu

278 Mogul Empire Established

1500   1510   1516   1519   1526   1533   1537   1541

264 St. Peter's Built in Rome

270 Thomas More Imagines Utopia

273 Magellan Sets Sail

279 Kingdom of Hungary Falls

285 Paré Innovates Surgery

266 Rudimentary Watch Constructed

287 Coronado Explores Southwest

269 Isthmus of Panama Crossed

277 Cubic Equation Solved

262 New World Maps Drawn

276 Cortés Overtakes Tenochtitlan

282 Pizarro Conquers the Inca

288 Sistine Frescoes Completed

An even stronger challenge to the authority of the Roman Catholic Church came from Martin Luther of Germany and other Protestant reformers who urged their followers to be guided by the Bible—which printing presses made widely available in translations—rather than by the teachings of the pope or Catholic clergy. "I cannot nor will not recant anything," declared Luther when asked to renounce his views, "for it is neither safe nor right to act against one's conscience." The Protestant Reformation caused turmoil in Europe, prompting persecution, religious wars, and a Counter-Reformation waged by Catholics, who upheld their beliefs by founding schools and missions.

Scholars such as the Dutch humanist Erasmus, a Catholic who urged tolerance and believed that faith could be reconciled with reason, served as forerunners of the Enlightenment, which took hold in Europe in the 17th century and allowed great minds expanded intellectual freedom and the room to pursue truth as they saw it. Analytical geniuses such as Sir Isaac Newton of England were no longer bound by religious preconceptions, and they launched a scientific revolution by expressing the laws of nature through mathematics.

Competing for Wealth and Glory

Some Europeans ventured to distant lands to spread their faith or gain religious freedom, but most went in search of spices, furs, precious metals, and other commodities that would enrich their own lives and the monarchs they served. The feats of Columbus and the conquistadores who followed him to the New World made Spain the world's largest and richest empire in the 16th century. But England, France, Portugal, and Holland competed for wealth and glory by launching their own trading and colonizing ventures to the

PREVIOUS PAGE | *An explorer from the Middle Ages ventures into new realms of knowledge.*

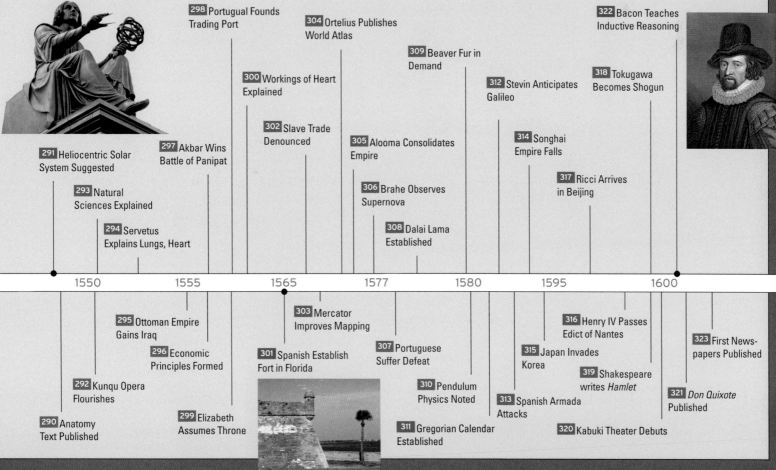

- **290** Anatomy Text Published
- **291** Heliocentric Solar System Suggested
- **292** Kunqu Opera Flourishes
- **293** Natural Sciences Explained
- **294** Servetus Explains Lungs, Heart
- **295** Ottoman Empire Gains Iraq
- **296** Economic Principles Formed
- **297** Akbar Wins Battle of Panipat
- **298** Portugal Founds Trading Port
- **299** Elizabeth Assumes Throne
- **300** Workings of Heart Explained
- **301** Spanish Establish Fort in Florida
- **302** Slave Trade Denounced
- **303** Mercator Improves Mapping
- **304** Ortelius Publishes World Atlas
- **305** Alooma Consolidates Empire
- **306** Brahe Observes Supernova
- **307** Portuguese Suffer Defeat
- **308** Dalai Lama Established
- **309** Beaver Fur in Demand
- **310** Pendulum Physics Noted
- **311** Gregorian Calendar Established
- **312** Stevin Anticipates Galileo
- **313** Spanish Armada Attacks
- **314** Songhai Empire Falls
- **315** Japan Invades Korea
- **316** Henry IV Passes Edict of Nantes
- **317** Ricci Arrives in Beijing
- **318** Tokugawa Becomes Shogun
- **319** Shakespeare writes *Hamlet*
- **320** Kabuki Theater Debuts
- **321** *Don Quixote* Published
- **322** Bacon Teaches Inductive Reasoning
- **323** First Newspapers Published

1550 1555 1565 1577 1580 1595 1600

Americas, Asia, and Africa, where old kingdoms collapsed and new one such as Dahomey (Benin) emerged and profited by selling captives to European slave traders. Profits from the traffic in slaves, spices, silver, gold, and other precious items went not only to European royalty but also to private investors, who formed companies and shared the risks and rewards of overseas ventures with other capitalists. Corporate capitalism and private enterprise bred a new commercial elite in Europe who grew more powerful than the old landed aristocracy, and financed the growth of cities, banks, and businesses.

The impact of Europeans on the New World was dramatic and devastating at the same time. Native Americans had no acquired immunity to diseases colonizers introduced, and no horses, firearms, or iron swords to match those of the invaders. Despite the ravages of disease and the swift destruction of the Aztec and Inca Empires by Spanish conquistadores, Indians endured in Spanish America and preserved elements of their culture even as they intermarried with Spanish colonists, adopted Catholicism, and acquired domesticated animals of European origin.

English, French, and Dutch colonization was largely confined to the Atlantic coast of North America. Tribes of the interior remained strong until settlers moved westward in later centuries. The first permanent English colony, Jamestown in Virginia, was nearly destroyed by defiant Indians of the Powhatan confederacy and by diseases such as malaria. Only by importing slave laborers from Africa with greater resistance to such diseases did the English succeed in colonizing the southeast coast of North America.

Rivals for Power

ELSEWHERE AROUND THE WORLD, EUROPEAN EXPANSION WAS thwarted or delayed by strong rulers who built their own

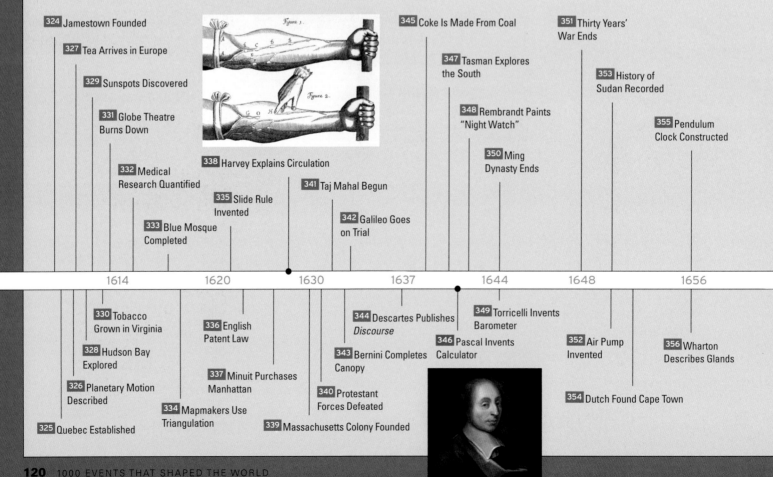

- 324 Jamestown Founded
- 327 Tea Arrives in Europe
- 329 Sunspots Discovered
- 331 Globe Theatre Burns Down
- 332 Medical Research Quantified
- 338 Harvey Explains Circulation
- 335 Slide Rule Invented
- 341 Taj Mahal Begun
- 333 Blue Mosque Completed
- 342 Galileo Goes on Trial
- 345 Coke Is Made From Coal
- 347 Tasman Explores the South
- 348 Rembrandt Paints "Night Watch"
- 350 Ming Dynasty Ends
- 351 Thirty Years' War Ends
- 353 History of Sudan Recorded
- 355 Pendulum Clock Constructed

1614   1620   1630   1637   1644   1648   1656

- 330 Tobacco Grown in Virginia
- 328 Hudson Bay Explored
- 326 Planetary Motion Described
- 325 Quebec Established
- 336 English Patent Law
- 337 Minuit Purchases Manhattan
- 334 Mapmakers Use Triangulation
- 344 Descartes Publishes *Discourse*
- 343 Bernini Completes Canopy
- 340 Protestant Forces Defeated
- 339 Massachusetts Colony Founded
- 349 Torricelli Invents Barometer
- 346 Pascal Invents Calculator
- 352 Air Pump Invented
- 354 Dutch Found Cape Town
- 356 Wharton Describes Glands

empires and kept foreign traders and missionaries at a distance. After seizing Constantinople, which they renamed Istanbul and took as their capital, Ottoman forces swept across the Balkan Peninsula and seized Hungary. At its height under Sultan Süleyman I in the mid-16th century, the Ottoman Empire extended from the Danube River to the Persian Gulf and covered much of North Africa. Süleyman's successors faced strong opposition both from European Christians—who defeated the Ottoman fleet at Lepanto off Cyprus in 1571 and repulsed Ottoman troops at Vienna in 1683—and from Shiite Muslims in Iran, ruled by shahs of the Safavid dynasty who denied the legitimacy of the Sunni sultans in Istanbul.

Another Muslim dynasty, the Mughals (or Moguls), took control of India in the 1500s and raised splendid palaces and monuments, including the majestic Taj Mahal. When Hindus rebelled and refused to pay taxes, Mughal rulers sought additional revenue through trade with the West and granted Europeans access to ports such as Bombay and Calcutta, where they began to colonize India.

In China, foreign traders were confined to a single port—Guangzhou (Canton)—and Catholic missionaries were banned for opposing the ancient Chinese custom of ancestor worship. Japan placed even stricter limits on contact with the outside world. Eventually, foreigners would break down these barriers, exposing Japan and China to Western influences and pressures. But Europeans, too, were influenced and transformed by their exposure to distant lands, acquiring new foods, including potatoes and tomatoes (transplanted from the Americas), new habits such as smoking tobacco and drinking coffee and tea, and new demands and challenges like battling rival colonial powers, dealing with defiant tribes, and incorporating within their imperial cultures people of other races and faiths.

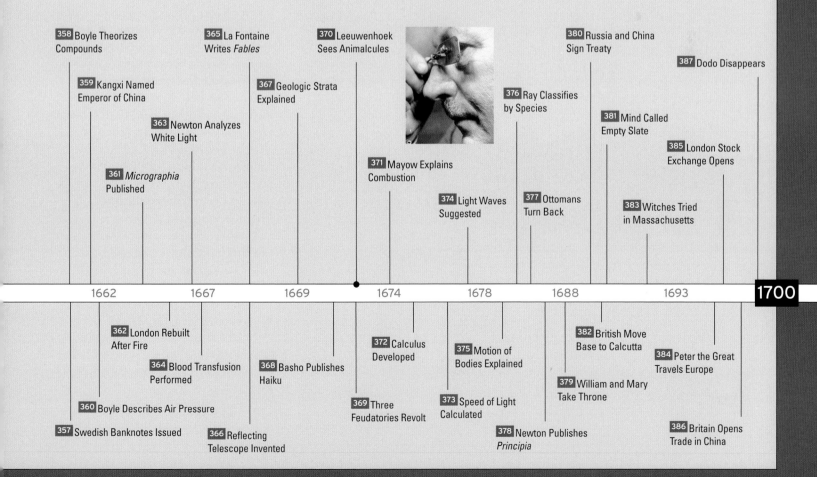

358 Boyle Theorizes Compounds

359 Kangxi Named Emperor of China

361 *Micrographia* Published

363 Newton Analyzes White Light

365 La Fontaine Writes *Fables*

367 Geologic Strata Explained

370 Leeuwenhoek Sees Animalcules

371 Mayow Explains Combustion

374 Light Waves Suggested

376 Ray Classifies by Species

377 Ottomans Turn Back

380 Russia and China Sign Treaty

381 Mind Called Empty Slate

383 Witches Tried in Massachusetts

385 London Stock Exchange Opens

387 Dodo Disappears

1662   1667   1669   1674   1678   1688   1693   **1700**

357 Swedish Banknotes Issued

360 Boyle Describes Air Pressure

362 London Rebuilt After Fire

364 Blood Transfusion Performed

366 Reflecting Telescope Invented

368 Basho Publishes Haiku

369 Three Feudatories Revolt

372 Calculus Developed

373 Speed of Light Calculated

375 Motion of Bodies Explained

378 Newton Publishes *Principia*

379 William and Mary Take Throne

382 British Move Base to Calcutta

384 Peter the Great Travels Europe

386 Britain Opens Trade in China

New World Maps Drawn

262 **1500** It did not take long after Christopher Columbus's voyages for European maps to start to represent these discoveries. In 1500, Juan de la Cosa drew the first navigational chart with the New World on it, depicting Columbus's voyages as well as Vasco da Gama's and John Cabot's expeditions. In 1507 Martin Waldesmüller went a step further and published a map with North and South America clearly detached from Asia. On it, he labeled the southern part of these new lands "America" after Amerigo Vespucci, the Italian who explored South America and the Amazon River.

St. Peter's Built in Rome

264 **1506-1626** When Pope Julius II decided to replace the crumbling basilica of St. Peter, he facilitated the creation of a building recognized throughout the world as a symbol of the Catholic Church and its power. Pope Julius II laid the first stone in April of 1506, but the structure wouldn't be dedicated until 120 years later, by Pope Urban VIII in 1626. As time passed, plans and architects changed, but the gigantic basilica remained true to Pope Julius's desire for a physical structure that conveyed the spiritual power of Christianity. And convey it did, surpassing structures of ancient Rome with its monumental almost 700-foot length (including the vestibule) and a facade longer than a football field.

Architects modified the original design to the three-aisled Latin cross with dome and extended nave found today. As chief architect, Michelangelo designed the striking dome, which became the gold standard in dome design. Inside are baroque and Renaissance treasures, including Michelangelo's "Pietà."

> **FOOTNOTE** St. Peter's was the largest Christian church in the world until 1989, when a basilica in Yamoussoukro, Côte d'Ivoire, surpassed it. St. Peter's can still hold more worshippers, however.

Safavids Build Persian Empire

263 **1501** The Battle of Shurer in 1501 set the stage for the beginning of the Safavid dynasty (1502-1736), which ushered in Shiite rule of Persia. Shah Ismail I, founder of the dynasty, defeated Alwand of the Ak Koyunlu (White Sheep) dynasty at Shurer, in Azerbaijan. The defeat of the Sunni Alwand brought Shiite rule to Azerbaijan and handed the White Sheep capital, Tabriz, in present-day Iran, to the Safavids.

By 1502, Shah Ismail controlled Persia and began to unify the region, ending a period of internal conflict. The dynasty faced formidable opponents in the Ottomans to the west and the Uzbek Tartars to the north and suffered a crushing defeat at the hands of the Ottomans in the 1514 Battle of Çaldiran, in present-day Turkey. The Ottoman sultan, Selim I (the Grim), took 50,000 men with him to defeat the Shiites. His reasons were religious, personal, and strategic: Selim, a Sunni, abhorred the Persian Shiites and Shah Ismail had supported Selim's brother against him and had been raiding Ottoman territory. Selim captured Tabriz, but his powerful janissary forced him to stop there. Ottomans took Kurdistan and Anatolia, and throughout the 17th century, the Safavids opposed the Ottomans on their eastern frontier.

Iranian Shiites pray at the Jamkaran Mosque, near the holy city of Qom in Jamkaran, Iran.

The 17th century saw the rise of Persia as a great world power, and by the century's end the Safavids' greatest ruler, Shah Abbas I, was creating a modern army with an eye toward revenging previous defeats by the Ottomans. After Abbas's death, the Safavid empire went into a period of decline until its 1736 demise with the ascension of Nadir Shah.

Portugal Wins Battle of Diu

265 **1509** With the 1509 victory at the Battle of Diu in the Indian Ocean, Portugal continued to expand its empire, becoming the dominant force in the Indian Ocean. In February of 1509, the Portuguese defeated a combined force of the Indian sultan of Gujarat and the Mameluke ruler of Egypt, Kansu al-Gauri, off the coast of Diu, located on the Kathiawar Peninsula in western India. The fleet commander, Francisco de Almeida, had become the first Portuguese viceroy of the Indian subcontinent in 1505.

Diu was not Almeida's first battle, though. After rounding the Cape of Good Hope, he began conquering the African city-states of today's Kenya, Mozambique, and Tanzania. By 1509, Portugal dominated African and Indian trade, and the defeat of the combined Indian and Egyptian forces brought a period of Portuguese control and expansion in the Arabian Sea and East Indies. A year after Diu, Goa fell to the Portuguese and became the capital of Portuguese India and a chief trading port. In 1511 the Portuguese defeated the Muslim principality of Malacca and controlled the Indian spice trade as well as the entrance to the South China Sea. Europeans, led by Portugal, exercised maritime control over the international spice trade.

In 1595, the Dutch would put an end to Portuguese control of the East Indies.

264 | *The dome of St. Peter's Basilica in Rome, designed by Michelangelo, set the standard for dome design.*

Rudimentary Watch Constructed

266 **ca 1510** Peter Henlein used a small mainspring to make the first known clock that could easily be carried around in about 1510. Henlein's invention allowed for small, portable timepieces, and he made the first pocket watches in Germany—even though other watches preceded his. A balance spring powered the "watch," which takes its name because it benefited sailors who had to remain on watch for a set amount of time. While not very precise (Henlein's watch only had an hour hand, lacking a minute hand), his invention advanced watchmaking technology.

Portuguese Capture Goa, India

267 **1510** Portuguese success in the Indian Ocean assured control over trade routes that had been controlled by Middle Eastern powers for centuries. Already active in the region, in 1510 a Portuguese force led by Afonso de Albuquerque seized Goa on the western coast of India from the sultan of Bijapur. Goa became the Portuguese capital of India and a chief trading port, and Albuquerque became the second viceroy of Portuguese India. Goa's strategic location gave Portugal control over merchant bases.

■ **FOOTNOTE** Palaces and churches from the Portuguese colonial period remain in Goa. Perhaps the most notable is the Church of Bom Jesus—which contains the tomb of St. Francis Xavier, a 16th-century Catholic missionary.

Machiavelli Writes *The Prince*

268 **1513** In 1513 Florentine statesman Niccolò Machiavelli wrote *Il Principe* (*The Prince*) as a manual on effective leadership. The book was not published until 1532, five years after Machiavelli's death. Since his book didn't discuss moral or religious codes of conduct, today it is remembered as the ultimate treatise on practical power politics.

Machiavelli wrote from experience. A Florentine foreign minister, Machiavelli took part in numerous political disputes before writing *The Prince* and even served time in prison, accused of complicity in a conspiracy to overthrow the powerful Medici family. Once published, the book was soon translated, ensuring that Machiavelli would be remembered as advocating almost any action in the name of retaining power.

Machiavelli's other political work, *Discourses on the First Ten Books of Livy*, gives voice to his ideas of an elected prince working for the common good. His legacy as a political theorist assured, Machiavelli's ideas continue to influence leaders today.

Isthmus of Panama Crossed

269 **1513** Spanish explorer Vasco Núñez de Balboa crossed the isthmus of Panama to claim the Pacific Ocean and all the lands it touched for the Spanish crown in 1513, becoming the first European to see the vast expanse separating Asia and the New World. He set out on September 1 with 190 men and hundreds of native porters. The party cut through dense forest, but diplomatic treaties Balboa made with Panamanian tribes allowed for their safe passage.

In less than a month Balboa spotted the Pacific Ocean, calling it the South Sea. Balboa didn't set out to find the Pacific, instead wanting to find gold. He had arrived in the New World as a stowaway and quickly ended up in debt. His political fortunes proved better. In 1511 Balboa and some colonists forced the Spanish governor to return to Spain. Balboa also founded the port of Panama, which opened up travel up and down the Pacific coast. Balboa requested the governorship of the colony, but the king only named him "Admiral of the South Sea," and appointed Pedro Arias de Ávila. The two got along for a few years but then Balboa fell out of favor. Accused of treason, he was executed by Spain on January 12, 1519. For the former stowaway, now remembered as one of the most famous of explorers, even finding the vast Pacific Ocean wasn't enough to save him.

Balboa claims Pacific Ocean for Spain. He trained his dog to attack and kill natives.

Balboa founded the first Spanish colony on the American mainland, Santa María la Antigua, in 1510. Another famous explorer was part of his expedition: Francisco Pizarro.

Thomas More Imagines Utopia

270 **1516** When Sir Thomas More published *Utopia,* he took his place in a long tradition of philosophical thought on how to make the world a better place. While Plato's *Republic* is a forerunner, it was More who contributed both a noun and adjective to describe an ideal state of social and political harmony.

Divided into two parts, *Utopia* dealt with the real problems of 16th-century England and described an ideal world where these problems were solved. More's fictional character Raphael Hythloday had traveled with Amerigo Vespucci and seen Utopia firsthand. Hythloday related the story of a land both communitarian and tolerant. But being still the 16th century, Utopia was a patriarchy where slaves cooked the meals (supervised by women). Everyone worked, though, and thieves were jailed instead of put to death as they were in England at the time. Quickly translated from the Latin (by 1551 into English), Utopia resonated with a Europe divided between self-interested powers.

More did not lead a Utopian life, however. He was jailed in the Tower of London and executed by Henry VIII when he would not renounce the authority of the pope. The Catholic Church canonized More in 1935, and some of his Utopian ideas have come into practice (reform of the severe English penal code for instance).

Ottomans Gain Strongholds

271 **1516-1517** Two battles enlarged Ottoman control in the early 16th century. The Ottoman sultan Selim I (the Grim) retained his sights on Persia in 1516, but the Egyptian sultan (aligned with Persia) took his forces to Aleppo in present-day Syria, attracting the Ottoman ruler. The August 1516 Battle of Marj Dabik resulted. Both Aleppo and Damascus surrendered, to be followed by the Battle of Ridanya near Cairo in January 1517. At the end, the Ottomans had conquered Egypt and controlled the holy places of Arabia. Under Selim's rule, the Ottoman Empire doubled in size.

■ **FOOTNOTE** The Egyptian sultan Kansu al-Gauri died at the Battle of Marj Dabik. The Ottomans sacked Cairo after four days of street battles that led to a massacre with estimates of 50,000 dead.

Luther Posts 95 Theses on Door

272 **1517** When the German friar and theologian Dr. Martin Luther formulated his "Ninety-Five Theses," he was reacting to a Dominican friar who preached that purchasing indulgences from the Catholic Church was a way to earn forgiveness for sinful acts. This troubled Luther, and he wanted to start a discussion within the church. Instead he started the Protestant Reformation by, as history has it, nailing his treatise to the door of his church, the Castle Church in Wittenberg, Germany. As his beliefs took shape, Luther articulated the idea of justification by faith alone, where through faith, and by the grace of God, humans achieve salvation. This ran counter to Catholic teachings.

A new invention—the printing press—made it much easier for Luther's ideas to reach a wide audience, and once they did, there was no turning back. His ideas also became a catalyst to spread education in order to educate Protestant church leaders as well as to give Protestants the ability to read the Bible for themselves. This was important to the Protestant Reformation, and Luther completed his German translation of the Bible in 1534. The Reformation also helped to usher in one hundred years of warfare, which ended with the most deadly European conflict before the 20th century, the Thirty Years' War (1618-1648). It didn't take long for Luther's ideas to take hold, and by the mid-17th century Protestants dominated Scandinavia, England, Scotland, northern Germany, and many Swiss towns. Protestants could be found in central Europe and France. Christendom would never be the same.

Magellan Sets Sail

273 **1519** The Portuguese explorer Ferdinand Magellan commanded the voyage that first circumnavigated the globe and provided distances to help sailors navigate their routes.

When snubbed by the Portuguese king, Magellan renounced his citizenship and obtained Spanish funding. Magellan wanted to reach the Spice Islands (the Moluccas) by sailing west from Spain, and Spain hoped the voyage would entitle it to the lucrative Spice Islands trade.

Magellan believed that the 1494 Treaty of Tordesillas gave the islands to Spain. To prove it, he set sail with five ships on September 20, 1519. He stood to make a

274 | *Armed guards escort slaves to work in Portuguese Zambesiland in southeastern Africa.*

fortune. Along the way he quelled a rebellion, saw men desert a ship and another wreck, and ultimately lost his life in the Philippines. But in November of 1520 he navigated the strait that now bears his name.

Only one of Magellan's ships, *Victoria,* completed the voyage and only 18 crewmen returned on September 8, 1522, to announce their discovery. Spain wasn't able to capitalize on the route Magellan pioneered given its inherit dangers, and five years after *Victoria*'s return, Spain gave up its claims to the Spice Islands for a cash settlement. But Magellan's legacy lives on, his voyage an attestation to human courage and the quest for knowledge.

■ **FOOTNOTE** The Magellanic penguin (*Spheniscus magellanicus*), named after Magellan, breeds along the coasts of southern South America. Perhaps it is fitting that the sea-tested explorer has a bird with flippers named for him.

Transatlantic Slave Trade Begins

274 **1519** Slavery has existed throughout time, and Europeans enslaved Africans from the beginning of the 14th century. The first explorers to the New World brought slaves with them. The beginning of the transatlantic slave trade can be traced to around 1519, when the first slave

ship likely arrived in the New World after sailing directly from Africa. The ship disembarked in Puerto Rico. With this landing a force had begun that would move more than ten million people involuntarily. One hundred years later, in 1619, 20 Africans arrived in Jamestown, Virginia, as "indentured servants" or slaves.

Goods traveled from Europe to Africa, slaves were carried from Africa to the Americas, and sugar, rum, and other colonial products were shipped back to Europe. The importance of slave labor cannot be underestimated, for it was with slave labor that the economies of the New World functioned and prospered. But the slave trade was truly a global phenomenon—moving people, goods, and capital as never seen before.

In 1501 Spain approved using enslaved Africans in the Americas, but Spain was not the largest carrier of slaves. That superlative fell to Portugal and England. These two countries transported 75 percent of all slaves. During the Middle Passage—the horrendous crossing of the Atlantic—slaves suffered incredibly high death rates, as much as 20 percent. New scholarship suggests that slaves staged a mutiny on one out of every ten voyages.

273 | *Magellan holds globe and protractor.*

Süleyman Becomes Sultan

275 **1520** Süleyman I became sultan when his father, Selim I, died. During his reign (1520-1566) Ottoman power reached its height of greatness, and Süleyman epitomizes a just Islamic ruler. Known for his leadership, his name in the Islamic world, Süleyman the Lawgiver, stems from his codification of Ottoman laws, which provided a legal code that was applied across his realm. Süleyman also possessed an exceptional military mind, battling the Safavids in Persia and European powers on their home turf and in naval battles as far away as the Indian Ocean. Early in his reign he succeeded in conquering the strategically important cities of Rhodes and Belgrade, sending a symbolic message of his abilities. Among other locations, the Ottomans expanded into Yemen, which offered a buffer against the Portuguese in India. Süleyman's court was a cultural center, and accomplishments in art and architecture also mark his rule. At times German princes and French kings had looked to ally themselves with him. His rule witnessed the height of Ottoman power on an international stage.

Ottoman sultan Süleyman I epitomized effective leadership.

With slavery and resistance came brutality, but also eloquence, strength, and eventually freedom. It is impossible to underestimate the social, economic, cultural, and political repercussions of the slavery practiced from the early 1500s to the late 19th century.

Cortés Overtakes Tenochtitlan

276 **1521** The famed Spanish conquistadore Hernán Cortés died far away from the Aztec Empire he conquered for Spain. In 1518 Diego de Velázquez, secretary to the Spanish governor of Cuba, sent Cortés to Mexico for conquest and riches. Cortés landed near Veracruz, Mexico, with nearly 600 men and a number of horses. To distance himself from Velázquez, he burned all of his ships except one, which sailed to Spain to explain that Cortés was in the sole service of Spain.

Cortés followed a difficult route to the Aztec capital of Tenochtitlan (today's Mexico City) in order to avoid Aztec spies or militia. Once there he was welcomed (albeit hesitantly) into the city but was called away to confront Panfilo de Narváez, who was under orders to replace Cortés, who was wanted for treason. While Cortés was away from the Aztec capital dealing with Narváez (Cortés defeated Narváez and persuaded most of his group to join his forces), the city revolted. Cortés returned to Tenochtitlan but was thrown out after Moctezuma died in unclear circumstances.

The retreat, known as the Night of Sorrows, saw a third of the Spanish forces cut down. Cortés would not be deterred, though, and after re-massing he besieged the city. Dwarfing the Spanish deaths, some 15,000 Aztecs died during the final attack. Tenochtitlan fell in August of 1521, helped in part by the smallpox arriving with the conquistadores. Cortés secured Mexico for Spain, but fell out of favor and died as a private citizen in Spain.

Cubic Equation Solved

277 **1526** Scipione del Ferro first solved the depressed cubic equation and advanced higher mathematics during the 16th century. Ferro, a professor at the University of Bologna, passed his notebooks to a student in 1526, the year he died. The notebook contained the proof. Girolamo Cardano first published Ferro's solution in his 1545 masterpiece on algebra, *Ars magna,* and showed how Ferro's solution also applied to the general cubic equation.

Ferro was preceded by the Chinese mathematician Wang Xiaotong in the seventh century and the Persian poet Omar Khayyam, who solved cubic equations using conic sections in the eleventh century. Khayyam wrote that he hoped an algebraic solution could be found. Ferro's work on the cubic equation would advance mathematics, leading to group theory and complex numbers.

FOOTNOTE An Italian mathematician, Niccolò Tartaglia, won a contest by solving cubic equations. Girolamo Cardano only included Scipione del Ferro's proof in his *Ars magna* after he realized Ferro's proof had preceded Tartaglia's work.

Mogul Empire Established

278 **1526** The Mogul Empire traced its beginnings to the victory of the Muslim ruler of Kabul, in present-day Afghanistan, at the first Battle of Panipat near Delhi, India. The victor, Zahir-ud-din Muhammad (Babur), founded an empire that controlled much of India for almost 200 years until European imperialism ended its power.

In April 1526, Babur's outnumbered forces faced Ibrahim Lodi, the sultan of Delhi. Lodi was killed in the battle, and his forces defeated. Babur protected his defensive line of soldiers by using carts chained together against the larger Hindustan army, which used as many as a thousand elephants. When the elephant drivers were shot off their mounts, the uncontrolled elephants wreaked havoc in the ranks.

Babur's grandson, Akbar, reconquered lands in the second Battle of Panipat in

1556 and extended the boundaries of the empire. Babur himself is recalled as a great military leader after outwitting larger armies in three battles in northern India. He also wrote poetry and his memoirs. The first victory at Panipat gave Babur, a descendant of Genghis Khan and Timur (the Lame), Delhi and Agra, and the world a dynasty that would rule northern India until 1761 and survive in minimized fashion until 1857.

Hernán Cortés

LETTER FROM MEXICO, 1519

After we had walked a little way up the street a servant of his came with two necklaces, wrapped in a cloth, made from red snails' shells ... And after he had given me these things he sat ... and addressed me in the following way:

"Because of the place from which you claim to come, namely, from where the sun rises, and the things you tell us of the great lord or king who sent you here, we believe and are certain that he is our natural lord, especially as you say that he has known of us for some time. So be assured that we shall obey you and hold you as our lord in place of that great sovereign of whom you speak; and in this there shall be no offense or betrayal whatsoever.... I also know that they have told you the walls of my houses are made of gold, and that the floor mats in my rooms and other things in my household are likewise of gold, and that I was, and claimed to be, a god; and many other things besides. The houses as you see are of stone and lime and clay."

Then he raised his clothes and showed me his body, saying, as he grasped his arms and trunk with his hand, "See that I am of flesh and blood like you and all other men, and I am mortal and substantial. See how they have lied to you? It is true that I have some pieces of gold left to me by my ancestors; anything I might have shall be given to you whenever you ask. Now I shall go to other houses where I live, but here you shall be provided with all that you and your people require, and you shall receive no hurt, for you are in your own land and your own house."

276 | *A painted panel depicts explorer Hernán Cortés being greeted upon his arrival in Mexico.*

Kingdom of Hungary Falls

279 **1526** The Ottoman Empire achieved a decisive victory over the Hungarian army at the Battle of Mohács in August 1526. The Hungarian king died during battle, and most of Hungary came under Ottoman control under János Zápolya. The Battle of Mohács marked the end of the Hungarian monarchy and ushered in the division of Hungary between the Ottomans and the Habsburgs. Hungary had stood between the Ottomans and Habsburg imperialism. In 1529, the Ottoman sultan, Süleyman the Lawgiver, attacked Vienna but suffered defeat. A brilliant leader regardless, Süleyman focused his attention on maintaining his empire and improving his navy. Süleyman died in 1566—while in Hungary.

Castiglione Writes *The Courtier*

280 **1528** Baldassare Castiglione wrote the Renaissance classic on courtly behavior, and *Il Cortegiano* (*The Book of the Courtier*) quickly became popular throughout Europe after its 1528 publication. Beginning in 1507, the Italian Castiglione served in the court of the Duke of Urbino, a court known for its intellectual refinement. More than an etiquette manual, the book offered a vision of the ideal society. Its courtier demonstrated political, cultural, and knightly skills. The book closes by discussing the popular conception of love, which progressed from physical to spiritual attraction and culminated by joining with the divine.

■ **FOOTNOTE** Translated into English in 1561, *The Courtier* helped shape the ideals of Elizabethan England and influenced higher education as well. The great Renaissance painter Raphael even painted a portrait of Castiglione.

Potatoes Brought to Europe

281 ca 1530 The Columbian Exchange —the term for the transfer of species between the New World and Old World—shaped global diet patterns and outlasted all the riches taken by the Spanish Empire. The exchange of foodstuffs also changed human diet and history, as illustrated by the simple potato. Records are imprecise, but soon after Pizarro conquered the Inca in 1532, potatoes began to make their way on board ships and were being grown by Basques in northern Spain. By the end of the century, the potato appeared in a book by John Gerard.

Pizarro Conquers the Inca

282 **1532** Francisco Pizarro's daring exploits in the New World subdued the Inca Empire but not without a price, helping to fuel severe inflation in Europe and continuing a legacy of conquest and oppression. In 1524 Pizarro started exploring down the western coast of South America. In 1530, Pizarro set out from Spain to conquer the Inca. His expedition used cunning and superior weaponry to defeat the Inca ruler Atahualpa and an estimated 30,000 men in November of 1532. Many Inca were killed, and Atahualpa was captured. Riches from the empire arrived for his ransom, but after a hasty trial Atahualpa was put to death.

Pizzaro continued to lay claim to what the Spaniards called New Castile and founded Lima, the present-day capital of Peru, in 1535. Pizarro died in Lima in 1541, but the colonists persevered to send riches back to Spain.

Ivan Crowned as First Tsar

283 **1533** After assuming power in 1533 at the age of three, Ivan IV

CONNECTIONS

The Columbian Exchange
New World plants revolutionize Old World culture

Christopher Columbus may not have found spices on his voyage toward what he called the Spice Islands, but he did lead the way to the discovery of a plethora of plants and animals unknown in the Old World. Likewise, plants and animals traveled from Europe to the Americas. This transfer continued for more than a hundred years after Columbus's original voyage, and it came to be known as the Columbian Exchange.

From the Americas came chocolate, maize, potatoes, tomatoes, squashes, pumpkins, peanuts, pineapples, and tobacco. Soon animals joined the trade, and the turkey made its way to the Old World. From Europe westward to the North American natives came cabbage, grapes, rice, sugarcane, wheat, coffee, and olives from the plant kingdom; cattle, pigs, sheep, and horses from the animal. Some items, like the turkey, gained popularity soon after reaching European shores, while others, such as the potato, took significantly longer to earn a place in Old World cuisines.

Columbus found cacao beans, the main ingredient of chocolate, in 1502, but he did not discover their use in a drink. Hernán Cortés, in the 1520s, discovered those properties of what explorers referred to as "black almonds." By the end of the 16th century, the citizens of Spain had grown immensely fond of drinking chocolate.

Native Americans gave Europeans the tomato.

Despite its strong cultural ties with Ireland in the popular imagination today, the Spanish discovered the potato in 1537 while exploring an abandoned village, They found maize, beans, and another plant product that they took to be some sort of truffle. In fact, the product was not a fungus at all, but the potato. While the potato reached Spain in the mid-16th century, not until after 1600 did it begin to appear in the farm fields of Spain. Eventually the potato traveled through Italy and reached northern Europe, including Ireland.

The pineapple originated in Brazil. Its appearance fascinated the European explorers, and its Old World acceptance was swift and widespread in Europe. By the early 16th century, pineapples were being grown throughout Europe, people delighting in its strange form and sweet flavor.

Coffee was one of the plant products that traveled from east to west. Originally a product of Arabian regions, it had swept through Europe by the end of the 16th century. During the next century coffee plants—often labeled a trap of Satan in the Old World—were transplanted into the Americas. Soon it was discovered that South and Central America provided the best climates for coffee growing. The story of the Columbian Exchange highlights how many associations we make today between food products and their countries of origin can represent cases of historic shortsightedness.

282 | *Engraved portrait of Francisco Pizzaro*

became the first ruler crowned tsar (from the Latin *caesar*) of Russia in 1547. His grandfather, Ivan the Great, first used the title, and Ivan IV's crowning symbolically connected Russia to the Byzantine Empire and consolidated the preexisting idea of Russia as the third Rome (following Rome and Byzantium). During his reign, Russia suffered an economic crisis as nobles and peasants fled. Ivan's nickname "the terrible" is better understood as "the mighty," even though he killed his own son. Years of political turmoil followed his death.

■ **FOOTNOTE** Ivan IV's attempt to protect trade along the Volga River failed in the face of raids by Tartars and other nomads from the east. Policies during his reign that aimed to keep peasants tied to their lands led down the road to serfdom.

Paracelsus Influences Medicine

284 **1536** The Swiss-German doctor Paracelsus (in full: Philippus Aureolus Theophrastus Bombastus von Hohenheim)—the father of medical chemistry—gave medicine a chemical foundation and helped change treatments such as bloodletting to chemical-based ones. For centuries Western physicians conceived of the body as being composed of four humors (black and yellow bile, blood, and phlegm), and their imbalance the cause of disease. Paracelsus conceived

of the mineral "spirits" of salt, sulfur, or mercury in the body as the cause of disease. Instead of accepting the ancients, most notably the ideas of the Greek doctor Galen of Pergamum who synthesized medical practice in antiquity, Paracelsus sought out commoners—miners and peasants—and developed his own drugs using minerals such as sulfur and mercury to treat patients.

Paracelsus also pushed alchemy to be used to create medicines instead of trying to change metals into gold, and he was the first doctor to treat syphilis with mercury and conceive of the benefits of chemotherapy. Importantly, Paracelsus saw mental illness as a disease and not as simply possession by demons.

Paracelsus reacted against Galenic medicine and offered a mystical, religious, and antiestablishment alternative. His medical system—Paracelsianism—broke away from Galen's system completely. Known to reduce his opponents in offensive tirades and to burn canonical texts, as well as his belief in the possibility of creating new human life in a laboratory, Paracelsus nonetheless took medicine down a new and effective track by advocating a medical philosophy with a chemical foundation.

Paré Innovates Surgery

285 **1537** French physician Ambroise Paré's advancements in 16th-century medical science have led some historians to consider him the father of modern surgery. As an army surgeon, Paré helped his suffering patients. In 1537, when he ran out of his supply of boiling oil to treat gunshot wounds—a common practice since the wounds were considered poisonous—he used a mixture of rose oil, turpentine, and egg yolk instead. These patients' wounds healed better, and in 1545 Paré published a report on his practices.

Paré also improved the techniques used for amputations, which were often performed to avoid the risk of complications or death from infection. More of Paré's patients survived

their amputations after he reinstated the Roman custom of tying off the vein or artery during surgery to limit bleeding—an improvement over the custom of cauterizing (burning) the incision. While many surgeons continued with their old ways, Paré was recognized in his time, becoming surgeon to four French kings.

■ **FOOTNOTE** Paré's written works were criticized by some physicians. At this time a surgeon was considered inferior to a physician because a surgeon worked with his hands and had to meet less stringent educational requirements.

Music Conservatories Built

286 **1537** Santa Maria di Loreto, built in 1537, represents the first musical conservatory in Naples. Conservatories had existed, but the milieu in Naples encouraged their growth as a place for training beyond that of religious music. Italian conservatories had been attached to church-run

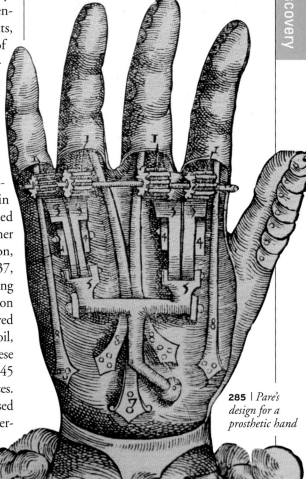

285 | *Paré's design for a prosthetic hand*

orphanages and used to train the children in music. As the interest in commercial music expanded in the early 1600s, musical conservatories took their place in popular culture training famous singers and musicians.

Coronado Explores Southwest

287 **1540-1542** Spanish exploration of North America continued with Francisco Vásquez de Coronado who traveled throughout the American Southwest for two years, beginning in 1540, as he searched for the riches of the seven cities of Cíbola. Riches of the material sort weren't found, but members of his party became the first Europeans to witness the grandeur of the Grand Canyon while others located the mouth of the Colorado River.

His party traveled through Zuni territory and present-day Arizona, Texas, and Kansas, but failed to locate the fabled cities.

When Coronado returned to his governorship of Nueva Galicia, he faced a Spanish inquiry into his expedition. Disappointed with the lack of wealth, Spain failed to see the real strength of Coronado's expedition—a clear understanding of the geography of the American Southwest—and indicted Coronado. Coronado died in Mexico, and the area he explored would have to wait until the end of the 16th century for colonists to arrive.

■ **FOOTNOTE** Coronado was cleared of charges relating to his expedition but found guilty of atrocities committed against American Indians under his control. He resigned his post as governor in 1544 and died ten years later.

Sistine Frescoes Completed

288 **1541** There can be no doubt that Michelangelo understood his own artistic genius, and the frescoes he painted on the Sistine ceiling showcase his talents and mark a high point in the Western artistic tradition. When Pope Julius II commissioned Michelangelo (Michelangelo di Lodovico Buonarroti Simoni) to paint the ceiling, Michelangelo suspended his work on the pope's tomb. Perhaps in a rush to return to the tomb, the artist completed the frescoes in just four years, finishing the masterpiece in 1512. The central scenes all come from Genesis.

Frescoes by other Renaissance painters adorn the chapel in the Vatican Palace, but Michelangelo's artistry transcends even these masters. Michelangelo envisioned the human body as a physical prison of the soul, and the soul immediately comes to mind in the ceiling's "Creation of Adam." The fresco captures the moment when the divine spark passed to Adam.

288 | *Michelangelo's Sistine Chapel (Vatican City) paintings were inspired by the Book of Genesis and took four years to complete.*

Michelangelo painted the "Last Judgment" (1534-41) on the altar wall, not the ceiling, but this work completed his portrayal of a theological history from creation to the end of time. Michelangelo started painting the "Last Judgment" 22 years after the ceiling frescoes, during the Reformation. This painting illustrates historical changes. Instead of the radiance of the ceiling, the viewer sees a scene showing huddled people begging for mercy before God.

Michelangelo's sculpture, painting, and architecture catapulted him into the top tier of the world's most revered artists. The vivid and timeless scenes of the Sistine Chapel also mark an unparalleled achievement in Western art.

■ **FOOTNOTE** A restoration of the Sistine Chapel began in 1979. Solvents were used on Michelangelo's frescoes, revealing the spectacular colors hidden beneath years of grime. Pope John Paul II inaugurated the chapel in 1999.

Brazilian Falls Discovered

289 **1541** Spanish explorer Álvar Núñez Cabeza de Vaca spent time in Europe, North and South America, and Africa. In 1528, Cabeza de Vaca's group set out from Tampa Bay, Florida, only to become detached from their supply vessels and then from each other. Cabeza de Vaca spent the next eight years traveling through the American Southwest, where he and his companions were passed as slaves between Native Americans. In 1536 a Spanish slaving expedition found him, and Cabeza de Vaca related tales of fabulous cities of wealth—the seven cities of Cíbola. His descriptions led to more Spanish exploration (see event 287).

In the mid-16th century, Spain wanted to exploit its newfound colonies, and to do so effectively it needed strong administrators. In late 1541 Cabeza de Vaca set out from Santos, Brazil, to Asunción, Paraguay, to replace the despotic governor Irala of the Rio de Plata colony. En route his party became the first Europeans to see Iguazú Falls on the Iguazú River. In Asunción Cabeza de Vaca enacted reforms and set out to explore the Paraguay River. Irala's

supporters saw that Cabeza de Vaca was deposed and sent back to Spain in 1545, where he was banished to Africa.

Anatomy Text Published

290 **1543** Belgian anatomist Andreas Vesalius published his textbook on human anatomy, *On the Fabric of the Human Body,* in 1543 and ushered in the beginnings of modern anatomy. Vesalius helped overturn the teachings of the Greek physician and philosopher Galen of Pergamum, whose ideas had dominated medical science for centuries. Vesalius brought a clinical thoroughness to his work, and his discoveries were incontrovertible in the face of hard evidence.

While Galen had to dissect animals to arrive at his anatomical ideas, the prejudice against using human corpses was just beginning to lift during Vesalius's time. When teaching anatomy at Padua University, Vesalius had a steady supply of criminal corpses to dissect and some executions even were timed to coincide with his lectures. Vesalius's anatomy textbook, with all its unflinching detail, firmly set anatomy as a scientific discipline.

Heliocentric Solar System Suggested

291 **1543** Nicolaus Copernicus placed the sun in the center of the solar system in his 1543 work *On the Revolution of Heavenly Bodies* (*De revolutionibus orbium coelestium*), overturning the Ptolemaic model that had shaped people's ideas of an unmoving Earth for 1,400 years. His idea recalled the work of the Greek astronomer Aristarchus who had suggested around 280 B.C.E. that the sun was the center of the universe. Copernicus took the idea one step further and attempted to work out the mathematics of a heliocentric universe by mapping planetary orbits. His work helped launch the scientific revolution.

An amateur astronomer, the Polish Copernicus was a canon (one of the administrators) of the cathedral in Frauenberg, Germany, since 1499. He circulated his revolutionary idea by 1514, but only in a small pamphlet passed among scholars. Concerned over how the Church would receive his work, Copernicus delayed its publication. When finally published, it contained a dedication to Pope Paul III. At the time, his ideas were considered mathematical in spirit, but the Catholic Church reacted by forbidding the book in 1616. Martin Luther assured the curious that Scripture clearly states that the sun moved, not the Earth.

While Copernicus's most famous work came out the same year as his death, it would be almost nine more decades before Galileo would publish his own work on a heliocentric universe. The year Copernicus died—1543—was a big one for scientific works. Andreas Vesalius also published his anatomy textbook (see event 290). Vesalius changed how people saw themselves, but it is the Copernican system that changed how people saw their place in the world.

Copernicus, although remembered as an astronomer, also wrote on Poland's currency, clearly in tune with another big change occurring at the time—the stirrings of capitalism.

Copernicus holds a model of the solar system in Warsaw, Poland.

293 | *Sea serpent and ship from* Historiae animalium

Kunqu Opera Flourishes

292 **ca 1550** The *kunqu* form of Chinese opera rose to dominance in the mid-16th century during the Ming dynasty and dominated Chinese opera late into the 18th century. Kunqu involved intricate vocalizations and articulations and required a mastery of complicated dance movements.

The regional operas of the time used folk songs to entertain commoners, but kunqu appealed to an educated audience. A commercial expansion in the Yangtze region accompanied the dominance of this form, which saw a revival in the early 20th century under state encouragement by the People's Republic of China. The Cultural Revolution and decreased state support for the arts sent kunqu into decline, and today it has more than likely reached the end of its theatrical tenure.

Natural Sciences Explained

293 **1551** Konrad von Gesner helped to provide the foundations of both zoological and botanical science when he published *Historiae animalium* (the first volume appeared in 1551, the fifth volume in 1587) and the posthumous *Historiae plantarum*. While books describing plants and animals existed during the Middle Ages, these herbals and bestiaries contained magical, religious, and legendary information. A Swiss naturalist, Gesner corresponded with naturalists all over the world who sent him descriptions of animals, which he then published in *Historiae animalum*. The compendium contained direct observations of animal behavior (with a few oddities thrown in). He died in 1565 from the plague, which still caused large numbers of deaths in Europe during the 16th century.

Servetus Explains Lungs, Heart

294 **1553** The Spanish physician and theologian Michael Servetus proposed pulmonary circulation in 1553, but this knowledge failed to reach the medical community because of his heretical views. In 1546 Servetus had sent a manuscript, "Christianismi Restitutio," to John Calvin, who had rejected its unorthodox ideas. Secretly published in 1553, the work contained the idea that the divine spirit could be found in the blood. Servetus also explained how blood travels from the right side of the heart to the lungs and then back to the heart's left side—otherwise known as pulmonary circulation.

Servetus questioned the existence of the Trinity, causing both Catholics and Protestants to view him as a heretic. He escaped the Inquisition and his trial for heresy by the Catholic Church but was later tried in Geneva. Servetus was convicted and burned at the stake in 1553. An Egyptian physician in the 13th century understood pulmonary circulation, but this knowledge failed to reach Europe, and Servetus's heretical beliefs again meant it was not shared. The anatomist Matteo Realdo Colombo would "rediscover" it six years later.

■ **FOOTNOTE** The trial and burning of Servetus led to criticism of the practice and influenced the founder of Unitarian views, Laelius Socinus. Unitarians, also known as Polish Brethren, did not believe in the doctrine of the Trinity.

Ottoman Empire Gains Iraq

295 **1555** Although concerned with the Safavids to his empire's east, the Ottoman sultan Süleyman I recognized that he should not overextend his military or financial resources in war against the Safavids. Süleyman waged three campaigns against the Safavids, and in 1534 the Ottomans captured Baghdad for good, illustrating their territorial goals in the region. In 1555 the Safavid ruler Shah Tahmasp recognized Ottoman control in the Treaty of Amasia. The treaty gave Safavid control over the Caucasus and Azerbaijan, and Ottoman control

Servetus

CHRISTIANISMI RESTITUTIO, 1553

From these things it is sufficiently clear that that soft mass of the brain is not properly the seat of the rational soul, since it is cold and lacking in sensation. But it is like a bolster for the aforesaid vessels lest they be broken, and like a custodian of the animal spirit lest it blow away when it must be communicated to the nerves; and it is cold that it may temper that fiery heat contained within the vessels.

Hence also it happens that the nerves serve the tunic of the membrane in the internal cavity, which is common to the aforesaid vessels as a faithful guardian of the spirit, and they hold this [away] from the thin meninx just as they hold another from the thick. Also those empty spaces of the ventricles of the brain which puzzle philosophers and physicians contain nothing else but the spirit.

...Finally, because we perceive the intellect exerting itself there when, as a result of concentrated thought, those arteries are pulsating as far as the temples. He who has not seen this thing will scarcely understand. Those ventricles were made for a second reason, that a portion of the inspired air penetrating through the ethmoid bones to their empty spaces, attracted by diastole from the vessels of the spirit, may refresh and ventilate the animal spirit contained within and the soul. In those vessels are mind, soul, and fiery spirit requiring constant fanning; otherwise, like an eternal fire which has been covered up, there would be suffication. As in the case of ordinary fire, there is required not only fanning and blowing upon so that it may take fuel from the air, but also that it may discharge its sooty vapors into the air. And just as this common external fire is bound to a thick earthy body, because of a common dryness and because of a common form of light, so that which has the liquid of the body as its food is blown upon, supported and nourished by the air; thus that fiery spirit and our soul are similarly bound to the body, making one with it and having blood as food...

over Iraq and eastern Anatolia, creating boundaries that would remain in place for centuries.

> ■ **FOOTNOTE** Both the Ottomans and the Safavids had to pay attention to stirrings from the north. Safavid raids to the north netted tens of thousands of prisoners, and Süleyman I faced challenges in the Caucasus and Black Sea.

Economic Principles Formed

296 **1556** The University of Salamanca in Spain was home to a lively school of economics in the 16th century. One of its leaders, Martín de Azpilcueta (also known as Navarrus), observed that the influx of gold and silver from the New World caused increased prices and wages in Spain in his 1556 work, *Commentario resolutorio de usuras*. Since many riches reached Spain first, it made sense to Navarrus that Spain would have higher prices than the rest of Europe. He advanced the idea that a currency's value increases as the amount of it decreases. The theory also applied to goods: when goods are in strong demand and scarce supply, their value increases. This "scarcity theory of value" would shape later economic thought.

A Dominican priest, Navarrus also believed that money changing and usury were important economic tools and refuted the need for any kind of price control. Navarrus was the first economist to write about purchasing power parity, the idea that when money is scarce it is worth more.

Akbar Wins Battle of Panipat

297 **1556** Babur's grandson, Akbar, fought to regain Mogul control over northern India in the second Battle of Panipat in November 1556. Akbar, only a teenager at the time, fought the more numerous Hindu army under General Hemu for control of Delhi. Luck would be with Akbar when Hemu was wounded in battle, allowing the Mogul victory. He had to fight his half-brother Mirza

Hakim for control of Afghanistan, which he secured in 1581. As a ruler, Akbar repealed discriminatory taxes on non-Muslims and was known for his fairness and keen strategy of expansion and consolidation of his empire, as well as tolerance of the diverse religions practiced by his subjects. Akbar died in 1605.

Portugal Founds Trading Port

298 **1557** Portuguese traders had been using Macau on the eastern coast of China since 1516 as a port and staging location, and in 1557 China agreed to the Portuguese establishment of the trading center, the oldest European presence in the Far East. At the time, China believed it

297 | *Afghan general Akbar returned Mogul rule to northern India.*

retained sovereignty. Portugal named its first governor in 1680, and European control lasted until December 1999, when Portugal returned Macau to China. The territory has special status within the Chinese government.

Elizabeth Assumes Throne

299 **1558** When Queen Elizabeth assumed the English throne, she was no stranger to political intrigue. Before she was three years old, her father, King Henry VIII, had her mother, Anne Boleyn, put to death. Elizabeth succeeded her sister Mary, who wanted to place England in the Catholic fold. When Mary died, the tactically brilliant Elizabeth reestablished Protestantism. She inherited a divided country served by a weak military, but her expanded navy defeated the Spanish Armada in 1588.

Elizabeth quieted critics who thought only men could be effective rulers. Intrigue over whether Elizabeth, the Virgin Queen, would marry gave way to a flourishing arts and commercial culture. Elizabeth came to symbolize the English destiny, and she encouraged her image as a queen wedded to her country. At least for a time in the 16th century, girls did rule.

> ■**FOOTNOTE** Queen Elizabeth's reign saw English colonization in newly discovered lands. The New World's first English settlers arrived at Roanoke Island in 1585, but the settlement didn't survive and the colonists' fates remain unknown.

Workings of Heart Explained

300 **1559** The Italian anatomist Matteo Realdo Colombo, who was recognized by his contemporaries as discovering pulmonary circulation, published his anatomy text, *On Anatomical Matters* (*De re anatomica*), in 1559—shortly before his death. Colombo's work built on his teacher Vesalius's discovery that blood does not pass between the right and left sides of the heart. Pulmonary circulation, the circulation of blood through the lungs, was discovered in the 13th century by an Egyptian doctor, but

Spanish Establish Fort in Florida

301 **1565** To protect its colonial exploits, Spain founded St. Augustine, Florida. The Spanish explorer Juan Ponce de León first arrived in the region and claimed it for Spain in 1513. When the French built a fort nearby, Spain sent conquistadore Pedro Menéndez de Avilés to counter the threat. He founded St. Augustine and massacred the inhabitants of the French fort. The Spanish Empire used St. Augustine as its principal northern military base, and no other European settlement in the U.S. has been continuously occupied longer.

Castillo de San Marcos in St. Augustine, Florida, is now a national monument.

Battles with the local Indians and administrative and location changes occurred as St. Augustine grew into a colonial town, but one not high on the priority list of the Spanish crown. When the English founded Charleston in 1670, Spain took notice, and in 1672 started to build the Castillo de San Marcos, the oldest masonry fort in North America. Its outer walls consist of coquina rock, a form of limestone that has the advantage of absorbing or deflecting the impact of cannonballs instead of shattering.

St. Augustine can also claim another superlative: the first free black settlement in North America, begun at Fort Mose in 1738. Fort Mose formed part of the settlement's outer defenses. St. Augustine passed to English control in 1763 after the Seven Years' War but Spain returned in 1784. Florida became a U.S. territory in 1821.

this information was unknown in Europe. The Spanish doctor Michael Servetus proposed the concept of pulmonary circulation in 1553, but he was burned at the stake for his heretical beliefs, and his knowledge failed to reach the European medical community.

So it took Colombo to rediscover that blood circulated from the heart's right ventricle to the lungs and then returns to the heart's left atrium. He noted that this returning blood was brighter and redder than blood entering the heart from the body. Colombo also correctly understood the motion of the heart to contract and push blood into the arteries. The great English doctor William Harvey recognized Colombo as the discoverer of pulmonary circulation and then went on himself to advance the idea of general circulation.

Slave Trade Denounced

302 **1569** Along with the growth of the slave trade came a growing body of literature about its legality. In 1569, the Spanish cleric and economist Tomás de Mercado denounced how the slave trade was carried out in *Practices and Contracts of Merchants*. In a work written in 1587 de Mercado said, "A thousand acts of robbery and violence are committed in the course of bartering and carrying off Negroes."

Perhaps most famous are the writings of Bartolomé de las Casas, a Spanish bishop of Chiapas, who published *The Black Legend* in 1542. He condemned the violent devastation and murders carried out by the Spanish, arguing that African slaves provided an alternative to the labor provided by the indigenous population of the Americas. De las Casas would later lament any part he played in the slave trade. Slavery in the Americas would not be outlawed completely until Brazil prohibited the practice in 1888.

■ **FOOTNOTE** In 1556, Domingo de Soto, a Spanish theologian, accepted enslavement if people were enslaved for a "just cause" but considered forced enslavement to weigh on the conscience of those involved.

Mercator Improves Mapping

303 **1569** Gerardus Mercator published an important map —a map of the world based on a new projection. He also published a collection of maps in 1585 that he called an atlas, but his name would be best remembered for inventing the Mercator projection. Instead of having to take compass readings over and over to make sure they remained on track when sailing long distances, the Mercator projection allowed seafarers to plot

303 | *Gerardus Mercator revolutionized navigation.*

their course using straight lines. Accurate navigational charts would benefit anyone who took to the seas—and greatly aid their navigation.

The Mercator projection combines equally spaced longitude lines with latitude lines that become wider apart farther away from the Equator. When using a compass, the projection renders lines of constant bearing. One drawback is that the projection distorts the size of lands near the poles (e.g., Greenland appears to be as large as South America, when it is closer to the size of the Arabian Peninsula). Regardless, the Mercator projection has dominated maps ever since.

■ **FOOTNOTE** Mapping using latitude and longitude did not begin in the 16th century. The second century C.E. geographer and astronomer Ptolemy used grids as a way to map the world, taking into account its spherical shape.

Ortelius Publishes World Atlas

304 **1570** Fast on the heels of Gerardus Mercator's world map, Abraham Ortelius published what is considered

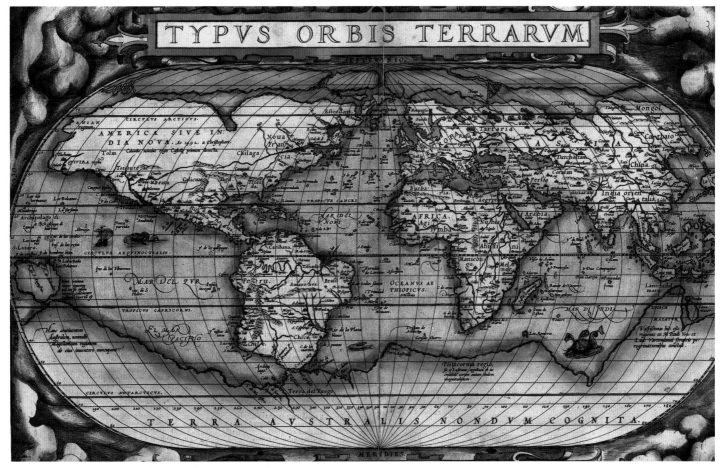

159 | *A copperplate engraving from Abraham Ortelius's* Theatrum Orbis Terrarum

to be the first modern atlas, the *Theatrum Orbis Terrarum,* in 1570. The Flemish Ortelius credited his friendship with Mercator with attracting him to the life of a cartographer, since he began his career as an engraver. Born in Antwerp, Ortelius published a map of the world using a heart-shaped projection in 1564, but his collection of world maps made him famous.

> ▪ **FOOTNOTE** Cartography continually changes, and the Library of Congress, for example, houses more than 53,000 atlases in its collection. These atlases take their place in the largest collection of maps in the world.

Alooma Consolidates Empire

305 **ca 1571** The Kanem-Bornu Empire in modern-day Chad and Nigeria consolidated its power during the reign of Mai (King) Idris Alooma. A pious Muslim, Alooma based his legal reforms on Islamic law. Alooma's military reforms included fixed camps and the use of a scorched-earth policy, and he gained firearms from the Ottomans. An epic poem even describes his success in more than a thousand battles. Kanem-Bornu's wealth came from its control over trans-Saharan trade routes (including ivory, nuts, and importantly slaves). After Alooma's death the empire held on to power, but it began to decline by the mid-17th century.

Brahe Observes Supernova

306 **1572** A supernova gave the Danish astronomer Tycho Brahe the chance to overturn the Aristotelian idea of an unchanging universe (in Aristotle's view our moon and any other celestial event that changed took place in Earth's atmosphere).

Turning his attention to the skies, Tycho (as with Galileo, he is most often referred to by his first name) observed an exploding star in the Cassiopeia constellation, which he recorded for 15 months. Chinese astronomers also recorded the supernova.

Tycho published his findings in 1593 in *De Nova Stella,* which presented evidence of a star outside our solar system that was not immovable and overturned Aristotelian ideas. He continued to record celestial events—including a 1577 comet, which enabled him to confirm (using parallax) that the comet was an event in our atmosphere.

By this time, some states were supporting scientific research, and Frederick II, King of Denmark, led the way. He gave Tycho the island of Hven, where he built a modern observatory known as Uraniborg. In Tycho's model of the solar system,

---

CONNECTIONS

Atlas of the World
Getting one's bearings facilitated in age of exploration

The age of exploration instigated great changes in geographic knowledge and the science of mapping, represented in the 16th century by Flemish cartographers Gerardus Mercator and Abraham Ortelius. The first modern atlas came about in the period. An engraver, Ortelius also sold maps. Mercator had made a map of the world in 1569 using his new projection with lines of latitude and longitude that could be used by navigators as constant bearing, but it was somewhat unwieldy. A trader asked Ortelius to create what we would today call an atlas, and his friend Mercator's map and influence proved invaluable to his work.

Collections of maps predated both men, with examples being found in Renaissance Europe. In Italy in the mid-16th century so-called map books were made to order, but in these collections the buyer determined the makeup. However, a year after Mercator's world map, in 1570, Abraham Ortelius published what is considered to be the first modern atlas, the *Theatrum Orbis Terrarum (Theater of the World).* The collection showcased 70 maps and the work of 33 different cartographers. Ortelius also listed almost 90 geographers—or all the ones he knew. Ortelius reduced the maps in his collection to a uniform size, which he compiled and edited, adding narrative text and source notes.

Ortelius's painted map of Asia

Ortelius's addition of text is notable, for it provided the reader with context and explanations. He also kept the atlas up to date, bringing out seven editions by the end of the century. After Ortelius's death in 1598, the atlas continued to be published until 1612, for a total of 31 editions.

Mercator also started a collection of world maps. It included some of the maps of Claudius Ptolemaeus (Ptolemy), the second-century Egyptian geographer whose maps took into account Earth's spherical shape and whose work greatly influenced early Renaissance cartographers. Mercator called his collection an atlas, named for the Titan in Greek mythology who had to hold up the world. Mercator first published his atlas in 1585.

From these beginnings, modern atlases quickly began to take off. Cartographers in Italy collected maps between 1556 and 1575 in the *Lafréri Atlas.* Ortelius introduced historical maps in his 1579 edition, illustrating his idea of the importance of geography for history. The popularity of atlases demonstrated the public's increasing interest in the wider world. Subsequent cartographers found much to work with (and to improve), as new and better knowledge made previous atlases outdated.

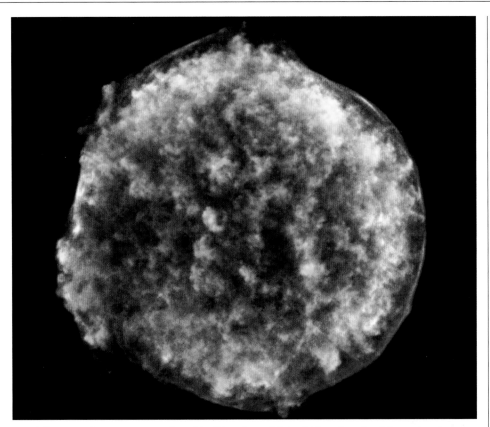

306 | *Remnant of a supernova reveals multimillion-degree debris within casing of rapidly moving electrons.*

the planets rotated around the sun, but the sun and moon rotated around Earth. His theory held sway in the early 17th century, only to fall to the correct Copernican model. Tycho remains the most observant astronomer in the pretelescope age and left his brilliant student, Johannes Kepler, to continue his work.

> ▓ **FOOTNOTE** Tycho called his star a "nova," known today as a supernova. He stressed accurate observations and made sure his instruments were correctly calibrated. His observatory, Uraniborg, was destroyed during the Thirty Years' War.

Portuguese Suffer Defeat

307 **1578** King Sebastian of Portugal looked across the Strait of Gibraltar to Morocco and wanted to conquer and convert its Muslim population to Christianity. Moroccans had been resisting Portuguese control in the region, and in August 1578 Sebastian's forces, aligned with the deposed Moroccan sultan, met those of the current sultan, Abd al-Malik. King Sebastian drowned during the defeat, and lacking an heir, the Spanish took control of Portugal. The victorious Muslims gained a new ruler since al-Malik died the day after the battle. Europe would leave Morocco alone for three centuries.

Dalai Lama Established

308 **1578** Buddhists believe that the incarnations of the Dalai Lama preceded Sonam Gyatso, but he was the first Tibetan Buddhist spiritual leader to receive the title Dalai Lama, bestowed upon him by the Mongol ruler Altan Khan in 1578. Considered the third Dalai Lama ("oceanic teacher"), Sonam Gyatso converted the Tumet Mongols from shamanism to Buddhism. In 1617, the fifth Dalai Lama, Losang Gyatso, combined spiritual authority with secular power and initiated a monastic bureaucracy. The Manchus in China welcomed the ability of the Dalai Lama to control the Mongols. In 1950 China invaded Tibet, and nine years later the 14th Dalai Lama fled Tibet for exile in India.

Beaver Fur in Demand

309 **ca 1580** Two commodities—fish and fur—helped shape the settlement of North America in the 16th century. European countries sent fishermen to the rich waters of the Grand Banks, which naturally led to contact with the indigenous inhabitants. Fur quickly became an important trade good for the French, as well as for the English and Dutch. The French began trading in beaver in the 1500s, and demand grew as the 17th century began.

Beaver fur is excellent for making felt, and although Europe had its own beaver species, by 1600 the Russian hat industry had decimated European supplies. Felt hats worn by Swedish cavaliers during the Thirty Years' War encouraged the style, and demand for hats caused the North American trade in beaver fur to explode in the early 17th century. The luxury trade encouraged alliances with Native Americans. These relationships embroiled indigenous groups in regional conflicts (for instance the 1649 defeat of the Huron by the Iroquois) and international conflicts (the French and Indian War in 1754).

The fur trade encouraged New France's reliance on export markets, and after fur was depleted lumber, wheat, and minerals would follow. By the late 18th century, the North American beaver populations would be decimated.

Pendulum Physics Noted

310 **1581** The life of Italian scientist Galileo Galilei represents the full flowering of the Scientific Revolution. Galileo discovered astounding things by simply observing the world around him. As the authority of the ancients collapsed, the way was cleared for a new scientific understanding of the world.

By 1581, while still a teenager (Galileo was born in Pisa in 1564), the story goes that Galileo watched the motion of a moving chandelier during a church service and noticed that no matter its arc (large or small), the chandelier took the same amount of time to complete a swing. He went home and performed a few experiments to prove the accuracy of his observations. This observation aided the accuracy of timekeeping.

Galileo then went on to bigger things, inventing a rudimentary thermometer in 1592 using a bulb and tube and a container of water. As the air in the bulb warmed, water was drawn into the tube, giving Galileo an idea of the relative warmth or coldness of the air.

In 1610 he published *The Starry Messenger* (*Sidereal Messenger*), and using the newly invented telescope (which he improved, naturally), he observed the phases of Venus, mountains on the moon, and some of the many satellites of Jupiter. The universe as envisioned by Aristotle was no

more. Galileo realized the importance of accurate scientific measurements and worked to invent tools that could be used to aid scientific research. Galileo advanced the idea that nature is written in the language of mathematics, which helped to alter the course of science by stressing the importance of experimental data over qualitative mathematics to explain the workings of the world.

Gregorian Calendar Established

311 **1582** Imagine having the power to erase days. Pope Gregory XIII did, in 1582, when he reformed the Julian calendar. The new science helped usher in more accurate timekeeping by stressing the importance of accurate measuring devices. The Julian calendar

was accurate for the big picture, but a year averaged 365.25 days, since an extra day was added every four years. Over centuries dates started to slip, particularly noticed by religious officials since Easter's date depended on the date of the vernal equinox, which fell earlier and earlier as the years passed.

In 1582, Pope Gregory XIII convened a meeting to discuss reforming the calendar. The group of scientists and theologians decided to cut ten days from the calendar—October 4 would be followed by October 15, 1582. The Gregorian calendar omits leap years every 400 years in order to keep the system aligned. The calendar was immediately accepted by Catholic nations such as France, Italy, Spain, and Portugal. Protestant countries took longer; Great Britain did not switch to the Gregorian system until 1752.

Stevin Anticipates Galileo

312 **1585** During the scientific revolution, theories and ideas would seem almost to be in the air. In 1586 the Flemish mathematician and engineer Simon Stevin published a little recognized work. His thesis that two lead balls of different weights fall 30 feet in the same amount of time supported theories advanced by Giovanni Battista Benedetti, also a mathematician and engineer. Galileo would first write on gravity three years later. In 1608, Stevin published a work supporting Copernicus's heliocentric universe. Instead of writing scientific works in Latin, which was the standard of the time, Stevin encouraged using the vernacular, which helped to spread information.

> ■ **FOOTNOTE** Stevin introduced the decimal system to Europe in his 1585 work, *De Thiende* (*The Tenth*). He believed that coinage, measurements, and weights would soon be represented using the system.

Spanish Armada Attacks

313 **1588** In 1588 the Catholic king of Spain, Philip II, launched an armada of 130 ships in an attack on Queen Elizabeth I and Protestant England.

179 | *From his papal throne, Gregory XIII instructs followers in the use of his new calendar.*

Spain suffered from privateer attacks and knew of English support for the rebels in the Spanish Netherlands, and the king wanted to combine an amphibious assault with an armed force from the Spanish Netherlands to take England. The fleet sailed from Lisbon in the spring of 1588 and was sighted off the Cornish coast on July 29. The English attacked as the flotilla sailed to Calais, proving the superiority of their guns (many of the Spanish used guns designed for use on land). The Spanish army was blockaded, and the English used ships for night-time attacks on the Spanish fleet. After the Battle of Gravelines Spanish commanders decided to return home, but by way of the treacherous North Sea. The fleet encountered severe storms and lost 63 ships, but the biggest loss of the campaign was to the Spanish reputation. England benefited from the battle expertise and leadership of her privateers, and the defeat showcased the vulnerabilities of

313 | *England's* Ark Royal, *one of many frigates that defended the British against the Spanish Armada.*

naval warfare to storms and to resupply during this period, no matter the military brilliance.

Songhai Empire Falls

314 | **1591** Located in Mali and Western Sahara, the Songhai kingdom (and later empire) had been in existence since around 500 C.E. when Morocco invaded in 1582. Moroccan fighters carried muskets and wore armor, and they easily stood up to the bows and arrows of the Songhai, ushering in the end of the empire. In 1591, at the Battle of Tondibi, the main cities of Timbuktu and Gao fell and the emperor fled into exile. Guerilla raids continued into conquered territory, but the Songhai's cultural center of Timbuktu came under Moroccan rule. By the mid-17th century the empire was reduced to weak states in part of its former territory.

Japan Invades Korea

315 | **1592** Under the leadership of Toyotomi Hideyoshi, Japan launched an invasion into Korea in 1592. Japan sought to expand its territory and had its sights on China. Hideyoshi first asked Korea to join them, but Korea refused. Korea received aid from the

Chinese Ming dynasty and benefited from the technical advances of Yi Sun-sin—a Korean admiral who invented warships that are considered the first ironclads, *kobukson* or "turtle ships." The Imjin War ended with Japanese withdrawal in 1598 after the death of Hideyoshi. Japan and Korea soon resumed a diplomatic relationship. In short order Korea suffered another invasion—this time by the Manchus (Qing dynasty).

> ■ **FOOTNOTE** The first battle between ironclads occurred in March 1862 during the American Civil War, when the U.S.S. *Monitor* and the U.S.S. *Merrimack* (renamed *Virginia* by the Confederates) met, ending in a stalemate.

Henry IV Passes Edict of Nantes

316 | **1598** England's King Henry IV effectively ended the French wars of religion that had been raging for almost half a century and passed the Edict of Nantes. The edict illustrated a new idea: the importance of allowing the religious freedom to avoid civil unrest. Henry IV, the first Bourbon king, granted Huguenots (French Calvinists) religious freedom to worship and many of the same civil rights as Catholics in France. Freedom of worship only applied to

299 More Details on Queen Elizabeth I

Speaking to the ambassador of the Duke of Würtemberg, Queen Elizabeth I said, "I would rather be a beggar and single than a queen and married." Indeed, the Virgin Queen made it well known that her loyalty rested with her country, publicly turning away many noteworthy suitors. Her devotion and strength as a ruler guided England into one of its most prosperous and memorable eras; its spectacular military strength was matched by a cultural renaissance that gave us Shakespeare and Milton.

Elizabeth I remains one of her country's best loved monarchs, and today her legacy is captured continually in film, television, and literature. Yet little is known about the personal life of the queen aside from her steadfast determination to excel on a man's throne. Her father, King Henry VIII, had wanted a son so badly that he rewrote the laws of the church, divorced his first wife, and married Anne Boleyn, only to gain yet another daughter, Elizabeth, as an heir. It was not until the passing of both her illegitimate brother Edward VI and her elder sister Mary I that Elizabeth took the throne, inheriting a country weak with religious strife and uncertain of its place on the world stage.

> "I have but the body of a weak and feeble woman; but I have the heart of a king."
> —Queen Elizabeth I

Elizabeth's first major act as queen was to reinstate the Protestant Church in England, and she showed a respectable compassion for her Catholic adversaries. Her popularity soared, and her public image was enhanced by her engagement in English culture and her well-known patronage of the arts, especially theater. She surrounded herself with the brightest minds of the day, including Sir William Cecil and Sir Francis Walsingham, which added to her credibility and perspective. But her political genius is most visible in her famous defeat of the Spanish Armada in 1588, which proved her might as a ruler and her country's power. As she famously said on the eve of the Spanish attack, "I know I have but the body of a weak and feeble woman; but I have the heart of a king, and of a king of England, too."

Queen Elizabeth I is shown in procession with her courtiers in an illustration from Memoirs of the Court of Queen Elizabeth.

places where Protestants had recently worshipped, and they were not allowed to worship in Paris. The edict also restricted new growth in Protestantism. Louis XIV revoked the edict in 1685, persecuting Protestants, and hundreds of thousands left France.

> ■ **FOOTNOTE** Before revoking the Edict of Nantes, Louis XIV started to strictly enforce its conditions. Five years before it was finally revoked, an edict forbade a Catholic to convert to Protestantism.

Ricci Arrives in Beijing

317 **1598** When the Jesuit missionary Matteo Ricci first arrived in the city of Beijing in 1598, he brought with him more than the word of God. He also brought knowledge coming from Western science and technology, lecturing the Ming imperial court. Jesuit missionaries began to convert some Chinese to Christianity, establishing contact between the Europeans and the Chinese. The Jesuits exercised the strongest influence on the elite and mainly missed the masses. Cultural accommodation was key to their success, which led to strong concerns from the Vatican.

Tokugawa Becomes Shogun

318 **1600** In the fall of 1600, the founder of the Tokugawa shogunate, Tokugawa Ieyasu, fought lesser lords for control of Japan—and won. The previous shogun, Toyotomi Hideyoshi had died two years earlier, throwing the country into civil war.

The Battle of Sekigahara pitted Ieyasu's eastern forces against rival western forces, and Ieyasu won the decisive battle, thanks in part to information provided by traitors from the other side. Ieyasu proclaimed the shogunate in 1603 that would rule Japan until 1868 from Edo (Tokyo), his military capital. Tokyo would become the economic and cultural center of Japan as well.

During the empire, Japan became isolated and politically conservative. Dissent, along with Christian beliefs, was suppressed. However, the period's stability encouraged the merchant class and ushered in a period of industrial and commercial growth. Confucianism flourished, and Japan saw a revival of lay learning. After two unsuccessful coups in 1651 and 1652, the Tokugawa shogunate did not face a major challenge to its rule until the 19th century.

Shakespeare Writes *Hamlet*

319 **1600** First performed at London's Globe Theatre in 1600, William Shakespeare's *Hamlet, Prince of Denmark* has gripped theater audiences, readers, and critics alike, establishing it one of the finest dramatic works ever written.

Renaissance drama usually presented well-drawn characters with clear dilemmas so the audience could predict how they'd react. Shakespeare's Hamlet, however, is a complex and philosophical hero. His father, the king, has been murdered by his own brother who then marries the queen, Hamlet's mother. Hamlet, confronted with awful circumstances, must decide if he should kill his uncle in revenge, even though he recognizes the act as evil. Hamlet's father even appears as a ghost, telling Hamlet of his murder and asking him to avenge it. Yet Hamlet finds himself unable to act, and the deaths in the play stem from this inability to fully carry out his own justice until the play's final act. Hamlet's actions cost him his life. A complicated hero, Hamlet broke the mold of a one-dimensional protagonist.

Shakespeare wrote at least 37 plays and numerous sonnets, but it is this

320 | *An 18th-century triptych, created from a woodcut, illustrates three scenes from a Kabuki performance.*

321 | *Don Quixote and companion Sancho Panza*

tragedy—one of the most famous of all his works—that continues to challenge us with its vivid portrayal of the human psyche even as we grapple with morality and mortality today.

> ■ **FOOTNOTE** *Hamlet* contains many well-known lines, including "The lady doth protest too much," spoken by Hamlet's mother, and "Neither a borrower nor a lender be," which Polonius offers as advice to his son.

Kabuki Theater Debuts

320 **ca 1600** Kabuki theater, still a popular genre in Japan today, traces its beginnings to the start of the 17th century. Kabuki combines music, drama, and dance. Historians believe that Japanese puppet theater inspired the form, and the first performances involved the actors striking a gong, dancing, and chanting Buddhist prayers. Soon, however, brothels adopted the entertainment, and by 1629 women were banned from performing Kabuki on stage. When young boys assumed the roles of the women, the government banned them as well in 1652. Then older men assumed the roles—as is still the case today. By 1700, the versatility and popularity of the form secured its firm establishment as a favorite Japanese art form.

Kabuki theater lacks directors, and its actors determine the interpretation of the play. The stylized dancing and singing serves as a platform to show off the actors' strengths. Kabuki has remained the main form of Japanese theater for 400 years.

Don Quixote Published

321 **1605** Spanish writer Miguel de Cervantes, perhaps the most famous Spanish writer of all time, published the first part of *Don Quixote* in 1605 and the second part ten years later. Many critics consider the work to be the first modern novel.

Cervantes's life reads like a novel. In the Battle of Lepanto against the Turks (the Turks lost), he lost the use of his left hand and was sold into slavery in Algeria, only to be released when he could pay for his freedom. No matter his personal hardships, Cervantes managed to write a masterpiece of European literature and achieved fame with *Don Quixote*. The novel owes its success in part to Cervantes's comic genius, whose title character has read a few too many romance novels and has gone mad because of them. After Don Quixote's adventures, he recovers his faculties and dies.

The first part underwent six editions in 1605 alone and was soon translated. Its influence continued past Cervantes's lifetime—traces can be found in the fiction of Daniel Defoe, Charles Dickens, and Fyodor Dostoyevsky, among others. Although ostensibly a satire, the novel poignantly portrays the human condition and shows what happens when a society cannot accommodate any deviant behavior. *Don Quixote* was a seminal work in the history of the modern novel and remains one of the greatest works in all of literature.

First Newspapers Published

323 **ca 1605** Long before newspapers were delivered to the doorstep,

Bacon Teaches Inductive Reasoning

322 **1605** Empiricist Sir Francis Bacon, accomplished as a lawyer, politician, and philosopher, offered a new foundation for the scientific method with his publication of *The Advancement of Learning*. In it he proposed three areas of human knowledge—history, poetry, and philosophy. The book dismissed the deductive reasoning of Aristotle; for Bacon, philosophy depended on reason, and reason on experience. By collecting facts, he said, new principles of the natural world would be discovered. Bacon also rejected Platonic forms as the essence of an object and believed instead that a form was a mechanical or geometric model.

Bacon conceived of Earth as the center of the solar system and believed that the advancement of scientific knowledge would return human beings to the ideal state found in the Garden of Eden. The incomplete *Instauratia magna* (*The Great Instauration*), published in 1620, offered the culmination of his ideas.

Portrait of British statesman and philosopher Sir Francis Bacon

Bacon was also a tireless advocate for the importance of collecting scientific data. For him, experience was everything, and so he is remembered as a champion of the inductive method and as a statesman and philosopher who greatly influenced the disciplines of science and philosophy.

news was posted in ancient Rome for the public to read and in China accounts of court affairs were read by civil servants. Beginning in the 15th century, Europeans stayed informed through news pamphlets and newsletters between powerful trading families. These commercial publications transformed in the early 17th century into the first newspapers. The forerunners are: *Nieuwe Tijdingen* from the Low Countries, first published in 1605; *Relation,* published in 1609 in Strasbourg; and *Avisa Relation oder Zeitung,* also published in 1609 in Augsburg. During this period, all newspapers had to navigate state censorship, which limited their development in Europe. The first daily newspaper in England was the *Daily Courant,* published in 1702.

Jamestown Founded

324 **1607** When the colonists of the Virginia Company of London arrived in Jamestown in May 1607, they founded the first permanent English colony in North America. Sent to make their investors money as well as to counter Spanish domination in the New World, the colonists almost abandoned the settlement for good in 1610, but a supply ship arrived just in time, and they stayed. Jamestown's first settlers faced starvation, a drought, diseases, hostile Native Americans, and ineffective leadership. They spent valuable time searching for riches instead of concentrating on their crops. But those who survived changed the course of history.

■ **FOOTNOTE** During the years from 1607 to 1625, only 20 percent of the settlers who arrived in Jamestown survived. In 1619, the colonists created a General Assembly whose members could own land and vote.

Quebec Established

325 **1608** European powers were racing to divide up the world by the time Samuel de Champlain founded Quebec in 1608. The French already had explored some of the area in the mid-16th century when Jacques Cartier claimed the region. Champlain's travels and cartographic work, however, provided detailed information for subsequent explorers over the next 200 years, and it is Champlain who is considered the crucial figure for French exploration in the New World.

He arrived in the spring of 1603 and began by exploring the Gulf of St. Lawrence. He then mapped an area spanning from Nova Scotia down the coast of what today is known as Cape Cod. In 1608, Champlain commanded an expedition of 32 colonists and founded Quebec. Only eight members besides Champlain would survive their first winter. A year later he discovered his eponymous lake.

The father of New France, Champlain's dependence on, and trust in, his native guides allowed him to gather important cultural and geographical information. His friendship with local groups ran counter to the experiences of indigenous people in most other parts of the Americas. Champlain consolidated French claims in the New World, and his alliances with the Montagnais and Huron helped secure

325 | *Natives port canoes for Samuel de Champlain and his fellow explorers.*

327 | *Workers in Kenya use large woven baskets to collect tea harvested from a tea plantation.*

those claims as well as facilitate the growing fur trade. Champlain spent the rest of his life administering the colonies, dying in Quebec in 1635. The other important French settlement—Montreal—was visited by Jacques Cartier in 1535-36, but it was not until 1642 that Paul de Chomedey founded the modern city.

■ **FOOTNOTE** Samuel de Champlain was no stranger to transatlantic travel, crossing the ocean nearly 30 times to explore New York State, Ontario, and surroundings. No complete artist's portrait of the well-traveled man remains.

Planetary Motion Described

326 **1609** The German astronomer Johannes Kepler accurately formulated the motions of the planets in 1609 by demonstrating that their elliptical orbits were not circular as the Greeks had believed. He published his first two "laws" of planetary motion in 1609 in *The New Astronomy*, and the third followed just ten years later in *Harmonies of the World*. The laws postulated planetary motion in relation to the sun, but Kepler still saw God's order in the universe, likening the sun to

God, the stars to the Son, and the space in between to the Holy Spirit.

Kepler wanted to decipher the real workings of the universe, and not just the abstract mathematics that had encompassed astronomy until his time. He even worked with the famed Danish astronomer Tycho Brahe (see event 306) on Mars's orbit before Tycho's death. Kepler, whose vision was damaged from smallpox when he was three years old, benefited from access to Tycho's keen observations. Although some of Kepler's ideas (celestial music and planetary souls) seemed odd to him even a few years later, he gave astronomy a sound physical footing and paved the way for Isaac Newton's theories and the discipline of celestial physics.

Tea Arrives in Europe

327 **ca 1610** When a ship from the Dutch East India Company arrived in Europe carrying tea from Macau early in the 17th century, it set off the beginnings of a new European habit. The habit, though, was not new. The Chinese began cultivating and using tea (at

first tea leaves were chewed) around 2000 B.C.E. Tea took its place alongside the foods of the Columbian Exchange, where New World and Old Word crops were introduced to foreign markets. Once established in Europe, both tea and its sister import coffee would become important trading commodities and the drink of choice for many Europeans.

■ **FOOTNOTE** Oliver Cromwell began taxing tea, an event that would eventually give Britain about a tenth of its tax income and help set the stage for the American Revolution and the Boston Tea Party of 1773.

Hudson Bay Explored

328 **1610** Searching for the Northwest Passage, Henry Hudson traveled the Hudson River in 1609 and the bay and strait that bears his name the following

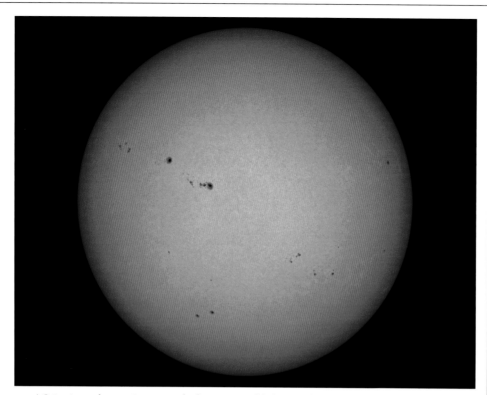

329 | *Scientists today continue to study the nature and behavior of sunspots.*

year. Many European powers wanted to locate the Northwest Passage, since once the passage was safely traversed, it would offer an alternative to the routes controlled by Spain and Portugal. The Iberian countries controlled all trade to Asia that used ships to sail around South America or Africa. It would take almost 300 years (and a three-year journey) before Roald Amundsen would navigate the frigid waters successfully and cross the Northwest Passage.

In 1609, while sailing for the Dutch East India Company, Hudson located the Hudson River. The river had been found in 1524 by a navigator from Florence, Giovanni da Verrazano. His exploits for the Dutch spurred the English government to request that Hudson and his English crew relinquish service to other countries. The next year Hudson sailed the *Discovery* on a voyage sponsored by two English trading companies—the Muscovy Company and the British East India Company. He sailed through the Hudson Strait to discover for England the immense Hudson Bay, where he and his crew overwintered. Tempers flared during the cold winter,

culminating in members of Hudson's crew accusing him of playing favorites (he probably did), then mutinying, and finally abandoning Hudson and any loyal crew members in a small boat to meet their fate. Their end remains unknown.

Hudson contributed greatly to the knowledge of northern North America, in spite of poor leadership. His voyages solidified the Dutch presence in the Hudson River area as well as gave the English the right to claim some of Canada.

> ■ **FOOTNOTE** During his 1609 voyage, Hudson sailed as far south as North Carolina. As his party traveled up the Hudson River, they realized it would not lead them to the Pacific. Hudson traveled upriver to present-day Albany.

Sunspots Discovered

329 **1610** While ancient astronomers noticed dark patches on the sun's surface, it was not until the invention of the telescope that scientists could look systematically at the sun. Historians believe that an English astronomer, Thomas Harriot, was the first to record sunspots in December 1610. Two astronomers, Christoph

Scheiner and Johannes Fabricus, started studying them in 1611. Galileo Galilei, a keen observer himself, debated Scheiner on their nature through letters to Marc Welser. Galileo drew the spots in his 1613 *Letters on Sunspots to Marc Welser,* and correctly theorized that these spots were on the sun and were not satellites orbiting the sun as Scheiner argued. Scheiner wanted to preserve the idea of an unblemished sun and continued to publish on sunspots, but eventually stopped advancing the idea that sunspots were satellites of the sun. Galileo also surmised that the sun rotated on its axis, which supported Copernican theory about Earth's rotation.

It would take more than two centuries before German astronomer Samuel Heinrich Schwabe would discern the sunspot pattern, now known to occur on an 11.1-year cycle, and it wouldn't be until the early 20th century that their magnetic fields and regular reversal of polarity would be discovered. Early in the 17th century, however, astronomers advanced an interest in these solar signatures.

Tobacco Grown in Virginia

330 **1612** John Rolfe arrived in Jamestown in 1610, three years after its first settlers. He found a starving population but started the settlement on its way to success when he planted tobacco from Trinidad and Venezuela around 1612. Tobacco had been used in the Americas for generations, but the native Virginia tobacco suffered from a bitter taste. Rolfe's imported tobacco thrived, and by 1616 the first major shipment arrived in England. Africans arrived in Jamestown in 1619 as either slaves or indentured servants; their legal status remains unclear today. What is clear is that by 1630 some 300,000 pounds of tobacco were shipped annually—and the cash crop continued to thrive.

The growing of tobacco brought economic prosperity to the settlement and environmental change to the landscape. Tobacco is a land-thirsty crop, and the settlers planted it on more and more land, leading to the displacement of native populations. Perhaps tobacco is an appropriate symbol for the Columbian Exchange, its pleasures tinged with the addictive qualities of nicotine and the use of slave labor. Tobacco, as well as other introduced plants and animals, also changed the North American environment and global diet.

Globe Theatre Burns Down

331 **1613** The performance of William Shakespeare's *Henry VIII* proved especially entertaining in 1613 when cannon fired during the performance lit thatch on fire and brought down the Globe Theatre, in which William Shakespeare himself had a stake in the profit. Remarkably, no one died, and only one patron had to use his ale to douse the flames from his pants. The theater was rebuilt the next year. The Puritans proved more dangerous than the flames, though, and they closed the theater in 1642, tearing it down in 1644. A rebuilt Globe Theatre opened in 1997.

■ **FOOTNOTE** The octagonal Globe Theatre rose three stories in the air and took its place among three other popular area theaters of its time—the Hope, the Swan, and the Rose. The Globe could seat some 3,000 theatergoers.

Medical Research Quantified

332 **1614** The physiology of the human body fascinated Italian doctor Santorio Santorio (Latin: *Sanctorius*), and he introduced quantitative procedures to medical research in an attempt to make medicine more certain. Santorio took careful measurements of everything he ate and drank, as well as everything he excreted, by weighing himself on a large scale, known as the weighing chair.

The scientific revolution saw all manner of human experience scrutinized, sometimes building from the ancients and sometimes refuting them entirely. Santorio analyzed the Greek physician Galen's theory that respiration occurred through the skin as "insensible perspiration." His experiments offer a prime example of how new scientific methods were used to test Galenic medicine, and Santorio was able to deduce the amount of weight he lost through respiration and perspiration. In 1614 he published *Ars de Statica Medicina* (*On Medical Measurement*), which provided a systematic analysis of basal metabolism. Santorio introduced physics into the study of medicine and demonstrated the importance of a rigorous experimental framework to the development of physiological science.

1500-1700 | Age of Discovery

CONNECTIONS

Environmental Effects of Introduced Species
As humans roamed the planet during the age of discovery, endemic species suffered

Although today's plants and animals shared ancestors on Pangaea 250 million years ago, after the continents split, species diversified into thousands of geographically distinct forms. Isolated areas developed unique ecosystems, such as the Amazonian rain forest, with its sloths and jaguars, and the Australian outback with its array of marsupials.

The European encroachment upon America kicked off an unprecedented era in which humans introduced "alien" species into established ecosystems. In the early 17th century, as John Rolfe planted tobacco in Jamestown, Virginia, other English settlers put European plants into the ground: peaches, apples, watermelon. The colonists had brought beehives from home—for honey. But unbeknownst to them the bees were also their crops' pollinators, and so the European insect and fruit proliferated together. Soon the insects swarmed over the countryside. Today, honeybees are the indispensable pollinators of American agriculture.

Smaller areas such as the Hawaiian Islands have suffered devastating consequences from species introduction. There, hooved animals such as pigs and deer have overgrazed endemic fauna and spread alien plant seeds through their dung. Many of the new grass species spread

Palm tree on desert island illustrates idea of isolated ecosystems.

wildfires, a phenomenon common where the grasses evolved but one that decimates Hawaiian fauna. Native bird populations such as the red-footed booby are heavily preyed on by introduced rats, mongoose, cats, and dogs. Today, fully half of Hawaii's endemic bird species are extinct.

Ecosystems worldwide suffer from imbalances brought on by invasive species. Among the most damaging animals is Australia's brown tree snake, which migrated to Guam as an airplane stowaway and has decimated the island's endemic bird population. An example of intentional introduction—with disastrous results—is the story of the Western mosquito fish, which was introduced internationally as a pest control but proved far more effective at decimating native fish populations than mosquitoes. And animals are not the only problem: Many plants, such as the South American water hyacinth, literally grow like weeds on new continents. The water hyacinth itself, which can double in size every two weeks, now clogs waterways and edges out native plants on five different continents. The combined effects of these and hundreds of other aliens are so great that species introduction is now Earth's second leading cause of extinction, outpaced only by habitat loss.

333 | *Soaring dome and rug-covered floor of the Blue Mosque in Istanbul, Turkey*

symmetry of his plan. Thousands of colored faience tiles in the interior give the interior a bluish cast and led visitors to name it the "blue" mosque. Located on the Bosporus, the breathtaking domes and the mosque's minarets punctuate the skyline and provide a lasting example of Ottoman classical architecture.

■ **FOOTNOTE** The mosque's design created some controversy at the time because its six minarets (four at the corners of the mosque and two at the ends of the attached courtyard) were seen as an attempt to rival Mecca.

Mapmakers Use Triangulation

334 **1617** As the world known to Europeans expanded, Europeans also wanted to know how to accurately map the world. Developments in cartography and exploration went hand in hand. A Dutch physician, Gemma Frisius, first explained geodetic triangulation in 1533. Using triangulation, a surveyor could plot a baseline and construct triangles from the baseline, using trigonometry to determine the length of the triangle's sides and therefore accurately plot distances.

Willebrord Snel, a Dutch physicist, has been called the father of triangulation since he applied Frisius's methods to map cities in Holland. Snel helped to provide the foundation for the mathematical measurements of large tracts of land and Earth's shape and curvature—geodesy. He published *Eratosthenes batavus* in 1617, which explained triangulation and used this method to determine the size of Earth. The 17th century saw increasing accuracy in physical measurements, with great strides occurring in surveying and cartography.

Blue Mosque Completed

333 **1616** The Mosque of Sultan Ahmet I, better known in the West as the Blue Mosque, in Istanbul, Turkey, exemplifies the brilliance of Islamic architecture in the 17th century. Begun in 1609, the mosque was completed by 1616. Ottoman mosques combined the styles of a Seljuk madrassa with the domed churches of Byzantium. When the Ottomans conquered Constantinople in 1453, their appreciation for the Hagia Sophia led to its plan influencing mosques built afterward.

These influences can be seen in the Mosque of Ahmet I, designed by architect Mehmet Aga. He refined the Hagia Sophia plan and reinvented it as a square. The mosque's domes highlight the form and

Slide Rule Invented

335 **1622** English mathematician William Oughtred invented the first true slide rule in 1622 using two rulers with logarithmic scales. A clergyman and mathematician, Oughtred greatly influenced English mathematics during the 17th century. Scottish mathematician John Napier had published his logarithms in a table eight years earlier, and he realized that by using exponents of numbers, multiplication could be reduced to addition and division to subtraction.

Napier coined the term logarithm ("proportionate numbers" in Greek) and greatly simplified complicated equations scientists were using in their work. Building on Napier's tables, Oughtred created both rectangular and circular slide rules, using moving parts to aid in computations. While improvements were made to the instrument, its basic design didn't change until the 20th century, when scientists would stop using slide rules, opting for computers instead.

> ■ **FOOTNOTE** In a 1630 publication, a former student of Oughtred's claimed to have invented the circular slide rule. This led to a bitter dispute over priority and Oughtred's 1632 book defending his priority, among other theoretical issues.

English Patent Law

336 **1623** England's Parliament passed the Statute of Monopolies in 1623, which declared monopolies to be illegal and allowed people to seek damages. The statute made an exception for inventions and allowed for patents. The law addressed Parliament's concerns over the granting of patents by Queen Elizabeth I and King James I as a way for them to reward favorites and solidify support among their allies.

Patents, however, were not new. They were granted in Europe in the 15th century. Venice, Italy, had a patent system in place to encourage inventors by late in the century. By 1641, even colonies were granting patents: the Massachusetts colony awarded a patent to Samuel Winslow for his method of extracting salt.

Other European countries took longer to establish a legal basis for their patent systems, for instance it wasn't until 1791 that France passed a formal statute. The newly formed United States Congress passed a patent law in 1793. Patents would prove important as they protected inventors but also benefited societies by encouraging the sharing and dispersal of information and technology.

Minuit Purchases Manhattan

337 **1626** The Dutch governor of New Amsterdam, Peter Minuit, met with American Indians in 1626 and purchased Manhattan for the Dutch West India Company with goods (cloth and trinkets) whose worth is estimated at less than two pounds of silver. A perfect location, near the mouth of the Hudson River, the island provided a gateway to the rich interior fur trade. It did not take long for hostilities to break out between the Dutch and the American Indians, however, but a peace began in 1645.

The rivalry between the English and the Dutch in North America continued, and in 1664 England's King Charles II bequeathed New Netherland to his brother, the Duke of York. The duke sent ships to New Amsterdam and asked for New Amsterdam's surrender. Advisers to Peter Stuyvesant, the Dutch director of the territory, feared a terrible loss. Stuyvesant surrendered. The English took control, renaming the city New York.

Massachusetts Colony Founded

339 **1630** When John Winthrop sailed to America in 1630, he spent some of his time composing a sermon that framed the colonists as joining in a covenant with God, founding "a Citty upon a Hill" as a theocracy, but one that embraced a representative government. Winthrop's leadership and faith in the colony gave it a successful beginning.

Harvey Explains Circulation

338 **1628** The English physician William Harvey revolutionized medical science when he advanced the idea of the heart as a pump in his 1628 work, *Exercitatio Anatomica de Motu Cordis et Sanguinis in Animalibus* (*On the Motions of the Heart and Blood in Animals*). He also overturned the estimable first-century Greek doctor Galen's idea that the liver and the heart produced blood, which then was absorbed throughout the body. In some ways Harvey's methods were as important as his discovery, since his use of experimental research became a model for subsequent generations. Harvey dissected countless organisms, including human corpses.

Harvey built on ideas advanced by other anatomists (see events 294, 300), but it was his experiments that confirmed that blood circulates throughout an animal's body in a one-way system, pumped by the heart. They also showed that blood flowed from the heart and then back to the heart in a closed system—general circulation. Harvey didn't have the

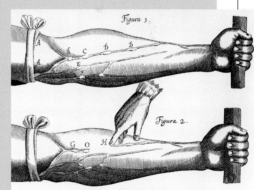

Engraving of Harvey's circulation discovery, the cyclical one-way flow of blood

technology to see capillaries, but he theorized that they existed and connected the arteries and veins. The discovery of capillaries would have to wait until 1660 when Marcello Malpighi placed a bat wing under a microscope and saw them firsthand.

Harvey relied on experience and not authority—a hallmark of the scientific revolution. While modern physiology conceives of the body as a machine, with its pumping heart, Harvey maintained a teleological view of the body's functions and believed that they depended on its soul. Medical advances in the period vastly altered existing ideas about how the body works. While Harvey remained true to Aristotelian ideas, he was instrumental in advancing the medical understanding of general circulation.

John Winthrop
TO HIS WIFE IN ENGLAND, 1630

My dear Wife,
Be sure to be warm clothes, and to have store of fresh provisions, meal, eggs put up in salt or ground malt, butter, oat meal, pease and fruits, and a large strong chest or 2: well locked to keep these provisions in; and be sure they be bestowed in the ship where they may be readily come by...

Be sure to have ready at sea 2 or 3 skillets of several size, a large frying pan, a small stewing pan, and a case to boil a pudding in; [and] a gallon of scurvy grass to drink ... with some saltpeter dissolved in it and a little grated or sliced nutmeg.

Thou must be sure to bring no more company than so many as shall have full provision for a year and half, for though the earth here be very fertile, yet there must be time and means to raise it; if we have corn enough we may live plentifully... The Lord will in due time let us see the faces of others again to our great comfort.

Remember to come well furnished with linen, woollen, some more bedding, brass, peuter, leather bottles, drinking horns etc.: let my son provide 12 axes of several sorts ... whatever they cost, and some augers great and small, and many other necessaries which I cant now think of, as candles, soap and store of beef suet, etc.: once again farewell my dear wife.

Thy faithful husband, Jo. Winthrop.

339 | *Pilgrims come ashore in forbidding weather on Plymouth Rock.*

Winthrop had gained a charter from Charles I, and he led about one thousand Puritans to New England as religious refugees. The Puritans were not separatists, however, and wanted to reform the Anglican Church. Since their charter didn't specify that shareholders had to meet in England (as was normal for the day), the colony exercised control from America until England annulled the charter in 1684.

> **FOOTNOTE** The Puritans who first made the trek to the Massachusetts Bay Colony were strong in faith but susceptible to the rigors of sea travel and colonization. Roughly a third of the settlers died at sea or soon after arrival.

Protestant Forces Defeated

340 **1631** Embroiled in the Thirty Years' War (1618-1648), Europe continued to see battles in 1631, including the defeat of the Protestant forces during the siege of the city of Magdeburg in present-day Germany. Magdeburg was a city fortress on the Elbe River and of strategic importance. Count Johan Tserclaus von Tilly, the Holy Roman Empire's top military commander, and his imperialist forces sacked the city, leaving only the cathedral standing. Their military victory, however, translated into a political defeat, since during the attack most of the city's 30,000 inhabitants were killed.

Magdeburg had held for some two months before Tilly's forces invaded. The massacre shocked Europeans and solidified Protestant support against the Catholic cause. Tilly had just come from defeating a Swedish force in New Brandenburg and would continue on to burn Halle and invade Saxony, but before the end of the year his forces were defeated at the Battle of Breitenfeld, by an army under the command of Sweden's King Gustavus II Adolphus. Breitenfeld, the first major Protestant victory, marked a turning point in the war. The battle badly wounded Tilly and showcased Gustavus's military genius. France and the Netherlands decided to support the German cause in part because of the battle. The Swedish king also made a number of advances in military techniques,

341 | *The Taj Mahal in Agra, India, immortalizes an emperor's love for his deceased wife.*

including reducing the weight of a musket by about half and providing professional training for his army.

Taj Mahal Begun

341 **1632** The Taj Mahal, one of the world's great architectural masterpieces, had its beginnings in 1631 after the Mogul emporer Shah Jahan's wife Arjumand Banu Begum (Mumtaz Mahal) died delivering their 14th child. The emperor requested plans for a mausoleum, and in 1632 architects from all over the Islamic world submitted ideas. It was completed in 1648.

The Taj Mahal combines Persian, Islamic, and Central Asian architectural styles. The complex, located on the Yamuna River outside Agra, India, houses the tombs of both Shah Jahan and his favorite wife. The brilliance of the white marble and the enormous onion-shaped dome greet the visitor. The dome, 58 feet

in diameter, and four minarets help give the complex its striking beauty.

Galileo Goes on Trial

342 **1633** Galileo Galilei's 1633 trial before the Inquisition became one of the world's most celebrated examples of the battle between science and religion. An Italian astronomer, Galileo had been observing the skies through telescopes, publishing his *Dialogue concerning the Two Chief World Systems, the Ptolemaic and the Copernican* in 1632.

Galileo knew the *Dialogue* would upset leaders of the Catholic Church, having previously been cautioned not to teach Copernicanism.

Galileo, though, was not easily dissuaded and decided to publish his *Dialogue* in Italian, not Latin, which brought his ideas to the public. The dialogue in Galileo's famous book takes place between a supporter of Ptolemy, one of Copernicus, and an outside observer.

Galileo knew that the Ptolemic system had started to fall out of favor—replaced by Danish astronomer Tycho Brahe's idea that Earth stood still, the sun rotated around Earth, and the planets rotated around the sun. Galileo didn't even give voice to Tycho's theory, considering it inadequate.

Galileo considered science to be distinct from religion, but the church did not. Even Galileo's renowned debating skills couldn't save him from being called to Rome to answer before the Inquisition. Threatened with torture, Galileo renounced the Copernican system.

Considered the first scientist of the scientific revolution, Galileo lived out his life outside Florence, under house arrest. His final work, the *Discourses of Two New Sciences,* had to be published outside of Italy. It came out in 1638. Galileo died in 1642.

Bernini Completes Canopy

343 **1633** The High Renaissance gave way to what is now considered a new style of European visual arts at the end of the 16th century—the baroque, represented in sculpture and architecture by the Italian artist Gian Lorenzo Bernini. He worked on a canopy over St. Peter's tomb from 1624 until 1633, and the resulting sculptural architecture is considered the first monument of the baroque. With superbly designed proportions, the canopy seems almost alive.

Bernini felt that art should inspire piety. He designed chapels and fountains in Rome and also sculpted a bust of King Louis XIV of France, who represents the power of an absolute monarch. Baroque art flourished in the paintings of Peter Paul Rubens, Caravaggio, and Jan Vermeer. Some scholars view the baroque as the final phase of the Renaissance, while others hold that it is a distinct development. In either view, the baroque period gave European art many of its finest works.

Descartes Publishes *Discourse*

344 **1637** René Descartes, a French mathematician and philosopher, published *Discourse on Method* in 1637. He argued that everything should be analyzed using the scientific method and that the only real object was human thought. For Descartes, the mind could arrive at certainty as long as the thinker no longer harbored any doubt. His work contained the famous phrase *Cogito ergo sum* ("I think, therefore I am"), which has become a mantra for individual knowledge.

Descartes's philosophical work encapsulated the 16th-century milieu and highlighted the importance of reason. In ways similar to how Copernicus and Galileo questioned religious doctrine by proposing a heliocentric universe, Descartes opened the floodgates to rigorous philosophical and scientific analysis. His philosophy greatly influenced modern thought and philosophers such as David Hume and John Locke.

Descartes also created analytical geometry (Cartesian geometry), which takes geometrical problems and solves them using algebra. This watershed event in the history of mathematics has been called "the greatest single step ever made in the progress of the exact sciences."

Coke Is Made From Coal

345 **1642** The importance of a cleaner-burning source of fuel led to advances in the smelting of coal, but the reasons at first had little to do with the industrial revolution. In Derbyshire, England, in 1642, coke was first made from coal. Coke is the residue of bituminous coal with low-sulfur content baked at high

The work of René Descartes is based on reason.

Pascal Invents Calculator

346 **1642** A child prodigy, the French mathematician and philosopher Blaise Pascal had proved himself at an early age by publishing on geometry when 16 and formulating his theorem. Pascal's theorem concerned how if the opposite sides of a hexagon inscribed in a conic are extended, the three points where they intersect will be on the same straight line. Pascal also invented a calculating machine for his father to use in his business. Interested in natural phenomena, physics, and how fluids act, Pascal contributed greatly to the natural sciences, especially in the burgeoning fields of hydrostatics and hydrodynamics.

Portrait of French mathematician and philosopher Blaise Pascal

Pascal experimented with mercury-filled tubes that became the forerunner for today's mechanical barometers and used his barometer to measure air pressure in different locations, including a French mountaintop. He figured out that the mercury remained at the same level regardless of the tube's shape or height, as long as the environment and elevation stayed the same. He also worked on the problem of a vacuum and formulated Pascal's law, which states that regardless of the area where pressure is applied to a confined liquid, the pressure remains constant throughout the liquid.

temperatures in an airless oven. When burned, coke emits little smoke, in conditions where coal creates much smoke.

In England at the time, deforestation meant that charcoal was becoming scarce. Coal offered an alternate fuel source, but a smoky one. In 1603 Sir Henry Platt suggested coal could be charred in the same way charcoal is made, but it wasn't until 1642 that brewers used coke as a way to roast their malt. In 1709, Abraham Darby first used coke-fired furnaces to smelt iron, setting England on its way to the industrial revolution.

FOOTNOTE Some brewers knew of a way around the poor taste of coal-cured malt. They used dampened logs on top of the coal to absorb the gases and created a "pale" malt. However, paler ales on a large scale were made using coke.

Tasman Explores the South

347 **1642** The Dutch navigator Abel Janszoon Tasman had an assignment from the Dutch East India Company. They wanted him to cross the Pacific and find a trade route to Chile, and to discern whether or not the disconnected sections of the Australian coast located previously by explorers were connected to form a great southern continent. In 1642 he set out from Indonesia to explore eastward and in the process found Tasmania and New Zealand. His expedition later located Tonga and the Fiji Islands. After ten months at sea, Tasman returned to Batavia in June 1643 having circumnavigated Australia but never setting eyes on the continent itself.

In the service of the Dutch trading company, Tasman set out again in 1644 to ascertain what this "South Land" really was, and landed in the Bay of Carpentaria, then continued to travel along the north and west coast of Australia. The wealth of this continent remained concealed, and Tasman left the Dutch East India Company a few years later.

Tasman added important geographic information to European knowledge of the "great South Sea," but his sponsors viewed his expeditions as failures since they didn't uncover economic wealth. Exploration was taking a back seat to trade during the 17th century, and the Dutch were focused on trade and taking power from the Portuguese in the East Indies.

FOOTNOTE It would take the voyages of James Cook aboard the *Endeavour* to accurately chart the region. Cook sailed from England in 1768 and went on to claim his discoveries for the British crown.

Rembrandt Paints "Night Watch"

348 **1642** Commissioned to paint a group portrait, Dutch master Rembrandt Harmenszoon van Rijn created "The Night Watch" (also titled "The Company of Captain Frans Banning Cocq") in 1642, a work that represents the baroque style. His ability to create moving scenes can be seen in this masterpiece, in which he highlighted movement, light, and shadow. Rembrandt's artistic independence and disregard for the conventions of his time can be traced to "The Night Watch." Deeply religious, Rembrandt conveyed the complexities of his world with sensitivity and grace. He produced more than 300 paintings, almost 300 etchings, and 1,000 drawings.

Torricelli Invents Barometer

349 **1643** Evangelista Torricelli invented the mercury barometer in 1643 and accurately described the physical force of atmospheric pressure. The Italian physicist knew that water could not be pumped out of a well below around 33 feet, and he wanted to understand the reasons for the phenomenon. Torricelli proposed that the atmosphere had weight and that its weight exerted pressure. He devised experiments using a tube, open at one end and filled with mercury. When he placed the open end of the tube in a dish of mercury, he theorized that a vacuum was formed at the

349 | *Drawing of first barometer*

tube's top and the atmospheric pressure balanced the pressure of the mercury. In the process he invented the barometer.

Ming Dynasty Ends

350 **1644** The ruling Ming dynasty came to an end in 1644, defeated by the invading Manchus, who entered Beijing and began their rule of China as the Qing dynasty. In northern China, the gentry welcomed the Qing—the last dynasty to rule China—since they ended the lawlessness of a popular rebellion. After consolidating their power, the Qing ushered in a period of stability that enlarged China's boundaries, reformed the tax system, and preserved Chinese culture. The Qing dynasty fell in 1912, unable to successfully confront internal problems and external powers.

End of Thirty Years' War

351 **1648** The Peace of Westphalia in 1648 ended 30 years of warfare on the European continent that had pitted Roman Catholics, Lutherans, and Calvinists against one another and unleashed mercenary armies that ransacked the countryside for supplies. By the time of the peace signing, European power had shifted dramatically. No longer would there be a Holy Roman Empire led by a Catholic pope as the major European power. France unseated Spain to become the dominant continental power, and another victor, Sweden, also gained territory.

The bloody conflict saw Europe embroiled in chaos as religious motivations gave way to political ones. Treaty negotiations began in 1641 with the signing happening seven years later. Negotiations included interested parties and not just the combative ones, which marked a distinct improvement in international agreements. From this point onward, European citizens placed their loyalty in their nation state and not in their religion.

Air Pump Invented

352 **1650** Otto von Guericke invented the air pump in 1650 to carry out experiments on respiration and combustion. In the process he opened the way for many other experiments and found that while light travels through a vacuum, sound does not. Four years after he invented the air pump, he demonstrated the force of air pressure by placing two copper hemispheres together and removing the air. Two teams of horses were unable to pull the bowls apart, as the force of the surrounding air held the sphere together.

The air pump provides another example of the drive to create accurate instruments during the scientific revolution. Robert Boyle used one as he formulated Boyle's law (see event 360) and created a vacuum to demonstrate that a feather and a coin would fall at the same speed. During this period, scientists began to understand the existence of vacuums. Guericke went on to invent the first electric generator by devising a machine that produced static electricity.

History of Sudan Recorded

353 **ca 1650** The Muslim scholar Abd-al Rahman as-Sadi saw the defeat of Timbuktu by the Moroccans in 1591, and his firsthand knowledge of the events led him to write the *Ta'rikh al-Sudan* in the mid-17th century. His history of the Sudan chronicled the Songhai Empire from the mid-15th century to the 17th century, and the book provided European colonizers and later historians studying the area and cities of Timbuktu and Djénné with important information. The *Ta'rikh al-Fattash,* another history by a different author, chronicled the earlier histories of the Mali and Ghana Empires of western Sudan. The *Ta'rikh al-Fattash* began to be compiled in 1519.

■ **FOOTNOTE** The Tuareg founded the fabled city of Timbuktu, today located in Mali, in the 11th century. A great center of learning by the time of the Songhai Empire, the city was taken by the French in 1894.

Dutch Found Cape Town

354 **1652** When the Dutch arrived in Cape Town, South Africa, in 1652, they found a few thousand Khoi hunter-gatherers and little else. It wasn't the Dutch, though, but the Portuguese

351 | *Seventy-seven Dutch and Spanish representatives ratify the Treaty of Münster in Westphalia in 1648.*

who were the first Europeans to step ashore at Table Bay, where Cape Town is located. Cape Town's location gave European ships a port to stop in on their way around the Cape of Good Hope. When survivors of a Dutch shipwreck noted the fertility of the region back home, the Dutch East India Company soon sent settlers. Jan van Riebeeck arrived in 1652 to set up a vegetable garden and fort.

Cape Town followed more the model of colonization in North America, where settlers arrived to claim land and make their homes. In other parts of Africa, colonization took the form of merchants and soldiers arriving to control the land and its inhabitants and extract its resources. The Dutch settlers pushed the Khoi out of their nomadic way of life, with many eventually joining the San and some working for the Dutch. The first slaves arrived six years after van Riebeeck arrived. The settlement grew and prospered, witness to colonial powers and the South African apartheid state. Today Cape Town is South Africa's legislative capital.

■**FOOTNOTE** Its beautiful setting and cosmopolitan ambiance has led Cape Town to become the leading tourist destination in South Africa—known for its vineyards along with the photogenic Table Mountain.

Pendulum Clock Constructed

355 **1656** Devices to keep time had been in use since sundials, but in 1656 Christiaan Huygens greatly advanced the science of timekeeping. A Dutch astronomer and physicist, Huygens used Galileo's discovery of the regular arc of a pendulum to develop a pendulum clock. It was the first timepiece accurate to a minute or better and aided scientists immensely. Since the pendulum's period is not exact except when it swings in a cycloid, Huygens developed a clock (also known as a grandfather clock) using weights and a pendulum swinging through a cycloid to keep the pendulum accurate. By 1659 he had perfected the design to make his pendulum clock accurate to within seconds.

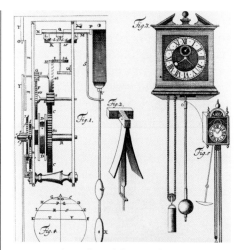

355 | *Weight and pendulum mechanisms*

Huygens and his brother also advanced the design of telescopes by improving the lenses. In 1655, he ascertained Saturn's rings and largest satellite, Titan. This discovery addressed Galileo's concern over his observations of the planet, which seemed to show an optical illusion (one of the criticisms of Galileo's work) on either side.

One of modern science's founders, Huygens tends to be overshadowed. He contributed to the understanding of the laws of motion and the wave theory of light, but arguably his most useful scientific contribution was an accurate timekeeper.

Wharton Describes Glands

356 **1656** In 1656, anatomist Thomas Wharton published the first work, *Adrenographia,* solely on the human glandular system. Wharton detailed the functions of different glands and differentiated between glands, such as the thyroid, and organs, such as the spleen. He discovered the submaxillary salivary gland and the connective tissue of umbilical cord, both of which carry his name today—Wharton's duct and Wharton's jelly. *Adrenographia* contained the first satisfactory account of the thyroid, a gland Wharton named himself.

A successful doctor and anatomist, Wharton remained in London to treat victims of the 1665 bubonic plague. It would take 200 years after Wharton's work for the study of glands to advance further.

Swedish Banknotes Issued

357 **1661** In 1661, a Swedish bank used the first banknotes (bills) and helped to change the face of currency. From antiquity, people had traded goods and services and used different methods to keep track of their resources and money. During the Middle Ages, coinage was exchanged at local markets and lent by pawnbrokers. Bills of exchange, credit, and deposits for one's bullion were known and practiced. Medieval banks, however, did not operate as today's banks, instead they mainly functioned as a depository.

Banks started to adapt at the beginning of the 17th century as overseas trade facilitated changes in markets and money. In 1609, the Bank of Amsterdam was established, with major European banks quickly following. The European age of coin lasted until the mid-18th century, but by 1661 the Stockholm Bank had started issuing banknotes, which could then be converted into coin. Sweden minted its coins from copper, mainly because of the large supply of the mineral available in the country. Historians trace the hindrance of copper coinage to the development of banknotes. These notes gained acceptance even though in 1667 the Stockholm Bank went bankrupt from overlending. The Bank of England (1694) and the Bank of Scotland (1695) started issuing banknotes, and today our wallets are lighter for it.

Boyle Theorizes Compounds

358 **1661** The Irish scientist, physicist, and chemist Robert Boyle published *The Sceptical Chymist* in 1661 and advanced modern chemistry by proposing that the world consisted of "perfectly unmingled bodies," or elements that could combine

356 | *Chromolithograph of nervous system from 19th century*

to form compounds. Boyle explained that particles of different sizes and shapes of matter formed chemical compounds, but he never took a stand on whether these building blocks were atoms. He published all his results, but shied away from making grand pronouncements. Regardless, his book is a foundational work in modern chemistry, and Boyle is known as the father of chemistry.

Kangxi Named Emperor of China

359 **1661** The second Qing emperor, Kangxi, was chosen to succeed his father in 1661. After a period of regency he ascended to the throne in 1669 at the age of 15. Kangxi held an interest in literature and the arts, as well as Western science as taught by Jesuit missionaries welcomed in his court. His rule lasted more than half a century. Kangxi also defeated the revolt of the three feudatories, conquered Taiwan in 1683, and invaded Tibet in 1717. His reign saw the Treaty of Nerchinsk (1689), which set much of the boundary between China and Russia and ushered in peace and trade.

■ **FOOTNOTE** The reign of Emperor Kangxi saw many accomplishments in the world of the arts and learning. He commissioned a dictionary in 1710 that remains in use today and can even be accessed on the Web.

Boyle Describes Air Pressure

360 **1662** The Irish scientist Robert Boyle worked closely with Robert Hooke to discover the properties of the law known as Boyle's law: Hooke built the air pump used by Boyle. They found that at a constant temperature, as the pressure of a gas increases, its volume decreases. During the scientific revolution scientists often worked together, either through correspondence or in groups and scientific societies. Ideas also were arrived at independently or at about the same time. Another scientist, Edme Mariotte, working on air pressure, also discovered the law.

Micrographia Published

361 **1665** Robert Hooke, an important force in advancing 17th-century science, published *Micrographia* (*Small Drawings*) in 1665. The book contained Hooke's drawings of his microscopic observations and included descriptions of the hair of a deer, a shell, a razor's edge, and a bee's stinger. When Hooke drew the structure of cork, he showed walls surrounding empty cavities and coined the

1500-1700 | Age of Discovery

CONNECTIONS

The Rise of Paper Money
Its popularity paralleled innovations in printing

Tangible money has taken many forms, in part because of its many roles in a wide number of cultures. Archaeologists trace the earliest evidence of money to China, between 1600 and 1000 B.C.E., in the form of cowrie shells. Minted coins began not long after, and China's Zhou state officially issued coins beginning in the late seventh century B.C.E. As the coin economy shifted, the coin itself changed shape, transitions generally occurring with a shift in dynastic power. A uniform coinage system, implemented and enforced by the early Song dynasty in the fifth century C.E., paved the way for a paper money economy.

China's role as the first culture to instate a system of paper money came naturally, considering that it was one of the first cultures to develop paper, using the bark from a mulberry tree. China's innovations in printing methods significantly influenced the history of paper money.

During the Song dynasty, between the 10th and 13th centuries, China's entire monetary system underwent dramatic changes, and the state began exerting control over the money in circulation. Initially these changes involved a move toward uniform coinage, with paper money used simply as receipts issued by merchants to indicate coins deposited with them. By 1024, the state monopolized distribution of paper money and prohibited its private issue. Made from mulberry bark paper and often the size of large napkins, the Chinese bills bore the emperor's seal and held a stated value of gold or silver. With such paper money, larger values could be carried at lower weights, with one bill equal in value to thousands of coins.

This system of paper money reached its peak during the 13th century, under the rule of the conquering Mongols. Kublai Khan encouraged the paper money system, which made for easier tax collecting and transport of state funds. Outlawing notes issued by the Song dynasty, he issued his own series of bills, convertible into silver. Under the Song, the paper system had paralleled the old system of coinage, but under the Mongols, bills took on a primary monetary role. Even foreigners, such as traveling merchants and tradesmen, had to trade in coins for notes.

In the 1350s, with the decline of the Mongol hold over China, the ruling government printed large amounts of paper money to fund debts, causing a swift period of hyperinflation. As paper money lost its value, its use began to decline. The Ming dynasty, following the Mongols, attempted to outlaw the use of coins, issuing new paper money, but this effort was eventually abandoned. With small exceptions, paper money would not resurface in China until the 20th century.

The euro represents the most recent form of paper money.

348 More Details on Rembrandt

The infamous myth of Danaë, mother of Perseus, had been illustrated twice by Renaissance artists Titian and Correggio, but it was Rembrandt's "Danaë" that became the most famous and unforgettable imagining of this story. Completed in 1636, the painting depicts the imprisoned daughter of King Acrisius of Argos as she welcomes Zeus, who has taken the form of a shower of gold. According to myth, this union gives them a son who has been fated to kill Acrisius; the king, hoping to escape his cruel destiny, sends his daughter and her child off to sea in a wooden casket. The prophecy, of course, is fulfilled years later, when the grown Perseus accidentally strikes Acrisius with a javelin.

Considered one of Rembrandt's masterpieces, "Danaë" embodies the artist's disregard for convention as well as his brilliant technical mastery of form, color, and light: Zeus is not a form but a presence in the room, a dramatic and radiant glow that envelops Danaë's bed. Also significant is the way Rembrandt captures the scene's emotion, evident in the startled but welcoming expression of Danaë's face and the natural manner in which she is posed, as if she has just been awoken from sleep. The female nude itself is a daring depiction for 17th-century Dutch painting, and the nude Danaë is portrayed here not just with exquisite form but with depth and individuality.

> "Danaë" embodies Rembrandt's disregard for convention as well as his technical mastery of form, color, and light.

The painting has resided in the State Hermitage Museum in St. Petersburg, Russia, since 1772, when it was acquired by Catherine II, and remains one of the museum's most celebrated pieces.

Unfortunately, Danaë's fame was reignited in 1985 by a terrible act of vandalism—a man slashed through the canvas twice with a knife before throwing acid on it. Remarkably, more than 70 percent of the painting's surface remained undamaged. A careful and tedious restoration process commenced immediately, resulting in the safe return of the masterpiece to the museum's walls.

Rembrandt's depiction of the mythical figure Danaë welcoming Zeus is the most celebrated version of this story.

term *cell* to describe the structure. The same year, studying spontaneous generation, Hooke observed spores in molds.

Hooke also discovered a star in the constellation Orion and drew sketches of Mars used by scientists two centuries later. He improved the design of the barometer, the microscope, and the telescope and invented the universal joint.

London Rebuilt After Fire

362 **1666** The devastating London fire of 1666 proved to be a positive development for astronomer and architect Sir Christopher Wren. The fire reduced more than half of London to rubble. Wren served on a commission charged with rebuilding the city, and he stepped in to work on parts of the city, including the ruined Gothic cathedral, St. Paul's. Wren had visited Paris and seen the Louvre, and he was familiar with continental architecture. Completed in 1711, Wren's architectural masterpiece contains baroque, neoclassic, and Renaissance elements. It is hard not to think of it as the Church of England's answer to St. Peter's Basilica in Rome.

363 | *Sir Isaac Newton*

Wren also took part in designing 52 other churches, the main gateway to Oxford University, Kensington Palace, and the library at Trinity College. The latter foreshadows the neoclassic movement of the next century.

A founding member of the Royal Society, Sir Christopher Wren was a baroque extension of the Renaissance scholar, interested in everything. His accomplishments were highly regarded by another knight, Sir Isaac Newton.

> ■**FOOTNOTE** Scientific experimentation also held an interest for Sir Christopher Wren. Early in his career he experimented with intravenous injections, and in 1656 injected a dog with wine until it became inebriated.

Newton Analyzes White Light

363 **1666** Sir Isaac Newton discovered that white light is a combination of different colors of light by passing light through apertures and prisms while a student at Cambridge. He also found that light rays bend at different angles when passed through a prism. When Newton used two prisms, the light recombined back into white light, and when he passed just one color of light through the prism the color remained intact. He first published his experiments in 1672. Scientists at the time thought that the process of refraction and reflection altered white light into colors, not that light itself contained colors. Newton's discovery changed the standard thinking.

In the 17th century, scientists debated whether light acted as a particle or a wave. Newton felt that light consisted of particles of different colors. His experiments also exemplify the new rigor of scientific experiments. Newton and other scientists designed and then repeated their experiments, publishing them so that others could attempt to duplicate the results.

Almost four decades after these experiments on light, Newton's great work on light, *Opticks,* was published. While the work dealt with the behavior of light and its spectrum, perhaps most useful were the questions Newton posed at the end

containing his speculations, which gave plenty of topics for 18th-century scientists to work on.

Blood Transfusion Performed

364 **1667** In 1667, an English doctor, Richard Lower, successfully transfused sheep's blood into a man, culminating a process begun with William Harvey's groundbreaking work on blood circulation. Once Harvey realized that blood circulated in a closed system (1615, published in 1628), it was a matter of time before a transfusion occurred. Lower worked with dogs first, transfusing blood directly from one dog's artery to the other's vein. In 1666 one dog lived after the transfusion. Lower performed his 1667 transfusion at the Royal Society on a man "crackd a little in his head." While this man lived, a French doctor performed an animal-to-human blood transfusion that caused the recipient's death. Because of the risk of death, transfusions were outlawed in England and France by the end of the 17th century.

Through his experiments, Lower also recognized that human blood became redder when exposed to air, as in the lungs.

La Fontaine Writes *Fables*

365 **1668** By the time the French poet Jean de la Fontaine wrote his *Fables,* Aesop was synonymous with a story that conveyed a moral message and often contained animals or inanimate objects with human characteristics. Aesop, however, was more than likely a legend. During the Middle Ages the tradition had developed into a "beast epic," an animal epic following a hero and his encounters. La Fontaine perfected the shorter form of these fables and shared his insightful awareness of human vanity and all its indiscretions. His fables showcased figures from Greek mythology, animals, and simple country people, and they also reflected East Asian influences.

Reflecting Telescope Invented

366 **1668** Following his experiments with light, Sir Isaac Newton built

366 | *Newton's wood and brass telescope*

the first reflecting telescope in 1668. Newton understood that the design of existing telescopes, which used lenses to refract light and then focus it, caused the chromatic aberrations and blurriness associated with the instruments. As scientists asked for better and better telescopes, the image distortions present in refracting telescopes became more pronounced. Telescopes with longer focal lengths were an improvement, but the length of the telescope made an unwieldy device.

Newton's refracting telescope used parabolic mirrors instead of lenses and operated using reflection, not refraction. While Newton's invention was a leap in instrument design, it would take half a century for reflecting telescopes to effectively be useful in scientific observation.

Geologic Strata Explained

367 **1669** Nicolaus Steno, the father of stratigraphy, wrote that the geologic record could be read chronologically—a breakthrough in the field of geology. After dissecting a shark's head, the Danish anatomist and geologist concluded that the shark's teeth were the same thing as glossopetrae, or "tongue stones," found in some rocks. He realized that the fossil teeth had changed chemical makeup (becoming petrified) without changing form. While other observers had made the connection between "tongue stones" and shark teeth, Steno's understanding of the connection led him to realize that rock layers are deposited horizontally. Steno later converted to Catholicism and no longer contributed to science, but his ideas are still in use today whenever scientists distinguish time differences in the geologic record.

Basho Publishes Haiku

368 **1672** Japan's foremost haiku poet, Matsuo Basho, published his first book of haiku in 1672. In *Covering Shells* he critiqued his own poetry and attempted to determine the wittiest poem about city life in the book. Basho figured prominently in Japanese classical literature, writing travel journals and essays in addition to his poetry, and attracting students along the way.

The writer changed his name to Basho, which means "banana tree," in 1680 and began studying Zen. Dissatisfaction with the material life led Basho to travel and grapple with achieving enlightenment and the beauty of the natural world.

■**FOOTNOTE** A form of linked verse that originated in the Tokugawa shogunate and known as *haikai* was the forerunner to haiku. Basho helped popularize northern Japan in the travel account *Narrow Road to the Deep North.*

Three Feudatories Revolt

369 **1673** The Qing dynasty in China faced a revolt beginning in 1673 from three semiautonomous regions known as the three feudatories. While northern China quickly aligned itself with the Qing, southern China proved more difficult, since, unlike the north, the southern areas were not in rebellion against the previous dynasty, the Ming. In 1673 Wu Sangui, a Ming general who had aligned himself with the Manchus of the Qing, led the rebellion when the Qing emperor Kangxi abolished the feudatories. After Wu Sangui's death in 1678 it took the Qing until 1681 to completely defeat the rebellion. By 1683 the dynasty had successfully countered all Ming resistance and brought Taiwan under its control.

Matsuo Basho

NARROW ROAD TO THE DEEP NORTH, 1689

I have always been drawn by windblown clouds into dreams of a lifetime of wandering. Coming home from a year's walking tour of the coast last autumn, I swept the cobwebs from my hut on the banks of the Sumida just in time for New Year, but by the time spring mists began to rise from the fields, I longed to cross the Shirakawa Barrier into the Northern Interior. Drawn by the wanderer-spirit Dosojin, I couldn't concentrate on things. Mending my cotton pants, sewing a new strap on my bamboo hat, I daydreamed. Rubbing moxa into my legs to strengthen them, I dreamed a bright moon rising over Matsushima. So I placed my house in another's hands and moved to my patron Mr. Sampu's summer house in preparation for my journey....

... I was moved nonetheless by the beauty of the natural world, rarely seen mountain vistas and coastlines. I visited the temporary hermitages of ancient sages. Even better, I met people who had given over their whole lives to the search for truth in art. With no real home of my own, I wasn't interested in accumulating treasures. And since I traveled empty-handed, I didn't worry much about robbers.

I walked at a leisurely pace, preferring my walk even to riding a palanquin, eating my fill of coarse vegetables while refusing meat. My way turned on a whim since I had no set route to follow. My only concerns were whether I'd find suitable shelter for the night or how well straw sandals fit my feet. Each twist in the road brought new sights, each dawn renewed my inspiration. Wherever I met another person with even the least appreciation for artistic excellence, I was overcome with joy. Even those I'd expected to be stubbornly old-fashioned often proved to be good companions. People often say that the greatest pleasures of traveling are finding a sage hidden behind weeds or treasures hidden in trash, gold among discarded pottery. Whenever I encountered someone of genius, I wrote about it in order to tell my friends.

Leeuwenhoek Sees Animalcules

370 **1673** Antonie van Leeuwenhoek liked to observe life through singles lenses he ground into microscopes. He also had unusually keen eyesight, and his skill at grinding lenses gave him an advantage over the compound microscopes in use during his time. Compound microscopes could magnify 20 or 30 times an object's actual size, but Leeuwenhoek's small, spherical lenses allowed him to see life at 200 times its actual size.

In 1673 the Dutch scientist started sending his observations to the Royal Society of London. He studied pond water underneath his microscope and observed what he called *animaeculae,* or animalcules. He called minute forms of life "wretched beast-

A look through Antonie van Leeuwen-hoek's microscope

ies." Leeuwenhoek observed protists, rotifers, and foraminifera and was the first to identify red blood cells. In 1677 he viewed sperm and confirmed a discovery made by Louis Dominicus Hamm. Leeuwenhoek understood that sperm carried a reproductive function; Hamm considered them to be diseased. Five years later Leeuwenhoek observed bacteria, and it would be more than a hundred years before scientists observed bacteria again.

Leeuwenhoek proved that weevil grubs hatching from eggs were found in wheat and not bred by the wheat itself. While he did not believe one of the prevailing ideas that life could spontaneously generate, it would take Louis Pasteur's work more than a century later to disprove it for good. In 1696 Leeuwenhoek published his findings in *Arcana naturae* (*Mysteries of Nature*).

If, as some historians suspect, Leeuwenhoek and the famous painter Jan Vermeer were friends, they both shared a love of careful observation. Leeuwenhoek made more than 400 lenses, but he never learned a language other than Dutch. Regardless, he was elected as a member of the Royal Society and his contributions to biology and his discoveries of microscopic life changed our view of the world forever.

Mayow Explains Combustion

371 **1674** John Mayow wrote on his experiments concerning combustion in an enlarged and corrected work published in 1674. The English scientist knew that combustion needed air—a theory similar to that of Robert Hooke's—but his experiments added more details and information. Mayow experimented with candles and mice in a closed system and discerned that "the nitro-aerial spirit" of air supported combustion and respiration.

While Mayow understood that air was made up of at least two parts, the nitro-aerial spirit and an inert part, his ideas were confused. He conceptualized this spirit as philosophical in nature and not gaseous. In the 18th century, Antoine Laurent Lavoisier, the French father of the chemical revolution, understood that air was made up of two gases, oxygen and the nonreactive nitrogen.

Calculus Developed

372 **1675** The scientific revolution saw great strides in mathematics, with mathematicians building on each other's works and sometimes arriving at the same breakthroughs at about the same time. This happened with calculus. The German mathematician Gottfried Wilhelm Leibniz puzzled out differential and integral calculus—necessary for higher mathematics—independently but a little later than Sir Isaac Newton. The dispute caused something of an international incident, leading the two mathematicians and their countries to argue over who came first in a spirited and rancorous debate. Today both men are given credit, but it is Leibniz who gave calculus the notations used today.

In 1672, Leibniz created a calculating machine that improved upon Blaise Pascal's, which could only add and subtract. Leibniz's machine could multiply and divide, as well as give square roots.

Calculus gave scientists a way to determine instantaneous rates of change, such as a planet's orbit, and the ability to sum up infinitesimal small factors into a whole, such as the volume of an odd-shaped object. This branch of mathematics often provides the first step in the study of economics, physics, biology, and chemistry.

■ **FOOTNOTE** Primarily remembered as a German philosopher, Gottfried Wilhelm Leibniz led an active intellectual life. He corresponded with some 600 people and actively encouraged scientific societies.

Speed of Light Calculated

373 **1676** Concerned with the nature of the universe, scientists during the scientific revolution theorized on light and its properties. Danish astronomer Ole Christiensen Römer recognized that light has a finite speed and determined that speed to be 140,000 miles a second in 1676 (modern methods increased this measurement to 186,282 miles a second). While working with astronomer Giovanni Cassini to predict when Jupiter's moons (discovered by Galileo) would be eclipsed by their planet, he realized that the predictions fell too early (by about ten minutes) when Jupiter was farther away from Earth. Using Cassini's estimate for the distance of Jupiter from the sun, Römer calculated the speed of light.

Römer's discovery wasn't immediately recognized, and even the estimable René

Descartes thought that the speed of light depended on the density of the medium it traveled through. It was not until 1729, when astronomer James Bradley confirmed the results, that Römer's achievement was largely accepted. Bradley's estimate of the speed of light, however, was more accurate.

Light Waves Suggested

374 **1678** The Dutch physicist Christiaan Huygens proposed that light travels in waves in 1678 and published his ideas in 1690. He thought that light traveled through "ether," which was everywhere. As light traveled, every point on the wavefront created weaker secondary waves. The theory, called Huygen's Principle, explained the reflection and refraction of light.

The principle also meant that light would travel slower through denser matter. Huygens's colleague, Sir Isaac Newton, believed that light behaved as a particle and that there was a vacuum between Earth and the sun, which wouldn't give a light wave anything to travel through. Newton also believed that waves wouldn't cast sharp shadows—which is true but at the time it was not possible to discern the subtle bending of light waves around sharp edges. Only in the 20th century would scientists understand the answer that light has characteristics of both a wave and a particle. Albert Einstein famously described this phenomenon in 1905.

■ FOOTNOTE A European Space Agency probe named for Huygens landed on Saturn's largest moon, Titan, in January 2005 during NASA's Cassini-Huygens mission. The probe confirmed that Titan's geology is similar to Earth's.

Motion of Bodies Explained

375 **1680-81** Giovanni Alfonso Borelli, an Italian physiologist, astronomer, and mathematician, published *De Motu Animalum* (*On the Motion of Animals*) in 1680-81. The work, divided into two parts, was the first to use physical laws to explain human motion. In the first part, Borelli offered a quantitative analysis of human motion, looking at muscles and the body as composed of levers. He showed the forces involved in activities such as lifting and running. The second part dealt with the physiology of bodily functions such as respiration. Borelli wanted "to investigate the properties of natural things … using the knowledge of artificial things." The work also discussed birds in flight and fish swimming in water.

Medical science in the 17th century continued to look toward ancient medicine as a model but also attempted to explain medicine and physiology in terms of the physical sciences. Borelli's text added an important contribution to the study of the human body.

Ray Classifies by Species

376 **1682** In 1682, the English naturalist John Ray published a classification of plants, *Methodus Plantarum Nova,* which led to a three-volume major work, *Historia Plantarum.* Ray and his friend, former student, and benefactor, Francis Willughby, decided to catalog all living things, with Ray working on plants and Willughby on animals. When Willughby died suddenly, Ray picked up his work and published catalogs on plants, birds, mammals, and fish.

Ray established the species as the fundamental unit in classification, and his works of flora and fauna helped bring order to an unruly system. Ray also understood that fossils were the petrified remains of once living organisms, but it would be a century before his idea was accepted. Considered the first modern naturalists, Ray and Willughby influenced scientists and brought order to taxonomic classification.

375 | *A 1680 illustration of Giovanni Borelli attempting to recycle his own breathing air underwater*

1500-1700 | Age of Discovery

Ottomans Turn Back

377 **1683** Ottoman forces attempted to advance into Europe in 1683 from a base in Transylvania. The struggle between the Habsburg and Ottoman Empires had reignited in 1662 when the Ottomans restored their control over Transylvania. By 1683 the Ottomans controlled almost all of Hungary and were ready to lay siege to Vienna. As the Ottomans, led by Pasha Kara Mustafa for Sultan Muhammad IV, marched toward Vienna, Austria and Poland formed an alliance. The siege began in July, and the city only needed a few additional fortifications to hold. Polish forces under John Sobieski aligned with Austrian-German forces to stop the Ottomans. This defeat marked the beginning of the end of Ottoman power. Vienna's defense depended on a pan-European cooperation, and the introduction of the Polish army ensured the Ottoman defeat.

■ **FOOTNOTE** The defeat proved costly for Pasha Kara Mustafa, who had aligned himself with rebelling Hungarian factions. Sultan Muhammad IV ordered his execution during the Ottoman retreat.

Newton Publishes *Principia*

378 **1687** In 1687, the English mathematician, astronomer, and physicist Sir Isaac Newton published his theories of natural philosophy based on mathematical principles and provided a foundation for physics for the next two centuries. *Philosophiae Naturalis Principia Mathematica* (or *Principia* for short) gave the world the laws of motion and the law of universal gravitation. His book explained the natural world in mathematical terms.

The work, considered by some the most important science book ever, had its beginnings when Edmund Halley encouraged Newton to put down his ideas about the shape of the planets' orbits. Halley edited the manuscript and paid for the printing. Originally published in Latin, *Principia* was translated into English in 1729.

Principia contains three books, one on gravitational forces and the laws of motion, one on the motions of fluids, and one on how gravity is proportional to mass. The laws offered principles that could be used to explain any number of actions, on Earth and in space. They also exemplified Newton's ability to explain seemingly contrasting actions using a uniform system. His three laws of motion explained the results

---

CONNECTIONS

Sir Isaac Newton
The great thinker's work was the apex of the scientific revolution

Sir Isaac Newton revolutionized humankind's view of the universe, developing an inclusive set of laws to explain how matter behaves in the heavens as well as on Earth. Newton's work confirmed the theories of his predecessors Copernicus, Kepler, and Galileo. Moreover, he was a formidable social figure in the world of European science, serving as president of the Royal Society in his final decades, with great influence on the generations of scientists who followed him.

But perhaps even more profound than Newton's specific advancements in optics, physics, and calculus was his development of what came to be known as the scientific method. Until Newton's time, philosophy and religion tangoed with science, often resulting in "laws" that had not been tested in any empirical way. Newton pioneered a new system, the one by which many scientists still study the natural world: carefully observe a phenomenon, form a hypothesis about its behavior, test it by applying known theories and develop new hypotheses based on the results.

Describing this method of experimentation in his 1704 work *Opticks,* Newton laid the groundwork for scientists of many disciplines to exponentially increase their knowledge. In the 18th and early 19th centuries, academics followed his model to study phenomena such as heat, electricity, magnetism, and

Newton developed the scientific method.

chemistry. They accepted Newton's mechanistic explanations for matter and motion, building their own theories on top of his formidable advancements from the *Principles* and the *Opticks*.

One notable group rejected Newton's universe and his concept that microscopic particles could explain macroscopic motion. These were the Romantics, or nature philosophers, a group that included the German thinker Immanuel Kant. Many of the nature philosophers did use Newtonian methods of experimentation to form their theories, but they argued that all matter is inextricably linked—a concept known as field theory—and that no phenomenon such as light, can be explained without a full understanding of heat, matter, and all other substances around it. In a cosmos where all particles are interrelated, the universe itself becomes a single, dynamic entity. Their work led to the discovery that energy is never truly created or destroyed—instead it transforms from state to state, such as from heat to electricity. This knowledge is the basis for today's theories on energy conservation.

In the 20th century, Albert Einstein would explode Newton's tidy universe. Einstein's theory of relativity changed physics forever, into a field focusing on the relationship between an observer and an event rather than the event itself.

379 | *Virginia's College of William and Mary, chartered in 1693, honored William III and Mary II.*

Russia and China Sign Treaty

380 **1689** It took less than 40 years after the founding of Nerchinsk, Russia, for the first European-Chinese treaty to be signed there in 1689. Russian explorers had begun pushing into China over land, and Emperor Kangxi sought to secure Qing, or Manchu, control with the Treaty of Nerchinsk. The treaty defined a boundary between Manchuria and Russia and allowed Russian caravan trade into Beijing. Nerchinsk grew as a trading center. The treaty also served to stop Russian assistance to the Mongol tribes. In 1696 Kangxi defeated Galdan, a Mongol ruler, to further consolidate his control.

■ **FOOTNOTE** Located in Siberia, Nerchinsk was founded in 1654 as a Russian outpost. The treaty stopped Russian expansion east but allowed trade, and it formed the basis for Chinese-Russian relations until the mid-19th century.

Mind Called Empty Slate

381 **1690** The great English empiricist John Locke saw human experience as the foundation of all knowledge, countering the rationalist René Descartes's idea that reason drives knowledge. Locke championed the idea of tabula rasa," or empty slate, an idea Aristotle discussed in the fourth century B.C.E. Locke gave the concept new currency in his 1690 *An Essay Concerning Human Understanding* and believed

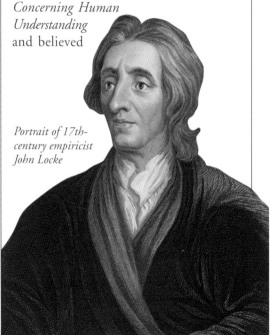

Portrait of 17th-century empiricist John Locke

of Galileo's experiments on falling bodies, Kepler's laws of planetary motion, and the ebb and flow of the tides. Newton's understanding of Kepler's laws helped him explain equatorial bulge (how centrifugal effect causes Earth to bulge around the Equator) and centripetal motion (the force a body exerts from its center that keeps it in orbit).

Newton's application of his equation for the gravitational force found between two bodies shattered the belief that celestial bodies followed natural laws distinct from those operating on Earth since the force applied to all matter in the universe. It wouldn't be until 1915 and Albert Einstein's general theory of relativity that Newton's explanation of gravity was altered. Einstein himself described Newton's genius as, "Nature to him was an open book, whose letters he could read without effort."

William and Mary Take Throne

379 **1688** A combination of events brought William III and Mary II to the English throne in 1688-89's Glorious (or Bloodless) Revolution. William of Orange, a Dutch prince, was married to the Protestant daughter of King James II of England, Mary II. The English kings and Parliament had been battling throughout the 17th century. The birth of King James's Catholic son—and heir to the throne—forced a confrontation. James fled to France and William and Mary assumed the throne. Their ascension secured governing powers for Parliament with the 1689 Bill of Rights, also a precondition to their rule. This document enumerated constitutional rights for English men while it also restricted Catholics from obtaining the monarchy. The threat of an absolute monarchy in England had ended.

in two kinds of experiences—those that come from the senses and those that stem from reflection. Any other awareness was "trifling." For empiricists, humans understand compound concepts by breaking them down into simple ones. Locke described the limits of human knowledge of God and self in his classic work, which is divided into four books and tackles innate notions, ideas, language, and the difference between knowledge and opinion.

Locke ushered in the 17th and 18th century Enlightenment in France and England but fled England to settle in Holland after the Catholic king Charles II came to the throne. Charles II added Locke's name to 83 other English citizens wanted for treason, and he returned to England only after the Glorious Revolution. Locke's contributions to philosophy and his advocacy of science are immeasurable. His ideas influenced American statesman Thomas Jefferson and French philosopher Voltaire, among others. Some philosophers trace the first modern idea of "self" to Locke's essay.

British Move Base to Calcutta

382 **1690** The British East India Company moved its regional base to Kolkata (Calcutta) in 1690 after disputes with the Moguls forced its director, Job Charnock, to leave his base at Hugli. Charnock established Kolkata as a trading post and fortified its fort, known as Fort William since 1700. By this time he had the approval of the Bengal viceroy. Britain used the city as its colonial capital from 1772 until 1912, when Britain shifted it to Delhi. The British government ended the East India Company's de facto rule of India in 1858 and took control. Kolkata provided a base for the expansion of British commerce and political control.

Witches Tried in Massachusetts

383 **1692** When a young girl fell ill in February 1692, conditions in the town of Salem, Massachusetts, led to witchcraft trials that saw 19 of its citizens hanged and one octogenarian pressed underneath stones. The victims were convicted in a trial where gossip was admissible in court, and the accused lacked legal counsel. With an Indian war near its borders, and the belief in witchcraft very real, historians think that property disputes and a schism within the village's Puritans led to mass hysteria. The blood-thirst soon faded, with all the accused exonerated by 1711. The trials, represented in American culture, symbolize American justice gone awry.

■ **FOOTNOTE** Pulitzer prize-winning playwright Arthur Miller set his play *The Crucible* during the Salem witch trials but used it to address McCarthyism of the 1950s. Miller was called before the Committee on Un-American Activities.

Peter the Great Travels Europe

384 **1697** Peter the Great, Tsar of Russia, set off in 1697 with an entourage to tour Europe and to solidify

383 | *Chaos prevailed at the trial of George Jacobs, accused of witchcraft in Salem, Massachusetts.*

384 | *Peter the Great, Tsar of Russia, in armor*

an alliance against the Ottomans (Russia was interested in controlling the Black Sea, under Ottoman control at the time). Peter also wanted to experience European culture and study Western development. This "Grand Embassy" provided valuable experience for the Russian tsar, whose interests in architecture, economics, military affairs, and even anatomy helped him to set his country on a modern path. A Russian reformer, Peter the Great served his country by assisting in the creation of a European power to be reckoned with.

Peter and his entourage's diplomatic efforts were not as successful as the enterprises he undertook incognito to learn shipbuilding and other scientific and technical advances. The Dutch and British governments were preoccupied with what would become the War of Spanish Succession and not interested in a Russian alliance. Peter's knowledge of European technologies, however, greatly benefited his country. He worked for four months in the shipyard of the Dutch East India Company and also invited European experts to Russia to help modernize industry. He returned to Russia in 1698 to suppress a revolt and consolidate his power, and turned his attention away from the Black Sea to the Baltic region. With Peter's leadership Russia saw great advances in technology, economics, culture, and education.

London Stock Exchange Opens

385 **1698** The first true modern stock exchange, as we think of stock exchanges today, was formed in 1698 in London. This stock market (stock is a shortened form of "loan stock") allowed for public debt and answered a financial need of England. The stock market allowed for capital to be concentrated and liquid, which aided government.

The stock exchange grew out of the produce exchanges (or bourses) of the Middle Ages, which were represented best by the Antwerp bourse. Merchants from many nations traded at Antwerp and created a truly international trading center. Exchanges of the Middle Ages dealt with commodities from the spice trade, and their volume swelled during the age of exploration, which altered traditional economic systems. The Reformation also helped by loosening the theological controls that tempered the accumulation of wealth. As the medieval emphasis on the importance of linking economics to social progress shifted, it began to allow for capitalist economies to grow. As a result, more stock exchanges soon followed the one in London.

■ **FOOTNOTE** Exchanges preceded the London market, and in 1460 an exchange was founded in Antwerp, Belgium, and traded mostly bonds. The Dutch East India Company founded an exchange in Amsterdam in 1602.

Britain Opens Trade in China

386 **1699** The British East India Company established a trading post at Quangzhou (Canton), China, in 1699 and started to institute trading practices that controlled Western contact with China. Other European countries soon followed, and the so-called Canton system was born. The ruling Qing dynasty in China managed foreign trade by restricting it to a monopoly held by a small number of Chinese firms who dealt with the Western traders. In this manner, the Qing contained Western contact with the Chinese population until the early 19th century.

Dodo Disappears

387 **1700** Hunted to extinction by both humans and animals in the 17th century, the dodo is a symbol of human rapaciousness and environmental change. Portuguese mariners stumbled upon the Indian Ocean island of Mauritius after rounding the Cape of Good Hope in 1507. The Dutch claimed the island in 1598 and settled there in 1644. Scientists estimate that the island's mainland likely had seen its last dodo by 1650. The flightless bird was no match for introduced animals such as feral pigs and hunting.

The 17th-century observations of dodo sightings are not as reliable as records from trained scientists today, and its exact extinction date is not precisely known. The dodo's demise, though, provides a cautionary tale for today.

FIRST PERSON

Increase Mather
CONCERNING EVIL SPIRITS, 1693

That there are Devils and Witches, the Scripture asserts, and experience confirms: That they are common enemies of Mankind, and set upon mischief, is not to be doubted: That the Devil can (by Divine permission) and often doth vex men in Body and Estate, without the Instrumentality of Witches, is undeniable: That he often hath, and delights to have the Concurrence of Witches, and their consent in harming men, is consonant to his Native Malice to man, and too Lamentably exemplified: That Witches, when detected & convinced, ought to be exterminated and cut off, we have God's warrant for...

Much debate is made about What is sufficient Conviction ... but this is a very dangerous, and unjustifiable tenet.... It is therefore exceeding necessary that in such a day as this men be informed what is evidence, and what is not.... In the case of Witchcraft we know that the Devil is the immediate Agent in the Mischief done, the content or compact of the Witch is the thing to be Demonstrated.

Revolutionary Era

1700-1850

1700-1850
The Rights of Man and Woman

The pace of historical change accelerated around 1700, as the scientific revolution set the stage for the industrial revolution, which coincided with political revolutions, first in England's American colonies and later in France and other countries. Together, industrialism and nationalism—or the transformation of kingdoms into nations and subjects into citizens—revolutionized Europe and deeply affected other regions colonized by Europeans or tied to them commercially.

In Latin America, colonies rebelled and won independence from their dominators, but they often lacked the political cohesion and economic power of leading European nations or the United States. In Asia and the Middle East, empires decayed and lost ground to Westerners whose industrial advances translated into military superiority.

Many factors contributed to the industrial revolution that began in England in the late 18th century, including significant theoretical breakthroughs in various fields of science, practical advances by inventors and mechanics, and the growth of capitalism, which allowed industrialists to invest in costly new technologies that paid dividends in the long run. The steam engine, perfected by James Watt in 1769, helped power this revolution, but large amounts of capital were required to exploit that new source of power and mass-produce goods that were once made by hand in cottages or shops. By applying steam power to locomotives and ships in the 19th century,

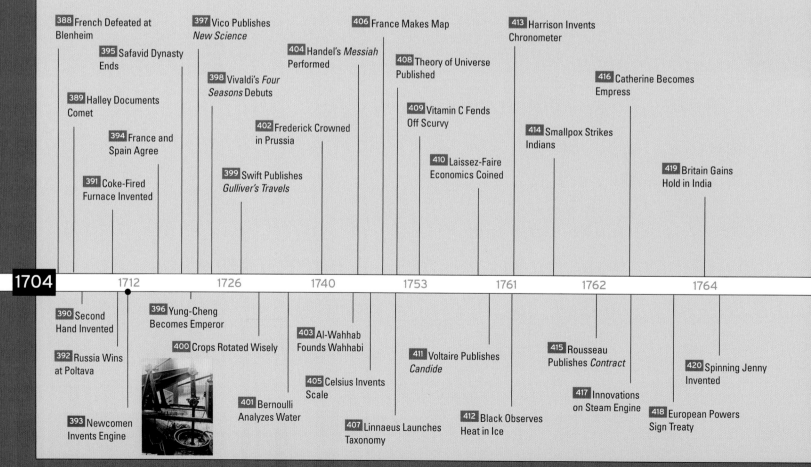

388 French Defeated at Blenheim

395 Safavid Dynasty Ends

389 Halley Documents Comet

394 France and Spain Agree

391 Coke-Fired Furnace Invented

397 Vico Publishes *New Science*

398 Vivaldi's *Four Seasons* Debuts

402 Frederick Crowned in Prussia

399 Swift Publishes *Gulliver's Travels*

404 Handel's *Messiah* Performed

406 France Makes Map

408 Theory of Universe Published

409 Vitamin C Fends Off Scurvy

410 Laissez-Faire Economics Coined

413 Harrison Invents Chronometer

416 Catherine Becomes Empress

414 Smallpox Strikes Indians

419 Britain Gains Hold in India

1704   1712   1726   1740   1753   1761   1762   1764

390 Second Hand Invented

392 Russia Wins at Poltava

393 Newcomen Invents Engine

396 Yung-Cheng Becomes Emperor

400 Crops Rotated Wisely

401 Bernoulli Analyzes Water

403 Al-Wahhab Founds Wahhabi

405 Celsius Invents Scale

407 Linnaeus Launches Taxonomy

411 Voltaire Publishes *Candide*

412 Black Observes Heat in Ice

415 Rousseau Publishes *Contract*

417 Innovations on Steam Engine

418 European Powers Sign Treaty

420 Spinning Jenny Invented

industrialists brought raw materials to their factories and shipped finished products to distant markets more quickly and efficiently, spurring the growth of yet other industries, such as the mining of coal and the manufacture of steel.

Rebels Against Royalty

THE INDUSTRIAL REVOLUTION WAS BARELY UNDER WAY WHEN colonies in America rebelled against King George III and won independence—a victory made possible in part by aid from France. The French had long been engaged in an imperial struggle with Great Britain, which embraced the united kingdoms of England, Wales, and Scotland. Having lost Canada to Britain in the Seven Years' War, which ended in the 1760s, King Louis XVI of France was only too glad to help Americans throw off British rule. But such costly campaigns abroad and lavish expenditures at home depleted King Louis's treasury and caused him to raise taxes, which angered peasants and the country's increasingly powerful middle class, or bourgeoisie. French radicals intent on ending the monarchy drew encouragement from the successful American rebellion and set out to create a republic based on the principles of liberty, equality, and fraternity. The French Revolution, which began in 1789 and claimed the lives of King Louis, Queen Marie Antoinette, and thousands of others associated with the old regime, left the country in turmoil until Napoleon Bonaparte took power in 1799.

Although Napoleon soon established himself as emperor and ruled by fiat, he promoted the idea that the French were now citizens rather than subjects and broadened their legal rights under his Napoleonic Code. Exploiting the rising spirit of nationalism in France, he formed a vast citizen army that conquered much of Europe before losing strength in Russia

PREVIOUS PAGE | *A lithograph entitled "Yankee Doodle, 1776" depicts three patriots leading troops into battle.*

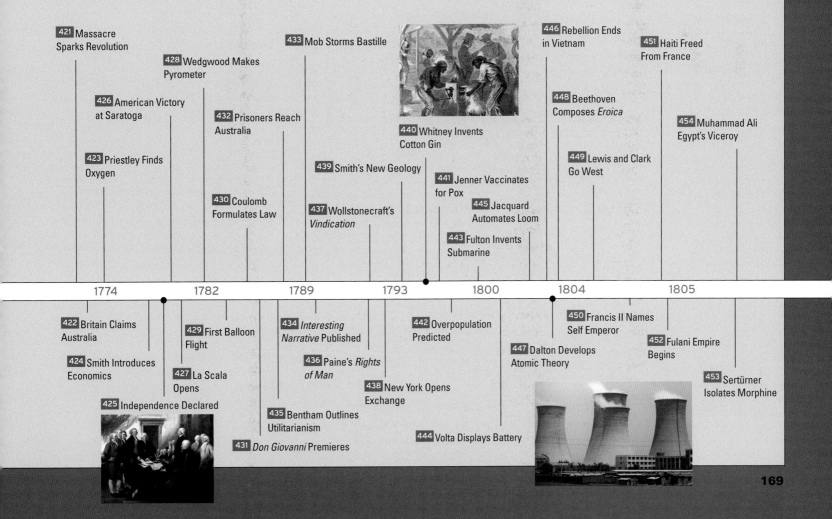

421 Massacre Sparks Revolution

428 Wedgwood Makes Pyrometer

433 Mob Storms Bastille

446 Rebellion Ends in Vietnam

451 Haiti Freed From France

426 American Victory at Saratoga

432 Prisoners Reach Australia

448 Beethoven Composes *Eroica*

454 Muhammad Ali Egypt's Viceroy

440 Whitney Invents Cotton Gin

423 Priestley Finds Oxygen

439 Smith's New Geology

449 Lewis and Clark Go West

441 Jenner Vaccinates for Pox

430 Coulomb Formulates Law

437 Wollstonecraft's *Vindication*

445 Jacquard Automates Loom

443 Fulton Invents Submarine

1774   **1782**   **1789**   **1793**   **1800**   **1804**   **1805**

422 Britain Claims Australia

429 First Balloon Flight

434 *Interesting Narrative* Published

442 Overpopulation Predicted

450 Francis II Names Self Emperor

424 Smith Introduces Economics

427 La Scala Opens

436 Paine's *Rights of Man*

447 Dalton Develops Atomic Theory

452 Fulani Empire Begins

425 Independence Declared

435 Bentham Outlines Utilitarianism

438 New York Opens Exchange

453 Sertürner Isolates Morphine

431 *Don Giovanni* Premieres

444 Volta Displays Battery

during the punishing winter of 1812 and suffering a crushing defeat at Waterloo three years later. As Napoleon demonstrated, nationalism was a force to be reckoned with. Many European monarchs acknowledged as much in years to come by allowing for the creation of elected legislatures with limited powers, thus making their subjects feel more like citizens—and more willing to fight and die for their country.

Those cautious reforms, however, did not satisfy the many people who found themselves alarmed by the convulsive effects of the industrial revolution and who sought radical changes in response. Rapid industrialization proved dangerous and demoralizing for workers, who toiled from dawn to dusk in squalid conditions. Working-class neighborhoods were breeding grounds for disease, and scourges such as cholera claimed many lives.

In Britain, which had a long tradition of representative government, reformers in Parliament placed restrictions on child labor and established a 12-hour-workday limit. That helped the British avoid revolution, but grievances in other industrialized nations boiled over and threatened the survival of monarchies. In 1848, the German political philosophers Karl Marx and Friedrich Engels published their "Communist Manifesto," and radicals took to the streets in Paris, Berlin, and other European cities, demanding governments that were truly responsive to the will of the people.

Industrial Benefits

The changes that were sweeping the world by the mid-19th century were not all disruptive or violent. The fast-growing middle classes in industrialized countries enjoyed fuller and healthier lives than their forebears did, thanks to advances in medicine, hygiene, education, and culture. Women emerged as prominent figures in literature and other arts and launched campaigns for political rights.

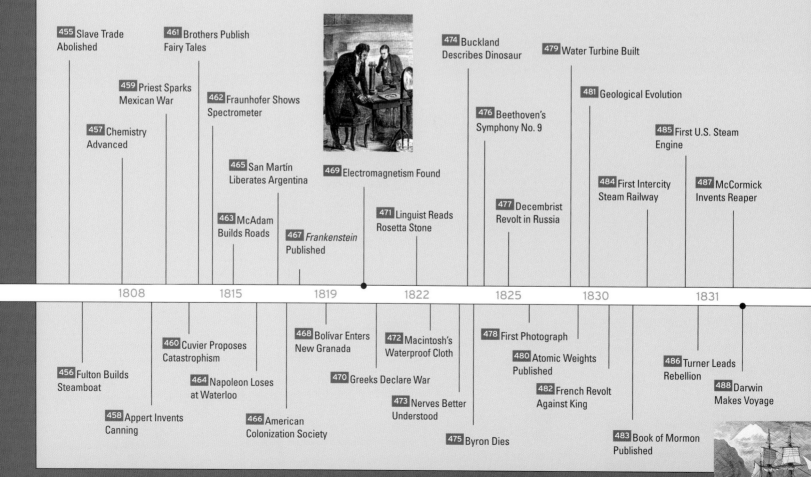

455 Slave Trade Abolished

461 Brothers Publish Fairy Tales

474 Buckland Describes Dinosaur

479 Water Turbine Built

459 Priest Sparks Mexican War

462 Fraunhofer Shows Spectrometer

481 Geological Evolution

457 Chemistry Advanced

476 Beethoven's Symphony No. 9

485 First U.S. Steam Engine

465 San Martín Liberates Argentina

469 Electromagnetism Found

484 First Intercity Steam Railway

487 McCormick Invents Reaper

471 Linguist Reads Rosetta Stone

477 Decembrist Revolt in Russia

463 McAdam Builds Roads

467 *Frankenstein* Published

1808   1815   1819   1822   1825   1830   1831

456 Fulton Builds Steamboat

460 Cuvier Proposes Catastrophism

468 Bolívar Enters New Granada

472 Macintosh's Waterproof Cloth

478 First Photograph

480 Atomic Weights Published

486 Turner Leads Rebellion

464 Napoleon Loses at Waterloo

470 Greeks Declare War

482 French Revolt Against King

488 Darwin Makes Voyage

458 Appert Invents Canning

466 American Colonization Society

473 Nerves Better Understood

483 Book of Mormon Published

475 Byron Dies

The invention of the telegraph accelerated communications and increased interest in newspapers and other periodicals, creating a public that was better informed and better prepared for citizenship.

Beyond Europe and fast-developing nations colonized by Europeans, such as the United States and Canada, however, few countries shared as yet in the benefits of industrialism and nationalism, and some lost strength and territory as a result. Economic and political development allowed established powers like France and Britain and emerging powers like Russia, Germany, and the United States to amass superior weaponry and stronger armies and navies than imperial rivals that lacked industry and political cohesion.

In 1821, Mexico, for example, emerged from its War of Independence against Spain as a sprawling empire extending from the Panamanian isthmus to what is now the American Southwest. Because it was economically weak and politically unstable, however, Mexico lacked the military clout to prevent Central American countries from seceding, and it lost California and other northern territories to the United States as a result of the Mexican-American War, which ended in 1848. A similar fate befell the once mighty Ottoman Empire, which lost Greece when that country won independence in 1829 and later surrendered Georgia and other territories around the Black Sea to Russia, Algeria to France, and Egypt to Britain.

No empire suffered more humiliating treatment at the hands of Western powers than China, whose rulers tried to prevent British merchants from importing opium to their country, where the addictive drug was traded for silk, tea, and other items prized in Europe. British gunships intervened and overwhelmed the antiquated Chinese fleet. In 1842, China was forced to sign a degrading treaty at Nanjing that perpetuated the ruinous opium trade and ceded to Britain the island of Hong Kong.

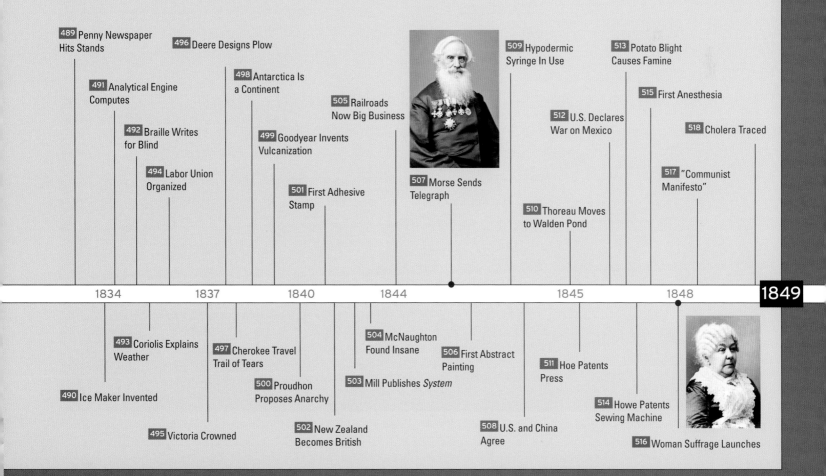

489 Penny Newspaper Hits Stands

496 Deere Designs Plow

509 Hypodermic Syringe In Use

513 Potato Blight Causes Famine

491 Analytical Engine Computes

498 Antarctica Is a Continent

505 Railroads Now Big Business

515 First Anesthesia

492 Braille Writes for Blind

499 Goodyear Invents Vulcanization

512 U.S. Declares War on Mexico

518 Cholera Traced

494 Labor Union Organized

501 First Adhesive Stamp

507 Morse Sends Telegraph

517 "Communist Manifesto"

510 Thoreau Moves to Walden Pond

1834   1837   1840   1844   1845   1848   **1849**

493 Coriolis Explains Weather

497 Cherokee Travel Trail of Tears

504 McNaughton Found Insane

506 First Abstract Painting

511 Hoe Patents Press

490 Ice Maker Invented

500 Proudhon Proposes Anarchy

503 Mill Publishes *System*

514 Howe Patents Sewing Machine

495 Victoria Crowned

502 New Zealand Becomes British

508 U.S. and China Agree

516 Woman Suffrage Launches

French Defeated at Blenheim

388 **1704** The Battle of Blenheim, on August 13, 1704, during the War of Spanish Succession, marked the French army's first major defeat in more than 50 years and the beginning of the decline of France and King Louis XIV. For decades Louis had been expanding France's borders and his power. The Holy Roman Empire (Austria) was on the verge of collapse. In response, the Duke of Marlborough and Prince Eugene of Savoy marched an army of some 52,000 Austrian and English troops and 60 cannon to the Danube River and met some 56,000 French and Bavarian troops with 90 cannon. France's Marshal Camille, comte de Tallard, was confident he had his enemy so outnumbered that he was caught off guard with a surprise attack. Coupled with tactical flaws, the French lost the battle after a bloody fight that ended in 20,000 French and Bavarian dead and 14,000 taken prisoner. The defeat took the wind out of Louis's sail.

Halley Documents Comet

389 **1705** British astronomer Edmund Halley predicted the return of the comet that we now call Halley's comet. He documented historic comet sightings and found patterns that led him to theorize that comets, which until then were considered baffling and even potentially dangerous because of their irregularity, actually had calculated orbits around the sun and would return periodically. He believed that the comets witnessed in 1531, 1607, and 1682 were actually the same comet and predicted it would return in 1758. Even though Halley died in 1742 the comet arrived on schedule and later became known as Halley's Comet. In 1717 Halley again made science history with the discovery that the so-called fixed stars in the night sky—that never seemed to move because the constellations always remained the same—actually were in motion. He looked all the way back to the observations of Ptolemy to compare data and saw that the stars had indeed moved but appeared fixed because they were so far from Earth. Halley is also known for his role in editing and publishing Sir Isaac Newton's *The Mathematical Principles of Natural Philosophy,* more commonly known as *Principia,* in 1687.

Second Hand Invented

390 **1707** The pendulum and hairspring added minute hands to clocks and watches, but it wasn't until English physician Sir John Floyer invented a windup pulse watch that ran for exactly one minute could people keep track of time to the second. That kind of precision

388 | *Armies clash in an 18th-century oil painting of the Battle of Blenheim on August 13, 1704.*

allowed doctors to count how many heartbeats their patients had per minute—a practice still considered essential.

> ■ **FOOTNOTE** Floyer, a physician, advocated cold baths for adults, children, and infants. He published several books, including one titled *An Enquiry into the Right Use and Abuses of the Hot, Cold, and Temperate Baths in England.*

Coke-Fired Furnace Invented

391 **1709** British ironmaster Abraham Darby began producing iron in a coke-fired blast furnace rather than using expensive charcoal as fuel. For more than 3,000 years iron smelting required the high temperatures of burning charcoal. But in England, charcoal grew expensive as deforestation became a significant problem. A Quaker and descendant of a nobleman, Darby found that using lumps of coke, the solid residue left over from low-sulfur coal heated to high temperatures, was stronger than charcoal and could support a larger charge of iron ore. Darby's method meant iron could be made in much larger furnaces and at a faster rate. Machinery made from iron could now be stronger and less expensive. Darby's ironmaking method would later be used for a cast-iron bridge and the first locomotive that used a high-pressure boiler. All of this set Britain up on its path to the industrial revolution.

Russia Wins at Poltava

392 **1709** Peter the Great's victory in 1709 at the Battle of Poltava marked the decline of powerful Sweden and the beginning of what would be Russia's supremacy in Europe. In the previous century, Sweden had compensated for a relatively low population with strong natural resources, enhanced by a growing Baltic empire. Sweden's previous failed invasion of Russia had weakened its army and artillery, but the determined King Charles XII once again besieged the Ukraine's Poltava in May 1709. The Russians, under Tsar Peter the Great, set up a countersiege and a month later overwhelmed the depleted Swedish forces.

Newcomen Invents Engine

393 **1712** The year 1712 marked the completion of the first Newcomen engine, an atmospheric steam engine. Thomas Newcomen, a blacksmith and ironmonger from Dartmouth, England, first worked for Thomas Savery, who had invented a steam-driven engine: a machine that used the force of built-up steam to generate mechanical motion and drive a water pump. Newcomen built a copy of Savery's engine, then used his own ingenuity to perfect the design.

At a time when coalfields were beginning to boom, there was a strong need for a machine to quickly pump water out of the mines. The atmospheric steam engine consisted of a cylinder fitted with a piston and attached to a counterweighted rocking beam, which was connected to a pump rod. Low-pressure steam pushed the piston up, and then cold water condensed the steam, creating a partial vacuum in the cylinder. Atmospheric pressure caused the piston to move up and down, creating a power stroke. Previous machines used dangerous high pressure to operate. Newcomen's engine was considered much safer than Savery's, in part because its strokes occurred slowly, not more than about ten per minute. Newcomen's engine design remained in place for at least the next 50 years, and it helped Britain gain a place of world prominence in science, technology, and industry.

Newcomen engine in 1908 at Rutherglen Farme Colliery in Scotland

France and Spain Agree

394 **1714** Between 1713 and 1714, France and Spain signed a series of treaties with other European countries in the Dutch city of Utrecht, marking the end of the War of Spanish Succession. The treaties, which became known as the Peace of Utrecht, led to the decline of France's power and the rise of Britain as the leader in world trade. Under the treaties a weakened France, bankrupted by war, gave Acadia, Newfoundland, and the territory around Hudson Bay (important colonies in the cod fish industry) to Britain; Spain agreed to recognize Louis XIV's grandson Philippe, Duc d'Anjou, as king, with the provision that Spain and France would never operate under one ruler; and Spain gave Britain the monopoly over supplying all of the Spanish colonies in America with African slaves for the next 30 years. The Peace of Utrecht established a new balance of power in Europe that would last for the next several decades.

> ■ **FOOTNOTE** With the signing of the Treaty of Utrecht, Gibraltar came under British rule. Only two square miles in size, the island has long been a desirable territory because of its strategic location between Europe and Africa.

Safavid Dynasty Ends

395 **1722** The Safavid's family rule began at the start of the 16th century and ended when a group of Afghanis captured the Persian capital of Esfahan and killed Safavid Sultan Hussein in 1722. Ismail I founded the Persian dynasty in 1501 and converted his people from Sunni Islam to Shiite Islam, which became a state religion. The Safavids greatly benefited financially because of their geographical location. They were at the center of the

396 | *A 19th-century engraving represents the life of Chinese emperors.*

trade routes between Europe and the Islamic civilizations of Central Asia and India. At the peak of its power the empire included much of present-day Iran, Iraq, Azerbaijan, Turkmenistan, and Afghanistan. It also warred extensively against the Ottomans and Moguls. Persia became an art and cultural center. Its mosques, architecture and parks impressed Europeans. But eventually trade routes began to shift away from Persia and there were ongoing threats at its borders. The Safavids declined in power and were easily taken over by an Afghan army in 1722, when the dynasty ended.

Yung-Cheng Becomes Emperor

396 **1722** Yung-Cheng became the third emperor of the Qing, or Manchu, dynasty of China in 1722 and at that point took the name Yongzheng. He was the fourth son of Kangxi, but when his brother, the heir apparent, became mentally unbalanced, Yung-Cheng saw an opportunity and after his father's death announced that he would be the next emperor. It was believed that Yung-Cheng had possibly

killed his father but managed to take the throne with the support of the Peking military. When he took power, he had several of his brothers imprisoned and set up an intricate system of spies and secrecy. One of his more substantial acts of mistrust was his removal of the imperial princes from the Eight Banners, a military organization begun by the Manchus when they began conquering China.

When Yongzheng took the throne, the Qing controlled three of the banners and imperial princes controlled the rest. Yongzheng seized the banners to prevent anyone from overtaking him. It is not surprising that the emperor insisted that all important decisions—executive, legislative or judicial—come from him, and he set his administration up to reflect that.

The Grand Council met with the emperor every day at dawn and kept him appraised of all affairs. All business was considered secret. This period was when the Qing was at the height of its power. The previous emperor had expanded the dynasty geographically, now commerce

was established and industries were doing well. It was during this time that art, specifically painting and porcelain work, flourished. Likely tied to his own accession to the throne, Yongzheng forbade the naming of a successor, saying the emperor should make the announcement on his deathbed. Yongzheng died in 1735. Some believe he was murdered, others believed he died peacefully. His son succeeded him. The Qing dynasty continued until the early part of the 20th century, but it began to wane in the mid-19th century with rebellions and defeats in the first Opium War and the Anglo-French War. The Qing dynasty ended with the beginning of the Republic of China.

■FOOTNOTE Although he exerted strict rules on his peoples, banning practices as disparate as Catholicism and tobacco, Yongzheng's reign, from 1722 to 1735, is considered a period of harmony and prosperity in Chinese history.

Vico Publishes *New Science*

397 **1725** Italian philosopher Giambattista Vico produced his groundbreaking book, *The New Science,* where he joins history and social sciences forming the science of humanity. Vico was born into poverty, but extremely interested in philosophy and was largely self-taught. While he went on to become a professor of rhetoric at the University of Naples, he remained relatively unknown until after his death, when a later edition of *The New Science* was translated into various languages and his thoughts were taken up by scholars of anthropology, history, sociology, and psychology. In *The New Science,* Vico outlines the principles of humanity and explains the stages common to the development of societies and language. He is now considered an early founder of cultural anthropology.

Vivaldi's *Four Seasons* Debuts

398 **1725** *Four Seasons,* the four-violin concerto composed by Italian Antonio Vivaldi, was performed in 1725. It would become one of the composer's best known pieces of work. Vivaldi, who was an ordained priest and was taught how to play the violin by his father, composed about 500 concertos in his lifetime, half of which were for solo violin, and some 45 operas. His concertos are known for their sequences: repeating the same patterns at different pitches. In *Four Seasons* each season is given a sound to represent it: songbirds for spring, thunderstorms for summer, harvesting for fall, and shivering for winter. Vivaldi published a set

Jonathan Swift
GULLIVER'S TRAVELS, 1726

In about ten weeks time, I was able to understand most of his questions; and in three months, could give him some tolerable answers. He was extremely curious to know "from what part of the country I came, and how I was taught to imitate a rational creature..." I answered, "that I came over the sea, from a far place, with many others of my own kind, in a great hollow vessel made of the bodies of trees: that my companions forced me to land on this coast, and then left me to shift for myself." It was with some difficulty, and by the help of many signs, that I brought him to understand me. He replied, "that I must needs be mistaken, or that I said the thing which was not;" for they have no word in their language to express lying or falsehood....

The word Houyhnhnm, in their tongue, signifies a HORSE, and, in its etymology, the PERFECTION OF NATURE. I told my master, "that I was at a loss for expression, but would improve as fast as I could; and hoped, in a short time, I should be able to tell him wonders." He was pleased to direct his own mare, his colt, and foal, and the servants of the family, to take all opportunities of instructing me.... Several horses and mares of quality in the neighbourhood came often to our house.... These delighted to converse with me: they put many questions, and received such answers as I was able to return. By all these advantages I made so great a progress, that, in five months from my arrival I understood whatever was spoken....

of sonnets with *Four Seasons* explaining the events that are portrayed. Vivaldi's work represented the progressive development of the late baroque period, and he would later influence Johann Sebastian Bach.

Swift Publishes *Gulliver's Travels*

399 **1726** *Gulliver's Travels,* written by Irish author Jonathan Swift, gained instant popularity and would later become a literary classic. The four-part story tells of an ordinary man, Gulliver, the lone survivor of a shipwreck, who has interactions with various races and societies in far away places. The adventure tale is considered an anti-Whig satire that reveals the political and social conditions of the time and also shows the pettiness of human nature.

Crops Rotated Wisely

400 **1730** English statesman Charles Townshend resigned from directing foreign policy and focused on agriculture. He developed the idea that farmers use a four-field crop rotation system where four different types of crops (wheat, oats or barley, clover, and turnips) are grown in four different fields but then rotated each year. Because each crop leached different nutrients from the soil, there was an overall decreased depletion of soil nutrients and a resulting increase in crop yields. It also meant land didn't need to rest. Townshend's system led to an agricultural productivity boom in Britain, which in turn supported the rapidly increasing population the country would see over the next century.

FOOTNOTE Crop rotation works in part because leguminous plants such as clover and soybeans actually collect and concentrate the essential mineral nitrogen in the soil, leaving more behind after a season of growing.

Bernoulli Analyzes Water

401 **1738** Dutch-born mathematician Daniel Bernoulli published *Hydrodynamica,* which presented theories on hydrodynamics (movement of water), and introduced what is now known as

Bernoulli's principle, still used today in designing boats, cars, and aircraft. Bernoulli's principle explained that when the velocity of a fluid increased, the pressure around it decreased. Bernoulli also helped scientists better understand the relationship between pressure and temperature and their behavior with gas and fluids. He realized that as temperature rises, atoms move faster, and when they collide, they move farther apart from each other. Thus the volume of a substance increases when its temperature rises, and its volume decreases as its temperature drops: an observation at the basis of the kinetic theory of gases.

FOOTNOTE Daniel Bernoulli's father, Jacques, was a professor of mathematics in Basel, Switzerland. Theoretical mathematicians today still study the exponential series he generated, called Bernoulli's numbers.

Frederick Crowned in Prussia

402 **1740** Upon his father's death, Frederick II, known as Frederick the Great, took the throne and led his people in a series of wars with Austria and other states, significantly increasing Prussia's territory and turning Prussia into one of the strongest military powers in Europe. Frederick's military was envied and looked to as a model by other European nations. But Frederick's interests were broader than war and strategy. As a child he was interested in the arts, and as king he was considered an enlightened monarch. He corresponded

400 | *Crops in southwest Kansas. The circles are caused by water-conserving central pivot irrigation.*

FIRST PERSON

Al-Wahhab

KITAB AL-TAWHID, N.D.

Allah says:
"And amongst mankind are those who take [for worship] others besides Allah, as equals [with Allah]: They love them as they should love Allah. And those who believe love Allah more [than anything else]. If only the wrongdoers could see, behold, they would see the punishment: That to Allah belongs all power, and Allah is Stern in punishment." (Koran 2:165)

Allah informs us in this verse that some of mankind set up for themselves deities which they love more than they love Allah, then He, Most Glorified explains that the Believers are stronger in their love for Allah than the polytheists because the Believers are pure and sincere in their love of Allah, Alone, while the polytheists divide their love between Allah and their false gods; and whoever was sincere in loving Allah, Alone, his love would be stronger than that of the polytheist who divides his love. Then Allah, Most Glorified, promises those who associate partners with Him that when they see the punishment which He has prepared especially for them on the Day of Resurrection, they will wish that they had not associated others with Allah, either in love, or in anything else. Then they shall know, with certain knowledge that all power belongs to Allah, and that Allah is Stern in enforcing His punishment.

403 | *A Saudi Arabian citizen asks a favor of the governor of Riyadh, Prince Salman.*

with artists and philosophers, constructed grand buildings that still stand today, and promoted religious tolerance. He is credited with bringing Prussia to Europe's forefront.

■ **FOOTNOTE** Frederick the Great undertook the construction of a grand opera house in the center of the city of Berlin. There he would enjoy the music of Carl Philipp Emanuel Bach, son of the great composer Johann Sebastian Bach.

Al-Wahhab Founds Wahhabi

403 **1742** Islamic theologian Muhammad ibn Abd al-Wahhab sets out his ideas for a Muslim puritan movement in 1736 in his *Book of Unity*. Believing that Islam had diverted from the original teachings of the Koran and the Hadith, al-Wahhab advocated for a return to Islamic roots. He rejected interpretation of sacred text and believed in the oneness and uniqueness of God. He believed that when people showed deep respect for heroes or saints it could lead to the belief in more than one god, and so denounced it. The Saudi family adopted the Wahhabi movement in 1744 and it spread. When Saudi Arabia was created in 1932, it was the established form of Islam there and remains so today.

Handel's *Messiah* Performed

404 **1742** In just three weeks, George Frideric Handel, a German-born English composer who at that time was considered the greatest organist and harpsichordist in the world, composed the *Messiah*. It was first performed in Dublin in 1742. Handel was a devout Christian and, although often associated with Christmas, only the first third of the *Messiah* is devoted to the coming of a Messiah and the birth of Christ. Much of the rest of the piece covers the Crucifixion and redemption. Combining baroque contrapuntal style with the dramatic qualities of the Italian opera, Handel borrowed from his and others' earlier work when he wrote the piece. The most famous movement is the "Hallelujah" chorus, which comes from the New Testament Book of Revelation. Nowadays, a Christmas concert would not

be complete if it did not include Handel's *Messiah,* considered the most famous of all oratorios.

Celsius Invents Scale

405 **1742** By 1742 the Fahrenheit scale had been firmly in place for 25 years, but there was a glitch that Swedish astronomer Anders Celsius could not let go: The freezing of water was set at 32 degrees. Celsius believed this was a rather odd number for the starting place of an important temperature that distinguished the difference between rain and snow or a liquid and a solid. Celsius's temperature scale put the melting point of ice at 0° and the boiling point at 100° (rather than 212° on the Fahrenheit scale). It was first called the Centigrade scale, Latin for "one hundred steps" because of the 100 intervals between freezing and boiling, but later renamed the Celsius scale in 1948. The scale has been adopted around the world except by the United States and a few other countries that still use Fahrenheit.

France Makes Map

406 **1744** The Cassini family, generations of distinguished astronomers, began making a detailed and accurate topographic map of all of France. Three generations of Cassinis had been named director of the Paris Observatory, and their discoveries included four of Saturn's satellites and the Cassinian oval. They employed the triangulation method—a technique used by astronomers to measure the size of the planets and the sun. Previous mapmakers worked from old material, duplicating inaccurate measurements, and did little fieldwork to gather new information. This meant when roads and canals were being prepared for construction the maps available were not useful and hindered projects. With the support of Kings Louis XIV (the Sun King) and XV (the Beloved), who wanted to show the world that France was not only a leader in military, art, and architecture, but also in science, the Cassinis spent decades surveying the country. Their maps were not

407 | *Carolus Linnaeus poses in Lapland attire.*

decorative, but they were precise. The Cassini map was the first accurate map of an entire nation. This and the subsequent atlas, produced by four generations of Cassinis almost 50 years later, became the standard for national topographic mapping.

■ **FOOTNOTE** Jacques Cassini's original map of France was drawn on a scale of 1:870,000. It was printed by copperplate engraving techniques, which allowed remarkably fine detail, onto 18 separate sheets of paper.

Linnaeus Launches Taxonomy

407 **1750** Throughout the 1740s and into the 1750s, botanist Carolus Linnaeus of Sweden collected, studied, and preserved hundreds of plant specimens from around the world. His work resulted in *Species Plantarum,* the first of 12 volumes proposing a new plant and animal classification system to replace Aristotle's method, used for more than 2,000 years. Since Aristotle knew relatively few plants and animals, they could only be grouped by simple traits, but by the 18th century explorers were adding so many new types of flora and fauna that the old system could not adequately distinguish them all. Linnaeus started by creating a hierarchical system that gave organisms a two-part or scientific name, a practice now known as binomial nomenclature. The first part, or genus, grouped organisms with similar qualities in categories such as anatomy, reproduction, and structure. The second part, or species, was often a descriptive term that set the organism apart. Each organism's name was given in Latin to avoid the potential for language complications. The system was widely accepted and grew more sophisticated with time; it remains in place today. Nowadays, the full seven ranks according to which a living thing is classified (scientific taxonomy) are: kingdom, phylum, class, order, family, genus, and species.

Theory of Universe Published

408 **1750** British astronomer Thomas Wright wrote in his work, *An Original Theory or New Hypothesis of the Universe,* that the stars were part of a flattened finite system—a vast spinning disk—and Earth was part of the system. Five years later German thinker Immanuel Kant drew similar conclusions. Kant believed the sun was one of many stars in a lens-shaped grouping, and that when we look up at the Milky Way, we are looking along the axis of this lens. He believed the spiral nebulae he observed were external galaxies, or "island universes" separate from the Milky Way. He did not have any evidence for this theory, and it would be 170 years before his theory could be verified by Edwin Hubble, using a high-powered telescope.

■ **FOOTNOTE** Wright worked as instrument maker to George, Prince of Wales. His calling card asserted that he "makes & sells all sorts of Mathematical Instruments for Sea & Land according to the best & latest Improvements."

Vitamin C Fends Off Scurvy

409 **1753** British physician James Lind determined that scurvy—a sailors' disease consisting of bleeding gums, loose teeth, aching joints, bleeding tissues, and anemia—resulted from a deficiency in vitamin C. He noted the similarity to diets of prisoners, who also suffered high rates of scurvy. Lind experimented by adding different foods to the diets of people who already had scurvy and found citrus fruits

408 | *Nebulae, interstellar dust and gas, form billowing, colorful clouds in outer space.*

were the most effective. Vitamin C was proved to prevent and treat scurvy. Lind's work was the beginning of the study of deficiency diseases and would eventually put an end to the age-old scurvy disorder.

Laissez-Faire Economics Coined

410 **1758** French physician and economist François Quesnay published *Tableau économique* (*Economic Picture*), which would become the foundation for the ideas of the physiocrats, who believed that land was the source of all wealth and that the natural law of economic order could be attained through unbridled competition. Quesnay, considered the founder of the physiocrat school of economics, believed industry and trade were necessary but wanted Louis XV, whom he was serving as a consulting

physican, to deregulate and reduce taxes surrounding French agriculture so France could emulate Britain. Quesnay coined the term "laissez-faire," referring to minimum governmental regulation in the economic business of people and society, a belief that would be further adopted by economist Adam Smith, who believed in free trade, and grow in popularity through the century. While Quesnay made an important contribution, laissez-faire economics waned in the next century because it could not meet the social and economic challenges that came with the rise of the industrial revolution.

Voltaire Publishes *Candide*

411 **1759** In 1759, Voltaire, the pen name for François-Marie Arouet, published *Candide,* his most widely read

book. Voltaire often wrote about injustices, especially religious prejudice. *Candide* is the story of a young man adventuring around the world, but it also ponders good and evil. Voltaire found himself in the Bastille prison twice—the first for almost a year after being accused of writing against the government and the second for engaging in an argument with a nobleman. He was one of the most popular European authors in the 18th century.

Black Observes Heat in Ice

412 **1761** Scottish chemist William Black noticed during studies of ice that when it melts, it takes up heat, even though it does not change temperature. While Black considered heat a subtle fluid, his findings led to modern thermodynamics. American-born British

---

CONNECTIONS

Internal Combustion Engine
The power source for everything from lawnmowers and cars to jets

As important as the steam engine was to the industrial revolution, steam power had its drawbacks. The bulk and inefficiency of steam engines made inventors wonder how much better an engine would perform if its fuel were burned inside the engine instead of outside. The result of their curiosity was the development of the internal combustion engine.

Experiments with exploding gases as far back as the 17th century finally had a payoff in the 1820s, when early gas engines were created in England. They exploded a hydrogen-air mixture in a chamber, which when cooled acted as a vacuum to move a piston. By the 1860s engines were burning a coal-air mixture, which was then compressed (instead of vacuumed) and ignited by a spark.

But the real breakthrough came in the late 1870s. Earlier internal combustion engines had relied on a two-stroke mechanism (a fuel intake stroke followed by a power stroke). A French scientist named Alphonse Beau de Rochas wrote a treatise on a four-stroke engine: intake (suction), compression, ignition/combustion, and exhaust. When the intake valve on such an engine opens, the piston moves down the cylinder; as it moves back up, it compresses the fuel-air mixture to make for a powerful

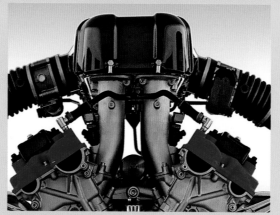

A naked engine of a very powerful sports car

explosion; at the very top of the piston's stroke, a spark ignites the fuel; the explosion forces the piston back down, which in turn makes the exhaust valve open. The motion then starts another cycle. Such repeating motion can be used to drive a crankshaft, which turns the piston's up-and-down motion into circular motion.

Beau de Rochas was a theoretician who never built his engine. It was left to German engineer Nikolaus Otto to seize upon the Frenchman's principles and devise a highly successful four-stroke engine. His countrymen Gottlieb Daimler and Karl Benz enhanced Otto's work and turned out a high-speed internal combustion engine in 1885, followed two years later by a motorcycle. They then adapted a horse-drawn carriage to handle a single-cylinder motor, and in 1889 he produced a two-cylinder automobile capable of traveling ten miles an hour. The world was never the same.

Today, automobiles are the main use for internal combustion engines. Instead of Daimler's two cylinders, modern cars have four, six, or eight cylinders, arranged in a line, a V shape, or in opposition. But their work is still the same—rotating the crankshaft. In addition to gasoline engines, diesel and jet engines also operate along internal combustion principles.

physicist Benjamin Thompson, later Count Rumford, studied the heat generated from boring cannon barrels with a drill. He weighed water and reasoned that if heat was a fluid, water would weigh more at a higher temperature. But since water weighed the same at both temperatures, either caloric heat was weightless or it did not exist. Thompson's work was not immediately accepted, but others continued it and were further able to prove that heat is a result of motion. Mechanical energy would later play an important role in the internal combustion engine.

■ **FOOTNOTE** Defined in 1863 as the amount of heat needed to raise one kilogram of water from 0°C to 1°C, the calorie was not a unit of measurement used in discussions of food and diet until the last years of the 19th century.

Harrison Invents Chronometer

413 **1761** British clockmaker John Harrison developed a balance-wheel system chronometer that could be taken aboard ships and proved to be accurate to within five seconds on a nine-week voyage from England to Jamaica. Its first sea trial was performed by his son, who took the chronometer aboard a ship that sailed the Atlantic in 1761.

Accuracy at sea—specifically knowing one's latitude and longitude—was becoming increasingly important as mariners were taking longer and longer voyages. Latitude was determined by measuring how high the North Star was on the horizon. But longitude required the use of a clock because it was best measured by the exact time on the ship compared to its starting point, like London. The difference in time would tell how far west or east the ship was. Although Harrison had completed his first chronometer in 1735, he continued to redesign it, coming up with innovations that would reduce friction, minimize the disturbances caused by a ship's movements through the water, and equalize the operations of the machine despite fluctuating temperatures. His fourth design was the notable success, allowing ships to navigate precisely and leading to fewer disasters at sea.

409 | *Vitamin C-rich citrus protected passengers and crew from the risk of death by scurvy.*

Smallpox Strikes Indians

414 **1761** European explorers and settlers brought to the New World deadly diseases that would have devastating effects on the American Indian population. The most significant disease was smallpox; it swept New England American Indian populations in the late 1700s, and subsequent outbreaks would continue for the next century until a vaccine was developed. The number of American Indians killed by smallpox is difficult to determine because there are no conclusive pre-Columbian population figures, but as many as 90 percent of some tribes died as a result of the disease.

Rousseau Publishes *Contract*

415 **1762** In 1762, the philosopher Jean-Jacques Rousseau, one of the most influential Enlightenment writers, published *The Social Contract*. The work opens with the revolutionary statement "Man was born free, but he is everywhere in chains," expressing Rousseau's underlying belief in the innate freedom of the human spirit—a principle underlying every revolutionary movement of the age. Leading thinkers of both the American and the French Revolutions echoed Rousseau's beliefs in their foundational documents. In *The Social Contract,* Rousseau outlined legitimate political order, defining government as a contract between the people and their leaders. He believed that humans give up freedoms in order to be governed by others because they more fully enjoyed rights, happiness, and property in a state preceding governance rather than in a state of social rules and strictures. Rousseau's

399 More Details on *Gulliver's Travels*

Travels into Several Remote Nations of the World by Lemul Gulliver first appeared on the London literary scene in November 1726. Published anonymously by Jonathan Swift, the surprise hit went into several more printings that year, appeared in translation the following spring, and has likely not gone out of print since. Known today as *Gulliver's Travels,* this riveting adventure tale—part political satire, part travel literature spoof—catapulted Swift to literary stardom.

Before the success of *Gulliver's Travels,* Swift was down and out, moving between London and Dublin, unsure where he stood politically, and unable to obtain the church appointment he desired. Though he had befriended famous literary folk in London, including Alexander Pope, Swift was losing favor with his audience due to his alignment with the failing Tory party. It was this discontent with the rampant political corruption in his homeland and, later, with England's efforts to constrain Ireland's economy and power that inspired Swift's biting satire and led to the stories that would make up *Gulliver's Travels.*

> Discontent with the rampant political corruption in his homeland inspired Swift's biting satire.

Told in four parts, the work recounts Gulliver's meetings with other peoples in fictitious remote countries, meant to represent various facets of European political culture. His meeting with the 72-foot-tall Brobdingnag farmer, for example, illustrated in the painting opposite, comments on power and ethics: Gulliver's diminutive size in relation to the Brobdingnags leaves him without a say in his fate, and he is virtually enslaved, forced to perform "tricks" in public for money. Profit comes at the expense of the powerless, Gulliver's tale teaches us, and newly achieved power can easily corrupt those who wield it recklessly. But as with his other travels, Gulliver hopes that his trials in Brobdingnag "will certainly help a Philosopher to enlarge his Thoughts and Imagination, and apply them to the Benefit of publick as well as private Life, which was my sole Design in presenting this and other Accounts of my Travels to the World."

Brobdingnag farmers peer in astonishment at Gulliver, in Jonathan Swift's satire Gulliver's Travels.

thoughts deeply influenced the British and European Romantics. When William Wordsworth wrote that children are born "trailing clouds of glory," he was expressing a Rousseau-inspired belief in the higher wisdom of innocence, untainted by worldly thoughts or concerns. Rousseau believed that education was best if it occurred naturally, inspired by the innate curiosity of the child, and his ideas influenced 20th-century educational philosophers including John Dewey and A. S. Neill.

> ■ **FOOTNOTE** Rousseau advocated belief in the noble savage, contending that primitive ways of life, before society, civilization, and governments developed, were essentially better because they were freer and more natural.

Catherine Becomes Empress

416 **1762** Catherine II, the daughter of an obscure German prince, proclaimed herself Empress of Russia in 1762 after she engineered the removal of her husband, Peter III, as emperor. She had married her cousin, heir to the Russian throne, and stood in the wings while the daughter of Peter the Great, Elizabeth, ruled Russia. After Elizabeth died and Peter

411 | *Portrait of French author and philosopher Voltaire, as a young man*

III was named emperor, Catherine gained the support of the army, which disagreed with Peter's alliances, and asserted herself as empress. Peter was assassinated shortly thereafter. Catherine ruled Russia for 34 years, expanding its territory and reorganizing its laws and administration. Before she rose to power Catherine intended to emancipate the serfs, which were the basis of the Russian economy, but knowing she would lose the serf owners' key support she actually strengthened the system, and the conditions for serfs worsened. Catherine promoted Russian culture, arts, and education and is considered to have played a key role in moving Russia to become a modern state.

Innovations on Steam Engine

417 **1763** In 1763, James Watt began improving upon Newcomen's steam engine, deemed extremely important but terribly inefficient. Watt was only one of a large group of technical innovators attempting to fulfill the promise of the steam engine. In order to improve it, new machines that would have lasting effects needed to be made. John Smeaton, considered the founder of British civil engineering, invented a cylinder boring machine in 1769 that would prove essential to manufacturing parts for the steam engine. His invention was improved upon in 1775 by Englishman John Wilkinson, who improved on the boring machine's precision, so that metal cylinders used as pistons could be manufactured more reliably. And Henry Maudslay, also of England, invented the screw-cutting engine lathe in 1797, which allowed accurate manufacture of standard screw heads.

European Powers Sign Treaty

418 **1763** Britain, France, and Spain, together with Portugal, signed the Treaty of Paris in 1763, ending the Seven Years' War and signaling the beginning of British dominance beyond western Europe. Called by Winston Churchill the first worldwide war, the Seven Years' War began in conflict between England and France

422 | *Capt. James Cook raises Britain's flag in New South Wales, claiming Australia for England.*

over control of territories in North America. The battles located there are identified as the French and Indian War, since native North Americans often aided the French in their efforts to keep the British from claiming North American lands as their colonies. At the signing of the Treaty of Paris, France and Spain gave, respectively, Canada and Florida to England.

> ■ **FOOTNOTE** Through this treaty, Britain gained control of the land between the 13 Colonies and the MIssissippi River. Territories in India, Africa, and the Caribbean also formed a part of the exchange.

Britain Gains Hold in India

419 **1764** In the Battle of Buxar, forces representing the British East India Company fought armies rallied together by several Indian leaders, including Mir Kasim, the nawab (governor) of Bengal; Suja-ud-Daula, the nawab of Awadh; and Shah Alam II, emperor of the

Mogul dynasty, which had dominated India for more than a century. British forces won a decisive victory at the town of Buxar, on the banks of the Ganges River, which secured the British East India Company control of the eastern portion of the Indian subcontinent—a big step toward Britain's colonization of the entire land.

Spinning Jenny Invented

420 **1764** In 1764, James Hargreaves invented the spinning jenny, which turned an ordinary spinning wheel into a multiple-spool wheel that allowed the work of eight people to be done by one. Spinning wheels had been used for centuries to turn wool or flax into thread or yarn. The spinning jenny allowed thread to be produced faster and cheaper, which drove the price of thread down. Fifteen years later Samuel Crompton improved the jenny with his spinning mule, making it possible for one person to operate more than 1,000 spindles. His machine's

method of drawing the fiber produced yarn that was as high quality as hand spinning and also allowed yarn to be spun fine or coarse. Yarn and high-quality thread could now be manufactured on a large scale. The inventions took what was a high labor, skilled industry and turned it into a high production, relatively unskilled labor industry. Heading into the industrial revolution, this meant wealth for the textile factory owners but unemployment for the workers whose jobs had been replaced by better equipment.

Massacre Sparks Revolution

421 **1770** Tensions had been building between the colonists of North America and the British troops in residence there. On March 5, 1770, soldiers of Britain's 29th Regiment mustered on a Boston street, drawing the ire of locals nearby. Some small matter escalated into a brawl, with colonists jeering and throwing objects at the soldiers, who eventually fired on the crowd. Five Boston citizens died as a result, including an African-American sailor named Crispus Attucks. The incident, now known as the Boston Massacre, galvanized colonial resistance to the British and is often considered the spark of the American Revolution.

■ **FOOTNOTE** Silversmith and printer Paul Revere soon distributed a color engraving of the Boston event, picturing a line of British redcoats firing on a group of colonists—an example of early American propaganda.

Britain Claims Australia

422 **1770** In 1770, on his first of three scientific expeditions of the Pacific, Lt. James Cook and his 94 crewmen and scientists on the *Endeavour* landed at the southeast coast of Australia. Though they were hardly the first Europeans to explore the continent, they claimed it for Britain, naming it New South Wales. Cook took on the navigational hazard of the Great Barrier Reef and surveyed 2,000 miles of the eastern coast. Also notable from this three-year journey was that none of the crew died from scurvy,

which was rampant on most ships during such a long voyage. This was due to the fact that Cook was adamant that the crew eat a proper diet including citrus extract, cress, and sauerkraut. He would later receive high honors for his success in keeping his crew free from the disease on multiple voyages. Cook's first expedition also included charting New Zealand and part of Australia and taking scientists to Tahiti to observe the transit of the planet Venus across the sun, establishing the practice of taking scientists aboard vessels for research. One of his main goals was also to find the great southern continent many believed must exist. He concluded Australia was not it and on future expeditions confirmed the great southern continent was a myth.

Priestley Finds Oxygen

423 **1774** In 1774, English chemist Joseph Priestley identified a strange gas that made mice frisky and caused him to feel light and easy when he breathed it—oxygen. While experimenting with heated red mercuric oxide, Priestley discovered that it gave off a colorless gas that he called dephlogisticated air. He noticed smoldering wood burst into flames when it came in contact with the gas. Priestley believed the gas was produced by plants. He shared his findings with French chemist Antoine Lavoisier, who repeated Priestley's experiments and was better able to define the role of the gas. He explained that substances burned by combining chemically with oxygen and that oxygen supported animal life respiration. He also noted that it was a contributor to rusting. Lavoisier renamed the gas oxygen. Priestley and Lavoisier's combined work on a gas that is critical to human life is considered to have revolutionized chemistry.

■ FOOTNOTE In part because of the company he kept, but also because of the philosophical implications of his findings, Joseph Priestley was considered an enemy of the British crown. Royalists destroyed his laboratory in 1791.

Smith Introduces Economics

424 **1776** In 1776, Scottish social philosopher Adam Smith published *An Inquiry into the Nature and Causes of the Wealth of Nations,* which became known as the bible of capitalism and was the first comprehensive system of political economy. His previous book, the well-received *Theory of Moral Sentiments,* published in 1759, had focused mainly on human nature and psychology, while *Wealth of Nations* broadened his focus to address factors of social evolution. He may

Independence Declared

425 **1776** The costly French and Indian War had ended in 1763, and Britain needed to recuperate its losses. It imposed new taxes and trade restrictions on the colonies, which the colonists resented, especially since they did not have representation in the British Parliament. King George III's failure to respond to the colonists' grievances led to the colonists' formation of the Continental Army, and in 1775 the American Revolution began.

On July 4, 1776, the Declaration of Independence was approved by the Continental Congress, announcing the separation of the 13 Colonies from Britain. It had become clear to the Continental Congress that separation from Britain was essential, and in June 1776 Thomas Jefferson was appointed to draft the declaration. He outlined the grievances the colonies had against the king, forming the justification for

Signers of the Declaration of Independence add their "John Hancocks" to the document in this U.S. Capitol painting.

separation. The document also declares individuals' "unalienable rights" of life, liberty, and the pursuit of happiness. It was signed by 56 delegates. The war ended in 1783, at which point Britain recognized the Colonies' independence. The Declaration of Independence is considered the founding document of the United States and a symbol of liberty for the country.

have developed his thinking through his association with members of the French Enlightenment, namely the economist François Quesnay. In *Wealth of Nations,* Smith, a moral philosophy professor, spoke harshly against the "mercantilist" system of his day where governments granted monopolies and protected their own farmers, merchants, and manufacturers against what they spun as unfair competition. Smith showed that free trade, competition, and choice increases economic development, decreases poverty, and even improves society's moral and social development for the greatest good of all. Although Smith believed humans were self-interested by nature, he wrote that competition in free trade kept prices low and forced the incentive for a variety of goods and services. This new philosophy, which was the beginning of classical

economics, helped pave the way for free trade and economic expansion.

American Victory at Saratoga

426 **1777** In 1777, the Continental Army's victories in the Battles of Saratoga marked a major defeat for the British and the turning point of the American Revolution.

Hoping to gain control of the Hudson River and take control of New York, Gen. John Burgoyne, considered the best British general in North America, marched about 8,000 British troops to the town of Saratoga, but he could not cross Gen. Horatio Gates's lines. In a second battle three weeks later, Burgoyne was met with a counterattack led by Gen. Benedict Arnold. Burgoyne's army had dwindled to around 5,000 and was short on supplies. He was forced to surrender.

The terms of the surrender at Saratoga required British troops to return to England for the remainder of the war. The American victory also secured the Hudson River and New York. Having proved themselves by defeating a renowned general, the Americans created an alliance with France, which allowed the 13 states to buy war supplies and pay soldiers—support that allowed the Revolution to continue longer than otherwise.

■ **FOOTNOTE** While Benedict Arnold's name is now synonymous with treason—he spied for the British by the end of the Revolutionary War—in the war's early years he was a general and an honored military hero.

La Scala Opens

427 **1778** In 1778, La Scala Opera house, or Teatro alla Scala, opened in Milan, Italy, replacing the Royal Ducal Theatre, which was destroyed by fire. Built by Empress Maria Theresa of Austria, which ruled Milan at the time, the neoclassic building would later be owned by the city of Milan. Surviving severe bombing during World II, the structure and its interior have been renovated several times over the past two centuries. The theater can accommodate some 3,000 spectators and has one of the largest stages in Italy. Some of the most famous operas written by 19th-century composers premiered at La Scala, including those of Giaochino Rossini, which helped position La Scala as one of the world's premier opera houses—a reputation still intact today.

Wedgwood Makes Pyrometer

428 **1782** In 1782, pottery designer and manufacturer Josiah Wedgwood of England invented the pyrometer, which measured high temperatures inside a kiln. Since opening his own firm more than 20 years earlier, Wedgwood had established himself as an innovator in different aspects of the process and materials in creating pottery. The pyrometer worked by measuring the radiation from the object whose temperature was being measured; therefore the object did not have to be touched. Prior to Wedgwood's thermometer the well-paid operator of a factory kiln had to possess the skill and knowledge to determine whether ware was properly fired. The pyrometer made the process a science.

First Balloon Flight

429 **1783** In 1783, physicist Jean-François Pilâtre de Rozier and François Laurent Marquis d'Arlandes became the first aeronauts in history, lifting off from the center of Paris in a hot air balloon designed by Joseph and Jacques Montgolfier. The flight covered five and a half miles and lasted 25 minutes. The Montgolfier brothers had built the first balloon to make a flight—unmanned, for ten minutes—earlier that year, but this was the first manned flight. The Montgolfiers believed that the balloon worked because a unique lighter-than-air gas was formed when the huge piece of cloth was filled with heated air, which in turn caused the balloon to rise. What they did not know

429| *Passengers including Joseph Montgolfier and Jean François Pilâtre de Rozier, ascend in "Le Flesselles."*

was the balloon inflated and rose because air is more buoyant when it is heated. The balloon flight was a success, but there was a problem. Once the air in the envelope of a balloon cools, the balloon descends. And keeping that air warm using the methods at that time was dangerous. Pilâtre de Rozier, for example, would later die attempting to cross the English Channel by balloon. Inventors would go on to experiment with different gases and develop safer

---

FIRST PERSON

Mary Wollstonecraft
VINDICATION OF THE RIGHTS OF WOMAN, 1792

Contending for the rights of women, my main argument is built on this simple principle, that if she be not prepared by education to become the companion of man, she will stop the progress of knowledge, for truth must be common to all, or it will be inefficacious with respect to its influence on general practice. And how can woman be expected to co-operate, unless she know why she ought to be virtuous? Unless freedom strengthen her reason till she comprehend her duty, and see in what manner it is connected with her real good? If children are to be educated to understand the true principle of patriotism, their mother must be a patriot; and the love of mankind, from which an orderly train of virtues spring, can only be produced by considering the moral and civil interest of mankind....

But, if women are to be excluded, without having a voice, from a participation of the natural rights of mankind, prove first, to ward off the charge of injustice and inconsistency, that they want reason, else this flaw in your NEW CONSTITUTION ... will ever show that man must, in some shape, act like a tyrant, and tyranny ... will ever undermine morality....

Let there be then no coercion ESTABLISHED in society, and the common law of gravity prevailing, the sexes will fall into their proper places. And, now that more equitable laws are forming your citizens, marriage may become more sacred; your young men may choose wives from motives of affection, and your maidens allow love to root out vanity.

---

hot air balloon techniques. Nonetheless, with Montgolfiers' balloon the fascination with human flight was born.

Coulomb Formulates Law

430 **1785** In 1785, French physicist Charles-Augustin de Coulomb published what is now known as Coulomb's law, one of the fundamental laws of electromagnetism—that electricity obeys the same laws as the planets in their orbits. More precisely, positive and negative charges attract each other and two like charges will repel each other with a force that is directly proportional to the amount of charge and inversely proportional to the square of the distance between them. A unit of electrical charge in the metric system is now named after Coulomb.

Don Giovanni Premieres

431 **1787** In 1787, *Don Giovanni,* an opera written by Wolfgang Amadeus Mozart with libretto by Lorenzo da Ponte, premiered in Prague. The opera portrays the medieval character Don Juan as a romantic hero for the first time. *Don Giovanni* juxtaposed tragedy and comedy, a first for an opera. In *Don Giovanni,* Mozart created what many people believe to be his greatest opera. It is still one of the operas performed most often today.

> ■ **FOOTNOTE** In *Don Giovanni* Mozart was choosing to retell the tale of the great Spanish lover Don Juan, whose escapades also formed the subject of poetry by Lord Byron in the 1820s and Aleksandr Pushkin in 1830.

Prisoners Reach Australia

432 **1788** In 1788, being a convict in England could mean a fate worse than prison. That year, 11 British ships—the First Fleet—carrying about 750 convicts and more than 200 marines and officers (to guard them) arrived at Port Jackson (today's Sydney Harbour), and established the first penal colony in Australia. The British needed to relieve overcrowding in their prisons and saw the vast land charted by Lt. James Cook 18 years earlier as an opportune place to house

them. Some believe the move was also part of a larger British plan to establish a launching pad for further economic endeavors in the South Pacific. Settling into the new colony did not come easy—the land was difficult to work, diseases were a persistent problem, and there were conflicts with the Aboriginal people, who had inhabited the continent for some 60,000 years. Nonetheless, over the next six decades another 160,000 convicts were shipped to Australia. It was not until the 1830s, when Australia's inland region became known as a prime spot for sheep rearing, did the non-convict British immigrant boom begin.

Mob Storms Bastille

433 **1789** On July 14, 1789, a mob stormed France's Bastille prison. King Louis XVI's troops ignored his order to fire on the citizens and as a result, the Bastille prison fell, beginning the French Revolution and the eventual toppling of the monarchy. The majority of France wanted a new government where the power didn't reside with a king or a god, but with the people. The first anniversary of the storming of the Bastille was celebrated by holding an event now called Bastille Day in English. Bastille Day is a national holiday, and much like the American holiday honoring the signing of the Declaration of Independence, it is a symbol of France's liberty and democracy.

Interesting Narrative Published

434 **1789** Olaudah Equiano, a Nigerian boy kidnapped at age 11 and eventually brought to the United States to work as a slave, detailed his life story in his 1789 book, *The Interesting Narrative of the Life of Olaudah Equiano.* Equiano was sold to a British Royal Navy officer and went on to travel the world and learned to read and write. He was bought and sold several times and eventually made enough money to buy his freedom. He chose to stay in London, where he became a prominent member of the abolitionist movement. His book, which went through nine English editions in his lifetime, made him a wealthy man

432 | *Prisoners—mostly the poor or petty thieves—arrive at Australia's Port Jackson penal colony.*

and was one of the first written by a former slave to speak out against the slave trade.

FOOTNOTE On a 1773 British expedition in search of a northwest passage to India, Olaudah Equiano sailed into the Arctic Circle. One of his shipmates was Horatio Nelson, who defeated Napoleon at Trafalgar in 1815.

Bentham Outlines Utilitarianism

435 **1789** English social theorist Jeremy Bentham published *An Introduction to the Principles of Morals and Legislation* in 1789, describing utilitarianism, which states that one's actions are right if they provide optimal happiness to all. Similarly, Bentham believed the government should promote the greatest happiness for the greatest number. Although his philosophies were criticized for being oversimplified, Bentham successfully argued for individual and economic freedom and was considered a pioneer of prison reform.

Paine's *Rights of Man*

436 **1791** British-born political philosopher Thomas Paine, who emigrated to America on Benjamin Franklin's urgings, published *The Rights of Man* in 1791, defending the French Revolution and republicanism. His work was banned in England, and he moved to France, where he spoke out against the Reign of Terror. He later wrote *The Age of Reason,* which was critical of organized religion. Although his writings were highly criticized at the time, Paine remains one of history's great political propagandists.

Wollstonecraft's *Vindication*

437 **1792** In 1792, British author Mary Wollstonecraft wrote *A Vindication of the Rights of Woman,* advocating that women have social and educational equality with men. Wollstonecraft wrote that if girls were given the same educational opportunities as boys they would not only improve at their traditional roles as mother and wife, but they would be capable professionals. This, in turn, would benefit society at large. Immediately successful, *Vindication* was considered a radical doctrine for its time, and Wollstonecraft, who was self-educated and briefly ran a school with her sisters, became known around the world for her passionate opinions. The nationwide educational reform for which Wollstonecraft argued was not embraced immediately, but her principles would later influence women's rights advocates in the next century, and *Vindication* would become known as the founding book of modern feminism.

New York Opens Exchange

438 **1792** A bell did not ring, but nonetheless the New York Stock Exchange began at an informal meeting under a buttonwood tree on what is now Wall Street in New York City. Twenty-four stockbrokers and merchants met to sign the Buttonwood Agreement, which allowed them to trade securities on commission. At first there were just five securities; now it is the largest stock exchange in the world by dollar volume. In the early 19th century, as the United States was becoming industrialized, the need for capital increased trade at the stock exchange. After the panic of 1837, where investors were hit with huge losses and the country suffered from one of its worst depressions, it was decided that companies could only offer stock on the exchange if they disclosed their financial information to the public. Reeling from the stock market crash of 1929, in 1934 the government established the Securities and Exchange Commission, which instituted new rules on buying and trading, and

437 | *Philosopher and author Mary Wollstonecraft*

eventually restored investors' confidence in the exchange.

Smith's New Geology

439 **1793** In 1793, William Smith, who would later become known as the founder of stratigraphy, studied rock layers, or strata, while surveying canal construction in England. He paid particularly close attention to the fossils and vertical changes within the layers. He sought out and examined more of these beds during subsequent years of travel and eventually recognized that each rock layer possessed fossils unique to it. He developed the principle of faunal succession—whereby strata can be identified and dated based on the fossils it contained. That means fossils from two different geologic time periods could not be found in the same layer of strata. In all of his spare time he tirelessly worked on what would become the first geologic map of England and Wales, appearing in 1815. Using improved topography, he used different colors for the various geological types, paying close attention to stratigraphic detail, which was valuable in the planning of canals, quarries, and mines. The stratigraphy theories and mapmaking techniques he introduced are still used today.

Jenner Vaccinates for Pox

441 **1796** In 1796, English physician Edward Jenner successfully administered a vaccination against smallpox that would lead him to become known as the father of immunology. Jenner had heard that milkmaids and farmers who had been ill from cowpox, a less harmful disease contracted from cattle, did not seem to contract smallpox. He tested this relationship by applying matter from a milkmaid's cowpox lesion to a young boy. The child became mildly sick but recovered fairly quickly Jenner then inoculated the boy with smallpox; he did not develop the disease. Jenner's peers at first couldn't believe the findings, so Jenner proved it again several times over. Once the vaccination was accepted by the masses and administered, smallpox death rates rapidly declined.

> ■ **FOOTNOTE** London's Royal Society honored Jenner not for his smallpox findings but for his discovery that when cuckoos take over another bird's nest, it is the newly hatched bird that pushes the host's eggs out of the nest.

Whitney Invents Cotton Gin

440 **1793** In 1793, engineer Eli Whitney, in the process of helping American farmers find a way to make cotton growing more profitable, invented the cotton gin. The type of cotton that was easy to separate from its seeds was only grown on the coast, which limited agricultural opportunities. The short-staple variety that grew inland in much of the South had sticky seeds that were difficult and time consuming to hand-separate from the cotton. While Massachusetts-born Whitney was visiting a plantation in Georgia, he heard about this difficulty and got to work. Whitney's solution: a four-part cotton gin that separated the seeds mechanically. His invention eliminated the tedious job of separating the cotton and opened the opportunity for mass production. By the middle of the next century the South would be producing three-quarters of the world's supply of cotton. Whitney patented his machine the following year and even formed a partnership with the Georgia plantation manager, Phineas Miller, to produce the gins. However, farmers weren't willing to pay him to have the machines serviced, and they pirated his design, resulting in protracted legal disputes.

An 1869 illustration of Whitney's first cotton gin in Harper's Weekly

Whitney never became wealthy as a result of his revolutionary invention, however, he did find some success in pioneering the manufacturing of interchangeable components of muskets. His cotton gin unintentionally led to profound social consequences: the elimination of the seed-separation problem spurred the growing of massive quantities of cotton, requiring a huge labor force to pick. This eventually led to the institutionalization of slavery in the United States.

The cotton gin was an important invention, but his invention of "interchangeable parts" was perhaps even more important to the advancement of manufacturing. He produced muskets for the U.S. that were made with uniform parts. That meant that when a rifle was broken in the field, a replacement piece could be on hand, rather than sending the whole thing in for repair. It was an advantage during the Civil War and a huge leap in the advancement of industry.

Overpopulation Predicted

442 **1798** In 1798, English economist Thomas Malthus published *An Essay on the Principles of Population,* arguing that humans are capable of overpopulating to the point of running out of their food supply, thus introducing the idea of overpopulation. Malthus believed that just like plants and other animals, humans by nature populate and overtake land, and if left unchecked, will leave nothing left for subsistence. He said that war, famine, and natural death control population growth, but he later wrote that there should be further self-imposed checks, including abstinence and late marriage, but only on the working class and poor, who he believed, should have no more children than they could support.

The agricultural revolution, which allowed food to be produced quickly and more economically, would throw a wrench in Malthus' theory. And fertility rates would go down as contraceptives became prevalent. However his ideas affected social policy, especially on the poor, and Charles Darwin would later be influenced by Malthus in his writing on natural selection.

Fulton Invents Submarine

443 **1800** In 1800, American inventor Robert Fulton first tested his creation, the *Nautilus,* a submarine to be used by the French in war against the British. The submarine and mines worked in several trials and impressed the French enough to fund Fulton's efforts. But when the craft tried to attack a British ship, the enemy was much faster and able to elude it. The French were no longer interested in the *Nautilus.*

Fulton would later work with the British to attack the French using the same submarine, and again the mission failed, this time due to defective mines. Fulton was defeated, but the submarine would eventually reemerge as an effective warfare machine. The United States named the first nuclear-powered submarine U.S.S. *Nautilus.*

■ **FOOTNOTE** After Fulton's disappointment with the *Nautilus,* he left France for his native United States, where he developed several successful steam-powered riverboats, a warship, and an engine manufactory in New Jersey.

Volta Displays Battery

444 **1800** Italian physicist Alessandro Giuseppe Volta demonstrated the action of the first electric battery. Volta observed the fact that when two metals that are dissimilar make contact, they produce a small electrical effect, and the fact that when metals make contact with certain fluids they also produce an electrical effect.

Taking it a step further, Volta put two dissimilar metals in contact and then joined them with water, completing the circuit and creating an electric current. He would subsequently go on to make a compact version of the battery by connecting stacks of small disks of copper, zinc, and paper soaked in salt with a wire that created a current when the circuit was closed. This set the stage for future chemists and physicists to study electromotive force and currents.

■ **FOOTNOTE** Volta's contemporary, Luigi Galvani, saw frogs' legs jerk with a spark and believed electricity to reside in their bodies. With his stacked chips of metal and brine—often called a Voltaic pile—Volta proved otherwise.

Jacquard Automates Loom

445 **1801** In 1801, Joseph Marie Jacquard created an automated loom that used a system of hooks and

444 | *Alessandro Volta demonstrates his battery to Napoleon Bonaparte (seated) and a group of scientists.*

needles to lift individual warp threads and perforated punch cards that could "remember" a pattern. The Jacquard loom could produce intricate woven patterns that were laborious if done by hand and the punch cards were interchangeable, so any pattern could be created on a single loom. Not only did Jacquard's invention allow interesting, complicated textiles to be produced quickly, the technology behind it would lead to one of the great inventions of the next century—the computer. A needle was allowed to go through the punch card if it lined up with a hole in a block of wood on the loom. If the holes didn't match up, the needle stopped and went on to the next hole. This is how a pattern was created. But it was also a primitive yes-and-no system that would become the basis for digital computers.

Rebellion Ends in Vietnam

446 **1802** The Tay Son Rebellion, considered one of the largest popular uprisings in Asian history up to that point, ended in 1802. The rebellion began in what is now south-central Vietnam under three brothers who came from a village named Tay Son. The Tay Son's mission was to seize property from the wealthy and redistribute it to the poor. With each village that came under their control, the oppressive landlords were punished and their property was reallocated. The leaders abolished taxes, freed prisoners, and gave food to the hungry. They managed to overthrow a 350-year-old imperial dynasty and successfully warded off the invading Siamese and Chinese. The rebellion helped break down the division between the Vietnamese living on either side of the Gianh River and is considered an important event in the transition of modern Vietnam.

Dalton Develops Atomic Theory

447 **1803** English chemist and physicist John Dalton in 1803 put forward his atomic theory stating that all elements are made up of tiny, invisible, indestructible particles called atoms and that atoms of an individual element are the same in size and weight. Dalton's groundbreaking work would become the basis of modern chemistry.

Dalton's early passion was meteorology. For nearly 60 years he kept a daily journal of the climate—the temperature, barometric pressure, rainfall, and dew point. This gave him the opportunity to ponder the composition of air, which is when he began theorizing that it was made up of minute particles. Then he began to consider that all matter, whether it was a solid, liquid or gas, was made of these particles.

Scientists have been studying atoms dating back to Democritus in 440 B.C.E., who called the particles *atomos,* which meant "invisible." But the Greeks, and many scientists thereafter, believed atoms varied in shape. Dalton said the atoms of one element were all alike but the atoms of a different element were distinctly different in size and weight. This idea of atomic weight meant that Dalton could give weights to the known elements, but Dalton did not have accurate values to assign them.

After Dalton presented his atomic theory he worked on devising a table of the atomic weights of the known elements. But there was not much known about molecular makeup, so his table was not accurate. Swedish chemist Jöns Jakob Berzelius labored extensively to come up with a better table and produced one in 1818. His method was not perfect, but his figures were fairly accurate. Dalton's work on atomic theory made chemistry a quantitative science and made Dalton one of the founding fathers of modern physical science.

John Dalton's atomic theory has led to the harnessing of atomic energy.

Beethoven Composes *Eroica*

448 **1803** Ludwig van Beethoven began composing his revolutionary third symphony, *Eroica,* in 1803, and completed it the year after. It would go on to be his most famous for its length and complexity, surpassing any symphony that had been composed previously. Originally called *Bonaparte* as a tribute to Napoleon, the title was supposedly changed when Beethoven became disgusted with the French revolutionary after he proclaimed himself emperor. *Eroica* redefined symphony. It was nearly twice as long as a typical symphony of the day and is considered by some to be the beginning of the Romantic era. Its first public performance occurred in Vienna in 1805.

> ■**FOOTNOTE** The *Eroica*'s second movement is often played at funerals and memorial services, including those for President Franklin Delano Roosevelt and for the victims of the terrorist attack during the 1972 Munich Olympics.

Lewis and Clark Go West

449 **1804** In 1804 U.S. President Thomas Jefferson sent Meriwether Lewis and William Clark on a two-year expedition of the West to find a northwest passage, map rivers, identify new plants and animals, build relationships with the native people, and open trade. The Louisiana Purchase had recently doubled the size of the U.S., and Jefferson was eager to find out more about this land. The expedition began in St. Louis, Missouri, and would cover 8,000 miles in 28 months. Some four dozen men originally made up the crew and along the way Lewis and Clark used a Shoshone Indian, Sacagawea, and her French-Canadian husband, Toussaint Charbonneau, as interpreters. Sacagawea carried her infant son on her back during the journey. While a coast-to-coast water route wasn't discovered, the expedition proved worthy for its scientific and geographic discoveries. It expanded the fur trade and since the explorers made it to Oregon and wintered on the coast, strengthened the U.S. claim to the Pacific.

Francis II Names Self Emperor

450 **1804** Habsburg monarch Holy Roman Emperor Francis II elevated Austria to the title of Austrian Empire in 1804 and changed his own title to Emperor Francis I to ward off the possibility that Napoleon Bonaparte or one of his followers might gain control over the land. Austria had been at war with France on and off again since 1792 and was not having success. Francis was opposed to the ongoing revolutionary movements that were occurring throughout Europe as a result of the French Revolution, and he deflected efforts at reform among his own people. In 1806, to ensure Napoleon could not be elected, Francis dissolved the Holy Roman Empire and renounced his own title.

■ **FOOTNOTE** Francis II had good reason to fear for his life during revolutionary times. His father's sister was Marie Antoinette, wife to Louis XVI, both of whom were killed by guillotine during the French Revolution in 1793.

Haiti Freed From France

451 **1804** Former slave and military leader François Dominique Toussaint-Louverture led the Haitian independence movement in the 1790s which would result in the establishment of the Republic of Haiti in 1804. Freed from slavery in 1777, Toussaint-Louverture assembled his own army and trained them in guerilla warfare. He at first aligned with Spain but later switched to France, because it had abolished slavery and Spain had not. He also negotiated treaties with the British. In 1801 he drove the Spanish out of Santo Domingo and freed the slaves there. The French removed Toussaint-Louverture from power in 1802. He died in prison. France, under Napoleon Bonaparte, who intended to restore slavery in Haiti, was defeated by an army led by one of Toussaint-Louverture's men and the French

448 | *Orchestras today continue to perform Beethoven's* Eroica.

449 More Details on Lewis and Clark

When Meriwether Lewis and William Clark set out to survey the American West, one of their objectives was to report on the situation of the native peoples there and build peaceful relations. With the Shoshone Indian Sacagawea as their guide and interpreter, the explorers made much progress toward that end, though their travels also helped to launch the westward expansion that would eventually cause conflicts over the land.

Tribes that once had hunted and roamed freely were now in competition with other natives for slowly shrinking resources. Hostility and strife were rampant as the forced migration brought tribes in close contact with one another. Yet white settlers pushed on, undeterred by the potential for conflict with natives. They claimed land for themselves and gave it boundaries—a foreign concept to the native peoples—as the frontier moved farther and farther westward.

> For a people unused to restrictions, the Prairie du Chien treaty and others like it were only a temporary fix.

The fragile state of the West, however, could not stand for long, and soon the U.S. government was stepping in to relieve conflict among Native American tribes in the hope that peace among tribes would mean peace for white settlers. Treaties were signed such as the one at Prairie du Chien, pictured here. William Clark was present for the 1825 negotiations, along with the Michigan governor Lewis Cass; the Sioux, Sac and Fox, Menominee, Ioway, Winnebago, and Anishinaabeg tribes also took part. The treaty attempted to fix the problem of intertribe aggression by drawing boundaries between each of the groups within which they could settle, hunt, and live out their day-to-day lives. But for a people unused to restrictions on their territory, the Prairie du Chien treaty and others like it were only a temporary fix to the larger problem of American settlements and land ownership. The U.S. government and the Native American tribes, in fact, would meet several times more to negotiate peace at Prairie du Chien, and the natives would be forced to migrate again.

Native Americans and members of the military meet at Prairie du Chien for the presentation of the peace treaty, in a lithograph painted on the scene.

Muhammad Ali Egypt's Viceroy

454 **1805** In 1805, Muhammad Ali, who has been called the father of modern Egypt, was named the Ottoman sultan's viceroy in Egypt. He went on to found the dynasty that ruled Egypt until 1953. France had occupied Egypt from 1798 to 1801, and the ambitious Muhammad Ali continued what the French had started by ending the region's traditional society and developing a strong economy and military. He eliminated the former ruling Mamluks, limited native merchant and artisan groups, and neutralized any peasant rebellions. He focused on agriculture, over which he believed the state should have a monopoly, and began exporting crops such as cotton, rice, and sugarcane. Muhammad Ali was also determined to expand. He invaded and occupied Syria until Britain, France, Russia, and Prussia allied with the Ottoman government and drove his armies out. Under an 1841 treaty, Muhammad Ali was forced to return all of his conquered territory except Sudan but was allowed to govern Egypt for life.

> ■ **FOOTNOTE** Muhammad Ali is buried in the grand Alabaster Mosque of Cairo, which he had built. It was not his first resting place, however; one of his successors had his remains brought to the mosque eight years after his death.

455 | *British illustration of the cruelty of Capt. John Kimber calls for "abolition of the slave trade."*

withdrew from Haiti. It became the second country, after the United States, to be free of colonial rule.

> ■ **FOOTNOTE** The name "Haiti" comes from *ayiti*, meaning "land of high mountains" in the language of the Arawak, indigenous to the island. It once referred to the entire island but now refers to its western half, the nation of Haiti.

Fulani Empire Begins

452 **1804** Fulani philosopher and reformer Usman dan Fodio engaged in a holy war from 1804 to 1808, which resulted in the formation of a new state, the Fulani empire, in present-day northern Nigeria.

Usman was a respected cleric living is the northern Hausa state of Gobir who had formed a community over which he presided according to the strict Muslim principles of law preached by the Qadiriyah. The kings in Gobir disapproved of Usman's independent community, leading Usman, who attracted both Fulani and Hausa as followers, to engage in a revolt against the Hausaland rulers in the name of Muslim revival and government reform. He hoped the new empire would be ruled by the principles and teachings of the Islamic tradition. Usman left much of the military decisions to his brother and son, who would become viceroys of the Fulani empire. The revolt was a success, and the empire that was created as a result of the jihad was the largest in Africa since the end of the 16th century. It inspired other related holy wars that would lead to the founding of the Islamic states of the Central African Republic, Chad, Ivory Coast, Mali, Senegal, and Sudan.

Sertürner Isolates Morphine

453 **1805** In 1805, German chemist F. W. A. Sertürner isolated a chemical from laudanum, an alcoholic extract of immature opium blooms, creating what would later become known as morphine—one of the most commonly used pain medications. Raw poppy juice could lead to overdose, since potency varied between batches, but the drug morphine could be prescribed in reliably regular dosages. The drug is still widely used as a painkiller for cancer patients but is extremely addictive. Sertürner's work was the start of alkaloid chemistry and the forerunner of the modern pharmaceutical industry.

Slave Trade Abolished

455 **1807** Under the Slave Trade Act, Great Britain's Parliament abolished the slave trade in the British Empire in 1807. The same year President Thomas Jefferson signed a bill prohibiting slaves from being imported into the U.S., which would take effect in 1808. Britain's slave trade dates back to the mid-16th century, but at the turn of the 19th century there was growing opposition by groups who found the practice immoral and inhuman. A large-scale organized boycott in the 1790s of sugar grown by Caribbean slaves sent a clear message that the people were willing to take a stand on the issue. Britain's Parliament would eventually sway, and the bill to abolish the slave trade passed, making it illegal for any of the British colonies to conduct in the trade of slaves. Britain knew the move would have an effect on its economy, so it put pressure on other nations to abolish their slave trade as well. In 1833, slavery was abolished throughout the British Empire. Although the United States put an end to the trade of slaves, slavery was still practiced until the 13th Amendment was passed in 1865. In Latin America the Spanish colonies were winning wars of independence in the early 1800s. Slavery was abolished when they were granted independence. Many other countries ended slavery by the late 1800s. Up until 1807 many parts of the world had some sort of system of slavery or serfdom. Slavery has not vanished, but the Slave Trade Act was the beginning of the system breaking down on a large scale and bringing awareness to the inhumanity of it.

Fulton Builds Steamboat

456 **1807** In 1807, American inventor Robert Fulton demonstrated the first commercially successful steamboat, which ran from New York City to Albany on the Hudson River at almost five miles an hour, propelled by paddle wheels driven by a Watt steam engine. The *North River Steamboat,* also known as the *Clermont,* made its first upriver 150-mile trip in 32 hours compared with the four days it took on sailing vessels. Fulton immediately began commercial service between the two cities and was given exclusive right to steamboat operations on the river. He patented the boat's design and would soon begin the commercial operation of steamboats on other major U.S. rivers. Fulton's steamboats reduced shipping costs and revolutionized transportation in the U.S. and in Europe.

Chemistry Advanced

457 **1808** In 1808, French chemist and physicist Joseph-Louis Gay-Lussac published his law of combining volumes of gases, which would give scientists a much deeper understanding of organic chemistry. Gay-Lussac's law, as it became known, showed that when gases form compounds they combine in simple proportions: hydrogen and oxygen must be combined by volume in the ratio of two to one to make water. Carbon monoxide and oxygen must be combined by volume two to one to make carbon dioxide. Gay-Lussac was also keenly interested in Earth's magnetic intensity. He took to the air in a hydrogen-filled balloon to conduct studies and in 1804 ascended four miles above sea level to collect samples of the atmosphere. He determined that the air and

CONNECTIONS

Psychoactive Drugs
Chemical substances can alter mood, consciousness, and behavior

Psychoactive drugs affect the perception and function of the mind through both the neurotransmitters and receptor sites of the brain, which control how the brain communicates with the rest of the body and itself. The core groupings are opiates, neuroleptics, mood modifiers, stimulants and sedatives, antianxiety drugs, and psychedelics. Typically, however, only the opiates, neuroleptics, mood modifiers, and antianxiety drugs serve medicinal purpose. Every category has been abused recreationally, however.

Derived from the juice of the poppy seedpod, opium was first used as a painkiller in the 2nd century by the Greek physician Galen. In the early 16th century Paracelsus, by dissolving opium in alcohol, produced a stronger derivative known as laudanum. By the mid-19th century, opium was obtainable as alcohol. This continued until passage of England's Dangerous Drugs Act, which required a prescription to obtain opium, morphine, and drugs such as cocaine.

In the 1950s, Henri Laborit, attempting to mix a sedative for his patients, discovered the existence of neuroleptic drugs like chlorpromazine. Eventually this primitive form evolved into Largactil and Thorazine. Although referred to as antischizophrenics, neuroleptics merely treat one of the disease's contributing factors, reducing patient agitation.

Psychoactive drugs lessen many disorders.

The first attempts at treating depression included using opiates or alcohol, but the effects of these proved too short-lived to be useful. In 1956, Nathan Kline began to treat his depressed patients with iproniazid, originally developed for tuberculosis. Since then, many other antidepressants have been developed. The addictive nature of most antidepressants, however, prompted the eventual development of Fluoxetine, or Prozac, which was introduced in 1987. The widespread use of Fluoxetine, even among nondepressive patients, has inspired controversy.

As the name implies, antianxiety drugs relieve general feelings of anxiety and the inability to relax, as well as relieve the physical symptoms of such panic attacks or tension. In the late 1940s Frank Berger, in attempting to develop the next stage of penicillin, found drugs that relaxed mice, though the rodents were still fully conscious. The drugs were tested on monkeys and then those with anxiety or muscle spasms. The results showed that mephenesin could reduce anxiety without inducing sleep. Leo Sternbach, in the late 1950s, further developed the drug into what would become known as Librium, followed closely by its derivative, Valium, introduced in 1963. The two drugs relieved anxiety, and, although producing some drowsiness, were found to be much less deadly than previous antianxiety drugs.

magnetic force at high altitude were the same as they were on land. It was during this study of air analysis that he began forming his law of combining volumes of gases.

Appert Invents Canning

458 **1810** The French government had offered a prize of 12,000 francs to the person who could find a way to preserve food for its Napoleon-led army. French chef Nicolas-François Appert received the cash prize in 1810 after publishing a paper on his method of heat-sealing food in glass jars. In 1812, he opened the first commercial cannery, known as House of Appert—the culmination of a 14-year quest for a mass food preservation technique. While he did not understand the science behind why his system worked, Appert is considered the father of canning.

> ■ **FOOTNOTE** Peter Durand, an English contermporary of Appert, devised a way to seal food inside metal containers—another step toward today's canning. He coated iron containers with a thin film of tin to prevent rusting.

Priest Sparks Mexican War

459 **1810** On September 16, 1810, Father Miguel Hidalgo y Costilla, who had grown increasingly determined to improve his parishioners' economic well-being, rang the church bell and delivered his famous Grito de Dolores, which called for a revolution against the Spanish. His words moved the people, many of whom were Indians and mestizos, and took his call for independence further, lashing out against Mexico's social and economic issues and the upper class. Tens of thousands joined Hidalgo, establishing an army and capturing several cities near Mexico City. The movement went all the way to the capital, but Hidalgo hesitated against the Spanish army and withdrew. Hidalgo lost his momentum and soon his followers. Fleeing to the United States, Hidalgo was captured and executed in 1811. Hidalgo is called the Mexican father of independence, and now Mexico celebrates its independence day on September 16.

461 | *The Grimm brothers' stories influenced later works, like* The Water-Babies *by Charles Kingsley.*

Cuvier Proposes Catastrophism

460 **1812** In 1812, French zoologist Georges Cuvier published *Inquiry Into Fossil Remains,* putting forth the thought that over Earth's time there were great catastrophes that eliminated certain creatures while enabling the emergence of more modern creatures. This view was called catastrophism, the opposite of uniformitarianism, whereby biological, physical, and chemical changes were thought to occur with general uniformity over a great length of time. But Cuvier did not buy into evolutionary thinking; in fact, he believed that any change in a life-form would destroy its delicate balance. Nonetheless, Cuvier was dedicated to classifying fossils the same way scientists were classifying animals living on Earth. He is considered the founder of paleontology.

Brothers Publish Fairy Tales

461 **1812** In 1812, Jacob and Wilhelm Grimm, known as the brothers Grimm, published the first of a two-volume collection of 200 stories generally known as *Grimm's Fairy Tales.* The work, taken mostly from oral sources, has been translated into more than 160 languages and is considered the basis for much of the children's stories and films enjoyed today. Working in a library in Germany, Jacob Grimm found medieval manuscripts of stories that were disintegrating and on the verge of becoming lost. The brothers

---

FIRST PERSON

Napoleon Bonaparte

MEMOIR BY LOUIS DE BOURRIENNE, 1815

Nothing could be more gloomy than Bonaparte's entrance into Paris. He arrived at night in the midst of a thick fog. The streets were almost deserted, and a vague feeling of terror prevailed almost generally in thecapital.... The capital never presented so melancholy s picture as: during those three months. No one felt any confidence in Napoleon's second reign, and it was said, without any sort of reserve, that Fouche, while serving the cause of usurpation, would secretly betray it. The future was viewed with alarm, and the present with dissatisfaction. The sight of the federates who paraded the faubourgs and the boulevards, vociferating, "The Republic for ever!" and "Death to the Royalists!" their sanguinary songs, the revolutionary airs played in our theatres, all tended to produce a fearful torpor in the public mind, and the issue of the impending events was anxiously awaited.

One of the circumstances which, at the commencement of the Hundred Days, most contributed to open the eyes of those who were yet dazzled by the past glory of Napoleon, was the assurance with which he declared that the Empress and his son would be restored to him, though nothing warranted that announcement. It was evident that he could not count on any ally; and in spite of the prodigious activity with which a new army was raised those persons must have been blind indeed who could imagine the possibility of his triumphing over Europe, again armed to oppose him.

invited storytellers into their homes, taking notes and then editing and rewriting the narrative. The Grimms' aim was to accurately reproduce the storyteller's words, emphasizing the fantastic and retaining the beliefs of the time. Their work was the first scientific collection of folktales.

Fraunhofer Shows Spectrometer

462 **1814** In 1814, German optician and physicist Joseph von Fraunhofer began plotting the more than 500 dark lines he observed in the spectrum of sunlight while working with prisms—work that would greatly affect the field of chemistry in years to come. Fraunhofer, who was manufacturing quality prisms and lenses, mapped the lines and gave them letters from A to K. He was not the first to discover the lines (noted in 1802 by a British physicist), but he was the first to document them. Nothing was done with his findings or his identification system until almost 50 years later, when scientists began to discover that each chemical element produced unique spectral lines. Once a matter like ore was heated to incandescence, it could be determined if a new element was present in it. The classification of spectra

quickly became an essential research tool for physicists and chemists and led to the discovery of many new elements.

> ■ **FOOTNOTE** Although Fraunhofer's discovery was to lead to greater understanding of the elements of Earth, he was a telescope maker, and his immediate interest was the variety of spectra emitted by the moon and planets.

McAdam Builds Roads

463 **1815** In 1815, Scottish engineer John Loudon McAdam became surveyor-general of the Bristol roads and began a new technique of roadbuilding in Britain that represented a complete shift from earlier methods and is still used today. Frustrated with his country's road conditions, McAdam worked to solve road deterioration problems caused by poor drainage. His durable paving method, known as macadamization, allowed for construction of lasting roads linking cities and thus quickly spread to the rest of the world.

Napoleon Loses at Waterloo

464 **1815** In 1815, Napoleon Bonaparte was finally defeated at the Battle of Waterloo, just south of Brussels in Belgium. The allied nations of Austria,

464 | *Currier & Ives lithograph of Napoleon fighting the Battle of Waterloo*

Britain, Prussia, and Russia had removed Napoleon from power the previous year, exiling him to the island of Elba in the Mediterranean, while Louis XVIII took the French throne. When the new king was not immediately favored by the French people, Napoleon mobilized another army, causing Louis to flee, and in March 1815 reclaimed his title as France's emperor. The allied nations were determined to oust Napoleon, but their armies were spread across Europe. Napoleon used this to his advantage and acted quickly. On June 18, 1815, 72,000 French troops battled 68,000 British, Dutch, Belgian, and German troops and 45,000 Prussians, but Napoleon would not prevail. The French suffered 25,000 casualties. Napoleon's defeat at Waterloo marked the end of 23 years of warfare between France and the other European powers.

San Martín Liberates Argentina

465 **1816** Holding true to his roots, Argentinian-born Gen. José de San Martín returned to his home country after fighting for Spain against Napoleon Bonaparte's army to win Argentina's independence in 1816. San Martín's parents moved from Argentina to their homeland in Spain when San Martín was a young boy, where he was educated and trained as an army officer. San Martín said he switched allegiance to fight the Spanish for Argentina as a calling of his native land. After his success in Argentina, San Martín perhaps took on his greatest physical battle. He led an army over a nearly 15,000-foot pass in the Andes to surprise the Spanish in the Battle of Chacabuco near Santiago, Chile, where he was victorious. A second battle a few months later won Chile's independence. Focused, San Martín pressed on toward Lima, Peru, where he would lead another revolution. Peru was eventually liberated by Simón Bolívar. San Martín was known for his military tactics, patience, and strong determination. He remains one of Argentina's greatest heroes.

American Colonization Society

466 **1816** The American Colonization Society, primarily made up of influential white men and slave owners but also some abolitionists, was founded in 1816 in an effort to return freeborn African Americans and emancipated slaves back to Africa. Some believe the group's efforts provided African Americans the opportunity to return to Africa, while others saw them as a refusal to let free African Americans integrate into white society. The ACS established a settlement named Monrovia, and by 1867 more than 13,000 African-American emigrants were placed there. Monrovia eventually gained its independence as what is now Liberia.

> ■ **FOOTNOTE** American supporters of the colonization movement included Daniel Webster, Andrew Jackson, Francis Scott Key, and James Monroe—hence the name for the African center founded for the cause, Monrovia.

Frankenstein Published

467 **1818** English novelist Mary Wollstonecraft Shelley anonymously published *Frankenstein* in 1818 and then published a revised version under her name in 1831. Shelley, who was the daughter of Mary Wollstonecraft, a women's advocate and author of *A Vindication of the Rights of Woman*, wrote *Frankenstein* as a Gothic novel, but it is also considered a philosophical work. Thought to be one of the first science-fiction novels, it tells the story of a scientist who creates a human being, a monster, which leads to horrifying consequences. The novel has been a source of philosophical and psychological discussion for nearly 200 years and has been made into classic horror films.

Bolívar Enters New Granada

468 **1819** South American soldier and revolutionary leader Simon Bolívar, known as the Liberator, led an army of 2,500 men over the treacherous Andes and through floodplains otherwise considered impassable on his way to an attack on New Granada in 1819. Bolívar

467 | *Frankenstein has become an unmistakable part of popular culture, an image of horror and sympathy.*

Electromagnetism Found

469 **1820** Because of some similarities between electricity and magnetism, scientists began experimenting to see if they could find a connection between the two. In 1820, Danish physicist Hans Christian Ørsted stumbled upon one, and throughout the following decade his experiments would be expanded upon to form the electromagnetism theory. Electricity and magnetism both have opposites—electricity has positive and negative and magnetism has a north and south pole. And with both of those, the opposites attract one another, and the similars repel one another. Mathematically, with both of them the strength of the attraction or repulsion decreases with the square of the distance.

Hans Christian Ørsted demonstrates his findings on electromagnetism.

Ørsted discovered that the electric current in a wire would deflect a magnetized compass needle. When he reversed the direction of the current, the needle pointed in the opposite direction. Ørsted left his research there, but a series of other scientists, interested in his findings, continued on his work.

A major breakthrough came when English physicist Michael Faraday experimented with moving a magnet through a coil of copper wire, causing electric current to flow in the wire. At the time, most scientists believed that electricity was some sort of fluid that flowed through the wire. Faraday speculated that it was vibration or force that was transmitted between two bodies because of tensions that are created. He found that if he turned a copper wheel and had its rim pass the holes of a horseshoe magnet, a continuous electrical current would flow. This is the basic principle of the electric generator. The copper wheel would one day be powered by a steam engine, capable of producing a large amount of electricity.

surprised the Spanish and defeated them at the Battle of Boyacá. He liberated the territory of Columbia and was made president and dictator. This was a substantial feat for the man who was born in Caracas into a wealthy family, schooled in Europe and had his beginnings in the Venezuelan independence movement. In 1822 he secured Ecuador's independence, and he became dictator of Peru in 1824. Under General Antonio José de Sucre, Bolívar's men overtook the Spanish at Ayacucho in 1824. Upper Peru, now named Bolivia, became a state in 1825. This was effectively the end of Spain's power in South America. Bolívar wanted to unite the South American republics as a confederation, but after centuries of oppressive rule, the people were not ready. There were various revolts, and Bolívar exiled himself in 1830. In all, Bolívar brought independence to six present-day nations. He is considered one of South America's greatest generals.

Greeks Declare War

470 **1821** A rebellion by the Greeks within the Ottoman Empire began in 1821. The Ottomans had ruled most of Greece for several centuries, but with the strong momentum of the French Revolution, Greeks sought out their own independence. They took control of the Peloponnesus, but the Turks later invaded and captured key cities. There were leadership problems within the Greek rebellion, and Egyptian forces were brought in to aid the Turks. But other European nations backed the idea of Greece's independence, and Britain, France, and Russia used their naval might to destroy Egypt's fleet. An 1830 London conference between the Greeks and Turks finally declared Greece an independent monarchial state.

Linguist Reads Rosetta Stone

471 **1822** In 1822, French linguist Jean-François Champollion began publishing papers of his work on the Rosetta Stone—the first deciphering of Egyptian hieroglyphs. The broken black granite stone, found 35 miles northeast of Alexandria, Egypt, in 1799, was engraved with Greek writing dating to 196 B.C.E. and two forms of Egyptian script. It was believed the inscription, honoring Egypt's King Ptolemy V, was the same in all three languages. Using the stone and drawing from his previous research, Champollion discovered that some of the Egyptian signs were alphabetic, some syllabic, and some represented a whole idea or object. This groundbreaking work represented the beginning of modern Egyptology.

FOOTNOTE Champollion worked from copies of the actual stone slab, discovered in 1799 by Napoleon's soldiers in Egypt. When the British defeated the French, the stone traveled to London. It is still in the British Museum.

Macintosh's Waterproof Cloth

472 **1822** Scottish chemist Charles Macintosh developed a waterproof fabric that would result in the world's first mass-produced raincoat. Working at a gasworks, Macintosh experimented with naphtha, a volatile liquid hydrocarbon, and he found that it had chemical properties that made it capable of dissolving rubber. He had worked with textiles earlier in his career and decided that this new liquid rubber might be used with fabric. He sandwiched the liquid rubber between two layers of wool cloth. Macintosh's invention led to the development of rainwear and other industrial applications.

■ **FOOTNOTE** As Macintosh perfected his technology, details leaked out, and he had to sue a competitor for patent rights. He won the suit—and went down in history. His name is still used commercially for rubberized cloth.

Nerves Better Understood

473 **1822** French physiologist François Magendie published a groundbreaking paper in 1822 on spinal nerves, distinguishing their separate motor and sensory roots. In a time when many scientists thought all matters relating to biology were controlled by vital forces that could not be explained scientifically, Magendie believed in uncovering facts through experimentation. Often his experiments were on animals, which led to an antivivisectionist movement and a demand to protect animals from experiments. As a result of his research, he discovered that strychnine injections reach the spinal cord by the bloodstream, not the lymphatic system, as previously believed. His experiments using strychnine, morphine, codeine, and quinine greatly contributed to pharmacology.

Buckland Describes Dinosaur

474 **1824** In 1824, British geologist and clergyman William Buckland became the first person to scientifically describe a dinosaur based on unearthed fossils in England (the term "dinosaur" would not be used for almost two decades). The *Megalosaurus*, or "great lizard," that Buckland found consisted mostly of a lower jawbone with some teeth, vertebrae, a hip, and hind limb. It would have been impossible for him to know what the creature would have looked like, except that it was big. Buckland hypothesized it

was an extinct lizard. Fossilized dinosaur bones were undoubtedly found throughout the ages, but it was not until the first half of the 19th century that they were scientifically noted. Englishman Richard Owen coined the term Dinosauria in 1842 after noting that the *Megalosaurus* and two other fossil finds were not lizards but a suborder of "saurian reptiles." From that point the quest began—and is still under way—to uncover, name, and discover more about these creatures that lived several hundred million years ago.

Byron Dies

475 **1824** Lord Byron, a popular poet and the personification of the English Romantic movement, died in 1824 after leading a colorful life of fame, fortune, travel, love affairs, and aid to the Greeks in their fight for independence against the Ottoman Empire. He inherited his title and fortune as a boy from an uncle and became well known as a writer after publishing his poetic travelogue, *Childe Harold's Pilgrimage*. His best known work is the unfinished satirical poem *Don Juan*.

475 | *Lord Byron, dressed in Albanian garb, shared his colorful life through his writing.*

477 | *Tsar Nicholas on horseback*

While he was writing that poem, he became interested in the Greek independence movement, and he had gone to Greece to support that cause when he grew ill and died, on the battlefield of Missolonghi. Byron's poetry had a wide range, but he consistently wrote about the need for people to have the freedom to choose their own life course.

■ **FOOTNOTE** As much as Byron traveled, he always kept a menagerie. Once his friend, the poet Percy Bysshe Shelley, reported finding "five peacocks, two guinea hens, and an Egyptian crane" on the stairs in his home in Italy.

Beethoven's Symphony No. 9

476 **1824** Ludwig van Beethoven's Ninth Symphony, also called the *Choral* Symphony, was first performed in 1824 and greeted with tremendous applause, although Beethoven, who was sitting in the audience, did not immediately respond because by this time in his life he was completely deaf. It is said that one of the soloist singers had to point out the audience's response, prompting him to bow. This was the last symphony Beethoven composed. What set it apart from his others was the use of chorus and solo vocalists in the finale. For the words, Beethoven chose part of Friedrich Schiller's poem "Ode to Joy," admiring its themes of freedom and brotherhood. The symphony would influence the great composers of the next era and continues to be appreciated today. It was performed by Leonard Bernstein during the fall of the Berlin Wall (with the words changed to "Ode to Freedom"), and it is the melody of the European Union anthem.

■ **FOOTNOTE** Beethoven, who was several measures off and still conducting at the symphony's end, received five ovations, two more than the imperial couple got on their entrance to the concert hall.

Decembrist Revolt in Russia

477 **1825** A group of 3,000 Russian officers and soldiers wanting a liberal constitution refused to swear their allegiance to their new tsar, Nicholas, and in December 1825 staged a revolt in the Senate Square in St. Petersburg. Their rebellion was easily suppressed by Nicholas and 5 people were executed, 31 sent to prison, and hundreds exiled to Siberia. The revolt had lasting effects on how Nicholas would rule and was the beginning of a revolutionary movement that divided the liberals and the government.

The Russian officers who had been at war during the Napoleonic Wars and in other parts of Europe came back with new ideas on human rights, opposed serfdom, and were interested in democracy. There were demands for a representative government by the upper class and officers and talk of overthrowing the government until Russia's Alexander I died in 1825. Alexander's brother Constantine was next in line, and the army swore allegiance to him, but he gave up his right to the throne. Nicholas, the younger brother of Alexander and Constantine, was named tsar, but the army largely still supported Constantine.

The revolt, while short and unsuccessful, was taken seriously by Nicholas. He would go on to form his Third Section, a secret police of spies and informants. The people were expected to abide by the Orthodox Church, and other religions were suppressed. Literature critical of Russia was censored. Russians lived under a harsh rule where they were expected to be loyal to Nicholas. The exiled

Lord Byron

THE DEATH OF BYRON, THOMAS MOORE, 1835

Prince Mavrocordato ... on the evening of the 19th issued this melancholy proclamation:—

The present day of festivity and rejoicing has become one of sorrow and of mourning. The Lord Noel Byron departed this life at six o'clock in the afternoon, after an illness of ten days; his death being caused by an inflammatory fever. Such was the effect of his Lordship's illness on the public mind, that all classes had forgotten their usual recreations of Easter, even before the afflicting event was apprehended.

The loss of this illustrious individual is undoubtedly to be deplored by all Greece; but it must be more especially a subject of lamentation at Missolonghi, where his generosity has been so conspicuously displayed, and of which he had even become a citizen, with the further determination of participating in all the dangers of the war.

Every body is acquainted with the beneficent acts of his Lordship, and none can cease to hail his name as that of a real benefactor.

Until, therefore, the final determination of the National Government be known, and by virtue of the powers with which it has been pleased to invest me, I hereby decree,—

1st, To-morrow morning, at daylight, thirty seven minute guns will be fired from the Grand Battery, being the number which corresponds with the age of the ... deceased.

2d, All the public offices, even the tribunals, are to remain closed for three successive days.

3d, All the shops, except those in which provisions or medicines are sold, will also be shut; and it is strictly enjoined that every species of public amusement, and other demonstrations of festivity at Easter, shall be suspended.

4th, A general mourning will be observed for twenty-one days.

5th, Prayers and a funeral service are to be offered up in all the churches.

(Signed) A. MAVROCORDATO.

GEORGE PRAIDIS, Secretary.

Given at Missolonghi, this 19th day of April, 1824.

1700-1850 | Revolutionary Era

revolutionaries were considered martyrs by the rebels who would later fight for a more liberal Russia.

First Photograph

478 **1826** Joseph-Nicéphore Niépce, a French inventor, created the first permanent photograph in 1826. Niépce was using a technique that required an 8- to 20-hour exposure time, which meant that photographs could be taken only of inanimate objects. French artist Louis-Jacques-Mandé Daguerre invented the first practical form of photography in 1839.

FOOTNOTE The world's first photograph—on display at the University of Texas at Austin—pictures a view out Niépce's window in Burgundy, France, with neighboring walls and rooftops and distant trees and pastures.

Water Turbine Built

479 **1827** In 1827, French engineer Benoît Fourneyron invented the water turbine, and its immediate success led it to overtake the old-fashioned waterwheel and within a few years the power industry in the United States and Europe. Fourneyron's teacher, Claude Burdin, coined the term "turbine" and conceptualized that water would run down a hub and out to the blades causing the wheel to whirl. Previous waterwheels hit the blades on the outside edge of the wheel. The new turbine would spin faster and deliver more power. Fourneyron's first turbine was a 6-horsepower unit, but within five years he would create one with 50 horsepower. In 1895, Fourneyron's turbines were installed at Niagara Falls to turn generators for electrical power. He considered that a turbine could be powered by a steam engine, but he lacked the materials for proper experimentation, and the steam-driven turbine would not be invented for another 50 years.

Atomic Weights Published

480 **1828** Jöns Jakob Berzelius, a Swedish chemist, determined that inorganic substances are made up of different elements in constant proportions by weight. Using this law of constant proportions, Berzelius in 1828 published a table of the relative atomic weights of all the known elements. He organized the table using letters from the alphabet as the elements, and numbers as the proportions. His ideas underlie the periodic table of elements used today. Berzelius also discovered the elements cerium, selenium, and

---

CONNECTIONS

Photography
Images from life—daguerreotype to Kodak

When French painter Louis Daguerre patented a technique in 1839 for capturing an exact image from the real world on paper, he gave the world a new technology. But his daguerreotype process had limits—the positive images could not be reproduced, thus they could not be printed in books or magazines. Subsequent pioneers would open up the field initiated by Daguerre and give us not only novel technology but also a new art form.

The year following Daguerre's patent, British inventor William H. Fox Talbot patented a process for producing negative images. These calotypes (or talbotypes) were made by exposing light-sensitive silver iodide paper in the camera, and then developing it in a solution of silver titrate and gallic acid and fixing it (making it permanent) with sodium thiosulfate. Talbot could then take the resulting ghostly negative and print it multiple times on a silver chloride paper to create positive pictures. His friend astronomer Sir John Herschel dubbed the new technique "photography."

Refinements in the 1840s and 1850s advanced photography well beyond the pioneer stage. Improved lenses made portraits more lifelike by gathering more light and thus reducing exposure time to a few minutes; landscape pictures had sharper focus. Then in 1851 a new developing technique was invented by British sculptor F. Scott Archer

Daguerreotype of unnamed stonecutter

that dramatically reduced exposure time and sharpened photographic detail. His wet-collodion process involved coating a glass plate with silver salts and a sticky material known as collodion. The wet plate was exposed for only a few seconds, then it was immediately developed.

The wet-collodion process yielded some of the world's most treasured photographs, including those of British journalist Roger Fenton from the Crimean War (1853-56) and of American journalist Matthew Brady from the American Civil War (1861-65). The inconvenience of the process was overcome by the introduction in 1871 of the dry-plate method, in which an emulsion of gelatin substituted for collodion—the gelatin dried on the plate without hurting the silver salts.

The next major advance put cameras in the hands of the masses. The gelatin emulsion allowed prints to be made by projection. So instead of the picture having to be the same size as the negative, the picture could be much larger. Now negatives, and thus cameras, could be much smaller. In 1888 dry-plate manufacturer George Eastman began marketing a small, cheap, lightweight device called the Kodak box camera. Amateurs and hobbyists could now record their memories. Meanwhile, the demands of serious photographers continued to push the new field of photography both technically and artistically.

481 | *Geological evolution seen in the splendor of Havasu Falls at Grand Canyon National Park*

thorium and isolated silicon and titanium. Berzelius is considered one of the founders of modern chemistry.

> ■**FOOTNOTE** Berzelius's early interest was in galvanism, or the presence of electricity in living things. For his medical degree, he wrote a thesis on the use of electric shock in the treatment of human diseases.

Geological Evolution

481 **1830** British geologist Charles Lyell continued on the work of James Hutton in his textbook *Principles of Geology*, establishing the theory of uniformitarianism—that Earth is shaped by a gradual, yet constant, geological process over millions of years. The opposing view of the time was catastrophism—the idea that Earth is shaped by sudden, violent supernatural events. By studying an ordinary process like the erosion of land from rivers, Lyell believed that these sorts of changes are uniform through time, and over the long term is what shaped Earth. He believed valleys were created by slow erosion from water and wind, not huge floods. He recognized that the process worked on a geologic time line, and concluded that Earth must be extremely old. His work, read by Charles Darwin, helped influence the study of evolutionary biology and became the basis of modern geology.

French Revolt Against King

482 **1830** The July Revolution of 1830 was a revolt against King Charles X of France and would bring Louis-Philippe, a bourgeois, to the throne. King Charles opposed the liberals, who had just won the majority in the recent legislature elections, and imposed his July Ordinances, which censored the press. He received about three-quarters of the electoral votes, and insisted on a new vote for the legislature positions. Workers, including middle-class professionals, revolted. Three days of uncontrolled fighting ensued, which forced King Charles to flee. Some of the insurrectionists wanted to form a republic, but Louis-Philippe, who was seen as more middle class than aristocratic, was named king. Workers were still disgruntled, but a more liberal constitution was instituted. The July Revolution was the start of a movement throughout Europe for social revolution. Belgium would become independent from the Netherlands in 1831, and Greece, which had already been fighting for independence from the Ottoman Empire, became a sovereign state in 1832.

> ■**FOOTNOTE** The 1830 Revolution occurred in three days—July 27 through July 29—by which date the red flags of the revolutionaries flew atop many buildings in Paris, including the Hôtel de Ville, or City Hall, and the Louvre.

Book of Mormon Published

483 **1830** The Book of Mormon, accepted as holy scripture alongside the Bible in the Church of Jesus Christ of Latter-day Saints and other Mormon churches, marked the beginning of the Mormon religion when it was published in 1830. The founder of the religion, Joseph Smith, an American, said an angel named Moroni told him where to find buried gold plates that were engraved with God's revelation. Smith translated the plates and published them as the Book of Mormon. He and his followers believed in the second coming of Christ followed by 1,000 years of peace ruled by Jesus and that through spiritual practice, a person could evolve into a god. They moved from New York, to Ohio, to Missouri, to eventually Illinois, where Smith was killed in 1844 by a mob because of his religious beliefs. In 1846, under new leader Brigham Young, a group of Mormons began a 1,100-mile migration to Utah and established what is now Salt Lake City in order to practice their religion without persecution. The Church of Jesus Christ of Latter-day Saints now has nearly ten million members worldwide.

First Intercity Steam Railway

484 **1830** The world's first intercity passenger railway operated by a steam engine opened between Liverpool and Manchester in Britain. The 30-mile

468 More Details on Simon Bolívar

From the grand statue commemorating him at the Sixth Avenue entrance to New York City's Central Park to the hundreds of memorials and murals scattered throughout his native Venezuela, Simon Bolívar is known and remembered throughout the Americas as an inspiring leader and revolutionary. His military efforts liberated much of South America from Spanish rule and spawned nearly a century of dramatic change, change that would take the continent through unstable governments and totalitarian rule until, finally, democracy began to emerge, most notably in Bolívar's home country. Here, in a Caracas slum, a large mural of Bolívar showcases the importance of his legacy to the Venezuelan people. An overwhelming majority of residents in this district—called "23 enero" in honor of the day in 1958 that dictator Marcos Pérez Jiménez was ousted—supported Hugo Chávez for president in 1999; the social movement Chávez began is referred to as the Bolivarian Revolution.

> "Neither Washington nor Bolívar was destined to have children ... so ... we ... might call ouselves their children."
> —**Venezuelan ambassador**

But Bolívar's last years saw the beginnings of fighting and strife, and his great dream of creating a united South America was lost as the people he helped to liberate turned against him. He resigned as president in the spring of 1830 and prepared for exile, sending crates of his belongings ahead to Europe, but he died of tuberculosis in Santa Marta, Colombia, before he could set sail. His last days are fictionalized in a 1989 novel by Gabriel García Márquez, *The General in his Labyrinth,* which imagines the once esteemed general as a weak and pitiful man now despised by his people. And though Bolívar's legacy is certainly fraught with controversy, his name today is on the boulevards and piazzas and government buildings of South America, and he has inspired revolutionaries throughout the world. While commemorating a statue of U.S. President George Washington in Caracas in 1920, a Venezuelan ambassador put it this way: "Neither Washington nor Bolívar was destined to have children of his own, so that we Americans might call ourselves their children."

A mural of Simon Bolívar looks out over a Venezualan district that supported Hugo Chávez—leader of the "Bolivarian Revolution"—for president.

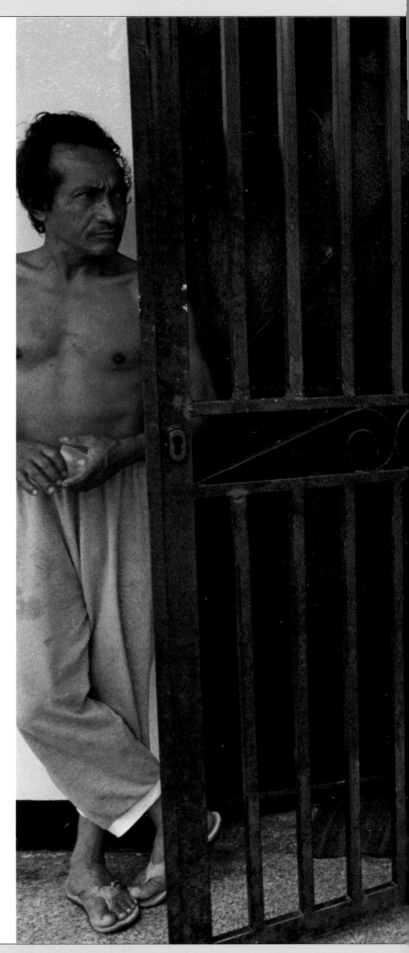

line was first powered by the *Rocket,* a steam locomotive designed by English engineers George Stephenson and his son Robert, which could reach speeds of up to 36 miles an hour and would become the model for later locomotives. The Liverpool and Manchester Railway was immediately deemed a success, and within 40 years Britain would have 13,500 miles of railways. This marked the beginning of the railway era, in which railways were built throughout the world, allowing people and goods to move quickly and efficiently. Railways were considered an impetus to the industrial revolution, and passenger railways, like the Liverpool-Manchester line, dominated transportation for nearly a century.

First U.S. Steam Engine

485 **1830** Dubbed *Tom Thumb,* America's first steam locomotive pulled out from Baltimore and traveled 13 miles to Ellicott's Mills. Clocked at 18 miles an hour, the train was the first steam locomotive to travel the rails of the United States. On its return trip, *Tom Thumb* raced a horse—and lost. But the miniature locomotive signaled the first use of the growing Baltimore and Ohio line, which connected the city of Baltimore with Ohio and the growing West.

FOOTNOTE *Tom Thumb* was designed by Peter Cooper, who also invented the gelatin soon commercialized as Jell-O. In 1859 Cooper founded a school "for the advancement of science and art": New York City's Cooper Union.

Turner Leads Rebellion

486 **1831** In 1831, Nat Turner, who was born into slavery in Virginia, led his famous slave revolt. Turner, whose parents and grandparents encouraged him to resist slavery, was a deeply religious preacher, said to have had visions. He believed it was his calling to free slaves from bondage and take over the armory in Jerusalem, Virginia. Turner first killed his master and his family and then led a group of some 70 men on a two-day march, killing more than 50 whites on their way to Jerusalem. A Virginia militia of 3,000 men captured and hanged many of the insurrectionists. Turner was on the run for six weeks but was eventually captured, tried, and then hanged. Some 100 slaves uninvolved with the march were murdered by angry mobs. As a result of the slave rebellion, the argument that slaves were content to be servants could no longer be used. At first the Virginia state legislature considered abolishing slavery, but the issue was defeated in a close vote. Word of Turner's slave rebellion spread throughout the South, igniting fear that it would happen again. As a result, legislation was drafted against free blacks and slaves, restricting their education, movement, and assembly. After Turner was executed, his lawyer, Thomas R. Gray, published *The Confessions of Nat Turner,* a pamphlet that was based on Gray's conversations with Turner before he went to trial.

FOOTNOTE Nat Turner said he heard voices and saw visions that encouraged him to rebel. When a full solar eclipse occurred in February 1831, he took it as a sign to mount his insurrection, which occurred six months later.

McCormick Invents Reaper

487 **1831** In 1831, American Cyrus McCormick invented his first mechanical grain-reaping machine, allowing farmers to harvest far more grain with less labor. The previous harvesting method was handheld scythes wielded by large numbers of laborers, who were only able to work up to three acres a day. By reducing the number of laborers and increasing the speed of the reaping process, McCormick's machine drastically increased profits. Another key component to McCormick's success was his business skills: He traveled door to door to sell his machine and offered money-back guarantees, fixed prices, and interchangeable replacement parts. The mechanical reaper caught the world's attention at the Great Exhibition of 1851 in London, and would soon be used by European farmers. McCormick was elected to the French Academy of Sciences for "having done more for agriculture than any other living man."

487 | *A 20th-century lithograph depicts Cyrus McCormick (foreground) and his reaping machine.*

Darwin Makes Voyage

488 **1831** Charles Darwin embarked on a five-year voyage aboard the H.M.S. *Beagle* to South America and the Pacific, collecting plants, animals, and fossils and making observations that would lead to his theory of evolution by natural selection. Darwin, an English naturalist, spent most of his time off-ship. During his time on the Galápagos Islands, he noted that the largest islands were far enough apart from each other to have developed their own unique flora and fauna. For instance, he noticed that finches on the different islands had developed different beaks adapted to the food available. This observation and others from the voyage led to his breakthrough theory of natural selection: Species that were better adapted to their environments would survive and produce stronger offspring. Species that weren't as adept had less success at survival. Darwin came home with his diary filled with 800 pages of writing and began to reflect on his five years of

An 1890 illustration of H.M.S. Beagle entering the Strait of Magellan, Mount Sarmiento in the background

research, which eventually led to his formation of the radical theory that species—including humans—were not immutable. Instead of being created in God's image, humans had evolved from ancient ancestors, just like other forms of life.

In 1839, Darwin published the results of his research during the voyage: *Journal of Researches into the Geology and Natural History of the Various Countries Visited by HMS Beagle, 1832-1836.*

Penny Newspaper Hits Stands

489 **1833** In 1833, advances in printing and papermaking engendered the penny press—cheap, politically independent newspapers that sold for a penny rather than six cents and made news accessible to everyday people. The *New York Sun,* founded by publisher Benjamin Day, is credited as having been the first successful penny paper, but many more soon followed, creating competition for "scoops." Stories focused on crime and human interest, unlike previous newspapers, which had primarily served as mouthpieces for political parties. The immediate success of the penny press caused newspaper circulation numbers to skyrocket. Before the *Sun,* the most popular New York paper sold about 4,500 copies daily. By 1835, New Yorkers were buying 15,000 copies of the *Sun* every day.

Icemaker Invented

490 **1834** In 1834, Jacob Perkins, an American inventor working in London, patented the first practical vapor-compression refrigeration system used for icemaking. His machine, which used the evaporation of sulfuric ether, had the same basic components that are found in refrigerators today: a compressor, a condenser, an expansion valve, and an evaporator. The natural-ice industry was already rooted in the United States, so Perkins's machine did not generate much interest, but 14 years later an improved design was introduced by an American doctor, John Gorrie, who developed a machine that made ice and provided cool air to his Florida hospital. Ice was hard to come by in the South, but Gorrie believed cool air would cure his patients, who were suffering from a malaria pandemic. He put all his efforts into

making his machine, and although it had flaws, Gorrie's and Perkins's pioneering refrigeration efforts paved the way for modern ice and refrigeration.

> ■ **FOOTNOTE** Jacob Perkins also invented a way to plate buckles, a machine that cut nails and made nail heads in one action, tools to measure water depth and vessel speed through water, and steel engraving plates for banknotes.

Analytical Engine Computes

491 **1834** In 1834, English mathematician Charles Babbage envisioned an "analytical engine"—a forerunner to the modern electronic computer. The device was to perform any mathematical function, based on programming from punch cards (similar to those of the Jacquard loom), and print the answer on paper. However, Babbage's governmental financial support to develop his machine—which, if built, would have been the size of a locomotive—was withdrawn in 1842. Even if Babbage had been granted the funds for his idea, modern computing was years away: Electronic switches had not been invented. The world would just have to wait for Babbage's idea to reach fruition.

Braille Writes for Blind

492 **1834** In 1834, Louis Braille perfected a code of raised dots on paper, making it possible for the blind to be able to read and write. The code, which is named after him, is read by a person lightly running his fingers over the embossed dots. Braille became blind at the age of three as a result of an accident and attended a school for blind children in Paris. While there he learned of a military writing system using a system of 12 raised dots that allowed soldiers to communicate quietly and at night. Braille simplified the system by arranging six dots in two columns of three. Sixty-three different patterns represent letters, numbers, and punctuation and can be written by hand or with a machine. The system has been adopted around the world and is credited as bringing literacy to the blind.

Coriolis Explains Weather

493 **1835** Gustave-Gaspard Coriolis first published his theories on the Coriolis force in 1835, providing a better understanding of Earth's winds and ocean currents. Earth's rotation has an effect on the path of anything traveling across its surface—from water, to wind, to missiles. A missile flies straight, but when watched from the rotating Earth, it appears to curve. The force also applies to weather and oceanography. Earth rotates under the air and ocean's currents, causing them to follow a curved path. In the Northern Hemisphere, the wind and currents turn to the right of their direction of motion; and in the Southern Hemisphere, they turn to the left. Coriolis articulated principles of physics that demonstrate that this deflection is caused by the motion of the object (such as the water or air), the motion of Earth rotating, and latitude.

> ■ **FOOTNOTE** While Coriolis's name is most often associated with meteorology, his work was in mechanics. His most important paper developed equations to describe the relative motion in rotating systems like waterwheels.

Labor Union Organized

494 **1836** The London Workingmen's Association was organized by radical William Lovett and others in 1836, creating an independent labor organization. Its core group was working-class men frustrated with the injustices that came with the industrial revolution in Britain. Out of this came a movement, called Chartism, named after the People's Charter, which was a bill drafted in 1838 demanding voting rights for all men and parliamentary reform. Slow economic times, high unemployment, and long factory hours were what stirred the working class to take action. An 1839 convention led to riots, and eventually many of the Chartist leaders were arrested. When the economy improved, the movement's momentum slowed, but most of the points in the original bill were eventually addressed. The Chartist movement showed that the working class could be organized on a massive scale, as would be proved in the following few decades.

Victoria Crowned

495 **1837** In 1837, Victoria became Queen of the United Kingdom of Great Britain and Ireland. She remained in power for 64 years, into the first year of the

---

CONNECTIONS

Native American Resettlement
How the West was won

Between the mid– and late 1800s, several hundred thousand American Indians were displaced or profoundly affected by massive waves of westward settlement. Indians east of the Mississippi were forced west, while those in the West were confined to ever smaller reservations. Some Indians, bowing to the inevitable, went peacefully, while others, mostly in the West, fought back for as long as they could.

Eastern Indians were the first to feel the white tide. During the 1830s and 1840s approximately 100,000 Cherokees, Choctaws, Creeks, Chickasaws, and Seminoles were forced from their homelands to the new "Indian Territory" beyond the Mississippi. President Andrew Jackson's Indian Removal Act of 1830 ultimately added 100 million acres of land to the public domain. But the Cherokee removal, the Trail of Tears, was an inglorious chapter in American history—some 4,000 Cherokees died from starvation and exposure.

Action against the western Indians took place mainly from the 1860s to the end of the century. Sioux rebellions against white settlement in Minnesota in 1862 and Wyoming in 1866 led Congress to enact a new Indian policy by the end of the decade. Indians were to stay in one of two large reservations north or south of the new transcontinental railroad corridor. But with the railroad came a wide market for the 35 million buffalo that roamed the Plains. Indians who made a living hunting buffalo had to range farther, well beyond their reservations. The spread of smallpox and other infectious diseases killed far more Indians than did armed conflicts. Alcoholism further weakened a dying way of life and made the Indians dependent upon the white man.

The Sioux annihilation of George Armstrong Custer and his 211 cavalrymen at Little Bighorn, Montana, in June 1876 shocked the nation during its centennial celebrations, but the flow of settlers and gold seekers was hardly checked. The Army continued to battle the Indians, herding them into smaller territories. Old treaties were broken and new ones made, often with Indians who had no authority to speak for the tribe. A massacre of more than 300 Sioux men, women, and children at Wounded Knee, South Dakota, in 1890 marked the end of real Indian resistance.

Forced to adapt to the dominant culture, Indians still managed to keep many of their languages and traditions alive. Today some 2.5 million live in the U.S.—the Cherokee, Navajo, and Sioux being the most populous tribes. About a third live on reservations or traditional tribal lands. More than 500,000 Indians live in Canada, and 45 million in Latin America.

Mandan and Arikara delegation to Washington, 1874

20th century. During her reign, called the Victorian age, Britain was involved in the Opium War in China; the Crimean War in Russia; and the Boer War in South Africa. The Victorian age was also the time when the British Empire saw great expansion, including Australia, Canada, India, New Zealand, large parts of Africa, and other regions around the globe. But it was the queen's prime ministers who were responsible for much of Britain's success, and Victoria realized that she needed to step back from power and take a more symbolic role as ruler. This was a change in the definition of the role of the queen (or king), but also allowed the British monarchy to remain in place to the present day.

■**FOOTNOTE** Victoria was 18 years old when she became queen, and her reign lasted until her death in 1901 at the age of 81. Her 64-year reign is the longest in British history, celebrated with both a golden and a diamond jubilee.

Deere Designs Plow

496 **1837** In 1837, John Deere (a name that now conjures up images of green-and-yellow tractors) began designing plows that would perform well in the dense prairie soil of the Midwest. These new plows provided vast improvements over the previous East Coast-made wood and iron plows used in his native Vermont. Deere, trained as a blacksmith but possessed of an inventor's mind, had discovered when moving from Vermont to Illinois, that his and the other homesteaders' cast-irons plows, which were productive with the sandy soils in New England, were useless on rich prairie soil. Plows had to be scraped clean of dirt constantly, making the work laborious and frustrating. In 1838, Deere developed a steel plow, using a broken saw blade that was self-scouring and easily cut through the soil. He named it the Grand Detour Plow. He immediately began manufacturing his plows and then taking them into the country to sell to farmers. In 1849 he and his business partners had a workforce that built more than 2,000 plows. By 1857, this number had risen to 10,000 plows per year.

495 | *Queen Victoria sits on her throne in royal pomp.*

His company would become a leader in making farm equipment, and his plow played a large role in opening up agricultural land in the western states.

Cherokee Travel Trail of Tears

497 **1838** In 1838, after gold was discovered on their tribal lands in the southeastern United States, the Cherokee Indians were forced to embark on the Trail of Tears, a thousand-mile journey to Indian Territory, in what is now known as Oklahoma. A minority of Cherokee had earlier agreed to the move and signed a treaty, but most did not want to leave their land and were forced out by U.S. Army soldiers. Some 16,000 Cherokee were gathered in camps while their homes were destroyed. The journey, which took place in fall and winter, was difficult, and about 4,000 died from inadequate food and shelter. About 1,000 Cherokee managed to escape the Army and established the Eastern Band of the

Cherokee in the Great Smoky Mountains. Today's Cherokee Nation Indians of Oklahoma are considered the descendants of the Cherokee that moved west.

> ■ **FOOTNOTE** In the years just before their relocation west, leaders among the Cherokee had developed a written language, called Talking Leaves, and had begun to publish a newspaper, called the *Cherokee Phoenix.*

Antarctica Is a Continent

498 **1838** In 1838, American naval officer Charles Wilkes set off on a four-year voyage to Antarctica. Others had previously sighted and charted parts of Antarctica, but because of its forbidding climate and icy waters it was difficult to reach, and explorers were unsure if it was a continent or a block of ice. In 1840, Wilkes sailed more than 1,500 miles along the coast. Exploration of the continent by land, air, and sea continued into the next century, and in the 1950s many countries built bases on Antarctica in order to conduct scientific research. Although multiple countries have claimed sovereign rights to the continent, the Antarctic Treaty of 1961 put all territorial claims on hold so no one country owns Antarctica, but all may access it.

Goodyear Invents Vulcanization

499 **1839** In 1839, Charles Goodyear invented the vulcanization process, which would eventually give the world countless usable rubber products ranging from vehicle tires to inflatable life rafts. Inventions using rubber, a chemical derived from a South American tree, had previously been limited by its temperature sensitivity. Goodyear, an American inventor, solved the problem one day by accidentally dropping a combination of rubber and sulfur onto a hot stove. The heated rubber was not sticky, and later, when chilled, it was not brittle. Weatherproof rubber was born. Vulcanization became wildly successful, and though he patented it in 1844, Goodyear struggled with patent infringements and died a debtor.

Proudhon Proposes Anarchy

500 **1840** In 1840, French socialist Pierre-Joseph Proudhon published *What Is Property?* which stated that "Property is theft!" Anarchism was an ancient term, but Proudhon helped make it a mass movement in the 19th century. Growing up in poverty, Proudhon believed in individual dignity and denounced ownership of property and exploitation of labor

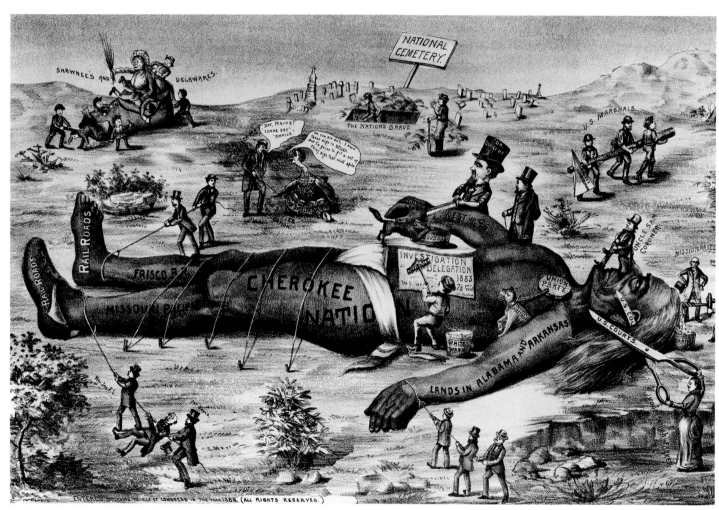

497 | *A caricature of the drawing and quartering of the Cherokee Nation*

498 | *Capt. Charles Wilkes*

while criticizing communism for denying human independence. His later writings were attacked by German political theorist Karl Marx, creating a split between anarchists and Marxists.

■ **FOOTNOTE** Proudhon's argument with Marx, as well as with Mikhail Bakunin, a Russian thinker of the time, arose from his beliefs in individual workers over a workers' collective and the possibility of peaceful social change.

First Adhesive Stamp

501 **1840** In 1840, the first adhesive stamp—called Penny Black and featuring a profile of young Queen Victoria—was issued in England, revolutionizing mail service around the world. Before Rowland Hill's suggestion of creating a prepaid postage stamp, postal charges were based on the weight of the letter and the distance it traveled. Postage was usually collected from the recipient upon delivery, and if that person refused the letter, it was returned unpaid. This meant that the post office had to assume the cost of the two-way trip. Hill suggested senders purchase a one-penny stamp for a half-ounce letter for delivery anywhere in Britain. He believed this lower rate would increase mail volume, thus increasing postal revenues. He was right. The system was immediately adopted by nations around the world as the best way to send mail.

New Zealand Becomes British

502 **1840** The implementation of the Treaty of Waitangi on February 6, 1840, made New Zealand a British colony and the native Maori subjects of Queen Victoria. The British promised that the Maori could maintain ownership of their land, fisheries, and forests as long as they wished, but difficulties arose. Debate over specific wording and provisions of the treaty led to large-scale conflict. The treaty is not considered part of New Zealand's domestic law, although the date of the signing is celebrated as a national holiday.

Mill Publishes *System*

503 **1843** In 1843, British writer, economist, and philosopher John Stuart Mill wrote *A System of Logic,* where he outlines five methods of experimental reasoning. Educated entirely by his father, James Mill, who instilled the ideas of social and political theorist Jeremy Bentham, the younger Mill believed in a world of equality and individual freedom, where people should be allowed to choose their own direction. He thought that individual determination was the path to personal happiness and that a fulfilled populace would contribute to the greater good of society. He therefore believed that one of the missions of public policy should be to promote the general happiness of people. In 1869, he wrote *The Subjection of Women,* where he discussed oppressive social patterns relative to women and made an analogy comparing marriage to slavery. Mill was the first man to speak in Parliament on behalf of women's rights. He was also a strong advocate for labor unions and farm cooperatives. He is considered one the most important British thinkers of the 19th century, and his work and writings are still of keen interest today.

McNaughton Found Insane

504 **1843** When Daniel McNaughton shot and killed the British prime minister's secretary, believing he was assassinating the prime minister himself, he became the first man in English law to be

FIRST PERSON

John G. Burnett

THE TRAIL OF TEARS, 1890

The removal of Cherokee Indians from their life long homes in the year of 1838 found me a young man in the prime of life and a private soldier in the American Army. Being acquainted with many of the Indians and able to fluently speak their language, I was sent as interpreter into the Smoky Mountain Country in May, 1838, and witnessed the execution of the most brutal order in the History of American Warfare. I saw the helpless Cherokees arrested and dragged from their homes, and driven at the bayonet point into the stockades. And in the chill of a drizzling rain on an October morning I saw them loaded like cattle or sheep into six hundred and forty-five wagons and started toward the west.

One can never forget the sadness and solemnity of that morning. Chief John Ross led in prayer and when the bugle sounded and the wagons started rolling many of the children rose to their feet and waved their little hands good-bye to their mountain homes, knowing they were leaving them forever. Many of these helpless people did not have blankets, and many of them had been driven from home barefooted.

On the morning of November the 17th we encountered a terrific sleet and snowstorm with freezing temperatures and from that day until we reached the end of the fateful journey on March the 26th, 1839, the sufferings of the Cherokees were awful. The trail of the exiles was a trail of death. They had to sleep in the wagons and on the ground without fire. And I have known as many as twenty-two of them to die in one night of pneumonia due to ill treatment, cold, and exposure. Among this number was the beautiful Christian wife of Chief John Ross. This noble-hearted woman died a martyr to childhood, giving her only blanket for the protection of a sick child. She rode thinly clad through a blinding sleet and snowstorm, developed pneumonia, and died in the still hours of a bleak winter night, with her head resting on Lieutenant Gregg's saddle blanket.

1700-1850 | Revolutionary Era

found not guilty by reason of insanity. His case became a precedent, the "McNaughton rule," holding that if medical experts find a criminal not to have known the difference between right and wrong, he can be deemed not guilty by reason of insanity and excused from the harshest punishment for the crime.

Railroads Now Big Business

505 **1844** In the 1840s, the United States' rapidly expanding railroad industry soon required professional mangers. In contrast to some parts of Europe, where dense railway networks could be state run or investor run, the expansive distances in the U.S. made for high operating, building, and maintenance costs. Large railroad companies, employing tens of thousands of workers, traded on the stock market and generated much needed revenue. But it quickly became clear that the method of managing a small company did not work for managing ones of this magnitude. Professional managers were brought in to organize what would become modern corporations. The managers adopted business models, such as organizational charts that created management hierarchy. This new form of corporation and business style led to the railways' success, and would be duplicated with equal success in other business beyond the railroads.

First Abstract Painting

506 **1844** In 1844, English Romantic landscape painter Joseph Mallord William Turner unveiled his "Rain, Steam, and Speed—the Great Western Railway" at the Royal Academy in London. The work was more abstract than Turner's earlier paintings, initiating new techniques that would be carried on by Impressionists at the end of the 19th and into the 20th century. Claude Monet is said to have carefully studied Turner's work. Besides its unique style, "Rain, Steam, and Speed—the Great Western Railway" also seemed to represent the time. Some equate it with the rapid changes that came with the industrial

Morse Sends Telegraph

507 **1844** When Samuel F. B. Morse, an accomplished American portrait artist, first heard about electromagnetism he immediately began studying how messages could be sent over a wire using electricity. In 1835, he developed prototypes of a telegraph but sought the help of colleagues with greater scientific knowledge to improve them. With this advice, he invented an electromagnetic relay system, which would make long-distance transmissions possible. In 1838, Morse created a system of dots and dashes to represent letters, numbers, and punctuation marks. Morse code, as this system came to be known, was how messages could be translated—a language of dots and dashes. Morse solicited Congress to make a transatlantic telegraph line and was rejected; however, in 1843 he received its support to create a line between Washington, D.C., and Baltimore. The first message, sent in 1844, said, "What hath God wrought!" And the American telegraph system was born.

Samuel F. B. Morse, heavily medallioned for his inventions, most notably, the telegraph

The impact soon reached around the world. By the end of the decade, telegraph systems were in use throughout Great Britain as a way to standardize time. Standardized time did not reach around the world, however, until the 1880s, at which point the hourly time zones—anchored at the Greenwich Royal Observatory in England and continuing in a progression around the world by longitude—were set.

Telegraphs tapped out current events in record time to newspapers. Printing telegraphs were originally called "tickers," for the tapping sound that they made—hence the term "ticker tape," which was the long, narrow rolls of paper onto which telegraphed messages were printed by the early years of the 20th century.

revolution, and its use of light and dark may represent past and present.

FOOTNOTE French Impressionists Claude Monet, Edgar Degas, and Auguste Renoir signed a declaration attributing to Turner the inspiration for the "fugitive phenomena of light" that characterized their paintings.

U.S. and China Agree

508 **1844** In 1844, under the Treaty of Wangxia, China opened five ports to the United States, beginning a

formal trade relationship with China. Before then, China had remained relatively closed to the European industrial revolution and colonialism. European countries, heavily involved in overseas trade, coveted such China goods as silk and tea. The Treaty of Wangxia was modeled after the Treaty of Nanjing, which marked the end of the First Opium War between China and Britain in 1842, but differed by allowing U.S. citizens to buy land in the five Chinese treaty ports and build churches and hospitals there to provide for Christian missionaries. It also gave Americans the right to learn Chinese, which was previously forbidden. Under the agreement, opium trade was illegal. China was soon flooded with an onslaught of foreign goods, which severely disrupted the old village economy, which had been the backbone to the Chinese systems for millennia.

FOOTNOTE Representing the U.S. in China was Caleb Cushing, a Massachusetts congressman who was later nominated (but not approved) as Chief Justice of the United States and who served as ambassador to Spain.

Hypodermic Syringe in Use

509 **1845** Irish physician Francis Rynd published an article in 1845 reporting that he had used an instrument to inject fluids underneath a patient's skin in Dublin's Meath Hospital. In the hopes of curing his patients of neuralgia, a painful attack on the nerves, Rynd injected morphine directly into his patient's bloodstream. Rynd did not describe the instrument he used for the injection, but it is considered a predecessor of the modern-day hypodermic syringe.

Thoreau Moves to Walden Pond

510 **1845** In 1845, American writer and philosopher Henry David Thoreau began his two-year experiment of solitary living at Walden Pond in Concord, Massachusetts. His book *Walden; or Life in the Woods* (published in 1854), a series of 18 essays, was the outcome of his time spent there, which Thoreau said was an experiment in living life simply and self-sufficiently. Thoreau built his own cabin, gathered wild fruit, and harvested beans that he planted. He fished, swam, meditated, and observed the surrounding flora and fauna. In *Walden,* he said if people could live more simply, they would have the time and energy for deeper life. In 1849, Thoreau wrote "Civil Disobedience," an essay seen as a social protest. He urged people to disobey laws that they believed unjust because there is a higher law than the civil one. He believed that higher law should be adhered to even if it meant imprisonment.

511 | *Visitors tour the London* Daily Telegraph *printing room, with a ten-feed rotary press, in March 1860.*

Thoreau's writings influenced civil rights activists, including Martin Luther King, Jr., and leaders such as Mahatma Gandhi.

Hoe Patents Press

511 **1845** In 1845, Richard Hoe, an American manufacturer, was developing the first high-speed printing press. His steam-driven rotary, or "lightning press," printed 8,000 sheets an hour—much faster than existing flatbed presses. Four cylinders fed large sheets of paper against one large cylinder laid with type. The *Philadelphia Public Ledger* was the first paper to be printed using the press. Hoe's invention, patented in 1847, would prove to be essential for the mid-19th-century development of newspapers.

U.S. Declares War on Mexico

512 **1846** A buildup of disagreements led the U.S. to declare war on Mexico on May 13, 1846, starting the two-year Mexican-American War. In 1836, the Republic of Texas had won its freedom from Mexico. But Mexico did not recognize Texas' independence, and when the U.S. annexed it as a state in 1845, Mexico ended U.S. relations. President James K. Polk was interested in expanding the U.S. westward, and a dispute began over the Texas-Mexico border. The U.S. believed the Texas border ended at the Rio Grande. Mexico said the border was the Nueces River. There was also growing interest to claim California as U.S. territory. Polk wanted to give Mexico more than $25 million for agreeing to the Rio Grande border and selling New Mexico and California to the U.S., but Mexico's president refused to see Polk's negotiators, prompting the war declaration. The war lasted nearly two years and ended with the Treaty of Guadalupe Hidalgo, under which the U.S. paid $15 million for nearly all of present-day California, Nevada, Utah, Arizona, New Mexico, Texas, and western Colorado.

Potato Blight Causes Famine

513 **1846** The second growing season after the appearance of the mysterious potato blight in Ireland began gloomily in 1846, with Britain instating efforts to stave off hunger and unemployment. Potatoes had become a staple in the Irish diet, but only a few varieties were grown, risking the entire crop if a problem occurred. That problem was a specific fungus that ruined the leaves and roots of the potato plant. Potato crops failed across the country for four consecutive years. The Irish potato famine caused a massive decline in Ireland's population through emigration and death. Some 1.5 million Irish immigrated to America and other parts of Britain for a new beginning. And more than one million died from starvation or disease during the famine.

Howe Patents Sewing Machine

514 **1846** Elias Howe patented the first usable sewing machine in 1846, revolutionizing the garment and shoemaking industries. It is said that as a young boy Howe was told that the person who invented a machine that could sew would be made rich. Determined, Howe worked for three years to meet the challenge. Using an eye-pointed needle and a double-thread stitch, his machine worked far faster than anyone could by hand. But it didn't immediately catch on in the U.S., and Howe moved to England, where he made improvements to his machine and used it to sew leather for shoes, but he did not become the wealthy man he had hoped. He returned to the United States and discovered countless patent infringements on his machine. After a long legal battle, he was given the right to all royalties on sewing machines that used his features, and eventually he found his fortune. In 1860 alone more than 110,000 sewing machines were manufactured in the United

States, and ready-to-wear clothes and shoes became abundant in stores.

> ■ **FOOTNOTE** When Howe returned to the U.S., he discovered that one competitor in particular was successfully marketing sewing machines with needles that moved up and down, not sideways. His name: Isaac Singer.

First Anesthesia

515 **1846** In 1846, American dentist and physician William Thomas Green Morton was the first person to publicly demonstrate the effectiveness of ether anesthesia during an operation at Massachusetts General Hospital in Boston. The search to find a better way to prevent and control pain had been ongoing throughout the ages. In the 19th century it was discovered that diethyl ether (commonly called ether) and chloroform caused unconsciousness, during which there was

515 | *Dentist William Morton's first anesthesia patient was grateful for his invention.*

Woman Suffrage Launches

516 **1848** In 1848, Elizabeth Cady Stanton's Declaration of Sentiments—demanding more rights for women in education and jobs and the right to vote—was signed at the first women's rights convention in Seneca Falls, New York. Sixty-eight women and thirty-two men signed the document, modeled after the Declaration of Independence. "The history of mankind is a history of repeated injuries and usurpations on the part of man toward women," it read, "having in direct object the establishment of an absolute tyranny over her."

Elizabeth Cady Stanton believed "The heyday of woman's life is the shady side of fifty."

One of the document's motivations was an event that occurred eight years earlier at an international antislavery meeting in London. American Lucretia Mott had been denied access to speak although she was an official delegate. The frustrated Mott met Elizabeth Cady Stanton, and the two pledged to work for women's rights, going on to organize the Seneca Falls convention. Although women held their place in the reform movements of the 19th century, they were rarely allowed to take leadership roles or politically lobby for their causes and goals. The document did not immediately change the society's entrenched mind-set regarding women, but it defined the new women's rights movement and guided its efforts during the next 70 years before women were granted the right to vote.

The places significant to this historic event, including the site of the Wesleyan Chapel where meetings were held and Elizabeth Cady Stanton's home, are now part of the Women's Rights National Historical Park in Seneca Falls, New York.

no pain. Morton experimented with ether on himself and animals and then successfully extracted a patient's infected tooth by having him inhale ether. While several others had used ether as an anesthetic a few years earlier, their surgeries weren't publicized. Newspapers immediately reported on Morton's surgery, and although Morton tried in vain to keep other people from using what he felt was his own ether anesthesia, it was immediately used in Europe for a variety of surgeries. The success of ether in surgery greatly improved pain management for patients and opened the door for what could be done in operating rooms.

■ **FOOTNOTE** Morton administered ether through an inhaler he had designed and named "Letheon" after the River Lethe of ancient Greek mythology. Crossing the Lethe, according to myth, evoked a state of forgetfulness.

"Communist Manifesto"

517 **1848** German philosopher Karl Marx and German economist Friedrich Engels wrote the "Communist Manifesto," a pamphlet which outlined their basic ideas on communism and became one of the most widely read documents over the next century, inspiring the revolutionary communist movement.

Marx studied history and the class struggles between the ruling class and the ruled, and believed that rulers who hold economic power will not willingly give up that power and force their will on the people. This, he said, inevitably leads to unrest. He related to the low pay and difficult, unhealthy conditions workers experienced over the past 150 years during the industrial revolution in Europe and concluded that the only way for society to be harmonious was to put workers in control. He called for the end of capitalism, where wealth is in the hands of a few, and the majority of the middle class turn into workers with a decrease in the quality of living conditions. This, he theorized, will lead to revolt, where the workers will be the ones to take over the government and set up a classless society. Eventually there would be no government or police and people would live in freedom with peace.

■ **FOOTNOTE** The first "Communist Manifesto" was a 23-page pamphlet printed in Liverpool with many typographical errors. It sped across Europe, reprinted over and over. Some say only the Bible has been reprinted in more versions.

Cholera Traced

518 **1849** In 1849, British doctor John Snow published an essay theorizing that cholera—which we now know is an acute infectious disease of the small intestine caused by bacteria—was not transmitted by disease-containing "clouds," but rather it enters the body through the mouth. Snow put his theory to the test in 1854 when Great Britain was suffering from a cholera pandemic that would ultimately take the lives of 23,000 people. Snow plotted cholera cases on a map, identifying a single water pump contaminated by a nearby sewer pipe as the source of the disease. He had the pump's handle removed, and the cholera cases immediately decreased. Though his work would not be accepted for several decades, it would eventually prove the important connection between improved hygiene and disease prevention.

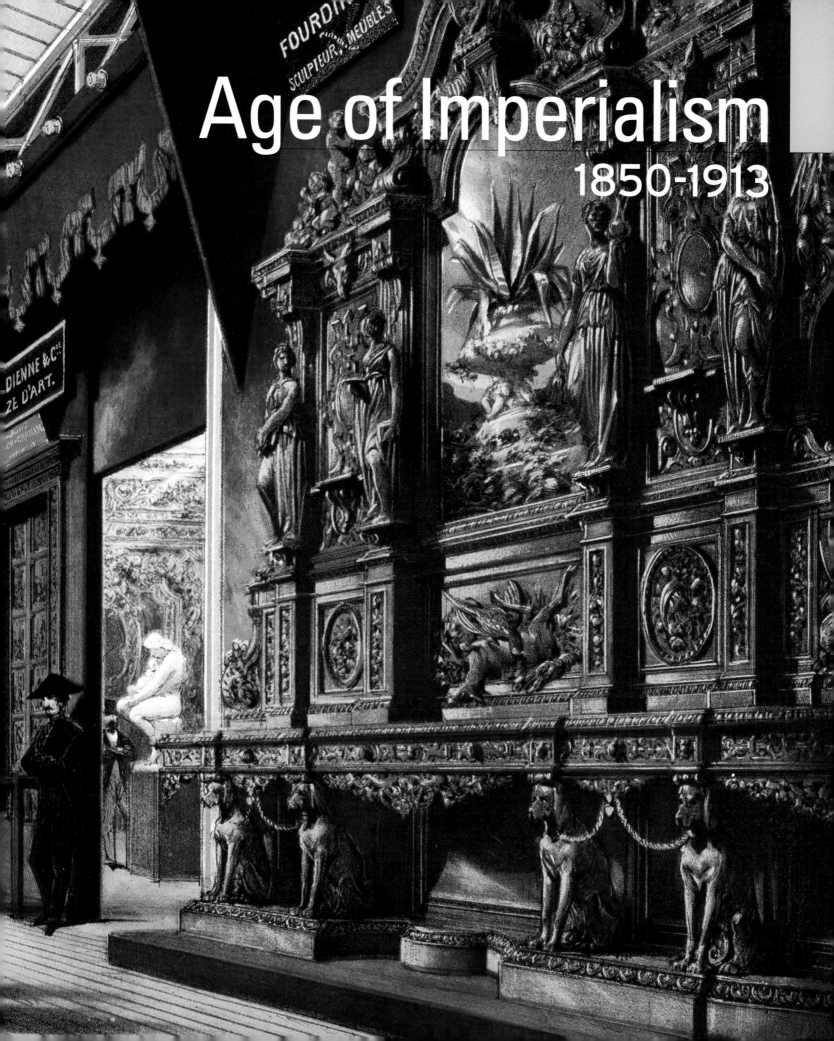

Age of Imperialism
1850-1913

1850-1913
Trade and Technology Rule

S ince ancient times, empires have risen and fallen, sometimes collapsing within decades and sometimes enduring for centuries. In the 1800s, however, a relentless new form of imperialism arose, powered by industrial development and technological innovations that gave the world's leading powers enormous advantages over less-developed societies. Equipped with modern weapons like machine guns and modern modes of communication such as telegraphs, telephones, steamships, and railroads, imperialists encompassed the globe and imposed their will on kings, sheiks, sultans, and tribal chieftains.

It was no accident that Great Britain was both the birthplace of the industrial revolution and the greatest power of this new imperial age. Although the British Empire originated in the 16th century, it experienced an explosion of growth in the mid-19th century as industrialists looked abroad for new sources of raw materials and new markets in which to sell their manufactured goods.

Capitalism was now so well developed in Britain that corporations like the East India Company and the British South Africa Company, founded by diamond magnate Cecil Rhodes, were strong enough themselves to dominate countries in which they operated, sparing the British government much trouble and expense.

In 1857, however, after Indian troops called sepoys rebelled against the East India Company that employed them, the

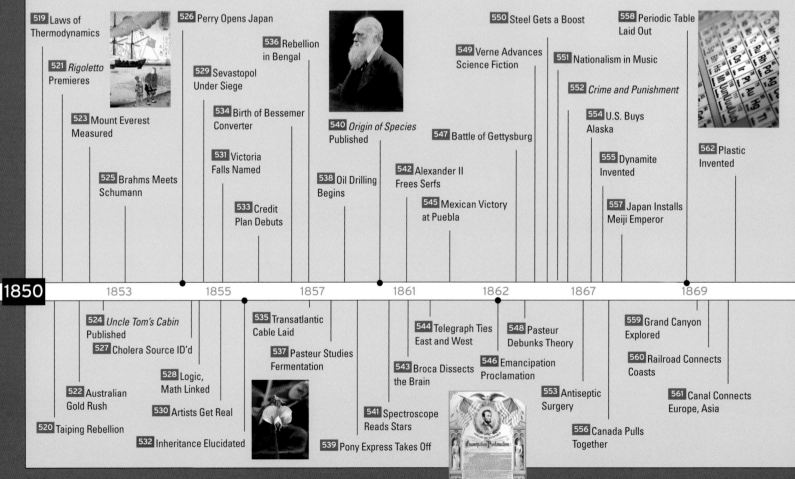

519 Laws of Thermodynamics

521 *Rigoletto* Premieres

523 Mount Everest Measured

525 Brahms Meets Schumann

526 Perry Opens Japan

529 Sevastopol Under Siege

536 Rebellion in Bengal

534 Birth of Bessemer Converter

531 Victoria Falls Named

533 Credit Plan Debuts

538 Oil Drilling Begins

540 *Origin of Species* Published

547 Battle of Gettysburg

542 Alexander II Frees Serfs

545 Mexican Victory at Puebla

550 Steel Gets a Boost

549 Verne Advances Science Fiction

551 Nationalism in Music

552 *Crime and Punishment*

554 U.S. Buys Alaska

555 Dynamite Invented

557 Japan Installs Meiji Emperor

558 Periodic Table Laid Out

562 Plastic Invented

1850   1853   1855   1857   1861   1862   1867   1869

524 *Uncle Tom's Cabin* Published

527 Cholera Source ID'd

528 Logic, Math Linked

522 Australian Gold Rush

530 Artists Get Real

520 Taiping Rebellion

532 Inheritance Elucidated

535 Transatlantic Cable Laid

537 Pasteur Studies Fermentation

544 Telegraph Ties East and West

543 Broca Dissects the Brain

541 Spectroscope Reads Stars

539 Pony Express Takes Off

548 Pasteur Debunks Theory

546 Emancipation Proclamation

553 Antiseptic Surgery

556 Canada Pulls Together

559 Grand Canyon Explored

560 Railroad Connects Coasts

561 Canal Connects Europe, Asia

British Army stepped in and took charge of India, which served as a source of cotton for British textile plants and as a market for cloth produced there.

To speed trade with India, China, and other Asian countries, the British built the Suez Canal and occupied Egypt and Sudan to secure that vital conduit between the Mediterranean and Red Seas. By 1900, nearly all of Africa had been carved up and taken over by Britain, France, or other imperial powers.

A Widening Gap

IMPERIAL EXPANSION WAS BASED ON TECHNOLOGICAL ADVANCES that brought industrialized nations power and wealth, which in turn funded further research and development, moving those nations further ahead of the rest of the world. Even breakthroughs in medicine and public health, which promised universal benefits such as chlorinating water, pasteurizing milk, and sanitizing surgical instruments, served to widen the gap between wealthy nations that applied those measures and poor countries that lacked the know-how or resources to do so and remained prey to dreadful epidemics and infections. Industrialization and the growth of cities were facilitated by advances in medicine, sanitation, transportation, and engineering that allowed millions of people to live and work together in close proximity safely and productively.

Increased efficiency in these teeming industrial centers brought profits that helped businesses expand and also supported hospitals, universities, and laboratories where further technological progress was made. Some of the leading inventors of this era, including Alexander Graham Bell and Thomas Alva Edison, were largely self-taught. But they drew on scientific research conducted at institutions endowed by

PREVIOUS PAGE | *Visitors enjoy the Great Exhibition in the Crystal Palace, the glass-and-iron building designed by Joseph Paxton, at Hyde Park, London.*

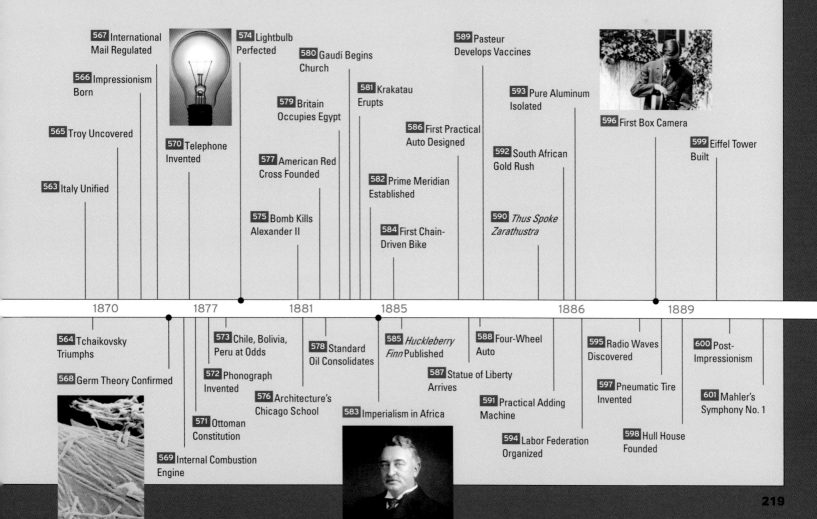

567 International Mail Regulated

566 Impressionism Born

565 Troy Uncovered

563 Italy Unified

574 Lightbulb Perfected

580 Gaudí Begins Church

581 Krakatau Erupts

579 Britain Occupies Egypt

570 Telephone Invented

577 American Red Cross Founded

575 Bomb Kills Alexander II

589 Pasteur Develops Vaccines

586 First Practical Auto Designed

593 Pure Aluminum Isolated

592 South African Gold Rush

582 Prime Meridian Established

590 *Thus Spoke Zarathustra*

584 First Chain-Driven Bike

596 First Box Camera

599 Eiffel Tower Built

1870   1877   1881   1885   1886   1889

564 Tchaikovsky Triumphs

568 Germ Theory Confirmed

573 Chile, Bolivia, Peru at Odds

572 Phonograph Invented

571 Ottoman Constitution

569 Internal Combustion Engine

578 Standard Oil Consolidates

576 Architecture's Chicago School

585 *Huckleberry Finn* Published

583 Imperialism in Africa

588 Four-Wheel Auto

587 Statue of Liberty Arrives

591 Practical Adding Machine

594 Labor Federation Organized

595 Radio Waves Discovered

597 Pneumatic Tire Invented

598 Hull House Founded

600 Post-Impressionism

601 Mahler's Symphony No. 1

wealthy businessmen like steel magnate Andrew Carnegie and used funds invested by such capitalists to found companies that made telephones and electric power widely available in industrialized nations, while poorer countries remained technologically in the dark.

No nation progressed more rapidly during this era than the United States, whose astonishing industrial growth and agricultural bounty made it the world's most productive nation in the 20th century. Few Americans thought of themselves as imperialists, and many opposed the idea of acquiring colonies overseas, fearing involvement in foreign wars. But in 1850 the nation was in fact a continental empire, including a vast area acquired by force from Mexico.

The Civil War that erupted in 1861 originated as a dispute between North and South over whether slavery would be permitted in the nation's western territories and led to the abolition of slavery by the victorious North. Yet the reunited Union still faced the huge task of colonizing the West by subduing defiant Indians, building railroads, and settling the country. By the time that process was completed in the late 1800s, American expansionists were looking overseas and pressing for annexation of the Polynesian kingdom of Hawaii and Spanish colonies such as Cuba and the Philippines, claimed by the United States in the Spanish-American War of 1898.

America's overseas possessions were small compared with those of Britain or France, but the consequences of acquiring them were huge. Holding the Philippines involved American troops in a brutal war with Filipinos seeking independence and later drew the United States into a horrific struggle with Japan for mastery of the Pacific.

New Contestants for Supremacy

JAPAN'S ASCENT PROVED THAT WESTERNERS WERE NOT THE ONLY ones who could play the modern imperial game. After

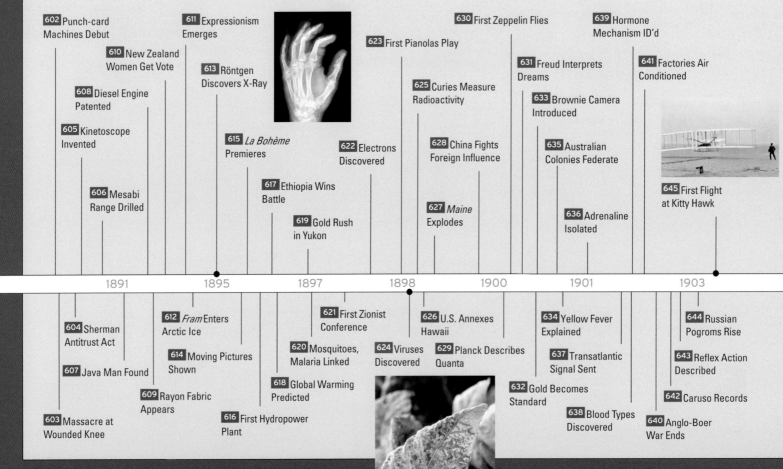

602 Punch-card Machines Debut

610 New Zealand Women Get Vote

608 Diesel Engine Patented

605 Kinetoscope Invented

606 Mesabi Range Drilled

611 Expressionism Emerges

613 Röntgen Discovers X-Ray

615 *La Bohème* Premieres

617 Ethiopia Wins Battle

619 Gold Rush in Yukon

623 First Pianolas Play

625 Curies Measure Radioactivity

622 Electrons Discovered

628 China Fights Foreign Influence

627 *Maine* Explodes

630 First Zeppelin Flies

631 Freud Interprets Dreams

633 Brownie Camera Introduced

635 Australian Colonies Federate

636 Adrenaline Isolated

639 Hormone Mechanism ID'd

641 Factories Air Conditioned

645 First Flight at Kitty Hawk

1891   1895   1897   1898   1900   1901   1903

604 Sherman Antitrust Act

607 Java Man Found

603 Massacre at Wounded Knee

612 *Fram* Enters Arctic Ice

614 Moving Pictures Shown

609 Rayon Fabric Appears

616 First Hydropower Plant

621 First Zionist Conference

620 Mosquitoes, Malaria Linked

618 Global Warming Predicted

624 Viruses Discovered

626 U.S. Annexes Hawaii

629 Planck Describes Quanta

634 Yellow Fever Explained

637 Transatlantic Signal Sent

632 Gold Becomes Standard

638 Blood Types Discovered

640 Anglo-Boer War Ends

644 Russian Pogroms Rise

643 Reflex Action Described

642 Caruso Records

Commodore Matthew C. Perry of the U.S. Navy ended Japan's isolation by entering its waters uninvited in 1853 and demonstrating the superiority of steamships and other modern technology, Japan held its own against Western powers by rapidly industrializing and building up its own navy and army. Led by Emperor Meiji, who had broad powers under the country's new constitution, Japan won victories over Russia and China—which continued to lose power during this era—and gained control of Korea and other territories.

Defeat by Japan came as a humiliating blow for Tsar Nicholas II of Russia, whose country was beginning to industrialize and at the same time was undergoing political upheaval much like that experienced by western European countries in 1848. After quashing a revolution in Russia in 1905, Nicholas sought to bolster his weak regime by cementing an alliance with two great powers, France and Britain. Those former enemies were now united in their desire to contain Germany, which had risen to prominence through the efforts of Otto von Bismarck of Prussia, who forged a formidable new German empire and placed Kaiser Wilhelm I on the throne.

Bismarck once stated that the fate of nations was determined by "blood and iron"—warfare and technology. Those words appeared prophetic as the imperial powers of Europe formed entangling alliances in the early 1900s. Little did they know that their decisions were moving toward a catastrophic conflict that would result in a devastating world war a generation later.

The same technological advances that made nations prosperous and powerful—including such recent innovations as the internal combustion engine, automobiles, and aircraft—would soon be used to shatter empires and destroy life and property on a scale few people could imagine before the shooting started.

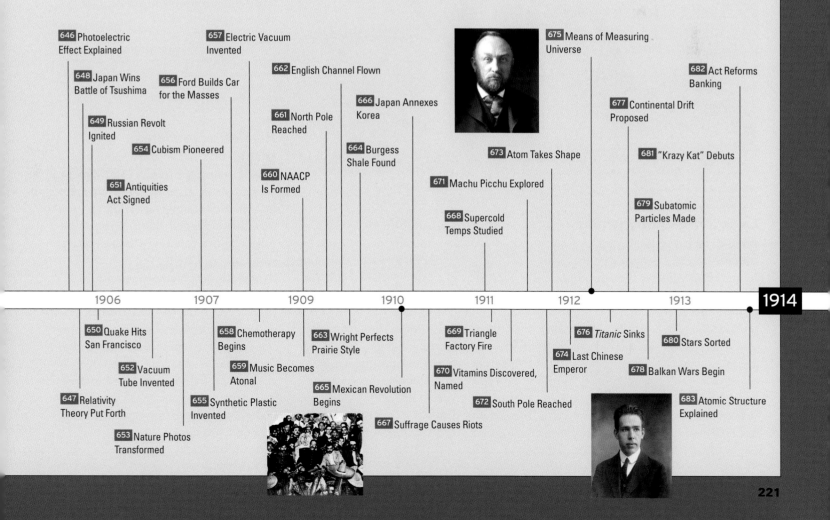

646 Photoelectric Effect Explained

657 Electric Vacuum Invented

675 Means of Measuring Universe

648 Japan Wins Battle of Tsushima

656 Ford Builds Car for the Masses

662 English Channel Flown

682 Act Reforms Banking

649 Russian Revolt Ignited

661 North Pole Reached

666 Japan Annexes Korea

677 Continental Drift Proposed

654 Cubism Pioneered

664 Burgess Shale Found

673 Atom Takes Shape

681 "Krazy Kat" Debuts

651 Antiquities Act Signed

660 NAACP Is Formed

671 Machu Picchu Explored

679 Subatomic Particles Made

668 Supercold Temps Studied

1906   **1907**   **1909**   **1910**   **1911**   **1912**   **1913**   **1914**

650 Quake Hits San Francisco

658 Chemotherapy Begins

663 Wright Perfects Prairie Style

669 Triangle Factory Fire

676 *Titanic* Sinks

680 Stars Sorted

652 Vacuum Tube Invented

659 Music Becomes Atonal

674 Last Chinese Emperor

678 Balkan Wars Begin

670 Vitamins Discovered, Named

647 Relativity Theory Put Forth

655 Synthetic Plastic Invented

665 Mexican Revolution Begins

672 South Pole Reached

683 Atomic Structure Explained

653 Nature Photos Transformed

667 Suffrage Causes Riots

523 | *Climber on the Lhotse face at 25,000 feet, heading toward Mount Everest's summit in 1963*

Taiping Rebellion

520 **1851** Beset by drought and famine, unable to fend off Western armies and Western opium imports, many Chinese were ready to hear words of hope from an unlikely prophet: Hong Xiuquan, the self-proclaimed younger brother of Jesus. Hong's visions had convinced him that he was sent to Earth to eradicate demons and establish the Heavenly Kingdom of Great Peace, or the Taiping Tianguo. In the process, he planned to overthrow China's Qing rulers. With his promises of economic and social equality, Hong attracted large numbers of followers, whom he pulled into a well-disciplined military organization. Beginning in 1851 and continuing for 14 destructive years, Hong's armies attacked towns and villages across China, occupying the city of Nanjing in 1853. Eventually his organization began to disintegrate and Hong himself withdrew from daily command. The rebellion ended with Hong's suicide in 1864. An estimated 20 to 30 million people had died in one of the bloodiest civil wars in history.

■ **FOOTNOTE** Hong's remarkably progressive philosophy recognized women as men's social and economic equals; he condemned slavery, concubinage, footbinding, torture, and opium smoking.

Rigoletto Premieres

521 **1851** On March 11, the first of Giuseppe Verdi's great middle-period operas, *Rigoletto,* had its premiere in Venice. The three-act work about a cursed court jester was a showcase for Verdi's talents, featuring a strong emphasis on drama, libretto, and melody. With its smooth integration of recitatives and arias into the action, the opera was emblematic of the way Verdi was moving on from the bel canto singing styles and stop-and-start action of earlier operas. *Rigoletto* and other great Verdi operas, such as *Aida* and *La Traviata,* were highly influential in establishing the grand opera tradition of high drama, big sets, and a broad use of the orchestra.

Laws of Thermodynamics

519 **1850** The proliferation of heat-powered engines in the 19th century allowed some thoughtful physicists to draw conclusions about the nature of heat and energy. In 1850, German physicist Rudolf Clausius first stated what would become the second law of thermodynamics, that "heat cannot pass from a colder to a hotter body." In other words, in the absence of outside sources of energy, entropy increases: Hot coffee grows cold, but cold coffee never becomes hotter.

Scottish scientist William Thomson, Lord Kelvin, formulated another version of this law at about the same time and often shared credit for the second law. The articulation of this law followed on the heels of the discovery of the first law of thermodynamics by James Prescott Joule and Herrmann von Helmholtz. This law, often known as the conservation of energy, states that energy can neither be created nor destroyed; the generation of power is simply the conversion of energy from one form to another.

525 | *Johannes Brahms, a year before his death*

Australian Gold Rush

522 **1851** Portly and ambitious, Australian Edward Hargraves learned the craft of panning for gold during an unsuccessful trip to America's goldfields in 1850. Recognizing that the California terrain resembled that of Australia, he returned home determined to find gold in his native country. In 1851, he traveled to Bathurst in New South Wales with a guide, telling him (according to his memoirs): "This is a memorable day in the history of New South Wales, I shall be a baronet, you will be knighted, and my old horse will be stuffed, put in a glass case, and sent to the British Museum!" Hargraves did indeed find a few grains of gold in a creek—and the rush was on.

Over the next few years, gold was also discovered in Victoria and other parts of Australia. Immigrants flooded in: In two years, Victoria's population alone grew from 77,000 to 540,000. The economy boomed as railroads and telegraph lines followed the miners into the field, and the wave of newcomers, particularly Chinese immigrants, permanently transformed Australian society.

Mount Everest Measured

523 **1852** Lost among the towering, frigid spires of the Himalaya, Peak XV was just another tall mountain until the Great Trigonometric Survey of India caught up with it. The Survey, which had been systematically measuring the Indian subcontinent for decades, reached Peak XV in 1852 and found it to be 29,002 feet high. The measurement, taken manually using a massive theodolite, was remarkably close to the height of 29,028 feet established 100 years later with more advanced technology. It was, and is, the tallest mountain in the world and the highest point on Earth. In 1865, apparently unaware that the mountain had the Tibetan name Chomolungma, the British surveyors renamed the mountain in honor of Sir George Everest, head of the Survey from 1830 to 1843.

FOOTNOTE Surveyors continue to revise Everest's official height. In 1954, it was declared to be 29,028 feet; in 1999, 29,035 feet. The mountain is also moving northeast at 2.4 inches a year.

Uncle Tom's Cabin Published

524 **1852** Originally published in 40 weekly installments in the antislavery weekly *The National Era, Uncle Tom's Cabin* became an instant best seller when it appeared in book form in March 1852. Written by Harriet Beecher Stowe, daughter and sister of famed Congregational preachers, the sentimental novel depicting the cruelties of slavery sold 10,000 copies in the first week and two million copies by the 1860s. The tale and its characters appeared in plays, songs, poems, even in games and on decorative plates. The influential book is credited with stoking national abolitionist fervor and contributing to the outbreak of the Civil War in 1861.

Brahms Meets Schumann

525 **1853** In April, 20-year-old German composer and pianist Johannes Brahms embarked on a musical tour of Germany in which he met composers Robert and Clara Schumann. Greatly impressed with the young man, Robert Schumann wrote an article that hailed Brahms's talents as a composer and launched his career. Brahms was heralded in the musical world as a champion of the classical tradition established by Mozart and Beethoven and an opponent of the Romantic and modernist tendencies exemplified by Lizst, for example. Brahms's profound and expressive compositions, such as his First Symphony and the *German Requiem*, wedded a new richness of harmony and tonal color to a classical sense of rhythm and structure.

FIRST PERSON

Harriet Beecher Stowe

UNCLE TOM'S CABIN, 1852

The cabin of Uncle Tom was a small log building, close adjoining to "the house," as the negro *par excellence* designates his master's dwelling. In front it had a neat garden-patch.... The whole front of it was covered by a large scarlet bignonia and a native multiflora rose, which, entwisting and interlacing, left scarce a vestige of the rough logs to be seen....

A table, somewhat rheumatic in its limbs, was drawn out in front of the fire.... At this table was seated Uncle Tom, Mr. Shelby's best hand, who, as he is to be the hero of our story, we must daguerreotype for our readers. He was a large, broadchested, powerfully-made man, of a full glossy black, and a face whose truly African features were characterized by an expression of grave and steady good sense, united with much kindliness and benevolence. There was something about his whole air self-respecting and dignified, yet united with a confiding and humble simplicity.

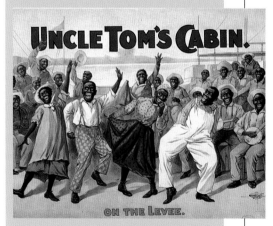

524 | *Poster advertising an 1899 theatrical production of* Uncle Tom's Cabin

1850-1913 | Age of Imperialism

Perry Opens Japan

526 **1853** Japan in the mid-19th century was virtually closed to foreigners, and had been that way for more than 200 years. Only a few Dutch and Chinese traders entered Japanese harbors. So observers in Edo (Tokyo) Bay were shocked when, on July 8, 1853, four black ships bristling with guns and emitting smoke cruised

Surprised onlookers watch American steamship entering Japanese harbor.

into the harbor. The boats were commanded by Commodore Matthew C. Perry of the United States, who bore a letter from President Millard Fillmore to the emperor of Japan, requesting a treaty. Perry refused Japanese orders to leave the harbor, insisting that he would deliver the letter by force, if necessary.

Having finally handed the letter to a reluctant pair of Japanese princes, Perry departed, leaving word that he would return for an answer. By the time he came back in 1854 with an even larger fleet, the Japanese government had realized it would have to concede the terms of the treaty. Without its own navy, Japan simply could not withstand an American attack.

The ensuing Treaty of Kanagawa opened up Japan to trade from the West and forcibly ended its self-imposed isolation. In the treaty, the Japanese agreed to admit U.S. ships to two ports, to allow American ships to pick up supplies and fuel in Japan, to give aid to any shipwrecked American sailors, and to accept the presence of a U.S. consul in their country. Subsequent treaties with other Western nations followed, leading to a series of social and economic changes that would bring modernization to Japan.

Cholera Source ID'd

527 **1854** An outbreak of cholera brought English anesthesiologist John Snow to London's Soho neighborhood in August. Snow had long held the unpopular belief that cholera was transmitted by unclean drinking water, rather than by "miasmas" in the air. By mapping the location of each case of cholera, Snow was able to tie the outbreak to a contaminated well on Broad Street as well as to the pipes of the Southwark and Vauxhall Company, a major water supplier. After his findings were presented to local officials, the Broad Street outbreak was ended by the simple method of removing the well's pump handle. Snow published a letter in the *Medical Times* that August that named the water company associated with the outbreaks, pointing out that

a rival company filtered its water "much better than the Southwark and Vauxhall Company, and no doubt rid it to a much greater extent of the cholera evacuations which pass down the sewers into the Thames."

Snow was a pioneering advocate for filtration and sanitation in public water, although widespread use of chlorine and other cleansing agents did not begin until the early 20th century. His systematic approach to isolating the source of the disease, using statistics and mapping, was a model for future health officials; he is generally viewed as the father of modern epidemiology. The advent of sanitary water supplies is also considered one of the greatest health advances of recent centuries and was a major contributor to greatly increased life expectancies in the developed world during the 20th century.

Logic, Math Linked

528 **1854** George Boole, an English mathematician, was the son of a tradesman and largely self-taught, but by the time he was in his 20s he was contributing important papers on differential equations and linear transformation to the *Cambridge Mathematical Journal.* In 1854 he published *An Investigation of the Laws of Thought, on Which Are Founded the Mathematical Theories of Logic and Probabilities.* In this book he pointed out that logical statements can be expressed mathematically, with algebraic symbols representing logical forms. This symbolic logic, now known as Boolean algebra, took on new life in the 20th century when it was shown that true-false statements could be represented by the on-off states of switches in electronic circuits: the basis for computer logic. Today, Boolean logic is used to expedite Internet searches, among many other applications.

■ **FOOTNOTE** Boole married his student, Mary Everest, niece of Sir George Everest, after whom the mountain is named. Their daughter, Alice Boole Stott, grew up to publish important papers on four-dimensional geometry.

Sevastopol Under Siege

529 **1854** The central battle of the short-lived but bloody Crimean War, the siege of Sevastopol lasted from October of 1854 to September of 1855. The war had begun in 1853 when Tsar Nicholas I declared the Christians living in the Ottoman Empire to be under his protection. Fearing a Russian incursion into the region, Britain and France allied to drive the Russians back. Fifty thousand French and British troops laid siege to the vital Russian naval base of Sevastopol on the Black Sea, holding on despite heavy casualties in a winter for which they were ill prepared. After a year of bombardments and trench warfare, Russian troops sank their own ships in the harbor, blew up their fortifications, and left the city. The end of the war came soon afterward in 1856, with the Russians, at least temporarily, pushed back behind their borders.

Artists Get Real

530 | **1855** French artist Gustave Courbet submitted 11 paintings of ordinary people—villagers, roadworkers, artists, and writers—to the Universal Exposition in Paris. When the exposition's jury rejected the simply executed, gritty paintings, Courbet set up his own rival Pavilion of Realism nearby, becoming the standard-bearer for the school of art known as realism. Courbet's 1861 manifesto that "painting is an essentially concrete art and can only consist in the representation of real and existing things" rejected the Romantic and idealized art of recent decades in favor of an everyday, truthful representation of life. Other realists of the era included the satirical Honoré Daumier and Jean-François Millet, as well as Édouard Manet and Edgar Degas in their early works. England's pre-Raphaelites owed something to realism, though in a more ethereal form, as did American realists Thomas Eakins and James Whistler. By 1880, the movement was fading as Impressionism took hold.

■ **FOOTNOTE** Courbet's canvas "The Artist's Studio" was an allegory of his professional life. In it he is painting in a crowded room, some of whose occupants ignore him, while others are enthralled. A nude model languishes at his back.

Victoria Falls Named

531 | **1855** Scottish missionary David Livingstone came to Africa in 1841 determined to spread Christianity and open up the continent's interior to commerce. In decades of hard-won travel from coast to coast, Livingstone filed dispatches to newspapers back home and also wrote several books about his travels, becoming the public face of African exploration. One of his key discoveries took place on November 17, 1855, when he and his African guides reached massive waterfalls, known as "the smoke that thunders," on the Zambezi River.

"In looking down into the fissure," Livingstone wrote later, "on the right of the island, one sees nothing but a dense white cloud, which, at the time we visited the spot, had two bright rainbows on it. From this cloud rushed up a great jet of vapor exactly like steam, and it mounted 200 or 300 feet high; there condensing, it changed its hue to that of dark smoke, and came back in a constant shower, which soon wetted us to the skin."

It was, Livingstone, wrote, "the most wonderful sight I had witnessed in Africa." The patriotic missionary named the torrent Victoria Falls. His accounts of this discovery and many others before

529 | *Croat laborers photographed by Roger Fenton, whose depiction of the Crimean War earned him the title of first war photographer*

Inheritance Elucidated

532 **1855** The middle of the 19th century saw two of the most important discoveries in the history of life science: Gregor Mendel's enunciation of the principles of inheritance and Charles Darwin's explanation of natural selection. However, the first of these discoveries, Mendel's, did not reach public ears until well after his death.

Gregor Mendel was a brilliant and nervous Austrian monk with a background in mathematics, physics, and botany. In the 1850s the abbot of his monastery in Brünn asked him to apply his considerable scientific skills to the study of crossbreeding, in hopes that the monastery could improve its own stock of Merino sheep. Mendel decided to experiment with the fast-growing pea plants in the monastery garden.

At that time, most people believed that inherited traits were blends of parental traits: Red flowers and white flowers would produce pink flowers, for instance. However, when Mendel began carefully crossbreeding pea plants, the results surprised him. Instead of producing even blends of the two parental traits, the daughter plants in the first generation possessed a single trait only. For instance, a smooth pea plant crossed with a wrinkled pea plant would produce all smooth pea plants. Even more remarkably, when those first generation plants were allowed to pollinate among themselves, they produced smooth and wrinkled plants at a ratio of three to one.

From 1854 to 1856, Mendel studied 34 varieties of pea. Using combinatorial mathematics, he then outlined the laws of inheritance he observed. Rather than blending parental properties, the plants inherited two separate factors—now called genes—for each characteristic, one from each parent. One factor would be dominant and the other recessive. Furthermore, traits were inherited separately and were not influenced by the others. Mendel presented his findings in 1865 to a natural history society in Brünn, where they received little attention. Only in 1900, 16 years after Mendel's death, did other scientists rediscover his work and realize that the rules he had outlined would explain the inheritance of characteristics in evolution.

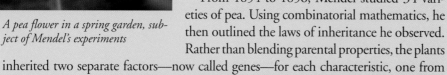

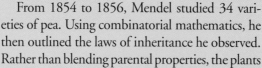

A pea flower in a spring garden, subject of Mendel's experiments

his death in 1873 were influential in encouraging European intervention, well-meaning and otherwise, in the interior of Africa.

Credit Plan Debuts

533 **1856** At $125, Isaac Singer's newly invented sewing machines were out of the reach of the average American consumer. So in 1856 Singer's company became the first to offer an installment credit plan, allowing buyers to pay for expensive items in affordable installments over time. Other merchants began to extend installment credit as well. In the years to come the practice allowed a wide range of consumers to raise their standards of living (and debt) by purchasing furniture, automobiles, and household appliances over time.

Birth of Bessemer Converter

534 **1856** A prolific inventor, British engineer Sir Henry Bessemer garnered more than 110 patents in his lifetime, but the invention for which he is most famous is the steelmaking furnace now known as the Bessemer converter. Until the mid-1800s, the metal used in machinery, bridges, and weaponry was typically either cast iron or wrought iron; steel could only be produced through a slow, impractical process.

Bessemer experimented with the furnaces producing cast iron and discovered that a blast of air directed through the molten metal would burn out the impurities and separate the purified metal from the slag. He announced his discovery before the British Association for the Advancement of Science in 1856. Although it was several more years before the process became foolproof, the technology of the Bessemer converter spread throughout Great Britain and the United States, aiding the spread of industrialization, and is still used in a modified form in today's steel mills.

FOOTNOTE Among Bessemer's other inventions were a telescope, a technique for forming graphite for pencils, a machine to extract juice from sugarcane, an artillery shell, gold paint, and a swinging boat cabin to counter seasickness.

Transatlantic Cable Laid

535 **1857** Before the invention of electric telegraphy, messages across the Atlantic typically took weeks to arrive. After Samuel Morse laid the first telegraph lines in 1844, the potential for using the new technology to communicate almost instantaneously across the ocean was apparent. In 1856, American Cyrus Field and Englishmen Charles Bright and John and Jacob Brett formed a company to lay down the first transatlantic telegraph cable.

In 1857, two ships, American and British, loaded up 2,500 nautical miles of cable and set sail from Ireland. Four hundred miles into the trip, the cable snapped. A second try in 1858 succeeded in laying only 140 miles before the cable snapped again. Finally, on August 5, 1858, the two

537 | *French chemist Louis Pasteur*

Pasteur Studies Fermentation

537 **1857** Louis Pasteur, a French chemist, became one of the leading scientists of the 19th century with a series of breakthrough discoveries about molecular chemistry and microorganisms. The son of a tanner, he had a keen interest in the application of scientific principles to industrial processes, and in the 1850s he began to study fermentation in substances ranging from beer to milk. In 1857, after analyzing compounds produced during fermentation, Pasteur announced that the process was not strictly a chemical one, as had been previously thought: It involved minute living organisms, or "germs." The discovery led in the 1860s to the process now known as pasteurization, in which harmful microorganisms in food are killed through the application of heat.

Oil Drilling Begins

538 **1859** The petroleum industry began in the wooded hills of northwestern Pennsylvania in August 1859, when American entrepreneur Edwin L. Drake struck oil in the little town of Titusville. Building the first well specifically designed to find oil, Drake tapped into a petroleum deposit that yielded about 20 barrels a day. Drake's oil well became the first of many as the petroleum industry spread around the world in the second half of the 19th century.

FOOTNOTE Neither safety nor conservation was an issue in the early days of oil drilling. Thick forests of oil derricks sprang up in Titusville, draining resources and prompting fires. Drake's first well burned to the ground soon after being built.

Pony Express Takes Off

539 **1860** Before the advent of coast-to-coast telegraphy in the United States there was, briefly, the Pony Express. Begun in April 1860 by the Central Overland California and Pike's Peak Express Company, the enterprise delivered mail between St. Joseph, Missouri, and Sacramento, California, using a nonstop relay system of horses and riders. Riders covered more than 1,900 miles in ten days, on average, crossing the states of Kansas, Nebraska, Colorado, Wyoming, Utah, Nevada, and California. The rider changed every 75 to 100 miles, but the horses had to be swapped for fresh ones every 10 to 15 miles at more than 100 stations located along the route. Riders were young, for the most part, and lightweight, and included among

ships reached their ports on opposite sides of the Atlantic without mishap. The message "Glory to God in the highest, and on Earth, peace, good will to men" was sent across the ocean.

Even this success was short-lived, however. Within a few weeks the cable, stressed by high voltages, failed. Not until 1866 did a reliable transatlantic cable go into operation.

Rebellion in Bengal

536 **1857** Britain dominated India by the 1850s, exerting its control through the East India Company. Believing in the loyalty of the local troops (sepoys) that they had trained, company army officers were stunned when the sepoys in northern India rose up in revolt in 1857. The immediate cause of the mutiny was the new kind of cartridge issued for the sepoys' Lee-Enfield rifles. Rumors had spread that the cartridges, which had to be bitten open, contained pork and beef fat, the first anathema to Muslims and the second to Hindus. Indian troops killed British officers and took over the city of Delhi as the rebellion spread across the country. Bloody massacres and equally bloody reprisals took place on both sides before the British finally suppressed the revolt the following year and replaced East India Company control with direct rule by Britain.

539 | *Pony Express mail carrier, taking shortcut through Indian burial grounds, Indians in pursuit*

Origin of Species Published

540 **1859** In the 1830s and '40s, two perceptive young British naturalists traveled the world and drew radical conclusions about what they saw there. The first was Charles Robert Darwin, who spent five years aboard the H.M.S. *Beagle* in the 1830s observing the flora and fauna of South America and the Pacific. He was struck, in particular, by the animals of the isolated Galápagos Islands and their specialized adaptations to ecological niches. Upon his return to England, Darwin resolved to take his time in writing up his new theory: that species evolve through natural selection, random variations within a group allowing certain individuals an advantage over others in survival and reproduction.

Meanwhile, a younger naturalist and admirer of Darwin's, Alfred Russel Wallace, spent four years in the 1840s exploring the Amazon River Basin, followed by eight years in the Malay Peninsula. Independently of Darwin, he came to the same conclusions regarding natural selection. In June 1858, he wrote to the older scientist, enclosing an essay on the "tendency of varieties to depart indefinitely from the original type." Darwin, in reply, suggested that the two of them publish an article jointly, which they did that year in the *Journal of the Linnean Society.*

Wallace's discoveries prompted Darwin to move forward rapidly with the book he had been so carefully developing, containing detailed arguments and hundreds of examples. In

Charles Darwin, in later life. Reports that he had renounced evolution on his deathbed were refuted.

1859 he published *On the Origin of Species by Means of Natural Selection.* Every copy sold out the first day. Most scientists were impressed; much of the public was outraged at the removal of God from the evolutionary process and the implication that humans had descended from a "lower" animal. Today, the book is regarded as one of the great works of scientific thought and is enormously influential in all areas of the life sciences.

Bunsen—discovered that a simple laboratory device could reveal the secrets of the sun and other stars. Bunsen, the inventor of the Bunsen burner, and his physicist colleague were attempting to identify chemicals through the colors with which they burned. Kirchhoff suggested passing the light through a spectroscope: an etched glass lens, invented earlier in the century by Joseph von Fraunhofer, that split light into a spectrum of colors and dark lines. To date, no one had quite understood what the patterns in the spectrum meant. Bunsen and Kirchhoff realized that each element as it burned gave off its own characteristic array of bright colors—emission lines—and dark spaces—absorption lines. From there it was but a small but vital step to realizing that sunlight and starlight passed through a spectroscope would yield a pattern of emission and absorption lines that identified the elements in the stars' atmospheres. Kirchhoff went on to name key elements in the sun's gases, including one never before seen on Earth, which he named "helium," from *helios,* for "sun."

■ **FOOTNOTE** Robert Bunsen was not afraid to take risks. Earlier in his career he specialized in studying arsenic compounds, a pursuit that nearly poisoned him and cost him his right eye when a compound exploded in the laboratory.

Alexander II Frees Serfs

542 **1861** Russia's defeat in the Crimean War galvanized its new tsar, Alexander II. It was clear that his country must modernize in order to survive. The industrial and social revolutions sweeping through Europe and North America had barely touched Russia, which was dependent on an agricultural economy run by landowning aristocrats. Farming the land of those aristocrats was a population of serfs 20 million strong, virtual slaves who owed dues and labor to the landed gentry.

By the 1850s, progressive elements among nobility and peasants alike were agitating for emancipation, and as Alexander II commented, "It is better to abolish

their ranks William "Buffalo Bill" Cody and Robert "Pony Bob" Haslam.

Dashing and romantic, the fleet-footed mail service captured the public imagination even as it lost large sums of money. Some credit it for encouraging the state of California to remain in the Union. However, when the transcontinental telegraph was completed in October 1861, the Pony Express ceased to be necessary. The business folded, leaving its founders $200,000

in debt, but living on in the growing mythology of the Wild West.

■ **FOOTNOTE** A newspaper ad read: "The undersigned wishes to hire ten or a dozen men, familiar with the management of horses, as hostlers, or riders on the Overland Express Route via Salt Lake City. Wages $50 per month and food."

Spectroscope Reads Stars

541 **1859** Two German scientists— Gustav Kirchhoff and Robert

serfdom from above than to wait until the serfs begin to liberate themselves from below." In March 1861 he signed an emancipation edict freeing the serfs. Like the U.S. emancipation proclamation two years later, the document was hedged about with political compromise. The government allotted land to the freed serfs in return for redemption payments spread out across 49 years. The system would not only compensate landowners for their property, it would also tie the former serfs to the land, preventing them from turning into a free-floating army of disaffection.

This compromise frustrated many former serfs, who did not have enough land to make their payments, and the payment system was eventually abolished in 1907. Nevertheless, the emancipation of the serfs was the first and most visible step in a series of Russian reforms in the 1860s and 1870s that expanded banking, established local parliamentary bodies, brought in railroads, and modernized the army.

Broca Dissects the Brain

543 **1861** French physician Pierre Paul Broca published the results of an autopsy he had conducted on the brain of a 51-year-old patient. The man, known as "Tan" because that was the only syllable he could produce, had been without the power of speech for some 30 years. Broca's autopsy

543 | *Broca identified brain's speech center.*

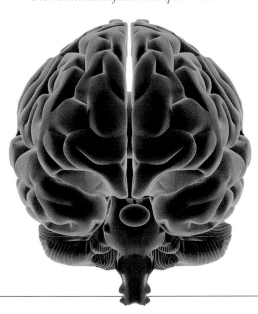

544 | *A young boy operates a telegraph machine in the early 20th century.*

revealed a lesion on the man's left frontal lobe: This case and other observations led the doctor to believe that the brain possessed a particular area (in the left frontal lobe) devoted to articulate speech—a region now known as Broca's area. It was the first proof that different regions of the brain are devoted to different functions.

Broca's work was supported by that of German neurologist Carl Wernicke, who in 1874 discovered the region of the temporal lobe responsible for speech comprehension—now called Wernicke's area.

Telegraph Ties East and West

544 **1861** Dozens of telegraph companies competed for American business in the 1850s, sending messages throughout the eastern half of the U.S. The Western Union Telegraph Company consolidated several of these companies in

1856 and embarked on an ambitious project to connect the end of the lines, in Omaha, Nebraska, to Carson City, Nevada. Starting from the eastern and western ends and stringing lines toward the midpoint of Salt Lake City, Utah, workers completed the telegraph in October 1861. Stephen Field, the chief justice of California, sent a message to Abraham Lincoln stating that the line "will be the means of strengthening the attachment which binds both the East and the West to the Union."

Mexican Victory at Puebla

545 **1862** In 1861, while America's attentions were focused on its Civil War, the forces of France, Spain, and Britain invaded Mexico, seeking repayment of loans they had issued to the cash-strapped government of President Benito

Juárez. Spain and Britain, at odds with France, soon withdrew from the country, but French troops pushed forward toward Mexico City.

On May 5, 1862, Frenchman Gen. Charles Latrille Laurencez led his 6,000 troops against a motley collection of some 4,000 Mexican soldiers under Gen. Ignacio Zaragoza at the city of Puebla. Brashly attacking the center of the Mexican lines, Laurencez was unable to dislodge the defenders and was eventually forced to surrender the field and retreat toward the coast.

The Mexican victory at Puebla was hardly the end of the war. French forces eventually succeeded in capturing Mexico City, where Napoleon III installed a puppet ruler, Maximilian of Austria. Only in 1867 did the Mexican Army under Gen. Porfirio Díaz retake the capital and restore Mexican rule. The Battle of Puebla is commemorated today by the holiday of Cinco de Mayo.

Battle of Gettysburg

547 **1863** Until the summer of 1863, the outnumbered Confederate troops had more than held their own against the Union Army in the American Civil War. By July 1, the Army of Northern Virginia under the brilliant Gen. Robert E. Lee had frightened the North by advancing into Pennsylvania. There, in the town of Gettysburg, they were met by the Army of the Potomac under Gen. George Meade.

Meade's 88,000 men held the high ground south of town, and this as much as anything ensured their eventual victory. Lee, with 75,000 men, tried but failed to outflank Meade's position on July 2. On July 3, Gen. George E. Pickett led his 15,000 Confederate men across an open field in a gallant but virtually suicidal attempt to break through the center of the Union line. Less than an hour later, only 5,000 remained. On July 4, Lee retreated, having lost more than one-third of his troops. The defeat was the high-tide mark of the South's advance and the beginning of the end for the Confederate Army.

> ■ **FOOTNOTE** Gettysburg National Cemetery was dedicated four months after the battle. Statesman Edward Everett's oration lasted two hours. President Abraham Lincoln, a last-minute addition, spoke for two minutes.

Emancipation Proclamation

546 **1863** Although the abolition of slavery was one of the Union's goals in the American Civil War, it was nevertheless a controversial subject in both North and South. It was not until July 1862, more than a year into the war, that President Abraham Lincoln started drafting an emancipation proclamation. After meeting several times during the year with his Cabinet in order to polish the document, Lincoln issued it formally as the next year was born. It began:

A lithograph created in 1888 celebrates the composition of the Emancipation Proclamation.

That on the first day of January, in the year of our Lord one thousand eight hundred and sixty-three, all persons held as slaves within any State or designated part of a State, the people whereof shall then be in rebellion against the United States, shall be then, thenceforward, and forever free….

The proclamation was not a blanket abolition of slavery. It applied only to slaves in rebellious states, leaving those in loyal border states untouched. It also exempted Confederate states that had already fallen under Union military control. Only when a Union victory was complete would all slaves become free.

Despite its limitations, the proclamation had considerable moral and political force. It dissuaded Great Britain from entering the war on the side of the Confederacy, even though it meant Britain had to give up the cotton it depended upon from the South. And hundreds of thousands of black soldiers were allowed for the first time to enroll in the Union Army, where they played a heroic role.

Pasteur Debunks Theory

548 **1864** The idea that life can arise via spontaneous generation—appearing without precursors from nonliving matter—had survived repeated attacks for a good 200 years by the time French scientist Louis Pasteur confronted it in the 1860s. In January 1860, the French Academy of Sciences offered a prize to anyone who could disprove the theory. Pasteur, experimenting with flasks of sugared yeast solutions, showed that the contents of flasks whose necks opened straight into the air would become spoiled with microorganisms, while those whose contents were protected by cotton plugs or bent necks did not. Clearly, the source of life in the flasks had come from the outside. In 1864, he claimed the French Academy's prize, and took biology further down the path to recognizing the germ origin of disease.

547 | *A Currier & Ives rendering of the Battle of Gettysburg in Pennsylvania*

Verne Advances Science Fiction

549 **1864** With its publication, Jules Verne's novel *A Journey to the Center of the Earth* became the first modern "novel of imagination." The journey of Professor Liedenbrock and his nephew Axel across Iceland and deep into the earth takes them into prehistory and the origins of humanity. Verne's blend of adventure and science—the book was filled with geological facts—proved popular in novel after novel and set the standard for the new genre of science fiction.

Steel Gets a Boost

550 **1864** The rapidly expanding steel industry of the 19th century got another boost with the advent of open-hearth technology. Carl Siemens, a German-born British engineer, devised a way to heat the waste air in the steelmaking furnace to extraordinarily high levels by passing it back and forth through a brick chamber. Pierre and Émile Martin of France then became the first to use the technique in 1864.

The Siemens-Martin open-hearth process was slower than the Bessemer system, but less wasteful and more flexible, able to use scrap iron, cold pig iron, and iron ore to make steel. The open-hearth method and the Bessemer process were both used widely around the world well into the 20th century, when they were replaced in more developed countries by basic oxygen steelmaking.

FOOTNOTE Pig iron took its name from the way it was formed: molten cast iron ran from the blast furnace into a trough of sand, from which extended a number of smaller, perpendicular troughs, looking like a litter of nursing piglets.

Nationalism in Music

551 **1866** Composers in Russia, Bohemia (now the Czech Republic), and Scandinavia, tired of German domination of their music, began in the 1860s to create works that reflected their own national heritage and folk traditions. Leading the way in musical nationalism was *The Bartered Bride,* a comic opera by Bedrich Smetana that had its premiere in Prague in 1866. The rollicking opera, involving Bohemian villagers, an arranged marriage, and a man in a bear suit, employed the syncopated rhythms and melodies of Bohemian folk music to great effect.

Smetana was joined in his quest for national expression by his countryman Antonin Dvořák, in Russia by the composers César Cui, Mily Balakirev, Aleksandr Borodin, Modest Mussorgsky, and

FIRST PERSON

Fyodor Dostoyevsky

CRIME AND PUNISHMENT, 1866

On an exceptionally hot evening early in July a young man came out of the garret in which he lodged in S. Place and walked slowly, as though in hesitation, towards K. bridge. He had successfully avoided meeting his landlady on the staircase. His garret was under the roof of a high, five-storied house and was more like a cupboard than a room. The landlady who provided him with garret, dinners, and attendance, lived on the floor below, and every time he went out he was obliged to pass her kitchen, the door of which invariably stood open. And each time he passed, the young man had a sick, frightened feeling, which made him scowl and feel ashamed. He was hopelessly in debt to his landlady, and was afraid of meeting her.

This was not because he was cowardly and abject, quite the contrary; but for some time past he had been in an overstrained irritable condition, verging on hypochondria. He had become so completely absorbed in himself, and isolated from his fellows that he dreaded meeting, not only his landlady, but anyone at all. He was crushed by poverty, but the anxieties of his position had of late ceased to weigh upon him. He had given up attending to matters of practical importance; he had lost all desire to do so. Nothing that any landlady could do had a real terror for him. But to be stopped on the stairs, to be forced to listen to her trivial, irrelevant gossip, to pestering demands for payment, threats and complaints, and to rack his brains for excuses, to prevaricate, to lie—no, rather than that, he would creep down the stairs like a cat and slip out unseen.

The heat in the street was terrible: and the airlessness, the bustle and the plaster, scaffolding, bricks, and dust all about him, and that special Petersburg stench, so familiar to all who are unable to get out of town in summer—all worked painfully upon the young man's already overwrought nerves....

Nikolay Rimsky-Korsakov—known as "the Five"—and in Scandinavia by Edvard Grieg, Carl Nielsen, and Jean Sibelius. Their important works on national themes include Mussorgsky's *Boris Gudonov* (1874), Dvořák's *Slavonic Dances* (1878), and Grieg's *Peer Gynt Suite* (1876).

> ■ **FOOTNOTE** One of the shortest and most popular pieces of music inspired by nationalism is Rimsky-Korsakov's "Flight of the Bumblebee" from *The Tale of Tsar Saltan,* in which the young hero is turned into a bumblebee to visit his father.

Crime and Punishment

552 | **1866** The year 1866 saw the publication of one of the great works of modern literature, Fyodor Dostoyevsky's *Crime and Punishment.* The tale of a young intellectual, Raskolnikov, who kills an old woman for a complex variety of reasons, was a psychological tour de force. Dostoyevsky's portraits of characters tormented by guilt and hidden desires, and his antihero's contention that "superior" people have the right to transgress moral laws, anticipated many of the philosophical and psychological debates of the late 19th century. His novels heavily influenced such thinkers as Friedrich Nietzsche, Jean-Paul Sartre, and Sigmund Freud, as well as paving the way for the dystopian novels of writers such as George Orwell and Aldous Huxley.

Antiseptic Surgery

553 | **1867** British surgeon Joseph Lister, operating on accident victims in the Glasgow Royal Infirmary in the 1860s, was dismayed to find that 45 to 50 percent of patients undergoing amputations died afterward of sepsis—infection of

555 | *A quarry blaster uses dynamite. The explosive, though dangerous, reduced the cost of construction work.*

the bloodstream. Learning of Pasteur's theories about the transmission of germs, Lister decided that microorganisms in the air were infecting the patients' open wounds. In 1867, he began to spray the operating room air and wash his hands, surgical instruments, and catgut with carbolic acid, an antiseptic formerly used in sewage treatment. He also insisted on clean aprons for operating room personnel and on keeping open wounds protected from the air. With these precautions, the mortality rate in his operations dropped to 15 percent.

Lister's methods caught on quickly around the world, particularly in military hospitals. Together with the work of Ignaz Semmelweiss, Louis Pasteur, and Robert Koch, his contributions to antisepsis saved untold thousands of lives.

U.S. Buys Alaska

554 **1867** On March 30, U.S. Secretary of State William Seward purchased the territory of Alaska from Russia. At 7.2 million dollars for 586,412 square miles of land, the price amounted to a thrifty two cents per acre; nevertheless, a derisive public labeled the territory the "polar bear garden," "Seward's icebox," and "Seward's folly." The mockery would vanish in the 1890s with the discovery of gold in the region.

■ **FOOTNOTE** The purchase of Alaska increased American territory by 20 percent but American population by very little. By the 1880 census, Alaska's population numbered a little over 33,000, almost all native inhabitants.

Dynamite Invented

555 **1867** Swedish physicist Alfred Nobel, looking for a more stable alternative to nitroglycerine, invented the blasting explosive dynamite in 1867. Nobel found that he could make the explosive by stabilizing nitroglycerine in a mixture with kieselguhr, a powdery rock made primarily of silica. He also invented a blasting cap, filled with gunpowder and ignited by a fuse, that could be used to detonate the explosion. The invention greatly reduced the cost of construction work

around the world. Nobel became a rich man and a philanthropist whose will established the funds for five Nobel Prizes.

Canada Pulls Together

556 **1867** Wary of the United States' increasing military and economic power, and eager to secure the northwest for expansion, leaders of Canada's disparate colonies agreed to form a union. In 1867, the British North America Act joined Nova Scotia, New Brunswick, and Canada East and West (now Quebec and Ontario) into the Dominion of Canada. The new central government had a British-style parliamentary system; it guaranteed the legal rights of French-speaking Quebec and divided powers between the federal government and the former colonies, now provinces. In 1869, the Northwest Territories were added to the mix, and in 1871 British Columbia also joined the union.

Japan Installs Meiji Emperor

557 **1868** The shocking appearance of Commodore Perry's four warships in Edo Bay in 1853 shook the foundations of Japan's isolationist government. For centuries, Japan had been ruled by a military aristocracy headed by a shogun, powerful regional lords—daimyos—and the samurai, formerly a warrior class. The emperor had become a figurehead. With the advent of Western forces on their

Periodic Table Laid Out

558 **1869** Throughout the 1800s, chemists had been new adding elements to the list of those already known: iodine, lithium, aluminum, and so on, until by 1860 about 60 or 70 had been identified. The symbols for denoting elements that John Dalton had devised in his work (see event 447) had been replaced by the one- or two-letter system in use today, but scientists in different countries called the elements by different names, and they could not agree on the atomic weights of many of them or on how to write out formulas or depict molecules. In 1860, the First International Chemical Conference, in Karlsruhe, Germany, clarified many of these issues, resulting in a general agreement on how to order the elements according to atomic weight.

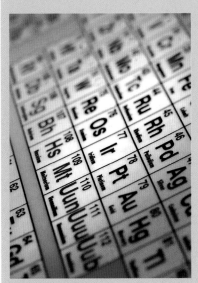

The periodic table organizes chemical elements by atomic number.

It took the work of Siberian chemist Dmitry Mendeleyev, however, to reveal a deeper relationship among the elements. A devoted solitaire player, Mendeleyev wrote the names, atomic weights, and properties of all the elements on cards and then arranged them according to atomic weight. As he moved the cards about, he realized that elements with similar properties would occur at regular intervals, or periods. (British chemist John Newlands had made a similar observation in 1864 but was widely ridiculed at the time.) Mendeleyev rearranged the cards into columns of similar elements: the first periodic table, published in 1869. He was so confident of his conclusions that he even left gaps in the table where he predicted (correctly) new elements would appear. Although Mendeleyev's idea was not accepted immediately, over the next two decades he was vindicated. Today, the periodic table has well over 100 elements but retains Mendeleyev's organization.

539 More Details on the Pony Express

It was the discovery of gold in Sutter's Mill, California, in 1848 that first created the demand for a swift and efficient cross-continental mail service. The Pacific Mail Steamship Company was the first to be contracted for this mammoth task, carrying mail from New York to San Francisco (via the Isthmus of Panama) by ship. This took three to four weeks, at best.

The Overland Mail Company attempted to improve upon this time by running a stagecoach route across the southern U.S. between Tipton, Missouri, and San Francisco, but the advertised delivery time of 28 days more often took several months. The citizens of California, for example, did not learn that their state was accepted into the Union until almost six months after the fact.

When this southern route through the states was threatened by the prospect of Civil War, a new route—and a new type of service—was needed. Enter the short-lived but legendary Pony Express, which used an elaborate but remarkably efficient system of stations and riders to cut the cross-country delivery time down to 10 days in summer, 12 to 16 days in winter.

> The riders, often not more than 20 years old, embodied the rugged, individualistic spirit of the American West.

The riders, often not more than 20 years old, took an oath "not to use profane language, not to get drunk, not to gamble, not to treat animals cruelly and not to do anything else that is incompatible with the conduct of a gentleman." They were paid 100 dollars per month to carry mail on horseback from St. Joseph, Missouri, to Sacramento, California, along the new "central route." Riding at all hours of the day, in all seasons of the year, they embodied the rugged, individualistic spirit of the American West, proving that sheer manpower could achieve what technology had yet to accomplish.

Though the cross-continental telegraph would eventually render the Pony Express obsolete just a year and a half after it began, the Express became an icon of the frontier, one that still captures our modern imagination.

"Pony Express Rider" by W. H. Jackson. The back says: "This courier of the first fast mail is speeding up the Valley of the Sweetwater in what is now Wyoming."

shores, Japanese bureaucrats and military rulers began an internal struggle between those who wanted to open to the West and modernize and those who clung to the status quo. In 1866, some samurai even armed themselves with American Civil War cannon to fight forces of the shogunate. Eventually, in 1867, the last shogun, Yoshinobu, resigned. In 1868 the reformers installed a new emperor, Mutsuhito, who was called Meiji—"the Enlightened One."

A centralized government replaced the old shogun system and the capital was moved from Kyoto to Tokyo (formerly known as Edo). Further reforms would follow, including the abolishment of feudalism and the samurai class, industrialization, modernization of the military, and the beginnings of compulsory education.

Grand Canyon Explored

559 **1869** John Wesley Powell, geologist and ethnologist, was a Civil War veteran who went on to study both the geology of the West and American Indian languages. In 1869 he led the Powell Geographic Expedition, which traveled by boat through the Grand Canyon. He heralded the hazardous trip

561 | *Ships moored at Port Said, entry to the Suez Canal, circa 1860*

559 | *John Wesley Powell, explorer and ethnologist of the American West*

in his diary: "We have an unknown distance yet to run; an unknown river yet to explore. What falls there are, we know not; what rocks beset the channel, we know not; what walls rise over the river, we know not. Ah, well!" Powell's surveys and expeditions provided vital information about the land and people of the West to the U.S. government.

> ■ **FOOTNOTE** Powell was the first to use the name "Grand Canyon" in published writings about the area. Local Paiutes called the canyon's plateau Kaibab, meaning "mountain lying down."

Railroad Connects Coasts

560 **1869** For much of the 19th century, the U.S. government and private entrepreneurs alike had dreamed of a transcontinental railroad connecting the western United States to the established rail lines of the East. In 1862, their wishes began to be fulfilled when the Pacific Railway Bill established two railroads—the Central Pacific and the Union Pacific—to work together to build a railroad from

Council Bluffs, Iowa, where eastern lines left off, to Sacramento, California. To support the immense undertaking, the federal government gave the two companies 24 million acres of public land and loans totaling 64 million dollars.

The Central Pacific built eastward, the Union Pacific westward. Every machine, locomotive, and piece of rail had to be shipped over the Isthmus of Panama or around Cape Horn. The vast number of workers involved eventually included 12,000 Chinese immigrants, who proved to be an extraordinarily hard-working group despite suffering from lower wages and the prejudices of the other workers. Together the two companies laid some 1,700 miles of track across mountain, prairie, and desert, finally meeting at Promontory, Utah, on May 10, 1869. The railroad became a major factor in bringing settlers to the West—and contributed as well to the removal of American Indians to reservations and to the demise of the great bison herds of the Plains.

Canal Connects Europe, Asia

561 **1869** In August, Egyptian and European laborers completed work on one of the engineering marvels of the modern world: the Suez Canal. Spanning 101 miles of the Isthmus of Suez in Egypt, the canal connects the Mediterranean and Red Seas, providing a shipping route between Europe, East Africa, and Asia.

Engineers of various nationalities had speculated for centuries about building a canal across the desert isthmus. In 1854, the viceroy of Egypt, Sa'id Pasha, granted an act of concession to French diplomat Ferdinand de Lesseps, authorizing him to construct the canal. A second concession, in 1859, gave the mostly French-owned Suez Canal Company the right to operate the canal for 99 years. De Lesseps himself dug the first hole in 1859, but it took tens of thousands of Egyptian laborers, unwillingly drafted, to finish the route ten years later. The canal greatly boosted international commerce and tourism between Europe and points east and provided a route as well for European colonial ventures in Asia and East Africa.

■ **FOOTNOTE** In July 1956, Egypt seized control of the canal from its European owners; after battling Israeli, British, and French forces and sinking 40 ships to block the canal, the country negotiated a final purchase of the waterway in 1958.

Plastic Invented

562 **1869** John Wesley Hyatt, an American printer and inventor, was searching for an affordable substitute for ivory in the making of billiard balls when he invented the first plastic, celluloid, in 1869. He knew that English chemist Alexander Parkes had managed to convert the explosive chemical nitrocellulose into a nonexplosive, malleable substance. Hyatt's successful variation on this invention combined cellulose nitrate and camphor to produce a strong, moldable, versatile material—celluloid—that was made not only into billiard balls, but into an almost infinite variety of items ranging from combs and collars to film and dental plates. Though not explosive, Hyatt's invention was nevertheless flammable, and eventually newer and safer forms of plastic came to dominate the market.

Italy Unified

563 **1870** For centuries a patchwork of separate city-states and kingdoms, Italy in the 19th century began to

---

CONNECTIONS

Plastic
The many shapes of modern life

The industry touched off by John W. Hyatt's search for a better billiard ball has come to affect the everyday lives of people around the globe. In 1879, the New York printer patented a material he called celluloid, made from cellulose, nitric acid, and pyroxylin. The world's first synthetic plastic could be shaped under pressure and heat to make any number of things besides billiard balls, but it unfortunately tended to catch fire easily. Researchers in the early 1900s came up with a less flammable material called cellulose acetate, which is still used in making film, fibers, and molded objects.

Next came the invention of Bakelite by the New York chemist Leo Baekeland, who was trying to make a synthetic shellac. Combining carbolic acid with formaldehyde had always resulted in an explosive mixture. Baekeland was able to control the reaction. The resulting phenolic resin was not the shellac he had hoped for, but he christened it Bakelite in 1907 and the material soon proved highly valuable in pot handles, telephones, and many other objects.

The next few decades saw an explosion in plastics. Made of polymers, long chains of repeating molecules, plastics have the wondrous ability of being shaped in seemingly endless ways; they also come in

Bakelite plastic and AM radios, both new in the 1920s

a variety of forms—some polymers make for rigid plastics, others for flexible and even soft plastics. Scientists in the 1920s and 1930s manipulated these polymers and invented nylon, acrylics, polystyrene, and polyvinyl chloride (PVC). Nylon found application in clothing and, later, in molded gears; acrylic was employed in airplane windows; polystyrene found its way into toys, tiles, clocks, radios, and containers; and PVC was (and is) used in pipes, hoses, and insulation.

In the 1940s and 1950s new plastics added to a list that seems now to include almost every conceivable household, office, and industrial item. Silicones are used as lubricants and body implants; polyethylene can be turned into artificial flowers, dishes, plastic bags, and squeeze bottles; and epoxy resins make for good adhesives. In 1953, the Chevrolet Corvette became the first automobile with a plastic body. Today, industries such as space, medicine, architecture, and electric power would be impossible without plastics. Despite their usefulness, long-chain polymers do not break down readily, and thus plastics contribute heavily to environmental waste. Current solutions are recycling and the creation of biodegradable plastics, first introduced in the 1970s.

566 | *Paul Cézanne's "Rideau, Cruchon et Compotier" fetched $60.5 million at a Sotheby's auction in New York in May 1999.*

move toward unification. Led by politician Camillo Benso di Cavour and soldier Giuseppe Garibaldi, Italian patriots began to expel Italy's Austrian and French rulers in the 1850s and 1860s—in some cases with diplomacy, and in others by force. By April 1860, a large part of central Italy had united under Italian leadership. In 1870, the last section was added to the Italian boot when King Victor Emmanuel II (previously king of Piedmont-Sardinia) took over Rome, formerly held by France. Italy was finally a single nation.

Tchaikovsky Triumphs

564 **1870** Russian composer Pytor Ilyich Tchaikovsky, having written three unsuccessful orchestral pieces, experienced his first musical triumph in March 1870 with the premiere of the *Romeo and Juliet* overture-fantasy. The one-movement, sonata-form piece showcased the singable melodies and sweeping romanticism that were his hallmark. In the years to come, Tchaikovsky would become one of the world's most popular composers.

■ **FOOTNOTE** Although he is best remembered for only a handful of them, in the course of his 53-year life Tchaikovsky composed well over 100 works, spanning numerous genres. His output included 8 symphonies (one unfinished), 3 ballets, 11 operas, 11 overtures, and more than 100 songs and piano pieces.

Troy Uncovered

565 **1870** German archaeologist Heinrich Schliemann began to dig into a mound called Hisarlik in northwestern Turkey. He was convinced that the site held the ruins of the legendary city of Troy, immortalized in Homer's epic poem, *The Iliad*. The mound turned out to contain nine cities of different eras built on top of one another; a citadel stands in the middle and a wall surrounds the city. Finding a wealth of gold, silver, and jewelry in the second level from the bottom, Schliemann declared that he had found the lost city and the jewels of Helen of Troy. Archaeologists today believe that the Homeric Troy was in fact the sixth or seventh level from the bottom.

Impressionism Born

566 **1874** Rebelling against the conventional, "salon" style of French painting in the 1860s, with its emphasis on literary themes and carefully prepped studio art, a group of influential French painters held a controversial exhibition in 1874 in the studio of a photographer. Among the paintings exhibited was Claude Monet's "Impression: Sunrise," which led an unimpressed critic to dub the group the "impressionists."

The name was an apt one, accurately describing the new style of painting employed by Monet, Camille Pissarro, Edgar Degas, Pierre-Auguste Renoir, Paul Cézanne, and Édouard Manet, among others. In their art, the Impressionists attempted to convey the immediate visual experience in terms of transient effects of light and color. Impressionists often worked outdoors, capturing the passing light with rapid brushstrokes. Its artists went on to divergent careers, but their visual style came to affect not only art but also music, as in the compositions of Claude Debussy, and literature, such as the novels of Henry James.

■ **FOOTNOTE** Impressionist painting took hold in America as well, exemplified in the light-filled canvases of such artists as Mary Cassatt, James McNeill Whistler, William Merritt Chase, and Childe Hassam.

International Mail Regulated

567 **1874** By the 19th century, mail delivery among European and American countries had become a tangled web of bilateral agreements, with postal rates and weights varying from country to country. In the fall of 1874, the Swiss government convened a meeting in Bern, Switzerland, to establish a single postal territory with uniform rates and weight standards. On October 9, representatives of 22 nations signed the Treaty of Bern, creating the General Postal Union. Within three years, the Union had gained more members and changed its name to the Universal Postal Union.

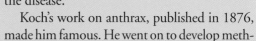

Germ Theory Confirmed

568 **1876** Throughout the 1800s, the work of scientists such as Ignaz Semmelweis, Joseph Lister, Casimir-Joseph Davaine, and Louis Pasteur had been leading to the conclusion that disease was transmitted by "germs"—tiny living entities invisible to the naked eye. This theory was finally confirmed in the 1870s through the solid scientific detective work of German physician Robert Koch.

Koch was living in a town in Germany when local farmers asked for his help in fighting an outbreak of anthrax that was killing their cattle. Working in a small laboratory in his home, the young doctor was able to identify the rod-shaped bacillus that appeared to cause the disease. Pasteur, viewing the microbes through a microscope, confirmed his findings. Koch then injected many generations of mice with the bacilli, which indeed infected them with the disease. He was also able to cultivate the microbe and observe that it formed spores, which could remain dormant in the earth and infect animals for years. Pasteur, in turn, created a vaccine for the disease.

Germs, magnified in a color-enhanced scanning electron micrograph

Koch's work on anthrax, published in 1876, made him famous. He went on to develop methods for cultivating a variety of microbes in the lab, later discovering the cholera bacillus and the tubercle bacillus (which causes tuberculosis). His systematic approach to proving the germ-borne transmission of disease is summarized in the four rules known as Koch's postulates:

• A specific microorganism is always associated with a given disease.
• The microorganism can be isolated from the diseased animal and grown in pure culture in the laboratory.
• The cultured microbe will cause disease when transferred to a healthy animal.
• The same type of microorganism can be isolated from the newly infected animal.

Koch won the Nobel Prize in 1905. His work, with that of Pasteur and many other 19th-century physicians, transformed the study of disease and contributed to the huge advances in sanitation and medicine that boosted life spans around the world in the next hundred years.

Internal Combustion Engine

569 **1876** Steam engines powered the early industrial revolution, but they had their drawbacks. Heavy and inefficient, they required a separate furnace and a water source. In the 1800s, several inventors proposed variations on an internal combustion engine; they included French engineer Alphonse Beau de Rochas, who outlined the basic principles of the four-stroke engine cycle. It was German engineer Nikolaus Otto, however, who built the first practical internal combustion engine in 1876. Running on coal gas, a flammable distillate of coal, it used the four-stroke cylinder-and-piston cycle that is still in use today. Though heavy and unwieldy by today's standards, the engine was an instant success, and Otto's company sold about 50,000 of them at

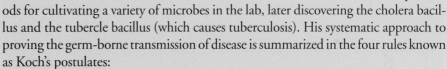

one to ten horsepower each before being overtaken by more modern, gasoline-powered engines.

> ■ **FOOTNOTE** Coal gas and petroleum were not the only fuels proposed by early tinkerers with internal combustion engines; other designs involved gunpowder, a hydrogen/oxygen mix similar to rocket fuel, and kerosene.

Telephone Invented

570 **1876** The inventor of the telephone was a Scottish-born elocution teacher who knew little of engineering. Alexander Graham Bell was the son of a famed speech expert who had devised a system for teaching the deaf to speak. The younger Bell followed in his father's footsteps, becoming a teacher of the deaf at Boston University in the 1870s. As part of his research into sound, Bell began to toy with the idea of transmitting sound via electricity, realizing that the electrical signal would have to reproduce the undulating form of sound waves. Teaching by day and working in his spare hours with a young American mechanic, Thomas Watson, on March 7, 1876, Bell finally filed a patent for "the method of, and apparatus for, transmitting vocal or other sounds telegraphically, as herein described, by causing electrical undulations." On March 10, 1876, he set up his latest design, containing a liquid transmitter, and spoke through it to his assistant down the hall: "Mr. Watson, come here, I want you."

Within a year, the first private telephone lines had been strung; by 1881, private telephone exchanges were in place in most major cities and towns in the United States.

Ottoman Constitution

571 **1876** The Ottoman Empire, once a great power, was embattled from without and within in the middle of the 19th century. Factions within the government argued about whether the empire could strengthen itself by establishing Western-style reforms and institutions, with advocates of reform usually winning out. By the 1870s, railroads, newspapers, and university education had been established within the empire. On December 23, 1876, the reforms came to a head with the first Ottoman constitution—indeed, the first formal constitution in any Islamic country. Although the document safeguarded many of the sultan's powers, it nevertheless provided for a national assembly and guaranteed the rights of its citizens without regard to ethnicity or religion.

CONNECTIONS

Telephonic Communication
Trillions of words spoken on hundreds of millions of telephones, make the world seem a smaller place

On March 10, 1876, Boston inventor Alexander Graham Bell spoke the words "Mr. Watson, come here, I want you" to his assistant after spilling battery acid on himself. Watson rushed into the adjacent room, and the two of them realized the invention they'd been tinkering with—the transmission of the human voice through an electrical current—worked.

Bell was not the first person with the idea for a telephone (from the Greek for "far" and "sound"). Since the 1830s, scientists had understood that vibrations in iron or steel could be turned into electrical impulses and hence that sound itself could travel over a wire. Yet it took an inventor who saw the commercial possibilities of telephony to carry out the work. In 1875 Bell noticed that when Watson was trying to fix a metal reed in their experimental harmonic telegraph, he could distinctly hear the sound—the electrical current had mimicked the variations Watson was making. Excited by the prospects, he went on to patent the telephone in less than a year.

Bell then had to sell his idea. It took more than a year of demonstrations before he could interest the public in his newfangled apparatus. He used a telegraph line to show how the device could work over several miles. It was not long before separate telephone lines were being strung. Those earliest lines connected individual phones—each connected to every single one. To cut down on the tangle of wires, centralized switchboards were set up. Until the early 1900s, switchboard operators manually connected all telephone calls.

Alexander Bell demonstrates telephone

By 1880, the United States had 138 telephone exchanges, connecting 30,000 subscribers. Seven years later there were nearly 1,200 exchanges and 150,000 subscribers, linked by some 146,000 miles of wire. Transcontinental telephone lines connected New York with San Francisco by 1915, and in 1927 people in New York could talk with people in London via radiotelephone (transmitted by radio waves). An actual undersea telephone cable from Europe to North America commenced operation in 1956.

In 1980 fiber-optic lines began carrying local calls in Atlanta, Georgia. Made of hair-thin filaments of light-transmitting glass, fiber-optic lines can carry more information than copper wires and require less amplification; they are also less subject to electrical interference. By the end of the 1980s, fiber-optic lines crossed both the Atlantic and Pacific. At the same time wireless cellular telephone service, transmitted via satellite, was available in most cities in the United States. Today a vast telecommunications network links people instantaneously in all but the most remote places on Earth.

Phonograph Invented

572 **1877** The invention of the phonograph followed closely on the heels of the invention of the telephone. Working in his laboratory in Menlo Park, New Jersey, Thomas Alva Edison was attempting to create a device that would graphically transcribe messages sent over a telegraph or telephone. He found that a diaphragm and stylus vibrating with the transmitted sounds could emboss a pattern on rotating cylinder covered with paraffin paper. Surprisingly, when the indented paper was pulled back beneath the stylus, it produced a reproduction of the original sounds.

In December 1877, Edison filed for a patent on his phonograph machine, now employing tinfoil instead of paraffin paper. That month, the editors of *Scientific American* wrote, "Mr. Thomas A. Edison recently came into this office, placed a little machine on our desk, turned a crank, and the machine inquired as to our health, asked how we liked the phonograph, informed us that it was very well, and bid us a cordial good night." Both Edison and Alexander Graham Bell separately worked to improve the phonograph over the next decade, arriving at the wax-cylinder model that took the device into the 20th century.

■**FOOTNOTE** Among the first recordings in the early decades of phonography were scores of cylinders containing surprisingly bawdy songs, recitations, and limericks. Agents of anti-vice crusader Anthony Comstock, who obtained passage of the legislation bearing his name, which bans "obscene, lewd, and/or lascivious" material from the mails, destroyed most of them.

Chile, Bolivia, Peru at Odds

573 **1879** Many Latin American countries in the late 19th century were dependent on exports, a fact that made both natural resources and access to ports especially valuable. In 1879, war broke out among Chile, Bolivia, and Peru over the rights to valuable nitrate deposits (used in fertilizers and explosives) in the desolate Atacama Desert. Chile invaded

572 | *Inventor Thomas Alva Edison poses in his laboratory.*

Bolivia's port city of Antofagasta on February 14; Bolivia, in return, called on Peru for assistance. By 1881, Chilean naval forces had taken control of the coast and entered the Peruvian capital of Lima.

Peruvian forces resisted for two more years, but the War of the Pacific finally ended in 1883 with the Treaty of Ancón, which granted Chile the rights to the nitrate deposits as well as the Peruvian province of Tarapacá and the Bolivian province of Antofagasta. The loss was a particularly severe blow to Bolivia, permanently separating it from the sea. Chile's size grew by one-third, while governments were toppled in Peru and Bolivia.

Lightbulb Perfected

574 **1879** Thomas Alva Edison was not the first person to conceive of the idea of an incandescent electric light, but he was the first to make it practical. A number of inventors, notably the English physicist Joseph Swan, had produced sim-

ple electric lights in the 19th century. Swan's used a filament of carbonized paper in an airless bulb; when electricity passed through the filament, it glowed, producing light. Swan could not find a reliable electric source, though, and had difficulty maintaining a vacuum in the bulb. (In the presence of air, the filament burned away.)

Edison took up these challenges in 1878. He and his assistants spent months testing materials for the filament before arriving at a carbon filament made from burned sewing thread. With that, a lower electrical current, and a better globe for the vacuum, Edison had a light that would burn for hours.

Edison developed not just a practical lightbulb but also many elements necessary to installing electric lighting in multiple households. They included the parallel circuit, safety fuses, and light sockets with on-off switches. In December 1879 he demonstrated his success by lighting up his laboratory in Menlo Park, New Jersey. He soon went on to develop an entire distribution system for electric lighting and built the first commercial power station on Pearl Street in Manhattan in 1882, serving 59 customers.

The first lightbulb was made by Joseph Swan, but Edison made it practical.

575 | *Russian tsar Alexander II*

Bomb Kills Alexander II

575 **1881** Tsar Alexander II's many reforms in the 1860s and '70s fueled a great societal upheaval in Russia, turmoil that was not always favorable to Alexander's regime. A new generation of intelligentsia, often educated in the West, began to agitate for more radical reforms in education and the press. Some went further and advocated anarchism, the total abolition of all government, starting with the tsar. After surviving previous assassination attempts, Tsar Alexander II was finally killed by a bomb in St. Petersburg in 1881: an event that only stepped up further repression and social unrest in Russia.

Architecture's Chicago School

576 **1881** The fruitful partnership of young Chicago architect Louis

Henry Sullivan and Dankmar Adler, begun in 1881, changed the face of modern architecture. Along with several other architects and engineers, they formed what is now known as the Chicago School of architecture, emphasizing simplicity of structure and technical prowess. Using a new iron-and-steel frame for their construction, members of the Chicago School built the first skyscrapers in that city, including the ten-story Home Insurance Company Building of 1884-85 and Sullivan's ten-story Auditorium Building (1889).

> ■ **FOOTNOTE** One of Sullivan and Adler's most promising assistants was a young drafts-man named Frank Lloyd Wright. Wright became Sullivan's chief assistant and worked for the company from 1887 until 1893.

American Red Cross Founded

577 **1881** Clara Barton, born in Oxford, Massachusetts, became famous as the "angel of the battlefield" for her volunteer work in bringing medical supplies to wounded soldiers during the American Civil War. In 1870, she was caught up in the Franco-Prussian War while on a trip to Europe. Throwing herself into the relief effort in France, she saw firsthand the effective aid given by the newly formed International Red Cross. When she returned to the United States, Barton lobbied three successive Presidents—Rutherford B. Hayes, James Garfield, and Chester Arthur—to sign a treaty establishing an American branch of the relief group. Arthur finally signed the treaty in 1881. Barton became its first president and, among other early ventures, rode on the first train to help the victims of the Johnstown Flood in 1889.

Standard Oil Consolidates

578 **1881** The United States before the Civil War was a land of small farms and small businesses. After the war, savvy business owners realized that the time was ripe for "combination": the consolidation of many competing businesses into a few corporations and trusts. Leading the way was John D. Rockefeller's Standard

Oil Company. Standard Oil's lawyers created a trust in 1882, setting up a board of trustees and persuading stockholders of competing oil companies to turn over their stock in return for trust certificates. Efficiency increased, competition faded, profits soared, and Rockefeller became immensely rich as the head of America's first great monopoly. Other industries followed suit, including cottonseed oil, whisky, sugar, and tobacco. By 1904, 319 industrial trusts had engulfed 5,300 previously independent businesses.

Britain Occupies Egypt

579 **1882** Egypt's rulers (known as khedives), struggling to modernize their ancient country and fend off bankruptcy while resisting European influence, faced challenges from within during the 1880s. After the government attempted to save money by disbanding Egyptian regiments, young officer Ahmad Orabi led a revolt in the summer of 1882. Egypt's khedive asked for British military aid, a move that further angered his opponents. Riots broke out in the city of Alexandria. Worried that they would lose ground in such a strategic location, the British sent a fleet to Alexandria, bombarded the port, and then sent an expeditionary force ashore in September to end Orabi's rebellion. The British now occupied Egypt and took firm control of the country's government and finances, beginning decades of dominance in the Islamic heartland.

Gaudí Begins Church

580 **1883** Antoni Gaudí i Cornet, a Spanish (Catalan) architect, became famous in his lifetime for his eccentric, fantastical, organic design. His distinctive buildings, almost all in Barcelona, also became prominent symbols of a Catalan culture trying to break away from Castilian domination. Most notable among them is the still unfinished Sagrada Família, or Church of the Holy Family, a towering, intricate, quasi-Gothic sandcastle of a building first commissioned in 1883. Gaudí eventually abandoned all his other work to concentrate on the religious structure, even going out into the streets to solicit funds from passersby, but was struck down by a trolley car when he was 75 and the church only partially finished. The architect and his greatest building remain a potent symbol of imaginative design.

■ **FOOTNOTE** Gaudí's buildings were among the most important symbols of the Catalan Renaixença, a late-19th-century nationalist movement that sought to restore the language and cultural identity of Catalonia within Spain.

1850-1913 | Age of Imperialism

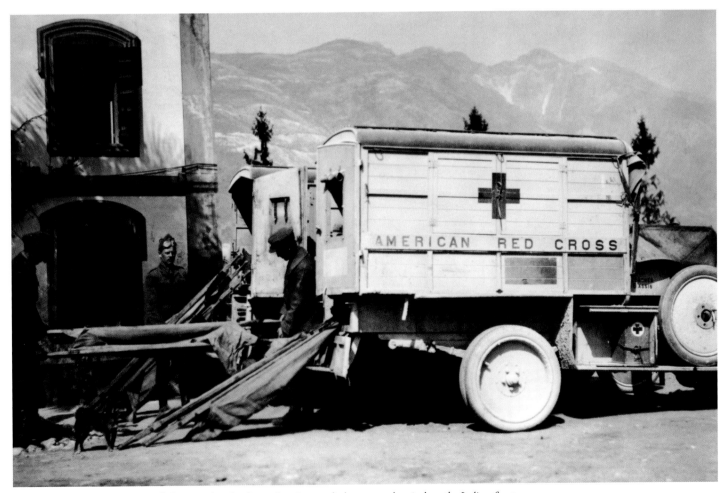

577 | *World War I American Red Cross workers load stretchers into ambulances at a hospital on the Italian front.*

Krakatau Erupts

581 **1883** On Sunday, August 26, 1883, thundering cannonlike noises began to boom from the volcanic Indonesian island of Krakatau. A black, ashy cloud rose 22 miles above the island as the blasts continued; the sounds culminated the next day with four massive roars, the final one a gigantic eruption that blew the island apart. The sound of the last blast was heard more than 2,800 miles away, making it the loudest sound in recorded history.

As two-thirds of the island collapsed into an undersea magma chamber, the eruption triggered enormous tidal waves, tsunamis up to 130 feet tall that spread across the Sunda Straits. Some nearby islands were completely submerged, while others lost all vegetation and habitation along their coastlines. When the eruptions and tsunamis subsided, more than 36,000 people were dead, some killed by the pyroclastic flows of the eruptions, but most (about 90 percent) by the deadly waves.

FOOTNOTE On August 11, 1930, a new volcanic island rose above the waves in place of the destroyed Krakatau. The new island, named Anak Krakatau, or "child of Krakatau," has already begun violent eruptions.

Prime Meridian Established

582 **1884** In a conference held in Washington, D.C., in October, 41 delegates from 25 nations met at the International Meridian Conference to agree upon standards for measuring longitude and for establishing a universal day. The delegates agreed that the line of longitude passing through the center of the transit instrument at the Observatory of Greenwich, England, would be the prime meridian, or 0 degrees longitude. The meridian became the reference from which all other lines of longitude are measured, east and west. It also became the baseline for 24 standard time zones around the world, a measure that greatly simplified long-distance transportation and telecommunications.

Imperialism in Africa

583 **1884** Powered by modernizing industry and telecommunications and looking for new markets and new territories, European powers turned their eyes toward the African continent in the late 19th century. In the 1870s, King Leopold II of Belgium read that the Congo Basin held untold riches waiting for "any enterprising capitalist." Leopold's formation of the International African Association, which set up trading stations along the area's rivers, drew protests from other European countries. Britain and Portugal then mutually agreed to reserve navigation rights on the Congo River. In late 1884, Germany's Otto von Bismarck called for an international conference in Berlin to lay out ground rules for European intervention on the continent. Representatives of every European nation except Switzerland, as well as the United States, attended—but none from any African country. The agreement hammered out in Berlin recognized Leopold's control of the Congo Basin, allowed international freedom of navigation along key rivers,

Leopold shared the dream of South African Cecil Rhodes to "annex the planets if I could."

and validated a British claim to Egypt, among other matters. In order to claim a territory, the treaty stipulated, a foreign power would have to actually occupy the land.

The Berlin Congress, which concluded in 1885, effectively declared the African continent to be open for the taking to European powers, and take it they did, controlling all but two countries by 1914.

First Chain-Driven Bike

584 **1885** Bicycling was a popular pastime for the fit and reckless throughout much of the 19th century. Velocipedes of various makes were produced in Europe and the United States, including "boneshakers," with their iron-rimmed wheels, and "penny-farthings" with enormous front wheels. Most were propelled by pedals attached directly to the front or rear wheels. By the 1880s, bicycles began to take on the features seen in today's models: In particular, the 1885 Rover Safety, designed by English inventor John Kemp Starley, was probably the first to combine a modern chain drive, 30-inch wheels with rubber tires, and front-mounted steering.

Huckleberry Finn Published

585 **1885** Mark Twain's *Adventures of Huckleberry Finn,* published in the United States in 1885, was a landmark in American literature. Told in the casual dialect of a young boy from Missouri, it describes the adventures of Huck Finn and the runaway slave Jim as they float down the Mississippi River looking for freedom. Twain contrasted the natural condition of the two people on the river and their intrinsic moral sense with the hypocrisy of the middle class on shore to devastating effect. Sharply funny and critical of American society, the book was praised at its publication—the *San Francisco Chronicle* called Twain "the Edison of our literature"—even while it aroused controversy among the reading public. It continues to do so today, despite Twain's notice up front that "PERSONS attempting to find a motive in this narrative will be prosecuted; persons attempting to find a moral in it will be banished; persons attempting to find a plot in it will be shot."

584 | *Bicycling company advertisement, 1890s*

First Practical Auto Designed

586 **1885** German engineer Karl Benz, having worked for years to build a "motor carriage" with the four-stroke engine earlier devised by Nikolaus Otto, succeeded in early 1885. Like modern automobiles, Benz's motorcar was powered by gasoline and had electrical ignition, a water-cooled engine, and differential gears. Unlike cars of today, it had only a single seat and three wheels on a horseshoe-shaped frame; it operated at 250 rpm. In 1886, Benz was granted a patent for his automobile, the Patent-Motorwagen. He began selling his invention that summer, redesigning it to a four-wheeled version in 1893. Eventually he merged his automobile company with that of another automotive pioneer, Gottlieb Daimler.

■ **FOOTNOTE** The first Daimler-Benz Mercedes automobiles were built in 1900. They were racing cars named after the daughter of one of their first promoters, Austrian businessman Emil Jellinek.

Statue of Liberty Arrives

587 **1885** Broken down into 350 pieces and packed in 214 crates, the Statue of Liberty—officially, "Liberty Enlightening the World"—arrived in New York Harbor on June 19 aboard the French frigate *Isere*. Designed by French sculptor Frédéric-Auguste Bartholdi, it was a gift from the people of France to those of the United States in honor of the centennial of the Declaration of Independence. President Grover Cleveland dedicated the statue in 1886. Facing east toward the ocean, it has become a symbol of freedom to millions of immigrants entering the United States for the first time through New York.

■ **FOOTNOTE** Emma Lazarus's poem "The New Colossus"—"Give me your tired, your poor, your huddled masses yearning to breathe free"—was originally composed as part of the efforts to raise funds for the statue's pedestal.

Four-Wheel Auto

588 **1885** Even while Karl Benz was devising his three-wheeled motorcar, his compatriot Gottlieb Daimler was pursuing a similar aim with his partner, Wilhelm Maybach. Together the men built the first high-speed internal combustion engine with a carburetor; it was capable of running at 900 rpm. After testing it on a bicycle frame in 1885, they added their engine to a former horse carriage, creating the first four-wheeled automobile. By 1889, Daimler had built an automobile from scratch. The four-speed vehicle had its engine in the rear and was steered by a tiller. Daimler founded his own automobile company, Daimler-Motoren-Gesellschaft, in 1890, and built the first Mercedes in 1900.

Pasteur Develops Vaccines

589 **1885** Proceeding from one important discovery to another, Louis Pasteur saved some of the best for last. Searching for a way to systematically develop vaccines, he and a colleague injected some chickens with an old culture of chicken cholera, and then injected that group and a control group with a fresh culture of cholera germs. The inoculated chickens survived, while the unexposed fowl died. Pasteur then performed similar tests on sheep using a weakened anthrax culture as a vaccine: Again, all the inoculated animals became immune to the disease. But the first human test of Pasteur's vaccine-making skills came unexpectedly in 1885. A local boy, Joseph Meister, had been bitten by a rabid dog. Knowing that the boy would certainly die without treatment, Pasteur injected him 13 times with weakened cultures taken from the spinal cord of a rabid rabbit. The boy survived. Pasteur's technique of using weakened cultures

FIRST PERSON

Krakatau
WIFE OF CONTROLLER, KETIMBANG, 1883

Suddenly, it became pitch dark. The last thing I saw was the ash being pushed up through the cracks in the floorboards, like a fountain. I turned to my husband and heard him say in dispair "Where is the knife ... I will cut all our wrists and then we shall be re-leased from our suffering sooner." The knife could not be found. I felt a heavy pressure, throwing me to the ground. Then it seemed as if all the air was being sucked away and I could not breathe. . . . I felt people rolling over me. . . . No sound came from my husband or children . . . I remember thinking, I want to . . . go outside . . . but I could not straighten my back . . . I tottered, doubled up, to the door . . . I forced myself through the opening . . . I tripped and fell. I realized the ash was hot and I tried to protect my face with my hands. The hot bite of the pumice pricked like needles. . . . Without thinking, I walked hopefully forward. Had I been in my right mind, I would have understood what a dangerous thing it was to . . . plunge into the hellish darkness . . . I ran up against . . . branches and did not even think of avoiding them. I entangled my-self more and more. . . . My hair got caught up . . . I noticed for the first time that [my] skin was hanging off everywhere, thick and moist from the ash stuck to it. Thinking it must be dirty, I wanted to pull bits of skin off, but that was still more painful . . . I did not know I had been burnt.

was unquestionably successful, even though no one at the time knew exactly why. Pasteur went on to head an institute bearing his name and devoted to developing a treatment for rabies.

■ **FOOTNOTE** Joseph Meister, the boy Pasteur cured of rabies, later became caretaker of Pasteur's tomb at the Pasteur Institute in Paris. In 1940, when the Nazis invaded Paris, Meister committed suicide.

Thus Spoke Zarathustra

590 **1885** German philosopher and classical scholar Friedrich Wilhelm Nietzsche wrote his seminal works between 1872 and 1888, but it was only after his death in 1900 that his philosophy became widely known. Perhaps his most famous book was *Thus Spoke Zarathustra*, published between 1883 and 1885. In it,

his protagonist Zarathustra returns from a ten-year stay in the wilderness to preach a new philosophy, one that rejects traditional religion. "Once the sin against God was the greatest sin, but God died," he says, enjoining each man to rise above the masses as a superman who will pursue self-mastery, creativity, and individuality, leaving behind standard conventions of good and evil.

Nietzsche's writing became hugely influential in the early 20th century, when it inspired philosophers, writers, dramatists, and psychologists including Sigmund Freud and Carl Jung. His concepts were also adopted and greatly distorted by the growing anti-Semitic movement in Germany.

Practical Adding Machine

591 **1885** Working as a bank clerk in New York, William Seward

Burroughs resolved to invent a machine that could automatically perform the tedious addition tasks involved in business. After poor health led to his going to work in a machine shop in St. Louis, Missouri, Burroughs patented his first calculating machine in 1885 and organized the American Arithmometer Company in 1886 with two partners to sell the devices. An improved version of the machine, invented in 1891, began to sell widely to banks. Operators entered the digits to be added on a keyboard, then pulled a crank to add the number to previous entries and print the total. By 1926, the company, now named the Burroughs Corporation, had sold a million units of the adding machine. By 1986, the corporation merged with Sperry Univac to form the computer company Unisys.

CONNECTIONS

Karl Benz
The open road, the busy highway

The invention of the automobile took place gradually over several years, with the involvement of many people working independently. Yet once the car became established as a consumer good in the early 1900s, it became firmly embedded in American and European culture. Perhaps more than any other invention, the automobile has changed the way we live.

The first steam-powered vehicle appeared in France in 1769, and, in fact, steam cars would hang on until the demise of the Stanley Steamer company in 1924. With their bulky, noisy engines, steam cars were a dead end in automobile evolution. A battery-powered electric car was successfully brought out by American inventor William Morrison in the 1890s. It had the advantage of quietness, ease of operation, and lack of noxious fumes; sadly, its top speed was only 20 miles an hour and it had to be recharged every 50 miles.

What made the automobile industry take off was the invention of the internal combustion engine. When such engines were adapted to carriages by German engineers Karl Benz and Gottlieb Daimler in 1885, the automobile found a road to the future. It was ten years later that the French rubber manufacturer Michelin began selling pneumatic tires (tires with compressed air). Now equipped with a gasoline-powered engine and pressurized

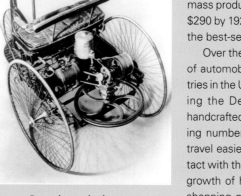

Benz three-wheeler, 1885

tires, the automobile industry was primed for a boom. Two major things happened to spur the industry. First, oil was discovered in Texas in 1901—its abundance meant a ready source of cheap fuel. Next, assembly-line production methods were applied to the manufacture of automobiles by Ransom Olds in 1901 and Henry Ford a few years later; suddenly nearly everyone could afford a car.

The Model T Ford, or Tin Lizzie, was first available in 1908 for $825, but through perfecting of mass production Ford was able to drop the price to $290 by 1924. For nearly 20 years the Model T was the best-selling car on the market.

Over the next several decades the manufacture of automobiles became one of the leading industries in the United States and abroad. Except for during the Depression, both mass-produced and handcrafted luxury cars were sold in ever increasing numbers. The car culture made independent travel easier, brought isolated areas in closer contact with the outside world, and led to tremendous growth of highways and their attendant suburbs, shopping malls, motels, and drive-in restaurants and similar businesses. Now automobile traffic and pollution have become major problems in urban areas. Future cars may employ clean-burning hydrogen fuel cells in hybrid cars that—like today's hybrids—have more than one power source.

South African Gold Rush

592 **1886** South Africa's economy, population, and politics were all dramatically affected by the 1886 discovery of the world's largest goldfields. Found in a rocky ridge called the Witwatersrand, the gold pulled in large numbers of immigrants and investors, many of them British. The boomtown of Johannesburg sprang up nearby to accommodate the throngs of miners, growing to a city of 100,000 within the decade. The influx of British fortune-seekers and financiers further aggravated existing tensions between British and Boer settlers in the country, pushing them down the road to the Boer War.

Pure Aluminum Isolated

593 **1886** It is the third most abundant element in Earth's crust, but until the 1880s aluminum was considered a precious metal, rarely seen in its pure form because it was bound so tightly to its ores. In 1886, shortly after graduating from college, Ohio chemist Charles Martin Hall discovered how to isolate pure drops of aluminum metal from cryolite and aluminum oxide by electrolysis. In 1888, Hall formed the Pittsburg Reduction Company to produce the metal; it was renamed Aluminum Company of America (Alcoa) in 1907. Between 1859 and 1914, the price of the formerly precious metal dropped from 18 dollars a pound to 18 cents. The lightweight metal, a good conductor of electricity and capable of forming strong alloys, became a vital part of the shipbuilding, aircraft, and electrical power industries.

▓ **FOOTNOTE** Paul-Louis-Touissant Héroult of France discovered the identical method of producing aluminum at the same time as Hall, but did not pursue its development as quickly as the American inventor did.

Labor Federation Organized

594 **1886** As small businesses merged into big corporations in the late 19th century, workers responded by forming the first large labor unions.

593 | *Rotary, oil-fired melting furnaces at Aluminum Industries were used in 1942 to make war materials.*

Largest and most powerful of these was the American Federation of Labor (AFL), founded by Samuel Gompers in 1886. Gompers, the son of a British immigrant, began his working life at the age of ten as a cigar-roller. At 14, he joined a local craft union in New York; by 1881, he had pulled together a variety of trade unions into the Federation of Organized Trades and Labor Unions, reorganized five years later as the AFL, with Gompers at its head. Organized into local chapters based on trades or crafts, the AFL was a relatively nonpolitical group that advocated for higher wages and shorter hours as well as such issues as sanitation and limitations on child labor. By the 1920s, the organization's membership had grown into the millions.

Radio Waves Discovered

595 **1888** Following up on the work of Scottish scientist James Clerk Maxwell, who had theorized that light is just one form of electromagnetic radiation, German physicist Henrich Hertz resolved to study and even measure these invisible waves. In 1888, he built a receiver that could detect the signal produced when an electrical spark jumped a gap in a circuit. He confirmed that the signal had a wave form with a length of about a foot—and that it moved at the speed of light, confirming that it was a form of electromagnetism.

What Hertz had measured were radio waves. It would not be long before they were put to use by inventor Guglielmo Marconi in his landmark transmission across the Atlantic.

First Box Camera

596 **1888** American inventor George Eastman, head of the Eastman Dry Plate and Film Company, revolutionized the photography business when he introduced his Kodak box camera to the public in 1888. The lightweight, handheld camera was a tightly sealed wooden box containing a simple lens and a 100-exposure roll of film. It was far easier to use than the wet-plate or dry-plate versions that preceded it: Users simply advanced the film with a click of a button and mailed the entire camera back to the Eastman company for processing and reloading when the film was used up. Eastman's slogan became famous: "You press the button, we do the rest."

Photographer using a box camera in 1909. Lightweight and easy to use, it allowed everyone to take pictures.

The Kodak box camera brought snapshot photography to the masses, a trend that led one newspaper to declare, in a foreshadowing of the Internet age: "The sedate citizen can't indulge in any hilariousness without the risk of being caught in the act and having his photograph passed around among his Sunday School children." Meanwhile, Eastman introduced roll film in 1889 and reorganized his enterprise as the Eastman Kodak Company in 1892. His company came to dominate the photographic business and made Eastman a fortune, half of which he gave away.

Pneumatic Tire Invented

597 **1888** John Boyd Dunlop, a Scottish veterinarian, was just looking for a way to make his son's tricycle ride more comfortable when he filled an old garden hose with air and fitted it to the tricycle's wheels. The commercial potential of his invention was not lost on Dunlop, however, and he filed for a patent on his rubber pneumatic tire in 1888. First used on bicycles, the pneumatic tire was soon adapted by Michelin & Company for use in the newly invented motorcar, boosting both the sales of the automobile as well as the fortunes of the rubber industry.

Hull House Founded

598 **1889** Inspired by a "settlement house" she had seen in London in the 1880s, American social reformer Jane Addams, together with Ellen Gates Starr, founded Hull House in a poor area of Chicago in 1889. Staffed by middle-class social workers, almost all of them women, the neighborhood center provided education, athletics, and employment aid for 2,000 impoverished locals a week. In an era when millions of immigrants were pouring into urban tenements, Jane Addams and her supporters publicized the plight of the poor and pressed for reform. In Illinois she helped bring in the first eight-hour law for working women, the first child-labor law, and the first juvenile court. Addams went on to become an international advocate for peace; in 1931 she won the Nobel Peace Prize.

■ **FOOTNOTE** Hull House grew to include an art studio, coffee shop, music school, library, drama group, employment bureau, book bindery, swimming pool, gymnasium, and labor museum.

Eiffel Tower Built

599 **1889** When the Eiffel Tower was built in Paris in 1889, more than a few critics considered it an aesthetic affront. Today, its strong, yet lightweight and airy design is seen as heralding a new era in architecture.

The structure was commissioned by the French government in honor of the 100th anniversary of the French Revolution, its plan chosen from more than 100 submitted. The designer, bridge builder Alexandre-Gustave Eiffel, constructed the open-lattice wrought-iron tower from 18,000 pieces of iron in 21 months. At 984 feet high, it was the tallest building in the world and one of the first to include passenger elevators. Although it was an instant tourist attraction, it was nevertheless scheduled to be torn down in 1909; it was saved because its antenna could be used for military purposes.

■ **FOOTNOTE** Gustave Eiffel went on to use the tower for his experiments in wind resistance, and aerodynamics (building a wind tunnel at the foot of the structure), and for meteorological observations.

Post-Impressionism

600 **1889** Dutch painter Vincent van Gogh painted "The Starry Night" in June 1889, just a year before his death. Its thick, sweeping brushstrokes, sense of violent movement, and emotional intensity were emblematic of the vivid, subjective, non-naturalistic direction in painting known as post-Impressionism.

Except for van Gogh, almost all post-Impressionist artists were French: Paul Cézanne, Paul Gauguin, Henri de Toulouse-Lautrec, Georges Seurat, and Auguste Rodin were among the style's most prominent practitioners.

Mahler's Symphony No. 1

601 **1889** The late 19th century saw the symphony taken to new and monumental extremes. No composer better typified the movement away from classicism than the Czech-born Austrian Gustav Mahler. Mahler conducted his own first symphony, originally called *Symphonic Poem in Two Parts,* in November 1889 before a largely uncomprehending Budapest audience. The work included birdcalls, children's tunes, and dramatic outbursts from horns and percussion. Despite the piece's poor reception, Mahler went on to compose a succession of long, ecstatic, songlike, and orchestrally huge symphonies—nine in all, with a tenth unfinished. The so-called *Symphony of a Thousand,* his eighth, required multiple orchestras as well as three choirs. The works abandoned standard tonal rules to move from key to key, without necessarily ending in the home key as classical structure demanded. In these innovations, Mahler presaged the modernist works of such composers as Arnold Schoenberg.

Punch-Card Machines Debut

602 **1890** Another step in the development of computing machines was taken in 1890 when American inventor Herman Hollerith devised a machine that could automatically tabulate the data for that year's U.S. census. Workers fed punched cards one by one into a card-reading station. Metal pins dropped down through the holes and made contact with tiny wells of mercury, closing an electric circuit. Results of the tabulations were then shown on dials mounted on a wooden desklike machine.

Hollerith's success with his tabulating machine led him to found the Tabulating Machine Company in 1896, a company that eventually led to the International Business Machines Corporation (IBM).

■ **FOOTNOTE** Punch-card technology proved surprisingly durable. Widely used in early computer programming, it was still employed in voting machines and library filing systems into the 21st century.

Massacre at Wounded Knee

603 **1890** The last major conflict of America's Indian wars, the massacre at Wounded Knee spelled a grim end to the Plains Indians' resistance to assimilation. It began with the messianic vision of Paiute holy man Wovoka, who told his followers that they could be reunited with the dead in a paradise free of white people by means of a mystical Ghost Dance. News of the Ghost Dance spread through South Dakota's desperate Lakota Sioux community, already displaced and on short rations on four reservations. The death of Sioux leader Sitting Bull, shot in an altercation with police in 1890, increased tensions between the Indians and the U.S. Army. In late December 1890, Sioux Chief Big Foot and 350 of his followers left their homes, fleeing through the Badlands in desperately cold weather on toward the Pine Ridge reservation. U.S. soldiers caught up with the Sioux near the banks of Wounded Knee Creek on December 28. On the 29th, as a blizzard approached, the soldiers demanded the Indians hand over any arms; when a Sioux resisted and his gun went off, shooting broke out on both sides. Nearly 300 Indians, mostly women and children, as well as Big Foot,

599 | *The Eiffel Tower, shown in 1900, seems to stand astride the Trocadero, behind.*

603 More Details on Wounded Knee

In 1890, for the first time in American history, the U.S. census could report no land free of white settlement in the West. In other words, the frontier—long a source of controversy, inspiration, and cultural legend—had ended. It is no coincidence that 1890 also marked the tragic massacre at Wounded Knee, where U.S. troops defeated once and for all the brave resistance of the Plains Indians. The West, it seemed, was finally safe for the white man.

But this fragile safety came at the expense of American Indian lives and culture. The forced assimilation and resettlement that the U.S. government imposed upon the country's native peoples caused hardship and suffering long before the violent military clashes brought resounding defeat. The reservations, initially meant to keep American Indians out of the way of white settlers (and vice versa), soon became places where natives were taught to become "civilized." Traditional tribal roles were reversed or eradicated as the men, stripped of their hunting lifestyle, depended on the women to collect government food rations.

> "You ask me to cut grass and make hay and sell it, and be rich like white men! But how dare I cut off my mother's hair."
>
> —Smohalla

The government hoped to transition the tribes to a farming way of life, giving them property of their own to cultivate. But property ownership was a white value that the Plains Indians did not share, and farming was far from what they considered a noble way of life. As Smohalla, a Wanapum spiritual leader, stated in a speech: "You ask me to cut grass and make hay and sell it, and be rich like white men! But how dare I cut off my mother's hair."

And so, by the time of the Wounded Knee massacre, the Plains Indians were a hungry, disheartened people who barely had the strength to continue fighting for their culture. A fierce blizzard swept onto the plains, as if to mark the end of the battle, and it was three days before U.S. soldiers began the mass burial captured in this photograph.

Bodies of Sioux Indians are unceremoniously piled into a mass grave in the frozen soil after the tragedy at Wounded Knee, South Dakota.

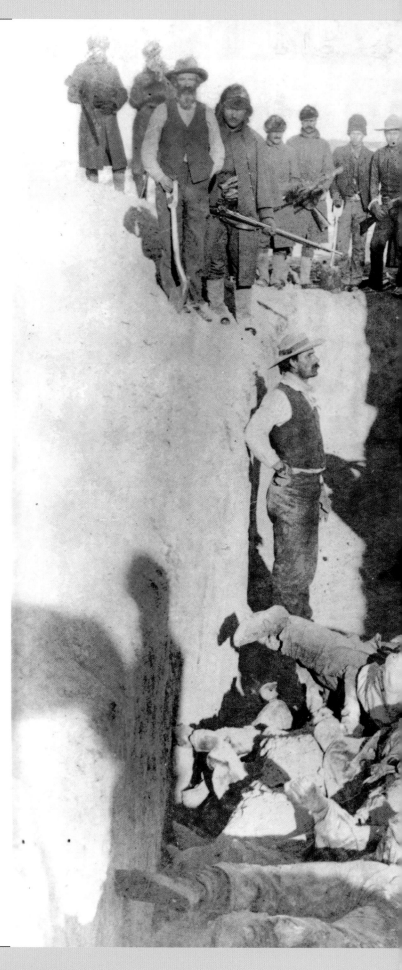

Burial of the Dead
at the Battle of Wounded Knee S.D.
NorthWestern Photo Co
Chadron Neb

were killed as they tried to run from the scene. Sioux holy man Black Elk, who was present, later said, "I can see that something else died there in the bloody mud, and was buried in the blizzard. A people's dream died there."

FOOTNOTE The massacre took place 14 years after Custer's defeat at Little Bighorn. Survivors said that soldiers called out "Remember the Little Bighorn" as they hunted down fleeing Indians in the snow.

Sherman Antitrust Act

604 **1890** Responding to the rapid consolidation of many small businesses into a few large and monopolistic ones, the American Congress passed the Sherman Antitrust Act on July 2. Its first sentence read: "Every contract, combination in the form of trust or otherwise, or conspiracy, in restraint of trade or commerce among the several States, or with foreign nations, is hereby declared to be illegal." Many of the targeted trusts managed to evade the law for years; finally President Theodore Roosevelt put some muscle behind the act to break up several large monopolies in the early 1900s.

Kinetoscope Invented

605 **1890** After a visit by Eadweard Muybridge, the stop-action photographer, American inventor Thomas Edison became sufficiently intrigued by the idea of a motion-picture camera that he patented an idea for a "kinetoscope" in 1888, without having a clear idea of how such a machine would be made. The work of developing the device fell largely to Edison's assistant William Kennedy Laurie Dickson. The machine that Dickson and his colleagues unveiled in May 1891 passed a 35mm strip of film (celluloid from the Eastman Company) in front of a shutter. Light flashing through the shutter lit each frame briefly, giving the appearance of motion. Kinetoscope parlors sprang up across America in the 1890s; patrons paid five cents to look, one by one, through a viewer at a 30-second motion picture.

Mesabi Range Drilled

606 **1890** The seven Merritt brothers of Duluth, Minnesota, drilled their first successful iron mine—the Mountain Iron Mine—in the 110-mile-long Mesabi Range of northern Minnesota. The rich mines expanded and drew in immigrant labor from northern and eastern Europe; the high-grade ore they dug

CONNECTIONS

Railroads
The glory days of the iron horse and beyond

Although the first railroads date back to the mid-16th century as horsedrawn mining vehicles, it was in the early 1800s when they began to really proliferate and push the industrial revolution into high gear. As an efficient means of carrying freight and passengers, trains still rank higher than most other means of transportation. The relative lack of friction of flanged (rimmed) wheels on steel rails means freight trains require only one horsepower to haul one ton; a tractor-trailer truck requires about ten. A train's fuel economy boasts a comparable advantage. Although passenger travel in the U.S. is now primarily by air and highway, railroads continue to dominate as freight carriers here and in the rest of the industrialized world.

English inventor Richard Trevithick presented the first successful steam locomotive in 1804, and by 1830 the world's first steam passenger railroad was in operation, carrying people the 30 miles between Liverpool and Manchester, England. It was in the 1830s that rail lines began to spread across the United States. By 1835 the United States had more than 1,000 miles of tracks, and by mid-century there were railroads operating in or under construction in every state east of the Mississippi.

With settlers pushing ever westward, the U.S. Congress began granting land for the development of railroads in 1850. Then, during the Civil War, the Union's superiority in railroads and locomotives gave it a decided edge over the Confederacy in its ability to transport troops and supplies. In the meantime, work on the first transcontinental railroad began. Chinese and European immigrants, joined by Civil War veterans, pushed the work to completion in May 1869, when west-going tracks from the Union Pacific Railroad met east-going tracks from the Central Pacific at Promontory, Utah. Four more transcontinental lines spanned the country by century's end.

Major rail lines stitched the European countryside together by around 1870, some of them spectacular feats of engineering, involving Alpine tunnels and bridges. Rail lines crisscrossing South America in the late 1800s helped strengthen the Latin American economy. In 1916, the world's longest continuous rail line was completed—the 5,600-mile Trans-Siberian railroad took 25 years to build.

Trains were gradually increasing their ability to travel fast in the late 1800s. The American steam locomotive No. 999 was the first to travel 100 miles an hour in 1893. Diesel-electric trains, introduced in the 1920s, increased fuel efficiency; the streamlined diesel-electric *Zephyr* set sustained speed records on runs between Chicago and Denver, on which it averaged 76 miles an hour. Today France's *TGV* passenger train can reach 186 miles an hour.

Steam locomotive

for an engine in which the fuel was ignited by the heat of compressed air. One early prototype of the diesel engine, as it came to be called, exploded. However, by 1897 Diesel had produced a successful version, an efficient engine that ran on liquid petroleum. Diesel engines caught on immediately in many industries looking to move away from steam and coal; eventually they were found in everything from automobiles to boats (including submarines) and in a wide variety of factories.

■FOOTNOTE Rudolf Diesel, whose invention made him a very wealthy man, died mysteriously in 1913, vanishing from the deck of the mail steamer *Dresden* as it crossed the English Channel. His body washed up a few days later.

Rayon Fabric Appears

609 **1892** The first practical artificial fabric for clothing, viscose rayon, was invented by British chemists Charles Cross, Edward Bevan, and Clayton Beadle in 1892. The fabric, made from cellulose, had several incarnations before the version produced by Cross and his colleagues. Most notable was the fabric known as Chardonnet silk, invented by the comte de Chardonnet in 1889; however, this form was highly flammable. The Cross fabric was produced by dissolving cellulose xanthate in sodium hydroxide. The solution was then forced through spinnerets to form tiny filaments, which were dried. Heavy and silky in appearance, the fabric became popular in clothing in the 20th century.

609 | *Closely nested spools of brilliantly colored rayon thread*

608 | *A diesel engine locomotive rounds a bend in the mountains of Colorado.*

was then sent by rail to ports on Lake Superior for transport around the country. The vast amount of iron the mines supplied helped to fuel the powerful young iron and steel industry of the United States; the range produced 60 percent of the nation's iron between 1900 and 1980, including 600,000 tons during World War II.

■FOOTNOTE So great was the demand for the Mesabi range's high-grade ore that many of its reserves were depleted after World War II. Mining companies then turned to extracting iron from lower-grade taconite rock.

Java Man Found

607 **1891** Hoping to find fossils of a "missing link"—an ancestral creature midway between ape and human—Dutch anatomist Eugène Dubois traveled to Indonesia in 1887. While working as a military surgeon, Dubois pursued his search in Sumatra and Java. Working near the Solo River at Trinil in 1891, he found first a fossilized

skullcap and then a fossil femur of an apelike creature. The skull was relatively small and apelike, indicating a cranial capacity of about 900 cc, but the femur was humanlike, indicating that the possessor had walked upright.

Convinced that he had found an early human ancestor, Dubois named his find *Pithecanthropus erectus,* "erect ape-man." But his findings, published in 1894, met with great resistance from scientists and the public alike. Angry, Dubois withdrew his fossils from public view for decades. In the 1930s, with further discoveries of early humans in Asia, it became clear that Java Man was in fact a human ancestor, a specimen of *Homo erectus.*

Diesel Engine Patented

608 **1892** An alternative to the spark-ignited internal combustion engine appeared, at least on paper, in 1892. In that year, Rudolf Diesel, a French-born son of Bavarian immigrants, filed a patent

1850-1913 | Age of Imperialism

New Zealand Women Get Vote

610 **1893** Led by Kate Sheppard of the Women's Christian Temperance Union, 30,000 women signed a petition sent to the New Zealand parliament demanding the right to vote. Despite considerable opposition on the Legislative Council, the persistent efforts of the suffragists pushed through the Electoral Act of 1893, granting women (including Maori women) the right to vote in all elections. Kate Sheppard remarked dryly: "It does not seem a great thing to be thankful for, that the gentlemen who confirm the laws which render women liable to taxation and penal servitude have declared us to be 'persons.'" New Zealand became the first self-governing country to grant full suffrage to women.

■ **FOOTNOTE** Despite winning the right to vote in 1893, women in New Zealand were not allowed to stand for public office until 1919; the first woman was elected to the New Zealand Parliament in 1933.

Expressionism Emerges

611 **1893** Psychological intensity, anxiety, cold eroticism, and death emerged as dark themes of European painting as the 19th century ended. Possibly the darkest of all the major artists of the time was Norwegian painter Edvard Munch. He painted his most famous work, "The Scream," in 1893. Its anguished figure in a nightmarish landscape was a major departure from the Impressionist pastorals or idealized figures of earlier art.

Munch's intensely personal, imaginative art inspired a younger group of European artists—many of them German—to develop a style that came to be known as expressionism, emphasizing personal experience and emotion. Vincent van Gogh and Belgian painter James Ensor were also major early influences; their bold colors, rough lines, and sometimes grotesque subject matter marked a clear departure from Impressionism.

Expressionism reached its fullest development in the early years of the next century. A group of German artists known as Die Brücke, which included Ernst Ludwig Kirchner, Erich Heckel, and Fritz Bleyl, produced paintings and woodcuts marked by violence, harsh colors, and jagged lines. Oskar Kokoschka, Egon Schiele, and Käthe Kollwitz were other prominent expressionists whose work reflected the increasingly anxious atmosphere of Germany and Austria in the years before World War I.

Fram Enters Arctic Ice

612 **1893** Norwegian explorer and oceanographer Fridtjof Nansen advanced scientific understanding of the ocean by taking his schooner, the *Fram,* deep into the Arctic ice. Launched in 1893, the *Fram* was a strong and ungainly boat specifically constructed to withstand the crushing pressures of the ice pack.

611 | *Edvard Munch's "The Scream" has become a staple of pop culture.*

Röntgen Discovers X-Ray

613 **1895** German physicist Wilhelm Conrad Röntgen discovered x-rays by accident. On November 8, 1895, he was studying cathode-ray emissions from a vacuum tube when he saw that a plate several feet away had begun to glow. Röntgen knew that cathode rays were too weak to penetrate the aluminum walls of the vacuum tube; some other form of radiation must be causing the plate to fluoresce. He soon discovered that objects interposed between the cathode-ray tube and a photographic plate would show up as variably transparent shadows on the plate. Placing his wife's hand over the photographic plate created an image of her bones and ring, with the flesh palely outlined around them.

Röntgen named the rays "x-rays," the "x" standing for the unknown since their source and nature were still mysterious. (Because the rays did not behave like visible light, he did not see a connection between the two. It was only in 1912 that German physicist Max von Laue performed experiments in which x-rays were diffracted while passing through crystals, proving that x-rays were in fact a form of electromagnetic radiation.) Röntgen's papers on the enigmatic rays, published in the next two years, were important contributions to the fields of both physics and medicine. For his discovery, Röntgen won the 1901 Nobel Prize in physics.

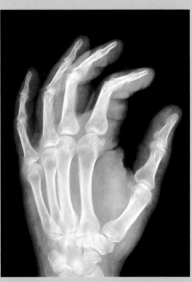

X-ray of a left hand. The bones almost glow, while skin fades to a shadow.

Nansen and his crew sailed her from Norway around Siberia and deliberately into the pack ice, allowing her to become frozen into place. Nansen was then able to study the currents that moved both ice and boat across the Arctic. In 1895, Nansen and a companion left the boat and attempted to reach the North Pole via dog sled, reaching 86°14' before returning. Back on the *Fram,* Nansen and his crew conducted experiments as the boat drifted, finally being released by the ice near Spitsbergen in 1896. The explorer was hailed as a hero upon his return to Norway and became an icon to subsequent Arctic and Antarctic explorers.

Moving Pictures Shown

614 **1895** In 1894, photographer Antoine Lumière was invited to see Thomas Edison's amazing new kinetoscope in Paris. He described the device to his adult sons, Louis and Auguste, who owned a factory for producing photographic plates, and the two brothers determined to create their own motion-picture machine. In 1895, they introduced the *cinématographe,* a hand-cranked movie camera that could take photographs and project film at 16 frames a second. The device caught on immediately, and soon audiences could see such short films as *The Sprinkler Sprinkled* or a sequence showing workers leaving the Lumière factory. Unlike Edison's machine, the cinématographe movies could be viewed by several people on a large screen, like the commercial films to come.

La Bohème Premieres

615 **1896** Conducted by Arturo Toscanini, Giacomo Puccini's opera *La Bohème* premiered in Turin on February 1. It was an immediate success and was performed around the world in the following years. The tale of starving artists in a Paris garret exemplified the new verismo (realistic) school of opera, a movement that reflected in music the trends toward naturalism seen elsewhere in painting and literature. Puccini was the school's most popular and successful exponent: His colorful, sentimental stories, gift for characterization, and memorable melodies made *La Bohème* and his other major operas, such as *Madame Butterfly* and *Tosca,* into mainstays of the operatic repertoire.

■ FOOTNOTE Other notable verismo operas include Mascagni's *Cavalleria rusticana,* Leoncavallo's *Pagliacci,* Giordano's *Andrea Chénier,* Puccini's *Tosca,* and Wolf-Ferrari's *I gioielli della Madonna.*

First Hydropower Plant

616 **1896** Long recognized as a potential source of power, the immense waterfalls at Niagara Falls became the site of the first major hydroelectric plant in the world in 1895. In August of that year, the Adams Number 1 generating station of the Niagara Falls Power Company began supplying electricity to local businesses. The company then contracted with the Westinghouse Company, pioneers in the use of alternating current transmission, to supply power to the city of Buffalo, New York. In 1896, the first long-distance commercial transmission of electrical power began between the hydroelectric plant at Niagara Falls and Buffalo.

Ethiopia Wins Battle

617 **1896** A rare exception to the pattern of European conquest in Africa took place in Ethiopia under its canny emperor Menelik II. Recognizing that European power derived primarily from its modern weaponry, the Ethiopian ruler managed to buy arms from both Italy and France. Italy then claimed that its arms treaty with Ethiopia meant that the African country had become an Italian protectorate. Menelik disagreed and became determined to rid himself of the outsiders, who were "burrowing into the country like moles." At a decisive battle near the town of Adowa on March 1, 1896, 18,000 Italian soldiers faced 100,000 Ethiopian troops armed with the same modern weapons. The Ethiopian Army easily defeated the outnumbered and outgunned Italians, who retreated, losing not only men but large numbers of rifles and artillery. Italy and other European states were forced to accept Ethiopia as a sovereign power, leaving it one of the few independent countries in Africa.

Global Warming Predicted

618 **1896** Swedish chemist Svante Arrhenius, mulling over the causes of ice ages, began to wonder if increases or decreases in the amount of carbon dioxide in the atmosphere would lead to a corresponding increase or decrease in world temperatures. French scientist Jean-Baptiste Fourier had already shown, in 1824, that Earth's atmosphere trapped warmth next to the planet's surface. In 1859, English physicist John Tyndall identified both water vapor and carbon dioxide as the key gasses in this process. After long months of penciled calculations, Arrhenius concluded that a doubling of atmospheric CO_2 would lead to an increase of 5°C to 6°C (9°F to 11°F). Arrhenius presented his paper on what he called the "hothouse" effect to the Swedish Academy in 1896. He was not particularly worried about this effect; carbon dioxide emissions in 1896 were negligible compared with modern rates, and in his Scandinavian view, a little warming might be a pleasant thing. Still, his calculations were the first to provide a clear model for the effects of human activity on climate.

■ **FOOTNOTE** Arrhenius said that it would take 3,000 years for atmospheric carbon dioxide to double. However, that was at contemporary rates; atmospheric CO_2 has already increased from 280 ppm in Arrhenius's day to about 380 ppm today.

Gold Rush in Yukon

619 **1897** Gold was first discovered in a tributary of the Yukon River in northwestern Canada in August 1896, but word of the find did not reach the outside world until the summer of 1897. "Gold Gold Gold!" read the headline in the Seattle newspaper, and "Stacks of Yellow Metal." Another gold rush was on as thousands trekked to the frigid northern goldfields. Railways and towns sprang up along the route of the gold seekers. Vancouver

---

CONNECTIONS

Global Warming
Living in a greenhouse world

Swedish chemist Svante Arrhenius calculated that a large increase in atmospheric carbon dioxide (CO_2) would create a "hothouse" effect that would raise the Earth's temperature. That was back in 1896 when his work was simply an effort to determine the cause of ice ages. Little could he know that more than a century later the planet would have entered a real hothouse period, caused, according to most climatologists, by man's release of CO_2 into the atmosphere.

A tremendous increase in the burning of fossil fuels has occurred since the 19th century. These fossil fuels—coal, oil, and natural gas from cars, buildings, power plants, and factories—release CO_2, which acts as a hothouse or greenhouse gas by trapping heat. Adding to the problem is deforestation—with fewer trees to absorb the CO_2, more of it goes into the atmosphere, where it can take hundreds of years to break down.

Serious scientific debate today swirls around the rate of global warming, its consequences, and possible fixes. Some predictions have the Earth's average temperature rising between three and eight degrees Fahrenheit by 2100 and polar ice disappearing (at current rates of decline) by 2060. Among other problems, increase in ocean temperature will lead to more catastrophic storms. With polar ice loss, sea levels would rise enough to inundate coastal areas several miles inland; polar bears and other species would vanish. Already, rising temperatures have put stress on numerous plant and animal species. For instance: Two-thirds of Costa Rica's harlequin frog species have disappeared in the past 30 years; millions of acres of forest in western Canada and the U.S. are under assault by pine beetles taking advantage of warm winters; forests have retreated up to 100 feet upslope to avoid the heat of lower areas.

In 1997 delegates from 160 countries met in Japan to discuss the issue of global warming. The resulting accord, the Kyoto Protocol, calls for the voluntary reduction of greenhouse gas emissions between the years 2008 and 2012. The U.S., which contributes about 25 percent of CO_2 emissions, abstained from the agreement. But since then, state and local leaders have worked independently to control the problem. The mayors of more than 200 cities have signed the U.S. Mayors Climate Protection Agreement, pledging to meet the Kyoto target—cutting greenhouse gas emissions to 1990 levels by the year 2012. Such efforts will not be likely to stop some climate changes already set in motion but may help slow the problem until a better solution can be reached.

Windmills provide an alternative source of power generation.

619 | *Book written in 1897 features the gold rush.*

and Edmonton boomed. A few people made millions; many more pocketed only hundreds. Nevertheless, the riches that flowed out of the north, particularly through the waystation city of Seattle, helped to lift the United States out of the depression that had been affecting the country since the early 1890s.

> **FOOTNOTE** Among those who traveled to the Yukon during the gold rush were American writer Jack London and Canadian poet Robert Service ("There are strange things done in the midnight sun/By the men who moil for gold...")

Mosquitoes, Malaria Linked

620 **1897** British doctor Ronald Ross became interested in malaria while working as a surgeon in India in the 1890s. During a period of home leave, he consulted with English tropical disease expert Patrick Manson, who told him that he believed malaria was transmitted by mosquitoes. Ross returned to India determined to find out if this was true. On the 20th of August, he discovered the malaria parasite in the stomach of a dissected *Anopheles* mosquito. He went on to trace the life cycle of the parasite through its mosquito and human hosts. For this discovery, Ross won the Nobel Prize in 1902 and was knighted in 1911.

First Zionist Conference

621 **1897** European Jews faced a rising tide of anti-Semitism in the late 19th century. Pogroms in Russia drove many Jews into western Europe, where they were greeted with suspicion during a time of economic hardship and unemployment. Established Jewish families in France and Germany also aroused resentment for their perceived dominance of banking and journalism. Reacting to the pervasive persecution, Austrian Jew Theodor Herzl, a journalist, became a leader in the movement to establish a separate Jewish state. On August 29, 1897, Herzl convened the First Zionist Conference in Basel, Switzerland. Delegates from 16 countries agreed upon a program to create a homeland for the Jewish people in the ancient land of Israel, bolstering the emigration of Jews to Palestine as the modern Zionist movement gained momentum.

Electrons Discovered

622 **1897** English physicist Joseph John Thomson was the first scientist to show that the atom, formerly thought to be the smallest indivisible entity in matter, was in fact made up of even tinier particles. Studying cathode rays in 1897, he saw that not only could they be deflected by an electrical field, but that they could not be made up of electrically charged atoms, as had been previously thought. The particles had only a tiny fraction of the mass of atoms. Thomson announced that he had found a "negative corpuscle," a new "subdivision of matter": the subatomic particles later called electrons.

> **FOOTNOTE** Many scientists doubted Thomson's findings. He noted: "I was even told ... afterwards by a distinguished physicist who had been present at my lecture at the Royal Institution that he thought I had been 'pulling their legs.' "

First Pianolas Play

623 **1898** American engineer and pipe organ expert Edwin Votey began marketing his first pianolas—automatic pianos that play using a perforated music roll—in 1898. His early models were

Viruses Discovered

624 **1898** Thanks to Louis Pasteur, Robert Koch, and others, 19th-century biologists had built up at least a small body of knowledge about bacteria, fungi, and protozoa by the end of the century. However, some diseases seemed to have another, unidentified source. Several scientists began to focus their attentions on tobacco mosaic

Beijerinck squeezed leaves to discover a new kind of infectious agent, later called a virus.

disease, a destructive condition that spread from leaf to leaf among tobacco and other plants. In the early 1880s, German scientist Adolf Mayer demonstrated that an extract from a diseased leaf could spread the disease to a healthy plant and theorized that the infectious agent was a bacterium. In 1892, Russian scientist Dmitri Ivanovsky cast doubt on this theory, showing that the infection could pass through a porcelain filter fine enough to screen bacteria.

Next to attempt the problem was Dutch botanist Martinus Beijerinck, the son of a tobacco dealer, who turned his attention to the disease in the 1890s. Pressing the leaves of infected plants to release their juices, he tried unsuccessfully to see the bacteria in the residue. Attempts to grow bacteria in a culture also failed. Beijerinck passed the liquid through a filter so fine that it would block any bacteria; the filtered liquid still infected other plants. In 1898, Beijerinck published his conclusions that the disease was caused by a new kind of infectious agent, which he called a *contagium vivum fluidum*. The pathogen, later called a virus, was too small to see, and it would be another generation or so before scientists began to understand its nature.

contained in cabinets placed up against a standard piano; air passing through the holes in the music roll activated wooden levers that pressed the piano keys. Later versions were built into the piano itself, evolving into the player piano of the early 20th century. In the days before gramophones, these popular instruments brought a wide range of music into middle-class homes, including performances by such musicians as Ignacy Paderewski, George Gershwin, and Claude Debussy.

> ■ **FOOTNOTE** The earliest pianolas were mechanical in sound. In 1904, however, a piano was invented that reproduced the dynamics, pedaling, and rubato of the pianists who made the original rolls, creating a more artistic effect.

Curies Measure Radioactivity

625 **1898** Wilhelm Röntgen's discovery of x-rays thrilled physicists all over the world. One of the first to follow up on his findings was French physicist Henri Becquerel, who discovered that uranium gave off a radiation, different from x-rays, that exposed photographic plates. At about the same time, the brilliant young Polish-born physicist Marie Curie began studying the unknown radiation—which she called "radioactivity"—as well. Assisted by her husband, distinguished French chemist Pierre Curie, she was able to measure levels of radioactivity, learning that it was in proportion to the amount of uranium in the radioactive material. The element thorium, she found, was also radioactive. In 1898, the two Curies isolated small amounts of two more radioactive elements from pitchblende, a uranium ore: they named the new elements polonium, after Marie Curie's homeland, and radium.

U.S. Annexes Hawaii

626 **1898** The Hawaiian Islands, valuable producers of sugar and pineapples, came under increasing U.S. control in the late 19th century. In 1891, Queen Liliuokalani came to the Hawaiian throne with the intention of throwing off foreign domination. U.S. planters on the islands persuaded American marines to come ashore and demand Liliuokalani's abdication, which she did reluctantly, issuing a formal protest that read, in part: "Now to avoid any collision of armed forces, and perhaps the loss of life, I do under this protest and impelled by said force yield my authority until such time as the Government of the United States shall … reinstate me in the authority which I claim as the constitutional Sovereign of the Hawaiian Islands." The new U.S. President, Grover Cleveland, was inclined to support the queen, but the issue remained in dispute until proexpansionist President William McKinley came into office. In 1898, he signed a treaty that formally annexed Hawaii to the United States.

> ■ **FOOTNOTE** In 1993, 100 years after Hawaii's annexation, President Bill Clinton signed a congressional resolution that formally apologized to the native Hawaiian people for the overthrow of their government.

Maine Explodes

627 **1898** The explosion of the U.S. battleship *Maine,* anchored in Havana Harbor on February 9, 1898, was almost certainly an accident. This did not, however, prevent the incident from triggering a war between the United States and Spain, the country then in control of the island. Feelings in the United States had been running high against the Spanish rule of Cuba, which was marked by considerable brutality. Cuban patriots in the U.S. also helped to spur support for the islanders, with the yellow press of New York City fanning the flames. In April, war broke out between the U.S. and Spain. It lasted all of ten weeks, in the course of which the United States not only fought

Spain in Cuba, but also took over the Spanish territory in the Philippines. In the treaty that ended the war in December 1898, Spain granted Cuba's independence and ceded the rights to the Philippines, Guam, and Puerto Rico to the United States.

> ■ **FOOTNOTE** Among the war's strongest advocates was Undersecretary of the Navy Theodore Roosevelt. When the war started, he resigned his post to take command of the Rough Riders, who fought in the Battle of San Juan.

China Fights Foreign Influence

628 **1899** Supported by China's conservative Qing dynasty, the secret Society of Harmonious Fists (also known as the Boxers) launched attacks on foreign intruders, including European missionaries and Chinese Christians. On August 14, 1900, troops from Britain, France, the U.S., and Japan invaded and captured Beijing, defeating the Boxers. Dowager Empress Cixi and her court fled the city; in September 1901 her government agreed to pay reparations to the foreigners.

Planck Describes Quanta

629 **1900** The theory that radiation flows in an unbroken stream—a basic premise of traditional physics—was overturned in 1900 by German physicist Max Planck. At the end of the 19th century the scientist took up the study of blackbody radiation. A blackbody is an ideal substance that absorbs radiation at all frequencies; when heated, it should also emit radiation at all frequencies. But the distribution of the wavelengths in the radiation thus emitted didn't match what physicists expected. After puzzling over the problem for six years, Planck hit upon a radical idea: Perhaps energy, like matter, was divisible into discrete packets—or quanta, as he came to call them (from the Latin meaning "how much"). He also found that the ratio between the temperature of the radiating body and the energy emitted—the size of each quantum—was a constant, h, now known as Planck's constant. Planck published his findings in 1900, giving birth to the field of quantum physics.

First Zeppelin Flies

630 **1900** Named for its designer, German army officer Ferdinand, Graf von Zeppelin, the first zeppelin took flight over Lake Constance, Germany, on July 2, 1900. The cloth-covered, rigid airship was 420 feet long and was propelled by two 15-horsepower Daimler internal combustion engines. The hydrogen-filled dirigible flew only 3.7 miles before being forced to land in the lake. Nevertheless, its success was persuasive enough that zeppelins were later developed for use as bombers in World War I.

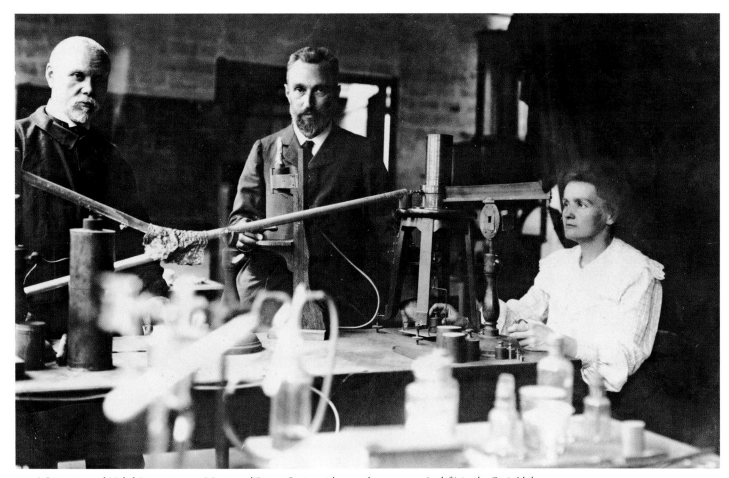

625 | *Scientists and Nobel Prize-winners Marie and Pierre Curie, with an unknown man (at left) in the Curies' laboratory*

Freud Interprets Dreams

631 **1900** Austrian psychiatrist Sigmund Freud published his masterwork, *The Interpretation of Dreams*, in 1900. Ignored by most and derided by a few when it was released, the book later became profoundly influential as the first exposition of Freud's radical new theories of the unconscious.

By the time he published *The Interpretation of Dreams*, Freud had already begun treating patients using psychoanalysis, particularly through the technique of free association, in which (he believed) the patient's random words and associations would reveal memories or conflicts—particularly sexual memories or impulses—that had been blocked from the conscious mind. In the course of analysis, patients often mentioned their dreams, and this, combined with Freud's interest in his own dreams, led him to the theory that dreams themselves are, as he put it, "the royal road to the unconscious." In *The Interpretation of Dreams*, Freud stated that dreams had a hidden meaning, a "latent content," that revealed forbidden desires. Dreams were wish fulfillment, an imaginary way to fulfill those desires.

Freud's ideas about free association, dream analysis, and sexuality gradually began to pull in adherents, until Freudian psychoanalysis became a major technique of psychiatry. Although many of his conclusions have since been disputed, his insights into the unconscious motivations of the human mind have spread through the science, art, and literature of the 20th century, permanently altering the understanding of human behavior.

■ FOOTNOTE Freud went on to publish many other groundbreaking books, including *Psychopathology of Everyday Life* (1904), *Beyond the Pleasure Principle* (1920), *The Ego and the Id* (1923), and *Civilization and its Discontents* (1930).

631 | *Freud was obsessed with forbidden desires.*

Gold Becomes Standard

632 **1900** Debate raged in the United States during the late 1800s over whether the country should convert to a gold standard—that is, link the value of its currency to a fixed price for gold—or peg it instead to silver, which was more plentiful at the time. With the influx of gold from Australia and the Klondike goldfields, the balance tilted in favor of the gold standard. On March 14, 1900, President William McKinley signed the Gold Standard Act, formally making gold the standard for the nation's currency and setting the price of gold at $20.67 per ounce.

Brownie Camera Introduced

633 **1900** Selling for one dollar apiece, Kodak Brownie cameras entered the marketplace with a boom in 1900. In the first year, 150,000 of the simple box cameras were shipped. Named for a popular cartoon character as well as for its creator, Frank Brownell of Eastman Kodak, the box camera was so easy to use that children could and did use it for snapshots. It was the first camera that was truly accessible to the masses, and came to be used for everything from Ansel Adams's first photographs to snapshots of the wreckage of the *Titanic*.

Yellow Fever Explained

634 **1900** Yellow fever was a feared scourge of the tropics until the dawn of the 20th century. Epidemics of the infectious disease regularly swept through the West Indies and coastal North and South America, particularly in

---

FIRST PERSON

John Moran

MEMOIRS OF A HUMAN GUINEA PIG, N.D.

When Major Reed terminated his mission in Cuba, on or about February 15, 1901, the following conclusions became part of his findings: Feeding of the mosquito on a case of yellow fever had to take place during the first three or four days of the attack. The mosquito so infected could not transmit the disease to a non-immune until twelve to fourteen days thereafter, during which period the yellow fever virus or germ was incubating.... After that period the insect would be a menace to every non-immune while it lived.... Such infected mosquitoes could silently carry death to untold numbers throughout their life cycle. The yellow fever carrier is ... a domestic insect, usually doing its feeding in the dark and biding its time until the victim is wrapped in the arms of Morpheus, seeing not being ... essential to its existence. Its only fatal weakness is that of overloading on human blood, if not disturbed, sometimes ... almost to the bursting point, thus making it indolent and an easy prey to a slap from its victim. It is ... possible that one or more of the mosquitoes which bit me in November ... matured some days later on, thus reaching the infectious stage. I did not follow them through to the end of their careers, nor have I been able to discover their subsequent activities.... I have a keen recollection ... that their performance on me was a disappointment to Major Reed and myself, happily overcome when fifteen of their tribe gave me yellow fever as a Christmas gift in the last days of the 19th Century.

by a virus). With that knowledge, public health officials were able to virtually eliminate the disease from much of the world.

In the process of investigating the transmission, Dr. Jesse Lazear himself developed yellow fever and died. His notebooks, which were subsequently lost, suggested that he may deliberately have exposed himself to the mosquitoes as part of the experiment.

■ **FOOTNOTE** Yellow fever persists primarily in tropical regions of Africa (90 percent of cases) and South America (10 percent), affecting about 200,000 people each year. Vaccines have now been developed to prevent the disease.

Australian Colonies Federate

635 **1901** Looking for free trade with other British colonies, and seeing a need for a stronger centralized defense in an imperialistic age, the six independent colonies of Australia formed a federation as the 20th century began. It had taken years of conferences and conventions to bring the colonies to agreement on a national constitution, but a draft was finally approved in 1899, and on January 1, 1901, New South Wales, Victoria, Queensland, Western Australia, South Australia, and Tasmania became states within the Commonwealth of Australia. The newly created federal government incorporated elements of both British and American government, with a House of Representatives and a Senate containing an equal number of representatives from each state. The central government gained control of defense, immigration, customs, and other national issues. Women (but not Aborigines) were granted the right to vote in 1902.

Adrenaline Isolated

636 **1901** Little was known about human hormones at the beginning of the 20th century—indeed, the term "hormone" had not yet been coined —when Japanese biochemist Jokichi Takamine isolated adrenaline. Earlier biochemists had shown that the adrenal glands secreted a substance that raised

634 | *Cartoon from 1873 shows Florida being attacked by "Yellow Jack" as Columbia calls for help.*

such port cities as Philadelphia and New York. In 1881, Cuban epidemiologist Carlos Juan Finlay published a paper suggesting that the disease was carried by the *Aedes aegypti* mosquito. For the next 19 years, he experimented by inoculating human volunteers—a process that convinced him of the mosquito-borne transmission, but failed to win over outside

experts. Finally, the U.S. Army yellow fever board sent several doctors to Havana, including Walter Reed and Jesse Lazear. Working with Finlay's mosquitoes and volunteer subjects, the U.S. scientists came to the same conclusion in 1900 that Finlay had reached earlier: that *Aedes aegypti* mosquitoes were the only vector for the disease (later found to be caused

630 More Details on the Zeppelin

On May 6, 1937, ground spectators near Lakehurst, New Jersey, were witness to a horrific event in the sky above them: the explosion of the *Hindenburg*. The luxury passenger airship, which ran a scheduled air service from the U.S. to Frankfurt, Germany, had carried hundreds of passengers and thousands of pounds of mail since its inaugural flight just one year before. But on this, its 11th roundtrip journey, the *Hindenburg*'s hydrogen ignited, causing a fire that killed 35 out of 97 people on board and ended, once and for all, the commercial promise of the airship.

The airship was the brainchild of Ferdinand, Graf von Zeppelin, who made the first successful dirigible flight in 1900. His company, Luftschiffbau Zeppelin, gained a contract to build airships for the German government, and in June 1910 they launched the world's first commercial airship. Between 1910 and 1914, ten zeppelins flew passengers and crew around the country. But the start of World War I in 1914 saw the zeppelin shift from luxury commercial liner to military asset, and the LZ-38 became the first zeppelin to bomb a foreign target on May 31, 1915. By 1918, 67 zeppelins had been constructed for the sole purpose of war.

> The *Hindenburg* ... took passenger luxury to a new level with a ... dining room, library, grand piano lounge, and large windows.

The Treaty of Versailles, which marked the end of World War I, not only required the Germans to turn over their 16 surviving zeppelins to the Allies but also prevented Germany from manufacturing any kind of planes or airships. It was not until the late 1920s that German zeppelins arrived back on the flight scene, and they arrived in style—the *Graf Zeppelin*, considered the finest airship ever built, became the first of its class to circle the globe in 1929. The *Hindenburg*, which followed in the footsteps of the *Graf Zeppelin*, marked the height of Zeppelin's company's success and took passenger luxury to a new level with a lavish dining room, library, grand piano lounge, and large windows. But its success and luxury were soon to be overshadowed by its tragic explosion, and the era of airship travel came to an abrupt and sudden close.

The Zeppelin airship, which was named for inventor Graf Zeppelin, on display for curious crowds

blood pressure. Takamine and an assistant, working in the United States, managed to purify the secretion in crystalline form. The scientist presented his findings in a 1901 paper and received a trademark for the name Adrenalin; the chemical went on to find uses in treatments for everything from heart disease to asthma. Today, it is more commonly known by its generic name, epinephrine.

■ **FOOTNOTE** Takamine devoted much of his free time to improving relations between the Americans and the Japanese. He paid for the 1912 gift of the Japanese cherry trees that encircle Washington, D.C.'s Tidal Basin.

Transatlantic Signal Sent

637 **1901** He flunked out of secondary school and failed the entrance exams for the Italian Naval Academy and the University of Bologna, but Guglielmo Marconi loved to tinker with machines. In 1895, the clever Italian youth read about Heinrich Hertz's experiments with the transmission of radio waves. Working at his father's country house in Italy, he began to experiment with sending radio waves wirelessly from a transmitter to a receiver, steadily increasing the distance until he could transmit for a mile and a half.

Traveling to England, Marconi received the world's first patent for wireless telegraphy. He started his own wireless telegraph company, sending signals from England to France in 1899. But his greatest achievement, and the one that truly marked the beginnings of long-distance wireless communication, came on December 12, 1901. Critics had claimed that transatlantic signals would not conform to the curvature of Earth and would instead simply shoot straight into space. They were wrong. Marconi set up a receiving station at Signal Hill, St. John's, Newfoundland, and prepared to receive Morse code signals sent from a transmitter in Cornwall, England. As he wrote later, "I heard, faintly but distinctly, pip-pip-pip. I handed the phone to Kemp: 'Can you hear anything' I asked. 'Yes,' he said. 'The letter S.' " The signal had traveled nearly 2,000 miles.

Blood Types Discovered

638 **1901** Before the 20th century, occasional attempts to transfuse blood from one person to another (or from an animal to a human) most often met with failure and the death of the recipient. In 1901, Karl Landsteiner, an Austrian physician with an interest in immunology,

---

CONNECTIONS

From Wire to Wireless
How the age of radio began

It had been only 25 years since the world's first telephone conversation when an event even more astounding occurred. Italian inventor Guglielmo Marconi's reception of a transatlantic signal in 1901 marked the beginning of the wireless age. For the average person, the transmission of sound through wires was miracle enough, but that messages could travel practically instantaneously with no wires at all was too much to comprehend.

Marconi had experimented for years with wireless signals, receiving a patent for a wireless telegraph in 1896. He was expanding on the work of scientists who preceded him. In 1864, British physicist James Clerk Maxwell had theorized the existence of electromagnetic waves that travel at light speed, and the experiments of German physicist Heinrich Hertz two decades later proved Maxwell right. It was then up to an

Researcher Irving Langmuir and Marconi, 1922

inventor to find a practical use for the science. Marconi's wireless telegraph became a valuable communication tool, especially for ships in distress. Signals sent by sinking ocean liners helped save thousands of lives.

While Marconi's signals were in the form of telegraphic code, it was not long before other engineers were figuring out how to send the human voice itself through electromagnetic waves. Marconi's telegraph employed radio waves, or electromagnetic waves with a radio frequency (between audio and infrared on the spectrum). The invention of vacuum tubes in the early 1900s improved the detection and amplification of radio waves, and in 1906 Canadian physicist Reginald Fessenden made the first radio broadcast of voice and music—from Massachusetts to ships in the Atlantic.

The radio era was up and running. Woodrow Wilson, speaking to his troops in 1919, became the first U.S. President to broadcast on the radio. Commercial radio stations started up in the 1920s, and the middle of that decade saw the beginnings of a golden age of radio broadcasting that was to last until well after World War II. News, family entertainment, and soap operas kept listeners tuning in. Programs featured such entertainers as Tommy Dorsey, Benny Goodman, and the comedy duo of George Burns and Gracie Allen; serialized shows like *The Green Hornet* and *The Shadow* helped instill a popular culture carried forward by television.

The rise of television has not diminished the appeal and usefulness of radio. Small, portable radios and car radios have kept the radio broadcasting industry growing as wider audiences continue to listen to their favorite music, news, and talk shows.

642 | *Opera star Enrico Caruso, in costume*

discovered that the blood serum of some people would attack the blood of certain other people, and that this transfusion reaction was a natural, immunological property. Within a few years, Landsteiner and colleagues had identified four basic blood types—A, B, AB, and O—based on their reactions to one another. By 1907, this knowledge was put to use in the first successful transfusion in Mt. Sinai Hospital, New York. For his contribution, Landsteiner was awarded the Nobel Prize in physiology or medicine in 1930.

■ **FOOTNOTE** In 1940, Landsteiner discovered another critical blood antigen: Rh factor, named for his studies of rhesus monkeys. Rh-factor incompatibility explained why some infants born to Rh-negative mothers had health problems.

Hormone Mechanism ID'd

639 | **1902** British physiologists Ernest Starling and William Bayliss conducted a simple and effective experiment that demonstrated the existence of chemical messengers in the blood. Working on anesthetized dogs, they cut all nerves leading to the pancreas, finding that it still secreted digestive juices when the intestines received food. What could be signaling the pancreas, if the nervous system was not involved? The two men found that acid in the small intestine caused the intestine to release a substance they later named secretin. Injected into the dog's bloodstream, secretin caused the pancreas to release its own secretions seconds later. "Then it must be a chemical reflex," remarked Starling.

The two men's experiments showed that the body's functions were controlled by chemicals in the bloodstream as well as by the nervous system. In 1905, Starling named these messengers "hormones," from the Greek for "I arouse to activity."

■ **FOOTNOTE** Bayliss and Starling's findings contradicted those of Ivan Pavlov, who believed the pancreas was controlled by the vagus nerve. Upon reading their paper, though, Pavlov is said to have remarked, "Of course they are right."

Anglo-Boer War Ends

640 | **1902** Tensions between Dutch settlers in South Africa, known as Boers, and the British colonists who controlled the Cape Colony and Natal kept the two groups in conflict for much of the 19th century. The British wanted a unified colony and the end of slavery in the region; the Boers wanted to retain control of their farms and their indigenous workers in their independent states of the Transvaal and the Orange Free State. (And the Bantu people, native to the country, resented both European occupiers.) The discovery of diamonds north of the Orange Free State and gold in the Transvaal further exacerbated hostilities; the British annexed the diamond-bearing land and attempted, unsuccessfully, to do the same in the Transvaal.

In 1880-81 and again in 1889, war between the British and the Boers embroiled the area. The British sent more than 250,000 soldiers to its South African colony, finally defeating the well-armed Boer forces in 1902. The treaty that followed eventually led to the unification of the various states in South Africa, with the Union of South Africa becoming part of the British Commonwealth in 1910; it also retained the race-based social structures of the Boers.

Factories Air Conditioned

641 | **1902** The first air-conditioning machines were intended to dehumidify, not cool, the air. In 1902, American engineer Willis Haviland Carrier devised such a system for a printing plant in Brooklyn, New York; high humidity was causing the paper to stretch. After contemplating the nature of humidity and condensation, Carrier came to realize that cold water sprayed through humid air would cause the water vapor to condense out of the air, both drying and cooling it. In 1911, Carrier presented his calculations to the American Society of Mechanical Engineers, and the modern air-conditioning business began. In 1915, he formed the Carrier Engineering Corporation.

Caruso Records

642 | **1902** Not long after the gramophone business began, young opera star Enrico Caruso recorded ten songs in Milan for the Gramophone Company of London. Although the company's executives were horrified by Caruso's fee of 150 pounds, the recordings went on to sell more than a million copies. Previously the realm of novelty songs and comedy routines, the recording industry moved quickly into the world of classical music after the Italian tenor's breakthrough sales, and, in fact, classical music outsold any other type. Opera singers, violinists, and symphony orchestras began to issue recordings on 7-, 10-, and 12-inch wax discs that held only a few minutes of music apiece. Musicians had to record directly into a horn, lacking electronic amplification during the recording process, so the recording quality was necessarily poor. Nevertheless, the business flourished as the technology improved quickly over the next decades.

Reflex Action Described

643 | **1903** Russian physiologist Ivan Pavlov was already known as a prominent researcher in the field of digestion when he made his serendipitous discovery of conditioned reflexes. Working at the Institute of Experimental Medicine, he was studying the digestive process in dogs when he observed that the animals would begin to salivate in anticipation of being fed. This led to Pavlov's famous experiment, in which he would precede each meal given to the dogs with the ticking of a metronome. In time, the dogs began to salivate merely at the sound of the metronome, whether the food was present or not. The salivating reflex would stop, though, if it proved wrong often enough—that is, if no food followed the stimulus.

At a 1903 conference, Pavlov presented a paper entitled "The Experimental Psychology and Psychopathology of Animals," which introduced the concept of a conditioned reflex, linking psychology to physiology. Pavlov's work earned him the 1904 Nobel Prize in physiology or medicine and was a major influence on the upcoming field of behavioral psychology.

■FOOTNOTE Pavlov first developed the idea for his famous experiments when he observed that the dogs—who were always fed by assistants in lab coats—began to salivate every time they saw anyone wearing a lab coat.

Russian Pogroms Rise

644 **1903** Waves of pogroms—mob attacks against Jews—swept through Russia in the late 19th and early 20th centuries. The first wave occurred after the assassination of Tsar Alexander II in 1881. A second, and even more destructive round of attacks occurred in the years from 1903 to 1906, during the turbulent era of the first Russian revolution. One of the most notorious of these took place in the town of Kishinev in April 1903. Prompted by the false rumor that Jews had murdered a Christian baby, mobs swept through the town, looting and destroying more than 1,000 homes and businesses and killing 45 Jews. Neighbor turned on neighbor in the bloody scene; a contemporary describes how the town glazier "rushed out, but they seized him and dragged him on to the roof of the outhouse, where they finished him off with sticks and cudgels on the spot which is still

First Flight at Kitty Hawk

645 **1903** Orville and Wilbur Wright, brothers and bicycle shop owners from Dayton, Ohio, spent four years carefully building, testing, and crashing models and gliders before they were ready to construct their first powered airplane. From 1899 to 1903—much of the time spent in a workshop in Kitty Hawk on the Outer Banks of North Carolina—they systematically worked out the tricky problems of controlling a heavy machine in the air. To perfect the airfoil curvature, they tested as many as 200 wing shapes in a wind tunnel they built themselves. After observing the flight of buzzards, they devised a glider with rudders and warpable wings, allowing it to turn. Their designs underwent constant trials and refinements.

In 1903, after constructing three unpowered gliders, the brothers built the *Flyer*. Twenty-one feet long, with a 40-foot wingspan, the flying machine was powered

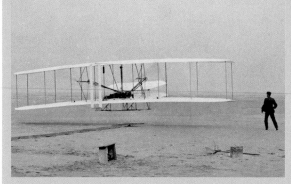

by a simple four-cylinder engine that the brothers had designed. Without a pilot on board, the whole contraption weighed 605 pounds. On December 17, watched by four men and a boy, the *Flyer* lifted off its launching rail on the windy sands of Kitty Hawk and flew for all of 12 seconds before thudding into the ground 120 feet away. It did not travel far, but it succeeded in making the first

Orville Wright takes off at Kitty Hawk, North Carolina, flying 120 feet in 12 seconds. Wilbur runs alongside to steady the craft.

controlled, piloted flight of a heavier-than-air machine. Three more flights that day increased the *Flyer*'s distance to 852 feet before an errant gust of wind wrecked the machine.

The public was skeptical at first about the practicality of the flying machine, but the methodical Wright brothers perfected the design over the next two years, increasing the machine's stability to the point where it could be flown in a circle and stay in the air for as long as 39 minutes. A patent on their invention—for the earlier, glider version—was granted in 1906. Wilbur Wright began to demonstrate his airplane in Europe to great acclaim, and the era of flight had truly been launched.

stained with his blood. When the widow was asked if she really recognized the murderer … she replied with conviction: 'I held him in my arms when he was an infant.' " The attacks, combined with the already harsh restrictions on Jews in Russia, prompted a wave of emigration to western Europe, Palestine, and the Americas.

Photoelectric Effect Explained

646 **1905** In the first of three papers, all published in one issue of *The*

Annals of Physics in 1905, German-born Swiss physicist Albert Einstein solved the mystery of the photoelectric effect. Until Einstein's paper, scientists had been unable to understand why light falling on certain metals would cause electrons to be emitted. Knowing of Planck's contention that light emits energy in packets, or quanta, Einstein took quantum theory one step further. He said that light itself traveled as quanta (later called photons); therefore, when a quantum of light struck an atom of metal, it essentially knocked loose an electron, one with the same fixed energy content as the photon.

Einstein's paper, "On a heuristic point of view concerning the production and transformation of light," marked the beginning of the field of quantum mechanics, the science that describes the behavior of matter and energy at the subatomic scale.

Relativity Theory Put Forth

647 **1905** In yet another of his revolutionary papers published in 1905, Einstein overturned classical physics by showing that space and time were not absolute, but would vary relative to an observer. The theory he proposed is called the special theory because it applies only in special cases involving motion in a straight line at a constant speed—although its implications spread far beyond that.

Einstein's paper is based on the assumption that the speed of light in a vacuum is a constant and can never be exceeded. From this assumption flow a number of other, counterintuitive findings, including the fact that time will flow more slowly for a person moving at very high speeds than it will for a stationary person. Mass will also change relative to velocity, increasing as objects approached the speed of light. Furthermore, mass and energy are simply different forms of one thing, and the relationship between them can be expressed by the elegantly simple equation $E=mc^2$, where E is energy, m is mass, and c is the speed of light (a constant).

Einstein's mind-boggling paper attracted the attention of noted physicist Max Planck, and his fame grew even as physicists around the world began to revise everything they thought they knew about how the universe worked.

> ■**FOOTNOTE** At the time Einstein published his landmark papers, he was a patent clerk in Bern, Switzerland. He had recently been turned down for a promotion because of an insufficient understanding of mechanical engineering.

Japan Wins Battle of Tsushima

648 **1905** A rapidly modernizing Japan clashed with Russia over control of Korea and Manchuria in the beginning of the 20th century. The resulting Russo-Japanese War began in 1904 when Japanese forces attacked the Russian naval squadron at Port Arthur on the Liaodung Peninsula in southern Manchuria. After a year of often bloody combat on land and sea, the two sides met in a naval battle in the Tsushima Strait in May 1905. The Japanese naval fleet, commanded by Adm. Togo Heihachiro, used its superior speed and new weapons, torpedoes, to destroy the Russian Baltic fleet. The war ended in the fall of 1905 with the Treaty of Portsmouth, which gave Japan control of the Liaodung Peninsula as well as Korea. The battle marked the first time in modern history that an Asian power had defeated a European one.

Russian Revolt Ignited

649 **1905** Unrest among urban workers and peasants alike grew throughout the end of the 19th century and into the 20th in Russia. Chafing against the autocratic rule of Tsar Nicholas II and demanding a host of reforms, a worker's union—the Assembly of Russian Workingmen—supported a series of strikes in St. Petersburg. On January 9, 1905, demonstrators marched peacefully toward the Winter Palace bearing petitions for the tsar (who was not in the city). When the marchers reached the palace, they were fired upon by police, who killed more than one hundred of the demonstrators.

The massacre, which came to be known as Bloody Sunday, kicked off the Russian Revolution of 1905. Strikes swept through the country, peasants led their own uprisings, and even the crew of the battleship *Potemkin* mutinied. Although Russian forces eventually quelled the rebels and arrested their leaders, the Russian government did institute reforms. It created a national parliament, the Duma, and allowed peasants to buy and sell land. In the long run, though, these changes were not enough to satisfy the revolutionaries, who eventually ended the tsarist regime the following decade.

649 | *Police shot scores of striking workers in St. Petersburg, igniting the Russian Revolution of 1905.*

1850-1913 | Age of Imperialism

San Francisco Quake

G. A. RAYMOND, PALACE HOTEL, 1906

I awoke as I was thrown out of bed. Attempting to walk, the floor shook so that I fell. I grabbed my clothing and rushed down into the office, where dozens were already congregated. Suddenly the lights went out, and every one rushed for the door.

Outside I witnessed a sight I never want to see again. It was dawn and light. I looked up. The air was filled with falling stones. People around me were crushed to death on all sides. All around the huge buildings were shaking and waving. Every moment there were reports like 100 cannons going off at one time. Then streams of fire would shoot out, and other reports followed.

I asked a man standing next to me what happened. Before he could answer a thousand bricks fell on him and he was killed. A woman threw her arms around my neck. I pushed her away and fled. All around me buildings were rocking and flames shooting. As I ran people on all sides were crying, praying and calling for help. I thought the end of the world had come....

At places the streets had cracked and opened. Chasms extended in all directions. I saw a drove of cattle ... rushing up Market Street. I crouched beside a swaying building. As they came nearer they disappeared, seeming to drop out into the earth. When the last had gone I went nearer and found they had indeed been precipitated into the earth, a wide fissure having swallowed them. I was crazy with fear and the horrible sights.

How I reached the ferry I cannot say. It was bedlam, pandemonium and hell rolled into one. There must have been 10,000 people trying to get on that boat. Men and women fought like wildcats to push their way aboard. Clothes were torn from the backs of men and women and children indiscriminately. Women fainted, and there was no water at hand with which to revive them. Men lost their reason at those awful moments. One big, strong man, beat his head against one of the iron pillars on the dock, and cried out in a loud voice: "This fire must be put out! The city must be saved!" It was awful.

Quake Hits San Francisco

650 **1906** One of the most shocking earthquakes of modern times struck the San Francisco Bay area at 5:12 a.m. on April 18. The quake, now estimated to have been around 7.7 on the Richter scale, was felt from Los Angeles in the south to Coos Bay, Oregon, in the north. It not only knocked down buildings throughout San Francisco but also triggered fires that rapidly burned out of control, destroying almost five square miles of the city. Estimates of the dead range from 700 to 3,000. As destructive as it was to lives and property, the earthquake did much to further the young science of seismology; studies of the 1906 quake led to the elastic-rebound theory that remains an important model for the earthquake cycle.

Antiquities Act Signed

651 **1906** Alarmed by looting and destruction at such precious archaeological sites as Chaco Canyon and the Casa Grande ruins in Arizona, archaeologists in the late 19th century began to lobby for laws to protect valuable historical and scientific locations. The movement found a sympathetic ear in President Theodore Roosevelt. The American Antiquities Act, which Roosevelt signed on June 8, 1906, prohibited the vandalism of historical monuments or ruins on federal lands, gave the President the power to designate national monuments, and established a process for archaeological permits. Devil's Tower in Wyoming became the first designated national monument that year; hundreds of millions of acres have since gained protection under the act.

Vacuum Tube Invented

652 **1906** American physicist Lee De Forest gave a powerful boost to the infant electronics industry when he invented the Audion, a triode vacuum tube, in 1906. Although earlier varieties of vacuum tube were already in use in electronics, De Forest's three-electrode version was the first to effectively amplify wireless signals. The new tube allowed for

651 | *Theodore Roosevelt protected antiquities.*

the coast-to-coast transmission of telephone signals and later took its place in radios as well.

> ■ **FOOTNOTE** Transistors have largely replaced Audion tubes; however, vacuum tubes are still used in military equipment that would otherwise be disabled by the electromagnetic pulse of an atmospheric nuclear explosion.

Nature Photos Transformed

653 **1906** George Shiras III, lawyer and congressional representative from Pennsylvania, launched the field of wildlife photography in the beginning of the 20th century. His images often featured animals photographed at night with a large-format camera and a hand-operated flash. In 1906, NATIONAL GEOGRAPHIC magazine first published his photographs of animals in the wild; two National Geographic Society board members resigned in protest, claiming the magazine was becoming a "picture book."

Cubism Pioneered

654 **1907** Spanish painter Pablo Ruiz y Picasso took the traditional subject of the nude female form and broke it up into a puzzle of planes, angles, and sharp curves. "Les Demoiselles d'Avignon" (a portrayal of women in a local brothel) was the forerunner of cubism, an art movement in which the subject and the space itself in the painting are rendered as geometric shapes, disassembled and reassembled in a two-dimensional plane.

Picasso and French painter Georges Braque, working in Paris between 1907 and 1914, were the pioneers of cubism. Braque's "Houses at L'Estaque" (1908), for instance, transformed buildings into a tumble of gray and gold blocks. Painters Juan Gris, Robert and Sonia Delaunay, and Marcel Duchamp, among others, further developed the style in the early part of the century. The movement spread from painting into sculpture and architecture, coming to dominate modern art and lead it toward complete abstraction.

Synthetic Plastic Invented

655 **1907** Belgian-born chemist Leo Hendrik Baekeland was already a successful inventor when he devised the world's first synthetic plastic. His invention of Velox, a photographic paper that could be developed in artificial light, brought him $750,000 when he sold the rights to George Eastman in the 1890s. With some of that money, he built a laboratory and began looking into developing a substitute for shellac, used as an electrical insulator. At the time, shellac had to be harvested from beetles in Southeast Asia, and demand for the substance was outstripping supply.

In 1907, experimenting with different approaches, Baekeland devised not a shellac, but a synthetic polymer—an artificial molecule made by linking smaller molecules together. Mixing carbolic acid and formaldehyde, the inventor produced a hard, translucent, malleable substance that could be dyed bright colors and molded. It could indeed be made into an insulator—and also into gears, buttons, plates, handles, knobs, and an almost endless number of other objects. Bakelite, as the plastic was named, became the first big success in the 20th century's booming plastics industry.

■ **FOOTNOTE** Genuine Bakelite items from the early 20th century have now become collector's items. Bakelite jewelry, such as brooches, dress clips, and earrings, can fetch thousands of dollars from antiques dealers.

Ford Builds Car for the Masses

656 **1908** "The way to make automobiles," Henry Ford once said, "is to make one automobile like another automobile, just as … one match is like another match when it comes from a match factory." The Ford Motor Company did just that with the production of the Model T in 1908. Although mass production techniques were not new, Henry Ford put them to use on a scale never seen before as he built the first car simple, sturdy, and cheap enough that the average middle-class family could afford one. At $825, more than 10,000 Model Ts were sold in the first year, a new record. The car's immense popularity led to such a demand that within a few years Ford perfected the assembly line system that would allow his company to dominate the world automobile market.

Electric Vacuum Invented

657 **1908** James Murray Spangler, an asthmatic janitor in Canton, Ohio, invented the electric vacuum cleaner in order to have a less dusty method of cleaning carpets in his employer's department store. Spangler's first model was made from a broomstick, a pillowcase, and a box containing an electric motor that ran a fan and a rotating brush. He patented his machine, the "suction sweeper," in 1908.

654 | *In 1907, Pablo Picasso used a new art form, cubism, in "Les Demoiselles d'Avignon."*

1850-1913 | Age of Imperialism

After his wife's cousin, William Hoover, saw the device, he invested in Spangler's company. It was renamed the Hoover Company in 1922.

Chemotherapy Begins

658 **1908** Like many discoveries, Paul Ehrlich's began with an intuitive leap. The German doctor was expert at staining cells to make their structures visible under the microscope. It occurred to him that the pathogens that cause infectious disease might be targeted in the same specific fashion as his stained cells—if only the correct chemical could be found.

Ehrlich determined to find a substance that would seek out and kill bacteria. After testing 605 unsuccessful preparations, in 1908 he found that number 606 did the trick. The drug was the arsenic-containing arsphenamine, potent against the scourge of syphilis. It became, for a while, the most widely prescribed single drug in the world. Ehrlich had found his "magic bullet," as he called it, and with it began the field of chemotherapy (a term he also coined).

> ■ **FOOTNOTE** In the centuries before the discovery of arsphenamine 606, the most widely prescribed treatment for syphilis was the highly toxic element mercury, applied as an ointment or ingested.

Music Becomes Atonal

659 **1909** Austrian composer Arnold Schoenberg, though heavily influenced by the music of Wagner and Brahms, broke away from standard harmonies and key signatures with the first of his truly atonal works, the Three Piano Pieces, opus 11 (1909). With its dissonant intervals and emphasis on the equal value of every note and motive, the work marked a radical new direction in composition

NAACP Is Formed

660 **1909** Horrified by reports of race riots in Springfield, Illinois, that resulted in lynchings and the destruction of black-owned homes and businesses, a small group of black and white reformers gathered in New York in 1909 to form a new organization that would vigorously fight for civil rights. The group issued a call to action in newspapers on Abraham Lincoln's birthday, February 12: "Hence we call upon all the believers in democracy to join in a national conference for the discussion of present evils, the voicing of protests, and the renewal of the struggle for civil and political liberty."

CONNECTIONS

Abstract Art
Wild beasts and 12-tone music

In the early 20th century, artists in all fields were experimenting with new forms in an attempt to break free of the traditional modes of expression. With the weight of the great Romantic and post-Romantic composers (Beethoven, Brahms, Tchaikovsky, and so forth), the heavy-hitting Victorian and Russian writers, and the likes of the Impressionists on their backs, new artists sought to explore the limits of their art, not simply to break free but also to give voice to a rapidly changing world that was increasingly urban-industrial and in which the individual often felt alienated from his time and place.

It was a logical progression in the evolution of Western music for Austrian composer Arnold Schoenberg to manipulate the traditional 12-tone harmonic system and create a composition of completely atonal music in 1909. With no clear key, or tonic note, and no resolution, such compositions gave equal emphasis to all 12 tones.

In painting, the early 1900s was a time for investigations into abstract art. Broadly speaking, abstract art has no clear subject matter. Also called nonrepresentational, nonobjective, or nonfigurative art, such paintings seek to abstract the essence of a traditional figure or landscape. Several movements within this broad umbrella popped up in the early 20th century. Matisse and other fauvists (from "wild beasts") did not break completely with objectivity, but their free hand with color and distortion of form were considered radical. Some

Schoenberg concert poster, 1913

fauvists went on to practice cubism, developed by Pablo Picasso and Georges Braques, which was also partially representational—objects and figures were reduced to simple geometric forms to try to show several aspects of the figure all at once. Meanwhile, the German expressionist movement, including Edvard Munch and Paul Klee, delved into the inner reality or emotional content of a subject; the emphasis was on expressing ideas and ethical concerns, no matter how disturbing, instead of worrying about beauty and harmony. Its theories were a direct counterpunch to Impressionism.

Literature had corresponding adherents. Cubist doctrines conceived by poet Guillaume Appolinaire and others resulted in experiments with imagistic, cubist poetry, which served as a forerunner to the work of Jean Cocteau and other surrealists. The expressionist school attracted such lyric poets as Ernst Stadler and several playwrights, including Georg Kaiser and Bertolt Brecht. These and other movements influenced each other and inspired artists in succeeding generations. By the late 20th century, however, many artists felt that experiment in form for its own sake was less important than developing a personal aesthetic freely drawn from a variety of styles and movements. It was a world in which purely abstract artists like Jackson Pollock and Willem de Kooning existed side by side with pop artists such as Andy Warhol.

661 | *Explorer Robert Peary, wearing heavy furs in bracing winds on deck of steamship* Roosevelt

discredited. In the 1980s, examinations of Peary's diaries also cast some doubt on his achievement, revealing that he may have missed the Pole by a few miles.

English Channel Flown

662 **1909** Hoping to win a £1,000 prize and a place in history, French aviator Louis Blériot flew his monoplane, the Blériot XI, from Calais to Dover across the English Channel on July 25, 1909. The plane lacked navigational instruments, so Blériot found his destination by following ships below him heading to port. After 37 minutes he landed successfully in Dover, despite damaging his propeller and landing gear. Blériot became an international hero and his Blériot XI model one of the most popular aircraft of its time.

FIRST PERSON

Robert Peary
JOURNALS, 1909

Tues-Wed. Apr. 21-22
Still the finest weather. Surprising. ....Passed Captain's igloo end of 7 hours. Recent bear track, hare track, several fox tracks....Sun so hot & blinding now practically impossible to travel in day time, yet temp from -16° to -20°.

Wed.-Thurs. Apr. 22-23
My life work is ended accomplished. The thing which it was intended from the beginning that I should do, the thing which I believed could be done, & that I could do, I have done. I have got the North Pole out of my system. After 23 yrs of effort, hard work, disappointments, hardships, privations, more or less suffering & some risks, I have won the last, great geographical prize, the North Pole, for the credit of the U.S., the Service to which I belong, myself, & my family. My work is the finish, the cap & climax, of 300 years of effort, loss of life, & expenditure of millions, by some of the best men of the civilized nations of ... the world; & it has been accomplished with a clean cut dash, spirit, & I believe thoroughness, characteristically American. I am satisfied.

Officially named the National Association for the Advancement of Colored People (NAACP) in the following year, the organization drew in W. E. B. DuBois's Niagara Movement, an existing civil rights group with similar aims. In the years to come it would gather members across the country and lead legal battles and public protests against segregation and discrimination.

North Pole Reached

661 **1909** American naval officer Robert Peary, already known for his expeditions in Greenland, set his sights on one of exploration's last frontiers: the North Pole. In March 1909, Peary set out over the Arctic ice with 23 men, 133 dogs, and 19 sleds. On April 6, Peary, his associate Matthew Henson, also a naval officer, and four Inuit companions—Oatah, Egingwah, Seegloo, and Ookeah—reached their target and planted an American flag.

Upon his return, Peary learned that another American, Frederick A. Cook, claimed to have reached the Pole before him. This claim was eventually

667 More Details on Woman Suffrage

Nearly a century of protest and dedicated activism gave U.S. women what property-owning men had possessed from the start: the right to vote. The passage of the 19th Amendment in 1920, which officially granted suffrage to women, ended what had been one of the more controversial issues of the day while launching an even more inspired women's liberation movement. The leaders of these early drives for equality—Susan B. Anthony, Elizabeth Cady Stanton—are now household names, and though the idea of women's equality has since taken a variety of shapes and sizes, today's women activists, from the most conservative to the most radical, are all in debt to this first great constitutional victory.

In the early 1800s the voices in favor of women's suffrage were loud but few in number, and it was not until after the Civil War—when women had stepped up to take over for men who had gone off to fight— that more significant strides were made. The National Woman Suffrage Association (later the National American Woman Suffrage Association), started by Anthony and Stanton in 1869, advocated an amendment to the U.S. Constitution, organizing marches and public demonstrations as well as hearings before Congress. By 1900, major headquarters were established in New York City, increasing the movement's visibility, and the relatively new states of Wyoming, Colorado, and Utah had all given women the vote.

> Although American women had pioneered the suffrage movement ... they were late to receive the vote.

After two unsuccessful attempts in the Senate, the 19th Amendment was finally passed in 1920. Although American women had pioneered the suffrage movement in the previous century, inspiring movements in Europe and Canada, they were late to receive the vote; Finland, Norway, Denmark, Canada, Russia, Germany, and Poland all granted suffrage to women in the first two decades of the 20th century. Great Britain had given women over 30 the vote in 1918 but extended suffrage to all women in 1928. Lichtenstein became the last Western nation to give voting rights to women in 1984.

Suffragists enjoy a straw ride on "Great Suffrage Day." After nearly a century of struggles, women in the United States gained the right to vote.

Wright Perfects Prairie Style

663 **1909** Pioneering American architect Frank Lloyd Wright revolutionized architecture around the world with his clean, open, dramatically geometric design. He became the leading exponent of the Prairie style that reflected the flat, expansive landscape of the American Midwest. In 1909, he completed one of the most famous examples of Prairie-style architecture, the Robie House in Chicago, Illinois. With its sweeping horizontal lines, open floor plan, dramatic overhangs, and brick construction, it became an icon of modern architecture.

Burgess Shale Found

664 **1909** Geologist Charles D. Walcott of the Smithsonian Institution was traveling on horseback through the Burgess Pass in Canada's Rocky Mountains when, legend has it, his path was blocked by a pile of rocks. According to the story, Walcott stopped to move the rocks and was surprised to discover in them a rich trove of fossils.

The Burgess shale is now known as one of the world's most important and best preserved fossil formations. Its fossil specimens date from the middle Cambrian period, a time when the land that is now Canada was just south of the Equator and life was confined to the oceans. It includes rare examples of soft tissue from worms, crinoids, and sea cucumbers. Since Walcott's day, more than 60,000 unique fossils have been found in the formation, providing an unusually complete picture of a moment in the evolution of life on Earth.

Mexican Revolution Begins

665 **1910** Porfirio Díaz had been in power in Mexico for more than 30 years by 1910. Under his dictatorship, large holdings of land had fallen into the ownership of a few and corruption was endemic. When a moderate political opponent, Francisco Madero, opposed him in the elections that year, the dictator had him imprisoned until the rigged elections declared Díaz the winner yet again. When Madero was released, he called for a national uprising, and a revolution began.

Leaders of the Mexican Revolution Pancho Villa and Emiliano Zapata with followers

Two leaders emerged in the rebellion: Emiliano Zapata in the south, whose motto was "*Tierra y Libertad*—Land and Liberty," and former bandit Pancho Villa in the north. By 1913, Madero had lost control of the revolution and was assassinated by a new dictator, Gen. Victoriano Huerta. Chaos reigned for the next several years as Villa and Zapata and government forces fought each other across the countryside. Villa led raids into the United States, which supported the Mexican rulers. The U.S. responded by chasing Villa through northern Mexico but failing to capture him.

In 1917, Venustiano Carranza became president and called for a constitutional convention. Reformers managed to push through a redistribution of property and educational programs, as well as restrictions on the power of the Catholic Church. By 1920, Zapata had been killed by one of Carranza's agents and the revolution had ended. About 1.5 million people had died.

Japan Annexes Korea

666 **1910** Already a Japanese protectorate, Korea fell under further Japanese control when its army was disbanded and it was annexed by Japan in 1910. The repressive Japanese government modernized transportation and communications in Korea but stifled freedom of speech and education while attempting to assimilate Korean citizens into Japanese culture. Japan's control of Korea lasted until the end of World War II.

FOOTNOTE The Japanese annexation ended Korea's Choson (or Yi) dynasty, which had ruled for more than 500 years. The last adult emperor, Kojong, was forced to abdicate in 1907 after he sought help from outside nations against Japan.

Suffrage Causes Riots

667 **1910** Nowhere were the supporters of woman suffrage more passionate than in England in the early 20th century. Led by suffragist Emmeline Pankhurst, the Women's Social and Political Union (WSPU) pulled in thousands of followers who gathered in vocal demonstrations for voting rights. On November 18, 1910, suffragists marched on Parliament to demand the vote; when police ordered them to return home, the women fought for six hours. Many were injured and arrested.

That day, known as Black Friday to members of the movement, marked the beginning of increasingly violent demonstrations in favor of woman suffrage. Suffragists broke windows and set fire to homes, following Pankhurst's declaration that "it is through property that we shall strike the enemy." For the next several years, suffragists were imprisoned and brutally force-fed when they attempted hunger strikes. Only the advent of World War I would quiet the conflict; after the war, British women were granted limited suffrage, with equal voting rights arriving only in 1928.

Supercold Temps Studied

668 **1911** Dutch physicist Heike Kamerlingh Onnes was fascinated

663 | *The Frank Lloyd Wright-designed Frederick C. Robie House at 5757 Woodlawn Avenue in Chicago*

by the behavior of materials at very low temperatures. In 1908, he became the first person to produce liquid helium, achieving this at temperatures only one degree above absolute zero. He then turned to studying metals at supercold temperatures in an effort to solve a controversy: Would the metals become less resistant to electrical current, as some people believed, or would their resistance approach the infinite, as others (including Lord Kelvin) contended?

In 1911, Onnes managed to chill pure mercury to 4.19 kelvins. To his amazement, electrical resistance suddenly vanished. Onnes went on to name the phenomenon "superconductivity." Although Onnes could not explain why it had occurred, the discovery clearly had vast potential in industries using electrical transmission, as well as in other realms of science. Today, superconducting materials are used in maglev trains, MRI machines, and other applications.

Triangle Factory Fire

669 **1911** On March 25, 1911, a Saturday afternoon, fire broke out on the ninth floor of the Triangle Shirtwaist Factory in Manhattan. The workers, mostly immigrant women and some as young as 15, overwhelmed the single fire escape as they fled; others pounded unsuccessfully on locked stairwell doors. Observers on the street saw many jump to their deaths from ninth-floor windows. When the fire was over, 146 of the 500 employees had died.

In the wake of the disaster, protests erupted over unsafe working conditions in the factory and in other sweatshops that exploited immigrant workers. The recently formed International Ladies' Garment Workers' Union led the way in demanding legislative protection for the working class. Within five years, new safety laws had been passed in New York State. Frances Perkins, who had watched girls clasp their hands in prayer before jumping from the burning building, later became secretary of labor under Franklin D. Roosevelt and helped to enact a wide range of worker reforms.

Vitamins Discovered, Named

670 **1911** By the beginning of the 20th century, English biochemist Frederick Gowland Hopkins had discovered that humans had to ingest certain amino acids in their food in order to live. Even so, some diseases, such as scurvy or rickets, seemed linked to diet and yet not to amino acids. Polish scientist Casimir Funk was pursuing the secrets of nutrition as well. He had discovered that pigeons with polyneuritis, a nerve disorder, could be cured with a diet containing rice bran (now known to contain thiamin). In 1911, Funk suggested that some diseases were caused by the absence of a vital nutrient in the diet, a nutrient he called "vitamines," from "vital amines." Later, it was shown that the nutrients did not need to be amines, and the "e" was removed from the word.

■**FOOTNOTE** In addition to polyneuritis, diseases or syndromes caused by vitamin deficiencies (and cured by the appropriate vitamins added to the diet) include scurvy, beriberi, pellagra, anemia, and rickets.

Machu Picchu Explored

671 **1911** Yale history professor Hiram Bingham was searching for the ancient Inca capital of Vilcabamba in July when his Peruvian guide took him up a steep slope in the Andes mountains. Two thousand feet up was an astonishing sight: an ancient city of houses, temples, towers, steps, and terraces buried beneath jungle vegetation. Bingham, sponsored by Yale University and the National Geographic Society, returned several times over the next few years to clear the city of vegetation and study its structures. The historian hoped that he had uncovered the legendary "lost city of the Incas," birthplace of that civilization. In fact, archaeologists now believe Machu Picchu was a royal retreat for Inca ruler Pachacútec. A World Heritage site, it remains one of the best preserved sites in South America.

South Pole Reached

672 **1911** Both Roald Amundsen and Robert Falcon Scott set out to be the first to reach the South Pole in 1911. Only Amundsen's party returned. Traveling by sled dog, the experienced Norwegian explorer and his four companions were aware that they were racing the British expedition to the goal. Pushing through blizzards and traversing crevasses, they reached the pole on December 14, 1911, and took up the Norwegian flag they had brought with them. "Five weather-beaten, frost-bitten fists they were," wrote Amundsen later, "that grasped the pole, raised the waving flag in the air, and planted it as the first at the geographical South Pole." Scott's group arrived a month later and died, disappointed but stoical, in dangerous storms on the return trip.

Atom Takes Shape

673 **1911** Ernest Rutherford, an energetic New Zealand physicist, advanced the young field of atomic physics with a combination of clever experimentation and insight in 1911. In order to study atomic structure, Rutherford had been bombarding gold foil with positively charged alpha particles. According to the current theory, the atom was a diffuse cloud of positively charged matter evenly studded with electrons—the "plum pudding model." Particles shot at this type of atom would pass through easily, with only a slight deflection. And yet in Rutherford's experiment, some of his alpha particles bounced vigorously off the foil. "It was almost as incredible," he said, "as if you fired a 15-inch shell at a piece of tissue paper and it came back and hit you." Rutherford deduced that the atom must contain a tiny, dense concentration of positive matter—its

nucleus—around which the electrons orbited like planets. It was a far more accurate picture of the atom than William Thomson's, though one that would soon be modified by quantum theory.

Last Chinese Emperor

674 **1912** It is said that when China's last emperor, three-year-old Puyi, was taken to the imperial throne room, he shouted "I don't want to stay here, I want to go home!" He got his wish three years later when the 268-year-old Qing dynasty was overthrown.

The last imperial government of China had been tottering for years. China's humiliating loss to Japan in the Sino-Japanese War was just one more blow to a regime beset by repeated rebellions. Finally, in 1911 a host of secret societies, student groups, and military groups all rose in revolution, and in 1912 the imperial family, ruled by

a little boy, was forced to abdicate in favor of a nominally republican government.

Titanic Sinks

676 **1912** When the luxury liner R.M.S. *Titanic* sank in the early morning of April 15, the disaster gripped the public imagination with a hold it has never released. The passenger ship was on its maiden voyage from Southampton, England, to New York City when it went down. One of the largest ships in the world, it was said to be unsinkable due to a double-bottomed hull divided into 16 watertight compartments. Among its first passengers were many society figures of the day, including millionaires John Jacob Astor and Benjamin Guggenheim and philanthropist Margaret Tobin Brown, later known as "unsinkable" Molly Brown.

Just before midnight on the 14th, the Titanic struck an iceberg some 400 miles

Means of Measuring Universe

675 **1912** Harvard astronomer Edward Pickering hired women for the painstaking job of measuring stars on photographic plates because he could pay them less than men, and he believed they were better suited to the picky work of analyzing dim dots in a photo. Well suited they were: Several of his hires went on to make major contributions to astronomy. One of them was Henrietta Swan Leavitt, a graduate of what would become Radcliffe College. Reserved and hearing-impaired, Leavitt was also brilliant. By 1908 she had analyzed more than 1,000 variable stars (those that wax and wane in brightness). Many were in formations called the Magellanic Clouds (actually nearby galaxies). Knowing that the stars in her sample were all at roughly the same distance from Earth, in 1912 Leavitt published a paper that outlined the mathematical relationship between the absolute magnitude (intrinsic brightness) of variable stars and their cycle. Once the absolute magnitude of a star was known,

Harvard astronomer Edward Pickering inadvertently launched women's astronomy careers

astronomers could then compare that to its brightness as seen from Earth (its apparent magnitude) to determine its distance. Leavitt had provided the world of astronomy with the first yardstick for measuring the distance of any variable star via its luminosity—and thus the first indications of the true size of the universe.

676 | *Bow of the* Titanic *lies where it sank with 1,500 passengers south of Newfoundland in 1912.*

south of Newfoundland. At least five of the watertight compartments ruptured, and as water rushed in, the weight pulled the bow of the ship under. The ship had only 1,178 lifeboat spaces for its 2,224 passengers; women and children were loaded into the lifeboats first, but in the chaos many boats were launched only partially full. At 2:20 a.m. the *Titanic* sank. Wireless operator Harold Bride, washed off the deck, watched the boat go down:

"She was a beautiful sight then. Smoke and sparks were rushing out of her funnel … the ship was turning gradually on her nose—just like a duck that goes for a dive.…The band was still playing. I guess all of them went down. They were playing 'Autumn' then. I swam with all my might. I suppose I was 150 feet away when the *Titanic,* on her nose, with her after-quarter sticking straight up in the air, began to settle—slowly."

About 1,500 people died on the boat and in the frigid waters. The survivors were picked up toward dawn by the liner *Carpathia.* The tragedy gave birth to many reforms in sea travel, including rules calling for a lifeboat seat for every passenger on board; regular lifeboat drills; and round-the-clock radio watches on all ships (a nearby liner, the *Californian,* had not heard the *Titanic*'s distress signals because its radio operator had gone to bed). It also led to the establishment of the International Ice Patrol to warn of icebergs in the North Atlantic.

Continental Drift Proposed

677 **1912** German meteorologist Alfred Lothar Wegener proposed a theory that was at once so obvious and so outlandish that it was roundly ridiculed for decades. While browsing through scientific papers, he had found examples of fossil organisms that were identical on both sides of the Atlantic. Geologically, too, the landforms on either side of the ocean seemed to fit like puzzle pieces. Not only did the coastlines roughly match, but formations such as the Appalachian Mountains and rock strata in South Africa could be fitted to their counterparts across the sea.

Wegener gave a lecture and presented papers outlining his hypothesis about these coincidences: Around 200 million years ago the world's continents were joined into a single supercontinent, Pangaea; they had reached their present positions by moving through the ocean floor. As solid as his evidence was, Wegener could not adequately explain the mechanism behind this "drift," and his theory was greeted with derision by virtually the entire scientific community. Only in the 1960s, long after Wegener's death, did increasing knowledge of Earth's geology bring geologists around to his viewpoint, now embodied in the science of plate tectonics.

■ **FOOTNOTE** By the late 20th century, scientists filled in the missing part of the continental drift puzzle by showing that continents and ocean floors float on top of a layer of viscous rock known as the asthenosphere.

Balkan Wars Begin

678 **1912** The Ottoman Empire, steadily losing its territory and its hold over eastern Europe, suffered another blow when members of the Balkan League—Serbia, Montenegro, Greece, and Bulgaria—attacked the empire in October. Rapid victories for the Balkan forces in Turkey and Macedonia led to an end to the first Balkan war and a peace treaty in

FIRST PERSON

Eva Hart
TITANIC PASSENGER, 1912

My father went away and spoke to one of the sailors and came back and said "We've hit an iceberg … they're going to launch the lifeboats but you'll all be back on board for breakfast."…

The panic seemed to me to start after the boats had gone … then we could hear the panic of people rushing about on the deck and screaming and looking for lifeboats … I was terrified…the bows went down first and the stern stuck up in the ocean what seemed to me like a long time … and then keeled over and went down, you could hear the people screaming and thrashing about in the water.…

Finally the ghastly noise of the people thrashing about and screaming and drowning, that finally ceased. I remember saying to my mother once, "How dreadful that noise was" and … she said, "Yes, but think back about the silence that followed it" … because all of a sudden the ship wasn't there, the lights weren't there and the cries weren't there.

680 | *Spiral galaxy NGC 4414, as seen through the Hubble telescope, lies about 60 million light-years away.*

May 1913. The empire yielded almost all its territory in Europe to its opponents.

The second Balkan war began soon afterward when Bulgaria quarreled with its allies over the division of land in Macedonia. On June 29, 1913, Bulgaria attacked Greek and Serbian forces in Macedonia; soon, Romania and the Ottoman Empire joined the opponents of Bulgaria and helped to defeat it. The Treaty of Bucharest, signed in August 1913, gave most of Macedonia to Greece and Serbia. Albania was made an independent state. Perhaps more significantly, tensions from the years of conflict were to erupt again with the assassination of an Austrian archduke in Sarajevo and the beginnings of World War I.

Subatomic Particles Made

679 **1912** Scottish physicist Charles T. R. Wilson, impressed by the beauty and structure of clouds, decided to re-create them in the laboratory. In 1912, filling a chamber with water vapor, he attempted to force the saturated air into condensing by passing radiation through it. He found that as the charged particles passed through the cloud chamber, the vapor condensed into water droplets along their paths. For the first time, the course of subatomic particles could be seen and even photographed. Wilson's chamber later allowed physicists to identify both electrons and positrons. Wilson himself won the Nobel Prize in physics in 1927.

Stars Sorted

680 **1913** In a rare example of scientific good will, two astronomers on opposite sides of the Atlantic agreed to share credit for their independent discoveries about the nature of stars.

Ejnar Hertzsprung, a Dane, and Henry Norris Russell, an American, both studied the relationships among the temperature, brightness, and color of stars. Both realized that stars could be organized onto a chart according to their luminosity and spectral class (a category that classifies stars according to their spectrum). The resulting chart shows that most stars fall along a main sequence, with hot, luminous bluish stars at top left and dim reddish stars at bottom right;

supergiants and dwarfs cluster at top right and bottom left.

Russell presented his findings to the public first in 1913, but acknowledged that Hertzsprung had reached the same conclusions earlier. The resulting chart, now a mainstay of astronomy, is known as the Hertzsprung-Russell diagram.

■FOOTNOTE Earth's sun lies in the middle of the main sequence in the Hertzsprung-Russell diagram, with a surface temperature around 6,000 kelvins and a luminosity of 1 (the sun is the standard for solar luminosity).

"Krazy Kat" Debuts

681 **1913** Beginning in 1913, the comic strip "Krazy Kat," created by George Herriman, began running as a daily feature in Hearst newspapers across America. The surrealistic strip, featuring the love triangle of Krazy Kat, Ignatz Mouse, and Offissa Pupp, took place in a strangely shifting Arizona landscape. The language varied from Yiddish to Spanish to oddly spelled Shakespearean English.

The strip had a devoted core of intellectual fans. The critic Gilbert Seldes called it "the most amusing and fantastic and satisfactory work of art produced in America to-day." It was the subject of a jazz ballet by John Alden Carpenter, an essay by e. e. cummings, who referred to the strip's "frank frenzy (encouraged by a strictly irrational landscape in perpetual metamorphosis)," and a tribute by writer Jack Kerouac, who named it "an immediate progenitor of the Beat Generation." Hailed as a serious work of art, and highly influential with later generations of comic artists, the strip baffled most readers, although it continued to run until 1944.

Act Reforms Banking

682 **1913** Haunted by a series of financial panics over the previous few decades, in 1913 U.S. bankers and Congress alike were in the mood for reform. In the panic of 1907, for instance, depositors learned that some financial institutions were failing after attempting to corner the copper market; the resulting runs on those banks and others created a crisis of confidence as some banks closed and others had to call in their loans. Only the intervention of one of the nation's richest men, J. P. Morgan, who organized private banks to pool their funds and back the failing institutions, prevented a financial disaster.

It was clear that the federal government needed some sort of central bank to cope with these sorts of credit crises—as well as to keep power out of the hands of a few powerful private bankers. In 1913, Congress passed the Federal Reserve Act. The act, promoted by newly elected President Woodrow Wilson, reformed the national banking system by enabling the government to control bank reserves and thus the money supply. The 12 regional banks of the Federal Reserve System would be administered by a board of governors in Washington, D.C. The system contributed to the stability of the economy and was key to helping the U.S. deal with the demands of World War I.

Atomic Structure Explained

683 **1913** Quantum theory, as mind-boggling as it was, allowed physicists to resolve some basic issues in atomic physics. One was the mystery of the atom's structure. Ernest Rutherford's model of the atom had its electrons orbiting the nucleus like planets circling the sun. However, scientists knew that electrically charged particles gave off radiation if diverted from a straight path. Therefore, electrons should gradually lose energy as they orbited, eventually spiraling into the atomic nucleus and collapsing the atom.

In 1913, the brilliant Danish physicist Niels Bohr, working with Rutherford in Manchester, England, solved the problem using the quantum theory recently developed by Planck and Einstein. Instead of moving about in an almost infinite number of orbits, as Rutherford's theory demanded, Bohr stipulated that the electrons were contained only within certain stable orbits, or shells, in which they do not radiate. If they absorbed radiation, in the form of quanta, they would jump from one orbit to a higher one; releasing radiation, they would jump to a lower orbit. (This was the "quantum leap"—a transition from one point to another without moving through the intervening space.) The quanta, or photons, that the electrons released when moving to a lower orbit could be observed as the characteristic radiation given off by every element: a finding that went some way to explaining the spectral lines emitted by glowing gases such as hydrogen.

The young Danish physicist Niels Bohr described the quantum leap.

Bohr's new atomic model also helped to solve the mystery of the structure of the periodic table. Elements that fell into the same column in the periodic table, and had similar properties, turned out to have the same number of electrons in their outer shells. Bohr's radical revision of atomic structure was a triumph for quantum physics and a milestone in the science of the 20th century. For his work deciphering atomic structure, Niels Bohr won the Nobel Prize in physics in 1922.

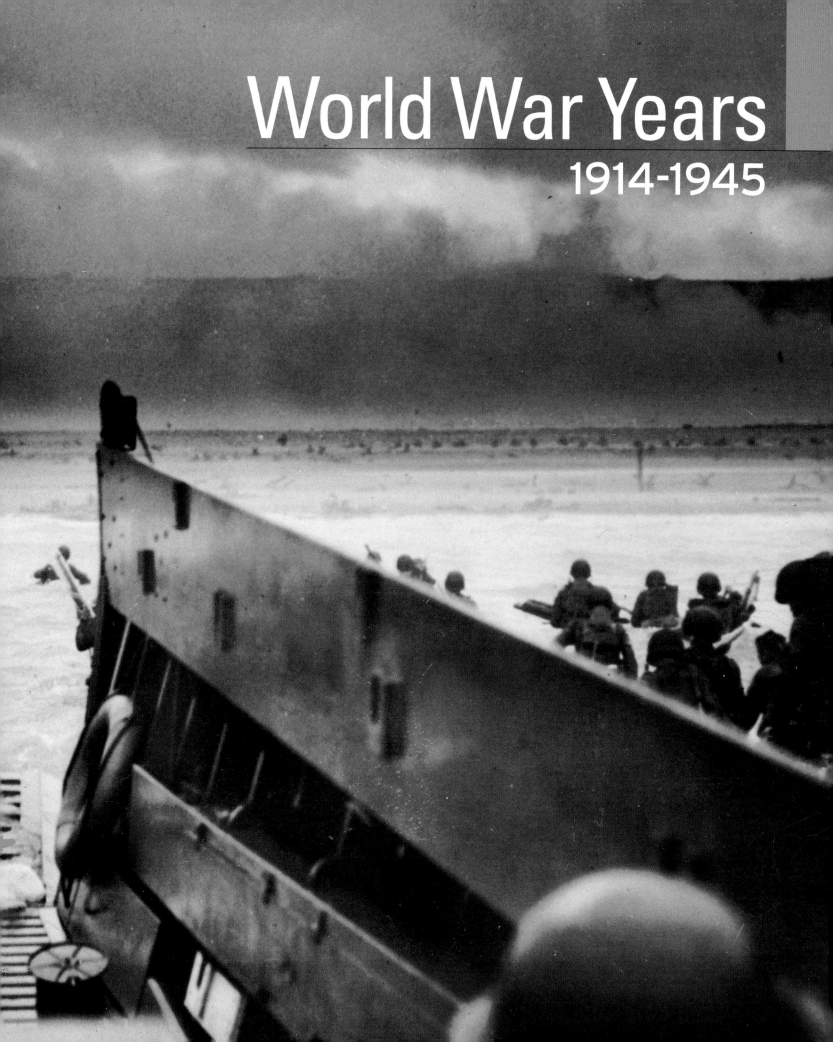

World War Years

1914-1945

1914-1945
Conflicts Escalate

During the first half of the 20th century, two wars of unprecedented fury convulsed the world, killing tens of millions of people and leaving few, if any, lives unaffected by distress and hardship. Even the years separating those conflicts were marked by tension and strife as nations recovering from the First World War were wracked by the Great Depression and suffered political unrest that brought extremists to the fore, shattering hopes for peace. During this tumultuous era of the early 20th century, defined by two massive eruptions of violence and many smaller upheavals, stresses that had long been simmering as empires expanded and converged were released with cataclysmic effect.

The First World War originated in the Balkans, where the assassination of Austrian Archduke Franz Ferdinand in 1914 caused conflict between Austria-Hungary and Russia, two troubled empires with powerful allies. Germany moved quickly to support Austria-Hungary by declaring war on Russia and its ally, France. Great Britain then entered the conflict on the side of France and Russia, which gained support from many other Allied nations around the world, including the United States, which joined the war belatedly after American ships carrying supplies to the Allies in Europe were attacked by German submarines. Germany and its partners Austria-Hungary and the Ottoman Empire, known collectively as the Central Powers, lost the support of Italy,

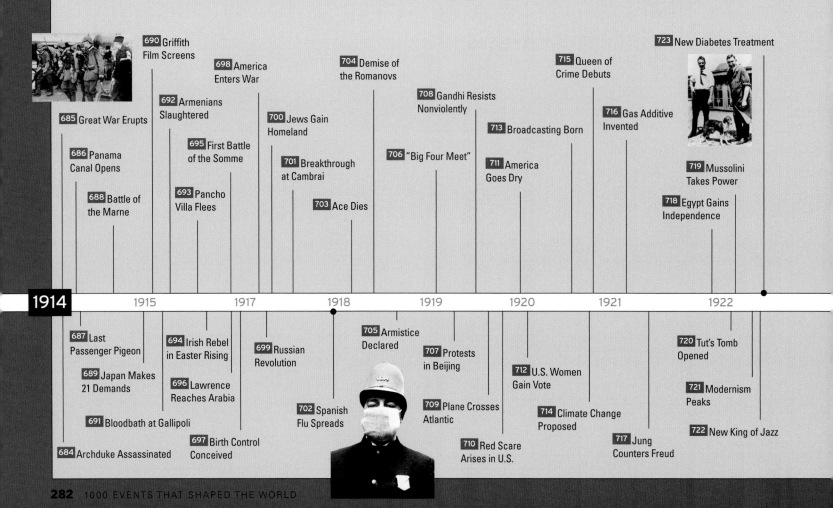

690 Griffith Film Screens

698 America Enters War

692 Armenians Slaughtered

685 Great War Erupts

686 Panama Canal Opens

688 Battle of the Marne

695 First Battle of the Somme

693 Pancho Villa Flees

700 Jews Gain Homeland

701 Breakthrough at Cambrai

703 Ace Dies

704 Demise of the Romanovs

706 "Big Four Meet"

708 Gandhi Resists Nonviolently

713 Broadcasting Born

711 America Goes Dry

715 Queen of Crime Debuts

716 Gas Additive Invented

723 New Diabetes Treatment

719 Mussolini Takes Power

718 Egypt Gains Independence

1914   1915   1917   1918   1919   1920   1921   1922

687 Last Passenger Pigeon

694 Irish Rebel in Easter Rising

699 Russian Revolution

705 Armistice Declared

707 Protests in Beijing

720 Tut's Tomb Opened

689 Japan Makes 21 Demands

696 Lawrence Reaches Arabia

712 U.S. Women Gain Vote

721 Modernism Peaks

691 Bloodbath at Gallipoli

702 Spanish Flu Spreads

709 Plane Crosses Atlantic

714 Climate Change Proposed

722 New King of Jazz

684 Archduke Assassinated

697 Birth Control Conceived

710 Red Scare Arises in U.S.

717 Jung Counters Freud

which switched sides, and waged an increasingly desperate struggle to stave off the Allies and keep their sagging imperial regimes intact.

A Sobering Victory

THE ALLIES EVENTUALLY WON THE WAR, BUT THE FIGHTING WAS so brutal and destructive that both sides found themselves drained and demoralized. Battles on the western front, in France and Belgium, raged for months on end and claimed hundreds of thousands of casualties without achieving any decisive outcome.

On the eastern front, the Russians suffered such costly defeats that Tsar Nicholas II was forced to abdicate in 1917 and communists known as Bolsheviks seized power. That revolution stunned the Allies and threw a pall over their 1918 victory. After waging a civil war against anticommunists, the Bolsheviks reconstituted the old Russian Empire as the Soviet Union and governed it as a one-party state while lending support to communist movements abroad.

At the opposite end of the political spectrum in Europe were fascists: ultraconservatives who favored dictatorial rule to crush communism and other forms of dissent they considered alien or subversive. Benito Mussolini exploited chaotic postwar conditions in Italy to impose a fascist regime there in 1923. He hoped to build an empire that would rival those of Britain and France, which retained their colonies and acquired new mandates in the Middle East following the collapse of the Ottoman Empire.

In the mid-1920s, prospects for lasting peace improved as Germany and other war-ravaged European nations stabilized with the help of investment from the United States, where the economy was booming. A new international mass

PREVIOUS PAGE | *Soldiers wade toward uncertain fates in the D-Day storming of Omaha Beach at Normandy on June 6, 1944.*

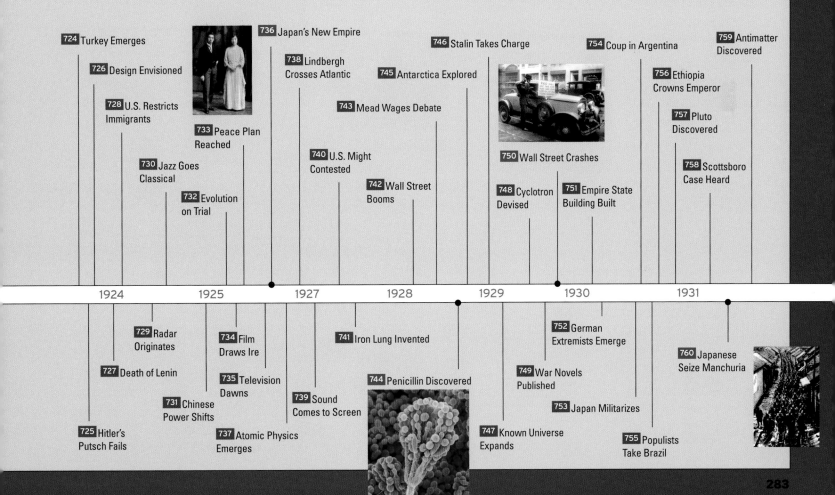

724 Turkey Emerges

726 Design Envisioned

728 U.S. Restricts Immigrants

730 Jazz Goes Classical

732 Evolution on Trial

733 Peace Plan Reached

736 Japan's New Empire

738 Lindbergh Crosses Atlantic

740 U.S. Might Contested

742 Wall Street Booms

743 Mead Wages Debate

745 Antarctica Explored

746 Stalin Takes Charge

748 Cyclotron Devised

750 Wall Street Crashes

751 Empire State Building Built

754 Coup in Argentina

756 Ethiopia Crowns Emperor

757 Pluto Discovered

758 Scottsboro Case Heard

759 Antimatter Discovered

1924   1925   1927   1928   1929   1930   1931

725 Hitler's Putsch Fails

727 Death of Lenin

729 Radar Originates

731 Chinese Power Shifts

734 Film Draws Ire

735 Television Dawns

737 Atomic Physics Emerges

739 Sound Comes to Screen

741 Iron Lung Invented

744 Penicillin Discovered

747 Known Universe Expands

749 War Novels Published

752 German Extremists Emerge

753 Japan Militarizes

755 Populists Take Brazil

760 Japanese Seize Manchuria

culture emerged with the appearance of radio, cinema, and phonographs, and jazz music of African-American origin came to define the times. Epic flights by Charles Lindbergh and other aviators inspired visions of a world where technology fostered international cooperation rather than conflict. But such optimism quickly faded when the boom on Wall Street ended in 1929 with a crash that reverberated around the world.

In Germany, the loss of American investment deepened the Depression and doomed the Weimar Republic, whose leaders had tried to bring Germany in line with other Western democratic nations. In 1933, Germany underwent a fascist revolution as Nazis led by Adolf Hitler took power. Hitler's aim was to avenge Germany's defeat and subsequent humiliation at the Paris Peace Conference in 1919 by rearming in defiance of the Treaty of Versailles and forging a new German empire called the Third Reich through conquest and the use of intimidation. Unlike other imperialists who sought to unite various factions and ethnic groups under their authority, Hitler planned to create a racially and ideologically pure empire by eliminating communists and Jews, for whom he had a pathological hatred. "We may be destroyed," he told his Nazi followers, "but if we are, we shall drag a world with us—a world in flames."

Breaking the Peace

IN 1936, HITLER JOINED FORCES WITH ITALY'S MUSSOLINI AND intervened in the Spanish Civil War against Republican forces there backed by the Soviet Union. In Asia a year later, Japan launched a major offensive against China, where nationalists and communists reached a truce in their ongoing civil war and joined forces against the Japanese.

Japan felt it had as much right to expand through conquest as Western powers did and later joined Germany and Italy in

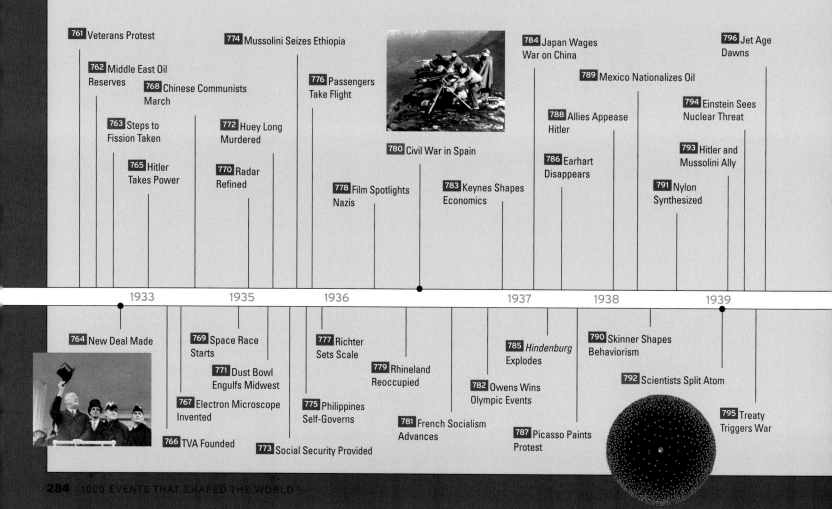

761 Veterans Protest

762 Middle East Oil Reserves

768 Chinese Communists March

763 Steps to Fission Taken

765 Hitler Takes Power

774 Mussolini Seizes Ethiopia

776 Passengers Take Flight

772 Huey Long Murdered

770 Radar Refined

780 Civil War in Spain

778 Film Spotlights Nazis

784 Japan Wages War on China

789 Mexico Nationalizes Oil

788 Allies Appease Hitler

786 Earhart Disappears

783 Keynes Shapes Economics

796 Jet Age Dawns

794 Einstein Sees Nuclear Threat

793 Hitler and Mussolini Ally

791 Nylon Synthesized

1933   1935   1936   1937   1938   1939

764 New Deal Made

769 Space Race Starts

771 Dust Bowl Engulfs Midwest

767 Electron Microscope Invented

766 TVA Founded

777 Richter Sets Scale

779 Rhineland Reoccupied

775 Philippines Self-Governs

773 Social Security Provided

781 French Socialism Advances

782 Owens Wins Olympic Events

785 *Hindenburg* Explodes

787 Picasso Paints Protest

790 Skinner Shapes Behaviorism

792 Scientists Split Atom

795 Treaty Triggers War

the Axis because it shared their view of Britain, France, and the United States as imperial rivals. Western democratic leaders, for their part, saw Axis aggression as a danger to the world, not just to their own interests, but did little to respond to the growing threat.

Haunted by memories of the last war, both France and Britain hesitated to challenge Hitler or to seek an alliance against him with the Soviet dictator Joseph Stalin, who was dreaded for the murderous purges he had carried out against his own people. That allowed Hitler to arrange a cynical nonaggression pact with Stalin, which cleared the way for the invasion of Poland in 1939. Britain and France promptly declared war on Germany, but now as in the last war the United States held back. President Franklin Roosevelt had to contend with isolationists and moved cautiously to aid the embattled British, left to fight alone after Germany conquered France in 1940.

Turning the Tide

THE TIDE OF BATTLE TURNED IN LATE 1941, WHEN GERMANY invaded the Soviet Union and failed to take Moscow, and when Japan launched attacks on American bases in the Pacific. This brought two giants—the Soviet Union and the United States—into the struggle against the Axis and transformed them into superpowers.

When the war ended in 1945 with the conquest of Berlin by the Soviets and the dropping of atomic bombs on Hiroshima and Nagasaki by American forces, the empires of Japan, Germany, and Italy lay in ruins. Among the victorious Allies, power had shifted decisively from the original participants, France and Britain—who would soon lose their colonies—to the latecomers, the United States and the U.S.S.R. Americans and Soviets scarcely had time to celebrate victory before they found themselves locked in a global struggle for supremacy that threatened a third world war.

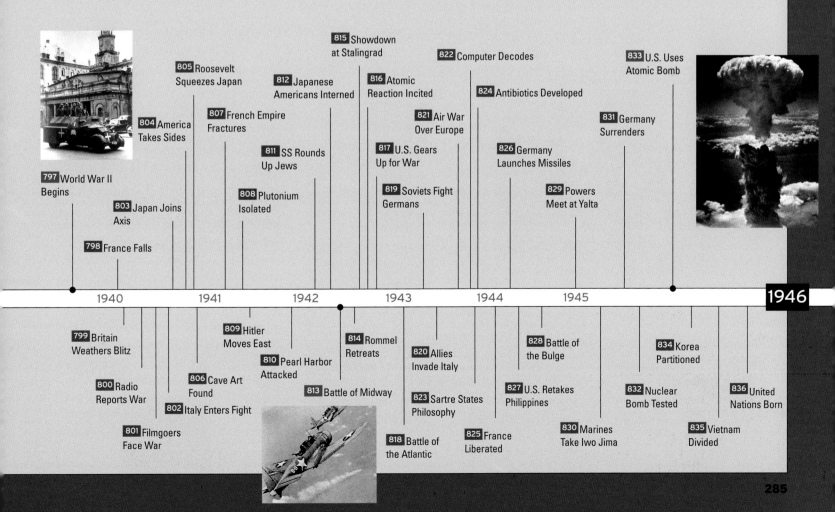

815 Showdown at Stalingrad

805 Roosevelt Squeezes Japan

822 Computer Decodes

833 U.S. Uses Atomic Bomb

812 Japanese Americans Interned

816 Atomic Reaction Incited

824 Antibiotics Developed

807 French Empire Fractures

821 Air War Over Europe

831 Germany Surrenders

804 America Takes Sides

811 SS Rounds Up Jews

817 U.S. Gears Up for War

826 Germany Launches Missiles

797 World War II Begins

808 Plutonium Isolated

819 Soviets Fight Germans

829 Powers Meet at Yalta

803 Japan Joins Axis

798 France Falls

1940   1941   1942   1943   1944   1945   **1946**

799 Britain Weathers Blitz

809 Hitler Moves East

814 Rommel Retreats

828 Battle of the Bulge

834 Korea Partitioned

810 Pearl Harbor Attacked

820 Allies Invade Italy

800 Radio Reports War

806 Cave Art Found

813 Battle of Midway

827 U.S. Retakes Philippines

832 Nuclear Bomb Tested

836 United Nations Born

802 Italy Enters Fight

823 Sartre States Philosophy

801 Filmgoers Face War

818 Battle of the Atlantic

825 France Liberated

830 Marines Take Iwo Jima

835 Vietnam Divided

Archduke Assassinated

684 **1914** On June 28, 1914, in the Bosnian capital of Sarajevo, a gunman fired two shots that stunned the world and led to the deaths of millions. The assailant was 19-year-old Gavrilo Princip, a member of a Serbian terrorist group called the Black Hand who hoped to free Bosnia from Austro-Hungarian rule and unite it with neighboring Serbia. His target was Archduke Franz Ferdinand, heir to the Austro-Hungarian throne, who was slain along with his wife as they rode in an open car. Princip was seized and sent to prison for life. As a direct result of the killings, exactly one month later World War I began.

Great War Erupts

685 **1914** Austria-Hungary blamed Serbia for the attack that resulted in the assassination of the heir to that nation's throne. Serbia was issued an ultimatum. Russia pledged to defend Serbia. Other countries would soon be drawn into the conflict, for Russia, France, and Great Britain were linked as Allied powers while Austria-Hungary, Germany, and the Ottoman Empire would unite as Central Powers. On July 28, after Serbia accepted most but not all of its demands, Austria-Hungary declared war. Informed of the move by that country's ambassador, the Russian foreign minister warned prophetically: "You are setting Europe alight."

By backing Austria-Hungary against Serbia, Germany placed itself in a bind. When Russian troops began mobilizing in opposition, German commanders faced the grim prospect of war on two fronts against Russia and its ally, France. Hoping to avoid that, they adopted the aggressive Schlieffen Plan, which called for German forces to advance swiftly through neutral Belgium and defeat France before turning on the Russians. On August 3, 1914, two days after declaring war on Russia, Germany declared war on France and invaded Belgium, which had been promised British support if it came under attack. When Britain entered the contest a day later, all the major European powers were involved. Known as the Great War, this struggle would convulse the world for more than four years and set the stage for an even greater conflict a generation later.

Woman helps a German soldier with his pack as he and his comrades make their way toward the war front in 1914.

Panama Canal Opens

686 **1914** In August 1914, the Panama Canal was opened to shipping with little fanfare. Newspapers in the U.S. devoted more attention to the fighting abroad than to the successful conclusion of a massive American construction campaign that lasted ten years and cost more than 5,000 workers their lives as a result of accidents or disease. Cutting through the rugged Panamanian isthmus, the canal reduced an ocean voyage of 8,000 nautical miles around the tip of South America to barely 40 miles, promising enormous savings in time and fuel

687 | The passenger pigeon demonstrated the need for conservation.

to merchant ships and warships. Such was its strategic importance that the U.S. retained sole authority over the canal until 1979, when it began sharing control with Panama, which took charge on its own in 1999.

Last Passenger Pigeon

687 **1914** Shortly after noon on September 1, 1914, the last passenger pigeon in existence, named Martha for America's first First Lady, died in captivity at the Cincinnati Zoo at the age of 29. Her passing drew attention to the need for conservation by demonstrating how a species once numbering in the billions could be extinguished through overhunting and loss of habitat. Native to North America, passenger pigeons were noted for their astonishing migrations or passages, in which vast flocks darkened the skies. They had long been pursued as game but were not endangered until the mid-19th century when hunters using nets began wiping out colonies as they nested. Conversion of forest to farmland placed further stress on the species, and the preservation of small numbers in captivity failed to prevent extinction.

FOOTNOTE In the 1950s and early 1960s, the bald eagle was nearly wiped out by DDT and hunting. Following conservation efforts, by 2007 the bald eagle was removed from the Endangered Species list.

Battle of the Marne

688 **1914** By early September 1914, German forces were pouring into France and threatening Paris. To save his capital, French commander Joseph Joffre threw all available Allied troops into battle along the Marne River east of Paris. Six thousand soldiers were rushed from the city in taxicabs to join in the attack on September 6, which forced the invaders back to the Aisne River, where they dug in. Optimism in France and Britain faded as it became clear that the Germans were far from beaten. Recently, they had routed

688 | *French soldiers pose with equipment salvaged from German forces following World War I's Battle of the Marne.*

Russian troops at Tannenberg in East Prussia, showing that they were fully capable of waging war on two fronts. On the western front, a stalemate ensued as both sides dug trenches, protected by barbed wire and machine guns that rendered offensive action almost suicidal.

The use of poison gas, introduced by the Germans in 1915 and soon adopted by the Allies, made the fighting even deadlier.

Japan Makes 21 Demands

689 **1915** The First World War became a truly global conflict when Japan joined the Allies and seized German possessions in the Pacific and China, including a base on China's Shantung (Shandong) Peninsula. Germany was too heavily engaged in Europe to stop Japan, and China had long been subject to incursions by foreign powers. In 1915, Japan increased the pressure by presenting China with 21 demands, including recognition of Japanese interests in Shantung and Manchuria. China yielded to some of the demands but rejected others, leaving the two countries sharply at odds. Once a mighty empire, China was in political turmoil and made a tempting target for imperial Japan. The rivalry between the region's rising star and its past master would explode on the eve of the Second World War, engulfing many other countries.

■ **FOOTNOTE** The demands were annulled by 1922 by terms of the Washington Conference, attended by the U.S., U.K., Japan, Italy, and France, which aimed to limit buildup of naval weapons and bases in Southeast Asia and the Pacific.

Griffith Film Screens

690 **1915** In 1915, 50 years after the U.S. Civil War ended, director D. W. Griffith released one of the most provocative films ever made, *The Birth of a Nation,* focusing on the struggles of a Southern family from the eve of the rebellion through Reconstruction. Griffith based his silent-screen epic on a play glorifying Ku Klux Klansmen as noble ex-Confederates who protected white Southerners from scheming Northerners and insolent blacks. In one scene, Griffith portrayed a black man molesting a white woman and causing her death before being lynched by the Klan. The impact of such lurid imagery was heightened by Griffith's mastery of cinematic technique, and his movie proved hugely successful. The film contributed to a resurgence of the Ku Klux Klan and reinforced racist attitudes that kept African Americans from gaining the civil rights promised them during Reconstruction for another 50 years.

CONNECTIONS

Film History
From Edison to Kurosawa

Millions of people every week rent or buy tickets to movies, participating in the billion-dollar motion picture industry. What is now perhaps our most popular form of art and entertainment began when inventor Thomas Edison exhibited a commercial motion-picture machine, called a kinetoscope, in 1893. His 90-second black-and-white films of dancing girls and historical pageants were viewed through a peephole. It was not long before moving pictures—silent dramas accompanied by music or lectures—were projected on a screen for large audiences.

Those earliest movies were basically filmed plays, with a stationary camera taking the point of view of a spectator in the audience. Soon filmmakers began understanding the ways in which film could mimic the storytelling techniques of writers. The most masterly early film director, D. W. Griffith produced hundreds of films between 1908 and 1930. He revolutionized the cinema by altering camera angles, establishing close-up shots of faces and objects, shortening cuts, and crosscutting from one scene to another—such techniques allowed for shifting points of view, greater realism, and more psychological depth.

The next major turn in the motion picture story was the advent of talkies. The mid-1920s saw the release of the first movies presenting

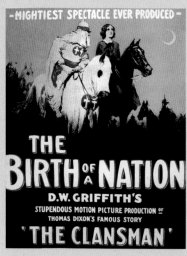

Nation *reinforced racist attitudes.*

sound synchronous with the picture. Partly silent and partly voiced, *The Jazz Singer* (1927) was the first talking picture show hit. Instead of a recorded disc playing separately, subsequent talkies took advantage of technology that recorded sound directly onto the filmstrip. For the first few years, the technical demands of sound held back the artistic advancement of filmmaking, but once the problems were overcome, the industry continued to make ever greater strides.

Some of the greatest films of all time were made in the 1930s, the decade of such classic comedies as *It Happened One Night* (1934) and horror films such as *Dracula* (1931). At the same time, filmmakers outside the U.S. were developing their own richly textured styles, including those of British director Alfred Hitchcock and French director Jean Renoir.

When the U.S. Supreme Court broke up the monopolies of major studios in 1948, the studios no longer had control of the industry from the top down. Production companies, film stars, distributors, and movie houses were now independent. Far fewer films were made—some 250 a year in the 1950s, compared with 550 before the war. Movie attendance declined with the rise of television, but a concurrent interest in art films followed, with quirky and complex productions by Federico Fellini, Ingmar Bergman, and Akira Kurosawa.

Bloodbath at Gallipoli

691 **1915** In early 1915, British forces set out to relieve pressure on Russia by seizing control of the Dardanelles (the strait between the Aegean and the Sea of Marmara) and capturing Constantinople

691 | *An Australian brings a wounded comrade to hospital during the Dardanelles campaign.*

from the Ottoman Turks, who were battling Russians in the Caucasus. The Ottoman Empire was in decline, and Allied leaders figured it would collapse under concerted assault. But they failed to reckon with the rising tide of Turkish nationalism that would lift Mustapha Kemal to power as Ataturk (Father of the Turks).

Turkish forces under Ataturk's command at Gallipoli—the gateway to the Dardanelles—withstood repeated amphibious assaults by ANZAC (Australian and New Zealand Army Corps) and other Allied contingents. Pinned down on blood-soaked beaches by Turks holding the high ground, the Allies suffered dreadful losses for months before pulling out. Victory at Gallipoli did not preserve the Ottoman Empire for long, but it helped propel Ataturk to leadership

of the Turkish republic that emerged from the ruins at war's end.

■**FOOTNOTE** Australia and New Zealand celebrate ANZAC Day in honor of their fallen soldiers at Gallipoli. The battle raised these countries' awareness of their identities as separate from the British Empire.

Armenians Slaughtered

692 **1915** During the Battle of Gallipoli, tensions between Muslim Turks and Christian Armenians in Anatolia (modern-day Turkey) reached a fever pitch. In 1915, Turkish leaders ordered nearly two million Armenians deported to Mesopotamia as enemies of the state. That exodus soon became a death march as Armenians of all ages were abused and attacked by guards and hostile civilians. In all, more than a half million people were killed or died of starvation. By engaging in ethnic cleansing on a vast scale, Turkish authorities set a deadly precedent for later regimes seeking to rid countries of targeted groups. The slaughter went largely unchallenged and unpunished, encouraging Adolf Hitler in his efforts to eliminate Jews.

FOOTNOTE Hitler believed his Final Solution for extermination of Jews would be ignored by world powers, saying "Who, after all, speaks today of the annihilation of the Armenians?"

Pancho Villa Flees

693 **1916** In March 1916, U.S. President Woodrow Wilson sent troops under Gen. John Pershing across the border in pursuit of Mexico's rebel leader Pancho Villa. This invasion came in response to attacks on Americans instigated by Villa, who was angered when Wilson recognized his rival, Venustiano Carranza, as Mexico's chief. Wilson's stated goal was to punish Villa, not to interfere in Mexican affairs. But the presence of American troops on their soil offended many Mexicans, including Carranza's forces, who clashed with some of Pershing's men at Carrizal in June. In early 1917, Pershing withdrew from Mexico without capturing the elusive Villa and began preparing American troops for battle in Europe.

Irish Rebel in Easter Rising

694 **1916** On Easter Sunday, April 23, 1916, Irish rebels seeking independence defied British authorities and took control of the General Post Office and other public buildings in Dublin. Although Ireland had recently been promised home rule under the crown, the militant Irish Republican Brotherhood refused to settle for anything less than complete independence and sought support from Germany, which shipped munitions to the rebels, hoping that their uprising would hamper the British war effort. That shipment was intercepted, leaving the rebels

693 | *Mexican revolutionary Pancho Villa taunts U.S. Gen. John Pershing in 1916 cartoon.*

outgunned and outnumbered when 20,000 British troops equipped with artillery surrounded their positions in Dublin. More than 3,000 people, many of them civilians, were killed or wounded before the rebels surrendered. Although some in Ireland hailed the rebels as heroes, they did not gain widespread support until the British cracked down on their movement. Only about 1,600 rebels had joined in the insurrection, but authorities arrested more than 3,500 men and women afterward and shipped more than half of them to England for internment. Suspected rebel leaders were court-martialed, and 15 were executed as traitors.

Angered by those repressive measures, Irish voters soon abandoned the moderate Irish Parliamentary Party and threw their support behind Sinn Féin, which worked politically for independence while a new organization, the Irish Republican Army (IRA), began waging war to achieve that goal. In 1921, after deadly clashes between the IRA and forces loyal to the crown, the British recognized two states—Northern Ireland, which remained linked with Great Britain as part of the United Kingdom; and the Irish Free State, a self-governing dominion within the British Commonwealth. Those fighting for independence had lost the battle in 1916, but they won the war in the long run when the Irish Free State became the autonomous Republic of Ireland on Easter Sunday in 1949.

FOOTNOTE Northern Ireland occupies one-sixth of the island it shares with the Republic of Ireland. Its capital, Belfast, once had a major ship-building industry, which built the *Titanic* and once employed more than half the workforce.

First Battle of the Somme

695 **1916** The futility of trench warfare on the western front was epitomized by the First Battle of the Somme, launched on July 1, 1916, by British commander Sir Douglas Haig. His aim was to relieve pressure on French forces at Verdun—where the Germans had mounted a massive offensive earlier in the year—by breaking through enemy lines along the Somme River. Haig preceded the attack with a week-long artillery barrage, which did little harm to the entrenched Germans. When British regiments emerged from their own bunkers and went over the top, they were riddled by machine-gun bursts and shellfire. Haig sent wave after wave of troops against the Germans but made little headway before finally halting the offensive in November. This calamitous battle, which cost the two sides more than a million casualties, helped the French hold the line at Verdun but failed to end the bloody stalemate on the western front.

Lawrence Reaches Arabia

696 **1916** In late 1916, a young British intelligence officer named T. E. Lawrence left Cairo to make his first visit to Arabia, the country with which his name would be forever linked. Lawrence's mission was to further an ongoing Arab revolt against the Ottoman Empire. He found an ally in Feisal, son of Emir Hussein of Mecca. Aided by Lawrence, Feisal led Arabs in a guerrilla campaign that played a small part in defeating the Turks. Lawrence's contribution to that Allied victory was exaggerated by journalist Lowell Thomas, who portrayed him as a great Arab hero and liberator. In fact, the campaign did not bring

695 | *British machine gun corpsmen in gas masks man a Vickers gun, First Battle of the Somme, 1916.*

FIRST PERSON

T. E. Lawrence
SEVEN PILLARS OF WISDOM, 1922

I was sent to these Arabs as a stranger, unable to think their thoughts or subscribe their beliefs, but charged by duty to lead them forward and to develop to the highest any movement of theirs profitable to England in her war. If I could not assume their character, I could at least conceal my own, and pass among them without evident friction.... Since I was their fellow, I will not be their apologist or advocate. Today in my old garments, I could play the bystander, ... but it is more honest to record that these ideas and actions then passed naturally. What now looks wanton or sadic seemed in the field inevitable, or just unimportant routine....

Bedouin ways were hard even for those brought up to them, and for strangers terrible: a death in life. When the march or labour ended I had no energy to record sensation, nor while it lasted any leisure to see the spiritual loveliness which sometimes came upon us by the way. In my notes, the cruel rather than the beautiful found place. We no doubt enjoyed more the rare moments of peace and forgetfulness; but I remember more the agony, the terrors, and the mistakes. Our life is not summed up in what I have written (there are things not to be repeated in cold blood for very shame); but what I have written was in and of our life. Pray God that men reading the story will not, for love of the glamour of strangeness, go out to prostitute themselves and their talents in serving another race.

Lawrence and Feisal the reward they hoped for—creation of an Arab state including Syria and Lebanon, which British officials conceded to their French allies after the war.

> ■ **FOOTNOTE** Lawrence wrote of his adventures in *Seven Pillars of Wisdom*, published in the 1920s. The 1962 movie *Lawrence of Arabia* dramatized his exploits and won seven Academy Awards that year.

Birth Control Conceived

697 **1916** Margaret Sanger founded the first birth control clinic in the U.S. in 1916, drawn to the cause as one of 11 children raised by a hard-pressed working-class woman who underwent 18 pregnancies. Later, as a nurse in New York's Lower East Side, Sanger witnessed the risks to which poor women were exposed by unwanted pregnancies and illegal abortions and became an outspoken advocate of contraception. Indicted for publishing information on birth control—classified as obscene material—she gained so much public support that the U.S. district attorney dismissed the charges. Although she later served 30 days in jail when her pioneering clinic in Brooklyn was shut down as a "public nuisance," she ultimately succeeded in overturning laws banning contraceptive devices and literature. Like Marie Stopes, who opened the first birth control clinic in England in 1921 and went on to promote family planning in Asia, Sanger advanced her cause around the world, becoming first president of the International Planned Parenthood Foundation.

America Enters War

698 **1917** In January 1917, Germany launched unrestricted submarine warfare in the Atlantic, exposing to attack American ships carrying supplies to the Allies. Then in February, British intelligence agents intercepted and made public a telegram from German Foreign Minister Arthur Zimmerman urging Mexico to oppose the U.S. if it went to war against Germany. Coming just months after General Pershing's troops clashed with Mexican forces below the border, this message alarmed Americans and increased anti-German sentiment.

In April, Wilson asked Congress for a declaration of war. Pershing was named commander of the newly formed American Expeditionary Force, which would help break the stalemate on the Western Front by bringing more than a million fresh troops into battle on the Allied side.

Russian Revolution

699 **1917** By 1917, the imperial regime of Tsar Nicholas II was near collapse. German forces were advancing deep into Russia, demoralizing the populace and discrediting the tsar. In March, faced with protests and mutinies, he abdicated in favor of a provisional government, which introduced democratic reforms while continuing the war effort. Opposing that government were radicals who formed revolutionary councils called soviets and urged an end to the war.

Amid the turmoil, the exiled Communist leader Vladimir Lenin returned to Russia through Germany with the aid of German authorities, who hoped he would take charge of the revolution and make peace on their terms. Lenin did just that. Promising the hungry, war-weary Russian masses peace, land, and bread, he and his Bolsheviks seized power in November and agreed to an armistice with Germany, which acquired vast areas from Russia in the peace settlement but suffered defeat on the western front before it could secure those gains.

> ■ **FOOTNOTE** The Romanov dynasty ended when Nicholas II's brother refused his offer of the throne—probably a smart move, since the former tsar, his wife, and five children were subsequently killed by the Bolsheviks.

Jews Gain Homeland

700 **1917** In November 1917, as British troops and their Arab allies wrested control of the Middle East from the Ottoman Empire, British Foreign Secretary Arthur Balfour declared in writing that his government favored "the establishment in Palestine of a national home for the Jewish people." The Balfour

697 | *Human rights advocate and nurse Margaret Sanger founded first U.S. birth control clinic.*

Declaration came in response to appeals by prominent Zionists such as Chaim Weizmann, an accomplished chemist who furthered the British war effort and used his influence to press for a Jewish homeland in what was once the biblical kingdom of Israel. Although Balfour promised to respect the rights of non-Jewish communities in Palestine, the Arab majority there felt betrayed.

Jews seeking refuge from persecution in Europe began arriving in substantial numbers. Weizmann's prediction that "Jewish settlement could proceed on a large scale without friction with the local population" proved mistaken, with Palestine remaining contested ground for generations to come.

Breakthrough at Cambrai

701 **1917** Grueling trench warfare on the western front spurred the development of tanks—armored vehicles with tracks capable of crossing rugged terrain, deflecting machine-gun fire, and plowing through barbed wire. Soon commanders massed them together to punch gaping holes in enemy lines and achieve quick victories.

The first such breakthrough was made by the British on November 20, 1917, at Cambrai, where several hundred tanks punctured enemy defenses, leading to the capture of thousands of Germans. This promising advance soon faltered, in part because the tanks were too slow and ran out of fuel. But the introduction in 1918 of faster tanks with greater range helped the Allies achieve lasting gains and defeat their opponents, who lagged behind in tank development. The lesson was not lost on the German military planners, who would strike back in 1940 with fast-moving armored divisions and overrun France in a blitzkrieg (lightning war).

Ace Dies

703 **1918** On April 21, 1918, the German fighter pilot Manfred von Richthofen, known as the Red Baron, died in action over France, ending the reign of the war's top ace, who shot down 80 enemy aircraft. Trained as a cavalryman, Richthofen realized that the days of heroic charges on horseback were over and found glory instead by taking to the air and dueling with Allied pilots. He and the men of his squadron, dubbed the Flying Circus, flew brightly colored Fokker triplanes and bedeviled opponents until the Allies introduced formidable warplanes of their own, like the Sopwith Camel, and evened the score. Credit for bringing down the Red Baron went to a Canadian pilot in the Royal Air Force, Capt. A. Roy Brown, but some denied that Richthofen had been bested by another ace and blamed ground fire.

Spanish Flu Spreads

702 **1918** One of the deadliest pandemics in history erupted in 1918 and spread swiftly around the globe. Known as the Spanish flu because Spain was one of the first countries to suffer massive mortalities, it may have originated in Asia, but the earliest documented outbreak occurred in March at an army camp in Kansas. The cases there were relatively mild, but when the flu reached Europe it grew deadlier.

In Germany, where people were already suffering from food shortages, the ravages of influenza compounded their misery and hampered their war effort. Around the globe overflowing hospitals turned away patients, government buildings temporarily closed, and many citizens stayed behind closed doors. In some places, sneezing or spitting in public were illegal; police in face masks were a common sight as they directed traffic or patrolled neighborhoods. By late 1918, the flu had returned with a vengeance to the U.S., where millions fell ill and more than 500,000 died. Surpassing the toll of the First World War, which cost the lives of some 15 million soldiers and civilians in the embattled nations, this global scourge left at least 25 million people dead before it subsided in 1919, vanishing as mysteriously as it had appeared and leaving scientists puzzled. The outbreak went down in history as the worst pandemic since the bubonic plague, which in the 14th century swept through Europe and decimated about one-third of the population: some 24 million.

Police officer wearing protective mask during Spanish influenza epidemic

Demise of the Romanovs

704 **1918** The Romanov dynasty had ruled Russia since the early 1600s. The long-lived dynasty came to a violent end in July 1918 when Tsar Nicholas II, Tsarina Alexandra, and members of their royal family, living together in the Impatiev House in Ekaterinberg, were shot to death by order of Vladimir Lenin.

Lenin and other Bolshevik leaders, now in power over Russia, had been considering placing Tsar Nicholas on trial. They took as their inspiration the revolutionaries in 18th-century France, who had tried and condemned King Louis XVI and Queen Marie-Antoinette to death in 1793.

Finally Lenin decided to eliminate Nicholas and his family promptly and without any legal proceedings. His decision was made in order to prevent White Russians, a contending political faction who were waging a civil war against his Red party, from rallying around the deposed Romanovs.

The decision also reflected Lenin's determination not to be bound by law in his efforts to remake Russian society. Concerned that the public might find the killing of Alexandra and her children repugnant, Bolshevik authorities announced only the death of the tsar and stated that others in the royal family had been "sent to a safe place."

■ **FOOTNOTE** Because of the secrecy surrounding the family's execution and remains, several women later claimed to be Anastasia. The mystery spawned numerous plays and movies, including the 1956 *Anastasia*.

Armistice Declared

705 **1918** Peace returned to Europe at the 11th hour of the 11th day of the 11th month in 1918 when Germany yielded and agreed to an armistice.

In Germany as in Russia, heavy losses in battle had led to mutiny and revolution, causing Kaiser Wilhelm to abdicate. Some Germans mistakenly blamed their defeat on the revolutionaries, who did not rise up until early November, when the war was already lost. That dangerous myth was

705 | *Men and women carry flags down New York City's joyous Fifth Avenue, celebrating Armistice Day, November 11, 1918.*

perpetuated by Hitler, an embittered veteran of the war who blamed the November uprising on Jews and made them scapegoats for Germany's defeat. Misreading history, Hitler concluded that Germany could avenge its humiliation and dominate Europe if it regained its will to victory and eliminated those he held responsible for dragging the empire down.

"Big Four" Meet

706 **1919** In January 1919, delegates met in Paris to redraw international boundaries following the collapse of the Central Powers. With Russia in turmoil and absent from the conference, the leaders of France, Britain, the U.S., and Italy—which had switched to the Allied side in 1915—made up the "Big Four" in Paris. Dominating the talks was Woodrow Wilson, who proposed a League of Nations to resolve

future disputes and self-determination for ethnic groups aspiring to nationhood.

Wilson's hopes for a just and lasting peace were not realized. He failed to win Senate approval for America's entry into the League of Nations, and it proved impossible to reconcile the demands of rival ethnic groups in newly formed nations such as Czechoslovakia and Yugoslavia. Peace terms imposed on Germany under the Treaty of Versailles weakened that nation's fledgling Weimar Republic, whose democratic leaders were denounced for accepting blame for the war and paying reparations that contributed to runaway inflation.

■ **FOOTNOTE** The League of Nations disbanded during World War II when it proved ineffectual against the aggression of Germany, Italy, and Japan. Following the war, the United Nations replaced the league.

Protests in Beijing

707 **1919** On May 4, 1919, thousands gathered in Tiananmen Square in Beijing to protest the Paris peace accord, which affirmed Japan's authority over the Chinese province of Shantung (Shandong). Among those involved in this May Fourth Movement was Mao Zedong, who would soon be among the founders of the Chinese Communist Party. For Mao, China's future ruler, communism was the means to an end—a strong and secure nation, free of foreign interference. He and his Communist successors viewed challenges to their authority as threats to national security and stifled dissent, including a pro-democracy rally in Tiananmen Square in 1989 that echoed the May Fourth Movement and ended tragically when Chinese forces opened fire, killing hundreds.

Gandhi Resists Nonviolently

708 **1919** Opposition to British rule in India crystallized in 1919 around the charismatic figure of Mohandas Gandhi, known to admirers as the Mahatma (great soul). Gandhi drew on his Hindu faith and other beliefs to propose satyagraha: a philosophy of nonviolent resistance using moral pressure to induce opponents to change their ways. Aroused by legislation denying legal rights to political prisoners, Gandhi called for peaceful dissent.

On April 13, British troops opened fire on unarmed demonstrators at Amritsar, killing nearly 400 people. Gandhi responded by organizing a boycott of British goods and institutions in India and urging acts of civil disobedience. True to his principles, he suspended that campaign in 1922 when protests turned violent. Radical foes of colonialism considered him too cautious, but Gandhi's nonviolent resistance movement gathered strength in years to come and placed mounting pressure on the

708 | *Mahatma Gandhi in about 1910*

British to part with the jewel in their imperial crown and grant India independence.

■ **FOOTNOTE** Gandhi was not an activist until he suffered discrimination while working as a lawyer in South Africa. He spent more than 20 years campaigning for Indian rights in South Africa before turning his focus to India.

Plane Crosses Atlantic

709 **1919** The world became a smaller place on June 15, 1919, when British aviators John Alcock and Arthur Brown completed the first nonstop flight across the Atlantic, reaching Ireland from Newfoundland in a Vickers-Vimy biplane in just over 16 hours. Their feat held out the promise of transatlantic passenger service, but as veterans of the Royal Air Force they knew that advances in aviation could also widen the scope of warfare. Most pilots during the First World War flew reconnaissance or tactical missions such as strafing enemy troops or dueling with rivals in aerial dogfights. A few pioneers like Alcock carried out short-range strategic raids on cities or factories in planes carrying small bomb loads. As aircraft increased in range and capacity after the conflict, however, strategists like Giulio Douhet of Italy envisioned future wars in which squadrons of heavy bombers would decide the outcome by spanning oceans and continents to obliterate cities and industries once safely out of reach.

Red Scare Arises in U.S.

710 **1919** Victory in Europe did little to reassure Americans who felt threatened at home by subversive movements of foreign origin such as communism and anarchism. The Bolshevik Revolution in Russia contributed to a Red Scare that swept the U.S. in 1919 when radical groups and foreigners linked to them were blamed for a series of bombings aimed at prominent figures such as Attorney General A. Mitchell Palmer, whose home was damaged. Raids launched by Palmer in January 1920 led to the arrest of several thousand suspected subversives, 500 of whom were deported. Even radicals born in America and engaged in legal activities faced reprisals. Labor leaders who organized strikes were denounced as Communists, and several assemblymen were barred from the New York state legislature because they were socialists.

The furor reached its peak when two anarchists from Italy, Nicola Sacco and Bartolomeo Vanzetti, were arrested in May 1920 and charged with murdering a guard and paymaster while robbing a shoe factory in Braintree, Massachusetts. Soon after they were indicted, a powerful bomb went off on Wall Street, killing 30 people—an attack that may have been carried out by anarchists who sympathized with Sacco and Vanzetti. Tried and convicted for the Braintree murders, the two men were executed in 1927 amid great controversy, with many protestors insisting that they had been denied a fair trial. By then, the Red Scare had subsided, but it would resurface after World War II, when Americans once again went from fighting enemies abroad to rooting out subversives at home.

■ **FOOTNOTE** Post-World War II McCarthyism picked up where the first Red Scare left off. In 1950 Senator Joseph McCarthy's list of 205 known Communists in the Department of State created a widespread witchhunt until his censure in 1954.

America Goes Dry

711 **1920** In January 1920, Prohibition became the law of the land in the U.S. following ratification of the 18th Amendment, banning "the manufacture, sale, or transportation of intoxicating liquors." Support for Prohibition was strong in rural areas, but many people in urban areas opposed the law, which was poorly enforced and easily circumvented. Far from encouraging sobriety, Prohibition ushered in the Roaring Twenties as unlicensed barrooms called speakeasies provided ready access to liquor distributed by mobsters such as Al Capone of Chicago. One critic of Prohibition, New York Congressman Fiorello La Guardia, estimated that federal and local governments were losing more than a billion dollars a year in taxes on liquor sold illegally and added: "This amount

712 | *Cartoon supporting the woman suffrage movement, 1915*

goes into the pockets of bootleggers and in the pockets of the public officials in the form of graft." The growing conviction that Prohibition was a costly failure led to its repeal in 1933.

U.S. Women Gain Vote

712 **1920** By adopting the 19th Amendment in August 1920, the United States became one of a dozen or so countries around the world allowing women to vote in national elections. Since the 1890s the National American Woman Suffrage Association (NAWSA) had been working to implement woman suffrage—first one state at a time, then by dramatic political tactics, including a 5,000-woman march on Washington, D.C., on the eve of President Woodrow Wilson's Inauguration in March 1913.

New Zealand, Australia, and a few other nations had extended voting rights to women before the First World War, but others waited until after the conflict, which saw women contribute significantly to war efforts as nurses, noncombat military personnel, factory workers, and heads of households and family businesses while their husbands were serving in uniform. Allied nations such as France, Great Britain, and the U.S., which touted the war as a fight for democracy, could no longer pretend that women were unqualified to vote or that elections restricted to male voters were truly democratic. Elsewhere, imperial regimes gave way to liberal or revolutionary governments that introduced political reforms, making women eligible to vote in Russia, Germany, Austria, Hungary, and other European nations.

CONNECTIONS

Aviation and the Military
From Chinese kites to supersonic missiles

Aviation has held a position within the military from its earliest conception, when the Chinese invented kites able to carry men for scouting and reconnaissance. The first powered, manned, and heavier-than-air flight occurred courtesy of the Wright brothers in North Carolina in 1903. By 1908 the U.S. government was concluding a contract for one of the Wright brothers' flying machines. Government and military interest in airplanes would propel the aviation industry forward through the 20th century.

After advancements like air mail and transcontinental flight in the Wright EX, aviation returned to serving the military. Bulgaria used planes militarily during the First Balkan War in 1912. Soon after, Charles Chandler tested the first machine gun mounted on an airplane. By 1914, Roland Garros solved the problem of gun steadiness, attaching a fixed machine gun to the front end of his plane. Throughout World War I, these aviators, known as aces, became famous for their intense air battles.

In the years after the war, engineers abandoned models of wood and canvas, with water-cooled gasoline engines, for aluminum models with radial air-cooled engines. To inspire further development, pilots setting flight records received prizes. Charles Lindbergh, for example, received $25,000 when he piloted the first solo, nonstop crossing of the Atlantic.

Poster celebrating John Alcock and Arthur Brown's first direct transatlantic flight, 1919

Competitive air shows also fueled the development of engine and airframe design. Pilots accomplished in-flight refueling, and a radio-controlled airplane was developed, leading to William Green's invention of the first automatic pilot in 1929. Simultaneously, pilots began setting new speed, distance, and endurance records. British and German engineers obtained patents for the first jet engines, and by 1939 the first functional jet plane, the Heinkel He 178, flew over Germany.

World War II initiated the development of long-range bombers and fighters whose purpose was to protect them. Advances included the development of the first cruise and ballistic missiles, although, since these first jets did not have effective speed, maneuverability, or aim, their role in the war was marginal.

Commercial aviation began to take off, and jetliners began to be patented, one of the first being the Avro C102 in 1949. Commercial flight would not come into its own, however, until the Boeing 707 in 1957. Many developments were still militarily based, such as crew ejection seats, the breaking of the sound barrier, and guided supersonic missiles. The Soviet Union developed long-range bombers capable of nuclear warfare, necessitating the invention of interceptor aircraft by the U.S. This stalemate pushed both the U.S.S.R. and the United States to focus upon the conquest of space.

1914-1945 | World War Years

Broadcasting Born

713 **1920** On November 2, 1920, radio station KDKA in Pittsburgh, Pennsylvania, launched commercial broadcasting in the U.S. by announcing results of the presidential election, won by Warren Harding. Amateur radio operators in various countries had been communicating by voice for more than a decade, but regular broadcasts of music and news did not begin until the First World War ended and governments eased restrictions on the nonmilitary use of radio.

In 1919, a station in Chelmsford, England, began transmitting opera music and other programs, and scheduled broadcasts were inaugurated in the Netherlands later that year and in Montreal, Canada, the following May. Commercial broadcasting was spurred in the 1920s by the introduction of radio receivers that did not require headsets and could be listened to by entire families. Along with motion pictures and phonograph recordings, radio formed part of the emerging technology of mass communications, bringing performers, politicians, and other public figures in touch with vast audiences.

FOOTNOTE In 1906, Canadian Reginald Fessenden, an inventor and former chief chemist for Thomas Edison, transmitted voices and music from a telegraph station near Boston to ships. Many call him the "father of radio broadcasting."

Climate Change Proposed

714 **1920** In 1920, Milutin Milankovitch, a Serbian-born mathematician and astronomer, published the first of many books and papers in which he related major climate changes, such as the onset of ice ages and periods of global warming, to small cyclical variations in Earth's orbit around the sun and in the tilt of Earth's axis in relation to the sun. His theory remained controversial during his lifetime but was later supported by sea sediment cores showing a correlation between the astronomical cycles he identified and past climate cycles. Those astronomical variations—known as Milankovitch cycles—are just one factor

contributing to climate change. Scientists have concluded that the rapid increase in average global temperatures in recent times cannot be explained by Milankovitch cycles or other natural factors and have placed the blame for global warming on human technology in the form of increased carbon dioxide emissions.

FOOTNOTE According to scientists, Europe's Alpine glaciers are half the size they were just 100 years ago; the Hudson Bay and Greenland are both two degrees warmer than they were just a few decades ago.

Queen of Crime Debuts

715 **1920** One of the most successful authors of all time made her first appearance in 1920 when Agatha Christie published *The Mysterious Affair at Styles,* introducing the fictional detective Hercule Poirot. This first effort sold only a few thousand copies, but Christie went on to become the world's most popular mystery writer.

Raised comfortably in the English seaside town of Torquay, she served as a nurse during World War I, acquiring clinical knowledge that helped her devise ingenious ways of committing fictional murder and concealing it from all but the shrewdest investigators, including her boastful hero Poirot and a quieter sleuth with whom she had more in common, the observant Miss Marple.

Gas Additive Invented

716 **1921** The mixed blessings of modern technology—offering comfort and convenience while posing environmental and health risks—were exemplified by the work of the American industrial chemist Thomas Midgley, who in 1921 developed tetraethyl lead, a gasoline additive that kept engines from knocking. Midgley knew the hazards of exposure to pure tetraethyl lead, which sickened him and killed several workers involved in producing it. But not until the 1960s did scientists conclude that even minute amounts of lead in gasoline could be harmful to humans over the long term.

713 | *Pittsburgh's KDKA radio station broadcasts presidential election coverage, November 2, 1920.*

Midgley also developed Freon, introduced in 1930 as the first nontoxic, nonflammable refrigerant and used as an aerosol propellant. In the 1970s, Freon joined tetraethyl lead on the list of notorious pollutants when it was identified as a threat to the ozone layer. Midgley, who was fond of saying that "the price of progress is trouble," died in 1944, before the full costs of his technological advances became clear.

Jung Counters Freud

717 **1921** In 1921, Swiss psychologist Carl Gustav Jung, once closely associated with Sigmund Freud, moved away from Freudianism with the publication of *Psychological Types,* concerned not with abnormal behavior but with how individuals adjust to society. Jung identified two basic personality types—the introvert and the extrovert—representing different psychological strategies for resolving tension between the outer world and

the inner world, or between what his contemporary, Sigmund Freud, called the superego (conscience or adherence to the rules of society) and the id (instinctive or unconscious urges).

Freud viewed unconscious urges as selfish and antisocial, often expressions of repressed sexuality. In contrast to those revolutionary ideas, Jung believed that the unconscious represented a more positive, life-enhancing repository of powerful psychological forces. He proposed the existence of a collective unconscious that can serve as a source of inspiration and creativity and strengthen social bonds through shared myths and beliefs. Dwelling within that collective unconscious were universally shared archetypes, mythic symbols packed with story and meaning that all human beings shared and understood in common. The goal of psychiatry in Jung's view was to promote what he called individuation, or a strong sense of one's identity in connection with society.

Egypt Gains Independence

718 **1922** After four decades under British occupation, Egypt achieved independence in February 1922 and established a constitutional monarchy, presided over by King Fuad. As an emerging nation, Egypt was shadowed by its colonial past. The British continued to exercise influence over its government and retained control of the Suez Canal. Political tensions between Fuad—who belonged to a dynasty installed by Egypt's former Ottoman rulers—and nationalists in parliament led to suspensions of the constitution and rule by decree. Fuad's son and successor, King Farouk, remained at odds with parliament and with dissidents of the Muslim Brotherhood, opposed to the monarchy and to interference by the British and other Western powers. Although Egypt entered the League of Nations in 1937, its foreign policy was still guided by Britain, which would reoccupy the country during the Second World War to keep it from falling into German hands.

FOOTNOTE Egyptian nationalism led to its participation in founding the Arab League, opposing creation of a Jewish state. Egypt was on the losing side of the Arab-Israeli War in 1949, and the State of Israel remains.

Mussolini Takes Power

719 **1922** Fascism took Italy by storm in October 1922 when Benito Mussolini's Blackshirts marched on Rome and propelled him to power.

A former socialist who shifted to the far right after the First World War, Mussolini exploited the fears and resentments of Italians who turned against Italy's democratic leaders when they gained little at the Paris Peace Conference for siding with the Allies and offered no cure for the nation's economic ills. Mussolini's remedy was to play Caesar and raise Italy to imperial glory.

His political party soon became known as the Fascist Party. The term "fascist" derived from ancient Rome—where bundles of rods called fasces were symbols of authority—as did the stiff-armed salute Blackshirts offered the man they called Il

FIRST PERSON

Benito Mussolini
THE DOCTRINE OF FASCISM, 1932

Fascism wants man to be active and to engage in action with all his energies; it wants him to be manfully aware of the difficulties besetting him and ready to face them. It conceives of life as a struggle in which it behooves a man to win for himself a really worthy place, first of all by fitting himself (physically, morally, intellectually) to become the implement required for winning it. As for the individual, so for the nation, and so for mankind. Hence the high value of culture in all its forms (artistic, religious, scientific) and the outstanding importance of education. Hence also the essential value of work, by which man subjugates nature and creates the human world (economic, political, ethical, and intellectual)....Life, as conceived of by the Fascist, is serious, austere, and religious .... The Fascist disdains an "easy" life.... Anti-individualistic, the Fascist conception of life stresses the importance of the State and accepts the individual only in so far as his interests coincide with those of the State, which stands for the conscience and the universal.... It is opposed to classical liberalism which arose as a reaction to absolutism and exhausted its historical function when the State became the expression of the conscience and will of the people. Liberalism denied the State in the name of the individual.... Never before have the peoples thirsted for authority, direction, order, as they do now. If each age has its doctrine, then innumerable symptoms indicate that the doctrine of our age is the Fascist.

719 | *Benito Mussolini, flanked by four generals, leads fascist troops marching on Rome in 1922.*

Duce (the Leader). When Italy's King Victor Emmanuel III yielded to the marchers and invited Mussolini to become prime minister, he obtained dictatorial powers temporarily, as rulers of the Roman Republic did in times of emergency. That dictatorship became permanent, serving as an example for Hitler and other Fascist strongmen around the world.

Tut's Tomb Opened

720 **1922** In November 1922, Howard Carter made one of the most spectacular archaeological finds of all time when he entered the tomb of Pharaoh Tutankhamun and discovered the young Egyptian king's mummified remains and golden death mask, among other treasures. Heaped in the tomb, Carter reported, were a "strange and wonderful medley of extraordinary and beautiful objects," including six chariots, a leopard-skin cloak, and jars of honey and wine left as offerings to the king's spirit.

This was not the first major discovery by the British archaeologist, who had earlier unearthed the tomb of Queen Hatshepsut. But Tutankhamun's crypt was exceptional because its contents had largely escaped tomb robbers, offering a dazzling view of the splendors of ancient Egypt. Public interest in Carter's find was heightened by groundless claims that he and others who entered the tomb were under a curse, but the enduring fascination with King Tut lay in the deathless beauty of his treasures, which later toured the world.

■ **FOOTNOTE** King Tut was only 10 years old—though already married—when he took the throne, and died when he was barely 20, of causes that are still under debate. He was buried in a borrowed sarcophagus and tomb.

Modernism Peaks

721 **1921** Modernism—a cultural movement of the early 20th century that saw writers and artists break with tradition and seek new forms of expression—reached a literary peak with the publication of James Joyce's novel *Ulysses* and T. S. Eliot's extended poem *The Waste Land,* both occurring in the year 1922.

Like Pablo Picasso and other modern artists, Joyce and Eliot borrowed themes and motifs from the past and radically reconfigured them to produce works of great originality. Eliot drew on Shakespeare, Dante, legends of the Holy Grail, and popular songs, among other sources, to create the poetic equivalent of a cubist painting, combining multiple perspectives. Joyce took Homer's epic hero Ulysses (Odysseus) as the model for his character Leopold Bloom, whose bold flights of imagination, captured by Joyce in interior monologues, enliven his otherwise-repressed existence with his unfaithful wife, Molly. While their writing styles differed tremendously, both took radical new steps away from the traditional styles of poetry and the novel of the Victorian era. Joyce's stream-of-consciousness writing style, introduced in *Ulysses* and pushed further in his next novel, *Finnegan's Wake,* influenced fiction writers for decades to come.

Overcoming obscenity charges, *Ulysses* emerged as one of the most influential novels of the 20th century and a monument to artistic freedom.

■ **FOOTNOTE** Modernism infused art, architecture, and design during World War I and the interwar years, developing simultaneously in a number of countries, characterized by geometric shapes, bold colors, and uncluttered lines.

New King of Jazz

722 **1922** When trumpeter Louis Armstrong arrived in Chicago in 1922 to join the band of Joe "King" Oliver, the stage was set for the emergence of a new jazz master who would soon reign supreme. Born in New Orleans—where jazz evolved from blues, ragtime, and other African-American traditions—Armstrong found a mentor in Oliver, a jazz pioneer who took his band north and invited young Armstrong to join him.

Within a few years, Armstrong was leading his own band and dazzling listeners with soaring improvisations that redefined

722 | *Louis Armstrong playing trumpet with Joe "King" Oliver's Creole Jazz Band in Chicago in 1923.*

New Diabetes Treatment

723 **1922** Three decades of medical research culminated in 1922 when Canadians Frederick Banting and Charles Best, working at the University of Toronto, found a treatment for diabetes by discovering insulin, a hormone from the pancreas secreted naturally by the body and essential in the digestion of food.

Frederick Banting and Charles Best with first diabetic dog to get insulin, 1921

Experiments on dogs in the late 1800s had shown that removal of the pancreas caused diabetes, or the inability of the body to regulate blood sugar levels. All attempts to identify the pancreatic substance responsible for regulating blood sugar failed until Banting, a physician, saw a surgeon's report stating that the insulin-producing "islets" in the pancreas remained intact even after the rest of the organ had shriveled. With Best, a medical student, he succeeded in preserving cells from the pancreas of a dog whose pancreatic ducts had been tied off. The team isolated the hormone insulin, which controlled diabetes when injected into animals suffering from the disease.

Their colleague, biochemist James B. Collip, determined a way to purify insulin for human injection; Banting and Best injected themselves first, to ensure its safety. In January 1922, the team treated a 14-year-old boy who was nearing a final diabetic coma. The boy's condition improved, and his case was recorded as the first juvenile diabetes ever controlled.

This breakthrough won swift recognition when Banting and J. J. R. Macleod, the lab director at Toronto, were awarded the Nobel Prize in medicine in 1923. Best, who had not yet received his medical degree, was overlooked, but Banting insisted he deserved to share in the honor and gave Best half his prize money.

jazz. One of the first African-American performers to achieve worldwide fame, he helped break down racial barriers in entertainment by appearing alongside white stars such as Bing Crosby.

Turkey Emerges

724 **1923** In July 1923 at the Swiss town of Lausanne, officials representing nations including France, Great Britain, Italy, and Greece, all of whom had allied against the Central Powers during the First World War, ended a bitter dispute over the fate of the former Ottoman Empire. Together they announced that they recognized the new nation of Turkey and, in so doing, settled its modern boundaries.

In signing the Treaty of Lausanne, Greece renounced claims to Turkish territory, including the capital city of Istanbul (formerly Constantinople) and the port city of Izmir (formerly Smyrna), where Greek troops had advanced against Turkish forces before being repulsed.

This international agreement granting Turkey status as an independent nation came as a victory for Ataturk, leader of the fight against the Greeks and founder of the Turkish republic. By abolishing the sultanate that had ruled the land for centuries, it also brought an end to the Ottoman dynasty. Although overwhelmingly Muslim, Turkey emerged as a secular state and established close ties with Western nations in years to come, serving as a bridge between Europe and the Islamic world.

Hitler's Putsch Fails

725 **1923** Adolf Hitler's reckless pursuit of power nearly came to an abrupt end in November when he tried to overthrow the Bavarian state government in Munich, Germany. He planned to follow this putsch by marching on Berlin with his Nazi Brownshirts and seizing power in the capital, much as Mussolini and his Blackshirts did in Rome a year earlier. He had manipulated Bavaria's state commissioner Gustav von Karl into joining him in declaring a new government and had enlisted war hero Gen. Erich Ludendorff as a figurehead but did not have a large party behind him or the support of the army and police. When he took to the streets with a few thousand armed followers, police blocked their way and shooting erupted. Sixteen marchers and several policemen died in the fighting, which ended the uprising.

Arrested and convicted of treason, Hitler could have been sentenced to death, but a sympathetic judge let him off. Commended for acting in a "pure patriotic spirit," Hitler ended up serving less than a year in prison, where he was allowed frequent visitors and began dictating his manifesto, *Mein Kampf* (*My Struggle*).

> ■ **FOOTNOTE** After the failed beer hall putsch and shooting in the streets, Hitler was said to be suicidal. He spent two nights before his arrest with his friends the Hanfstaengls, who reportedly talked him out of killing himself.

Design Envisioned

726 **1923** The basic principles of modern design were laid out in 1923 by the Swiss visionary Le Corbusier (born Charles-Édouard Jeanneret) in his book *Towards a New Architecture*. Influenced by modern art, Le Corbusier stressed simplicity and functionalism: spacious, open interiors and neat, geometrically precise exteriors framed in concrete, glass, and steel. Le Corbusier's ideas contributed to the development of the International Style,

1914-1945 | World War Years

which helped give cities around the world similar skylines dominated by monolithic high-rises.

Death of Lenin

727 **1924** When Vladimir Lenin died on January 21, 1924, he left a bitter legacy to Russia and other states such as Georgia and Ukraine within the recently formed Union of Soviet Socialist Republics. Despite its title, the Soviet Union was in fact an empire, controlled from Moscow by the Central Committee of the Communist Party and its ruling Politburo, consisting of Lenin and other high officials. This one-party system was solidified by Lenin after his Reds defeated conservative White Russians in a civil war that ended in 1921. Victory enabled him to reconstitute the old Russian empire under a new name and eliminate political opposition through surveillance by secret police and show trials of dissidents. Lenin saw one-party rule as legitimate, because Communists supposedly represented the masses. But he feared its consequences if control went to Joseph Stalin, who loomed as the likely successor to Lenin.

727 | *Vladimir Lenin in about 1920*

U.S. Restricts Immigrants

728 **1924** Before World War I, the United States had accepted nearly one million immigrants a year. In 1921, Congress significantly narrowed immigrant access to the nation. But America's reputation as a refuge for "your hungry, your tired, your poor"—symbolized by the Statue of Liberty—was tarnished in 1924 when Congress passed the National Origins Act, restricting immigration from eastern and southern Europe and banning immigration from Japan and other Asian nations. Using a quota system initiated in the 1921 law, the National Origins Act approved immigration from different national groups in proportion to their share of the existing American population. The act was prompted by bigotry and by fears among Americans of western European ancestry that immigrants from other areas might spread radical ideas or prove disloyal. With the exception of immigrants from American territories such as the Philippines, all Asians residing (but not born) in the United States had been declared ineligible for citizenship, and the ban on immigration came as a further insult to them and their countries of origin. In Japan, the government proclaimed a national day of mourning to protest the act. Some Japanese felt that only by becoming a superior military power would they prevent Westerners from dominating and discriminating against them.

Radar Originates

729 **1924** For British physicist Edward Appleton, who served as a signals officer with the Royal Engineers during the First World War, radio was more than an instrument for military communication or commercial broadcasting. It was a means of exploring the atmosphere.

In 1924, using a transmitter of the British Broadcasting Company (BBC), he conducted experiments designed to test the theory that radio waves were reflected by the ionosphere (a region of electrically charged particles located above the stratosphere). The results were so precise he was able to identify a

730 | *George Gershwin at his piano in 1938*

discrete layer within the ionosphere that reflected radio waves and measure its height above Earth's surface. His technique for measuring how far radio waves traveled before they were reflected back to Earth furthered atmospheric science and proved of great practical significance for aviation and air defense by leading to the development of radar.

■ **FOOTNOTE** The Appleton layer of the atmosphere, named after Appleton discovered it in 1926, lies 150 miles aboveground and carries a strong electrical charge, reflecting short waves around Earth.

Jazz Goes Classical

730 **1924** By the early 1920s, jazz had so permeated American popular culture that author F. Scott Fitzgerald entitled a collection of his short stories *Tales of the Jazz Age.* Few people took jazz seriously, however, until musicians gave it orchestral treatment.

In 1924, pianist and composer George Gershwin teamed with arranger Ferde Grofé and bandleader Paul Whiteman, whose orchestra helped popularize jazz, to produce *Rhapsody in Blue,* billed as "An Experiment in Modern Music." True to the jazz tradition, Gershwin's piece left room for improvisation and evolved as he and his collaborators interpreted it. Critics were lukewarm when it was first performed at a concert hall in New York, but audiences loved *Rhapsody in Blue,* and it became a classic.

Chinese Power Shifts

731 **1925** The death in March 1925 of Sun Yat-sen, leader of China's Kuomintang (Nationalist People's Party), triggered a power struggle that would convulse the country for the next quarter century. Two years before he died, Sun Yat-sen, who had spent time both in Japan and the U.S., distanced his ruling party from those two powers by seeking support from the Soviet Union. He was not a communist but welcomed Soviet aid as he struggled to subdue warlords and unite China under his authority. In return for Moscow's help, he granted several Chinese communists high positions in the Kuomintang. His ambitious aide, Chiang Kai-shek, went along with this sudden shift to the left and visited the Soviet Union as a military observer. After Sun Yat-sen's death, however, Chiang gained control of the Kuomintang with support from conservatives and broke with the Soviets, expelling communists from the Nationalist People's Party and entering into a long and bitter contest with them for control of China.

FOOTNOTE Sun Yat-sen, known as the father of modern China, went to college in Hawaii, was baptized a Christian, graduated from medical school in Hong Kong, and practiced medicine before heeding the call to politics in 1894.

Evolution on Trial

732 **1925** In July 1925, crusading lawyer Clarence Darrow defended John Scopes of Tennessee on charges he violated a state law that prohibited the teaching in public schools of evolution or any theory denying "the divine creation of man as taught in the Bible." Technically, Darrow had no case. He did not deny Scopes had broken the law but managed to place creationism on trial by calling to the stand lead prosecutor William Jennings Bryan, a prominent politician and strict fundamentalist.

Under questioning, Bryan had difficulty defending his literal interpretation of biblical passages that conflict with the laws of science, such as the verse stating that God prolonged the day for Joshua in battle by making the sun stand still. Scopes was found guilty and fined a hundred dollars, but his conviction was overturned on a technicality. Darrow's case helped erode public and legal support for creationism, culminating in a 1968 U.S. Supreme Court decision overruling state laws against teaching evolution.

CONNECTIONS

Immigration to the United States
The country achieves status as the Great Melting Pot

Since its beginnings, America was a nation of newcomers. From the first English settlers through today, immigrants have arrived on American shores and been greeted with mixed enthusiasm. The Indians (whose ancestors had themselves migrated to America thousands of years earlier) were not uniformly happy about foreigners with powerful weapons displacing them.

Nevertheless, the Europeans kept coming. Up through the early 19th century they came mainly from England; then from around 1820 to 1880 they came pouring in from Ireland and Germany. While the Irish generally arrived poor, the Germans often brought along a little money and a skill. They set up shop as printers, bakers, painters, and so on, and many of them established farming communities in the Midwest.

A second, larger, wave of immigrants streamed into the country from 1880 to the early 1920s. More than 25 million immigrants arrived during this period—the largest migration in world history—adding to a U.S. population that was only 50 million. Whereas the earlier wave was primarily from western and northern Europe, this wave was largely from eastern and southern Europe. Large numbers of Italians came, as well as Jews fleeing persecution in Russia and Poland.

Immigrants with their few belongings on pier

Around the same time, tremendous numbers of Chinese and Japanese were arriving through the West Coast. This steady influx of foreigners with a collage of languages, customs, religions, and appearances was difficult for established Americans to adjust to. Many worried that the low-paying jobs would be grabbed by the new arrivals. The Chinese Exclusion Act of 1882 attempted to stem the flow.

Since then a number of pieces of legislation have been passed to cope with immigration as the country reassesses what the ideal population mix and size should be. The Immigration and Naturalization Act of 1952 ended the ban against Chinese immigrants, and the quota system was abolished in 1965. Thirteen years later, a cap of 290,000 total immigrants per year was put in place, but illegal immigrants continue to swell such ceilings.

In recent years large numbers of immigrants have come from Mexico, the Philippines, the Dominican Republic, Jamaica, Cuba, El Salvador, Vietnam, China, India, Sri Lanka, Ukraine, and South Korea. In 2003, the foreign born were 11.7 percent of the U.S. population, a rising trend, though still below the 14.7 percent of 1910. Of that proportion, 53.3 percent were from Latin America, 25 percent from Asia, and 13.7 percent from Europe.

720 More Details on King Tutankhamun

Very little is known about the life of Tutankhamun, the boy king. What fascinates us is not his reign, relatively insignificant in Egyptian history, but the splendors of his tomb in the Valley of the Kings. Discovered in November 1922, the tomb was virtually intact, although evidence indicates that it was robbed twice shortly after burial. The English archaeologist Howard Carter was the first to enter King Tut's tomb in more than 3,000 years, and his remarkable find would forever change the face of ancient Egypt in our popular culture.

One of the most familiar stories surrounding Tut's tomb is that of the curse of the pharaohs. Popularized by newspapers in the United States and Europe shortly after Carter's discovery, the story describes the suspicious deaths of those who had been involved in the excavation. Lord Carnarvon, who had financed Carter's quest, fell severely ill a few months after entering the tomb, and according to legend, the lights in Cairo went out at the time of his death. By 1929, two of Carter's relatives and his personal secretary had also passed away. Still other deaths followed, and the grand total attributed to the curse reached as many as 21 people. Since that time, Egyptologists, museum exhibits, books, and documentaries have devoted extensive resources to disproving the curse, but it, like the tomb, is still an endless source of fascination.

> Howard Carter's remarkable find would forever change the face of ancient Egypt in our popular culture.

Also of interest is the death of Tutankhamun himself. Since the sarcophagus was opened and the mummy removed in 1924, many explanations have arisen, the most popular being that he was murdered by a rival. X-rays taken in 1968 supported this theory—a spot at the back of the skull indicated the possibility of a fatal blow. In 2005, a team led by Egyptian archaeologist Zahi Hawass ran a computed tomography scan on the mummy, providing the most scientifically advanced theory yet: A fracture in the left leg of the boy king became gangrenous, leading to his death only a few days later.

Pharaoh Tutankhamun speaks with his wife, Queen Ankhesenamun, in a gold relief on display at the Egyptian Museum in Cairo.

Peace Plan Reached

733 **1925** The big question left hanging at Paris in 1919—how to enforce the Treaty of Versailles and keep Germany in line—led European diplomats to renew talks in 1925 at Locarno, Switzerland, where they reached agreements that appeared to guarantee peace. Germany, dependent on foreign loans and eager to improve relations with its former enemies, agreed with France and Belgium to respect their borders and not to launch an attack except in self-defense. This helped restore international confidence in Germany, which entered the League of Nations.

Other provisions in the Pact of Locarno signaled trouble on the horizon. Germany still hoped to redraw its borders with Poland and Czechoslovakia, and though it promised to do so peacefully, those two countries secured a commitment from France to defend them against aggression. Britain, in turn, pledged to defend France and Belgium if they were attacked. Germany lashed out when Adolf Hitler rose to power in 1933. He denounced both treaties, built formidable military forces, and invaded the Rhineland demilitarized zone. In pursuit of peace, the diplomats at Locarno helped set the stage for the next world war.

FOOTNOTE In 1936, just over ten years after the pact, Germany sent an army into the to demilitarized zone of the Rhineland. Two years later, Hitler invaded Austria, followed by Czechoslovakia and Poland.

Film Draws Ire

734 **1925** Soviet filmmaker Sergei Eisenstein became an international cinematic sensation following the release in 1925 of his gripping film *Battleship Potemkin*. Portraying a mutiny by sailors during the Russian Revolution of 1905 and the ensuing massacre of civilians in the port of Odessa, the movie established Eisenstein as a master of the montage—a riveting sequence of shots assembled during the editing process to make a thematic point. To signal that a rebellion was brewing, for example, he juxtaposed images of hungry, dejected sailors with a simmering pot of rancid soup. His scene showing supporters of the mutineers being slaughtered by troops on the Odessa Steps ranks among the most celebrated and influential in cinematic history. Eisenstein caused controversy and drew critics, who dismissed his work as propaganda. Soviet authorities actually suppressed some of his films.

Television Dawns

735 **1925** The dream of transmitting live images over the airwaves became reality in 1925 when Scottish engineer John Logie Baird used a device he called a televisor to broadcast a recognizable picture of a human face to viewers watching a screen. The image was transmitted electronically, but Baird's televisor used mechanical technology developed in the late 1800s by Paul Nikow of Germany—a rotating disk with holes in it through which light reflected by the televised object activated a photoelectric cell made of selenium. This mechanical scanner required extremely bright light and produced images of lower resolution than electronic scanners using cathode-ray tubes (CRT), which were

Japan's New Empire

736 **1926** On December 25, 1926, Hirohito became emperor of Japan following the death of his father, Yoshihito. His reign was designated Showa, or "enlightened peace." As monarch, the shy, studious 24-year-old served as commander in chief of the armed forces and commanded the devotion of his people, who were taught to revere him as a god. Japanese emperors had not always been so exalted. For centuries,

Japanese Emperor Hirohito and Empress Nagako in Western-style attire, about 1925

they had been purely ceremonial figures, overshadowed by military rulers called shoguns, until a constitutional government was formed in the 1800s under Hirohito's dynamic grandfather, Emperor Meiji. His successor, Yoshihito, however, was frail and indecisive, and military leaders began reasserting authority. Top generals and admirals bowed to Hirohito as their ruler and commander, but they expected him to heed their advice and support their efforts to strengthen and expand the Japanese empire. In practice he simply ratified the policies that ministers and advisers designed. At times he objected and attempted to rein them in, but as the militarists grew in strength, it was obvious that any serious attempt to restrain them would have resulted in a coup—and Hirohito was determined to preserve the dynasty at all costs. For the most part he went along with their plans and served as a symbol of Japan's growing imperial might from 1931 to World War II, during which time, ironically, his era of enlightened peace was marked by a bloody military invasion of China, the decimating effects of WWII, and the unprecedented foreign occupation of his beloved nation.

735 | *John Baird tuning early television device*

developed independently in the U.S. in the 1920s by American Philo Farnsworth and Russian immigrant Vladimir Zworykin. Their technology won out, and in the 1930s Baird lost his bid to televise programs for the BBC. He remained a pioneer in the field, however, and went on to develop a high-resolution CRT scanner for color television.

> **■FOOTNOTE** The British Broadcasting Corporation (BBC) has operated under royal charter as a public corporation since its founding in 1927. It held the monopoly on British television until 1954.

Atomic Physics Emerges

737 **1926** British astrophysicist Arthur Stanley Eddington confirmed Albert Einstein's prediction that the sun's gravity bends light emitted by other stars and soon emerged as a leading theorist in his own right by proposing that stars were powered by the "transformation of elements," or nuclear fusion. If hydrogen atoms were fused under intense pressure and heat at the core of stars, he argued in his book *The Internal Constitution of the Stars,* they would form helium and release enormous amounts of energy in the process.

Eddington's theory appeared unlikely, because nuclear fusion was thought to require greater heat than could possibly exist within the sun. That objection was later removed by physicists who used quantum theory to show how fusion could

occur at lower temperatures and keep stars burning for billions of years. Scientific understanding of nuclear fusion led ultimately to a fearsome new weapon: the hydrogen bomb.

Lindbergh Crosses Atlantic

738 **1927** On the evening of May 20, 1927, American aviator Charles Lindbergh touched down at Le Bourget airfield outside Paris, France, completing the first solo flight across the Atlantic in 33 and a half hours. The feat earned Lindbergh a $25,000 prize and a hero's welcome from 100,000 admirers who mobbed the airfield in France and millions more who hailed him when he returned to the United States.

Lindbergh's marathon flight in the *Spirit of St. Louis* demonstrated the efficiency of monoplanes, which caused less drag than biplanes and would eventually render them obsolete. It also marked the start of Lindbergh's tumultuous career as a public figure, shadowed by the kidnapping and murder of his infant son in 1932—one of the most sensational crimes of the century—and

his controversial stand against American involvement in World War II.

Sound Comes to Screen

739 **1927** Motion pictures acquired a new dimension in October 1927 with the release of the first film with a full sound track, *The Jazz Singer,* starring Al Jolson. This technological advance came in a picture that had less to do with jazz than with older American musical traditions.

Jolson, a vaudeville performer, appeared in blackface in the film singing minstrel songs like "Swanee" and "Mamee." In between numbers, he regaled viewers with his catchphrase: "Wait a minute! You ain't heard nothin' yet." Blackface entertainment died out in decades to come as African Americans gained greater popularity on stage and screen and moved away from the stereotypes of minstrelsy.

But Jolson's film had a lasting impact on the movie industry by demonstrating the mass appeal of sound. A few stars such as Charlie Chaplin continued to make successful silent films. Indeed, Chaplin believed that silent films would win out

738 | *Charles Lindbergh with the* Spirit of St. Louis, *shortly before his solo transatlantic flight in 1927*

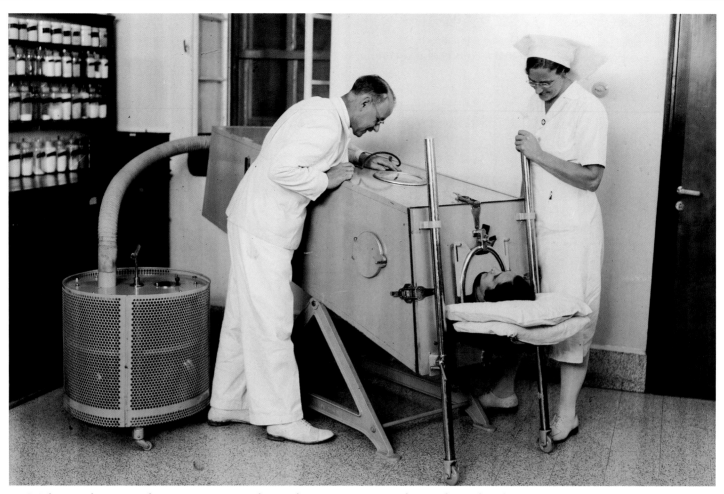

741 | *A doctor and nurse attend to a patient in an iron lung at the Scots Mission Hospital in Israel, March 1940.*

over the "talkies," since they could transcend language barriers and gain international audiences. In the long run, his opinions were ill founded, and the film producers, directors, and actors who followed him had either to adapt their talents to include voice and sound—or leave the business.

■**FOOTNOTE** Lon Chaney, the "man of a thousand faces," enjoyed wide stardom in silent films for his emotive facial expressions and diverse—sometimes gruesome—roles. He died two months after the release of his first talkie.

U.S. Might Contested

740 **1927** The U.S. Marines entered Nicaragua in April 1927 in response to the Nicaraguan government's pleas for U.S. aid to quell the unrest over upcoming elections. The right of the United States to intervene in Latin America was challenged by guerrilla leader August Cesar Sandino.

A liberal reformer, Sandino resented Americans for backing his conservative opponents, who had allowed the U.S. to collect revenues in Nicaragua used to repay debts owed to American banks. Hiding out in the mountains with his followers, Sandino eluded capture and became a hero to many in the region who harbored anti-American sentiments. Sandino agreed to lay down his arms in 1933 when the U.S. withdrew its troops and recognized the election of his political ally, Juan Sacasa. Unwisely, Sacasa entrusted command of the American-trained National Guard to the power-hungry Anostosio Somoza Garcia, who had Sandino seized and killed before taking control of Nicaragua. Sandino's resistance movement later inspired the Sandinistas, who forced out the last ruler of the Somoza family in 1979 and engaged in a long struggle with U.S.-backed opposition forces.

Iron Lung Invented

741 **1927** By the 1920s, poliomyelitis was one of the most dreaded scourges in developed countries such as the U.S. where advances in medicine and hygiene had brought other communicable diseases under control. Although the virus causing polio was discovered in 1908, no effective vaccine was yet available, and victims faced paralysis and possible death if their lungs ceased to function.

In 1927, Philip Drinker and Louis Agassiz Shaw of Harvard University developed the iron lung, a chamber that encased patients unable to breathe from neck to foot and kept them alive by rhythmically raising and lowering pressure to force air in and out of their lungs.

Wall Street Booms

742 **1928** During the Roaring Twenties, stock prices advanced steadily, then surged dramatically in 1928. In that year alone, the Dow Jones Industrial Average rose nearly 50 percent, and by mid-1929, it stood more than 400 percent above its low in 1921, far outstripping gains made by the American economy as a whole. Manufacturing output increased during the decade by 60 percent, for example, and per capita income rose by one-third. The prolonged bull market was fueled by easy credit for consumers and investors, who bought securities on margin—loans from brokers obtained with small deposits—confident that stocks would continue to rise. When loans to investors soared in 1928, raising fears of a crash, President Calvin Coolidge assured reporters that it was simply "a natural expansion of business in the securities market."

Mead Wages Debate

743 **1928** With the publication in 1928 of her book *Coming of Age in Samoa*, anthropologist Margaret Mead

743 | *Anthropologist Margaret Mead*

Penicillin Discovered

744 **1928** One of the great medical advances of the century resulted from an accident that occurred in 1928 in the laboratory of Alexander Fleming, a physician and bacteriologist at St. Mary's Hospital in London. One of Fleming's research assistants carelessly exposed a petri dish containing a bacteria culture and contaminated it, allowing mold to grow. Fleming noticed that the area around the mold was free of bacteria and realized that it contained an antibiotic, which he called penicillin. Although an extract he derived from the mold helped fight infections, he lacked sufficient training as a biochemist to isolate and refine the antibiotic. In the late 1930s, Howard Florey and Ernst Chain at Oxford University took up where Fleming left off and purified penicillin. In order to produce large quantities of the medicine, scientists experimented with growing the mold in large fermentation vats, using a strain of Penicillium found in an overripe

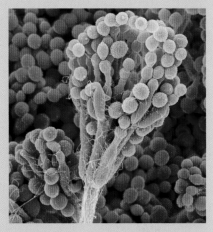

Closeup of common household mold used to produce cheeses and the antibiotic penicillin

cantaloupe. The drug was refined for clinical use and proved highly effective in treating bacterial infections during the Second World War. This wonder drug was so widely used in years to come that some forms of bacteria developed a resistance to it.

won fame and influenced opinion on a hot issue—whether nature or nurture played a larger part in determining such behavioral patterns as adolescent rebelliousness and gender roles. As a graduate student at Columbia University, she was guided by Franz Boas, who argued that culture rather than biology determined social behavior and distinctions. To test that thesis, the 23-year-old Mead went to American Samoa in 1925 to conduct fieldwork among adolescent girls. She found that cultural factors—such as tolerance of premarital sex—made adolescence less stressful for girls in Samoa than it was for girls in countries such as the United States, where greater restraints were placed on young people.

Critics questioned Margaret Mead's methods and conclusions, but she persisted in her vanguard work in anthropology, working at New York's Museum of Natural History well into the next decade. Margaret Mead's intellectual legacy spread

far beyond the field of anthropology: She did much during her career to advance the view that societies were not at the mercy of biological factors and could change behavior by altering their cultural assumptions and standards.

> ■ **FOOTNOTE** "Anthropology demands the open-mindedness with which one must look and listen, record in astonishment and wonder that which one would not have been able to guess." —Margaret Mead

Antarctica Explored

745 **1928** When American aviator Richard Byrd reached Antarctica in December 1928, it remained largely an unknown continent. Small areas near its margins had been probed by parties from various countries since Roald Amundsen reached the South Pole by dogsled in 1911, but Byrd and his team were the first to explore Antarctica systematically by air. His most celebrated feat came in November 1929, when he and several crewmen flew over the South Pole, but his larger accomplishment as the leader of this and three later expeditions was to map large parts of the continent using aerial photography and other tools. Territorial claims made by Byrd and explorers from other countries raised the possibility that Antarctica might become contested ground, but the U.S. agreed with other nations in the 1950s to reserve the continent for scientific research and other peaceful purposes.

■ **FOOTNOTE** Though Byrd won the Medal of Honor for his flight, questions arose after his death about whether he had reached the Pole or whether Roald Amundsen, who flew over it just three days later, was actually the first to do so.

Stalin Takes Charge

746 **1929** By 1929, Stalin had swept aside all rivals to power within the Communist Party and emerged as Soviet dictator. Determined to modernize the economy and crush resistance to Communism among enterprising peasants called kulaks, he pressed ahead with a ruthless Five-Year

746 | *Joseph Stalin in military dress*

Plan aimed at collectivizing agriculture and spurring industrialization. All land became the property of the state, and peasants were forced onto collective farms. Defiant kulaks were killed or imprisoned, and many collectivized farmers died of starvation when they were forced to provide so much food for the state they could not meet their own needs. Industrial output rose sharply, but laborers faced coercion and bosses who fell short of production quotas were punished. Dismayed by this chaotic Five-Year Plan, some in high positions grew critical of Stalin, who responded in the 1930s by launching murderous purges that spread beyond the ranks of the Communist Party and the Red Army, terrorizing Soviet society and claiming millions of victims.

Known Universe Expands

747 **1929** American astronomer Edwin Hubble offered a new view of the cosmos in 1929 by showing that the universe is expanding and calculating the rate of expansion, thus shedding light on the origin and age of the universe. This breakthrough was made possible by earlier advances, including the finding by Christian Doppler of Austria that light and sound waves shift frequency as they move toward or away from the observer.

Hubble used Doppler shifts in light from stars to determine how fast they are receding. He also benefited from a more recent discovery by American Henrietta Leavitt that stars called Cepheid variables grow brighter and dimmer at regular periods that can be used to calculate their distance.

Employing those techniques and the 100-inch reflecting telescope at the Mount Wilson Observatory, Hubble established that nebulae—once thought to be clouds of gas within the Milky Way—are in fact distinct galaxies, receding at a rate that increases with their distance from Earth. This led to the theory that the universe began with a big bang more than ten billion years ago.

Cyclotron Devised

748 **1929** Even as astronomers probed the outer limits of the universe,

FIRST PERSON

Joseph Stalin
SPEECH ON THE DEATH OF LENIN, 1924

For twenty-five years Comrade Lenin tended our Party and made it into the strongest and most highly steeled worker' party in the world. The blows of tsarism and its henchmen, the fury of the bourgeoisie and the landlords, ... the armed intervention of Britain and France, the lies and slanders of the hundred-mouthed bourgeois press—all these scorpions constantly chastised our Party for a quarter of a century. But our Party stood firm as a rock, repelling the countless blows of its enemies and leading the working class forward, to victory. In fierce battles our Party forged the unity and solidarity of its ranks. And by unity and solidarity it achieved victory over the enemies of the working class.

Lenin never regarded the Republic of Soviets as an end in itself. He always looked on it as an essential link for strengthening the revolutionary movement in the countries of the West and the East, an essential link for facilitating the victory of the working people of the whole world over capitalism. Lenin knew that this was the only right conception, both from the international standpoint and from the standpoint of preserving the Republic of Soviets itself. Lenin knew that this alone could fire the hearts of the working people of the whole world with determination to fight the decisive battles for their emancipation....

You have seen during the past few days the pilgrimage of scores and hundreds of thousands of working people to Comrade Lenin's bier. Before long you will see the pilgrimage of representatives of millions of working people to Comrade Lenin's tomb. You need not doubt that the representatives of millions will be followed by representatives of scores and hundreds of millions from all parts of the earth, who will come to testify that Lenin was the leader not only of the Russian proletariat, not only of the European workers, not only of the colonial East, but of all the working people of the globe.

that struggle: *All Quiet on the Western Front,* by Erich Maria Remarque, and *A Farewell to Arms,* by Ernest Hemingway. Both novelists had been wounded in the war, Remarque as a German soldier and Hemingway as an American medic driving an ambulance. And both transcended their own experience to convey the disillusionment of a generation whose heroic ideals were shattered by the conflict. Hemingway's main character attempts to leave the war behind—as many Americans did afterward by retreating into isolationism—but cannot escape anguish and loss. Remarque's narrator confronts the full horror of battle but stays in the fight to the bitter end, personifying the plight of Germans sacrificed for a lost cause.

749 | *Hemingway and bookseller Sylvia Beach, 1928*

physicists were seeking the fundamental particles at the heart of matter. Ernest Rutherford had succeeded in 1919 in releasing protons by bombarding nitrogen atoms with high-energy alpha particles from radioactive material. Further progress depended on accelerating charged particles to even higher energy levels and using them to delve deeper into the structure of the atom. In 1929, Ernest Lawrence at the University of California, Berkeley, learned of proposals in Europe for linear accelerators —which would have to be extremely long to produce sufficiently high energy levels— and conceived a practical alternative called the cyclotron. The device used electromagnets to propel charged particles released at the center in a long spiral path toward the perimeter, where they exited with great energy and caused a nuclear reaction.

■**FOOTNOTE** Ernest Rutherford was awarded the Nobel Prize in chemistry in 1908 for creating the framework for the field of nuclear physics. Ernest Lawrence won the Nobel Prize in 1939 for the cyclotron.

War Novels Published

749 **1929** In 1929, a decade after the nations engaged in the First World War made peace, two novels appeared testifying to the lasting impact of

747 | *Astronomer Edwin Hubble peers through the 48-inch Samuel Oschin Schmidt Telescope, 1949.*

Wall Street Crashes

750 **1929** The great stock market boom on Wall Street came to a shattering end in late 1929, ushering in the Great Depression. Alarmed by a speculative frenzy that sent share prices soaring over the summer despite signs of economic weakness—a construction slump, falling car sales, layoffs in auto plants—the Federal Reserve tightened credit severely in August by raising its discount rate a full percentage point. Some bullish investors kept charging into the market on borrowed money, but others backed out, causing prices to sag. On Black Thursday, October 24, shareholders panicked and began unloading at any price. More black days followed, and by month's end stocks had lost nearly half their value since early September. Investors who had borrowed heavily to buy stocks suddenly owed much more than they possessed.

Although the crash directly affected only some three million stockholding Americans, its impact went far beyond investors and sent the sputtering American economy into a tailspin. Within months America was crushed by the worst depression in its history. Many businesses lowered prices to stay afloat, failed to make a profit, then finally closed, leaving workers on the street. By 1930 some five million were unemployed; a year later the number was 13 million. Bad news for the U.S. was even worse news for foreign nations with lower standards of living that depended on American investment and trade.

A bankrupt investor trying to raise money by selling his car for $100 on October 30, 1929

Empire State Building Built

751 **1930** Conceived in the Roaring Twenties and constructed at the start of the Great Depression, the Empire State Building emerged as the world's tallest structure and a monument to high hopes that survived the crash on Wall Street. The driving force behind the project was financier John J. Raskob, a former executive at General Motors, who envisioned a structure that would tower over the planned Chrysler Building and all other rivals in Manhattan.

Work began on the 102-story office building in January 1930 and concluded 15 months later, three months ahead of schedule and well under budget thanks to the reduced cost of labor and materials in a slumping economy. Designed in art deco style, which recalled the elegance and flair of the prosperous 1920s and contrasted with the unadorned functionalism of later skyscrapers, the building evoked memories of good times in hard times and symbolized the heights to which Americans still aspired.

■ **FOOTNOTE** The Empire State Building, at Fifth Avenue and 34th Street, is one of New York City's main tourist attractions, with an observatory, restaurants and shops, a simulated helicopter ride, and a virtual-reality movie theater.

German Extremists Emerge

752 **1930** The financial crisis in the U.S. had a swift and devastating impact on Germany as nervous American investors demanded repayment of loans on which many struggling German firms depended. Some businesses and banks failed as foreign investors withdrew funds, and other companies survived only by laying off workers. By late 1930, nearly five million Germans were unemployed—twice as many as the year before. The Great Depression undermined faith in the nation's fragile democratic system and drove voters toward extreme parties with revolutionary goals.

In elections that September, the Communist Party increased its share of seats in the Reichstag from 54 to 77. Far bigger gains were made by Adolf Hitler's Nazis, who emerged as the second largest party in parliament by boosting their share from a paltry 12 seats to 107. Hitler disguised his intention to destroy democracy and rule as dictator by promising to achieve power by legitimate means.

■ **FOOTNOTE** Hitler also amassed power by recruiting young Germans. Starting as young as ten years old, uniformed youth attended rallies, collected money, and learned to revere Aryanism and Nazism.

Japan Militarizes

753 **1930** In Japan as in Germany, the global economic crisis had dire political consequences, weakening Japan's constitutional government and strengthening the military. As the Depression deepened, the United States raised protective trade barriers and other countries responded in kind, causing a sharp decline in agricultural prices since farmers could no longer export produce profitably.

In Japan, prices dropped disastrously, leaving some farmers so deeply in debt they sold their daughters into prostitution. Military service was the only refuge for many young men from impoverished families. Some Japanese were bitterly opposed when Prime Minister Hamaguchi Yuko attempted to place the military under firm civilian control and accepted a treaty limiting the Japanese navy to roughly two-thirds the strength of the American and British navies.

In November 1930, Hamaguchi was shot by an assassin and died a few months later. Similar attacks in years to come silenced political opponents of militarization and imperial expansion.

Coup in Argentina

754 **1930** Long troubled by political strife, Latin America grew more unstable with the onset of the Depression. In 1930, two of the region's largest nations, Brazil and Argentina, underwent revolutions led by men with quite different agendas.

In Argentina, José Félix Uriburu, a retired general, carried out a right-wing coup and repressed political dissent, allowing conservatives backed by the military and the nation's wealthy elite to dominate the country for more than a decade.

Populists Take Brazil

755 **1930** Brazil's Getulio Vargas led a populist revolution in which he offered laborers a minimum-wage law and other protections and granted voting rights to women. Although hailed as the "father of the poor," Vargas placed restraints on labor unions and used emergency powers to suppress communists on the left as well as fascists on the right. His long tenure as Brazil's populist strongman, which lasted until 1945, was emulated by Juan Perón, who launched a similar regime in Argentina a year later.

■ **FOOTNOTE** Perón leveraged labor unions to build his party's political power. He also enjoyed the support of women; his wife Evita's work on behalf of woman suffrage resulted in granting women the right to vote in 1947.

Ethiopia Crowns Emperor

756 **1930** The coronation of Haile Selassie as emperor of Ethiopia in 1930 was a unique demonstration of black political power in Africa, where other countries remained under white colonial rule. Although Ethiopia was a small empire, it consisted of many ethnic groups speaking different languages, and holding it together was an imposing task. Haile Selassie sought to modernize his realm by abolishing slavery, promoting education, and introducing other reforms. His reign was cut short when Ethiopia was invaded by Italy in 1935, but he returned to power with British aid during World War II and remained on the throne until deposed shortly before his death in 1975. He served as an inspiration for other African leaders in the postcolonial era and was revered in Jamaica and other countries by Rastafarians, or Rastas, who took their name from the title he held before he became emperor —Ras Tafari—and hailed him as a redeemer for black people around the world.

CONNECTIONS

History of Skyscrapers
Glittering towers of glass and steel

Scratching the clouds, the world's tall buildings have since the late 1800s been called skyscrapers, and they have come to define an individual city's skyline and symbolize its prosperity. The world's earliest skyscrapers were built in Chicago and New York City, with Chicago's ten-story Home Insurance Building (1885) usually claiming title to first.

Before super-tall buildings could be erected, a number of engineering innovations had to occur. Though the Home Insurance Building is not especially tall, it was the first to use a steel frame that carried the load. In earlier buildings the walls supported the load. With buildings higher than 40 stories, the wind load (the force of the wind against the building) is more important than the weight—the frame transfers the load to the foundation and thence to the surrounding rock or soil. In addition to a metal skeleton, elevators, water pumps, and reinforced concrete were necessary to make a tall building inhabitable.

With new building techniques in place, New York and Chicago began competing for the claim to world's tallest building. The 269-foot Auditorium Building in Chicago was superseded a year later by the 309-foot New York World Building. After Chicago imposed a height limit on buildings, New York wore the crown for years to come. Noteworthy skyscrapers included the

Empire State Building, ca 1931

792-foot neo-Gothic Woolworth Building (1913), the 1,046-foot art deco Chrysler Building (1930), and the 1,250-foot, 102-story Empire State Building (1931). Skyscrapers began to appear in Shangai, Hong Kong, São Paulo, and other major Asian and Latin American cities in the 1930s, with Europe and Australia joining in by mid-century.

For four decades the Empire State Building was the world's tallest, its reign ending in 1972 with the completion of the north tower of the World Trade Center (1,368 feet). In 1974, the Sears Tower in Chicago topped out at 1,450 feet. With a number of buildings competing for top billing, the accepted height of a skyscraper was measured from the sidewalk to the structural top, excluding flagpoles and antennas. Not until 1998 did a taller building appear on the scene—the Petronas Towers (1,483 feet) in Kuala Lumpur. Five years later, the soaring Taipei 101 in Taiwan was the world's tallest at 1,671 feet. With the destruction of the World Trade Center by terrorists in 2001, the Empire State Building is again New York's tallest.

Among super-tall buildings on the horizon are the Chicago Spire and Trump International Hotel and Tower, both in Chicago, and the Burj Dubai in Dubai, which is expected to become the world's tallest upon completion in 2009.

Pluto Discovered

757 **1930** In 1930, a 24-year-old self-taught astonomer named Clyde Tombaugh, working at the Lowell Observatory in Arizona, discovered Pluto, hailed at the time as the ninth planet in the solar system. So small and distant that observers using the most powerful telescopes were unable to distinguish it from its moon Charon until 1974, Pluto had an eccentric orbit like that of comets. Subsequent discoveries placed it within the Kuiper belt—a ring of small icy bodies orbiting at the outer reaches of the solar system—and led to the redesignation of Pluto in 2006 as a dwarf planet, distinct from the eight major planets.

■ **FOOTNOTE** Pluto, now also known as minor planet number 134340, is extremely cold, with temperatures ranging from -391°F to -346°F. NASA launched a spacecraft in 2006 that should reach Pluto in 2015.

Scottsboro Case Heard

758 **1931** One of the most sensational and significant legal cases in American history began in April 1931 in Scottsboro, Alabama, when nine African-American youths were hastily tried and convicted by an all-white jury on charges of raping two young white women. All but the youngest defendant, who was 12 years old, were sentenced to death.

The case against them was weak. Doctors who examined the women testified that there was no evidence of rape, and one of the two accusers later recanted. Lawyers with the American Communist Party came to the defense of the Scottsboro Boys, as they were known, and appealed to the U.S. Supreme Court, which ruled that the defendants had not received adequate legal counsel. When one of them was retried and found guilty, the appeal process resulted in another crucial decision by the Supreme Court, overturning the conviction because blacks had been systematically excluded from the jury—a landmark ruling that struck a blow against racial bias in the legal system.

Antimatter Discovered

759 **1931** In 1931, British physicist Paul Dirac proposed that electrons, the negatively charged particles spinning around the nucleus of atoms, must have positively charged twins of identical mass. That those antielectrons were not just figments of Dirac's mathematical imagination soon became clear when physicist Carl Anderson detected them in 1932 while studying the tracks of cosmic rays passing through a magnetic field in a cloud chamber at the California Institute of Technology. Positrons, as Anderson called them, left tracks identical to those of electrons except that they curved in the opposite direction in response to the magnetic field. In years to come, scientists using particle accelerators discovered other short-lived forms of antimatter, including antiatoms of hydrogen, detected by physicists in 1995 for less than a billionth of a second before they collided with regular hydrogen atoms and were annihilated.

Veterans Protest

761 **1932** In June, some 15,000 World War I veterans, many of

Japanese Seize Manchuria

760 **1931** Hopes that the horrors of the First World War would render another such conflict unthinkable faded in 1931 when Japan challenged China for control of Manchuria, igniting hostilities that alarmed the U.S. and other nations with interests in the region. Although Manchuria had long been part of China, Japan had won major concessions there in the early 1900s, including control of the Southern Manchuria Railway, which was guarded by Japanese troops.

Japanese soldiers march through streets of Manchuria, an act condemned by the League of Nations.

Acting on their own authority, Japanese officers staged an explosion along that railway in September 1931 and attacked Chinese forces whom they blamed for the incident. More Japanese troops then entered Manchuria from occupied Korea and widened the offensive, which Emperor Hirohito approved only after it began. China's Nationalist ruler, Chiang Kai-shek, gave priority to defeating communist forces in his country and did little to stop the Japanese takeover of Manchuria. Japanese conquerors gave Manchuria a new name, Manchukuo, and declared it an independent state; in truth, it was a colony of the Japanese Army. They then installed the malleable Puyi as the figurehead ruler. Known as the last emperor of China, Puyi had been deposed during childhood, in the overthrow of the Qing, or Manchu, dynasty in 1911.

Condemned for aggression, Japan left the League of Nations and continued on a path that would deepen its conflict with China and heighten tensions with the United States, eventually leading to Pearl Harbor and the World War II Pacific theater.

762 | *Camel herd moves across the desert of Nariya, Saudi Arabia. In choosing to develop its oil reserves, King Ibn Saud ushered in Westernization.*

them joined by their families, marched on Washington, D.C., demanding immediate payment of bonuses awarded by Congress that were not due in their entirety until 1945. Camping in a shantytown much like those inhabited by vagrants around the country—known derisively as Hoovervilles for President Herbert Hoover, who grew increasingly unpopular as the Depression deepened—the bonus marchers failed to sway Congress, which rejected their demand. Most left Washington at that point, but several thousand remained and took over vacant buildings near the Capitol.

In July, after veterans clashed with police, Hoover ordered the army to clear those buildings. Gen. Douglas MacArthur did more than that, sending in tanks and troops who torched the veterans' shantytown and drove them from the city at gunpoint—a show of force that appalled many Americans and further damaged Hoover's reputation.

■ **FOOTNOTE** Three years into the Great Depression, 1932 was a time of desperate poverty for many, especially the quarter of the U.S. workforce that was unemployed. Hoover's failure with the bonus marchers lost him the 1932 election.

Middle East Oil Reserves

762 **1932** In 1932, Iraq achieved nationhood, inspiring a major shift in world economics and politics as the Middle East's immense oil reserves were tapped. Iraq had been governed since 1918 by the British, who created the country by combining three provinces of the former Ottoman Empire: Mosul, Baghdad, and Al Basrah. Holding together this diverse land—divided ethnically between Arabs and Kurds and religiously between Shiite

and Sunni Muslims—was no easy task for Iraq's rulers. Revenues from vast oil fields at Kirkuk helped develop the country but heightened internal political rivalries and exposed Iraq to foreign pressure and intervention. In Saudi Arabia, embracing the holy city of Mecca, King Ibn Saud cast his lot with Americans early on by reaching an agreement with Standard Oil in 1933 to develop the nation's petroleum reserves. It took nearly 20 years for that deal to pay off in a big way, and the bonanza brought change and stress to this austere Islamic kingdom in the form of materialism and Westernization.

Steps to Fission Taken

763 **1932** By the early 1930s, physicists confronted growing evidence that the atomic model proposed by Ernest Rutherford—consisting of negatively

charged electrons orbiting more-massive positively charged protons in the nucleus—was incomplete. Not only were electrons shown to have antimatter counterparts called positrons that exist briefly at high-energy states, experiments also demonstrated the existence of lasting atomic particles that when released radioactively had greater penetrating power than electrons or protons.

In 1932, James Chadwick, a colleague of Rutherford's at Oxford University's Cavendish Laboratory, identified the missing piece in the puzzle as the neutron, an uncharged particle roughly equal in mass to the proton and bound to it in the nucleus of all elements heavier than hydrogen. This discovery led to nuclear fission, or the process of splitting the nucleus of heavy elements and releasing neutrons, which as uncharged particles are not repelled by protons as they approach other nuclei and have sufficient mass to split them, causing a chain reaction.

> ■ **FOOTNOTE** James Chadwick received the Nobel Prize in 1935 for discovery of the neutron, "a new building stone of matter playing the same fundamental part as the proton and the electron," according to the Nobel Committee.

Hitler Takes Power

765 **1933** On January 30, 1933, President Paul von Hindenburg of Germany named Adolf Hitler chancellor to lead a new cabinet and preside over the Reichstag, where his Nazis now formed the largest party. Having lost the presidential election to Hindenburg a year earlier, Hitler recognized that the democratic system could only take him so far and was ready to dispense with it. In late February, an opportunity arose when a former communist from the Netherlands torched the Reichstag. Portraying this isolated act as part of a broad communist plot, Hitler obtained an emergency decree from Hindenburg that suspended civil rights and exposed communists and other political opponents of the Nazis to assault and detention. As a result of that brutal crackdown, the Nazis increased their strength in the next election and passed an act enabling Hitler to rule by decree. Hindenburg was reduced to a figurehead and died in 1934, leaving Hitler as Germany's unchallenged führer (leader), with absolute power over the Reich.

TVA Founded

766 **1933** In May 1933, President Roosevelt established the Tennessee Valley Authority, a massive program of flood control and power production that drew fire from conservatives who felt the government had no business competing with private electric companies.

In years to come, the TVA constructed nine dams on the Tennessee River and eleven along its tributaries, improved water quality through soil conservation and reforestation, eradicated mosquitoes that carried malaria, and built hydoelectric plants that generated more power than Central and South America combined, providing affordable electricity across seven states and helping to raise the percentage of rural American households with power from one in ten in 1930 to one in four in 1939.

> ■ **FOOTNOTE** TVA plants produced power for U.S. weapon construction during World War II. In 1942, for example, about 28,000 people worked in the design or construction of 12 hydroelectric or steam plants.

Electron Microscope Invented

767 **1933** Drawing on recent advances in nuclear physics, Ernst Ruska of Germany in 1933 invented the electron microscope, a more powerful tool for medical and scientific research than conventional microscopes because electrons have a shorter wavelength than light, allowing for greater magnification.

New Deal Made

764 **1932** In November 1932, Democrat Franklin D. Roosevelt, promising "a new deal for Americans," was elected President in a landslide over Republican incumbent Herbert Hoover. With unemployment at 25 percent and trust in banks so low that people were stashing money away at home, many Americans felt that any deal would be better than the traditional government response of laissez-faire, or leaving the economy alone. Roosevelt, a polio victim who was usually confined to a wheelchair but stood in public with the help of leg braces, inspired confidence with his genial manner and reassuring words. Insisting in his Inaugural address in 1933 that the "only thing we have to fear is fear itself," he urged Americans not to lose faith in the banking system. Roosevelt knew that Americans needed a sense of energy and action. So a mere five days after his Inauguration he called Congress into session; that day they passed an emergency banking reform law. The ensuing push to regain equilibrium for the nation became known as the Hundred Days. During that time the President stabilized that system and went on to implement New Deal legislation that created federal programs and agencies designed to promote economic recovery, such as the Civilian Conservation Corps and the Tennessee Valley Authority. In decisive moves, Congress passed the Federal Emergency Relief Act, the National Industrial Recovery Act, and dozens of other laws.

Franklin Roosevelt waves to the crowd during his Inauguration ceremony, 1937.

768 | *Speaker addresses survivors of the 6,000-mile Long March from southeast to northwest China.*

Ruska's pioneering device was a transmission electron microscope (TEM), which sends a beam of electrons through a vacuum chamber and focuses it with electromagnetic lenses on a razor-thin section of the object under study, positioned above a fluorescent screen that reflects a magnified image to the observer. James Hillier of Canada produced an improved TEM in 1937 that could magnify objects 7,000 times, more than ten times the power of conventional microscopes. Magnifications of up to 250,000 times can now be achieved using a TEM or SEM (scanning electron microscope), which has a cathode ray tube like those in television cameras to scan solid objects that have not been sectioned.

Chinese Communists March

768 **1934** In October 1934, facing defeat by Chiang Kai-shek's Nationalists, more than 80,000 Communists fled Jiangxi province in southeast China and embarked on the Long March, an epic, 6,000-mile trek to sanctuary in the northwest that brought Mao Zedong to prominence. Convinced that Communists would prevail in China only by organizing peasants and waging guerrilla warfare, Mao opposed efforts by others in his party to ignite a Russian-style revolution among workers in cities and challenge Chiang Kai-shek's troops head on. Forced into exile, many Communists saw Mao's strategy as their only hope, and he emerged as their leader. Sickness, hunger, and pursuing Nationalists took a steep toll on his followers as they crossed rivers and mountain ranges on their grueling odyssey. Yet the 8,000 or so survivors who found refuge in Shaanxi province with other Communist fugitives in 1936 formed a dedicated cadre who would serve Mao well in years to come as he reached a truce with Chiang Kai-shek and targeted their common enemy—the Japanese.

■ **FOOTNOTE** Chinese Red Army marchers were hindered by the equipment they tried to salvage, including printing presses and typewriters. Half the army was killed when the Nationalists attacked them just over a month into the march.

Space Race Starts

769 **1935** In early 1935, scientist Robert Goddard and his team at Roswell, New Mexico, launched rockets fueled by a mixture of gasoline and liquid oxygen that reached altitudes of more than a mile at speeds up to 700 miles an hour, approaching the sound barrier. For Goddard, who had been ridiculed for suggesting that rockets would one day reach the moon, these tests offered hope that technology he developed, such as the use of gyroscopes to stabilize rockets, would ultimately allow them to leave the atmosphere. His efforts gave the U.S. a head start, but similar advances were made by rocket scientists elsewhere during the 1930s.

■ **FOOTNOTE** NASA named its space and earth science laboratory in Maryland after Robert Goddard. The Goddard Space Flight Center opened in Greenbelt, 10 miles northeast of Washington, DC, on May 1, 1959.

Radar Refined

770 **1935** Like other leading scientists of his era, Robert Watson-Watt of Great Britain shifted from research with peaceful applications to work of pressing military importance as the 1930s progressed and war loomed. After developing an early form of

weather radar used to detect thunderstorms, he wrote a memo to the Air Ministry in February 1935 in which he proposed using radio signals to locate oncoming warplanes.

He and his team were not the only ones working to develop radar precise enough to detect aircraft well beyond visual range. Similar efforts were being made by many of the world's major powers. But the British pursued their program more urgently than other nations when Hitler renounced the Versailles Treaty and began building a formidable air force. Watson-Watt knew that his was not the best possible system, but its rapid development and installation in a network of coastal radar stations called Chain Home helped save his country from defeat when war erupted.

Dust Bowl Engulfs Midwest

771 **1935** On Sunday, April 14, 1935, a mammoth dust storm struck a wide swathe of the Great Plains, from Kansas to Texas, turning day into night and enveloping people in dense clouds of grit that sickened thousands and darkened the skies in distant cities. This Black Sunday storm was among the worst of many to strike the Dust Bowl—a region that had been overcultivated in recent times and suffered catastrophic erosion when prolonged drought occurred in the 1930s and winds blew away the brittle topsoil. The state of Oklahoma was particularly hard hit and lost one fifth of its population.

Huey Long Murdered

772 **1935** The assassination of Huey Long in Baton Rouge, Louisiana,

---

CONNECTIONS

Manned Spaceflight
The race for supremacy continues

The path of manned spaceflight began in 1961 when Soviet cosmonaut Yuri Gagarin became the first man on Earth to enter space. While the U.S. managed to quickly meet this challenge, sending America's first man into space, Alan Shepard, in May of that year, catching up to the U.S.S.R. was not enough to raise American morale. On May 25, President John F. Kennedy officially declared that the United States' goal would be to land a man on the moon safely by the end of the decade. This indicated the beginning of the "space race" between the U.S.S.R. and the U.S.

In February 1962, John Glenn became the first American to orbit Earth. Soviet Valentia Tereshkova then became the first woman to enter space in June 1963, almost 20 years before the first American woman would leave Earth's atmosphere. The Soviets remained in the lead, achieving the first space walk with Alexei Leonov. America then passed the Soviets in December 1968 when Apollo 8, flown by Frank Borman, James Lovell, and William Anders, became the first manned spaceship to enter lunar orbit.

The race reached its climax in July 1969 when man first walked on the moon. Apollo 11, another of the American Apollo series, landed on the moon on the 20th, manned by Neil Armstrong and Edwin Aldrin. Kennedy's challenge was achieved one year before the deadline, and America had apparently won the space

Rocket scientist Goddard, 1926

race, although the rivalry between the U.S.S.R. and the U.S. in space continued long afterward.

Space travel was not without its risks, and disaster struck Apollo 13 when an explosion occurred in the oxygen supply. The crew made it home safely with little time to spare. Manned space travel was not slowed, however, and when Apollo 14 landed on the moon, the crew even hit golf balls, an amusing sight in the low gravity of the moon's atmosphere.

For the next decade, most space exploration developments centered upon unmanned probes and the early developments of space stations, both American and Soviet. In June 1983, however, Sally K. Ride became the first American woman to enter space. Soviet astronaut Svetlana Savitskaya then became the first woman to spacewalk the next year.

In 1998, John Glenn again entered space, for the last time, at age 77. In 2001, Dennis Tito became the first space tourist while on board the Soyuz TM-32.

In 2003, China became the third country with a manned flight, sending up Lt. Col. Yang Liwei. Although far behind Russia and the U.S., China hopes to achieve its first moon landing by 2024.

The future of manned spaceflight remains hopeful, despite tragedies, such as *Columbia*'s disintegration upon reentry in 2003. NASA hopes to have the first manned landing of an American spacecraft on Mars by 2037.

in September 1935 silenced one of America's most outspoken and controversial political figures, revered by some as a champion of the poor and reviled by others as a dictator. Elected governor of Louisiana in 1928, Long brought relief to that depressed state with a massive public works program that produced new roads, bridges, health, and educational facilities and was financed in part by taxes on inheritances and oil production, antagonizing powerful interests in Louisiana. Faced with opposition from legislators and public officials, he cracked down, bullying those who could not be bought and fastening a stranglehold on state and local agencies.

Long continued to boss the state through his chosen successor after entering the U.S. Senate, where he advocated a Share the Wealth program guaranteeing the poor a minimum income at the expense of the wealthy. His populist rhetoric appealed to millions of Americans in the depths of the Depression, and he was considering running for President when his volatile career came to a violent end. His legend lived on in Robert Penn Warren's memorable novel, *All the King's Men,* featuring a demagogue named Willie Stark bearing a strong resemblance to Long. All but forgotten was Long's own book, *My First Days in the White House,* published shortly before his death, in which he forecast his election as President and named his Cabinet. No great admirer of President Roosevelt—who considered Long one of the most dangerous men in America—Long demoted FDR in the book by appointing him secretary of the Navy.

■ FOOTNOTE Though Huey Long was a high school dropout, self-tutoring and a year of law school earned him a law degree. His populist slogan was "Every man a king," and he nicknamed himself "Kingfish."

Social Security Provided

773 **1935** In August 1935, Franklin D. Roosevelt carried his New Deal to new heights by signing into law the Social Security Act, providing old-age benefits to Americans with a program funded

771 | *A farmer and his two sons walk through a dust storm in Cimarron County, Oklahoma, April 1936.*

by contributions from employers and employees. Supplemented in years to come by legislation providing workers with disability and unemployment insurance, Social Security marked a dramatic departure for the U.S. government, which had left social welfare efforts to states, municipalities, and private charities while European countries developed ambitious federal programs. Germany introduced national health insurance and old-age benefits in the 1880s, for example, and Britain and other countries enacted similar plans in the early 1900s. In 1935, Roosevelt also signed the National Labor Relations Act, which upheld the right of workers to form unions and barred employers from firing those who did so. Critics labeled Roosevelt's New Deal socialistic, but voters registered their approval by reelecting him overwhelmingly in 1936.

Mussolini Seizes Ethiopia

774 **1935** In October 1935, Benito Mussolini defied the League of Nations and sent Italian troops into Ethiopia. By seizing that country and adding it to Libya and other Italian colonies in Africa, Mussolini hoped to rival major imperial powers such as Britain and France and counter concerns at home that his dictatorship had not brought Italians the prosperity and glory he promised them. "The war which we have begun on African soil is a war of civilization and liberation," he proclaimed as his army and air force targeted ill-equipped Ethiopian defenders with poison gas and rained bombs on soldiers and civilians alike.

Ethiopia's monarch, Haile Selassie, appealed to the League of Nations, but it failed to stop Italian troops from overrunning his country in 1936 and forcing him into exile.

■ FOOTNOTE Mussolini was kicked out of school for violent behavior and sent to a succession of strict boarding schools where he was expelled twice more—both times for stabbing and attacking students and teachers.

1914-1945 | World War Years

Philippines Self-Governs

775 **1935** The prolonged American involvement in the Philippines, which began in 1898 when the United States seized the islands from Spain, entered a new phase in November 1935 when the country became a self-governing American commonwealth. With this step, it became a slow evolution toward complete independence, promised by the United States to take place on July 4, 1946.

The American concession came partly in response to pressure from Filipinos, whose independence movement had revived after being suppressed by American troops early in the century. Fears in the U.S. that holding colonies overseas would entangle the nation in foreign wars also contributed to the granting of commonwealth status.

But by delaying the granting of independence to the Philippines for another decade, Americans remained responsible for defending a nation that was much closer to Japan and its fast expanding war fleet than to the U.S. naval base at Pearl Harbor. Despite assurances from the American Army commander, Douglas MacArthur, that the Philippines would be shielded against attack, President Manuel Quezon feared for his country if it was drawn into conflict between the U.S. and Japan and called for independence by 1940, a demand that was not met.

■ **FOOTNOTE** The Japanese invaded the island in 1942 during World War II, and a joint army of the U.S. and Filipinos fought for and regained its freedom in 1944-45. U.S. military bases were removed by the end of 1992.

Passengers Take Flight

776 **1935** When the Douglas DC-3 aircraft began carrying passengers in late 1935, many people still shunned flying as too dangerous or uncomfortable. The DC-3 altered that perception and spurred commercial service in the U.S., where the number of passenger miles flown increased fivefold by 1941. A sturdy all-metal monoplane, it had retractable landing gear that reduced drag and increased its range, which exceeded 1,500 miles. It could cross the country in under 18 hours, cutting more than 7 hours off the flight time between New York and Los Angeles. Skysleeper service, introduced in 1936 on DC-3s equipped with 14 berths, lured passengers accustomed to stretching out in railroad sleeping cars.

By 1939, DC-3s were handling the vast majority of commercial flights worldwide. Readily adapted for military use as the C-47 freight carrier and the C-53 troop carrier, this flying workhorse remained in service throughout the 20th century.

Richter Sets Scale

777 **1935** Scientists had no system for gauging and comparing the magnitude of earthquakes until Charles Richter and Beno Gutenburg of the Carnegie Institution's Seismological Laboratory in Pasadena, California, developed the Richter scale in 1935. Before then, earthquakes were rated by the damage they caused, on a scale devised by Italian geologist Giuseppe Mercalli. The Mercalli scale was imprecise and did not measure magnitude, which is just one factor responsible for earthquake damage along with the strength of buildings, the solidity of the

776 | *Eastern Airlines DC-3 soars over Miami Beach in 1941.*

material beneath them, and distance from the quake's epicenter. The Richter scale relies on readings from seismographs to quantify magnitude, providing seismologists with an essential tool for analyzing earthquakes and their underlying causes.

Film Spotlights Nazis

778 **1935** In 1935, German filmmaker Leni Riefenstahl won praise and condemnation for *Triumph of the Will,* portraying the massive Nazi party rally held at Nuremberg the year before. One of the few women to gain prominence in Nazi Germany, where motherhood and child-rearing were promoted as the feminine ideal, Riefenstahl moved from acting to directing and used innovative techniques such as the telephoto lens to capture the fervor of Hitler and his followers. Even those who dismissed the film as Nazi propaganda were impressed by the skill with which she drew viewers into the pageantry at Nuremberg and made them participants in the drama. Many critics would dispute that, but *Triumph of the Will* and her later work *Olympia,* portraying the 1936 Berlin Olympics, had a deep and lasting impact on filmgoers and filmmakers.

Rhineland Reoccupied

779 **1936** On March 7, 1936, Hitler sent troops into the Rhineland—a vital industrial area along Germany's western border—and repudiated the Treaty of Versailles, which declared the Rhineland a demilitarized zone. Eager to reclaim territory that belonged to Germany before the First World War, Hitler gambled that France would not resist the move and test his army, which was unprepared for war. German commanders had orders to withdraw from the Rhineland if French troops opposed their advance. Such a reversal would have been devastating for Hitler, but no one called his bluff. French commanders would not commit troops unless the government began mobilizing by calling up civilian reserves—a move sure to evoke bitter memories of 1914 and the carnage that followed. The French government, in

Civil War in Spain

780 **1936** The fragile peace in Europe was broken in July 1936 when a military coup against Spain's Republican government led to a sprawling civil war involving forces from many nations. Opposing the Republicans, whose ranks included liberals and democratic socialists as well as communists and anarchists, were right-wing Nationalists, monarchists, and a conservative Roman Catholic hierarchy that feared a Soviet-style regime in Spain and rallied behind Gen. Francisco Franco. The three-year civil war was brutal, with mass executions of prisoners and other atrocities common on both sides. The Nationalists received troops, tanks, and bomber squadrons from Germany and Italy, and Germany used Spain to test new air war tactics and technologies. The Republicans drew military aid from the Soviet Union and volunteers from various countries intent on fighting what they saw as fascist aggression. Among them was British author George Orwell, who came to dread communism as much as fascism. Returning home before Franco triumphed in 1939,

Spanish loyalists in Huesca, Spain, aim weapons at rebels during civil war, August 1936.

Orwell found people oblivious to the dangers of totalitarianism abroad and "sleeping the deep, deep sleep of England, from which I sometimes fear that we shall never wake till we are jerked out of it by the roar of bombs."

turn, would not mobilize without support from the British, who offered no assurances. Haunted by memories of the last war, the Allies lost a chance to rebuff Hitler before he provoked an even costlier conflict.

> ■ **FOOTNOTE** France was also distracted by its own national misery—while it had escaped the earlier years of a severe depression that had wracked many other countries, in 1936 it was suffering high rates of poverty and unemployment.

French Socialism Advances

781 **1936** The struggle in Spain posed a dilemma to Léon Blum, who became premier of France in June 1936. Assailed by right-wing extremists because he was Jewish and a socialist, Blum loathed fascism and sympathized with the Spanish Republicans. But his Popular Front coalition, which included communists, was regarded with suspicion by French officers, and he feared resistance from the army and civil strife if he intervened in Spain. His policy of nonintervention left France

vulnerable to an alliance between Franco's Spain and Hitler's Germany but allowed Blum to pursue ambitious social programs designed to relieve economic distress. Among his initiatives was the 40-hour work week, later adopted by many nations. Although Blum was no longer in power when Germany invaded France, he was charged with inciting conflict and sent to a concentration camp, from which he emerged alive at war's end to help rebuild a free French government.

Owens Wins Olympic Events

782 **1936** Hilter used the 1936 Summer Olympics in Berlin to glorify his regime and advance his theory of Aryan supremacy by showcasing the talents of German athletes. But the brilliant African-American athlete Jesse Owens defied Hitler's script and reigned supreme at the podium by capturing gold in four events: the long jump, the 100- and 200-meter dashes, and the 400-meter relay. Hitler

774 More Details on Haile Selassie

Horrific images of the Ethiopian famine of 1984-85 were broadcast around the world—emaciated children, a barren landscape plagued by draught, long lines of starved migrants—and they are often all we know of this East African nation. Inspired by the BBC's dedicated coverage and the Live Aid benefit concerts, the world rallied behind the Ethiopian cause, donating millions of dollars and urging governments to take action.

But Ethiopia was not always a symbol of hardship and inept government. In fact, throughout much of the 20th century, Ethiopia was known for Haile Selassie, emperor from 1930 to 1974 and one of history's most influential leaders. Known to his people by many titles, including Conquering Lion of the Tribe of Judah, Selassie ruled a strong and independent nation in a continent where much land remained under white colonial rule. When Italy invaded Ethiopia in 1935 he was deposed, only to return triumphantly to reclaim his country (with the help of Great Britain) in 1941; after this remarkable feat, he would forever be recognized as a symbol of independence in Africa.

> "We Africans ... know that we shall win, as we are confident in the victory of good over evil."
>
> —Haile Selassie

Haile Selassie advocated civil disobedience as a means to fighting injustice and counted Martin Luther King, Jr., Nelson Mandela, and even Dwight Eisenhower as his friends. His words inspired legendary musician Bob Marley, and he famously attended President Kennedy's funeral. He is the only leader in history to address both the League of Nations and the United Nations, giving stirring speeches against oppression. The arresting words he spoke at a meeting of the UN in October 1963 are among his most remembered: "Until bigotry and prejudice and malicious and inhuman self-interest have been replaced by understanding and tolerance and goodwill; until all Africans stand and speak as free beings, equal in the eyes of all men, as they are in the eyes of heaven; until that day, the African continent will not know peace. We Africans will fight, if necessary, and we know that we shall win, as we are confident in the victory of good over evil."

Ethiopia's last emperor, Haile Selassie, pets lion at home in Debre Zeit. He entered his country into League of Nations and created its first constitution, 1931.

supposedly snubbed Owens by refusing to shake hands with him. In fact, after shaking hands with some victorious German and Finnish athletes, Hitler was told by the head of the International Olympic Committee that he must treat all winners alike and decided to congratulate none of them.

Keynes Shapes Economics

783 **1936** With the publication of his book *The General Theory of*

FIRST PERSON

Hindenburg Explosion
RADIO DESCRIPTION, 1937

A thousand people have come out to witness the landing of this great airship....

Here it comes, Ladies and Gentlemen, ... the moment we have waited for so long. ...The back motors of the ship are just holding it just enough to keep it from—....

It's burst into flames! It burst into flames, and it's falling, it's crashing! Watch it! Watch it! Get out of the way! Get out of the way! ... It's fire—and it's crashing! It's crashing terrible! Oh, my! Get out of the way, please! It's burning and bursting into flames; and ... this is the worst of the worst catastrophes in the world....Crashing, oh! Four- or five-hundred feet into the sky and it—it's a terrific crash, ladies and gentlemen. It's smoke, and it's flames now; and the frame is crashing to the ground.... Oh the humanity!

785 | *Miraculously, many survived* Hindenburg*'s fiery blast in New Jersey, May 1937.*

Employment, Interest and Money, John Maynard Keynes emerged as the leading economist of his time, one whose call for increased government spending to counter recessions would be debated by Keynesians and their critics for generations to come.

As a British delegate to the Paris Peace Conference in 1919, Keynes had opposed saddling Germany with steep reparation payments. In the 1920s, he argued against adhering to the gold standard, which limited the amount of paper currency a government could issue. Nations abandoned the gold standard during the Depression, but many were reluctant to spend heavily on social programs for fear of inflation. Keynes argued that deflation and unemployment were greater threats than inflation and urged deficit spending to revive depressed economies—a policy easier to implement in totalitarian states, he noted, than in democracies where government intervention in the free market had long been shunned.

> ■ **FOOTNOTE** Keynesian economists advocated deficit spending to alleviate recession. Sometimes this backfired, as seen in the late 1960s and early 1970s, when deficit spending gave way to runaway inflation.

Japan Wages War on China

784 **1937** In early 1937, Chiang Kai-shek's Nationalists and Mao Zedong's Communists formed a united front against Japan, whose troops occupied Manchuria and were stationed in Chinese cities to protect Japanese residents. Tensions boiled over in July when Chinese and Japanese forces clashed at the Marco Polo Bridge in Beijing. Local commanders there soon reached a truce, but defiant words from Chiang Kai-shek, who vowed not to surrender "one more inch of our territory," were met by calls in Tokyo for Japan to launch a full-scale invasion. Assured that sending more troops to China would bring the situation there under control within months, Prime Minister Fumimaro Konoye and Emperor Hirohito authorized a war that would last years and prove disastrous for both countries. After

seizing the city of Nanjing in December, Japanese troops ran amok, raping and killing on a massive scale. The massacre lent weight to President Roosevelt's recent statement that nations should seek ways to "quarantine" foreign aggressors before the plague of war spread further.

Hindenburg Explodes

785 **1937** On May 6, 1937, the world's largest aircraft, the 804-foot-long German dirigible *Hindenburg*—which had soared over Berlin during the Olympic Games a year earlier—burst into flames as it landed in threatening weather at Lakehurst, New Jersey, after a transatlantic flight. Thirty-six of the *Hindenburg*'s 97 passengers and crew died in the fiery crash, which was caught on film and reported on radio by Herbert Morrison, who watched in horror as the giant airship was reduced to "a mass of smoking wreckage."

Earhart Disappears

786 **1937** The disappearance of Amelia Earhart over the Pacific in July as she was attempting to fly around the world in her Lockheed Electra remains a mystery. A last, faint radio broadcast while she was above the Pacific Ocean signaled that her fuel was running low. Then she was gone. A sea and air search that covered 500,000 square miles found no trace of the pilot or her navigator. Authorized by President Franklin Roosevelt, that four-million-dollar rescue effort was the largest operation of its kind conducted to date and testified to the high esteem in which Earhart was held both as an aviator and as an eloquent role model for women.

As the first woman to fly alone across the Atlantic and the first aviator of either sex to fly solo from Hawaii to California, Amelia Earhart was hailed as a pioneer, and she served as an inspiration for others, before and after her disappearance. As she herself had put it, she welcomed the chance to show that women could match men in any task demanding "intelligence, coordination, speed, coolness, and willpower."

787 | *Picasso's painting of a mother with dead child after Guernica bombing, Spanish Civil War, 1937*

Picasso filled a wall-size canvas with tortured figures looking skyward in terror. It became the centerpiece of the Spanish Pavilion at the 1937 World's Fair in Paris. A guidebook for German visitors to the exposition described "Guernica" as "a hodgepodge of body parts that any four-year-old could have painted." But sympathetic observers saw in its disjointed imagery a haunting reflection of a world fractured by systematic violence. After the fair, the piece toured Europe and North America, raising awareness about the threat of fascism. Today many consider it modern art's most powerful antiwar statement.

> ■**FOOTNOTE** Picasso lived in Paris during the German occupation in World War II. Nazis did not like his art, but they allowed him to continue working quietly in his studio, not detecting the bronze he smuggled for sculptures.

Allies Appease Hitler

788 | **1938** In 1938, after annexing Austria without opposition from France or Britain, Hitler went further by demanding that Czechoslovakia cede the Sudetenland, which like Austria had many German-speaking inhabitants. Czechoslovakia refused, and war appeared imminent.

Seeking to appease Hitler and avert hostilities, British Prime Minister Neville Chamberlain arranged a conference at Munich, where Britain and France accepted German occupation of the Sudetenland in exchange for Hitler's promise to make no more territorial demands. Chamberlain felt Britain was not ready for war and needed time to prepare its defenses. By touting the Munich accord as a triumph that promised "peace in our time," however, he raised false hopes and appeared so eager to avoid conflict that Hitler figured he would tolerate further aggression.

When German troops seized all of Czechoslovakia in early 1939, Chamberlain realized his mistake and joined France in pledging to defend Poland against attack, but Hitler continued to doubt Allied resolve and pursued a policy of forceful expansion.

Picasso Paints Protest

787 | **1937** The Paris International Exposition of 1937 was devoted to the wonders of technology, but on display at the Spanish Pavilion was a gripping testament to the horrors of modern technological warfare—Pablo Picasso's monumental painting "Guernica," commissioned by Spain's beleaguered Republican government.

A German air raid in April on the Spanish village of Guernica had left nearly one-third of its 5,000 inhabitants dead or wounded. Controversy continues over whether Guernica was a true military target or whether the attack was merely an exercise for the Luftwaffe, to hone its tactics for future air missions during World War II. Deeply horrified by the event,

790 | *Skinner and behavioral research subject*

Mexico Nationalizes Oil

789 **1938** President Lázaro Cárdenas of Mexico set a precedent for other developing countries in 1938 when he nationalized the country's foreign-owned oil companies after they refused to accept in full a court-ordered settlement of a labor dispute with oil workers. Mexicans hailed the move as a declaration of economic independence and rallied around Cárdenas, who sought to fulfill the promise of the Mexican Revolution by redistributing land to poor farmers, supporting organized labor, and asserting his nation's right to control its own resources.

▦ **FOOTNOTE** Mexico's successful oil fields became known as the Golden Lane for their yield of oil for consumers and riches for their owners and operators. In 1921, Mexico was the world's second largest oil producer.

Skinner Shapes Behaviorism

790 **1938** B. F. Skinner helped redefine psychology as an objective science in 1938 with his book *The Behavior of Organisms,* based on experiments conducted at Harvard University in which he shaped, or conditioned, the responses of animals to stimuli using rewards, or positive reinforcement.

Influenced by Russian physiologist Ivan Pavlov and American behaviorist John Watson—who argued that psychology should deal not with subjective thoughts or feelings but with objective behavior—Skinner concluded that if conditioning could be used to train animals with small brains, such as pigeons, to carry out useful tasks like pressing buttons to operate machinery, it could also be applied systematically to modify human behavior. His goal was to use positive reinforcement to improve education and the treatment of behavioral disorders.

His later books, including the utopian novel *Walden Two* and *Beyond Freedom and Dignity,* brought him fame as well as criticism from those who felt his vision of a highly programmed society left little room for individualism and self-expression.

Nylon Synthesized

791 **1938** In late 1938, the chemical company Du Pont announced one of the most significant advances in synthetics since the introduction of plastic early in the century—the artificial fiber Nylon, which proved so popular its trade name became a generic term. Strong and durable, nylon was formulated by a team of polymer chemists at Du Pont led by Wallace Carothers.

The commercial importance of nylon as the Second World War approached could hardly have been greater. When hostilities in Asia cut off exports of silk to the U.S., nylon hose took the place of silk stockings. As the war progressed, so much nylon was used to make parachutes and other military goods that nylon stockings became a luxury, sold on black markets at eight times their prewar price.

Hitler and Mussolini Ally

793 **1939** The bond between Hitler and Mussolini, who had been loosely allied as Axis partners since 1936, tightened in May 1939 when they reached

Scientists Split Atom

792 **1939** In January 1939, German scientists Otto Hahn and Fritz Strassmann startled the scientific world by announcing that they had achieved fission by splitting the nucleus of uranium. This breakthrough grew out of experiments conducted by Italian physicist Enrico Fermi, who found that beams of neutrons filtered through paraffin, which slowed them down, caused uranium to become radioactive. Fermi's team thought that the radioactive products were isotopes of new elements heavier than uranium.

But when Hahn and Strassmann repeated Fermi's experiment and their colleagues Lise Meitner and Otto Frisch analyzed the results, they came to the conclusion that the nucleus had been split, thus breaking down uranium into lighter elements and converting mass into energy.

Further tests showed that the energy that was released when uranium was bombarded by neutrons included additional neutrons, *Computer graphic of an atom. Otto Hahn and Fritz Strassman split a uranium atom's nucleus.* meaning that a chain reaction was taking place. This raised the possibility of processing uranium and producing highly fissionable material, capable of causing an explosive chain reaction and fueling a nuclear bomb.

a formal military alliance, known as the Pact of Steel. For Hitler, whose relentless efforts to expand the Reich had alienated Britain, France, and Poland, this pact with Italy promised to keep Germany's southern flank secure in the event of war. But Mussolini and his armed forces were weaker than they appeared and would provide Hitler with little support. Italy's recent occupation of Albania and its earlier conquest of Ethiopia were no test of its capacity to wage war on major powers. Its military budget was one-tenth that of its Axis partner, and its warplanes and tanks were outdated. Italians feared being dominated by Hitler and Germany, their enemy in the last war, and felt lingering ties to their former allies, including Britain and the U.S., which had many Italian immigrants.

Einstein Sees Nuclear Threat

794 **1939** On August 2, 1939, physicist Albert Einstein, who had fled to the United States to escape Nazi persecution, signed a letter to President Roosevelt warning that uranium might be used to produce "extremely powerful bombs." Germany had taken over uranium mines in Czechoslovakia, Einstein noted, and scientists in Berlin were doing work similar to that of American physicists, who were exploring the possibility of triggering "a nuclear chain reaction in a large mass of uranium." He urged the administration to secure supplies of high-grade uranium ore for the U.S. and obtain ample funding for nuclear research.

Presidential adviser Alexander Sachs added his own words of warning, and Roosevelt got the point. "What you are after is to see that the Nazis don't blow us up," he said to Sachs. "This requires action." The first small step taken by the board he established—a $6,000 research grant—led ultimately to the massive Manhattan Project and production of nuclear weapons.

Treaty Triggers War

795 **1939** On August 23, 1939, Germany and the Soviet Union agreed not to attack each other and to settle their disputes diplomatically. They called it a nonaggression pact, but it cleared the way for the invasion of Poland and set the world at war.

For Hitler and Stalin, ruthless dictators with starkly opposing ideologies, this ten-year treaty proved to be simply a brief truce that allowed them to deal with more pressing matters before battling each other for supremacy. Hitler was intent on conquering Russia, but he first had to reckon with Poland and its allies, France and Britain. Stalin had tried unsuccessfully to reach agreement with those two Western powers to contain Germany. This pact gave him time to rebuild the Red Army's officer corps, ravaged by his purges, and take on weaker opponents. In a secret protocol, he and Hitler drew lines of conquest, with Germany claiming western Poland while the Soviets targeted eastern Poland, the Baltic States, and Finland.

> ■ **FOOTNOTE** The pact specified that Poland would be divided between Russia and Germany roughly along the Narev, Vistula, and San Rivers, and that in southeastern Europe, Germany was not interested in Bessarabia.

Jet Age Dawns

796 **1939** A new technology of great military significance was introduced on the eve of World War II when a German test pilot made the first flight in a jet aircraft, the Heinkel He 178, on August 27, 1939. In place of propellers, twin turbines on this prototype compressed air to provide explosive thrust when fuel was ignited. Although Germany, Britain, and other warring countries raced to develop such jets, it took years to produce a model that could contend with swift and highly maneuverable propeller-driven fighters such as the British Spitfire, which topped 400 miles an hour. Not until 1944 did the first operational jet fighter, the Messerschmitt Me 262, enter combat for Germany.

FIRST PERSON

Albert Einstein

TO PRESIDENT ROOSEVELT, AUGUST 1939

Some recent work by E. Fermi and L. Szilard, which has been communicated to me in manuscript, leads me to expect that the element uranium may be turned into a new and important source of energy in the immediate future. Certain aspects of the situation which has arisen seem to call for watchfulness and, if necessary, quick action on the part of the Administration. I believe therefore that it is my duty to bring to your attention the following facts and recommendations: In the course of the last four months it has … become possible to set up a nuclear chain reaction in a large mass of uranium, by which vast amounts of power and large quantities of new radiumlike elements would be generated.…This new phenomenon would also lead to the construction of bombs, and it is conceivable—though much less certain—that extremely powerful bombs of a new type may thus be constructed.

794 | *Albert Einstein, ca 1947*

World War II Begins

797 **1939** An hour before midnight on August 21, 1939, radio programs in Nazi Germany were interrupted by the announcement that Germany and the Soviet Union—once the bitterest of enemies— had signed a peace pact. Peace in Europe was doomed. On September 1, 1939, Germany invaded Poland, igniting a conflict that would spread catastrophically and engulf much of the world. A few days later, France and Britain declared war on Germany, but they were not prepared to defend Poland. By then Nazi forces had infiltrated the nation, having advanced at such speed that a new phrase was coined: blitzkrieg or "lightning war." Poland's fate was sealed in mid-September when Soviet troops moved in from the east. Intent on wiping Poland off the map, Hitler had many of the country's military and civilian leaders executed. Jews were confined to ghettoes and later sent to concentration camps. The rapid conquest of Poland was followed by the "phony war," an eerily quiet interval as Hitler prepared for a showdown with the Allies to his west. To the east, however, there was hard fighting in late 1939 as Soviet troops invaded Finland. Scarred by Stalin's assaults on its top ranks, the Red Army performed "like a badly led orchestra," in the words of the opposing commander. It took a million Soviets to defeat a Finnish army of barely 200,000 men.

Five German soldiers ride in armored vehicle during occupation, Poznan, Poland, 1939.

France Falls

798 **1940** Eager to avoid the static trench warfare that led their nation to defeat in 1918, German commanders stunned the Allies in 1940 by unleashing a blitzkrieg—a swift advance by armored divisions that skirted the heavily fortified Maginot Line and doomed France. The campaign began on May 10 when German troops stormed into Belgium and the Netherlands. Allied forces moved north from France in response, only to be cut off when enemy tanks advanced furtively through the forested Ardennes and swept across northern France to the English Channel. Much of the British Expeditionary Force escaped by sea from Dunkirk, but more than a million Allied troops were captured.

On June 22, after Paris fell, Marshal Philippe Pétain surrendered occupied France to Germany, leaving a sector in the south to be administered by his compliant regime at Vichy. "The Battle of France is over," declared Winston Churchill, who replaced Neville Chamberlain as British prime minister. "I expect that the Battle of Britain is about to begin."

FOOTNOTE The Maginot Line, named after defense minister André Maginot, was the French border fortification insulating France from Germany. The fortification included concrete wall, tank obstacles, and gun posts.

Britain Weathers Blitz

799 **1940** Facing a defiant Churchill, who vowed never to surrender, Hitler in early August ordered his Luftwaffe to destroy the Royal Air Force (RAF) as a prelude to an invasion of Britain by sea. Although radar gave RAF fighter squadrons early warning of attacks, the Luftwaffe had far more pilots and warplanes and came close to winning the Battle of Britain by targeting opposing airfields, radar stations, and aircraft factories. But with little time left before autumn storms ruled out an amphibious assault, Hitler grew impatient and changed tactics. Responding to a bombing raid on Berlin in late August, he authorized massive attacks on London, hoping for a showdown that would shatter the RAF and force Churchill to seek terms or face defeat.

For two months the people of London endured constant bombing raids. They took to sleeping in underground stations for protection from the barrage.

The blitz exposed the Luftwaffe to heavy losses. In October, Hitler called off the invasion. It was the first great air battle in history—and the first demonstration that air power alone could not break the will of a determined opponent.

Radio Reports War

800 **1940** Many Americans felt safely removed from the fighting in Europe in 1940. As London came under assault, however, radio correspondent Edward R. Murrow brought the war home to them through riveting broadcasts in which the sounds of air raid sirens and bursting bombs were plainly audible. Listeners across the Atlantic admired the pluck and sympathized with the cause of Londoners during the blitz.

Filmgoers Face War

801 **1940** In an age of mass communications, Americans found it hard to remain detached from the struggle, even though it was going on across the Atlantic, far from home. Even filmgoers seeking comic relief were exposed to scenes of war and encouraged to take sides.

Among the Academy Award nominees for best picture in 1940 were two films by British directors playing on anti-Nazi sentiments—Alfred Hitchcock's *Foreign Correspondent,* the story of a reporter uncovering a German spy ring in London, and Charlie Chaplin's *The Great Dictator,* a satiric assault on Hitler, played by Chaplin in his first speaking role.

■ **FOOTNOTE** President Franklin D. Roosevelt created the Office of the Coordinator of Government Films and the Bureau of Motion Pictures to influence Hollywood to incorporate patriotic values into war and other feature films.

Italy Enters Fight

802 **1940** Despite his Pact of Steel with Hitler, Mussolini declined to join Germany in battle until France was nearly defeated, at which point Italian troops entered the fight but made little headway. Determined to match Hitler's gains with victories of his own, Mussolini advanced on two fronts in late 1940. In September, his forces crossed from Libya into Egypt, where they were overwhelmed by a smaller British army and surrendered in droves. In October, Italian troops advanced from Albania into Greece and were beaten back. As those twin defeats made clear, Mussolini had failed to prepare Italy for war either economically or militarily, leaving his forces ill equipped and

demoralized. Hitler would soon send troops to North Africa and the Balkans to repair the damage done by Mussolini, demonstrating that this was not an alliance of equals but a mismatch between a powerful dictator and a faltering one who could not bear to be overshadowed.

Japan Joins Axis

803 **1940** In September 1940, Japan allied itself with Germany and Italy by signing the Tripartite Pact, in which the three Axis partners pledged mutual military assistance if any one was attacked by a nation with which it was not already at war. This was aimed primarily at the U.S., which remained at peace but was aiding Britain against Germany and Italy and assisting China against Japan. As German Foreign Minister Joachim von Ribbentrop remarked, the pact was meant to discourage Americans from entering the war by showing that they would have to reckon with "three great powers as adversaries." But expansion of the Axis to include Japan served instead to alarm and antagonize Americans. Especially worrisome

804 | *"Big Three" in 1943: Joseph Stalin, Franklin Roosevelt, and Winston Churchill in Tehran*

to officials in Washington was the possibility that Japan might exploit recent German victories in Europe by attacking vulnerable British, French, and Dutch colonies in Southeast Asia, a move the U.S. could not oppose without placing its bases in the Pacific at risk.

■ **FOOTNOTE** During the peak of their World War II conquests, Japan invaded and captured many Pacific Islands, including the Philippines, Guam, Mariana Islands, Marshall Islands, Gilbert Islands, and Wake Island.

America Takes Sides

804 **1940** Unlike Hitler and Mussolini, Roosevelt and Churchill worked closely together to strengthen ties between their two countries and form an effective strategic alliance well before the U.S. officially entered the war. In December 1940, after Churchill informed him that Britain could no longer afford to pay for American military equipment it needed, Roosevelt proposed that aid be granted free of charge. Britain could repay the U.S., he suggested, by returning any equipment that remained serviceable at war's end. Roosevelt likened this to lending one's neighbor a garden hose to help put out a fire. Congress endorsed his proposal in March 1941 by passing the Lend-Lease Act, which provided billions of dollars worth of military aid to Britain, China, and other countries at odds with the Axis. This policy exposed American ships carrying supplies across the Atlantic to attacks by German submarines—

799 | *British military planes, Hawker Hurricane and Supermarine Spitfire, defend British skies, 1940.*

the same threat that had turned the U.S. against Germany in World War I.

Roosevelt Squeezes Japan

805 **1940** Following the invasion of the Soviet Union, Japanese leaders debated whether to join Germany in that struggle by invading Siberia or to move south from China through French Indochina—occupied in part by Japan in 1940—and seize British-ruled Malaya and the Dutch East Indies, a major source of oil, which Japan imported largely from the U.S.

In late July, Japan moved south and occupied all of Indochina. In response, President Roosevelt imposed an oil embargo on Japan and left its leaders with a stark choice. They could yield to American pressure and withdraw their forces from China and Indochina, in which case Roosevelt would lift the embargo, or they could secure oil and other vital resources by continuing to expand and risking war with the U.S. In October, Gen. Tojo Hideki became Japan's prime minister, bringing to power an officer who had no intention of yielding.

Cave Art Found

806 **1940** As Nazi officials tightened their hold on France in late 1940 and added insult to injury by confiscating precious works of art there, four French teenagers exploring a limestone grotto along the Vévère River made a discovery of inestimable value that escaped the ravages of war and became a world treasure—the Lascaux cave paintings, one of the richest troves

806 | *Prehistoric Lascaux cave paintings escaped Nazi destruction and inspire modern artists.*

of prehistoric art ever uncovered. Experts who studied the splendid animal paintings at Lascaux dated them to about 15,000 B.C.E. and linked them to other finds in western Europe, such as the Altamira cave paintings in Spain. Modern artists like Picasso found such work inspirational and tried to produce similar magic on canvas.

French Empire Fractures

807 **1941** Following the fall of France, Gen. Charles de Gaulle, in exile in Britain, emerged as leader of the Free French, who opposed German occupation forces and the Vichy regime that cooperated with them. De Gaulle's ultimate objective was to liberate his homeland by organizing a united resistance movement within France and by recruiting French volunteers abroad to help Allied troops retake the country. In the first few years of the war, however, he had little hope of loosening Hitler's hold on France and concentrated instead on winning over French colonies, some of which remained loyal to Vichy while others sided with de Gaulle.

In 1941, Free French troops joined a British campaign to secure the Middle East against German advances and helped defeat Vichy forces holding Syria and Lebanon. In return for backing the Allies, those two countries gained independence, signaling that times were changing and that victory for de Gaulle and his cause would not restore France to its former imperial glory.

■ **FOOTNOTE** Free France's flag was a red cross of Lorraine imposed on a red, white, and blue striped background. The cross, inspired by a 1300s double-barred cross reliquary, was said to symbolically combat the swastika.

Plutonium Isolated

808 **1941** In February 1941, a team of scientists led by Glenn Seaborg, using the cyclotron at the University of California, Berkeley, bombarded uranium with nuclear particles called deuterons and produced a new element they dubbed plutonium, heavier than uranium and destined to play a large

808 | *Gen. Erwin Rommel, the "Desert Fox," and aide in Africa, 1941*

part in the development of nuclear weapons and nuclear power. "We were excited that we'd discovered a new element," recalled Seaborg, but he and his colleagues did not think they were altering the course of history. As they continued working with plutonium, however, they produced the isotope plutonium-239, which turned out to be highly fissionable, meaning that the chain reaction triggered when its nucleus was bombarded with neutrons and split apart released vast amounts of energy. Seaborg's findings drew keen interest in Washington and he joined the Manhattan Project, seeking to isolate enough plutonium-239 to fuel a nuclear weapon while other scientists worked with the isotope uranium-235, which had similar potential.

Hitler Moves East

809 **1941** Thwarted in his efforts to conquer Britain, Hitler turned

east in 1941 and prepared to break his nonaggression pact with Stalin. But first he had to deal with crises in the Balkans and North Africa brought on by his ally Mussolini. Greek troops, with aid from Britain, had responded to Mussolini's recent attack on their country by advancing into Albania in pursuit of Italian forces. Fearing that the British might take this opportunity to occupy the Balkans, Hitler launched a preemptive strike to secure his southern flank before he challenged the Soviets. In April, Germany invaded Yugoslavia—whose leaders refused to cooperate with Hitler as those in Hungary, Romania, and Bulgaria did—and went on to defeat Greece in May despite British intervention. Meanwhile, German Gen. Erwin Rommel, sent to Libya to rescue Italian forces, was pressing opposing British forces back toward Egypt. By mid-1941, Hitler was ready to follow the fateful path of an earlier conqueror, Napoleon, by sending his forces into Russia.

In late June, some three million German troops invaded the Soviet Union. Hitler took this gamble for several reasons, including his desire to crush communism at its source, provide lebensraum (living space) for Germans in fertile areas such as Ukraine, and destroy or dispossess groups he despised, such as Jews and Slavs. He expected to defeat Stalin and his Red Army within months. "You have only to kick in the door," he told one of his top generals, "and the whole rotten structure will come crashing down." Those words appeared prophetic when German armored forces shattered Soviet lines and took millions of prisoners over the summer. But when autumn rains turned roads to mud, the invaders bogged down short of Moscow, giving their foes a chance to regroup. Late in the year, Stalin—armed with intelligence that Japan would not join Germany in attacking him—shifted divisions from Siberia to Moscow and forced the Germans onto the defensive.

> ■ **FOOTNOTE** The opera *War and Peace* by Sergei Prokofiev, based on Leo Tolstoy's book of the same name about Russia during the war against Napoleon, was begun in the summer of 1941, as Hitler's army invaded the Soviet Union.

Pearl Harbor Attacked

810 **1941** On Sunday, December 7, 1941, Japanese warplanes took off from six aircraft carriers near the island of Oahu and attacked Pearl Harbor, home to the U.S. Pacific Fleet. Despite warnings that Japan might initiate hostilities somewhere in the Pacific, the attackers achieved complete surprise, destroying two battleships and damaging more than a dozen other warships, wrecking nearly 200 aircraft, and killing more than 2,300 troops. At the same time, Japan attacked British forces in Hong Kong and Malaya and prepared to invade the Philippines by bombing American airfields there.

Calling it "a day which will live in infamy," Roosevelt promptly obtained from Congress a declaration of war on Japan. He knew many Americans were wary of widening the war to include Germany and waited for provocation from Hitler, who

obliged him on December 11 by declaring war on America. "We will always strike first!" vowed Hitler, who within six months had made enemies of the U.S. and the U.S.S.R.—the world's two emerging superpowers.

SS Rounds Up Jews

811 **1942** In January 1942, Reinhardt Heydrich of the SS, the organization responsible for enforcing Adolf Hitler's murderous racial policies, set in motion what he called "the final solution of the Jewish problem." At the time, SS death squads in occupied Soviet territory were shooting Jews and burying them in mass graves. Heydrich and his boss, Heinrich Himmler, considered that method of genocide inefficient. Henceforth, all Jews in areas under German control were to be sent either to concentration camps—where

---

FIRST PERSON

Franklin Roosevelt
ADDRESS TO CONGRESS, DECEMBER 8, 1941

To the Congress of the United States: Yesterday, December 7, 1941—a date which will live in infamy—the United States of America was suddenly and deliberately attacked by naval and air forces of the Empire of Japan.... The United States was at peace with that nation and, at the solicitation of Japan, was still in conversation with the government and its emperor looking toward the maintenance of peace in the Pacific.... The Japanese government has deliberately sought to deceive the United States....

As commander in chief of the Army and Navy, I have directed that all measures be taken for our defense.... With confidence in our armed forces—with the unbounding determination of our people—we will gain the inevitable triumph—so help us God. I ask that the Congress declare that since the unprovoked and dastardly attack by Japan on Sunday, December 7, a state of war has existed between the United States and the Japanese empire.

they would perform slave labor until they died of natural causes or were killed in gas chambers—or to extermination camps, where they would be put to death as quickly as possible. By war's end, six million Jews had been murdered by the Nazis, and they were not the only victims. Hundreds of thousands of Roma (gypsies) were killed as well, and several million other people died in confinement while serving as slave laborers.

Japanese Americans Interned

812 **1942** Acting on unsubstantiated claims that Japanese-Americans posed a security threat, President Roosevelt signed an executive order in February 1942 authorizing their removal from the Pacific coast to internment camps in the interior. No Japanese Americans had been charged with espionage or sabotage. But unlike Italian Americans and German Americans, who were not subject to internment, they were a small, stigmatized group, long

subject to racial discrimination, and lacked the political influence to counter charges that they were all "potential enemies," as one general put it. More than 110,000 of them were forced from their homes and sent to bleak camps in desolate surroundings, hemmed in by barbed wire and kept under guard. Despite the fact that American authorities "abused us and treated us like enemies," in the words of one internee, they were asked to affirm their loyalty to the U.S. Many did so, and some 20,000 Japanese Americans served in the armed forces during the war.

Rommel Retreats

814 **1942** Gen. Erwin Rommel had long bedeviled the British, but by October 1942 they had the "Desert Fox" pinned down at El Alamein in western Egypt. He had done his best to fulfill Hitler's master plan, which called for his tanks to advance through Egypt into the Middle East as German troops moved

down from Russia through the Caucasus. That could have proved decisive in a war that had as much to do with securing oil and other strategic resources as winning territory. But the farther Rommel advanced across the desert from his base at Tripoli, the harder it was for him to preserve his supply line and maintain momentum. Blocked at El Alamein by a larger British force, he could no longer outfox his opponents and came under their guns. "This battle will involve hard and prolonged fighting," Gen. Bernard Montgomery warned his officers before he attacked in late October. Applying relentless pressure, he forced Rommel to retreat in November and dealt the Axis a momentous setback.

> ■ **FOOTNOTE** General Montgomery's Operation Lightfoot plan included three stages: "the break-in, the dog-fight, and the final break of the enemy." The battle took place between October 23 and November 5, 1942.

Showdown at Stalingrad

815 **1942** Although the main German objective over the summer had been to advance southward through the Caucasus and capture Soviet oil fields, that effort lost steam when Hitler sent two armies involved in the campaign off to attack Stalingrad, an industrial city on the Volga River that was a symbol of Stalin's prestige and his efforts to keep Soviet industries running. The city was destroyed in fierce fighting, but defenders held out in the ruins and made the Germans pay dearly for every block they seized. Then in mid-November, Soviet reinforcements surrounded Stalingrad and trapped their opponents, who were ordered by Hitler to stand fast. More than 200,000 of his troops were killed or captured in this lost battle for Stalingrad, which set German invasion forces on the path to retreat and defeat.

Atomic Reaction Incited

816 **1942** In December 1942, scientists at the University of Chicago led by Enrico Fermi, a refugee from fascist Italy, achieved the first controlled, self-sustaining nuclear chain reaction,

Battle of Midway

813 **1942** In May 1942, Adm. Isoroku Yamamoto sent a Japanese fleet led by four heavy aircraft carriers to attack the U.S. base on Midway, northwest of Hawaii. He hoped this strike would lure within range of his bombers American aircraft carriers that had escaped his attack on Pearl Harbor. If he did not destroy those vessels soon and take command of the Pacific, the U.S. would achieve naval supremacy by turning out warships far faster than Japan could. For the first six months of the Pacific war, Japanese forces under Yamamoto had, in his own words, "run wild," winning supremacy over 20 million square miles of Asia and the Pacific, an area five times the size of Germany's conquests.

U.S. Navy fighter plane soars above burning Japanese ship under attack in the Battle of Midway, 1942.

Alerted to his plan by code breakers, bombers from three U.S. carriers surprised the Japanese off Midway in early June and sank all four carriers while losing just one of their own. This pivotal battle ended Japanese dominance in the Pacific and demonstrated conclusively that control of the seas, long determined by battleships, depended now on aircraft carriers.

showing that it was indeed possible to produce nuclear weapons and nuclear power. Using a squash court as their laboratory, Fermi and his team constructed what he called an atomic pile—a rudimentary nuclear reactor containing a critical mass of uranium and graphite, which served like paraffin in Fermi's earlier experiments to slow down emissions of neutrons, making a chain reaction possible. The reaction lasted less than an hour and produced a half watt of energy at its peak, but Fermi's aim was to control the process, not to produce an explosion.

U.S. Gears Up for War

817 **1942** The Allies made many strategic advances in 1942, but none was more significant than the gains made on the American home front as the world's largest economy mobilized for war. Still feeling the lingering effects of the Depression when the conflict began, American industry received a huge boost from increased military spending and turned out more tanks and aircraft in 1942 than the three Axis powers combined. American factories furnished the Soviets with hundreds of thousands of military vehicles during the war, and American farms provided Britain with nearly one-third of its food supply. Transformed by the war effort, the nation pulled together as never before and emerged with a productive capacity nearly equal to that of the rest of the world.

■ **FOOTNOTE** The War Advertising Council's Rosie the Riveter campaign, a cartoon drawing of an attractive woman in a work jumpsuit flexing her arm, recruited millions of women to work in factories from 1942 to 1945.

Battle of the Atlantic

818 **1943** America's war policy was Europe First, meaning that defeating Germany and Italy had priority over beating Japan. The prospects for victory in Europe looked bleak, however, so long as the sea lanes between the U.S. and Britain were haunted by German U-boats, which wreaked havoc in the winter of

817 | *Woman completes assembly work in wheel well of Vultee bomber at factory in Nashville, Tennessee, 1943.*

1942-43. Fortunately for the Allies, they had a secret weapon against those submarines, which prowled in "wolf packs" using coded radio signals. Polish cryptanalysts had mastered the Enigma machine, used to encode many German military messages, and had shared that intelligence with the British, whose experts sought keys to Enigma settings employed by Germany's various armed services. By 1943, they had cracked the U-boat code. That helped Allied forces—who were hunting wolf packs relentlessly now with radar-equipped aircraft and destroyers—sink more than 40 submarines in May, forcing the U-boat fleet to abandon the North Atlantic.

■ **FOOTNOTE** Early in the war, Allied convoys suffered high losses, but by 1945 the tide turned; U-boats expected to survive two patrols, and if they attacked, they could expect to sink only one ship before being sunk themselves.

Soviets Fight Germans

819 **1943** After their victory at Stalingrad in early 1943, Soviet troops pushed the German invaders back and reclaimed the Ukrainian city of Kursk, around which the opposing sides massed armor that summer in preparation for an epic tank battle. Throughout the war, Hitler had counted on his tank commanders to lead the way to victory. He expected no less from them now, but the Soviets were outproducing the Germans in tanks and other weaponry and had a larger population from which to draw soldiers, factory workers, and laborers, 300,000 of whom built tank barriers around Kursk. When the Germans attacked on July 5, Soviet commander Georgy Zhukov used those formidable defenses to wear them down before he struck back with overwhelming force. After fierce fighting involving nearly 6,000 tanks, the Germans retreated and went over to the defensive, hoping to stave off an invasion of their own homeland by a vengeful and increasingly powerful enemy.

Allies Invade Italy

820 **1943** By mid-1943, North Africa was controlled by the Allies, among them Americans who had landed in Morocco in late 1942. Where they should land next was a matter of sharp debate. Gen. George Marshall, U.S. Army Chief of Staff, argued that invading Italy would only divert strength from the planned invasion of France, which offered a shorter path to Germany. British and American forces were not ready to challenge the strong German defenses in France, however, and struck first at vulnerable Italy.

Landing on Sicily in early July, they soon won control there, helped by the fact that Italian support for Germany was crumbling. In late July, Mussolini fell from power. His successor sided with the Allies soon after they crossed to the Italian mainland, but reinforcements sent by Hitler in response kept them from breaking through to Germany before the war ended. As Marshall foresaw, this campaign was a diversion, but it toppled a dictator and aligned postwar Italy with the U.S., Britain, and other democratic nations.

Air War Over Europe

821 **1943** In late July of 1943, British bombers avenged deadly German air raids on London and other cities by targeting Hamburg and igniting a firestorm there that killed more than 30,000 people. That fearful toll would later be surpassed by the firebombing of Dresden, but such punishment was not enough in itself to win

---

CONNECTIONS

Transistors and Integrated Circuits
From the abacus to the microchip

The first primitive computer form, the abacus, was developed more than 4,000 years ago in the Middle East, but it was not until the 20th century that computers grew significantly in capability. Lee De Forest's invention of the vacuum tube in 1906 served as an amplifier for electrical signals and boosted phone and radio capabilities. In 1946 the world's first digital computer, ENIAC (Electronic Numerical Integrator and Computer), was completed. ENIAC, which was the size of a large room, weighed 30 tons and contained 18,000 vacuum tubes and 6,000 switches. Among other things, it was used to calculate bullet trajectories.

Vacuum tubes had problems, such as overheating and inefficient energy requirements, so William Shockley, Walter Brattain, and John Bardeen in 1947 invented the transistor, which allowed for faster, smaller, and more powerful computers. By 1954 the first mass-produced computer had been developed.

The transistor evolved in 1959 when Robert Norton Noyce invented the integrated circuit, placing multiple transistors on silicon, helping to eliminate the need for wires. It took only until 1962 before the first colleges added a Computer Sciences Department. In 1965, the first minicomputer, the DEC PDP8, was mass-produced, and IBM developed floppy disks on which to store information. The integrated circuit improved in 1967 as, for the first time, more than a thousand

Microchip detail, computer motherboard

transistors were placed onto one chip. This advance allowed a transistorized cable to handle 720 phone calls simultaneously.

In 1971, the microchip outstripped its predecessors. The number of transistors implanted onto the chip was so great that for the first time a single chip held the entire central processing unit of a computer. That same year the first pocket calculators were mass-produced and the prototype for electronic mail was developed. Over the next few years the first word-processing software was developed; the first commercial cellular telephone network was built; and IBM launched its first personal computer. By 1982 the word "Internet" had been coined in reference to a set of connected networks, and in 1985 IBM introduced the first megabit memory chips, which could store up to one million bits of data each.

As the 1990s began, the first commercial Internet dial-up access provider came online, digital cellular systems were introduced, the first portable computers were developed, the first Pentium chip was built, and miniaturization took hold of the technology industry. By the turn of the 21st century CDs would be exchanged for MP3 files, dial-up Internet access would be replaced by DSL, and computers would become faster. Scientists are researching the possibility of a transistor based on the movement of a single electron, a goal that has been accomplished in the laboratory.

the war. Beginning in 1942, the Allies combined the saturation bombing of German cities at night with more precise daytime raids on railroads, airfields, weapons factories, and other military and industrial targets. British and American air crews suffered heavy losses in the process, but their combined forces gained supremacy over the Luftwaffe before the Allies invaded France. By 1944, the Germans had only a few hundred fighter planes left there to contend with more than 10,000 Allied aircraft.

■ **FOOTNOTE** *Slaughterhouse-Five,* a widely read and now classic 1969 novel by Kurt Vonnegut, tells the story of an American soldier surviving the firebombing of Dresden as a prisoner of war in a slaughterhouse.

Computer Decodes

822 **1943** In late 1943, scientists at Bletchley Park, the British codebreaking facility, began using a huge electronic computer called Colossus to decipher German messages. The theoretical foundations for such digital computers—which process information using numbers, typically 0 and 1—had been laid in the 1930s by mathematicians such as Alan Turing, who served at Bletchley Park during the war. In the early 1940s, electronic computers capable of performing various mathematical functions were developed by Konrad Zuse of Germany and Americans John Atsonoff and Clifford Berry.

Colossus demonstrated the strategic significance of this new technology by allowing problems that expert code breakers had struggled with for weeks to be solved within hours. Similar advances were made during the war by American scientists, who produced high-powered computers such as ENIAC (Electronic Numerical Integrator and Computer), completed at the University of Pennsylvania in 1946 and used to perform calculations for physicists developing the hydrogen bomb.

Sartre States Philosophy

823 **1943** A former prisoner of war living in occupied Paris under the Nazis, Jean-Paul Sartre knew what it meant

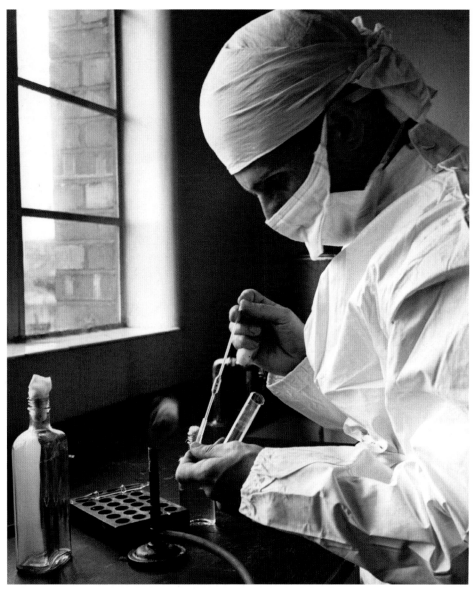

824 | *British pharmacist makes tuberculosis-curing streptomycin antibiotic in laboratory, 1946.*

to have freedom threatened. Yet in two works that appeared in 1943—*Being and Nothingness* and *The Flies*—he argued that freedom was absolute and inescapable and that people must make choices and live with the consequences. Man is "condemned to be free," he wrote. That applied not just to those living in free societies but to those in conquered lands like France, who had to choose whether to submit to the invaders or resist them, as he did. Drawing on his wartime experiences, Sartre gave existentialism—a philosophy stressing the unique and solitary nature of each person's existence—new meaning for those who

saw upholding freedom as both an individual and a social responsibility.

■ **FOOTNOTE** "Either man is wholly determined (which is inadmissible, especially because a determined consciousness—i.e., a consciousness externally motivated—becomes pure exteriority and ceases to be consciousness) or else man is wholly free."—Jean Paul Sartre

Antibiotics Developed

824 **1943** American microbiologist Selman Waksman discovered a lifesaving weapon, the antibiotic streptomycin, which offered the first effective medicinal treatment for tuberculosis, one

FIRST PERSON

Marie-Louise Osmont

NORMANDY, JUNE 6, 1944

Little by little the gray dawn comes up, but this time around, from the intensity of the aircraft and the cannon an idea springs to mind: landing! I get dressed hurriedly. I cross the garden, the men recognize me. In one of the foxholes in front of the house, I recognize one of the young men from the office; he has headphones on his ears, the telephone being removed there. Airplanes, cannon right on the coast, almost on us. I cross the road, run to the farm, come across Meltemps. "Well!" I say, "Is this it, this time?" "Yes," he says, "I think so, and I'm really afraid we're in a sector that's being attacked; that's going to be something!" We're deafened by the airplanes, which make a never-ending round, very low; obviously what I thought were German airplanes are quite simply English ones, protecting the landing. Coming from the sea, a dense artificial cloud; it's ominous and begins to be alarming; the first hiss over our heads. I feel cold; I'm agitated. I go home, dress more warmly, close the doors; I go get Bernice [a neighbor] to get into the trench, a quick bowl of milk, and we run—just in time! The shells hiss and explode continually....

Around six o'clock a lull. We get out and go toward the house to care for the animals and get things to spend the night underground. And then we see the first damage. Branches of the big walnut broken, roof on the outbuildings heavily damaged, a big hole all the way up, a heap of broken roof tiles on the ground, a few windowpanes at my place—hundreds of slates blown off the chateau, walls cracked, first-floor shutters won't close—but at Bernice's it's worse. An airplane or tank shell has exploded on the paving in her kitchen at the corner of the stairs, and the whole interior of the room is devastated: the big clock, dishes, cooking equipment, walls, everything is riddled with holes, the dishes in broken pieces, as are almost all the windowpanes. The dog Frick that I had shut up in the next room ... is all right and sleeping on a seat. But we realize that if we had stayed there, we would both have been killed.

of the worst scourges of modern times. Waksman's achievement grew out of his research at Rutgers University into microorganisms in soil that decompose organic material. One such enzyme, discovered by his gifted French laboratory assistant René Dubos, proved effective against pneumonia, prompting Waksman to seek other substances in soil that would serve as antibiotics, a term he coined.

The search was long and difficult because many antibiotics are highly toxic and destroy both harmful and healthful organisms within the body. After testing numerous substances, Waksman and his assistants Albert Schatz and Elizabeth Bugie found streptomycin, which gave doctors another proven weapon along with penicillin to destroy potentially deadly microbes without risking the patient's life.

FOOTNOTE Tuberculosis, also known as TB, is an infection, usually of the lungs, that spreads by coughing or sneezing. At one time, TB was the number one killer in the U.S. In 2005, TB caused only about 14,000 U.S. deaths.

France Liberated

825 **1944** On D-Day, June 6, 1944, Allied forces came ashore at Normandy, opening a new front in the war against Germany, which was already under intense pressure from Soviet troops to the east. Hitler and his generals had long expected an invasion of France, but the Allies kept them guessing as to where on the coast the blow would fall and used air power to impede German movements once the operation began. In the words of Allied Supreme Commander Dwight Eisenhower, this was the "greatest amphibious assault ever attempted," involving more than 6,000 ships and landing craft.

Americans landing at Omaha Beach on D-Day encountered fierce resistance from defenders holding the cliffs above but succeeded in linking up with troops in neighboring sectors to establish a bridgehead. By July, the Allies had a million men in Normandy. German armored divisions fought hard to contain them, but in August they broke out and reached Paris, entering the

828 | *American troops pass another American tank in Ardennes Forest during Battle of the Bulge.*

city to a jubilant reception with Free French troops in the lead.

Germany Launches Missiles

826 **1944** A frightening new chapter in the history of warfare opened in mid-June 1944 when German V-1 missiles struck London and vicinity. Although rockets had long served as tactical weapons, these were the first strikes by guided strategic missiles aimed at civilians. The British knew that Germans were developing such weapons at Peenemünde, an island in the Baltic Sea, and had bombed the facility there in 1943. But that did not halt development of the V-1— a cruise missile that flew at relatively low altitude—or the deadlier V-2, a ballistic missile with a bigger payload that rocketed into the stratosphere before descending on its target. First fired in September 1944, the V-2 was dreaded because it struck without warning and could not be defended against. Although it killed thousands of people, it was not the wonder weapon Hitler hoped for to avoid defeat. Missiles armed with nuclear warheads might have altered the war's outcome, but by 1944 Germany was

years behind the U.S. in developing an atomic bomb.

U.S. Retakes Philippines

827 **1944** "I shall return," vowed Gen. Douglas MacArthur when he was ordered to abandon the Philippines to Japanese invaders in early 1942. Not until October 1944 was he able to make good on that pledge by landing on the island of Leyte with American forces. The delay was due partly to fierce resistance by the Japanese—who considered it shameful to surrender and dealt harshly with Allied prisoners of war who did so—and partly to the fact that American commanders had a vast area in the Pacific to conquer and were not sure how best to reach and defeat Japan. MacArthur, based in Australia, favored an approach from the south that would take his army through New Guinea to the Philippines and on to Japan. Adm. Ernest King, chief of naval operations, and Adm. Chester Nimitz, the commander at Pearl Harbor, favored an approach from the east that involved seizing one small island after another in amphibious assaults.

In a strategic compromise, MacArthur and Nimitz divided the Pacific theater and proceeded slowly but surely toward Japan along separate paths that converged on the Philippines in 1944. By then, forces dispatched by Nimitz had captured the Mariana Islands, bringing B-29 bombers within range of Japan, and attacks by American submarines had greatly reduced the flow of oil and other vital supplies to Japanese bases. That did not guarantee victory, however, and Nimitz joined with MacArthur in seizing the Philippines as a prelude to a possible invasion of Japan. In late October, the U.S. Pacific Fleet won the largest naval battle in history, shattering the Japanese fleet in Leyte Gulf and shielding American troops as they gained possession of Leyte and retook the rest of the Philippines. For Filipinos, who resisted Japanese invaders as they had earlier resisted Spanish and American colonizers, the U.S. victory brought them what they had long sought—independence, granted as promised by Congress on July 4, 1946.

Battle of the Bulge

828 **1944** In December 1944, as Allied forces advanced from France into Belgium and prepared to invade Germany, they were staggered by a furious counterattack that represented Hitler's last desperate bid to turn the tide. By drafting all able-bodied men between 16 and 60 and shifting soldiers from noncombat duty to the front lines, he amassed two dozen divisions and launched them against the Allies in Belgium. Striking a weak point held only by infantry, German armor caused havoc and made a deep crease in the Allied line. But that bulge became a trap for many of the attackers when British and American forces rallied and hemmed them in under relentless air strikes. All Hitler achieved in the end was to delay for a few months an invasion from the west that proved merciful for his people compared to the dire threat to the east, where Soviet troops advanced relentlessly toward Berlin, raping and pillaging in retaliation for the German assault on their homeland.

Powers Meet at Yalta

829 **1945** When Roosevelt, Churchill, and Stalin met in early February of 1945 at the Soviet city of Yalta, they were assured of victory in Europe, but their alliance was crumbling and with it hopes for lasting peace. Churchill was deeply suspicious of Stalin and feared Soviet domination of eastern Europe. Roosevelt was in failing health and still had to defeat Japan. He could not risk a rupture with Stalin before that struggle was over and settled for vague assurances that governments in Poland and other countries under Soviet military control would respond to "the will of the people." Pending reunification at an unspecified date, Germany was to be divided into four zones—British, French, American, and Soviet—with the Soviet sector encompassing all of East Germany except for Berlin, which would become a divided city and a hot spot in the emerging Cold War.

Marines Take Iwo Jima

830 **1945** On February 19, 1945, U.S. Marines seized the air base on the island of Iwo Jima and used it as a stronghold against their Japanese enemy. This was the closest Americans had come to Japan, and opposition was fierce. Gen. Kuribayashi Tadamichi and some 20,000 Japanese troops fought to the finish.

For Americans back home, the rousing image of Marines raising their flag on

829 | *Winston Churchill, Franklin Roosevelt, and Joseph Stalin at Yalta, February 1945*

Iwo Jima promised victory, but the struggle to subdue Japan was far from over. In early March, U.S. bombers dropped incendiaries on Tokyo, igniting a firestorm that killed more than 80,000 people. On April 1, American troops landed on Okinawa, from which a massive invasion of Japan would be launched if its leaders refused to surrender. Seizing Okinawa cost the U.S. nearly 50,000 casualties, raising fears that as many as a million Americans might be killed or wounded taking Japan.

■ **FOOTNOTE** The Marine Corps memorial is a bronze statue of the six Marines who raised the U.S. flag on Iwo Jima. Three of the soldiers died in the war, so their 32-foot-high likenesses had to be created from measurements.

Germany Surrenders

831 **1945** On the night of April 30, 1945, as Soviet troops fought their way into Berlin, Hitler committed suicide in his bunker at the Reich Chancellery. His long-cherished ambition had been to avenge Germany's humiliating defeat in World War I. Instead, he had subjected his nation to a far greater disaster. In this one battle for Berlin, 125,000 Germans died. Millions had fled their homes as the Soviets advanced, seeking refuge in the British, French, or American zones before the dreaded Red Army engulfed them. The overriding concern of Hitler's successor, Adm. Karl Dönitz, was to allow as many German civilians and soldiers as possible to reach those zones before he surrendered. On May 8, the Allies celebrated V-E Day, for Victory in Europe—a bittersweet moment for troops aware that there were still battles to be won. "There were no celebrations or parties where we were," recalled an American soldier in Austria, who wondered if he would soon be fighting in the Pacific.

Nuclear Bomb Tested

832 **1945** Early on the morning of July 16, 1945, a mushroom cloud rose above the desert at Alamogordo, a restricted air base in New Mexico, signaling success for the Manhattan Project,

an intensive, nationwide effort to develop nuclear bombs. While the Oak Ridge facility in Tennessee and the Hanford Engineer Works in Washington produced nuclear fuel in the form of uranium-235 and plutonium-239, an elite team of scientists led by J. Robert Oppenheimer gathered at Los Alamos, New Mexico, to design the bomb, which worked by first imploding and pressing together a supercritical mass of nuclear fuel before exploding. Their feat gave President Harry Truman, who had taken office in April following Roosevelt's death, a fearsome new weapon in the war against Japan. Sticking to Roosevelt's policy of demanding unconditional surrender and taking into account the great risk to American troops if he had to order an invasion, Truman prepared to use that weapon soon if Japan did not heed Allied warnings and give up.

Korea Partitioned

834 **1945** On August 8, 1945, with Japan under nuclear attack by the U.S. and on the verge of defeat, the Soviet Union entered the war in Asia and advanced against Japanese forces in Manchuria and Korea. Although the U.S. had earlier urged the Soviets to join the fight against Japan to relieve pressure on American troops, this belated offensive raised fears in Washington that Stalin might send his forces beyond the 38th parallel in Korea, which had been negotiated as a boundary between the Soviet occupation zone in the north and the American zone in the south until Korea was reunified and granted independence. Though the Soviets adhered to that demarcation line, they widened the rift between north and south by establishing a communist government in their sector led by Kim Il-sung, whose

U.S. Uses Atomic Bomb

833 **1945** On August 6, 1945, a B-29 piloted by Col. Paul Tibbets released "Little Boy," a 9,000-pound bomb loaded with uranium-235, over the Japanese city of Hiroshima. Maneuvering to escape the blast, Tibbets felt a violent shock wave and looked back. "The city we had seen so clearly in the sunlight a few minutes before was now an ugly smudge," he wrote. "It had completely disappeared under this awful blanket of smoke and fire." The plane's tail gunner called the devastation "a peep into hell." In minutes thousands lay dead or dying from the ensuing shock wave, firestorm, and fallout. The White House called on Japan to surrender or "expect a rain of ruin from the air." Neither the first nuclear attack nor the threat induced surrender, so Truman ordered a second strike, directed at Nagasaki, where a bomb packed with plutonium-239 exploded on August 9. Nearly 120,000 lives were lost in the two blasts, and the death toll would rise as survivors exposed to radiation fell ill and died. On August 15, Emperor Hirohito yielded to the Allies to prevent the "ultimate collapse and obliteration of the Japanese nation." The surrender document was signed on September 2 in the presence of General MacArthur, who would rule conquered Japan as commander of occupation forces.

Nuclear bombs detonated over Japan effectively caused that country's surrender.

determination to bring all of Korea under his authority would make this the first major battleground in the Cold War.

■ **FOOTNOTE** Kim Il-Sung enjoyed a long reign, from 1948 to 1994, when he died, prompting widespread, almost hysterical national grieving. His reclusive son, Kim Jong-il, took over after his father's death.

Vietnam Divided

835 **1945** In late August 1945, shortly after Japan surrendered, indigenous communist forces entered Hanoi and proclaimed Vietnam independent. Their leader, Ho Chi Minh, had waged a long fight for independence, first against French colonial authorities and more recently against Japanese occupation forces. Although Ho Chi Minh was a dedicated communist with ties to the Soviet Union and Mao Zedong's forces in China, he was also a fervent nationalist, prepared to accept aid from any source that served the cause of Vietnamese independence—including the Office of Strategic Services (OSS), an American undercover organization formed in 1942. OSS agents reached Ho Chi Minh's headquarters north of Hanoi in July 1945 and gave the ailing rebel leader medical aid that may have saved his life. They also provided members of his organization, known as the Viet Minh, with weapons, explosives, and training in order to hasten the defeat of Japanese forces in Vietnam.

Based on that aid, Ho Chi Minh had reason to hope the U.S. would tolerate the Viet Minh if it came to power. He echoed sentiments of the American Revolution when he arrived in Hanoi in early September and proclaimed victory, declaring that all men are born equal and have the right to "life, liberty, and happiness." Hopes for peaceful accommodation between the Viet Minh and the victorious Allies were soon dashed, however, as American officials grew increasingly wary of the spread of communism in Asia and France moved to reassert authority over Vietnam. In October 1945, Gen. Jacques Leclerc reached Saigon with French forces and effectively divided

836 | *President Truman signs UN charter, flanked by Secretary of State James Byrnes, 1945.*

Vietnam by taking control of the south, where anticommunist sentiment remained strong. Ho Chi Minh then reached a compromise with the French that lasted only a few months before fighting erupted. That conflict led ultimately to U.S. military involvement in what Americans saw as a struggle against communism and Ho Chi Minh's followers continued to regard as a war for independence.

■ **FOOTNOTE** The Office of Strategic Services (OSS) was the first organized U.S. intelligence. The OSS was dismantled in 1945 and eventually replaced by the Central Intelligence Group, which in turn was replaced by the CIA in 1947.

United Nations Born

836 **1945** The United Nations was established in October 1945 to "save succeeding generations from the scourge of war." President Franklin D. Roosevelt is credited with coining the name, which came from a declaration signed by 26 Allied nations fighting the Axis powers. The UN replaced the League of Nations, which had failed to prevent the worst such scourge in history, World War

II, a catastrophe that claimed more than 50 million lives. The framers of the UN sought to make it more effective than the League of Nations by creating a Security Council with five permanent members—the U.S., the U.S.S.R., the United Kingdom, France, and the Republic of China—and authorizing that council to take forceful measures to preserve international peace and security. The permanent members each had veto power, however, making it difficult for the council to act when disagreements arose between the Soviet Union and the U.S. and other Western democracies opposed to the spread of communism.

Those ideological disputes grew sharper when communists led by Mao Zedong challenged Chiang Kai-shek's Nationalists for control of China and the right to represent that nation at the United Nations. Although the U.S. supported the Nationalists, leading to a boycott by the Soviet Union, an ally of Mao's People's Republic of China, in 26 years Resolution 2758 would vote to seat representatives of the People's Republic.

1914-1945 | World War Years

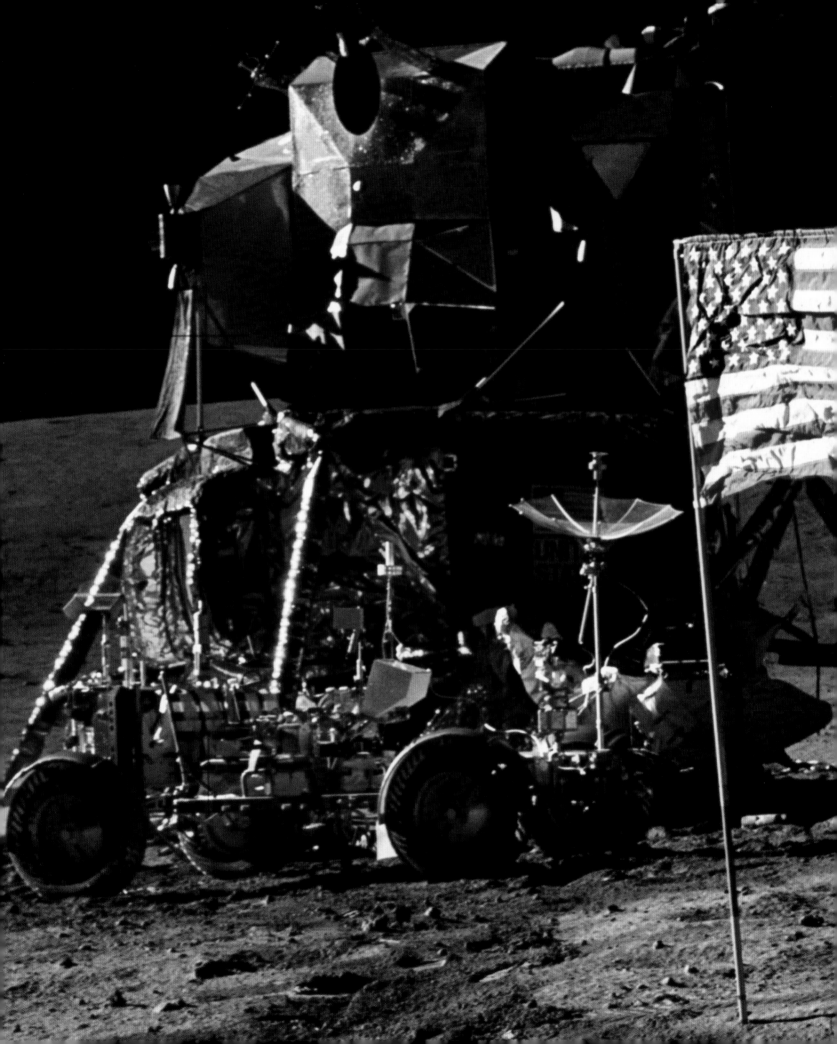

Modern Age
1946-Present

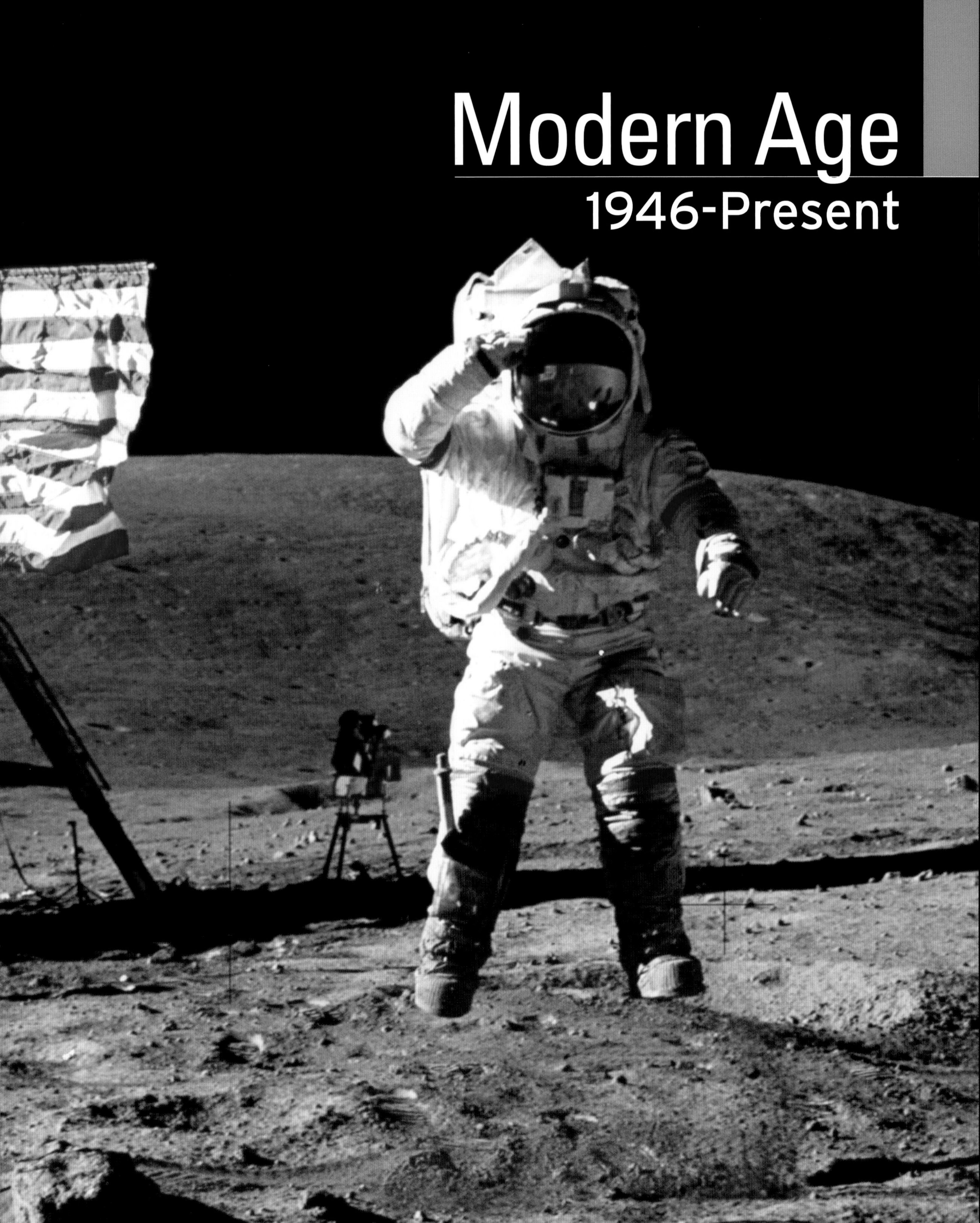

1946-Present

Stepping Into the Future

Following the Second World War, the process of globalization—or the integration of countries around the globe within an international economic or political system—gained momentum. A world once divided among many great powers was now dominated by just two: the United States, leader of the Western democratic bloc; and the Union of Soviet Socialist Republics (U.S.S.R.), leader of the communist bloc, which included the nations of Eastern Europe and other countries.

Despite the Cold War waged by those two nuclear superpowers, distant nations were linked more closely than ever by technology and trade—forces that eventually led China to abandon communist economic principles and develop close ties with the West. The collapse of the Soviet Union in the late 1900s seemingly cleared the way for a new world order based on free trade, free enterprise, and settlement of disputes by the United Nations and other international bodies. Yet resistance to globalization remained strong, and prospects for peace remained uncertain.

Decolonization and the Cold War

BEGINNING IN THE LATE 1940s, MANY COLONIES IN ASIA, AFRICA, and the Middle East once governed by Britain, France, or the imperial powers defeated in World War II achieved independence. Few countries made this difficult transition to nationhood without strife or turmoil.

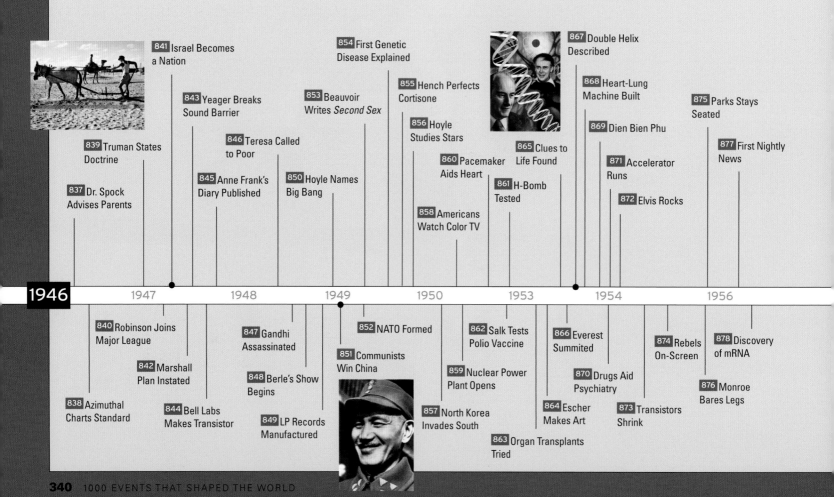

841 Israel Becomes a Nation

854 First Genetic Disease Explained

867 Double Helix Described

843 Yeager Breaks Sound Barrier

853 Beauvoir Writes *Second Sex*

855 Hench Perfects Cortisone

868 Heart-Lung Machine Built

875 Parks Stays Seated

839 Truman States Doctrine

846 Teresa Called to Poor

856 Hoyle Studies Stars

869 Dien Bien Phu

877 First Nightly News

837 Dr. Spock Advises Parents

845 Anne Frank's Diary Published

850 Hoyle Names Big Bang

865 Clues to Life Found

860 Pacemaker Aids Heart

871 Accelerator Runs

861 H-Bomb Tested

872 Elvis Rocks

858 Americans Watch Color TV

1946 — 1947 — 1948 — 1949 — 1950 — 1953 — 1954 — 1956

840 Robinson Joins Major League

847 Gandhi Assassinated

852 NATO Formed

862 Salk Tests Polio Vaccine

866 Everest Summited

874 Rebels On-Screen

878 Discovery of mRNA

842 Marshall Plan Instated

851 Communists Win China

859 Nuclear Power Plant Opens

870 Drugs Aid Psychiatry

876 Monroe Bares Legs

848 Berle's Show Begins

838 Azimuthal Charts Standard

844 Bell Labs Makes Transistor

849 LP Records Manufactured

857 North Korea Invades South

864 Escher Makes Art

873 Transistors Shrink

863 Organ Transplants Tried

When the British exited India, for example, conflict between Hindus and Muslims led to partition, with the predominantly Muslim nation of Pakistan emerging in the north. Decolonization proved deeply divisive as well for two other countries that found themselves caught up in the Cold War struggle and partitioned along ideological lines: Korea (recently under Japanese control) and Vietnam (a former French colony).

The Korean War began in 1950, one year after communists led by Mao Zedong took control of mainland China. Backed by China and the Soviet Union, North Koreans invaded South Korea, defended by American forces who clashed with both North Korean and Chinese forces before the conflict ended with the prewar boundary restored between the two Koreas.

In Vietnam, communists in the north followed their victory over the French in 1954 by waging a long and bitter struggle against the noncommunist south and its American defenders, who ultimately withdrew, leaving the nation united under communist rule.

Many other countries felt the jarring impact of the Cold War as the world's superpowers intervened to remove dictators or democratically elected leaders they considered hostile to their interests or backed opposing sides in regional struggles like the long-simmering conflict between Israel and its Arab neighbors. The Middle East was one of the hot spots of the Cold War, but no spot was hotter than Cuba, where the introduction of Soviet ballistic missiles in 1962 brought the superpowers close to nuclear war. After that high-stakes confrontation, tensions eased somewhat and talks were held, but the arms race and the Cold War that sustained it dragged on for decades.

PREVIOUS PAGE | *U.S. Apollo 16 astronaut John Young photographed on the moon by lunar module pilot Charles Duke in April 1972*

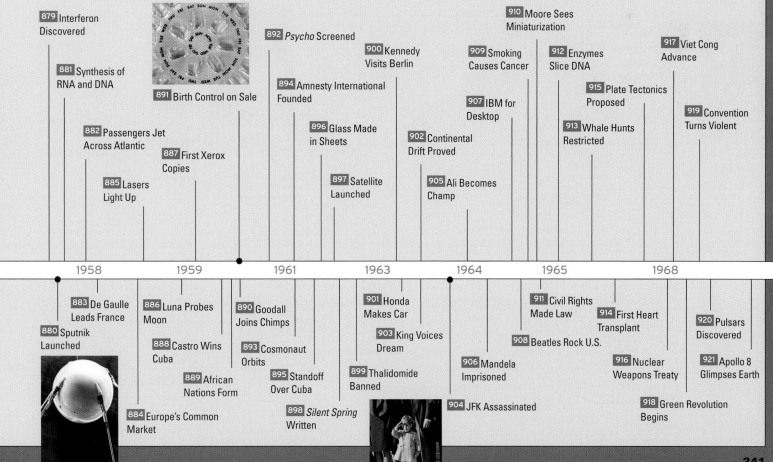

879 Interferon Discovered

881 Synthesis of RNA and DNA

882 Passengers Jet Across Atlantic

885 Lasers Light Up

887 First Xerox Copies

891 Birth Control on Sale

892 *Psycho* Screened

894 Amnesty International Founded

896 Glass Made in Sheets

897 Satellite Launched

900 Kennedy Visits Berlin

902 Continental Drift Proved

905 Ali Becomes Champ

907 IBM for Desktop

909 Smoking Causes Cancer

910 Moore Sees Miniaturization

912 Enzymes Slice DNA

913 Whale Hunts Restricted

915 Plate Tectonics Proposed

917 Viet Cong Advance

919 Convention Turns Violent

1958   1959   1961   1963   1964   1965   1968

880 Sputnik Launched

883 De Gaulle Leads France

884 Europe's Common Market

886 Luna Probes Moon

888 Castro Wins Cuba

889 African Nations Form

890 Goodall Joins Chimps

893 Cosmonaut Orbits

895 Standoff Over Cuba

898 *Silent Spring* Written

899 Thalidomide Banned

901 Honda Makes Car

903 King Voices Dream

904 JFK Assassinated

906 Mandela Imprisoned

908 Beatles Rock U.S.

911 Civil Rights Made Law

914 First Heart Transplant

916 Nuclear Weapons Treaty

918 Green Revolution Begins

920 Pulsars Discovered

921 Apollo 8 Glimpses Earth

Peaceful Revolutions

UNLIKE SOME PAST STRUGGLES BETWEEN GREAT POWERS, THE COLD War was not fueled by jingoism or war fever among Americans or Soviets. To the contrary, both the Western and Eastern blocs were swept periodically by protest movements that challenged the moral authority of the superpowers and called for a new world order. Far-reaching developments such as the emergence of television as a mass medium, increased travel on jet aircraft, space exploration, and a growing awareness of the impact of economic development on the global environment transcended national interests and boundaries—as did movements aimed at ending social injustice or inequality.

In pressing peacefully for desegregation in the South, for example, the African-American civil rights leader Martin Luther King, Jr., was inspired by Gandhi's nonviolent resistance campaign in India. The movement toward equality for women was an international phenomenon, as evidenced by the election of women as heads of state in Israel, India, and the United Kingdom. Peace movements like that directed against the American war effort in Vietnam were denounced by some critics as unpatriotic, but the capacity to tolerate protest and respond to it politically made the Western democratic system more resilient and more attractive internationally than the Soviet system, which left little room for dissent.

After crushing anticommunist uprisings by sending tanks into Hungary in 1956 and Czechoslovakia in 1968, Soviet authorities were hard-pressed to sustain the fiction that their Eastern European satellites were independent of Moscow. Economic woes made worse by an arms race the Soviet Union could ill afford—and glaring examples of mismanagement like the meltdown of the Chernobyl nuclear reactor in 1986— further discredited communism and helped foster resistance movements like Solidarity in Poland that were too broad to

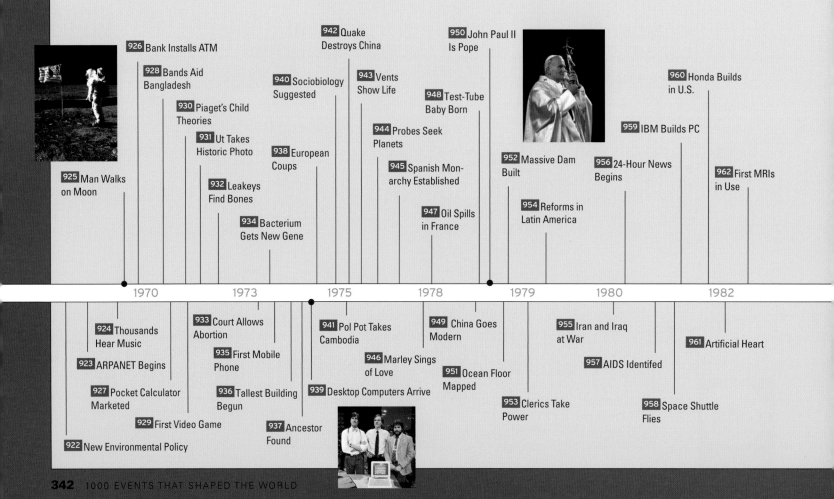

926 Bank Installs ATM

928 Bands Aid Bangladesh

930 Piaget's Child Theories

931 Ut Takes Historic Photo

932 Leakeys Find Bones

934 Bacterium Gets New Gene

938 European Coups

940 Sociobiology Suggested

942 Quake Destroys China

943 Vents Show Life

944 Probes Seek Planets

945 Spanish Monarchy Established

947 Oil Spills in France

948 Test-Tube Baby Born

950 John Paul II Is Pope

952 Massive Dam Built

954 Reforms in Latin America

956 24-Hour News Begins

959 IBM Builds PC

960 Honda Builds in U.S.

962 First MRIs in Use

925 Man Walks on Moon

1970   1973   1975   1978   1979   1980   1982

922 New Environmental Policy

923 ARPANET Begins

924 Thousands Hear Music

927 Pocket Calculator Marketed

929 First Video Game

933 Court Allows Abortion

935 First Mobile Phone

936 Tallest Building Begun

937 Ancestor Found

939 Desktop Computers Arrive

941 Pol Pot Takes Cambodia

946 Marley Sings of Love

949 China Goes Modern

951 Ocean Floor Mapped

953 Clerics Take Power

955 Iran and Iraq at War

957 AIDS Identifed

958 Space Shuttle Flies

961 Artificial Heart

be suppressed. The collapse of the Soviet empire, symbolized by the destruction of the Berlin Wall in 1989, was a largely peaceful revolution and left the nations of Eastern Europe free to align with the West and join the global economy.

After the Cold War

THE WORLD THAT EMERGED FROM THE COLD WAR WAS MORE cohesive and tightly knit than ever, linked electronically by computers and the World Wide Web. Globalization based not on American power but on principles of economic and political cooperation developed by the United States and allied nations seemed to promise an end to the relentless struggle for imperial supremacy that had long convulsed the world.

Skeptics, however, considered globalization a new form of imperialism, driven by multinational corporations and institutions that did not have to answer politically for the impact of their policies on advanced nations—which acquired cheap imported goods but lost manufacturing jobs—or developing countries, which expanded industrially but at the same time suffered cultural disruption and environmental degradation similar to that experienced by Western nations when they had earlier industrialized.

Resistance to the spread of Western political and cultural values around the globe was one factor contributing to the rise of the radical Islamic movement al Qaeda, whose stunning attacks in 2001 on the Pentagon and the World Trade Center—a towering symbol of globalization—triggered American military action abroad and dimmed hopes that the new century would witness the peaceful expansion of a new world order. That may yet occur; but not until the world withstands further shocks in the form of war, economic panic, or other unsettling events without losing cohesion can the recent trend toward global cooperation and integration be considered the start of a major new chapter in history.

963 Protocol Links Computers

971 Dalai Lama Awarded Nobel

978 Dial-Up Access

995 Euro in Circulation

969 Philippine Reforms

980 U.S. Storms Desert

988 GPS in Place

973 Berlin Wall Falls

986 Chunnel Opens

999 Climate Change Declared

968 *Challenger* Explodes

976 Gene Therapy Performed

984 Rabin Offers Peace

993 Genome Decoded

997 YouTube Debuts

965 Ozone Hole Spotted

974 Dissolution of Soviet Union

982 Books Online

990 Princess Diana Dies

1986   1989   1990   1992   1995   1997   2004   2007

967 Chernobyl Malfunctions

975 First Email

983 North America Trades

989 Sheep Cloned

996 U.S. Invades Iraq

970 Stocks Crash

985 Tomato Modified

977 Telescope Launched

991 Google Searches

998 North Korea Goes Nuclear

966 CD-ROMs Created

981 Web Worldwide

992 Crew Inhabits Space

964 Gorbachev Takes Over

972 Chinese Protest Quashed

979 Mad Cow Explained

987 New Quark Found

1000 New Planet Found

994 Terrorists Attack U.S.

Azimuthal Charts Standard

838 **1946** Azimuthal World Air Charts became the cartographic standard for air navigation in 1946.

In any cartographic application, the mapmaker's challenge is to reproduce the spherical surface of Earth on a flat piece of paper. Different types of projections have been developed to create maps for different purposes. An azimuthal map is made by projecting the globe onto a plane surface (such as a flat piece of paper) that touches the globe at one point. This map resembles a target, with lines of latitude forming concentric circles around the point of no distortion (the point where the plane touches the globe), and lines of longitude extending out from this point like spokes of a wheel.

Since "great circle" routes—the shortest route between two points over the surface of the Earth—appear as straight lines, the new maps helped pilots fly the globe more accurately.

■ **FOOTNOTE** The word azimuth comes from Arabic's *as-sumut,* meaning "the way" or direction, and its principles are used not only in mapmaking, but also for navigation, astronomy, surveying, and gunnery.

Truman States Doctrine

839 **1947** President Harry S. Truman articulated the Truman Doctrine, a policy of containment for dealing with the spread of communism that formed the rationale for the Cold War. On March 12, 1947, Truman convinced a joint session of Congress to appropriate $400 million to help Greece and Turkey repel communism. "It must be the policy of the United States," said Truman, "to support free peoples who are resisting attempted subjugation." He drew battle lines with his assertion that "every nation must choose between alternative ways of life." Truman did not mention the Soviet Union in his speech, but his point was clear: Communists had taken much of Eastern Europe, and other nations would fall to communism like dominoes.

840 | *Jackie Robinson was a Negro Baseball League star before becoming a major league player.*

Dr. Spock Advises Parents

837 **1946** Pediatrician Benjamin Spock published *The Common Sense Book of Baby and Child Care* in 1946, launching a new philosophy of child-rearing. Previously, experts had insisted that raising children with sternness would best prepare them for life. Dr. Spock, trained in psychiatry and child development, viewed these practices as contradictory to the instincts of parents and detrimental to children and society. He encouraged mothers and fathers to nurture emotional security by being affectionate and playful with their babies. "Trust yourself. You know more than you think you do," was Dr. Spock's gentle guidance and the first line of his book.

Robinson Joins Major League

840 **1947** Jack Roosevelt Robinson took the field for the Brooklyn Dodgers on April 15, 1947, breaking barriers of racial discrimination in major league baseball. Son of a sharecropper and grandson of a slave, Jackie Robinson was a star athlete at UCLA and served as an Army officer in World War II. After the war, he played in the Negro Baseball League. Pressure was growing for the major leagues to integrate, and Robinson was offered a tryout for the Boston Red Sox. He showed up—but the protesting manager and players did not.

In 1945, two years prior to his Red Sox tryout, Jackie Robinson had signed on with the International League's Montreal Royals, leading the team to both league and Little World Series titles.

Dodgers general manager Branch Rickey signed Robinson to a Detroit farm club in 1945. When he made it to the majors, the second baseman endured ugly threats with quiet dignity and soon awed the crowds by batting .297. Robinson was voted the league's first Rookie of the Year. Doors had opened: The season after his first game as a Dodger, he was one of three African-American All-Stars.

Marshall Plan Instated

842 **1947** U.S. Secretary of State George C. Marshall proposed a $13 billion aid package to help Europe recover from the ravages of World War II. As Chief of Staff of the U.S. Army, Marshall had been lauded by Winston Churchill as the "organizer of victory" during World War II.

In the war's aftermath, Western Europe was in severe economic distress, with many of its people facing starvation. The United States saw other threats as well: the loss of a valued trading partner and an opening for socialist and communist incursion into the struggling countries. Congress authorized the first payment in December 1947, with aid continuing until 1952. Considerable support went to Germany, the former industrial center of Europe, where the economic situation was extremely dire. The Soviets responded by blockading Berlin in June 1948, which created alarming shortages of food, coal, and other supplies. The United States, Britain, and other allies answered with the Berlin Airlift, a yearlong mission that brought 3.2 million tons of goods into the city.

■ **FOOTNOTE** One of the Berlin airlift pilots, Lt. Gail Halvorsen, became known as the Chocolate Flyer for dropping chocolate and candies—often using his own handkerchiefs and clothes—to Berlin children.

Yeager Breaks Sound Barrier

843 **1947** Capt. Charles Yeager, USAF, flew the Bell XS-1 rocket plane faster than the speed of sound on October 14. World War II fighters had almost achieved this milestone, but as they approached the speed at which sound travels through the air, the ride became severely rough and the plane hard to control. No one knew whether aircraft would break up or tumble out of control when—and if—that speed was ever achieved. When the rearward blast of exhaust propelled the XS-1 across the sky, the plane reached supersonic speed, and its pilot safely accomplished his mission—proving that the sound barrier was no barrier at all and ushering in a new age of air transportation.

Bell Labs Makes Transistor

844 **1947** Bell Laboratories announced the invention of the miniature transistor in 1947, revolutionizing electronic equipment by replacing the bulky vacuum tube with the first successful amplifying semiconductor device. The transistor—a tiny electronic switch that is far smaller and easier on power than the vacuum tube—was originally devised as a way to amplify and strengthen long-distance telephone signals. It soon found its way into other instruments, bringing transistor radios to remote lands, computers to space, and the Nobel Prize to its

Israel Becomes a Nation

841 **1947** The United Nations separated Palestine into Arab and Jewish states in 1947, granting Jews the homeland they longed for and spurring anguished dissent among Arabs in the region. Made urgent in the wake of the Holocaust, the partition sent many thousands of long-settled Arab Palestinians into refugee camps in Lebanon, Gaza, Jordan, and Syria. When Israel formally declared its independence a year after the UN action, war broke out between Israel and its Arab neighbors—setting the stage for decades of strife over territory and the Jewish nation's right to exist. Syria and Egypt amassed troops against Israel in 1967 and were defeated in the Six Day War; Israel gained territories, including Sinai, West Bank, Gaza, and Golan Heights. Compounding the complexity of relations, Israel's building of settlements in occupied areas made it difficult to exchange territory for peace. Hope for compromise has glimmered: Israel and Egypt signed the Camp David Accords in September 1978; 15 years later, President Bill Clinton stood between Israel's Yitzhak Rabin and the PLO's Yasser Arafat as they shook hands over the Oslo Accords. The Israel-Jordan Treaty of Peace, signed in October 1994, resolved territorial disputes between Israel and Jordan. Nevertheless, territorial conflict and human rights issues persist.

Jewish settler plowing his field in 1947 in what would become Israel

innovators—Walter Brattain, John Bardeen, and William Shockley.

Anne Frank's Diary Published

845 **1947** *The Diary of Anne Frank* was published in 1947, personalizing the horror of the Holocaust in World War II. Anne Frank was born in Frankfurt, Germany, in 1929 and raised in Amsterdam, where her family fled to escape Hitler's regime. When the Nazis began deportations from the city in 1942, the Franks—Anne, her father and mother, and older sister Margot—went into hiding in the back rooms of a warehouse they owned. Four other Jewish people hid with them, and friends smuggled in provisions. In her diary, the teenage Anne described everyday life and occasional dramas in their secret world, her impressions of the tumult outside, and her desire to be a writer. She continued until 1944, when the Gestapo burst in on August 4. Anne died of typhus at Bergen-Belsen concentration camp, never knowing that her dream would come true: The diary, held by a friend and given to Anne's father after the war, has evoked sadness, anger, and hope in millions of readers.

Teresa Called to Poor

846 **1948** Mother Teresa of Calcutta received permission from her superiors in 1948 to leave her teaching position and devote herself to working among the poorest of the poor. Born Agnes Gonxha Bojaxhiu in Skopje, Macedonia, she entered a Roman Catholic convent as a teenager and was eventually sent to teach girls at a school in Calcutta, India. There she received the "call within a call," as she described it, to serve the city's poor. Rome approved her mission, and in 1952 she opened the Nirmal Hriday (Immaculate Heart) Home for Dying Destitutes. The Missionaries of Charity, the order she established in 1950, grew to 3,000 women working in 87 countries. Petite in stature and keen of wit, Mother Teresa spoke out tirelessly for the downtrodden and helpless, often garnering attention from the rich and famous—which she used to generate help for her cause. Mother Teresa received the Nobel Peace Prize in 1979 and died in 1997 at age 87.

■ **FOOTNOTE** Of the 96 Nobel Peace Prizes given from 1901 to 1979, Mother Teresa was only the ninth woman to be so honored. It was a woman, Austrian peace activist Baroness Bertha von Suttner, who inspired Nobel's Peace Prize.

Gandhi Assassinated

847 **1948** Indian independence leader Mohandas K. Gandhi was assassinated in 1948, leaving unanswered the question of one India or two. Called Mahatma ("great soul") by his people, Gandhi led India's quest for independence from Great Britain by means of civil disobedience and passive resistance. In 1930 he organized a 240-mile walk to the sea, where thousands of Indians extracted salt from seawater to protest the oppressive British tax and monopoly on this plentiful natural resource. Championing the poor and living as an ordinary Indian, Gandhi endured arrest and imprisonment for his protests, always acting and reacting with nonviolence. He worked toward equality and tolerance between Islam and Hinduism and was dismayed when the longed-for independence came at great cost: partition of the country into a Muslim Pakistan and a Hindu India, with bloodshed on both sides. The following year, the Father of India

846 | *Catholic faithful holds image of Mother Teresa during Pope Benedict's Munich visit, September 2006.*

CONNECTIONS

Sound Recording Technology
From Edison to MP3

When Thomas Edison invented the phonograph in 1877, he gave the world the first machine that could record and play back sounds. It featured a diaphragm attached to a vibrating stylus that made grooves in a turning, tinfoil-wrapped cylinder. The depth of the grooves made a record of the sound waves; to play them back, the cylinder was spun again, with the stylus just touching the foil. For the first time in human history the human voice could be stored and reproduced.

Subsequent machines would improve upon the sound's fidelity—its likeness to the original. A wax cylinder was the first advance, followed in the late 1880s by a flat disc developed by German inventor Emil Berliner, who called his machine a Gramophone. Edison also began making discs and disc-playing machines, and by about 1915 they had replaced cylinders. The 78-rpm record could hold about 4.5 minutes of sound per side.

Early record players were cranked by hand, and a correct playback could occur only if the record spun at a consistent speed. Electric motors began replacing hand-cranked mechanisms by the late 1800s. The discs themselves evolved from wax (heavy-metal soap with a wax gel) to shellac on an aluminum base to vinyl by the 1940s. Then in 1948 Columbia brought

The long-playing record was supplanted by tapes and CDs.

out its 12-inch long-playing record. With 23 minutes of playing time per side at 33⅓ rpm, the LP soon replaced the 78 as the standard record.

Recording on magnetic tape started with U.S. and German patents in the late 1920s for a tape made by coating a strip of paper with magnetic particles; in the following decade engineers began devising magnetic recording equipment for moviemaking. By the late 1950s and early 1960s recordings in stereo sound on both disc and tape were being marketed to the public. Sales of cassette tapes began edging out those of discs by the early 1980s.

Phonograph records and early tapes relied on analog reproduction—they stored sound waves and then mimicked them on playback. In digital recording, waves are sampled at frequent intervals and then represented on the tape as pulses, almost eliminating pitch distortion and increasing frequency range. Digital tapes slowly began yielding to the longer-lasting compact discs (CDs) after their introduction in 1982.

Research in audio compression technology culminated in 1999 with the debut of portable MP3 players, which allow for the storage of much more data than CDs. Interfaceable with computers, MP3 players are capable of rapidly disseminating large audio files via the Internet.

---

was fatally shot by a Hindu fanatic who objected to Gandhi's attempts to bring peace and tolerance. Gandhi's teachings inspired such leaders as Martin Luther King, Jr., who used the principles of nonviolence throughout the American civil rights movement, and Nelson Mandela, who resisted apartheid in South Africa.

Berle's Show Begins

848 **1948** The debut of the *Texaco Star Theater* on television, with Milton Berle as its star, increased the sale of television sets to people across the country. Millions bought TVs for the first time ever, and plenty of those buyers made the purchase specifically to enjoy "Uncle Miltie" and his outrageous humor. Televisions had become available after World War II, and baseball's World Series was

broadcast in 1947, spurring fans to buy sets that year. The more sets, the more programming; hence *Texaco Star Theater,* a comedy/variety show that debuted on June 8, 1948. Berle's immediate popularity with viewers meant that "Mr. Television" soon became the show's permanent host.

> ■ **FOOTNOTE** The *Milton Berle Show* as it became known, hosted a number of now legendary performers from 1948 to 1956, including Boris Karloff, Kay Thompson, Danny Thomas, Peggy Lee, Elvis Presley, and Jimmy Durante.

LP Records Manufactured

849 **1948** Long-playing (LP) records replaced 78-rpm records when Columbia debuted its 12-inch records—with 23 minutes of playing time on each side—on June 26, 1948. They were made of vinyl, which enabled the new LPs to

hold more grooves and thus more material than before. Philco was enlisted to produce the new turntable needed to play them at the speed of 33⅓ rpm. Seven months later, RCA introduced its seven-inch "single," which became the jukebox standard in the 1950s.

Hoyle Names Big Bang

850 **1949** Scientist and popular author Fred Hoyle made a sarcastic reference to "this big bang idea," on a radio program in 1949, inadvertently naming a theory that negated his own beliefs and changed the way science viewed the creation of the universe. Hoyle conceived of a steady-state universe, unchanging over time. The big bang asserted the opposite. It grew from Albert Einstein's theory of relativity, which hinted that the

Communists Win China

851 **1949** Chinese Communist Party leader Mao Zedong expelled Nationalist Chiang Kai-shek from the mainland in 1949, establishing communist rule over the world's largest nation. Earlier in the century, the two had allied against powerful warlords who carved up China amid a period of political turmoil and social upheaval. But once the warlords were subdued, Chiang had turned on the communists and started a conflict that eventually led to his own expulsion. In 1949, he fled to Taiwan and established a Nationalist government. Mao's style of communism raised China from a failing empire to a strong and independent nation, and his disassociation from the Soviets helped to defuse the Cold War. The regime provided education and health care for the poor and rights and opportunities for women. But other policies failed: The Great Leap Forward diverted workers from

Nationalist Chinese leader Chiang Kai-Shek visiting army air force base in 1945

farm to industry and caused the starvation of 20 million people, and Mao's Cultural Revolution caused irreparable damage to education, history, and millions of lives.

Survivors of the roughly 700 million people who had been relocated to more than 25,000 communes had to try to rebuild their lives, while the hundreds of thousands of "backyard" furnaces had consumed coal needed by the railroad. Mao accepted responsibility for the catastrophe and abdicated his leadership to Liu Shao-chi.

universe had changed. The work of numerous scientists bolstered the big bang idea: Georges Lemaître theorized that all matter had been condensed into a vast body that exploded on an atomic level to create the universe; Edwin Hubble found that galaxies are receding from Earth; George Gamow envisioned a hot big bang and resulting "soup" that cooled and fused into elements; Arno Penzias and Robert Wilson discovered the cosmic radiation echo of the big bang; and Stephen Hawking showed theoretical proof. Through it all, Hoyle's uncomplimentary nickname for the event has stuck.

NATO Formed

852 **1949** In the world's first international partnership against communism, the United States and its European allies formed NATO, the North Atlantic Treaty Organization, as a defense against Soviet aggression. In its first peacetime military alliance since 1778, the U.S. joined with Canada, Great Britain, France, Italy, Denmark, Portugal, Norway, Iceland, Belgium, the Netherlands, and Luxembourg. Leaders saw a strong unified defense as the best strategy to counter the spread of communism. The United Nations Charter authorized the alliance under Article 15, which allows countries to make regional security plans. West Germany was admitted to NATO in 1955, a move that spurred the Soviet Union to form the Warsaw Pact with its Eastern European satellites. Alarmed by the prospect of an armed West Germany at the edge of the Iron Curtain, the Soviets used the situation to put troops in Eastern Europe—as much to control those nations as to defend from the West.

Beauvoir Writes *Second Sex*

853 **1949** Simone de Beauvoir published *The Second Sex* in 1949, heralding a new stage in the development of feminism. In her groundbreaking book, the French existentialist writer and philosopher asserted that men and women are different—yet that is no reason for inequality. She saw several keys to women's self-actualization: Women must realize that they don't need to be like men to be independent, and socialization norms must be changed so that women learn to accept risk and the necessity of risk.

The book was considered scandalous and indecent at the time of publication, but it came to be viewed, particularly in the 1970s, as an expression of feminist strategy for justice and change.

■**FOOTNOTE** Beauvoir, a brilliant intellectual and philosopher, was the youngest ever to pass the rigorous philosophy comprehensive exam in 1929, taking second place to Jean-Paul Sartre.

First Genetic Disease Explained

854 **1949** Linus Pauling uncovered the molecular flaw responsible for sickle-cell anemia, a devastating disease that primarily affects Africans and African Americans. After three years of study, Pauling announced in 1949 that the disorder was molecular in origin—the first time a disease was so characterized. Sickle-cell anemia is caused by a flaw in genetic encoding that leads the hemoglobin molecules in red blood cells to clump into long rods and warp the cells into a crescent shape. The misshapen cells block blood flow, causing pain, organ damage, and often, death. Affected cells have a shorter life span than healthy blood cells and cannot be replaced as fast as they die, leading to anemia.

Hench Perfects Cortisone

855 **1949** Cortisone was developed by Philip Hench and others, leading to treatment for rheumatoid arthritis and other autoimmune diseases.

In rheumatoid arthritis, an autoantibody called rheumatoid factor attacks tissue around the joints, causing severe pain, swelling, and deformity as the bones and connective tissue erode. Hench, a doctor at the Mayo Clinic, noted that the pain of rheumatoid arthritis was alleviated by certain changes in the body—pregnancy, jaundice, infection, and the postsurgical state—and hypothesized that it might come from adrenal hormones.

Hench collaborated with Edward Kendall, who had isolated several hormones from the adrenal cortex, to test Compound E—later called cortisone—on a severely debilitated 29-year-old patient. After four days of injections, she was able to walk. Hench, Kendall, and Tadeus Reichstein shared the Nobel Prize in 1950 for a treatment that helps millions who suffer from this and other disabling conditions.

Hoyle Studies Stars

856 **1949** Scientist Fred Hoyle developed the idea that nuclear reactions in stars could produce all the naturally occurring elements. In the late 1940s, Hoyle and his associates Hermann Bondi and Thomas Gold proposed the theory of the steady-state universe—a universe that does not change at all, throughout time. They accepted that galaxies are receding from Earth, however, and asserted that matter is continually being created, in very small amounts, to fill the widening gap. The elements from helium to iron, they theorized, could be created by nuclear activity within stars, while heavier elements could be created when stars run out of hydrogen, their nuclear fuel.

Hoyle's premise of an unchanging steady-state universe has been disproved, but most scientists endorse his theory that stars could be the source of the elements.

North Korea Invades South

857 **1950** North Korean communist troops, armed by the Soviets, surged across the 38th parallel in 1950 to invade South Korea. A Japanese colony

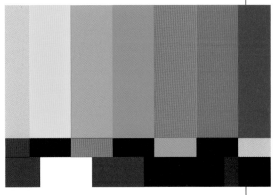

858 | *TV test pattern run during absence of programming on early analog TVs*

before the end of World War II, Korea had been split into communist and noncommunist nations in 1945 by the U.S. and Soviet Union. The Cold War turned hot as the North Koreans sought to unify the two countries under communist leadership. Within days of the invasion, President Harry S. Truman mobilized American ground troops under a UN mandate to protect South Korea. They pushed back the enemy, but their commander, Gen. Douglas MacArthur, was not satisfied with the settlement favored by Truman; he wanted nothing less than a World War II-style defeat. As he pushed on, North Korea's ally China entered the fray—killing thousands of American troops and driving the survivors south of the 38th parallel. Truman fired MacArthur, the conflict ended in stalemate, and a potentially greater crisis—war with China—was averted. Besides stabilizing the antagonistic powers in the region, Truman's firing of MacArthur—a general revered for his role during World War II—ended the tension between the headstrong general and the White House and reinforced one of the principles of the American Constitution: the subordination of even a five-star general to the civilian President.

Americans Watch Color TV

858 **1951** Color television was introduced in the United States in 1951. Devised by Peter Goldmark of CBS, the system was based on an earlier one demonstrated by British engineer John L. Baird in London. CBS used Goldmark's

857 | *In Hagaru-ri, Korea, U.S. Marines advance toward bomb set off to flush out enemy, December 1950.*

invention to make color broadcasts in June 1951. However, it did not catch on: While 10.5 million televisions sets had been sold in the U.S. by that time, virtually none of them were color—and Goldmark's innovation was short-lived. Meanwhile, RCA built a new system using shadow mask CRT technology and made a successful color broadcast in 1953. The first nationwide color broadcast, of the Tournament of Roses Parade, beamed coast to coast on January 1, 1954. Not until 1972, though, when the cost came down, did Americans buy more color than black-and-white TV sets.

> ■ **FOOTNOTE** In 1954, the first color television sets were manufactured by Westinghouse, RCA, GE, and Sylvania and all sold for more than $1,000. By 1955, larger screens were available for $800 to $900.

Nuclear Power Plant Opens

859 **1951** A nuclear powered reactor was used to generate electricity in 1951, when the lights in a plant built in Idaho by the federal Atomic Energy Commission were powered by nuclear fission. This process made more plutonium, a highly fissionable element, from less uranium, an element of limited quantity. Civilian nuclear power came about as a result of submarine research, an application in which a clean and long-lasting fuel was ideal. In nuclear fission, uranium atoms are split in a chain reaction that releases huge quantities of energy. The reaction produces heat, which is generally used to boil

water, with the resulting steam turning turbines to generate electricity. The process does not produce greenhouse gases. At the time of its debut, civilian nuclear power was the hope of the future—but plants proved expensive to build and maintain, and disposal of radioactive waste was problematic. Even so, nuclear fission produces about one-sixth of the world's power today.

Pacemaker Aids Heart

860 **1952** The first artificial pacemaker, invented in 1952 by Harvard's Paul Zoll, sent up to 150 volts to the heart through electrodes on the chest and, while lifesaving, left painful burns on the skin. In 1957, cardiologist C. Walton Lillehei hooked wires directly to the patient's heart, and electrical engineer Earl Bakken later developed a portable power source— a transistor box that could hang on the patient's belt. Today's artificial pacemakers are implanted in the chest and powered by batteries. They issue tiny painless electronic signals to regulate the heart's pumping.

> ■ **FOOTNOTE** Today's pacemakers are capable of sophisticated monitoring and recording, adjusting the heart rate according to the wearer's activity, as well as storing performance data and patient history.

H-Bomb Tested

861 **1952** Edward Teller and others developed the hydrogen bomb in 1952, raising the fear of a nuclear holocaust and increasing the heat in the Cold War. Many scientists had opposed this fearsome weapon on moral and practical grounds, while other experts, including members of the U.S. Cabinet, warned of disaster if the Soviets developed it first. Debating the question, President Truman asked his advisers, "Can the Russians do it?" When the answer was affirmative, Truman saw no other choice, and the bomb was built. With energy equivalent to 10 million tons of TNT—vastly more powerful than the World War II atomic bombs—the 65-ton thermonuclear device got its destructive power from fusing the nuclei of light atoms. When tested on November 1, 1952, the

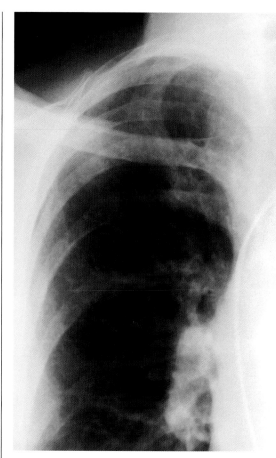

860 | *X-ray of a chest, showing spine, ribs, and implanted pacemaker*

bomb nearly obliterated a small South Pacific island, leaving a crater 2 miles wide. The U.S.S.R. soon followed, testing its own thermonuclear bomb and placing the two nations in a stable condition of armed truce.

Salk Tests Polio Vaccine

862 **1952** Jonas Salk, physician at the University of Pittsburgh, Pennsylvania, conducted test inoculations of children against polio in the early 1950s. He used "killed" inactivated strains of three viruses known to cause this crippling disease. During that era, many biologists thought that only live virus could trigger the human immune system to function against polio, yet tests of a live vaccine had led to several deaths. When Salk developed his killed-virus vaccine, he first inoculated himself to be sure of its safety. He then conducted field trials, which culminated in government approval and wide

861 | *Mushroom cloud of the first hydrogen bomb, set off in the Marshall Islands in 1952*

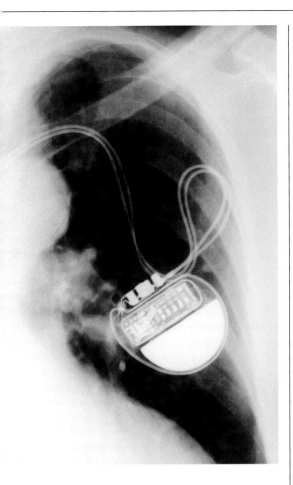

distribution in 1955 of this safe and effective vaccine. Tens of thousands were spared the debilitating effects of polio, which struck in warm weather and caused paralysis and death. By 1961, cases had dropped drastically; by 1995, the disease was thought to have been eradicated from the Western Hermisphere. Meanwhile, Albert Sabin was working to create a safe formulation using live weakened virus, and his new oral vaccine—famously administered in sugar cubes—later edged out Salk's as the popular choice.

Organ Transplants Tried

863 **1953** Called the father of transplantation biology, Peter Medwar made groundbreaking discoveries on tissue culture and nerve regeneration. During World War II, he helped treat a pilot for severe burns. The pilot's body rejected the donor tissue. Medawar found that animals exposed to foreign tissue while very young— at the fetal or neonatal stage—do not reject grafted tissue. He then found that such tolerance could be artificially reproduced.

■ **FOOTNOTE** The 1984 National OrganTransplant Act specified a national Organ Procurement and Transplantation Network to coordinate the donation—not sale—of healthy organs to needy recipients.

Escher Makes Art

864 **1953** In 1953 Dutch graphic artist M. C. Escher created "Relativity," one of his most famous images, along with other surrealistic woodcuts and lithographs. Mathematicians and scientists especially appreciated Escher's use of polyhedra and geometric distortions in stark yet complex creations. His images seemed to reflect the chaotic unpredictability and worlds within worlds that characterized the revolutionary scientific theories taking hold during the mid-20th century. Claiming that his art did not "say" anything, Escher made images that were, in his words, "results of a fascinating play of thoughts." He often experimented with light, shadow, and perspective to create imaginary situations that at first glance seem realistic but upon closer examination turn out to be physical impossibilities or optical illusions.

Clues to Life Found

865 **1953** Stanley Miller and Harold Urey made startling discoveries in 1953 about the possible origins of life on Earth, leading to further studies about our planet's beginnings. Using a closed and sterilized glass container, the two scientists attempted to reproduce the conditions of primeval Earth by circulating hydrogen, ammonia, and methane—the components of the earliest atmosphere—through water that represented the ocean. Arcs of electricity were passed through the gases to simulate lightning. After the experiment ran for one week, the resulting "soup" was analyzed. It contained fatty acids, urea, and four amino acids—the building blocks of DNA. Later the experiment was varied, with hot silica used to simulate lava flowing into the ocean and ultraviolet radiation to represent the sun shining on a young Earth with little atmospheric protection. Similar results were observed, prompting further theories and research about the processes at work during the first moments of life on our planet.

Everest Summited

866 **1953** Edmund Hillary and Tenzing Norgay reached the summit of Mount Everest, the world's highest mountain, on May 29, 1953. The New Zealand beekeeper and his Sherpa guide were members of British Brigadier Sir John Hunt's expedition, the eighth climbing party to attempt Everest since Tibet granted access to outsiders in 1921. They faced daunting odds: While Everest is not the coldest, windiest, or most technically difficult peak on Earth, its extreme altitude combines with these factors to create a formidable climb. In air that contains only one-third the

FIRST PERSON

Sir Edmund Hillary

NATIONAL GEOGRAPHIC, JULY 1954

Suddenly I realize that the ridge ahead doesn't slope up, but down. I look quickly to my right. There, just above me, is a softly rounded, snow-covered little bump about as big as a haystack.

The summit.

One last question concerns me: is the top itself just a large, delicately poised cornice? If it is, someone else can have the honor of stepping on it.

I cut my way cautiously up the next few feet, probing ahead with my pick. The snow is solid, firmly packed. We stagger up the final stretch. We are there. Nothing above us, a world below.

I feel no great elation at first, just relief and a sense of wonder.

Then I turn to Tenzing and shake his hand. Even through the snow glasses, the ice-encrusted mask, the knitted helmet, I can see that happy, flashing smile.

He throws his arms around my shoulders, and we thump each other, and there is very little we can say or need to say.

1946-PRESENT | Modern Age

Double Helix Described

867 **1953** British physicist Francis Crick and American biologist James Watson mapped the deoxyribonucleic acid (DNA) molecular basis of heredity in 1953, explaining for the first time the physical structure and information-carrying process

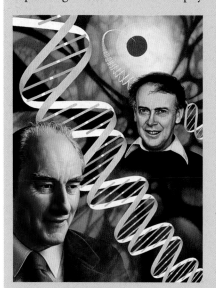

James Watson and Francis Crick explained the nature and behavior of DNA.

of the genetic code. Scientists knew that cells carried genes and that DNA determined genetic traits, but the process of "how" was a mystery. Crick and Watson hypothesized about the structure of DNA and confirmed their ideas with images of DNA molecules made by British scientists using the new technique of x-ray crystallography, which allowed the three-dimensional structure to be viewed. Crick and Watson then created a model from beads, wire, and cardboard that demonstrated how genes replicate and carry information during cell division: The ladderlike double-helical structure of the DNA molecule "unzips" to become the blueprint for new cells. Tangled like yarn and constantly twisting within the nucleus of each cell, long strands of DNA hold a set of biochemical instructions, encoded in sequences of proteins, for building the entire body.

British scientist Rosalind Franklin made great leaps in the understanding of DNA by using x-rays to unlock its finite structure. Some believe that had she lived she, too, would have shared the Nobel Prize for DNA's discovery.

amount of oxygen found at sea level, human vision blurs and the limbs become unbearably heavy. By the time of Hillary's attempt, at least 16 people had perished trying to summit Everest. Hunt's first assault team had reached 28,700 feet, but when their oxygen failed, Hillary and Tenzing took over and achieved the 29,028-foot summit. Upon their arrival back at base, the plainspeaking Hillary announced, "Well, we knocked the [expletive] off."

Heart-Lung Machine Built

868 **1953** John Gibbon, a Boston surgeon, unveiled a heart-lung machine in 1953 that enabled doctors to maintain blood circulation and oxygenation during cardiac surgery, so that the patient's own heart could be stilled and repaired. Gibbon had watched helplessly as a woman died during the six and a half

minutes it took for a blood clot to be removed from her lung, anguishing that if only he could have removed some of her blood and oxygenated it during that short time, the patient probably would have lived. Galvanized by the experience, Dr. Gibbon and his wife spent 20 years developing the first machine to take over the function of the heart and lungs. In 1953, he used it to implement a successful procedure on the heart of a teenage girl. Today the heart-lung machine is essential during routine surgeries to repair congenital holes in the heart wall and other conditions.

Dien Bien Phu

869 **1953** The Battle of Dien Bien Phu (1953-54) ended the French colonial experience in Southeast Asia. Trying to hold onto their colony in Vietnam, French commanders of *la guerre sale* (the

dirty war) planned to intimidate the communist Viet Minh forces with a show of military might. Instead, the Viet Minh—spearheaded by communist leader for independence Ho Chi Minh and backed by the Soviets and Chinese—surrounded the French in a valley near the Laotian border and began a two-month siege. France surrendered in 1954 and signed the Geneva Treaty, which split Vietnam into a northern zone controlled by the communists and a southern zone occupied by the French—who put anticommunist Vietnamese forces in charge. According to the Geneva agreement, an election would be held in 1956 to reunite the country under one leader. However, fearing that the charismatic Ho Chi Minh would win, the South Vietnamese leader canceled the election with U.S. approval. With that development, American involvement in Vietnam increased.

■ FOOTNOTE In 1976, Saigon, the former capital of South Vietnam and location of U.S. headquarters during the Vietnam War, was renamed Ho Chi Minh City in honor of the Vietnamese ruler.

Drugs Aid Psychiatry

870 **1954** Drugs were introduced to treat mental illnesses, breaking with protocols such as electroconvulsive therapy, lobotomy, and, in some cases, institutionalization. In the intricate workings of the brain, tiny amounts of chemicals—called neurotransmitters—cross gaps between cells and latch on to receptors, allowing cells to communicate with one another. Brain disorders can result from the subtlest errors in timing, intensity, or amount of chemicals in these interactions. In the 1950s, researchers began developing drugs that treated mental illnesses by influencing neurotransmitter activity. Thorazine, approved by the Food and Drug Administration in 1954, was a powerful antipsychotic that effectively controlled the symptoms of psychosis by inducing a detached state in patients. Librium, introduced in 1960, and its milder and more effective cousin Valium, introduced in

1963, both affected neurotransmitter sites, but were found to be addictive. A newer class, the selective serotonin reuptake inhibitors, are now the choice for a variety of conditions. Improved medications continue to be developed as scientists unlock the secrets of brain chemistry.

Accelerator Runs

871 **1954** The Organisation Européen pour la Recherche Nucléaire (European Organization for Nuclear Research), commonly known as CERN, was established by convention on September 29, 1954. At four miles long, it is the world's largest particle physics laboratory, situated near Geneva on the border of France and Switzerland. CERN provides the tools—enormous vacuum tubes called particle accelerators—for scientists to probe the structure of the atom. By accelerating particles almost to the speed of light and firing protons at the nuclei of atoms, physicists attempt to re-create states and forms of matter that may have existed only in the seconds after the big bang. In 2000, CERN made a new state of matter, quark-gluon plasma. Particle research has yielded new theories and understanding about the beginnings of our universe and important developments in cancer therapy, imaging, and manufacturing. The organization also created the first version of the World Wide Web in 1990.

■ **FOOTNOTE** CERN has been the site of a number of Nobel Prize-winning discoveries, such as physicist Georges Charpak's multiwire proportional chamber, and physicists Carlo Rubbia and Simon van der Meer's W and Z particles.

Elvis Rocks

872 **1954** On July 5, 1954, a shy but swaggering young truck driver recorded the song "That's All Right Mama" in Memphis, Tennessee—launching the career that made Elvis Presley one of the first rock-and-roll performers and the biggest star in the universe of popular music. Presley's sound was influenced by the rhythms of African-American gospel, soul, and blues—a sound that was crossing over to white radio stations because of

teen influence. His career also received a boost from the day's new technology: transistor radios, portable record players, television (a benchmark of Presley's career was his appearance on *The Ed Sullivan Show*), and car radios—which allowed teenagers to enjoy their music away from parental ears. His singing voice was melodious by any standard, and his smoldering good looks and controversial gyrations completed the package, helping to make Elvis a worldwide sensation. "The King" recorded more than 150 hit songs in his

23-year reign, and legions of fans mourned his passing in 1977.

■ **FOOTNOTE** The sideburned, sequined crooner also starred in 33 movies, including *Love Me Tender* and *Jailhouse Rock*. His Graceland estate in Memphis still attracts mourners, especially on the anniversary of his death.

Transistors Shrink

873 **1954** Gordon Teal developed a silicon-based transistor in 1954, making it possible for computers to handle large numbers of computations faster

872 | *Elvis Presley, at about age 20, flashes a smile as he strums his 12-string guitar.*

on small chips. In previous employment at Bell Labs, Teal had improved methods of growing pure germanium crystals for transistors. It was a slow process, and germanium transistors did not work well when circuits heated up because there were too many free electrons for proper functioning.

But when Teal later joined Texas Instruments as director of research, his experience with germanium served him well: He began working with silicon, the next element on the periodic table and the second most common element found in Earth's crust, and developed a transistor that performed consistently. In May 1954, he stunned a conference of radio engineers with his dramatic presentation of the world's first silicon transistor, which TI had already begun producing—making Texas Instuments an electronics giant and silicon the foundation of a high-tech revolution.

874 | *James Dean, Rebel Without a Cause, 1955*

Rebels On-Screen

874 **1955** *Rebel Without a Cause,* starring James Dean, revealed the torments of the youth culture emerging in America in the 1950s. Starring James Dean, Natalie Wood, and Sal Mineo, the visually and thematically notable film told the story of troubled teenagers growing up in Los Angeles, rebelling against a conformist, hypocritical world. It was based on a case from the 1944 book *Rebel Without a Cause: The Story of a Criminal Psychopath,* by Dr. Robert Lindner. Like some of the subsequent teen-angst movies it would inspire, *Rebel's* story followed classical lines—mirroring the conflict with parents, climactic test, and final tragedy of Shakespearean plots.

> ■ **FOOTNOTE** All three stars of Rebel died tragic deaths. Dean died in a head-on collision (just two hours after being pulled over for speeding) at the age of 24; Wood drowned at age 43; Mineo was murdered at age 37.

Parks Stays Seated

875 **1955** Rosa Parks refused to give up her seat on a bus to a white man on December 1, 1955. Exhausted from a long day's work in Montgomery, Alabama, the African-American seamstress waited for an uncrowded bus so that she could sit down. She took a seat in the black section near the back. When the bus filled, the driver ordered the first black row emptied so a white man could sit. Parks was the only person who refused to stand. Her arrest and conviction under state segregation laws spurred the black community to boycott the Montgomery bus system. A young minister, Martin Luther King, Jr., organized carpools so people could get to work as the protest continued. It reached a monumental conclusion in 1956: The U.S. Supreme Court overturned Parks's conviction and ruled the segregation of public transportation to be unconstitutional. This led to the Civil Rights Act, which criminalized segregation in nearly every aspect of American life.

Monroe Bares Legs

876 **1955** In 1954, Marilyn Monroe jetted to New York to film exteriors for *The Seven Year Itch*. When she walked onto a subway grate, her white halter dress billowed—and the night erupted with the repercussions of that playfully risqué moment. The character played by Monroe's costar, Tom Ewell, became smitten according to script. Photographers snapped from every angle, capturing iconic images that would continue to sell half a century later—and that the League of Decency, in 1955, would force theaters to remove from public display. The actress's husband, baseball star Joe DiMaggio, recoiled in horror at the sight of his wife so revealed. The couple screamed and fought that night, and their marriage ended soon after—a union of just 274 days. Monroe's star continued to rise, until it glimmered out one night in 1962.

First Nightly News

877 **1956** Chet Huntley and David Brinkley were teamed as news anchors to cover the American political conventions of 1956, a pairing that created the template for political and news coverage for other networks. Their convention coverage was well received, and on October 9, 1956, they replaced NBC's "Camel News Caravan"—a 15-minute news program supplied with footage from 50 cameramen around the world and anchored by legendary broadcaster John Cameron Swayze. It was a tough act to follow, but Huntley's straightforward style and Brinkley's wit won over the viewers. The first news team was one of the most popular in television history, seen by as many as 20 million viewers each night and winning eight Emmy Awards. During the 1964 Democratic National Convention they drew 84 percent of U.S. viewers. Huntley retired in 1970, ending his last report with "there will be better and happier news some day if we work at it!" The team format they perfected is an enduring standard in television news.

■ **FOOTNOTE** At the close of every Huntley-Brinkley report, Huntley and Brinkley delivered what became a well-known ending line: "Good night, Chet." "Good night, David." "And good night for NBC News."

Discovery of mRNA

878 **1956** Messenger RNA (mRNA) was identified in the early 1960s, establishing a fundamental principle of molecular genetics. In living cells, the nucleus holds DNA—the genetic material that contains the code for protein-making. When a protein is needed, a ladder-like strand of DNA unzips to reveal a set of instructions. However, DNA is locked in the nucleus. How, scientists wondered, did the instructions get from the DNA out to the protein-building structures known as ribosomes, which are in the cell's cytoplasm? The answer was mRNA. When DNA unzips, a "working copy"—mRNA—is created to carry the instructions. It is transported out of the nucleus to the ribosomes, which read the protein

876 | *Marilyn Monroe's dress billows up over subway grate while she films* The Seven Year Itch, *1954.*

code and gather amino acids to build proteins. This process was observed at Oak Ridge National Laboratory in 1956, and a multinational cadre of scientists later named mRNA and advanced the research. Knowledge of mRNA and its role in the DNA transcription process led to gains in diagnostic medicine, gene therapy, and other fields.

Interferon Discovered

879 **1957** Alick Isaacs and Jean Lindenmann discovered interferon, a substance with promise for fighting cancer, in 1957. Doctors had observed that patients suffering a viral infection rarely came down simultaneously with another one. Isaacs and Lindenmann, working at London's National Institute for Medical Research, investigated this "viral interference" by experimenting with the membranes found inside chicken eggshells. They soaked membranes in a nutrient solution and exposed them to an influenza virus. When other viruses were added, the membranes' cells resisted infection. Further, when new membranes were placed in the same solution, they too resisted infection through contact with the

875 More Details on Rosa Parks

Rosa Parks, speaking of her defiant act aboard a Montgomery, Alabama, bus, later said, "All I was trying to do was get home from work." And yet it was this single, ordinary protest that ignited the civil rights movement in the United States, launching the 381-day Montgomery bus boycott and establishing Martin Luther King, Jr., as the movement's national leader. At her funeral, held November 2, 2005, in Detroit, more than 4,000 mourners gathered to celebrate her life and achievement; her casket was then moved to Washington, D.C., where she became the first woman in U.S. history to lie in honor in the Capitol Rotunda. Celebrities, politicians, heads of state, and religious leaders spoke words on her behalf.

Parks was 42 years old and working as a tailor's assistant at a department store when she refused to surrender her seat to a white man. In the tense aftermath, Parks and her husband both lost their jobs, and an onslaught of harassment and death threats forced them to flee to Detroit. Meanwhile, around the country, black Americans launched scores of Parks-inspired, nonviolent protests. They staged sit-ins in white eateries and swim-ins in white public swimming pools. Most famously, in 1960, four black college students in Greensboro, North Carolina, sat down at a white-only Woolworth's lunch counter and refused to leave, even though they were denied service. They stayed from opening to close for five days, joined by hundreds of other protesters, and their act launched a black student movement whose participation grew into the thousands.

> "All I was trying to do was get home from work."
>
> —**Rosa Parks**

These nonviolent protests led to the voluntary desegregation of public spaces all over the South, gaining sympathy from white members of the community and from business owners worried about revenue. Even more significantly, they turned the cause for civil rights into a pressing moral issue. It was no longer simply the law that was at stake; it was human dignity. And the peaceful faces of Rosa Parks, of black college students sitting calmly at white lunch counters, inspired decades of dramatic change.

Rosa Parks riding bus in Montgomery, Alabama, where she refused to give up her seat to a white man, becoming "mother of the civil rights movement"

Sputnik Launched

880 **1957** The Soviet Union placed the first artificial satellite in orbit around Earth in 1957. Boosted into space by an intercontinental ballistic missile, Sputnik 1 ("traveling companion") weighed less than 200 pounds and was no larger

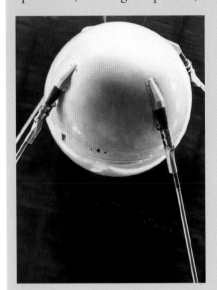

Russia's first satellite, Sputnik 1, the size of a basketball, weighed less than 200 pounds.

than a basketball. When news of its launch reached the United States, pandemonium ensued. This was the first event of the space race, and the prestige of victory—not to mention demonstration of the capacity to hit a distant target—went to the Soviets. Anxieties intensified when, just a month after Sputnik, the Russians launched Sputnik 2. The original Sputnik could carry 3.5 pounds, while Sputnik 2 could carry more, plus its canine passenger, a medium-size dog named Laika. The vessel was not designed to return, prompting protest from animal rights supporters. Satellite development in the United States had been delayed by disagreement in the Eisenhower Administration regarding which U.S. military branch should spearhead the project. The Navy took the lead until its satellite exploded on the launch pad; this "Kaputnik" resulted in the project reverting to the Army, where Wernher von Braun had a satellite almost ready. On January 31, 1958, Explorer 1 was successfully launched. The United States was playing catch-up in the space race and would continue to do so for some time.

antiviral chemical that stayed in the solution. The first virus had stimulated the cells to produce interferon—an anti-infective agent that kept other viruses from invading the cell. It was later discovered that the cells of many organs make interferons and that human cells secrete them. Inventor and scientist Sidney Pestka later developed methods to isolate and clone interferons for use in numerous medications.

Synthesis of RNA and DNA

881 **1957** During the 1950s, after Crick and Watson revealed the double helix, scientists learned more about ribonucleic acid (RNA) and deoxyribonucleic acid (DNA), the components of heredity DNA. Severo Ochoa, by working with enzymes to make them build up nucleic acids, created a synthetic form of RNA. His student Arthur Kornberg became the first to synthesize DNA molecules in a test tube.

Passengers Jet Across Atlantic

882 **1958** The first transatlantic passenger jet made its debut in 1958. Jet engines actually were first built and tested in the 1930s. England and Germany furthered the technology during World War II, but developments came too late to have much impact on aerial fighting and bombardment. However, this legacy of wartime would have a profound influence on travel for decades to come. On October 4, 1958, British Overseas Airways Corporation (BOAC) began operating the world's first transatlantic passenger jet service, flying between New York and London and completing in six hours a run that took nine in a propeller plane. Later that month, Pan American World Airways flew its Boeing 707 to Paris. The smooth start of passenger jet service gave a boost to the popularity of transatlantic travel, leading to a new social distinction for the well-heeled who could afford to fly to Europe: They became known as the Jet Set.

De Gaulle Leads France

883 **1958** Charles de Gaulle, a French hero of World War II, returned to power in France in 1958 and settled a colonial crisis. Almost the only member of the French government to resist the Nazis, General de Gaulle had organized the Free French forces during World War II and headed the postwar provisional government. In the 1950s, France was involved in a bloody struggle with its colony in Algeria. Guerrillas had attacked government facilities and urged Algerian Muslims to revolt against French rule. Many French citizens did not want to pay for a war—as the military and other officials favored—to hold onto a colony that had become a strain. Elected as president in large part due to his opposition to such a war, de Gaulle presented a new constitution that transferred decisive power from Parliament to the executive branch. As president, he allowed Algeria to leave French control and pursue independence, which was achieved on July 5, 1962. De Gaulle served as president of France until 1969.

Europe's Common Market

884 **1958** The European Economic Community (EEC), also called the Common Market, was established in 1957 to an effort to give European nations economic clout equal to that of the United States and the Soviet Union.

Forming the alliance were France, West Germany, Italy, Holland, and Belgium, in the hope that an economically stronger Europe could more effectively ward off global depression and, potentially, another world war. They eliminated trade barriers within the alliance and established a tariff for imported goods from outside the bloc. Within ten years, the members were trading four times as much as before. As time went on and political changes occurred, more countries joined the Common Market and other economic alliances came into being: In 1967, the Common Market merged with other groups to form the European Community, and three decades later, the 12-nation European Union was established, proving a strong competitor on the world economic scene.

883 | *Charles de Gaulle, ca 1942*

Lasers Light Up

885 **1958** The optical laser—a word created as an acronym for light amplification by stimulated emission of radiation—was theorized in 1958 and demonstrated in 1960 by physicist Theodore Maiman. Whereas a lightbulb converts energy into light of different wavelengths (colors) that spread in every direction, a laser converts energy into a pure wavelength in a narrow beam.

To build his laser, Maiman flashed a photographer's strobe through a little cylinder of ruby, creating pulses of pure red light packed with energy. With a precisely focused beam that can make a surface hotter than the sun, the laser lent itself to a variety of applications, from surgery to steel cutting.

Charles Townes had discovered the maser (microwave amplification by stimulated emission of radiation) in 1953; since it worked according to a similar principle, he claimed the patent for the laser.

■ **FOOTNOTE** Today lasers are used to measure distances in space, drill holes in diamonds, sense air pollution, cut or melt metal, determine movement of tectonic plates, transmit data, play DVDs, and conduct surgery.

Luna Probes Moon

886 **1959** The first successful space probe, Luna 1, passed near the moon in 1959. The Luna series was developed by the Soviet Union for lunar exploration, and on numerous missions over the next 17 years, the increasingly sophisticated probes successfully photographed, orbited, landed on, captured television images of, and collected samples from the moon. Luna 3 produced the first photographs of the far side of the moon.

First Xerox Copies

887 **1959** The first widely used commercial copy machine came on the market in 1959, introduced by the company that would become Xerox. Joseph C. Wilson of the Haloid Company had invested in a technology known

887 | *An office worker makes photocopies on a "compact copier" in 1965.*

as xerography ("dry writing") that made photographic copies on plain paper rather than expensive coated paper. Haloid introduced a xerographic machine in 1949, but it was slow, expensive, and messy. By 1959 the company had developed a better model, calling it the 914 xerographic copier for the largest size of paper it accommodated: 9 x 14 inches. Two years later, Haloid took the new name Xerox to reflect its groundbreaking technology. The company also made an electronic facsimile machine in 1966, advancing a concept more than a century old: A fax precursor was used for telegraphy in 1856, and a later device, the Belinograph, converted light into electric impulses that were read and printed out by a receiver—the basis of the Xerox fax machine and those in use today.

Castro Wins Cuba

888 **1959** On February 16, the 32-year-old Fidel Castro was sworn in as Cuba's prime minister in the Presidential Palace's cabinet room in Havana. This marked the culmination of years of leading resistance movements against the former president and military ruler, Fulgeneio Batista. His previous attempts to overthrow the government both ended badly. But with this victory, Castro cemented his authority and reforms in Cuba. He antagonized the U.S. until it levied an embargo, which, coupled with his style of rule, has impoverished the country and his people.

African Nations Form

889 **1960** Seventeen former European colonies became independent nations in what would be known as the Year of Africa—1960. Nigeria achieved independence from Great Britain, and the nation of Somalia was created from former British and Italian territories. Separating from France in 1960 were Niger, Mauritania, Mali, Senegal, Chad, Ivory Coast, Togo, Benin, Burkina Faso, Cameroon, Gabon, the Central African Republic, and Madagascar; by 1962, when Algeria won independence after an eight-year rebellion, the French colonial empire was virtually gone. Also in 1960, Jomo Kenyatta became president of the Kenya African National Union and helped negotiate a new constitution with Britain for his nation, which soon gained its independence. Soon after the Belgian Congo became the Republic of the Congo in 1960, a power struggle broke out between foreign entities. The American CIA-backed Col. Joseph Mobutu, who led a successful coup against Soviet KGB-supported Prime Minister Patrice Lumumba—was later murdered.

■ **FOOTNOTE** Despite progress, many African nations are still undeveloped, and many regions of the continent are beset by poverty, disease, famine, illiteracy, and ethnic, political, and tribal warfare.

Goodall Joins Chimps

890 **1960** Jane Goodall went into the African bush to study the chimpanzee population in 1960, and soon revealed the surprising discovery that humans were not the only tool users on the planet. In almost half a century among the chimps, Goodall created the Gombe Stream Research Centre in Tanzania and made groundbreaking discoveries about chimpanzee behavior. She documented chimps' ability to make and use tools, as evidenced by "fishing" for termites with a sharpened stick. Goodall also brought to world attention the chimps' use of facial gestures, body language, and vocalizations to communicate, and their dark turns toward murder and war. Groundbreaking

paleoanthropologist Louis Leakey encouraged Goodall's research, considering the study of primates to be important to the understanding of early man. Several other Leakey protégés conducted important work: anthropologist Biruté Galdikas, who observed orangutans; and Dian Fossey, who was murdered in Rwanda like so many of the mountain gorillas she tried to protect. Goodall's legacy lives on in her Jane Goodall Institute, which promotes and helps fund the work she began.

■ **FOOTNOTE** Fifi, a chimp Goodall studied when she first set up the Gombe Stream Research Center, was 46 years old when she disappeared in 2004. Her descendants make up more than a quarter of the center's population.

890 | *A chimp, familiar with Jane Goodall after her five years' work in Tanzania, holds her hand.*

Birth Control on Sale

891 **1960** Margaret Sanger coordinated the research and funding necessary to create the first human birth control pill, which was introduced in 1960. During an era when United States law prohibited the teaching or distribution of information about birth control, Sanger fought to gain women's reproductive control of their own bodies—a freedom she considered more empowering than the vote. Sanger opened clinics, founded the American Birth Control League in 1921, and later launched Planned Parenthood. Sensing that the public was ready, she enlisted respectable middle-class women and male doctors to support birth control—rather than the more radical elements who previously had been its main proponents. Sanger located biologist Gregory Goodwin Pincus and other scientists who would create the birth control pill, and convinced heiress Katherine McCormick to fund the work. The team produced a formulation of synthetic progesterone and mestranol that prevented ovulation. Within three years of its debut, 2.3 million women were on the pill.

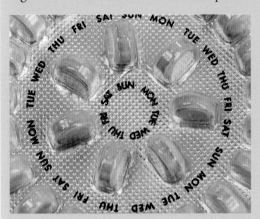

Birth control pills in plastic packaging on card, with weekdays marked next to each

Psycho Screened

892 **1960** *Psycho,* directed by Alfred Hitchcock and starring Anthony Perkins and Janet Leigh, used an Oedipal murder plot to become one of the century's top horror films, influencing a succession of later movies. But no lurid imitator could match the thematic complexity and masterful editing of the 1960 gothic thriller. Hitchcock used the film crew from his television show to make the black-and-white classic, which was his first horror feature.

Cosmonaut Orbits

893 **1961** Soviet cosmonaut Yuri Gagarin became the first human to orbit Earth, prompting U.S. President John F. Kennedy to announce a space program with an aggressive schedule.

Gagarin, a 27-year-old lieutenant in the Soviet Air Force, soared skyward in Vostok 1 on April 12, 1961. Gagarin claimed to feel no ill effects of weightlessness during the 108-minute event, in which he orbited Earth at altitudes of 109 to 188 miles. After a radio-controlled reentry, he ejected and parachuted to a safe landing.

Gagarin's flight shook the world and intensified the space race. The Soviet cosmonaut would not venture into space again: He died in the 1968 crash of a MiG-15 jet while training for a mission.

Amnesty International Founded

894 **1961** Amnesty International, an organization for the protection of human rights, was founded in 1961 by British lawyer Peter Benenson. He set out to gain amnesty for prisoners of conscience—nonviolent detainees arrested because of their convictions, race, faith, or ethnicity. Today Amnesty International has more than two million members and supporters in 150 countries and regions. The organization received the Nobel Peace Prize in 1977.

Standoff Over Cuba

895 **1962** The Cuban missile crisis brought the world perilously close to nuclear warfare.

On October 14, 1962, U-2 spy planes photographed Soviet missile sites in Cuba that targeted the United States. Soviet premier Nikita Khrushchev was installing the weapons to counter U.S. missiles in Turkey, as well as to protect its communist ally Cuba—which the previous year had repelled a U.S.-backed invasion attempt.

President John F. Kennedy demanded removal of the warheads and put up a naval blockade, at first keeping the situation secret from the American public. When he acknowledged the threat, frightened citizens stocked bomb shelters and schools held drills in which children practiced diving under their desks. Kennedy prepared to bomb the sites; Khrushchev threatened retaliation. Finally, the Soviets agreed to remove the sites in exchange for assurances that the U.S. would withdraw its missiles from Turkey and cease efforts to overthrow Cuban dictator Fidel Castro. After two weeks of suspense, the situation cooled.

FOOTNOTE Since Castro instituted communism in Cuba—the first communist state in the Western Hemisphere—more than one million Cubans have immigrated to the U.S. in search of economic and personal freedoms.

Glass Made in Sheets

896 **1962** The Pilkington Company invented a new method of producing glass, making possible very large, flat panes for skyscrapers, vehicles, and other purposes. Glassmaker Alastair Pilkington developed a method in which molten glass was floated in a bath of molten tin, spreading out and moving down a long "float line" until it cooled into an exceedingly pure, wide, flat ribbon of glass. The sheets could be made to order regarding dimensions, thickness, tint, and coating, with a high level of optical precision and a brilliant shine on both sides. His company received the first license for the process in 1962. Most of today's flat glass is float glass.

1946-PRESENT | Modern Age

John F. Kennedy

SPEECH, JUNE 26, 1963

I want to say on behalf of my countrymen ... that they take the greatest pride that they have been able to share with you, even from a distance the story of the last eighteen years....

While the wall is the most obvious and vivid demonstration of the failures of the Communist system, all the world can see we take no satisfaction in it, for it is ... an offence not only against history, but an offence against humanity, separating families, dividing husbands and wives and brothers and sisters and dividing a people who wish to be joined together.

What is true of this city is true of Germany. Real lasting peace in Europe can never be assured as long as one German out of four is denied the elementary right ... to make a free choice.

In eighteen years of peace and good faith this generation of Germans has earned the right to be free, including the right to unite their families and their nation in lasting peace with goodwill to all people.

You live in a defended island of freedom, but your life is part of the main. So let me ask you as I close, to lift your eyes beyond the dangers of today to the hopes of tomorrow, beyond the freedom merely of this city of Berlin and all your country of Germany to the advance of freedom everywhere, beyond the wall to the day of peace with justice, beyond yourselves and ourselves to all mankind.

Freedom is indivisible and when one man is enslaved who are free? When all are free, then we can look forward to that day when this city will be joined as one and this country and this great continent of Europe in a peaceful and hopeful globe.

When that day finally comes, as it will, the people of West Berlin can take sober satisfaction in the fact that they were in the front lines for almost two decades.

All free men, wherever they may live, are citizens of Berlin. And therefore, as a free man, I take pride in the words *"Ich bin ein Berliner."*

Satellite Launched

897 **1962** The Telstar communications satellite soared into orbit and relayed the first transatlantic television broadcast on July 10, 1962. Launched atop a Delta rocket, Telstar was a collaboration of NASA and AT&T. Bell Laboratories designed and built the satellite, while NASA contributed the launches and used them to support research experiments. "Live via satellite" flashed on screens as Telstar relayed television signals in near-real time to and from ground stations on either side of the Atlantic.

More would follow: The Communications Satellite Act of 1962 created COMSAT, which yielded international partnerships for satellite technology, and by 1965, commercial satellites were speeding information around the globe.

> **FOOTNOTE** Now satellites serve such wide-ranging uses as identifying terrorist bases and militia movement, predicting earthquakes, discovering and monitoring rare species, and tracking potential tsunamis.

Silent Spring Written

898 **1962** Rachel Carson published *Silent Spring*, focusing attention on the effects of chemical pesticides on land and water. The modern environmental movement arguably began with the publication of this meticulously researched volume.

Carson, former editor in chief of publications for the U.S. Fish and Wildlife Service and holder of a master's degree in zoology, championed the philosophy that humans can profoundly damage the natural world in the course of our attempts to control it. She equated chemicals with radiation in terms of damaging effects, and denounced the "barrage of poison" that chemical pesticides put into the earth. She warned that these insecticides not only killed every insect, good and bad, but also posed hazards for birds, fish, and ultimately the entire web of life on Earth.

Carson's landmark book spurred worldwide concern for preservation of the environment and the eventual banning, in numerous countries, of the chemical pesticide DDT.

> **FOOTNOTE** Because of the disastrous impact of DDT on the bald eagle, Carson wrote in *Silent Spring* that "The trend ... may well make it necessary for us to find a new national emblem."

Thalidomide Banned

899 **1962** Thalidomide, a sleeping pill and treatment for morning sickness during pregnancy, was taken off the market after being linked to devastating birth defects afflicting thousands of babies. Introduced by a German pharmaceutical company in 1953, it was sold over the counter in Europe and Canada beginning in 1958.

Dr. Frances Kelsey, a medical officer at the U.S. Food and Drug Administration, reviewed thalidomide in 1960. She questioned the manufacturer and managed to delay the process long enough to establish a link between thalidomide and severe birth defects in places where it was sold. The U.S. application was withdrawn. It was later found that even one dose of thalidomide could cause harm. This tragic incident led to improvements in the way drugs are tested.

Kennedy Visits Berlin

900 **1963** U.S. President John F. Kennedy made his "I am a Berliner" speech at the Berlin Wall, voicing the United States' commitment to keep West Germany and Berlin free from communism. On June 26, 1963, Kennedy spoke before more than 150,000 West Berliners in the Rudolph Wilde Platz (later renamed for Kennedy), praising their courage in the face of the division they had endured for 18 years and drawing a line in the sand concerning communist aggression. If people do not understand the difference between the free world and communism, he said, "Let them come to Berlin. Freedom has many difficulties, and democracy is not perfect, but we have never had to put a wall up to keep our people in." The most enduring passage of his speech

903 | *Martin Luther King, Jr., stirs listeners with his "I Have a Dream" speech at the Lincoln Memorial, 1963.*

was its conclusion, an expression of solidarity with the cheering citizens: "I take pride in the words '*Ich bin ein Berliner.*' "

Honda Makes Car

901 **1963** In 1963, Honda, known for high-performance motorcycles, launched its first production car in Japan: the S500 sports car, which produced 44 horsepower and weighed 1,500 pounds. This little four-speed transmission car could reach 80 miles an hour and sold for $1,275. In March 1964, Honda began manufacturing the S600, a slightly heavier vehicle with a greater engine capacity, and its first mass-marketed car. Honda began exporting in 1965 and reached the U.S. market in 1969 with the N600 in Hawaii, but sales lagged because of its small engine. In 1972, Honda introduced its Civic to the U.S., and Americans were hooked.

Continental Drift Proved

902 **1963** The theory of continental drift was confirmed in 1963 by comparing magnetic differences in rock. The concept was proposed in 1912 by meteorologist Alfred Wegener. In 1953 came the discovery of the Mid-Ocean Ridge—a long mountain ridge running through the world's oceans and containing the canyon-like Great Global Rift, whose breaks outline the edges of tectonic plates. Geologist Harry Hess theorized that as magma erupted, it pushed away the existing seafloor to create new surface and widen the ocean.

In 1963, a team including Fred Vine and Drummond Matthews discovered that the crust surrounding the Mid-Ocean Ridge had bands of opposite polarity—indicating that seafloor formed over time as the planet's polarity changed, causing the resulting rock to magnetize differently.

The theory was confirmed in 1966, when it was shown that Earth's polarity undergoes regular shifts.

■FOOTNOTE The Mid-Ocean Ridge and other undersea geologic formations are sometimes studied with the help of remotely operated vehicles that broadcast real-time transmissions of undersea activity to scientists and classrooms.

King Voices Dream

903 **1963** Reverend Martin Luther King, Jr., galvanized the American civil rights movement with his soaring "I Have a Dream" speech in 1963.

Activists had planned a march in Washington, D.C., to demonstrate multiracial support for the civil rights bill, which was blocked in Congress. On August 28, more than 250,000 people gathered near the Lincoln Memorial to hear speakers from all segments of society.

1946-PRESENT | Modern Age

JFK Assassinated

904 **1963** One of the most controversial assassinations of modern times is that of President John F. Kennedy, shot in Dallas, Texas, on November 22, 1963.

To a sorrowing nation, the sight of three-year-old John F. Kennedy, Jr., saluting his father's cortege placed yet another unforgettable image in our collective memory book of this beloved, bereaved family. The Kennedys had defined and demystified the U.S. Presidency through photographs. Perhaps her earlier work as a photojournalist had given First Lady Jacqueline Kennedy an understanding of the value and power of the image; she often requested photographers to document the events of her husband's Presidency and her family's life, from state occasions and foreign travel to the Kennedy children at play. Many iconic photos had been made during the family's White House years. Then came the indelible scenes from Dallas, from the plane ride home, from the days to follow. When the Kennedys gathered on a Washington avenue that sad November day in 1963, their image became a touchstone, yet again, of the value of what we had lost.

Three-year-old John F. Kennedy, Jr., salutes his father's coffin, 1963.

For many Americans, JFK's death left too many unanswered questions. President Lyndon Johnson tasked Chief Justice Earl Warren's commission to investigate the assassination and answer such questions as whether Lee Harvey Oswald acted alone. With the assassination of Oswald by nightclub owner Jack Ruby on national television, hope of extracting the truth—from Oswald, at least—disappeared. The Warren Commission conducted its investigation with secrecy that the government claimed was necessary due to the Cold War, but it only intensified public suspicion. The House Select Committee on Assassinations continued the investigation in 1978 and 1979, and in 1992 the JFK Act assembled and opened all the previously withheld records surrounding the case. Conclusive evidence of all events surrounding the assassination have never been irrefutably established.

As King ended his presentation, singer Mahalia Jackson urged him to "Tell them about the dream!" and King said: "I have a dream that one day this nation will rise up and live out the true meaning of its creed … that all men are created equal." He saw children of all races living in unity, judged only by "the content of their character." And he offered a glimpse into a future when Americans could live "Free at last!"

The Civil Rights Act was signed in less than a year, and other antidiscrimination laws followed. But in 1968, to the world's shock and sorrow, King was gunned down in Memphis.

Ali Becomes Champ

905 **1964** Muhammad Ali became heavyweight boxing champion in 1964, defeating titleholder Sonny Liston in the early days of a long and colorful career. Boxing under his birth name, Cassius Marcellus Clay, the Olympic gold medalist had fought only 19 matches and was not expected to win. But he danced around punches and returned them with speed. A rematch—which some considered staged in his favor—sealed the victory. Soon after, the champ converted to Islam and changed his name to Muhammad Ali—only to lose his title for refusing on religious grounds to perform military service during the Vietnam War.

Mandela Imprisoned

906 **1964** Nelson Mandela was sentenced to life in prison by the government of South Africa in 1964 for his opposition to the policy of apartheid, which had become law in 1948. Under the rule of descendants of the country's European settlers, known as Afrikaners, the nation enforced racial segregation in nearly every aspect of life. Discrimination against black people was expressed in law, jobs, and political representation.

Mandela was a lawyer and key leader of the African National Congress (ANC) for democratic reform, through which he advocated for nonviolent resistance to apartheid. His work led to his being sentenced to life in prison under charges of sabotage, treason, and conspiracy to overthrow the government. The imprisonment of Mandela galvanized anti-apartheid activists around the world, with trade and diplomatic sanctions levied against South Africa as international pressure grew.

Freedom came after 27 years, on February 11, 1990, when Prime Minister F. W. de Klerk legalized the ANC and released the world's most famous political prisoner.

Mandela became the first black president of South Africa in 1994, at the age of 75, after 16 million black citizens waited in mile-long lines to vote. For their "negotiated resolution" of apartheid, he and de Klerk shared the 1993 Nobel Peace Prize.

■ FOOTNOTE One law of apartheid, meaning "separateness" in Afrikaans, required South Africa's majority black population to carry identification cards that restricted their movement and dictated which jobs they could hold.

IBM for Desktop

907 **1964** IBM introduced the IBM System/360, the first family of computers to use interchangeable software and the first to handle both scientific and commercial work, on April 7, 1964: An announcement came from the IBM Data Processing Division, saying that the "new generation of electronic computing equipment combines microelectronic technology" with "significant advances in the concepts of computer organization."

The System/360 promised greater productivity at lower cost, improved circuitry through solid logic technology, expanded capabilities for a wider range of data processing applications, and a revolutionary idea in computer selection: Buyers now had a choice of five processors and 19 combinations of power, speed, and memory, and any version could use the same software and peripherals. Huge monolithic mainframe computers would soon become archaic.

■ **FOOTNOTE** Before the System/360, IBM's offerings included computers such as the 650, which had the first drum memory, cost more than $500,000, and could be programmed in decimal rather than binary.

Beatles Rock U.S.

908 **1964** The Beatles came to the United States for several concerts, bringing their Liverpool brand of rock-and-roll to international prominence. Television host Ed Sullivan encountered a hubbub at London's Heathrow Airport in 1963, and when it was attributed to a Beatles arrival, he booked the group—even though Beatlemania had yet to cross the Atlantic.

By February 9, 1964, "I Want to Hold Your Hand" was at number one—and 40 percent of the U.S. population tuned in for the Beatles' debut. With their effervescent music and soon-to-be-imitated hairstyles, the Fab Four charmed and entertained over the screams of teenage girls. Within two months, they owned the top five singles simultaneously—a feat that is still unmatched.

As the 1960s wore on, their music progressed, and eventually John Lennon, Paul McCartney, George Harrison, and Ringo Starr went their separate ways, never to reunite musically. A bullet ended that possibility when Lennon was murdered in front of his New York apartment building in 1980. George Harrison died in 2001.

Smoking Causes Cancer

909 **1964** The U.S. Surgeon General established that cigarette smoking is a cause of cancer and other diseases. The habit had been increasing in the United States since 1900. By 1963, the number of smokers in the United States had reached 70 million—39 percent of the population—and lung cancer deaths had grown almost in proportion to the rise in the number of smokers.

As early as 1946, a link between smoking and lung cancer was suggested. Dr. Luther Terry, U.S. Surgeon General, confirmed in 1964 that damage to body functions, organs, cells, and tissues occurred more frequently in smokers. American radio and television stations that carried cigarette ads soon were required to also include information about health risks. By 2000, the number of smokers had declined to 25 percent of the population.

Moore Sees Miniaturization

910 **1964** Gordon Moore predicted that the number of transistors that could fit on a silicon chip would double every two years, leading to ever faster, more powerful personal computers. Cofounder of chipmaking company Intel, Moore made his prediction in 1965. It came to be known as Moore's law, and, indeed, has characterized a trend of exponential growth in computing power: As transistors become smaller, computing performance rises while the cost goes down. However, Moore's law was a tad conservative. The actual pattern of growth has been a doubling every 18 months. What happens, though, when there is simply no more room on a chip? Currently under development is a replacement for the computer chip itself—a smaller version made from carbon nanotubes. Like transistors, these tubes function as tiny switches—but they are more than a thousand times thinner than a human hair. In terms of performance, carbon tubes do

908 | *Beatles McCartney, Harrison, Lennon, and Starr perform on* Ed Sullivan Show, *February 1964.*

not measure up to the standard of silicon-based transistors—yet.

> ■ **FOOTNOTE** Gordon Moore, a California native, was CEO of Intel until 1987 and became chairman emeritus in 1997. President George H. W. Bush awarded him the National Medal of Technology in 1990.

Civil Rights Made Law

911 **1964** The Civil Rights Act was signed into law by U.S. President Lyndon B. Johnson in 1964, outlawing segregation based on race, creed, national origin, or sex. Bolstered by Supreme Court cases that struck down segregation in public schools and public transportation, the bill had been in Congress for years but met continued resistance from Southern members. President John F. Kennedy belatedly voiced support for the bill in the early 1960s, prodded by the necessity of federal action to enforce the admittance of black students to state universities in Mississippi and Alabama. Martin Luther King, Jr., with his rousing appearances at Civil Rights demonstrations and his recent "I Have a Dream" speech at a national demonstration in Washington, D.C., helped to build momentum.

The bill became law after Kennedy's death, with Johnson and religious leaders summoning the needed support. The Civil Rights Act ended discrimination in public places, guaranteed equal voting rights, and created the Equal Employment Opportunity Commission. Soon to follow were the Voting Rights Act of 1965 and the Fair Housing Act of 1968. One hundred years after slavery, the nation pushed closer to equal treatment for all.

Enzymes Slice DNA

912 **1965** Werner Arber, one of the 1978 recipients of the Nobel Prize in medicine, first published his findings on research with bacteriophages (viruses that infect bacteria) in 1965. The Swiss microbiologist observed that these viruses not only caused a change in the bacteria they invaded but also underwent a genetic change.

Further study revealed the presence of protective enzymes in the bacteria that cut the invader's DNA and restricted its growth—without having the same effect on the bacteria. These became known as restriction enzymes, "chemical knives" that cut DNA into defined sections. Researchers used these tools to analyze DNA and determine the order of new combinations of genes.

CONNECTIONS

Civil Rights
Equal protection under the law

The U.S. Constitution guarantees the civil rights of individuals—that is, the rights of free speech, religious choice, property ownership, and fair and equal treatment by other individuals and groups. Yet throughout U.S. history various groups have not always enjoyed basic civil rights. Groups unfairly treated have included blacks, women, American Indians, Jews, Asians, Hispanics, homosexuals, and the handicapped.

Since the 1950s a number of legal cases and new laws have been aimed at protecting the civil rights of the nation's largest minority, African Americans. Particularly significant was the 1954 case *Brown* v. *Board of Education of Topeka,* in which the Supreme Court ruled that segregation in public schools was unconstitutional. A bus boycott in Montgomery, Alabama, the following year—initiated when a black woman refused to yield her seat to a white man—brought national attention to the unequal treatment of blacks and whites and made Rev. Martin Luther King, Jr., a leader in the civil rights arena.

One of King's models was Mohandas Gandhi, whose use of passive resistance (or civil disobedience)

Civil rights protester, Brooklyn, 1963

helped fight discrimination against Asian immigrants in South Africa and then, in the 1930s and '40s, won freedom for his homeland India. King's and Gandhi's philosophy was heavily influenced by the writings of Russian novelist Leo Tolstoy and American transcendentalist Henry David Thoreau, whose 1849 essay "Civil Disobedience" proposes that "it is not desirable to cultivate a respect for the law, so much as for the right."

During the late 1950s and early 1960s, U.S. schools and public places that had been segregated by race gradually began to integrate as the power of the law took hold and attitudes about what was fair shifted. A comprehensive Civil Rights Act was passed in 1964 after a 75-day filibuster in Congress, one of the longest in history. The bill outlawed discrimination by public businesses, employers, and unions.

Among other groups that have had recent successes with civil rights issues, the handicapped won a victory in 1990 when the U.S. Congress passed the Americans with Disabilities Act, requiring public buildings and mass transit be accessible to the disabled.

Elsewhere in the world various groups have likewise had to struggle for fair and equal treatment. Citizens in most western European countries have long been protected by constitutional democracies safeguarding civil rights. Communist nations such as China, on the other hand, while claiming civil, or human, rights, do not in fact allow the same freedom of speech enjoyed by the West. The government controls the press, and criticism of the Communist Party, which runs the government, is often met with punishment.

Whale Hunts Restricted

913 | **1966** To prevent species extinction, a general moratorium on the hunting of humpback whales was introduced in 1966 and is still in force today. Disappearance of these "singing whales" in the North Atlantic prompted the International Whaling Commission to prohibit their hunting in that area in 1955; the ban was extended to every ocean in 1966. With the establishment of the 1973 U.S. Endangered Species Act, all of the great whales—humpback, gray, bowhead, blue, fin, sei, and sperm—were placed on the endangered list.

> ■**FOOTNOTE** Ancient peoples hunted whales for subsistence for thousands years; Bering Sea Eskimos whaled with handheld harpoons in flimsy walrus-hide boats and, if they survived the hunt, were revered by their tribes.

First Heart Transplant

914 | **1967** Dr. Christiaan N. Barnard of South Africa performed the world's first human heart transplant operation in 1967. The surgery took place at Groote Schuur Hospital in Cape Town, South Africa. Working with a team that included Michael De Bakey, Adrian Kantrowitz, and black South African surgeon Hamilton Naki, Barnard placed in the chest of 55-year-old Louis Washkansky a donor heart from a young woman who had suffered a fatal car accident. Washkansky lived for 18 days before dying of a lung infection. World response to the surgery was mixed: Some people considered it an attempt to play God, while others approved.

The 1969 discovery of cyclosporine aided transplant success. Found in a Norwegian fungus by immunologist Jean-François Borel, cyclosporine suppresses the immune system against foreign tissue. By 1984, 80 percent of patients survived two or more years. Transplant operations have raised end-of-life issues concerning the death of donors, with death redefined as the cessation of electrical activity in the brain rather than the stilling of the heart.

913 | *Workers attach chain and cable to a humpback whale to cut the blubber loose from the body.*

Plate Tectonics Proposed

915 | **1967** Jason Morgan shaped the theory of plate tectonics with his discovery of "hot spots," or magma plumes, in 1967. The geophysicist sought to understand how volcanoes could occur on the Big Island of Hawaii, which is situated in the middle of the Pacific plate rather than at the edge, where upheavals would be expected. He theorized that convection zones deep in Earth's mantle caused hot magma to well up through the plate at certain spots and create volcanoes on the surface. Further, he postulated that these hot spots stay in one place while the plates move over them, creating chains of volcanoes in the vicinity.

Morgan found 20 hot spots across the globe; today, many more are known. His breakthrough greatly advanced geophysical science.

> ■**FOOTNOTE** It is now known that hot spots come in a variety of forms: hydrothermal vents—spouts of searingly hot water; seeps—gases or fluids leaking upward through porous mud; or seamounts—current-warmed mounds.

Nuclear Weapons Treaty

916 | **1968** The Treaty on the Non-Proliferation of Nuclear Weapons was opened for signing in 1968. This United Nations initiative got its start in 1953, when U.S. President Dwight D. Eisenhower's "Atoms for Peace" speech expressed the need for an international organization to prevent hostile use of nuclear technology and to disseminate peaceful applications.

The International Atomic Energy Agency was established in 1957 to serve as this safeguard system. Its main tasks are to conduct inspections in an effort to guard against weapons development and deployment; to help countries upgrade their nuclear safety and security; and to support cooperation toward constructive applications of nuclear science, such as energy production and medical treatment.

As support grew for an international, legally binding commitment, the Treaty on the Non-Proliferation of Nuclear Weapons was developed. Its objective is to prevent the

907 More Details on Computers

Today's sleek and powerful computers owe their existence to a machine that stood 51 feet long and 8 feet high, contained 530 miles of wire, and weighed nearly 10,000 pounds. The Mark I, unveiled by IBM in 1944 and given to Harvard University, was the world's first automatic computer and forever changed technology in the modern age. Though its top speed of three additions or subtractions in a second is shoddy by today's standards, this large-scale digital calculator—referred to as the Automatic Sequence Controlled Calculator (ASCC) by IBM—pioneered the use of machines in science and applied mathematics. "When this calculator returns to civilian use, it will be of the greatest importance in astronomy, atomic physics, radio research, investigations of the ionosphere, actuarial work, optics, and electronics," read a 1945 IBM brochure on the ASCC. "The apparatus will quickly solve statistical problems in which the manual labor has been enormous.... It will be the key to the solution of differential equations, the evaluation of integrals, and all phases of applied mathematics, yielding a speed and accuracy formerly beyond belief."

> "It will be the key to ... all phases of applied mathematics, yielding a speed and accuracy formerly beyond belief."
>
> —IBM brochure

The Mark I was conceived in 1937 by Harvard graduate student Howard Aiken, who needed a machine to help solve a set of nonlinear equations. IBM was tapped to fund and develop the project, and it was there that Aiken and a team of researchers spent nearly seven years fleshing out the machine's schematics. In the end, the machine consisted of seven major units and 765,299 total parts. It could multiply in 5.7 seconds and divide in 15.3 seconds; it could solve a logarithm or trigonometric function in just over one minute. It could store 72 numbers of up to 23 decimal digits each.

Though the Mark I astonished Harvard with its speed and potential, it was outdated merely four years later with the arrival of a machine more than 250 times faster. Technology advanced rapidly from that point forward, giving us computers whose speed and complexity would be barely believable to the Mark I's creators.

IBM's Automatic Sequence Controlled Calculator (ASCC), the first fully automatic computer, was 51 feet long, 8 feet high, and 2 feet deep.

spread of nuclear weapons and, ultimately, to attain complete disarmament. There are currently 190 nations enrolled, including five nuclear-weapon states.

Viet Cong Advance

917 **1968** The Tet offensive gave notice of the Viet Cong and North Vietnamese potential to dominate the conflict that raged in Southeast Asia. In late January 1968, a truce was declared in Vietnam's civil war to celebrate the Buddhist holiday Tet—but Viet Cong and North Vietnamese forces broke the cease-fire and launched massive strikes on cities throughout South Vietnam. In Saigon, the capital city, they entered the U.S. embassy compound in a failed attempt to capture it. The Viet Cong lost 40,000 soldiers, but the Tet offensive was a political triumph for the communists. It showed

that they were not on the brink of defeat as the U.S. military tried to portray. With antiwar sentiments intensifying in the U.S., President Lyndon B. Johnson's advisers urged him to deescalate. He halted bombing in parts of the war-torn region, denied Gen. William Westmoreland's request for 206,000 American troops, and began to turn the war effort over to the South Vietnamese.

> **FOOTNOTE** The Tet offensive also included attacks on Hue and the village of Khe Sanh near the Laotian border, where it was months, instead of hours, before the U.S. achieved a tactical victory.

Green Revolution Begins

918 **1968** The Green Revolution, a massive philanthropic and governmental effort, introduced high-yield grains and enhanced farming techniques,

irrigation systems, pesticides, and agricultural management in parts of Asia and Latin America in the 1960s and 1970s. While still underway, it could be said to have begun with the 1968 speech of Norman E. Borlaug, an American microbiologist who spoke at the International Wheat Genetics Symposium in Canberra, Australia, on wheat breeding in August 1968. For his work internationally, Borlaug received the Nobel Peace Prize in 1970.

While harvests and food supplies increased, the program caused unintended ecological effects, such as water quality problems, pesticide overuse, and waterlogged fields. In India, Green Revolution innovations enabled the country to grow enough food for its population of one billion; however, groundwater pumping resulted in depleted aquifers, groundwater shortages, and salt seeping into coastal wells.

918 | *Farmer with baskets on pole walks through terraced rice fields in Bali, Indonesia*

Today, the Alliance for a Green Revolution is under way in Africa, marking the first phase of a long-term plan to boost food security. The program emphasizes environmental awareness in conjunction with farming techniques and business practices.

Convention Turns Violent

919 **1968** Antiwar demonstrators at the 1968 Chicago Democratic Convention squared off against police for

---

FIRST PERSON

Apollo 8
'ROUND THE MOON AND BACK, NASA, 1968

Mission objectives: Demonstrate crew/space vehicle/mission support facilities during manned Saturn V/CSM mission. Demonstrate translunar injection, CSM navigation, communications, and midcourse corrections. Assess CSM consumables and passive thermal control. Demonstrate CSM performance in cislunar and lunar orbit environment. Demonstrate communications and tracking at lunar distances. Return high-resolution photographs of proposed Apollo landing sites and locations of scientific interest. All mission objectives were achieved.

Mission highlights: First manned lunar orbital mission. Maximum distance from Earth 376,745 kilometers. In lunar orbit 20 hours, with 10 orbits.

Apollo 8, the first manned mission to the Moon, entered lunar orbit on Christmas Eve, December 24, 1968. That evening, the astronauts—Cmdr. Frank Borman, Command Module Pilot Jim Lovell, and Lunar Module Pilot William Anders—did a live television broadcast from lunar orbit, in which they showed pictures of the Earth and Moon seen from Apollo 8. Lovell said, "The vast loneliness is awe-inspiring and it makes you realize just what you have back there on Earth." They ended the broadcast with the crew taking turns reading from the book of Genesis. Borman then added, "And from the crew of Apollo 8, we close with good night, good luck, a Merry Christmas, and God bless all of you—all of you on the good Earth."

---

five days when police attempted to move their protest to another location and when they blocked protestors from reaching the convention site. The August 26-29 convention played to an already unsettled nation, coming on the heels of the assassinations of Martin Luther King, Jr., in April and Robert Kennedy in June. George McGovern took Robert Kennedy's place and reached out to the protestors. Hubert Humphrey, President Lyndon Johnson's Vice President, was considered a shoo-in, however, and easily won the nomination. Meanwhile, the battling culimated in the streets, as protestors attempted to reach the convention via Michigan Avenue, eventually resulting in a total of 589 arrests, with injuries to 100 protesters and 119 police.

Pulsars Discovered

920 **1968** Jocelyn Bell discovered pulsars in 1968. While assisting professor Antony Hewish in the study of quasars, the Belfast graduate student picked up mysterious, regularly occurring signals through a radio telescope. After ruling out earthly broadcasts, the researchers concluded that the source of the transmissions must be extraterrestrial—and jokingly called the signals LGM1, for "little green men." Bell then found another transmission coming from a different part of the universe.

The team announced its discovery and solicited help from the scientific community in finding the source of the signals. Robert Oppenheimer suggested the idea of a collapsing star, and he was proved correct. The signals came from pulsars—rapidly spinning neutron stars that send out a narrow beam of energy from their north and south magnetic poles. When Earth is in the line of transmission from a pulsar, the radio waves are detectable. Hewish received the Nobel Prize in physics for the discovery.

Apollo 8 Glimpses Earth

921 **1968** For the crew of Apollo 8— the first humans to achieve lunar orbit—the sight of earthrise came as a stunning surprise. No plans had been made to

---

921 | *View of planet Earth from Apollo 8, moon in foreground*

photograph Earth from the perspective of the moon, but the astronauts managed to grab a free-floating camera, and Bill Anders captured this exquisite, iconic portrait—which photojournalist Galen Rowell called "the most influential environmental photograph ever taken." A television camera also traveled on the mission, to let Mission Commander Frank Borman, veteran astronaut Jim Lovell, and rookie Anders broadcast the astonishing views they experienced. It was December 24, 1968, the closing days of a turbulent year in the United States. As a rapt TV audience gazed at the stark, cratered moonscape passing beneath the spacecraft, the astronauts narrated with the Genesis account of creation. Borman closed the transmission with a wish of "good night, good luck, a Merry Christmas, and God bless all of you—all of you on the good Earth."

> ■ **FOOTNOTE** The backup crew for the Apollo 8 mission included later astronaut celebrities Neil Armstrong, Buzz Aldrin, and Fred Haise. Armstrong and Aldrin manned the Apollo 11 craft and were first to actually walk on the moon.

New Environmental Policy

922 **1969** The U.S. National Environmental Policy Act was created in 1969, establishing a broad national framework for environmental protection. It requires the U.S. government to consider the environmental consequences of any actions taken: Whenever facilities are built, resources harvested, or parklands purchased, federal agencies must undertake a study, report the potential environmental cost, and seek public comment. The act addresses the impact of population growth, urbanization, industrial expansion, resource exploitation, technological advances, and many other activities, with consideration for the health of air, land, water, wildlife, and the human population.

Further Earth-friendly legislation followed the NEPA: the Clean Air Act (1970) regulates emissions from area, stationary, and mobile sources; the Clean Water Act (1972, 1977) regulates the discharge of pollutants into waterways; the Superfund Act (1980) authorizes federal response action to the release of hazardous substances and established a trust fund for cleanup; and the Oil Pollution Act (1990) addresses catastrophic oil spills.

■ **FOOTNOTE** In response to the more than 2.1 million tons of waste dumped in the oceans between 1973 and 1974, the U.S. government instituted the Ocean Dumping Act, overseen by the Environmental Protection Agency.

ARPANET Begins

923 **1969** ARPANET, the forerunner of the Internet, was established by the U.S. Department of Defense—and the first message was sent through cyberspace.

In the 1970s, the Defense Advanced Research Projects Agency (DARPA) developed a computer networking system that sent messages via the technology of packet switching—breaking data into "packets" with addresses and return addresses, and forwarding them from computer to computer until they reached their addressed destination.

Thousands Hear Music

924 **1969** The Woodstock Music and Art Fair, in rural New York, attracted more than 300,000 enthusiasts. Its Manhattan promoters had planned to

hold the show—originally a benefit to fund a music studio—in Woodstock, New York. When that location didn't work out, Max Yasgur's dairy farm near Bethel hosted the defining event of the 1960s generation. Some 50,000 fans were expected to enjoy "three days of peace and music," with top acts such as Janis Joplin, Jimi Hendrix, Santana, Joan Baez, and Crosby, Stills, and Nash. But people arrived in the hundreds of thousands. Woodstock became a countercultural touchstone, a demonstration—to the participants as well as to their elders—of the potential power of youth, peace, and rock-and-roll.

■ **FOOTNOTE** Max Yasgur's son Sam persuaded his father to offer his fallow alfalfa field for the Woodstock festival. In 2004, Sullivan County awarded Max its History Maker Award for his role in making the festival possible.

Bank Installs ATM

926 **1970** The banking industry's automated teller machine (ATM) began to come of age, changing the way people do business with their banks and nationalizing bank access for customers. The idea arose in the 1930s, when Luther George Simjian created the Bankmatic. James Goodfellow received a United Kingdom patent in 1966 for a system with a machine-readable coded card and numerical keypad. John Shepherd-Barron installed a cash-dispensing ATM at a London bank in 1967 that used chemically treated checks for account identification. In the United States, Don Wetzel developed magnetic-strip cards and personal identification numbers (PINs), and John D. White patented a design in 1973 for a "Credit Card Automatic Currency Dispenser." Industry

Man Walks on Moon

925 **1969** American astronaut Neil Armstrong became the first human to set foot on the moon. The crew of Apollo 11—Armstrong, Buzz Aldrin, and Michael Collins—began their 240,000-mile journey on July 16, 1969. Four days later, Armstrong and Aldrin boarded the lunar module *Eagle* for the dangerous descent to the moon. Despite alarms blasting in the *Eagle* and boulders threatening on the lunar surface, Armstrong piloted the craft to a safe landing—with just 30 seconds of fuel remaining. On July 20, 1969, at 10:56 p.m., he stepped down onto the moon's surface as 600 million people watched or listened.

Astronaut Neil Armstrong snapped Buzz Aldrin on Apollo 11 mission to moon,

The crew returned to Earth with moon rocks and powdery dust; they left behind an American flag, a patch honoring the astronauts who perished in the 1967 fire of Apollo 1, and a plaque that read in part: "We came in peace for all mankind." That same year, two Mariner space probes captured more than 100 pictures of the surface of Mars.

By 1971, all three Apollo 11 astronauts had finished their astronaut careers with NASA and went on to highly successful careers. Armstrong became a professor of aeronautical engineering, Collins served as director of the Smithsonian Institution's Air and Space Museum, and Aldrin became a consultant, lecturer, and author.

924 | *Woman plays flute with drummer in crowd at Woodstock music festival, 1969.*

estimates place the number of ATMs in use today at 1.5 million worldwide.

Pocket Calculator Marketed

927 **1971** In 1965, Texas Instruments had set out to create a use for integrated circuitry that people would buy. Jack Kilby and other engineers were assigned to invent a miniature calculator capable of performing addition, subtraction, multiplication, and division—and small enough to fit in the palm of the hand. The 1967 prototype, code-named "Cal Tech," was 4.25 x 6.15 x 1.75 inches thick, and weighed almost 3 pounds. TI then partnered with the Japanese company Canon, leading to the 1970 debut of the market-ready Pocketronic. It resembled the prototype, but calculators would become ever smaller and more powerful as the new industry grew.

Bands Aid Bangladesh

928 **1971** The Concert for Bangladesh took place in 1971, raising support for refugees in India and inspiring future pop-music benefit performances. Ravi Shankar and George Harrison organized the Concert for Bangladesh, holding a star-studded show in New York and creating an award-winning album and feature film that earned millions of dollars for UNICEF refugee aid. In the 1980s, Bob Geldof and Midge Ure produced benefits for famine victims in Ethiopia: Band Aid gathered Irish and British musicians to record the song "Do They Know It's Christmas," and in 1985, Live Aid featured stadium concerts in London and Philadelphia and related events elsewhere. More than 150,000 people attended the performances, with 1.5 billion more watching live broadcasts. Donations totaled $245 million.

First Video Game

929 **1972** Nolan Bushnell created Pong, the original video game. A childhood inventor, Bushnell managed an amusement park as a teenager and studied computer graphics and engineering. He invented the game Computer Space in 1970, but it filled an entire room and had no commercial potential. Then came Pong, with its elusive moving blip and knob-controlled paddles.

Sensing a market, Bushnell and Ted Dabney founded Atari in 1972 with $500—and sold it several years later for $28 million. Atari had entered an agreement with Sears in 1975 to distribute a home version of Pong, marking the first interactive use of television sets.

FOOTNOTE In 1976 and 1977, Atari, responding to the Pong craze it had created, released Pong Doubles, Super Pong, Super Pong Ten, Super Pong Pro-Am, Super Pong Pro-Am Ten, Ultra Pong, and Ultra Pong Doubles.

Piaget's Child Theories

930 **1972** Jean Piaget pioneered studies in the cognitive development of children, making discoveries that form the basis of modern child psychology. The Swiss-born scientist had been a prodigy himself, with an early fascination in studies of nature. His work in psychology revolved around a "biological explanation of knowledge," as he called it. He studied cognitive processes by playing and talking with children and respecting the way they thought and learned. His 1972 *Psychology of the Child* outlined the developmental stages that children undergo as they grow.

Among his findings are the benchmarks so familiar to parents, teachers, and pediatricians: Babies learn by testing, e.g., putting things in their mouth; young children begin to think in symbolic terms, such as pretend play; older children's thoughts expand to the world beyond their own lives; and adolescents become able to process methodology and abstractions, such as algebra. In a 60-year career, Piaget changed how the world thought of children and influenced the fields of psychology, medicine, and education.

Ut Takes Historic Photo

931 **1972** When AP photographer Nick Ut headed out to cover a South Vietnamese Army engagement on

June 8, 1972, he captured an image that would personify the innocent victims of war—and he created it from a perspective that pulled viewers into the horrific scene as none had done before.

Bombs had hit a village, and though soldiers shouted for the children to run, the warning came too late. Now, injured villagers poured down the road. A young girl, severely burned by napalm, tore off her clothes in agony. The Vietnamese-born Ut documented the scene, and then, with his driver, rushed the child to a hospital and convinced doctors to care for her.

The film was delivered to the Associated Press—and thus to the world. The girl, Phan Thi Kim Phuc, recovered after two years of treatment and became a government-supervised symbol of war. In 1992, she and her husband defected to Canada. Today, the child once scarred by war has been named a UNESCO Goodwill Ambassador for Peace.

■ **FOOTNOTE** As long as Kim remained in Vietnam, because she was a national symbol of the war, she was monitored by the communist government, required to live in her home village, and cast in mandatory propaganda films.

Leakeys Find Bones

932 **1972** Mary Leakey discovered the world's earliest known hominid remains in Olduvai Gorge, Tanzania, spurring the idea that the human species originated in Africa. Excavating this rich deposit of fossils in 1959, the paleoanthropologist found teeth—large premolars—that her husband, Louis S. B. Leakey, agreed were distinctly human looking. They proved to be 1.75 million years old, from a species given the name *Australopithecus boisei.*

In 1972, Richard Leakey uncovered a 2.3-million-year-old skull from the earliest known member of the genus *Homo.* Mary Leakey found footprints made by two adolescent Australopithecines as they walked (upright) along a muddy river flat during a volcanic ash fall 3.6 million years ago. And in 1999, Meave and Louise Leakey unearthed an early homind skull

932 | *Archaeologist Mary Leakey with cast of 3.7-million-year-old footprints found in Tanzania in 1976*

and jaw that indicated a flat face, unlike the previous species discovered. Named *Kenyanthropus platyops,* this find provided yet another fascinating clue to the puzzle of human evolution.

Court Allows Abortion

933 **1973** The Supreme Court's *Roe* v. *Wade* ruling in 1973 established the legality of abortion in the United States, determining it to be a decision between a woman and her doctor.

In 1967, a Texas resident named Norma McCorvey, under the pseudonym Jane Roe, challenged antiabortion laws in her state. After losing in state and appeals courts, the case went to the U.S. Supreme Court on January 22, 1973. The Court voted 7-2, overturning the Texas law and legalizing abortion across the United States.

The court decreed that the state should not interfere in a woman's request for a first-trimester abortion; the decision was up to the woman's doctor. For the remainder of pregnancy, the state could regulate with consideration to maternal health.

Since the ruling, states have passed laws regulating specific aspects, techniques, and conditions of abortion. Controversies have arisen over numerous issues: interpretation of the high court ruling, partial birth abortion, embryonic research, the legal status of the unborn, waiting periods, parental notification laws for minors seeking abortion, the restriction on late-term abortion, and others. Debate continues along religious, political, and ideological lines on this polarizing issue.

Bacterium Gets New Gene

934 **1973** The first successful genetic engineering was achieved when a gene was transplanted into a common intestinal bacterium. Herbert Boyer, of the University of California at San Francisco, had the technology to cut DNA into specific segments. Stanley Cohen, of Stanford University, knew how to introduce circular pieces of DNA (known as plasmids) into bacteria that would then copy the gene.

The two met at a conference and decided to combine efforts toward gene-splicing. In 1973, they announced the world's first successful recombinant organism—a bacterium into which DNA from a virus had been inserted. This development signified the birth of genetic engineering and led to a wide range of applications in the new biotechnology industry: cloning, gene modification, the use of bacteria to manufacture insulin, and many more. Stanford managed to acquire a last-minute patent on the process, which earned $250 million in royalties, and Boyer founded the bioengineering company Genentech.

First Mobile Phone

935 **1973** In April 1973 Martin Cooper, an electrical engineer, unveiled the Motorola Dyna-Tac, the world's first portable telephone. The Dyna-Tac measured 9 x 5 x 1.75 inches and weighed 2.5 pounds. It took ten hours to build up its maximum charge, which would then power only a three-and-a-half-minute conversation. The phone's features were simple: dial, talk, and listen.

■ **FOOTNOTE** Martin Cooper placed the first cell phone call on April 3, 1973, from his 30-ounce cell phone on the streets of New York City. The then general manager at Motorola called his rival at AT&T's Bell Labs.

Tallest Building Begun

936 **1973** On February 6, 1973, work began on the CN (Canadian National) Tower, which at 1,815 feet is arguably the world's tallest building, tower, and freestanding structure. Construction first got under way on the foundation and

---

CONNECTIONS

Genetic Mapping
Cracking the code to aid everything from disease treatment to law enforcement

Since the discovery of the structure of DNA as a double helix by Francis Crick and James Watson in 1953, based on the x-ray photographs taken by Rosalind Franklin, human knowledge of genetic coding, especially its own, has grown by leaps and bounds. Only four years later, Matthew Meselson and Franklin Stahl were able to demonstrate the processes of DNA replication in detail, which, due to the process's dependence upon the double-helical shape, verified Crick and Watson's work. In 1961, Crick teamed up with South African chemist Sydney Brenne and discovered with him the function of base triplets in DNA as a reference for specific amino acids, as well as the fact that it is mRNA that conducts protein synthesis.

However, despite the obvious usefulness of such knowledge in working with genetic materials, it was not until 1969, when Jonathan Beckwith became the first to isolate a single gene, that the field of genetic mapping would begin to accelerate. By 1977, English biochemist Frederick Sanger had managed to investigate and describe the complete sequence of a virus. This was the first time that an entire genome had been fully sequenced. Alec Jeffreys then managed to discover the basis of simple-sequence DNA, which would lead to the

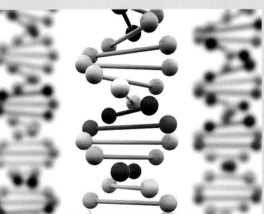

Colorful model of the double helix of DNA

development of an investigative technique known as DNA fingerprinting, a process that has become invaluable to law enforcement globally. Much like with a physical fingerprint, individual DNA samples are matched to make identifications. In 1989, the first three-dimensional visual image of a DNA molecule was obtained using a scanning tunneling microscope.

Genetic mapping as a field really began to prosper in 1990 with the launch of the international Human Genome Project, the goal of which was to map the genes of human chromosomes. While the project was still in progress, molecular biologist Craig Venter sequenced the full DNA of a bacterium, the first time the entire DNA of any organism had been sequenced. The full mapping of a multicellular animal, in this case a nematode worm, was then completed in 1998. By 2000 the scientists involved in the Human Genome Project had published the first draft of its results; by 2003 the project had been completed, and all papers analyzing individual chromosomes were published by 2006. As more is continually discovered about DNA, its structure, and its functions, the possibilities for the application of such knowledge continue to grow.

then moved on to the tower's three concrete legs. The tower itself rose at the rate of 18 feet per day, built using the slipform technique in which concrete was pumped into a form that slowly moved skyward as the concrete hardened. The crowning touch, a powerful broadcast antenna, was put in place by a Sikorsky helicopter. The tower functions as a telecommunications facility and a tourist attraction: Glass-walled elevators whoosh visitors to a glass-floored room more than a thousand feet up, and an even loftier level boasts the world's highest public observation gallery. On March 31, 1975, the *Guinness Book of World Records* proclaimed it the world's tallest freestanding tower. The American Society of Civil Engineers lists it as one of the seven wonders of the modern world.

> ■ **FOOTNOTE** Visitors can dine at 360, the CN Tower's restaurant that slowly rotates 1,151 feet aboveground. The menu includes regional Canadian dishes such as maritime lobster and Quebec ash-rolled goat's cheese.

Ancestor Found

937 **1974** Donald Johanson discovered "Lucy," providing clear proof that this human ancestor walked upright 3.2 million years ago. While excavating in Ethiopia in 1974, the paleoanthropologist saw an elbow protruding from the gravelly sediment. The partial skeleton had a combination of human and apelike features—long dangling arms, but pelvic and leg bones suited for walking upright. Named "Lucy," this *Australopithecus afarensis* was thought to have been female because it was petite—about three and a

937 | Australopithecus afarensis *skull*

half feet tall—compared with other fossils found in the area. Humanlike wisdom teeth indicated that Lucy was an adult.

In 2006, another astonishing find— the fossilized skeleton of an Australopithecine toddler—was nicknamed "Lucy's baby." This remarkably complete skeleton, actually 100,000 years older than Lucy, showed that these hominids apparently retained tree-climbing ability as evidenced by the structure of the baby's tiny shoulder blades. The Australopithecines gave rise to the highly adaptable, tool-using genus *Homo,* of which *Homo sapiens* is a member.

European Coups

938 **1974** In Portugal, the breakup of the nation's overseas empire caused an influx of 700,000 returning settlers, further straining a weak economy. A military coup ensued in 1974, ending more than six decades of repressive government and introducing democratic reforms. Portugal joined the European Union in 1986.

Greece, scarred by Nazi occupation and civil war, endured years of military dictatorship in the mid-20th century. The junta fell in 1974, and an elected government and new constitution followed—returning democracy to the land where it was conceived around 500 B.C.E.

Sociobiology Suggested

940 **1975** Edward O. Wilson proposed that animal behavior could be understood as a result of evolutionary adaptation. A biologist and Harvard professor, Wilson made observations of leaf-cutter ants that led him to theorize that they developed agriculture millions of years before humans did. The leaf-cutters chewed pieces of leaves to make a paste, which they fed to fungi, the mainstay of the ants' own diet. Cameron Currie, a graduate student, found that the leaf-cutter ants also produced an antibiotic to thwart a mold that threatened the fungi. Wilson called this relationship "mutualism," a type of symbiosis that developed through coevolution,

Desktop Computers Arrive

939 **1975** Bill Gates and Paul Allen built a BASIC compiler and started Microsoft Corporation; Steven Jobs and Stephen Wozniak built the first Apple computer in the Jobs family garage. In the early 1970s, calculator manufacturer Ed Roberts marketed a $500 build-it-yourself computer kit he called Altair. Though it had no screen, keyboard, or software, Altair was something of a sensation, because manufacturers then were building computers for industry and not for home use. In 1975, Harvard student Bill Gates and programmer Paul Allen offered to improve Altair by programming it in the computer language BASIC rather than its existing machine code. They used a Harvard computer to develop the software, which increased Altair's success and essentially launched the home computer industry. Gates and Allen went on to found Microsoft. Meanwhile, unable to afford an Altair, Steven Jobs and Stephen Wozniak built their own computer—Apple I—and marketed it through small retailers. When they introduced Apple II, with color graphics, their company grew faster than any other in American history.

Steve Jobs, John Sculley, and Steve Wozniak unveil Apple IIc in 1984.

and asserted that cooperation is an important force in the perpetuation of biodiversity because it benefits both species in a partnership. He later endorsed Darwin's idea that group selection—rather than collateral kin selection—is important to evolution, suggesting that simple animals such as ants can't recognize their own relatives and thus cannot act to favor their kin.

> ■ **FOOTNOTE** Mutualism, an arrangement in which the acts of one group promote both its own survival as well as that of another group, can also be found in fungus and alga living together as a lichen.

Pol Pot Takes Cambodia

941 **1975** The Khmer Rouge took control of Cambodia and massacred 1.7 million people, opening the world's eyes to this kind of internal cleansing. During the Vietnam War, relentless heavy bombing extended across the border into Cambodia and plunged the country into chaos.

The Khmer Rouge regime, headed by Pol Pot, seized control on April 17, 1975. These Maoist guerillas launched a campaign of terror in which they executed educated people, separated children from their parents, forced people of all ages into work camps or the armed forces, and tried to rid the country of all foreign influences—including books, medicine, and money. They idealized the peasant class and sought to revert the country to a simple agrarian society. The Khmer Rouge renamed the country Democratic Kampuchea and held power until the Vietnamese removed them in 1979. Civil war continued for almost a decade. Pol Pot died in 1998, and the Khmer Rouge surrendered. During their brutal reign, almost two million people died by execution, torture, or starvation.

Quake Shakes China

942 **1976** The most devastating earthquake in modern times struck Tangshan, China, early on the morning of July 28, 1976. China designated its magnitude as 7.8 on the Richter scale, with major aftershocks hours later.

943 | *Deep-sea tube worms thrive on edge of vent. Tube worms killed by eruption lie behind.*

The catastrophe occurred at 3:42 a.m. and killed or trapped many people in the ruins of their homes in this industrial area 200 kilometers east of Beijing. The quake and its aftereffects killed at least 240,000 people—the official estimate—with the actual toll possibly as high as 655,000.

Vents Show Life

943 **1977** Scientists discovered life around deep-sea vents in the Pacific Ocean where temperatures reach up to 760°F. In a 1977 exploration of the Galápagos Rift along the coast of South America, Robert Ballard piloted the Navy submersible *Alvin* over a field of hydrothermal vents—underwater volcanoes spewing superheated, mineral-rich water from cracks in the seafloor—at depths of about one and a half miles below the ocean's surface.

Abundant sea life animated the water near the vents: giant tube worms up to four feet long, acorn worms, giant clams, long-necked barnacles, and other species. Unique bacteria that adapt to the lack of sunlight form the foundation of the food chain, metabolizing large amounts of sulfur in the hot springs. Some scientists believe life on Earth began in a similar environment.

> ■ **FOOTNOTE** The three-person submersible *Alvin,* first launched in 1964, is named for Woods Hole Oceanographic Institution's Allyn Vine, a geophysicist and an inventor of deep-sea submersibles.

Probes Seek Planets

944 **1977** On August 20, 1977, Voyager 2 blasted off from Kennedy Space Center in Florida, followed weeks later by Voyager 1 on a shorter, faster trajectory. The unmanned spacecraft were designed for close-up study of Jupiter, Saturn, Saturn's rings, and both planets' major moons. Due to the success of those missions, the two were reprogrammed on the fly for further study. They explored all the giant planets in our solar system and 48 of their moons, as well as the solar wind. Both have now entered the vast heliosphere at the edge of interstellar space where the sun's influence ends.

Carl Sagan

MURMURS OF EARTH, 1978

The Voyager spacecraft hurtling through space as I write these words resembles a glistening cocoon carrying on it a gold record, a gift to all our intelligent counterparts inhabiting the universe. The greetings part of the record is a celebration of the human spirit, emphasizing our gregariousness ... expressing our desire to be thought of as eloquent in this, our first speaking engagement to the universe. We are saying that ... we would welcome—indeed, relish—a dialogue with another interlocutory civilization elsewhere in the cosmos....

Under a sun-drenched Florida sky, a few hundred people gathered, outfitted with special gear for the occasion—sunglasses, binoculars and cameras—to watch Voyager rise from Earth in a blast of white light, a puff of sunset-colored smoke and a sky-splitting roar. Watching Voyager flash out of our sight ... one hopes that, like Marco Polo, it will find itself at the gates of some ancient and great civilization. As our emissary, it will extend greetings and present our calling card (or disc, in this case), as any well-mannered Victorian guest would do when out visiting in the neighborhood....

Voyager has been compared to a bottle with a note inside tossed over the railing of a ship at sea.... We are tossing our bottle into the void of the sky. Whether it will ever be found by someone walking on a galactic beach will not be known by our generation. Our distant progeny will have this to look forward to.

In case they encounter life-forms, Voyager 1 and 2 carry a greeting—a 12-inch disk containing a carefully selected variety of the sounds and images of life on Earth.

Spanish Monarchy Established

945 **1978** Spain's Gen. Francisco Franco wielded power from 1936 until his death in 1975, when Juan Carlos became king. Three years later a new constitution confirmed Spain as a parliamentary monarchy—and after 1986, when the Socialist Party under Felipe Gonzáles Márquez led Spain into the European Community, the economy grew faster than any other member nation's.

> **FOOTNOTE** Spain, with its population of nearly 40 million, joined the European Community along with Portugal in 1986, raising the number of member countries to 12. These 12 signed the Treaty on European Union in 1992.

Marley Sings of Love

946 **1978** Bob Marley and the Wailers, along with other reggae artists, played the One Love Peace Concert at National Stadium in Kingston, Jamaica, on April 22, 1978. The show was arranged to benefit a youth employment project, but Marley seized the opportunity to endorse peace in his homeland of Jamaica, where rightist and leftist factions had clashed over control of areas of Kingston. Marley brought Jamaica's situation—as well as its irresistible music—to world attention.

Oil Spills in France

947 **1978** On March 16, 1978, the supertanker *Amoco Cadiz* ran aground in heavy seas, spilling 222,000 tons of oil that blackened some 200 miles along France's Brittany coast. Strong tides and winds contributed to the spread of pollution from the 1978 spill, in which 68.7 million gallons resulted in an oil slick that covered nearly 800 square miles.

More than a decade later, on March 24, 1989, the *Exxon Valdez* broke up off the coast of Alaska, spreading 11 million gallons of oil over 500 square miles. The wreck caused disastrous environmental damage and brought to world attention the

944 | *Collage of Voyager 1 photos of Jupiter and its moons, the Galilean satellites, March 1979*

ecological threat that large tankers presented. The *Exxon Valdez* ran aground in wildlife-abundant Prince William Sound. The cost to animals was enormous, with hundreds of thousands of birds and mammals killed. It was the largest spill and worst environmental disaster in U.S. history, and may have caused more damage to nature than any other spill in world history.

The 1989 disaster led to the passing of the Federal Oil Pollution Act and payment of $4.5 billion in damages by Exxon.

■FOOTNOTE The Exxon spill was so massive that cleanup was a tremendous undertaking. The three methods employed were burning (discontinued due to weather), mechanical cleanup, and chemical dispersants.

Test-Tube Baby Born

948 **1978** Louise Joy Brown, the world's first "test tube" baby, was born in England on July 25, 1978. The child, a girl, was conceived outside her mother's body through the process of in vitro fertilization (IVF), which was developed to aid couples who could not conceive naturally. In this procedure, the woman receives injections of hormones to stimulate her ovaries to ripen eggs, which are retrieved and mixed with sperm in a test tube or dish—hence the name in vitro, Latin for "in glass." The fertilized egg or eggs are implanted into the uterus, where a pregnancy can develop in the usual way. The procedure has spurred controversy over issues including donor eggs, multiple births, testing of embryos for genetic diseases, stem cell research on unused embryos, and the high cost of IVF, which can reach $17,000 per attempt. Despite these concerns, the procedure has helped many couples and is widely performed today. More than 50,000 children have been born as a result of in vitro fertilization.

China Goes Modern

949 **1978** In 1978, to support Chairman Hua Guofeng's recently announced Ten Year Plan, China relaxed its ban on receiving loans from foreign governments and took out $1.2 billion from a group of British banks. This change in policy was the result of a national desperation to advance and overcome the disastrous effects of the Maoist Cultural Revolution, which had shrunk the number of educated elite in China and reduced its competitiveness on the world stage. Success in the projects outlined under the plan would cost hundreds of billions of dollars. China quickly secured another ten billion dollars from foreign banks and sought financing for development projects from countries such as Germany and Japan, who shared some of the profits. Just one year into the plan, it became clear that the number of projects the government had begun in the first year was unrealistic, so thousands were halted. The Communist Party also began to relax economic and social controls, allowing factories to sell excess products for a profit and allowing individuals greater freedom to live where they pleased.

John Paul II Is Pope

950 **1978** The first non-Italian pope since 1523, Pope John Paul II, was elected to lead Roman Catholics in 1978. Athletic and charismatic, Karol Josef Wojtyla of Poland assumed the papacy at age 58 and took the name John Paul II in honor of his predecessor. His rise in the church hierarchy at first had met the approval of communist leaders, who considered him a moderate—a notion they regretted when John Paul II's visit to Poland in 1979 inspired a new nationalism and a trade-union movement that become an important catalyst in the fall of communism. Fluent in several languages, John Paul II jetted around the world in his efforts to support human rights and reach out to Catholics and non-Catholics alike, particularly in developing nations. He was the first pope to visit a synagogue and a mosque. John Paul II died in 2005 after a ten-year struggle with Parkinson's disease. Though not a theological reformer, he played a key role in one of the most significant social and political upheavals of the 20th century.

During John Paul II's papacy, the Catholic Church did not change any of its teachings on some of the controversial issues facing progressive, modern societies, including the ordination of women, divorce, contraception, and same-sex marriage.

Pope John Paul II says Mass at Yankee Stadium, October 2, 1979.

Ocean Floor Mapped

951 **1978** The Seasat satellite permitted oceanographic research on a global scale. Launched on June 28, 1978, Seasat was the first satellite designed for remote sensing of the world's oceans. It was developed for NASA by the Jet Propulsion Laboratory of the California Institute of Technology. Seasat flew in a nearly circular orbit at an altitude of 497 miles. It carried the first civilian spaceborne synthetic aperture radar (SAR), which monitored the global surface wave field and polar sea ice conditions. An array of sensors monitored sea surface temperature, coastal dynamics, pollution, and other features of clouds, water, and shoreline. Among other firsts, NASA proved the ability to measure Earth's wind speed and direction from space. Seasat operated for 105 days, until a massive short circuit in the electrical system ended the

949 More Details on China

Emerging as the de facto leader of China following Mao's death in 1976, Deng Xiaoping inherited a country still suffering from the repercussions of the Cultural Revolution. Education and industry had all but come to a halt, long-held customs and traditions had been displaced by revolutionary thought, and human rights violations were rampant. But Deng's particular brand of politics—which he called "socialism with Chinese characteristics"—was poised to lead China in a new direction.

In December 1978, Deng launched the Four Modernizations in the areas of agriculture, industry, science and technology, and national defense. Designed to make his country a world power by the start of the 21st century, the modernizations were part of an overall shift toward a market economy and a gradual loosening of national politics. On an individual level, citizens were encouraged to be economically self-reliant and entrepreneurial. Peasants were allowed to produce food for sale, and China saw its first surpluses in decades. New construction projects in the coastal cities drew workers from the countryside and paid them handsomely, and the standard of living among the majority of workers and peasants rose substantially. "To get rich is glorious," Deng famously proclaimed, and his words became a slogan in the campaign for continued progress.

> "To get rich is glorious," Deng ... proclaimed, and his words became a slogan in the campaign for continued progress.

On a national scale, foreign investment and open trade were encouraged. Technology from Japan and the West accelerated China's growth, and the newly liberalized market profited from the influx of foreign ideas and skills. Most notably, Deng opened diplomatic doors with the West, visiting U.S. President Jimmy Carter and British Prime Minister Margaret Thatcher.

Although the reforms and progress of Deng's era eventually became a source of contention and uprising—demonstrated most memorably in the events of the Tiananmen Square massacre of 1989—his insistence on a market economy and his open diplomacy launched China's transformation into a global economic power.

Neon lights and Chinese characters illuminate a crowded intersection on Nanjing Road, a popular shopping street and tourist destination in Shanghai.

955 | *March 1984 photo of Iraqi troops crouched behind sandbags during the Iran-Iraq war.*

mission. Its sensors performed as intended and led the way for new generations of instruments such as the U.S. Navy's geodesic satellite and the space shuttle's imaging radar.

> ■ **FOOTNOTE** After the devastating Indian Ocean tsunami of 2005, National Oceanic & Atmospheric Administration scientists measured the height of the wave by comparing images captured by four satellites.

Massive Dam Built

952 **1978** The Itaipú dam—one of the most ambitious hydroelectric projects in the world—was built in South America. A blast of dynamite in 1978 diverted the Paraná River to permit dam construction. Stretching some five miles along the border of Paraguay and Brazil, the Itaipú—structurally completed in 1984—is the largest hollow gravity concrete dam in the world, built so that the weight of the dam resists the force of the water. With ten million gallons of water surging through its spillway every

second, the Itaipú produces a significant percentage of the electricity used by Paraguay and Brazil.

Clerics Take Power

953 **1979** When U.S. President Jimmy Carter allowed the fleeing shah of Iran into the U.S. for medical treatment, Iran's militant students retaliated by attacking the U.S. Embassy. A revolutionary government headed by conservative Muslim cleric Ayatollah Ruhollah Khomeini had already taken control of Iran, establishing the world's first Islamic republic. Khomeini had been in exile for 14 years in Iraq and France for his opposition to the shah's regime. With his return and the U.S.'s sheltering of the shah, militants stormed the U.S. Embassy in Tehran on November 4, 1979, seizing dozens of embassy staff members and beginning a hostage crisis that would last 444 days. Khomeini supported their demand that the deposed shah be extradited to Iran in exchange for

the hostages' freedom. Diplomatic relations ended between the United States and Iran. Within weeks of the hostage-taking, female and African-American captives were freed. Another hostage was released because of illness, but the remaining 52 were held until January 20, 1981. As a result of negotiations mediated by Syria—and the unfreezing of eight billion dollars in Iranian assets—the captives were released hours after the end of Jimmy Carter's Presidency.

> ■ **FOOTNOTE** Conservatism in Iran governs the movement, education, behavior, and dress of women. Until 1997 unmarried women could not study abroad; married women may hold jobs only with their husbands' permission.

Reforms in Latin America

954 **1979** Sandinistas achieved victory on July 17, 1979, when they overthrew the government of President Anastasio Somoza Debayle and took over Managua, the Nicaraguan capital. The 42-year dictatorship had ended, but the Sandinistas' already poor relations with the newly elected Reagan Administration deteriorated rapidly. Civil war between the Sandinistas and the U.S.-funded rebels (known as contras) ended in 1988, and a democratic government was put in place. This heralded many other democratic reforms in Latin American countries and ushered in new rights and freedoms. Argentina suffered under a military junta from 1976 to 1983, during which some 30,000 people disappeared. Defeat by Britain in the 1982 Falkland Islands war loosened the regime's grip and led to increased freedom of the press and tolerance of opposition. Chile once enjoyed Latin America's longest tradition of political stability and civil liberty, but in 1973 a coup overthrew the elected Marxist government and ushered in 16 years of dictatorship. Democracy was restored in 1989. Guatemala's 36-year-long civil war ended in 1996, and the democratic government, though facing crime, illiteracy, and poverty, has made progress. Brazil, Paraguay, and Panama also saw democratic reforms during the late 20th century.

Iran and Iraq at War

955 **1980** The Iran-Iraq war split the Islamic world, with political and religious repercussions, when Iraq invaded Iran in 1980 as part of a territorial dispute. Iraqi leader Saddam Hussein also wanted to stop Iranian Shiite Muslims from influencing Shiite Iraqis against his Sunni Muslim regime.

While most Middle Eastern nations supported Iraq in the conflict, Libya and Syria sided with Iran. The United States, in an effort to gain freedom for American hostages held in Lebanon by Shiite militants, secretly supplied arms to Iran. However, when concern arose that extremist Iran might win control of the Persian Gulf, the U.S. gave satellite intelligence to Iraq. The war went on until the United Nations brokered a cease-fire in 1988.

More than one million people died in the long and bloody conflict, which set the stage for the 1991 Persian Gulf war: Iraq had acquired high debts after the cease-fire, and Kuwait's refusal to forgive them was ostensibly a reason for Iraq's invasion of Kuwait.

24-Hour News Begins

956 **1980** Cable Network News (CNN) signed on as the world's first around-the-clock global news television station on June 1, 1980. According to CNN's figures, the station reached 1.7 million cable TV households initially and is seen by nearly a billion people around the globe today. It claims the distinction of the first live broadcast from non-U.S. territory in Cuba by an American network since 1958. CNN's coverage of the first Persian Gulf war in 1991 set a standard for live, continuous coverage of breaking world events.

AIDS Identifed

957 **1981** On June 5, 1981, the Centers for Disease Control published a notice of a deadly pneumonia that seemed to target gay men and called it acquired immune deficiency syndrome (AIDS). Belgian doctor Peter Piot realized that a similar illness was striking people of all genders and ages in Africa. An international committee gave the name HIV (human immunodeficiency virus) to the microbe that causes this incurable condition, which robs the body of its defenses and makes victims vulnerable to a host of diseases.

Antiviral drugs have given new hope—and longer lives—to the HIV-positive.

CONNECTIONS

AIDS
Progress of a modern scourge

One of the most destructive of modern diseases, AIDS (acquired immune deficiency syndrome) targets the body's immune system, thus crippling its ability to defend itself from infections of all sorts. First reported in 1981 when young homosexual men developed strange cases of pneumonia and skin cancer, the disease is thought to have originated in Africa, possibly from monkeys. Since then, the disease has spread, mostly through heterosexual contact, and become an epidemic. Currently, nearly 40 million people worldwide have AIDS, and some 5 million new cases arise annually. The disease kills 3 million people a year. About 70 percent of all AIDS cases are in sub-Saharan Africa. In the United States, about 1 million people are infected with the virus that causes AIDS.

HIV (human immunodeficiency virus) is transmitted through body fluids, primarily through semen or vaginal fluid during unprotected sex. It can also be passed along by a contaminated syringe, such as that shared by intravenous drug users. Before routine blood screening for HIV in the mid-1980s, people receiving transfusions were at risk. The virus can also be spread through the placenta or breast milk of a mother. It is not spread by coughing or shaking hands, and although saliva, sweat, and tears can

South African woman cradles man dying of AIDS

carry the virus in low levels, scientists do not believe that transmission occurs through these fluids.

Once inside the body, HIV attacks the immune system's helper T cells, which orchestrate the body's entire immune response to pathogens. Inside a cell the virus drops its protective protein coat and begins its destructive work, hijacking the cell's engines to make an army of viruses.

The first stage of HIV infection generally results in a short, flulike illness. Symptoms include fever, fatigue, swollen lymph nodes, rash, sore throat, and joint pain. At this point the levels of HIV in the blood are still so low that an antibody test does not detect the virus. But within a few weeks, the immune system has created enough antibodies that a test can reveal HIV-positive status. For about ten years the virus will then continue to replicate, and the afflicted person will show no symptoms. But when the helper T cells decline to about 20 percent of normal levels, opportunistic infections begin occurring that the body cannot fight.

There is no cure or vaccine for an HIV infection, but there are a number of drugs that can slow its progress, and researchers continue to develop new treatments.

1946-PRESENT | Modern Age

958 | *STS-1* Columbia *launches from Kennedy Space Center in April 1981, for a 54-hour orbit of Earth.*

Organizations worldwide are distributing information about this stigmatized illness and campaigning to make the drugs, which are extremely costly, available in developing nations.

Africa is hardest hit by AIDS, with cases also increasing in China, India, Indonesia, and Russia. As of January 2006, the Joint United Nations Programme on HIV/AIDS (UNAIDS), which works in more than 75 countries, and the World Health Organization (WHO), which takes the lead within the UN system in the global health sector response to HIV/AIDS, estimate that AIDS has killed more than 25 million people worldwide since 1981, making it one of the most destructive epidemics in recorded history.

Space Shuttle Flies

958 **1981** The space shuttle *Columbia,* the world's first reusable spaceship, was launched by the United States on April 12, 1981. In the course of a two-day flight, the two-man crew completed 36 Earth orbits and a successful landing. The space shuttle program, called Space Transportation System (STS) by NASA, was designed for a variety of missions: deployment and retrieval of satellites, scientific and medical research, military reconnaissance, space construction projects, and studying the sun, universe, and Earth from an observation platform in space. A reusable spaceship had been a dream of NASA's for decades. The design could accommodate five to seven astronauts and

crew and was built to withstand 100 launches, or ten years' use. Space shuttles after *Columbia* have included: *Challenger* (1982), *Discovery* (1983), *Atlantis* (1985) and *Endeavour* (1991).

■ **FOOTNOTE** Before *Columbia,* spacecraft consisted of rockets several hundred feet long that would shed parts during flight, returning with only part of the original structure, leaving millions of dollars of "space junk" behind.

IBM Builds PC

959 **1981** When it introduced the 5150, its first personal computer, IBM launched a technological revolution. By 1980, when electric typewriters were still the norm, IBM's Displaywriter text processing system could store documents for revision and spell-check 50,000 words. But the following year, everything would change. A highly secretive plan known as Project Chess was under way, with a dozen engineers designing a new machine and Bill Gates enlisted to create software. The IBM PC burst onto the scene in 1981, with 25,000 units selling that year. By aggressively marketing this desktop tool through outside distributors such as Sears, IBM put its considerable reputation behind the concept of a PC on every desk, making computers a necessity in offices across the world. The PC was named *Time* magazine's 1981 Man of the Year.

■ FOOTNOTE IBM's first attempt at a PC, the IBM 5100 (code name "Project Mercury"), released in 1975 but cost $10,000, putting it well beyond reach of most individuals desiring a personal computer.

Honda Builds in U.S.

960 **1982** Thirty-four years after the Honda Motor Company was

Barney Clark

GEORGE RAINE, *NEW YORK TIMES,* 1982

A retired Seattle dentist suffering from inoperable heart disease underwent surgery ... for what was to be the first transplant of a permanent artificial heart.

Barney Clark, 61 years old, had been scheduled to receive the fist-sized polyurethane device Thursday morning ... but his rapidly deteriorating condition led doctors to begin an emergency operation .... Dr. Clark ... was among 10 prospective recipients of the revolutionary device, called the Jarvik-7.... Hundreds of animals have survived for up to nine months with the Jarvik-7 heart, but Dr. Clark is the first human recipient.... In recent months, while he was in better health, Dr. Clark visited the medical center to observe parts of artificial hearts in place in calves and sheep.... "His attitude prior to surgery was marvelous," said Dr. Chase N. Peterson, the vice president for health sciences at the University of Utah. "He turned to his wife, Unaloy, and said, 'I'm a little nervous.'"

established in Japan, Honda of America Manufacturing began making cars in Marysville, Ohio. The Honda brand was associated with reliability, low cost, and good fuel economy—an important factor for drivers who remembered 1970s gas lines. The first Honda produced at the Marysville plant was a four-door Accord; the Civic would start production in 1986. In 1990, the plant began making cars for export to Japan and produced the first Honda also designed in the U.S.—the Accord wagon. Honda production (and later design) in the U.S. reduced shipping costs, and Americans could alleviate any guilt they might have felt about not buying American-made cars. In its first nine years, the plant made 350,000 cars for U.S. drivers.

Artificial Heart

961 **1982** Barney Clark received the first permanent artificial heart on December 2. Ineligible for a heart transplant, the 61-year-old dentist lived for 112 days with a Jarvik-7 artificial heart implanted in his chest—and a washing machine-size compressor attached by a system of tubing that ran though his chest wall. William DeVries performed the procedure in Salt Lake City, Utah. Robert Jarvik had constructed the heart of plastic, aluminum, and Dacron polyester, but its hoses made the patient vulnerable to infections and blood clots. After a series of strokes, Clark died—yet the Jarvik-7 was still beating. Further attempts were made with other patients, but they suffered infections as well.

First MRIs in Use

962 **1982** The first magnetic resonance imaging (MRI) machines were tested in hospitals in 1982, representing a major medical advance through the use of superconductor technology.

Superconductor research advanced throughout the decade of the 1980s, with a wide range of applications envisioned. Superconductors are materials that conduct electricity perfectly, with no loss of energy to resistance. They repel magnetic

961 | *Robert Jarvik (right) with artificial heart*

fields, causing levitation. However, from their 1911 discovery until 1986, it was thought that the material had to be chilled almost to absolute zero (-460°F) to calm the ricocheting electrons that generate heat in the transmission of electricity. Scientists at IBM's Swiss laboratory made history by using a ceramic formulated with copper oxide, which worked at the slightly warmer temperature of -406°F.

Improved ceramic technology, higher temperature points, and the use of inexpensive liquid nitrogen for cooling have brought practical applications closer to reality. A hoped-for result is a superconductor replacement for conventional power lines, which lose significant amounts of electricity due to resistance. Research also continues on superconductors in satellite and maglev technology.

Protocol Links Computers

963 **1983** The switch from Network Control Protocol (NCP) to Transmission Control Protocol/Internet Protocol (TCP/IP) made the global Internet a reality. The former communication system allowed data-sharing only between computers that were connected within the same network, but new protocols allowed computers to share files with those in different networks. The National Science Foundation created a system linking the nation's computer science departments and adopted TCP/IP, the standard protocol for today's Internet, a decentralized worldwide network of computers.

> ■ **FOOTNOTE** The early National Science Foundation Network (NSFNET) connected research and information-sharing supercomputing centers on a high-speed network—with network speeds reaching 56 kbps.

Gorbachev Takes Over

964 **1985** On March 11, Mikhail Gorbachev succeeded Konstantin Chernenko as leader of the Soviet Union. Gorbachev's relative youth and vigor, in contrast to Chernenko's poor health, gave him an advantage in mobilizing support and proposing change. Gorbachev was initially thought by many to be a strict proponent of Soviet ideology, but he quickly showed a willingness to work with the West, and his glasnost, or policy of openness, transformed the Soviet Union. Eight months after he took office, Gorbachev met with U.S. President Ronald Reagan in Geneva—the first meeting between the two countries' leaders in six years. In 1991, President George H. W. Bush and Gorbachev signed the Strategic Arms Reduction Treaty, and in 1993 each country reduced its number of nuclear warheads by half. Under Gorbachev's perestroika—economic restructuring—Russia began the transformation out of Cold War-era communism toward a market economy. Gorbachev's progressive policies antagonized the old regime, which ultimately forced him to resign in December 1991. But just days after his resignation the Soviet flag was retired as the old republic gave way to a confederation of Soviet states.

Ozone Hole Spotted

965 **1985** A hole in the ozone layer was reported in 1985 by researchers of the British Antarctic Survey, a study begun in 1957 to monitor changes in Earth's stratosphere. For the survey's first two decades, ozone levels varied in a regular seasonal pattern. But in 1985 a measurable hole in the ozone layer was detected.

Ozone is Earth's sunscreen, a three-atom compound of oxygen created in the stratosphere between 6 and 30 miles above the planet's surface. Ozone absorbs solar

---

CONNECTIONS

Planetery Exploration
Probing ever farther in the solar system

When planetary exploration began, it focused on the moon. This exploration truly began in 1959 with the Soviet probe Luna 1, which was the first probe to pass near the moon. The second Luna then became the first man-made object to impact the moon. The series photographed more than half of the moon's surface. Also in 1959, America's Pioneer 4 probe became the first U.S. solar orbiter. Not until 1964 would the world glance at close-range images of the moon from the American probe Ranger 7.

Soon the scope of exploration expanded. The first close-range images of Mars arrived in 1965 from the American Mariner 4. The Soviets impacted Venus in March 1966 with Venus 3 and accomplished their first full moon orbit with Luna 10. The American Lunar Orbiter 1, in August that year, captured the first image of Earth from the moon's orbit.

Rover in Nevada field tests to simulate conditions on Mars

In November 1971, Earth's probing reach extended farther, with the first orbit of another planet. American Mariner 9 reached Mars, orbiting the red planet and documenting its entire surface. Expansion continued two years later with the first close-ups of Jupiter from the American Pioneer 10. Pioneer 10 simultaneously became the first probe to travel through the asteroid belt.

The Soviets focused their efforts on Venus. In October 1975, they received the first pictures of its surface from Venera 9 and Venera 10. In March 1982, Venera 13 became the first probe to land on the surface. Pioneer 11 reached Saturn in September 1979, sending the first close-range images of it. At the same time, the U.S. put together the Voyager project, consisting of two probes, Voyagers 1 and 2, whose goal was to gather data from the far reaches of the solar system. Should extraterrestrials come across the probes once they left range, a package of information, language, sounds, and images of Earth was included. The Voyagers reached Jupiter in 1979 and Saturn the year after. Six years after encountering Saturn, Voyager 2 passed Uranus and continued into deep space.

The new millennium became the time for discoveries. In 2004, probes reported information indicating that, in the past, significant volumes of Martian rock were located underwater. The red planet no longer shows any capability of life, but the presence of water would indicate that at some point it might have. In 2005, a potential new planet with a mass larger than that of Pluto was discovered. The mass, nicknamed Xena, was officially labeled as a dwarf planet. The next year Pluto would lose its status as a planet, also becoming classified as a dwarf planet.

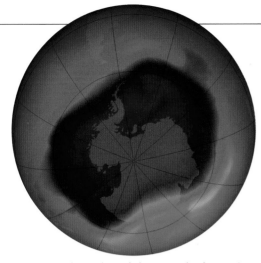

965 | *Blue and purple low ozone levels, 2006*

ultraviolet radiation, which can damage our very DNA if it reaches life-forms on Earth. When scientists sought reasons for the decrease in ozone levels, they ultimately pinpointed a class of chemicals known as chlorofluorocarbons (CFCs) used as refrigerants, solvents, and propellants. Studies revealed that CFCs break up ozone molecules and, worse yet, are so stable that they can linger in the atmosphere for a century or more. An international mandate led to CFCs being replaced with less harmful chemicals.

■ **FOOTNOTE** Ozone can cause respiratory distress to humans and animals within the ground-level atmosphere. At much higher levels, however, it acts as a filter, preventing ultraviolet light from penetrating.

CD-ROMs Created

966 **1986** Sony and Philips jointly introduced the CD-ROM (compact disc–read-only memory) in 1986. This breakthrough in computer-related technology enabled digital storage and retrieval of vast amounts of data—including sound, text, and pictures—on one small disc. Sony and Philips had previously collaborated in the early 1980s on the launch of the CD-DA (compact disc-digital audio), which reproduced sound in superb quality and virtually replaced long-playing records made from plastic. Applications of the new CD-ROM technology included not only audio, but also digital storage of computer content that included text and images. CD-ROM became a standard feature on most computers in the mid-1990s.

Chernobyl Malfunctions

967 **1986** A partial meltdown of the Soviet nuclear power plant at Chernobyl released radiation over wide areas of Ukraine, Belarus, and Russia in 1986. Workers had been conducting a test in the early hours of April 26, with the emergency water-cooling system shut down. Mounting pressure blew the lid off the container of the No. 4 reactor, spewing radiation and flaming particles into the environment. Thirty-one people died from exposure shortly after the incident, and as fires raged, toxic clouds carried high levels of radiation to millions more. The secretive Soviet government waited two days before alerting the public.

Cancers and other health problems still plague the region, and children in western Ukraine and Belarus are still monitored for lingering traces of exposure.

Challenger Explodes

968 **1986** The space shuttle *Challenger* broke apart 73 seconds after liftoff, killing all seven crew members. At 11:38 a.m. on January 28, 1986—an unusually cold morning in Florida—the 25th shuttle mission was launched from Cape Canaveral. Among the crew was Christa McAuliffe, a New Hampshire high school teacher selected as the first to teach from space. Millions watched, and their exuberance turned to horror as the disaster unfolded.

Shuttle launches were immediately suspended as NASA investigated every aspect of shuttle operation to find the cause of the tragedy. An impulsive act by a member of the specially appointed presidential commission—dropping a small O-ring gasket into a glass of ice water—led to the conclusion that O-rings on the rocket boosters had become brittle in the cold weather and failed, causing fuel tanks to explode. These findings resulted in redesign of the seals and creation of a crew escape system.

■ **FOOTNOTE** Besides Christa McAuliffe, the *Challenger* crew of seven included: Mission Commander Francis Scobee, plus Michael Smith, Judith Resnik, Ronald McNair, Ellison Onizuka, and Gregory B. Jarvis.

Philippine Reforms

969 **1986** "People power" brought reform to the Philippines, a nation of 7,107 Pacific islands that gained

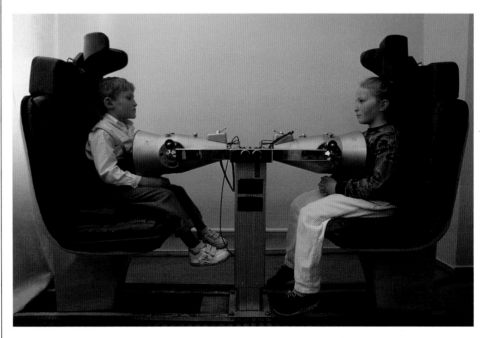

967 | *Russian children scanned for carcinogenic radioisotope eight years after Chernobyl meltdown*

independence in 1946 when Japanese occupation ended. In the ensuing decades, widespread poverty, political corruption, and insurgent attacks sparked unrest. The dissatisfied populace demanded in 1986 that heavy-handed President Ferdinand Marcos stand election. Opposing him was a reluctant yet determined candidate— Corazon Aquino, widow of assassinated opposition leader Benigno Aquino. Marcos tried to rig the election and claim victory, but key government officials mutinied. In an extraordinary demonstration of "people power," hundreds of thousands of unarmed citizens stood up to Marcos' military action and pushed the despot into exile. Corazon Aquino made lasting changes as leader of the troubled government, creating a new constitution to prevent dictatorship, freeing political prisoners, and working toward economic recovery and peace among fighting factions within the country. The Philippine government continues to make progress in negotiations with Muslim rebels.

■ **FOOTNOTE** Ferdinand Marcos's wife, Imelda, symbolized his decadent presidency with her shopping excesses. She reportedly protested an inaccurately high estimate of her shoe collection, saying that she had only 1,060 pairs.

Stocks Crash

970 **1987** A stock market crash in New York, larger than the one in 1929, shocked the world in 1987.

971 | *Dalai Lama at press conference at Kaohsiung Airport in Taiwan, 1997*

During the week of October 14-19, stock prices dropped off drastically, which culminated in a new Black Monday on October 19: The Dow Jones Industrial Index fell 508 points in one day, with a record 604 million shares traded. Stock prices plummeted 22 percent on that day alone. Unlike in the 1929 crash, however, Black Tuesday did not ensue. The next day saw a record gain of 102.27 points. The U.S. Federal Reserve Board flooded the market with money by buying government securities. Banks took this as a good sign and resumed lending to securities firms. Several companies bought back their own stocks.

Analysts attribute the cause of this crash to several factors, including a high U.S. trade deficit, inflated stock prices, and volatile interest rates in Europe. Investors lost billions of dollars in stock value, but the economy bounced back.

Dalai Lama Gets Nobel

971 **1989** Tenzin Gyatso, 14th Dalai Lama of Tibet, gave a Nobel acceptance speech in 1989. Identified at age 2 as the next Dalai Lama ("ocean of wisdom"), Tenzin Gyatso was placed on the throne three years later, in 1940, in the capital city of Lhasa. He became Tibet's head of government in 1950. When China overtook the country in 1959, the Dalai Lama was driven into exile in India. From there, he serves as the spiritual leader of millions of Tibetans and works toward the liberation of his homeland and a peaceful agreement between Tibet and China. He was awarded the Nobel Peace Prize in 1989 for his constructive philosophy of nonviolence, problem-solving, and reverence for living things.

The Dalai Lama has written a number of books on topics ranging from the spiritual to the secular. He is a popular speaker and proponent of freedom for Tibetans.

■ **FOOTNOTE** The Dalai Lama is recognized as the leader of Tibetan Buddhists and a spiritual figure even by many non-Buddhists, but his authority does not extend to other Buddhist traditions, such as those in Thailand or Japan.

973 | *Graffiti-covered Berlin wall, symbol of communism, before it was removed.*

Chinese Protest Quashed

972 **1989** A student protest for democracy was brutally put down by the Chinese government in Beijing's Tiananmen Square. The protest began in April 1989, when students and teachers gathered to honor the late Hu Yaobang, an official who crusaded against corruption. City workers and others added their voices to the call for greater freedoms. To coincide with an upcoming visit by Soviet president Mikhail Gorbachev, protesters began a hunger strike in May—and China's leader, Deng Xiaoping, brought down the hammer. He imposed martial law and sent tanks to the square, where almost a million protesters had amassed. Overnight on June 3-4, a 50-truck convoy crushed protesters as they slept. Others were cut down by soldiers with assault rifles. The movement ended as the bloody suppression killed hundreds, if not thousands, of protesters. China's relations with the horrified

West were damaged, and Zhou Ziyang was removed as head of the Chinese Communist Party for his sympathetic stance. The regime held onto its power.

Berlin Wall Falls

973 **1989** On November 9, the Berlin Wall came down, reuniting a city divided since the end of World War II and providing a powerful symbol of the fall of the Soviet bloc. The East German government bowed to massive demonstrations and allowed free access by opening the Berlin Wall, which the Soviets had constructed in 1961 to cut off East Berliners' access to the West. On November 11, jubilant crowds sang "Wir sind ein Volk—We Are One People" as East Germans breached the barricade. One year later, the wall was officially dismantled—and Germany was reborn as one country.

With the opening of the wall, East Berliners would no longer have to go to the desperate measures many took to escape East Germany. It is estimated that, during the 28 years of the wall's existence, about 10,000 people attempted to cross the wall to freedom. About half of them were successful, while the other half were caught by East German authorities and 191 people were actually killed during the attempt.

■ FOOTNOTE A year after the wall fell, former Pink Floyd singer Roger Waters staged a rock opera, *The Wall: Live in Berlin,* to raise funds for the city. A quarter million attended and 500 million people in 52 countries watched it on TV.

Dissolution of Soviet Union

974 **1989** In the 1980s, against long-standing communist policy, reform-minded Soviet President Mikhail Gorbachev had instituted glasnost (openness), allowing citizens to speak more freely. Communist regimes were put down in Bulgaria, Czechoslovakia, Romania, and Hungary, with the latter opening its borders to East Germans fleeing Communist control. The Communist Party of the Soviet Union (CPSU) had been the authoritarian ruling body, dating from the Russian Revolution in October 1917. The name of the party—originally Bolshevik—went through several changes before becoming the CPSU after the U.S.S.R. was formed in 1952. Though the government and CPSU technically were separate bodies, members of government were also CPSU members, and thus CPSU ideology dictated government policy. A series of general secretaries maintained strict adherence to communist ideals. And yet the charismatic, reform-minded Gorbachev eventually assumed the role of general secretary after Konstantin Chernenko's death. Not without opposition, Gorbachev established relationships with Western powers and reform within the country. In 1990, opposition parties were legalized, CPSU membership declined, and free, multiparty elections were held. After the increasingly desperate CPSU attempted to oust Gorbachev, it lost its hold over the government and military. Although Gorbachev was finally forced to resign in December 1991, the hammer and sickle lowered for the last time on December 25, 1991.

The 14th Dalai Lama
NOBEL PRIZE ACCEPTANCE SPEECH, 1989

I feel honored, humbled and deeply moved that you should give this important prize to a simple monk from Tibet. I am no one special. But I believe the prize is recognition of the true value of altruism, love, compassion and non-violence which I try to practice, in accordance with the teachings of the Buddha and the great sages of India and Tibet

I accept the prize with profound gratitude on behalf of the oppressed everywhere and for all those who struggle for freedom and work for world peace. I accept it as a tribute to the man who founded the modern tradition of non-violent action for change: Mahatma Gandhi, whose life taught and inspired me. And, of course, I accept it on behalf of the six million Tibetan people, my brave countrymen and women inside Tibet, who have suffered and continue to suffer so much. They confront a calculated and systematic strategy aimed at the destruction of their national and cultural identities. The prize reaffirms our conviction that with truth, courage and determination as our weapons, Tibet will be liberated.

As a Buddhist monk, my concern extends to all members of the human family and, indeed, to all sentient beings who suffer.... We need to cultivate a universal responsibility for one another and the planet we share. Although I have found my own Buddhist religion helpful in generating love and compassion, even for those we consider our enemies, I am convinced that everyone can develop a good heart and a sense of universal responsibility with or without religion.

As we enter the final decade of this century I am optimistic that the ancient values that have sustained mankind are today reaffirming themselves to prepare us for a kinder, happier twenty-first century.

I pray for all of us, oppressor and friend, that together we succeed in building a better world through human understanding and love, and that in doing so we may reduce the pain and suffering of all sentient beings.

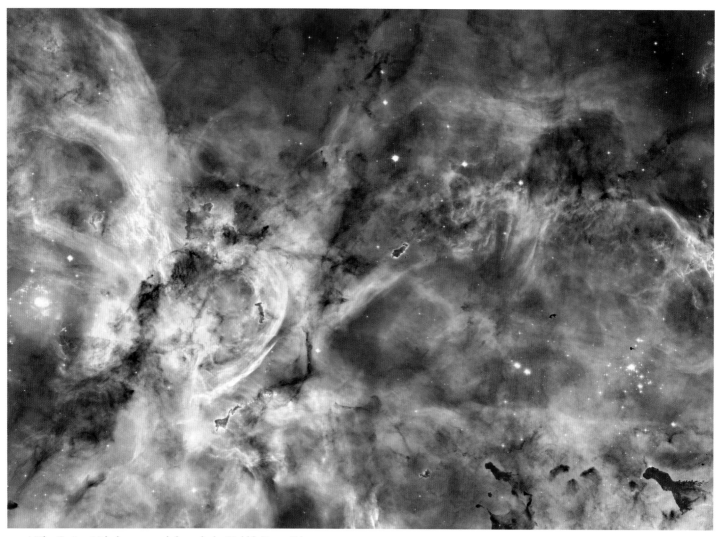

977 | *The Carina Nebula, captured through the Hubble Space Telescope*

First Email

975 **1989** Electronic mail, or email, was originally developed in conjunction with the U.S. Department of Defense's computer-based messaging system, ARPANET. Computer engineer Ray Tomlinson, a consultant from the firm Bolt Beranek and Newman who worked with ARPANET, made it possible to transfer files among several computers on a network. Considered the "father of email," he created email addresses using the now-familiar symbol @ (chosen because this character would not be part of someone's name), and sent the world's first email message—probably a meaningless string of letters such as "QWERTYUIOP," the top row of an American keyboard.

Gene Therapy Performed

976 **1990** The first successful gene therapy on a human was performed in 1990 at the U.S. National Institutes of Health. The patient, four-year-old Ashanti DeSilva, suffered from severe combined immunodeficiency (SCID), in which a defective gene left her body unable to produce an enzyme crucial to immune system functioning. Doctors from the National Heart, Lung, and Blood Institutes and the National Cancer Institute drew Ashanti's blood, treated some of her white blood cells with viruses carrying healthy copies of the defective gene, and reinjected the cells into her body.

While periodic repeat treatments were indicated in Ashanti's case to keep her enzymes at the correct level, she was the first to show positive—though not permanent—results from gene therapy. Several other patients with the same condition were similarly treated but did not survive, succumbing to infection caused by the gene-carrying virus or leukemia from genetic mutation.

■ **FOOTNOTE** The goal of gene therapy is to cure inherited conditions—such as hemophilia, cystic fibrosis, or Huntington's disease—by isolating faulty genes and replacing them with healthy ones.

Telescope Launched

977 **1990** The Hubble Space Telescope was deployed by NASA from the space shuttle *Discovery* on April 25, 1990.

Named for astronomer Edwin Hubble, it peers across light-years and back in time to capture high-resolution images of galaxies that thrived one billion years ago.

The bus-size Hubble is the first orbiting observatory built to be serviced in space; it includes fixtures designed specifically for capture by the space shuttle's robotic arm and has undergone repairs in this manner. With three cameras, two spectrographs, and fine guidance sensors, the Hubble has provided many remarkable sights: a comet's collision with Jupiter; exploding stars and gamma-ray bursts from the early universe; evidence of Einstein's "dark force," a repulsive form of gravity; and the stunning births of stars in cloud-like nebulae.

■ **FOOTNOTE** Astronomer Edwin Hubble (1889-1953) discovered the existence of numerous galaxies besides ours and developed the theory that the farther apart galaxies are, the more quickly they move away from one another.

Dial-Up Access

978 **1990** In 1990, the first commercial dial-up service—called The World and addressed "world.std.com"—became available to consumers. Soon the use of the Internet exploded, as consumers used home computers and fast modems to access an ever growing array of online services. Broadband and high-speed technologies aided this boom, enabling users to send and receive data much more quickly and efficiently, and in higher volume, than with dial-up access. From 2000 to 2007, the use of the Internet grew 214 percent worldwide.

Mad Cow Explained

979 **1991** As a medical resident, Stanley Prusiner had treated a patient suffering from Creutzfeldt-Jakob disease, a "slow virus" infection with devastating neurological effects. Prusiner questioned whether a virus really was the cause. Making a major step forward by isolating a gene probe in 1984, Prusiner discovered a new class of disease-causing agent, which he called a prion, for "proteinaceous infectious

particle." Further research showed that prions are usually harmless cell proteins, but can convert to forms that cause always-fatal illnesses including Creutzfeldt-Jakob; scrapie, which affects sheep and other species; and bovine spongiform encephalopathy, also known as mad cow disease. All of these cause the sufferer's brain tissue to become spongy as nerve death progresses. Early on, fellow scientists doubted Prusiner's work. Receiving the Potamkin Prize for neurological advances in 1991, he began to receive more credit. He won the Nobel Prize in medicine in 1997.

U.S. Storms Desert

980 **1991** On January 17, a U.S.-British air campaign struck Iraq military targets, in fulfillment of a deadline issued by the UN Security Council to Saddam Hussein to remove Iraqi soldiers from Kuwait. Ground forces followed, attacking on February 24. By February 27, the Iraqis had retreated, Kuwait City was liberated, and the next morning at eight o'clock, a cease-fire halted the war.

The tensions leading up to the war lasted longer than the war itself. Hussein's Iraqi Republican Guard troops invaded Kuwait on August 2, 1990. As the UN condemned Iraq's invasion of Kuwait, the U.S. began mobilizing forces. On August 7, American troops deployed to the region to restore Kuwait's government and to protect oil resources—those of Kuwait, but especially those of neighboring Saudi Arabia, on whose oil the U.S. and many nations depended. The UN gave Hussein an ultimatum: Remove Iraqi troops from Kuwait by January 15 or coalition forces would attack. Hussein did not budge and was quickly overwhelmed by airstrikes followed by ground forces. When it became evident that it could not win, Iraq began to retreat, first attempting to destroy Kuwait's oil supply by burning its oil fields. The U.S. did not succeed in one of its goals, which was to replace Iraqi leadership.

Web Worldwide

981 **1991** The World Wide Web, one of the most significant advances in the development of the Internet, was released in 1991. It owed its early existence to a number of organizations, including the Defense Advanced Research Projects Agency, universities, and political support. Early users were primarily engineers, librarians, and scientists for applications such as defense planning, cataloging, and information-sharing. The Web was invented at CERN, the European Laboratory for Particle Physics, when software engineer Tim Berners-Lee needed a computer system to keep his files organized in a "brainlike way." He devised software that created links among all related files in his computer, and soon linked many computers so users could share files with no central database or manager. The Internet was already running, primarily as a means for email messages, and Berners-Lee built the World Wide Web on that foundation—making the technology public so that anyone with Internet access could retrieve and contribute information. HTML (hypertext markup language) was invented as the code creating links to files, and HTTP (hypertext transfer protocol) was created to move them in and out of the Web. Within five years of the Web's debut, the number of Internet users rocketed from 600,000 to 40 million.

Yahoo!'s updated Web page, with older version in background

1946–PRESENT | Modern Age

983 | *President Bill Clinton addressing a Chamber of Commerce group on the benefits of NAFTA*

However, the major victory in this war, the rapid deployment, overwhelming attack, and quick victory was made possible for the first time by heavy reliance on technology.

■ **FOOTNOTE** Patriots on the home front tied yellow ribbons around trees to support the U.S. troops abroad. When the war ended, Gen. Norman Schwarzkopf led tanks down Constitution Avenue in Washington, D.C., in a victory parade.

Books Online

982 **1992** Project Gutenberg, a gargantuan effort to digitize important works of literature, was launched in 1992. Founder Michael Hart began the project in 1971 when he received a lot of free computer time and decided to create something of value—the online capability for storage, search, and retrieval of the treasures held in libraries. His first entry was the Declaration of Independence. Today, legions of volunteers type or scan in books whose copyrights are no longer in force; a work enters the public domain 50 years after the lifetime of its author. At least 20,000 free titles are available in the world's first and largest online collection.

North America Trades

983 **1993** The United States, Mexico, and Canada formed the North American Free Trade Agreement (NAFTA) in 1993, creating the world's largest and wealthiest trading bloc. The agreement removed most barriers to trade and investment among the three countries, with remaining tariffs to be phased out by 2008. NAFTA's supporters favored trade liberalization as a way to increase national wealth; ease arbitrary rules for farmers, workers, and manufacturers; and provide lower prices and more choices for consumers. The controversial agreement had its critics as well, with trade unions and environmentalists protesting that NAFTA would reduce wages in the U.S., take jobs to Mexico, and undermine safety standards regarding food, health, and the environment. Effects have not been as drastic as feared, and the office of the U.S. Trade Representative reports that for the years from 1993 to 2005, trade among the three countries went up 173 percent—from $297 billion to $810 billion.

■ **FOOTNOTE** NAFTA promoters included corporations, while its opponents included labor unions, environmentalists, religious groups, and consumer advocates who believed it would lower standards and erode jobs.

Rabin Offers Peace

984 **1993** Israeli Prime Minister Yitzhak Rabin addressed the Palestinian people in his "Enough of Blood and Tears" speech, signifying his nation's willingness for peace and compromise in the region.

The onetime warrior, together with Palestinian Liberation Organization leader Yasser Arafat and former Israeli Prime Minister Shimon Peres, had forged the Oslo Accords—a historic treaty granting land and territory to the Palestinians. When Arafat offered a gesture of goodwill at the 1993 White House ceremony, Rabin participated in the historic handshake. His speech implored, "Enough of blood and tears.... We, like you, are people: people who want to build a home, to plant a tree, to love, to live side by side with you in dignity."

The three leaders won the Nobel Peace Prize, but within a few months, extremists on both sides resumed fighting—and two years later, as he left a peace rally, Rabin was assassinated by an Israeli student who feared that the prime minister was giving away too much in his quest for peace.

Tomato Modified

985 **1994** The Flavr Savr tomato, the first whole food developed by genetic engineering and the first genetically modified food sold to the public in the United States, was approved in 1994 by the U.S. Food and Drug Administration. To create a tomato with a longer shelf life, scientists removed a gene that affected the gradual softening that fruits undergo as they age, and reinserted it backward. The altered tomato ripened well and resisted softening—but was removed from the market because its cost was too high for the product to be profitable.

Chunnel Opens

986 **1994** The English Channel Tunnel between England and France was formally opened in 1994, another step in the union envisioned by many European countries. The two nations agreed in 1964 to construct the "Chunnel," which spans 31 miles from Coquelles, France, to Folkestone, England. Workers took three years to bore through the chalky earth from both ends. This complex system is engineered to carry massive double-decker trains in two five-foot-thick concrete tunnels, with a third tube in between for maintenance and emergencies, and water pipes running alongside the tracks to cool them. Ducts open and close to relieve the pressure that builds before the fast-moving trains. Passengers plunge beneath the Channel at 100 miles an hour. By linking Great Britain with continental Europe, the Chunnel marks the fulfillment of a centuries-old dream. The American Society of Civil Engineers named it one of the seven wonders of the modern world.

Opening the Chunnel was accompanied by great pomp. France's president, François Mitterrand, and Queen Elizabeth II conducted ribbon-cutting ceremonies, and a number of other high-ranking officials attended. Despite high expectations, the Eurotunnel-operated Chunnel was initially extremely unprofitable, and the company recorded one of the greatest UK corporate losses to date. Since then, usage has steadily increased and, with the exception of a six-month service shutdown to repair damage from a fire, the Chunnel, with its 20-minute ride from England to France, has become a popular mode of transportation.

FOOTNOTE The Chunnel marks the modern physical link of two age-old rivals, a marked truce after such historic battles as the Hundred Years' War's Battle of Crecy in 1346, in which King Edward III invaded France near Cherbourg.

New Quark Found

987 **1995** The last of the six quarks that make up protons and neutrons was detected. In the orders of magnitude that govern matter, the atom—once thought to be the smallest possible unit—can be split into protons, neutrons, electrons, and other particles. Protons and neutrons are further composed of quarks.

CONNECTIONS

Genetically Modified Food
From Gregor Mendel to the Flavr Savr tomato

When Gregor Mendel discovered the methods of crossbreeding among plants and the laws of heredity in the mid-19th century, he could not have realized that nearly 200 years later his much more natural method of genetic manipulation would develop into genetic modification. The DNA of genetically modified (GM) crops is altered synthetically with the use of recombinant DNA technology. When applied, this method allows a gene from one organism's DNA to be cut and spliced into the sequence of another organism's DNA. Genetic modification should not be confused with crossbreeding, which consists of interbreeding species of organisms to achieve specific characteristics.

The first genetically modified organism was released by the U.S. Department of Agriculture in 1986, in the form of a virus. Meanwhile researchers were testing the first GM crop, a high-yield tobacco plant. Soon scientists were able to produce potatoes from the United Kingdom that were inserted with genes to increase their protein content, new baking yeasts, and the Flavr Savr tomato, produced by the molecular biologists at Calgene Inc.

The public greeted these revolutionary products with suspicion, however, often viewing them as potentially dangerous and generally unnatural—the product of science gone mad. Some, such as Dr. Arpad Pusztai,

Insect-resistant corn has been produced.

claimed to have obtained proof that such creations cause permanent internal damage. Other claims regarding "Frankenfood" worry that it may promote food allergies, that the natural nutrient levels will be lost, or that it might cause a future resistance to antibiotics. Some wonder whether these plants, due to their foreign properties, might cause damage to the soil and the surrounding environment. Ultimately, however, no decisive proof, either negative or positive, has yet been provided.

Yet GM crops have become a very real part of agriculture. By the end of the 20th century several pharmaceutical drugs were approved by the FDA that were recombinant in nature, and Chymosin, a GM enzyme used in the production of cheese, made its way into use. While the Flavr Savr tomato, perhaps the most publicized GM crop to date, was approved as safe, supplies and sales remained too low to support its continued production. However, the government's widespread approval of the innovative tomato served as a precedent, and GM products are slowly making their way into the agricultural market. While most are simply small ingredients, such as yeast, insect-protected corn and cotton have gained increasing acceptance and use. But although the concept of genetically enhanced products has lost some of its shock value, the prospect of GM animals continues to raise many ethical concerns.

980 More Details on Gulf Wars

On January 17, 1991, a coalition of UN forces, led by the United States, launched a campaign to liberate Kuwait from an Iraqi invasion. The resulting Persian Gulf war, known also by its U.S. name, Operation Desert Storm, was a swift and successful operation, with minimal casualties on the side of the coalition. The damage to Iraqi and Kuwaiti infrastructure, however, was substantial, and the fires that raged on Kuwaiti oil fields, set by retreating Iraqi forces, produced some of the most haunting and memorable images of the conflict.

The decision in favor of military action was based as much on the territorial integrity of Kuwait as on the Western world's economic interest in the region. The Iraqi invasion of Kuwait on August 2, 1990, threatened economic giant and longtime U.S. ally Saudi Arabia, and on August 7, the U.S. launched a separate defensive mission, Operation Desert Shield, to protect the Saudis from an Iraqi attack. The war was overwhelmingly supported on the home front; major media outlets, too, looked favorably on military action and the leadership of President George H. W. Bush and provided unprecedented television coverage. The war was further justified by well-publicized information about the human rights abuses of the Iraq regime and by Iraqi President Saddam Hussein's nuclear ambitions. But the U.S., after freeing Kuwait and securing Saudi Arabia, refrained from deposing Hussein, citing the enormity of the military effort it would take and the strain of a long-term commitment in Iraq.

> The fires that raged on Kuwaiti oil fields ... are some of the most haunting ... images of the conflict.

Just over one decade later, however, spurred by the September 11 tragedy, the U.S. would renege on this strategy and overthrow the Iraq regime, beginning a long and exceptionally controversial military engagement in the region. The new Iraqi government today faces a country torn apart by civil war and terrorism, and the stability of the surrounding region has drastically deteriorated. Military and civilian casualties are high, as the insurgents' suicide bombing tactics present unprecedented military challenges. A U.S. withdrawal looms on the horizon, but the fate of the new Iraq remains in question.

Iraqis set the oil fields outside Kuwait City ablaze after coalition forces arrived during Operation Desert Storm.

Diana, Princess of Wales

EULOGY BY EARL CHARLES SPENCER, 1997

I stand before you today the representative of a family in grief, in a country in mourning before a world in shock. We are all united not only in our desire to pay our respects to Diana but … in our need to do so. For such was her extraordinary appeal that the tens of millions of people taking part in this service all over the world via television and radio … feel that they too lost someone close to them…. It is a more remarkable tribute to Diana than I can ever hope to offer her today.

Diana was the very essence of compassion, of duty, of style, of beauty. All over the world she was a symbol of selfless humanity. All over the world, a standard bearer for the rights of the truly downtrodden, a very British girl who transcended nationality. Someone with a natural nobility who was classless and who proved in the last year that she needed no royal title to continue to generate her particular brand of magic….

Diana explained to me once that it was her innermost feelings of suffering that made it possible for her to connect with her constituency of the rejected. The world sensed this part of her character and cherished her for her vulnerability whilst admiring her for her honesty.

The last time I saw Diana was on July 1, her birthday, in London, when typically she was not taking time to celebrate her special day with friends but was guest of honour at a special charity fund-raising evening. She sparkled of course, but I would rather cherish the days I spent with her in March when she came to visit me and my children in our home in South Africa. I am proud of the fact that apart from when she was on display meeting President Mandela we managed to contrive to stop the ever-present paparazzi from getting a single picture of her….

I would like to end by thanking God for the small mercies he has shown us at this dreadful time. For taking Diana at her most beautiful and radiant and when she had joy in her private life. Above all we give thanks for the life of a woman I am so proud to be able to call my sister, the unique, the complex, the extraordinary and irreplaceable Diana….

Electron-scattering experiments at Stanford and MIT hinted at the existence of these pointlike objects, which have fractional charges. They were named "quarks" for a passage in James Joyce's novel *Finnegan's Wake*. Six kinds of quarks have been discovered and given equally whimsical names—up, down, strange, charm, bottom, and top. Up and down quarks make up most of the world's matter. These enigmatic particles are virtually weightless, but they move around so fast that they give weight. Their mass comes from their motion and the powerful force field between them: 15 tons of force holds two quarks together. The largest quark and final one predicted to exist—the up quark—was discovered by the Fermi National Accelerator Laboratory in 1995.

■ **FOOTNOTE** Quark is also a type of central European curd cheese, as well as the name of a software program widely used for desktop publishing, including design, layout, and editing.

GPS in Place

988 **1995** The satellite-based global positioning system (GPS) was envisioned in 1973 and became operational in 1995. The system uses 24 orbiting satellites arranged so every point on Earth is always in contact with 4 of them. The GPS receiver picks up each satellite's position and the exact time as determined by ultraprecise atomic clocks and uses that information to calculate its own position within a hundred feet. There are actually two GPS signals: a civilian signal, and a more precise one that only the military can decipher. The civilian system is used in fields such as mapmaking, commercial shipping, emergency response, seismic monitoring, aviation, and automobile technology.

GPS, increasingly known as global navigation satellite system (GNSS), is also being used for more mundane infrastructure tasks such as locating buried utility cables to speed construction projects and repairs. The military uses GPS for security, surveillance, hazardous materials monitoring, warfare, space exploration, aviation,

989 | *Cloned sheep Dolly, originally called 6LL3*

precision guidance, and navigation. Europe is currently constructing a new civilian-owned and -operated network of 30 satellites, known as Galileo. This will alleviate its reliance on the military-controlled U.S. GPS or the Russian global navigation satellite system (GLONASS).

Sheep Cloned

989 **1997** British scientist Ian Wilmut announced the successful cloning of a sheep, a process in which DNA from a single cell was coaxed to develop into a living genetic replica of the entire animal. The team took a cell from one female sheep and an unfertilized egg from another, removed both nuclei, and, with a spark of electricity, fused the nucleus from the cell into the denucleated egg—which began to develop as though fertilized. It was implanted in the womb of a third ewe, where a pregnancy progressed. Dolly the cloned sheep met the world in February 1997, becoming an instant media darling and the focus of volatile controversy over the ethics and safety of cloning. The complex process can go fatally wrong at any stage, and many governments quickly moved to ban human cloning. Several groups of secretive scientists have claimed to be working on such a project, but this has not been verified. Since Dolly's birth, numerous other mammal species have been successfully cloned.

Monkeys, calves, pigs, cats, mice, goats, and mules have been cloned successfully using nuclear transfer. Studying and creating clones helps scientists hone treatments for genetic disorders and reproduce certain characteristics, such as high milk yield in cattle.

■FOOTNOTE There are three types of cloning: recombinant DNA technology (commonly used in molecular biology), reproductive cloning (the type used in Dolly's origins) and therapeutic cloning (used to harvest stem cells for research).

Princess Diana Dies

990 **1997** A year after her divorce from Charles, Prince of Wales, Princess Diana died in a car crash in Paris on August 31, 1997. Also killed were Diana's companion, Dodi Fayed, and their driver, who had tried to outrun paparazzi. The world reacted with shock and sorrow: The caring, spontaneous personality Diana projected had contrasted with the formal ways of England's royal family, and the stylish princess was widely admired. Her funeral—a farewell planned by both the royals and Diana's family—reflected her unique position as the divorced mother of the heir to England's throne as well as her prominence as a charity activist and beloved symbol. More than a million people lined London's streets as the cortege passed, with an estimated 2.5 billion watching on TV to pay respects to the "people's princess."

Ten years after Diana's death, audiences flocked to see *The Queen,* a movie dramatizing Diana's death from Queen Elizabeth II's perspective. For her portrayal of the queen, Helen Mirren was named best actress of 2007 in both the U.S. (where she won the Oscar) and the U.K., where she was honored by the British Academy of Film and Television Arts Awards.

On the tenth anniversary of her death, Diana's sons, William and Harry, hosted a memorial service at Guards' Chapel, Wellington Barracks, with speakers from Diana's charities. Earlier, on what would have been her 46th birthday—July 1—thousands attended a Concert for Diana at Wembley Stadium.

990 | *From left, Prince Charles, Prince Harry, Earl Spencer, Prince William, and Prince Philip face Lady Diana's coffin at Westminster Abbey, September 1997.*

1946-PRESENT | Modern Age

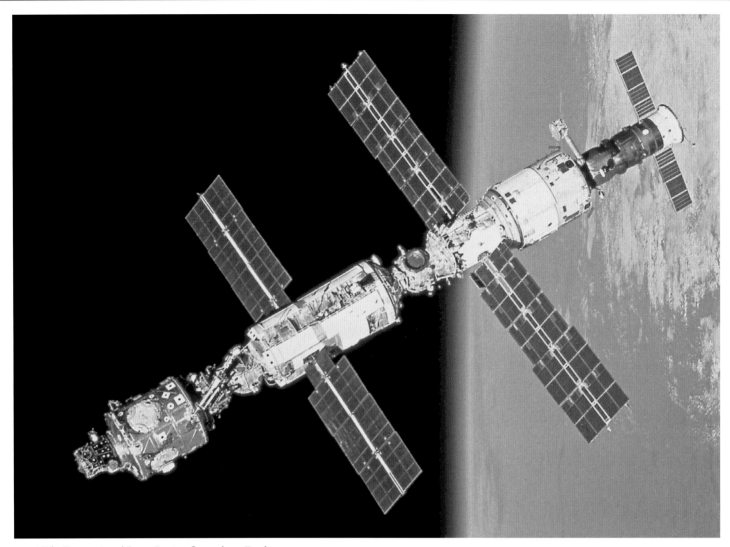

992 | *The International Space Station floats above Earth.*

Google Searches

991 **1997** Internet search engine Google opened its doors in 1998 and became so popular that its name is now a verb. Google founders Larry Page and Sergey Brin created an algorithm for the search engine as a graduate school project. Working in a friend's Silicon Valley garage, they founded their company and named it for the numeral 1 followed by 100 zeros—a googol. Google now handles 45 percent of all Internet searches. The company went public in August 2004, and by the end of 2005 its worth had topped $100 billion. Google's revenue—$1.5 billion in 2005—comes primarily from advertising, which is targeted to the topics that users search and the sites they visit. With an offbeat corporate culture that encourages innovation and individualism, the company has expanded its services to include shopping, email, digital photo management, and Google Earth satellite imaging of any address. Google and other search engines have put an almost limitless array of information at users' fingertips and opened a gigantic new medium for advertisers.

■ **FOOTNOTE** Meta search engines or meta-crawlers do not search themselves but aggregate results of search engines such as Google and Yahoo. They include: Dogpile, Vivisimo, Kartoo, Mamma, SurfWax, and Clusty.

Crew Inhabits Space

992 **2000** The first long-term crew reached the International Space Station (ISS) on November 2, 2000, marking the beginning of a permanent human presence in space. Originally planned as a NASA project, this longtime dream became reality as an international effort. It includes 16 partners: the U.S., Russia, Canada, Japan, and Brazil, plus European Space Agency members Belgium, Denmark, France, Germany, Italy, the Netherlands, Norway, Spain, Sweden, Switzerland, and the U.K. Since the arrival of the first crew—Bill Shepherd, Yuri Gidzenko, and Sergei Krikalev—at least two people have inhabited the ISS, usually working six-month rotations. They study health and safety issues relating to travel and life in space, grow plants in a greenhouse, and work on new technologies with immediate application for life on Earth. The ISS has docking for three types of vehicles: the U.S. space shuttle, the Russian automated resupply craft Progress, and the Russian Soyuz space ferry, which carries crew members to and from the ISS. It is considered one of the most complicated feats ever accomplished.

> ■ **FOOTNOTE** A daily schedule for the space station astronauts includes morning inspection at 6 a.m. GMT, 90 minutes of physical exercise, a daily planning conference, maintenance, cleaning and testing, and lights out at 9:30 p.m.

Genome Decoded

993 **2001** The Human Genome Project successfully decoded human DNA, identifying the 30,000 genes and 3 billion DNA base pairs that make up the human species. This huge undertaking began in 1990, with the ultimate goal of making a "map" of the genome—all our genes combined—available to medical science for better treatments, diagnostics, and preventions. To carry out the study, scientists recruited an internationally diverse group of volunteers to donate blood, from which DNA was extracted. DNA is made

up of four different bases that pair up in specific combinations. The project determined the order of these pairs to identify every possible combination and sequence that makes a gene. The work was performed at universities and research centers in a consortium of countries—the U.S., the United Kingdom, France, Germany, Japan, and China. A draft of the findings appeared in 2001, and two years later came the final result—an "instruction manual" for how the human body is built, with the potential for better health and wellness through deeper understanding of the building blocks.

Terrorists Attack U.S.

994 **2001** On September 11, 2001, the U.S. suffered the worst terrorist attack in its history. Nearly 3,000 people died as four commercial jetliners were hijacked and crashed into several targets. Two planes hit the twin towers of New York's World Trade Center. Rescue personnel rushed in to evacuate the burning skyscrapers, but as people tried to escape down the stairwells, many lost their lives when the buildings collapsed shortly after the attacks. Search-and-rescue teams found few survivors in the rubble. A third jetliner hit the Pentagon near Washington, D.C., where the U.S. Department of Defense is headquartered, and a fourth plane was brought down by passengers in rural Pennsylvania. All on the planes were killed, as well as scores of people at work in the Pentagon. Suspected orchestrator of the attacks is Osama bin Laden, an exiled Saudi Arabian who funded the al Qaeda terror network and the extremist Taliban regime in Afghanistan. The U.S. military struck and weakened the Taliban, but bin Laden remains at large. The Department of Homeland Security was created in 2002 as a Cabinet-level department to identify and prevent terrorist attacks on the U.S.

> ■ **FOOTNOTE** Following the attacks, people in countries all over the world held candlelight ceremonies in support of the U.S., and for months afterward mourners could be seen standing near the sites of the three crashes.

994 | *Fireball at World Trade Center's south tower*

Red Cross Volunteer

SEPTEMBER 11, 2001

I was sent to the National Headquarters of the American Red Cross to help in answering the overwhelming number of calls to the hot line. Half way through the training someone came in and named 20 people, to go to the Pentagon and 20 to go to New York City (NYC), the World Trade Center (WTC), [and] I was on the Pentagon's list. At lunch several people were going over the new plan and I over heard an older gentlemen saying that he could not go to NYC it would be too hard.... I said I would trade trips and go to the NYC WTC. ... I was assigned to a special unit there of only 8 caseworkers.... Our team of ARC caseworkers worked side by side with the Fire Department of New York (FDNY) counseling unit and the New York Police Department (NYPD) Staten Island Special Units Department.... One day six out of the eight of us had been asked "have you been down to the WTC site?" ... The FDNY counseling unit and the NYPD Staten Island Special Unit Dept. made arrangements for the eight of us to go down to ground zero inside the perimeters because they also agreed that those of us working so closely to the FDNY and the NYPD families should have an understanding or at least have a feeling of what the atmosphere is like.... I will never forget the feelings that took place inside of me ... as I stood at the platform that was built for the families to come and view the recovery efforts. The Lieutenant motioned for us to follow and we began to walk the grounds as they pointed out what buildings once stood there. The workers at the site were so nice as we passed by and some would just nod and say thank you. Others would be kneeling on the ground or sitting in chairs receiving drinks or having their eyes washed out or just taking a moment to reflect.... The flags flew over this trailer office, on top an American flag, the United Mohawk Steelworkers Association flag, and the United States Marines flag flew over head. I stood there in a silent shock ... [and the] cranes and the flags floating in the wind gave off a vision that I will not ever forget.

Euro in Circulation

995 **2002** Many countries in Europe went to a single official currency—the euro—in 2002, signaling another step toward economic unity. Twelve European Union member nations made the change: Austria, Belgium, Finland, France, Germany, Greece, Ireland, Italy, Luxembourg, Netherlands, Portugal, and Spain. Nonmembers Monaco, San Marino, and the Vatican City also adopted the new system. While some feared that cultural identities would be blurred or that a shared system would not suit all countries' economies, the prevailing attitude was that a common currency would stabilize exchange rates and control inflation, boosting Europe's economic power on the world stage. Following more than a decade of preparation—which included a public relations campaign to educate 300 million people about the new system—the euro went into use on January 1, 2002. Banknote designs, chosen through a competition, depict European architectural styles from classical to modern. The adoption of the euro signified the largest currency conversion in history.

The euro bill comes in seven denominations, ranging from 5 euro to 500, and each has a different color.

With the transition to the euro, 12 currencies were simultaneously retired. The euro replaced the Austrian schilling, Belgian franc, Finnish markka, French franc, German mark, Greek drachma, Irish punt, Italian lira, Luxembourg franc, Netherlands guilder, Portugese escudo, and Spanish peseta. In preparation for the transition to the new currency, mints produced 14.5 billion banknotes and 56 billion coins over a period of two and a half years. There are seven bills, ranging from the 5-euro bill to the 500-euro bill (worth more than 680 U.S. dollars in September 2007). Lesser amounts—the 1- and 2-euro denominations—are two-tone silver and gold coins. There are also coins for euro cents, in amounts of 50, 20, and 10 (gold colored) and 5, 2, and 1 (copper colored). Coins have a common design on one side and a national design (surrounded by the 12 EU stars) on the other. In January 2007, Slovenia adopted the euro, and Cyprus and Malta are scheduled to begin using the euro in January 2008.

U.S. Invades Iraq

996 **2003** The Iraq war, also known as the second gulf war (U.S. military code name Operation Iraqi Freedom; United Kingdom military code name Operation TELIC), started in 2003. U.S. President George W. Bush had received information that Iraqi ruler Saddam Hussein was concealing weapons of mass destruction. Bush also tried to tie Hussein to the terrorist group al Qaeda, which had attacked the U.S. on September 11, 2001.

Despite opposition to the use of military force expressed by such countries as France, Germany, and Russia, a coalition force led by the U.S. and the U.K. invaded Iraq in March 2003. The only other countries that politically supported the invasion were Spain and Bulgaria.

The U.S. employed a strategy of what top leadership called shock and awe, military doctrine known as "rapid dominance." The goal was to overwhelm and paralyze the enemy, preventing an organized response and securing a quick victory.

Hussein was captured and later executed, but no weapons of mass destruction were found. Meanwhile, Iraqi insurgent groups launched attacks on coalition forces. As of spring 2007, there had been more than 3,500 casualties of coalition forces.

■ **FOOTNOTE** Saddam Hussein was tried by an Iraqi court and sentenced to death for crimes against humanity. He was executed by hanging on December 30, 2006, in a Shiite district government building in Baghdad.

YouTube Debuts

997 **2005** YouTube launched in August 2005 with a video-sharing format that trumped previous sites in its ease of use. Even the least technologically inclined could upload a video, simply through an email attachment. Almost immediately, amateur video artists and aspiring performers made home movies using digital cameras, camcorders, and cell phone camcorders in their basements, backyards, sports fields, schools, and bedrooms.

In October 2006, powerhouse search engine company Google bought YouTube for $1.65 billion. At that time, YouTube viewers were watching more than 100 million videos on the site every day.

North Korea Goes Nuclear

998 **2006** North Korea asserted its status as a nuclear state in 2006 with the testing of nuclear missiles. At the time, it was thought that the United States' recent support of nuclear reactors in Iran (for nonwarfare purposes)—support which it had denied Pyongyang under any conditions—was the final straw that prompted the nuclear tests. The world had known for a decade that the authoritarian socialist regime possessed a nuclear reactor. At the revelation of a nuclear weapons program in 2002, foreign aid was reduced.

North Korea, regarded as one of the so-called axis of evil countries (along with Iran and Iraq) by President George W. Bush, agreed in 2005 to abandon its nuclear program in exchange for aid, which it relies on to feed its people and arm its military. However, North Korean assets in a Macau bank were frozen in 2005 after the United States contended that the $25 million had come partly from illegal activities. The following year, an angered North Korea tested nuclear missiles. The country's leader agreed in February 2007 that in exchange for aid and normalized relations with the U.S., North Korea would close its reactor as the first step toward nuclear disarmament and allow the International Atomic Energy Agency to inspect. These measures are due to be implemented by the end of 2007 if Korea is to receive the humanitarian, economic, and energy aid it so desperately needs. However, the frozen assets remained a sticking point.

Climate Change Declared

999 **2007** Most scientists agreed on the reality of global warming—and many saw it as a dangerous result of pollution and other human activity. In 2007, the Intergovernmental Panel on Climate Change (IPCC) of the United Nations and the World Meteorological Organization linked human activity to Earth's warming temperatures, rising seas, more intense storms, loss of Arctic ice, and other environmental symptoms. Hundreds of climate experts and government representatives from 113 countries joined in the prediction that global temperatures will increase between 2°F and 11.5°F over preindustrial levels by century's end. Sea levels were projected to rise between 7 and 23 inches. These increases could go on for centuries even if greenhouse gas emissions were stabilized today. The 1990s indeed was the warmest decade since recordkeeping started; however, over the past million years Earth has fluctuated between colder and warmer periods, with changes sometimes occurring rapidly.

999 | Greenhouse gases from cars contribute to global warming.

Scientists hope that these ancient events can tell us more about the current state of climate change.

■ **FOOTNOTE** In 2006, moviegoers flocked to see a documentary of a reputedly stiff politician giving a PowerPoint presentation. *An Inconvenient Truth* became a hit and drove home the reality of global warming.

New Planet Found

1000 **2007** Astronomers discovered the first known planet beyond the solar system that could harbor life as we know it—Gliese 581 c. The most Earth-like planet yet found, it orbits a red dwarf star—Gliese 581—and may contain liquid water. The planet is estimated to be 50 percent larger than Earth, making it the smallest yet known outside the solar system, and is located in the constellation Libra, some 20.5 light-years away. Because Gliese 581 c is 14 times nearer to its star than Earth is to the sun, a year there lasts just 13 days. However, because red dwarf stars are relatively small and dim, Gliese 581 c lies within the relatively cool habitable zone of its solar system. It was discovered in 2007 by European scientists working in Chile with the High Accuracy Radial Velocity Planetary Searcher (HARPS), which detects the wobbling caused by the gravitational pull of an unseen planet on the star it orbits. Gliese 581 c will likely become a target for missions in search of extraterrestrial life. The surface of the planet is unknown, but the surface temperature is thought to be roughly 32°F to 104°F.

996 | Saddam Hussein statue toppled in Baghdad in wake of U.S.-led invasion, April 9, 2003

FURTHER READING

Adovasio, J.M., and Jake Page. *The First Americans: In Pursuit of Archaeology's Greatest Mystery.* The Modern Library, 2002.

Alcock, Antony. *A Short History of Europe: From the Greeks and Romans to the Present Day.* Macmillan, 2002.

Applebaum, Wilbur. *The Scientific Revolution and the Foundations of Modern Science.* Greenwood Press, 2005.

Asimov, Isaac. *Asimov's Chronology of Science and Discovery.* HarperCollins, 1994.

Bahn, Paul G. *Archaeology: The Cambridge Illustrated History.* Cambridge University Press, 1996.

Barnes, Harry Elmer. *An Economic History of the Western World.* Harcourt, Brace, 1937.

Barzun, Jacques. *From Dawn to Decadence: 1500 to the Present.* HarperCollins, 2000.

Bentley, Jerry H., and Herbert F. Ziegler. *Traditions and Encounters: A Global Perspective on the Past,* Vol. 1., 2nd Ed. McGraw Hill, 2003.

Bergin, Thomas G., and Jennifer Speake. *The Encyclopedia of the Renaissance,* Market House Books, 1987.

Bix, Herbert P. *Hirohito and the Making of Modern Japan.* HarperCollins, 2000.

Black, Jeremy. *European Warfare, 1494-1660.* Routledge, 2002.

Bokenkotter, Thomas. *A Concise History of the Catholic Church.* Doubleday, 1990.

Boorstin, Daniel J. *The Discoverers,* Random House, 1983.

Bowman, John S. *Columbia Chronologies of Asian History and Culture.* Columbia University Press, 2000.

Boyden, David. *An Introduction to Music.* New York: Alfred A. Knopf, 1970.

Brendon, Piers. *The Dark Valley: A Panorama of the 1930s.* Vintage, 2000.

Brinkley, Alan. *American History: A Survey.* McGraw-Hill, 1999.

Bunch, Bryan. *The History of Science and Technology.* Houghton-Mifflin, 2004.

Butterfield, Roger. *The American Past.* Simon and Schuster, 1957.

Cantor, Norman F. *The Civilization of the Middle Ages.* HarperCollins, 1993.

———. *In the Wake of the Plague,* Perennial, 2002.

Carey, John, ed. *Eyewitness to History.* Avon Books, 1987.

———. *The Faber Book of Science.* Faber and Faber, 1995.

Clodfelter, Michael. *Warfare and Armed Conflicts,* 2nd Ed. McFarland and Co., 2002.

Conquest, Robert. *The Great Terror: A Reassessment.* Oxford University Press, 1990.

Conrad, Lawrence I., Michael Neve, Vivian Nutton, Roy Porter, and Andrew Wear. *The Western Medical Tradition: 800 BC to AD 1800.* Cambridge University Press, 1995.

Daniels, Patricia, and Stephen G. Hyslop. *National Geographic Almanac of World History.* National Geographic Society, 2003.

Davidson, Basil. *Africa in History.* Macmillan, 1968.

Davies, Norman. *Europe: A History.* Oxford University Press, 1996.

Davis, Paul K. *100 Decisive Battles: From Ancient Times to the Present.* Oxford University Press, 2001.

Des Forges, Roger V., and John S. Major. *The Asian World, 600–1500.* Oxford University Press, 2005.

Ellis, Richard. Aquagenesis: *The Origin and Evolution of Life in the Sea.* Penguin Books, 2001.

Eugene, Toni. *Mysteries of the Ancient World.* National Geographic Society, 2005.

Evans, Richard J. *The Coming of the Third Reich.* Penguin, 2003.

Fairbank, John K., Edwin O. Reischauer, and Albert M. Craig. *East Asia: Tradition and Transformation.* Houghton Mifflin, 1989.

Figes, Orlando, *A People's Tragedy: A History of the Russian Revolution.* Viking, 1996.

Fortey, Richard. *Life: A Natural History of the First Four Billion Years of Life on Earth.* Alfred A. Knopf, 1998.

Green, Peter. *Alexander of Macedon, 356-323 B.C.: A Historical Biography.* University of California Press, 1991.

Harley, Sharon. *Timetables of African-American History.* Simon and Schuster, 1995.

Hindley, Geoffrey, ed. *The Larousse Encyclopedia of Music.* Hamlyn, 1971.

Hitchcock, Susan Tyler. *Geography of Religion.* National Geographic Society, 2004.

Hoyt, Edwin P. *The Rise of the Chinese Republic: From the Last Emperor to Deng Xioping.* McGraw-Hill, 1989.

Janson, H. W. *History of Art,* 3rd Ed. Prentice Hall, 1986.

Johansen, Bruce. *The Native Peoples of North America,* Vol. 1, Praeger, 2005.

Keegan, John. *The Second World War.* Penguin, 1989.

Keegan, John, and Andrew Wheatcroft. *Who's Who in Military History From 1453 to the Present Day.* Routledge, 1996.

Kunitz, Stanley K., and Vineta Colby, eds. *European Authors: 1000-1900.* H. W. Wilson and Company, 1967.

Langer, William. *An Encyclopedia of World History,* 5th Ed. Houghton-Mifflin, 1980.

Lee, John. *The Warlords: Hindenburg and Ludendorff.* Weidenfeld and Nicholson, 2005.

Littleton, C. Scott. *Mythology: The Illustrated Anthology of World Myth and Storytelling.* Duncan Baird Publishers, 2002.

Magill, Frank, ed. *Masterpieces of World Literature,* Harper and Row, 1989.

MacMillan, Margaret. *Paris 1919: Six Months That Changed the World.* Random House, 2001.

Manchester, William. *American Caesar: Douglas MacArthur, 1880-1964.* Little Brown, 1978.

Mankiewicz, Richard. *The Story of Mathematics,* Princeton University Press, 2000.

McCullough, David. *The Path Between the Seas: The Creation of the Panama Canal, 1870-1914.* Simon and Schuster, 1977.

McGrath, Alister. *Reformation Thought: An Introduction.* Basil Blackwell, 1988.

McLeish, John. *The Story of Numbers,* Fawcett Columbine, 1994.

Meyer, Michael C., William L. Sherman, and Susan M. Deeds. *The Course of Mexican History,* 7th Ed. Oxford University Press, 2003.

Millar, David, Ian Millar, John Millar, and Margaret Millar. *Cambridge Dictionary of Scientists.* Cambridge University Press, 1996.

Morgan, Kenneth, ed. *The Oxford Illustrated History of Britain.* Oxford University Press, 1995.

Nevins, Allan, and Henry Steele Commager. *A Pocket History of the United States.* Pocket Books, 1992.

Norwich, John Julius. *Great Architecture of the World.* Bonanza Books, 1979.

Overfield, James H., and Alfred J Andrea. *The Human Record: Source of Global History,* Vol. 2. Houghton-Mifflin, 2001.

Palmer, Douglas. *Atlas of the Prehistoric World.* Discovery Books, 1999.

Parker, Steve. *Medicine.* DK Publishing, 1995.

Payne, Robert. *The Dream and the Tomb: A History of the Crusades.* Stein and Day, 1984.

Porter, Roy. *The Greatest Benefit to Mankind: A Medical History of Humanity.* W. W. Norton, 1997.

Powell, Barry B. *Classical Myth,* 3rd Ed. Prentice Hall, 2001.

Quataert, Donald. *The Ottoman Empire: 1700-1922.* Cambridge University Press, 2005.

Reader, John. *Africa: A Biography of the Continent,* Knopf, 1998.

Reichhold, Klaus, and Bernard Graf. *Buildings That Changed the World.* Prestel Publishing, 1999.

Roberts, J. A. G. *A Concise History of China.* Harvard University Press, 1999.

Roberts, J. M. *History of the World.* Oxford University Press, 1993.

Rossabi, Morris. *Khubilai Khan: His Life and Times,* University of California Press, 1988.

Scarre, Chris. *Timelines of the Ancient World: A Visual Chronology From the Origins of Life to A.D. 1500.* Dorling Kindersley, 1993.

Spangenburg, Ray, and Diane K. Moser. *The History of Science from 1895 to 1945.* Facts on File, 1994.

Spick, Mike, *Milestones of Manned Flight: The Ages of Flight From the Wright Brothers to Stealth Technology.* Smithmark, 1995.

Stearns, Peter, Stuart B. Schwartz, Marc J. Gilbert, and Michael Adas. *World Civilizations,* Vol. 2. Addison-Wesley, 2001.

Suplee, Curt. *Milestones of Science.* National Geographic Society, 2000.

Thomas, Hugh. *The Story of Mankind From Prehistory to the Present,* Rev. Ed. HarperCollins, 1996.

Toland, John. *The Rising Sun: The Decline and Fall of the Japanese Empire, 1936-1945.* Modern Library, 2003.

Vidal-Naquet, Pierre. *The Harper Atlas of World History.* Harper and Row, 1987.

Viola, Herman J., and Carolyn Margolis. *Seeds of Change: Five Hundred Years Since Columbus.* Smithsonian Institution Press, 1991.

Wilford, John Noble. *The Mapmakers: The Story of the Great Pioneers in Cartography—From Antiquity to the Space Age.* Rev. Ed. Vintage Books, 2001.

Winkowski, Frederic, and Frank D. Sullivan, *100 Planes 100 Years.* Smithmark, 1998.

Winter, Jay, and Blaine Baggett. *The Great War and the Shaping of the 20th Century.* Penguin, 1996.

ABOUT THE AUTHORS

Dan O'Toole (Chapter 1) has written for a number of projects with National Geographic, including *Concise History of the World, Complete Birds of North America, and Encyclopedia of Space.* He holds a degree in classical languages from Georgetown University and works in the fields of archaeology, paleontology, and geology, conducting fieldwork in North America, South America, and Europe.

Elizabeth Towner (Chapter 2) is a former staff editor with NATIONAL GEOGRAPHIC magazine. Now a freelance writer and editor, she has written for National Geographic Online, National Geographic's *100 Best Pictures Unpublished,* and the magazine's international editions. She holds degrees in anthropology and medieval literature.

Michelle R. Harris (Chapter 3) calls Florida's First Coast home. She is a freelance researcher, editor, and writer who has worked primarily for the National Geographic Society, AARP, the Center for Public Integrity, and Congressional Quarterly. Her research and writing for National Geographic includes many of the WildCam sites and the Discover Antarctica site.

Julie Cederborg (Chapter 4) is a freelance writer, editor, and researcher based in northern California. She is a former staff researcher for NATIONAL GEOGRAPHIC and a former editor for *Health* and has written for National Geographic Online, *Health, Backpacker, Runner's World, Child, and* BabyCenter.

Patricia Daniels (Chapter 5) is an author and editor who has written extensively on history, geography, and science. Among the books she has written for are *National Geographic Almanac of World History* and *Body: The Complete Human.* She lives in State College, Pennsylvania, with her husband and two sons.

Steven G. Hyslop (Chapter 6 and Chapter Introductions) is the author of *Eyewitness to the Civil War: The Complete History from Secession to Reconstruction, Bound for Santa Fe: The Road to New Mexico and the American Conquest, 1806-1848,* and *National Geographic Almanac of World History* (co-written with Patricia Daniels). Formerly an editor at Time-Life Books, he has contributed to many volumes on American and world history. His articles have appeared in *American History, World War II,* and the *History Channel Magazine.*

Teresa Barry (Chapter 7) During her decade-long tenure as an editor on staff, and since launching her freelance career, award-winning writer Teresa Barry has contributed to a wide range of National Geographic publications: atlases, reference books, travel guides, and more. She also has written for Special Olympics, Inc.; the Smithsonian; public radio; and several branches of the U.S. government. Assignments often reflect her interest in children's issues, animal welfare, and environmental concerns. She lives with her family in Fairfax, Virginia.

Peter Stearns (Consultant) is a historian and provost at George Mason University in Fairfax, Virginia. He is the author of a number of books, including *The Battleground of Desire: The Struggle for Self-Control in Modern America,* and *World History: Patterns of Change and Continuity.* Stearns also is editor of the six-volume *Encyclopedia of European Social History from 1350 to 2000* and the general editor of the sixth edition of the *Encyclopedia of World History.*

Contributors to this book also included:
Stephanie Hanlon
Karin Kinney
Kathryn Pond
Lauren Pruneski
Susan Straight
John Thompson

ILLUSTRATION CREDITS

Losevsky Pavel/Shutterstock; 192-193, MPI/Getty Images; 194, Library of Congress; 195, Library of Congress; 196, Library of Congress; 197, Library of Congress; 198, John Kobal Foundation/Getty Images; 199, The Granger Collection, NY; 200, John Kobal Foundation/Getty Images; 201, The Art Archive/CORBIS; 202, Library of Congress; 203, Michael Nichols, NGP; 204-205, John Van Hasselt/Sygma/CORBIS; 206, Library of Congress; 207, Bettmann/CORBIS; 208, Bettmann/CORBIS; 209, W. & D. Downey/Getty Images; 210, Bettmann/CORBIS; 211, Bettmann/CORBIS; 212, Library of Congress; 213, CORBIS; 214, Time Life Pictures/Mansell/Time Life Pictures/Getty Images; 215, Library of Congress; 216-217, Hulton Archives/Getty Images; 222, Barry Bishop; 223 (UP), Hulton Archive/Getty Images; 223 (LO), Library of Congress;224, Library of Congress; 225, Library of Congress; 226, Vasiliy Koval/Shutterstock; 227 (UP), Library of Congress; 227 (LO), Library of Congress; 228, CORBIS; 229 (UP), Library of Congress; 229 (LO), iStockphoto.com; 230, Library of Congress; 231, Library of Congress; 232, Evans/Three Lions/Getty Images; 233, Steve Cole/Getty Images; 234-235, MPI/Getty Images; 236 (UP), Library of Congress; 236 (LO), CORBIS; 237, Tom Hahn/iStockphoto.com; 238, AFP/Getty Images; 239, Science Source/Photo Researchers, Inc.; 240, Bettmann/CORBIS; 241, Library of Congress; 242 (UP), Loke Yek Mang/Shutterstock; 242 (LO), Library of Congress; 243, CORBIS; 244, W. & D. Downey/Getty Images; 245, Library of Congress; 246, Library of Congress; 247, Library of Congress; 248, Library of Congress; 249, Library of Congress; 250-251, MPI/Getty Images; 252, Jan Paul Schrage/iStockphoto.com; 253 (UP), Darin Echelberger/Shutterstock; 253 (LO), DJM-Photo/Shutterstock; 254, Burstein Collection/CORBIS; 255, iStockphoto.com; 256, Stephen Strathdee/Shutterstock; 257, Library of Congress; 258, Norm Thomas/Photo Researchers, Inc.; 259, Fox Photos/Getty Images; 260, Hulton Archive/Getty Images; 261, Library of Congress; 262-263, Library of Congress; 264, Library of Congress; 265, Library of Congress; 266, Library of Congress; 267, Hulton Archive/Getty Images; 268, Library of Congress; 269, Buyen-large/Buyenlarge/Time Life Pictures/Getty Images; 270, Imagno/Getty Images; 271, Library of Congress; 272-273, Library of Congress; 274, Underwood & Underwood/CORBIS; 275, Library of Congress; 276, Science Source/Photo Researchers, Inc.; 277, Emory Kristof; 278, NASA; 279, Library of Congress; 280-281, Robert F. Sargent/Getty Images; 286 (UP), Bettmann/CORBIS; 286 (LO), Three Lions/Getty Images; 287, Topical Press Agency/Getty Images; 288 (UP), Hulton Archive/Getty Images; 288 (LO), CORBIS; 289, Library of Congress; 290, General Photographic Agency/Getty Images; 291, Library of Congress; 292, Hulton-Deutsch Collection/CORBIS; 293, Hirz/Getty Images; 294, Imagno/Getty Images; 295 (UP), Library of Congress; 295 (LO), Hulton Archive/Getty Images; 296-297, Hulton Archive/Getty Images; 297 (LO), Keystone/Getty Images; 298, Frank Driggs Collection/Getty Images; 299, Hulton Archive/Getty Images; 300 (UP), Renato Toppo/Getty Images; 300 (LO), Library of Congress; 301, Library of Congress; 302-303, Kenneth Garrett; 304, Bettmann/CORBIS; 305 (UP), Bettmann/CORBIS; 305 (LO), Hulton Archive/Getty Images; 306, Library of Congress; 307 (UP), Visuals Unlimited/CORBIS; 307 (LO), APA/Getty Images; 308, Swim Ink/CORBIS; 309 (UP), Tallandier/Getty Images; 309 (LO), Boyer/Roger Viollet/Getty Images; 310, Bettmann/CORBIS; 311, Lewis W. Hine/George Eastman House/Getty Images; 312, Keystone/Getty Images; 313, W. Robert Moore; 314, Thomas D. Mcavoy//Time Life Pictures/Getty Images; 315, Hulton-Deutsch Collection/CORBIS; 316, NASA; 317, Library of Congress; 318, Robert Yarnall Richie/Time Life Pictures/Getty Images; 319, Time Life Pictures/Pictures Inc./Time Life Pictures/Getty Images; 320-321, Genevieve Chauvel/Sygma/CORBIS; 322, Bettmann/CORBIS; 323, Burnstein Collection/CORBIS; 324 (UP), Nina Leen/Time Life Pictures/Getty Images; 324 (LO), Kenneth Eward/Photo Researchers, Inc.; 325, Library of Congress; 326, CORBIS; 327 (UP), Hulton-Deutsch Collection/CORBIS; 327 (LO), Fox Photos/Getty Images; 328, Ralph Morse/Time Life Pictures/Getty Images; 328-329, Hugo Jaeger/Timepix/Time Life Pictures/Getty Images; 330, Time Life Pictures/US Navy/Time Life Pic-tures/Getty Images; 331, Library of Congress; 332, Javier Fontanella/iStockphoto.com; 333, Hulton-Deutsch Collection/CORBIS; 334-335, George Silk/Time Life Pictures/Getty Images; 335 (LO), Library of Congress; 336, Bettmann/CORBIS; 337, Hulton-Deutsch Collection/CORBIS; 338-339, NASA; 344, Photo File/MLB Photos/Getty Images; 345, Zoltan Kluger/GPO/Getty Images; 346, Carsten Koall/Getty Images; 347, CYLU/Shutterstock; 348, CORBIS; 349 (UP), Tara Urbach/Shutterstock; 349 (LO), National Archives and Records Administration; 350 (LO), Time Life Pictures/Us Air Force/Time Life Pictures/Getty Images; 350-351, Dario Sabljak/Shutterstock; 352, Ned Seidler; 353, Hulton Archive/Getty Images; 354, John Kobal Foundation/Hulton Archive/Getty Images; 355, Bettmann/CORBIS; 356-357, Bettmann/CORBIS; 358, NASA; 359 (UP), Harold M. Lambert/Lambert/Getty Images; 359 (LO), CORBIS; 360, Hugo Van Lawick; 361, Brent Melton/iStockphoto.com; 363, Bettmann/CORBIS; 364, Bettmann/CORBIS; 365, Bernard Gotfryd/Getty Images; 366, Library of Congress; 367, Library of Congress; 370, Grosvenor Collection, NGS; 371, NASA; 372, NASA; 373, Bill Eppridge/Time Life Pictures/Getty Images; 374, Kenneth Garrett; 375, Eugene Kuklev/iStockphoto.com; 376 (LE), VILEM BISCHOF/AFP/Getty Images; 376 (RT), Bettmann/CORBIS; 377, Emory Kristof; 378, NASA; 379, Dirck Halstead/Time Life Pictures/Getty Images; 380-381, Justin Guariglia; 382, Peter Jordan/Time Life Pictures/Getty Image/Getty Images; 383, Brent Stirton/Getty Images; 384, NASA; 385, Jim Pozarik/Liaison/Getty Images; 386, NASA; 387 (UP), NASA; 387 (LO), Gerd Ludwig; 388 (LO), David Hartung/Liaison/Getty Images; 388-389, Alexander Hafemann/iStockphoto.com; 390, NASA; 391, Justin Sullivan/Getty Images; 392, Diana Walker/Time Life Pictures/Getty Images; 393, Tischenko Irina/Shutterstock; 394-395, Department of Defense; 396, Getty Images; 397, Jayne Fincher/Getty Images; 398, NASA; 399, Spencer Platt/Getty Images; 400, Matt Trommer/Shutterstock; 401 (UP), Jodi Cobb, National Geographic Photographer; 401 (LO), Mirrorpix/Getty Images.

INDEX

Blast furnaces, development of 105
Blenheim, Battle of 172, **172**
Blood transfusion 158
Blood types, discovery of 264–265
Blue Mosque, Istanbul, Turkey 148, **148**
Bohr, Neils 279, **279**
Bolívar, Simon 198–199, 204, **204–205**
Bonaparte, Napoleon 169–170, **189, 197,** 197–198
Book of Mormon 203
Booke, George 224
Books: censorship 104; first English book 113; online collection 392
Boston Massacre 183
Bow and arrow, development of 21
Boyle, Robert 154–155
Brahe, Tycho 136–137, 145, 151
Brahms, Johannes 223, **223,** 270
Braille, Louis 207
Brazil: hydroelectric dam 382; populist revolution 311
Broca, Pierre Paul 228
Bronze Age: dynasties of China 31
Brown, Arthur 294
Buckland, William 200
Buddha: birth of 46; wall mural **67**
Buddhism, origin of 15
Buddhist temple, earliest 60
Bulge, Battle of the **334–335,** 335
Bunsen burner 228
Burgess Shale, British Columbia, Canada 274
Burnett, John G. 211
Byrd, Richard 307–308
Byron, Lord **200,** 200–201
Byzantine Empire 65, 66, 70, 71, 77, 128

C

Cabeza de Vaca, Álvar Nuñez 130–131
Cabot, John 115

Caesar, Julius 58, **58,** 59, 70
Calculator, pocket 373
Calculus, development of 160
Cambodia: Pol Pot regime 104, 377; *see also* Angkor Wat
Camel, Battle of the 80
Cameras: box cameras 248, **248;** Brownie cameras 260; motion-picture machine 255
Canada: union of 233; *see also* Burgess Shale; CN Tower; Hudson Bay; Quebec; Yukon River
Cancer: linked with smoking 365
Candide (Voltaire) 178, 183
Canning, invention of 196
Canterbury Tales (Chaucer) 90, 92, 107, **107**
Cape Coast Castle, Ghana **113**
Cape Town, South Africa: founding of 153–154
Carbon nanotubes 365–366
Carson, Rachel 362
Carter, Howard 298, 302
Caruso, Enrico 265, **265**
Caste system 40–41
Castiglione, Baldassare 127–128
Castro, Fidel 359, 361
Catherine II, Empress (Russia) 182
Caxton, William 113
CD-ROMs, introduction of 387
Celsius scale, invention of 176
Celts, appearance of 42
Cervantes, Miguel de 143
Cézanne, Paul 239, 248; painting by **238**
Challenger (space shuttle) 384, 387
Champlain, Samuel de **144,** 144–145
Charlemagne 71, 82; reliquary **82**
Charles, Prince of Wales 397, **397**

Charles X, King (France) 203
Chaucer, Geoffrey 90, 92, 107
Chavín cult 41–42
Chemistry: advancement of 195–196; compounds theorized 154–155; presaged 87–88
Chemotherapy 270
Chernobyl, Russia: nuclear accident 342, 387
Cherokee Indians 208, 209–210, 211
Chiang Kai-shek 348, **348**
Chicago, Ill.: protest at Democratic Convention 371; *see also* Hull House; Robie House
Chicago School of architecture 242
Chichén Itzá, Mexico: Maya pyramid **88**
Chickasaw Indians 208
Child psychology 373
Chile: settlement of southern 21
Chimu people 113
China: earliest Buddhist temple 60; foreign influence fought 171, 259; gunpowder discovered 72, 83, 86; last emperor 276; Long March 315, **315;** map printed on press 93; mass book burning 104; modernization 379, 380; paper money 154; tea cultivation 145; three feudatories revolt 159; trade with U.S. 212–213; war with Japan 322; waterwheel technology 100; wood-block printing 78; WWI 287; *see also* Beijing; Manchuria; Tangshan
Chivalry 92, 95
Choctaw Indians 208
Cholera 215, 224
Christianity: foundations of 15, 60; Inquisition launched 97–98; promotion by Paul 60; writings of St. Augus-

tine 75; *see also* Crusades; Jesus Christ
Christie, Agatha 296
Chronometer, invention of 179
Chu state 44
Civil Rights Act 354, 364, 366
Civil War, U.S. 220, 230, **231,** 242, 252
Clark, Barney 385
Clark, William 190–191, 192
Cliff Palace, Mesa Verde, Colorado **63**
Climate change: declared 401; proposed 296; *see also* Global warming
Clinton, Bill **392**
Clocks: chronometer 179; pendulum clock 154; second hand 172–173
Cloning, development of 396–397
Clovis culture 22
CN Tower, Toronto, Ontario, Canada 375–376
Coal mining: beginning of 98; Newcomen engine 173, **173**
Coins, first 44
Coke: coke-fired furnace 173; first made from coal 151
Cold War: aftermath of 343; decolonization and 340–341; peaceful revolutions 342
Colosseum, Rome, Italy 60–61, **61**
Columbia (space shuttle) 316, 384, **384**
Columbian Exchange 114–115, 128
Columbus, Christopher 112, 114, **114,** 115, 128
Combustion, explanation of 161
Compasses, use of 95
Computers: analytical engine 206; CD-ROMs 387; chip technology 322, 365–366; code-breaking 333; first email 390; first fully automatic computer

368–369; first personal computer 384–385; IBM System/360 364–365; standard protocol switch 385–386; transistors and integrated circuits 332, 353–354
Concrete, development of 57
Confucius 40, 48, **48**
Constantine, Emperor (Roman Empire) 60, 66
Constantinople: Islamization 111; Roman Empire 70; seized by Ottomans 73, 121
Continental drift, theory of: proposed 277; proved 363
Cook, Frederick A. 271
Cook, James 152, **182–183,** 183–184, 186
Copernicus, Nicolaus 87, 91, 131, **131,** 151
Coríolis force 208
Corn: domestication of 25; insect-resistant **393**
Coronado, Francisco Vásquez de 130
Cortés, Hernán 126
Cortisone, development of 348–349
Cotton gin 188, **188**
Creation myths 17, 25, 88
Credit plan, first 226
Creek Indians 208
Crete (island), Greece 13, 30, 31, 32, 37–38
Crick, Francis 352, **352,** 358
Crimean War 224, 225
Crusades 72, **91,** 91–92, 94–95
Crystal Palace, London, England **216–217**
Cuba: independence 259; missile crisis 341, 361
Cubic equation, solution of 126
Cuneiform tablet **26**
Curie, Marie and Pierre 258, **259**
Custer, George Armstrong 208
Cuvier, Georges 196
Cyclotron 308–309

human activity 401; predicted 256
Globe, world's oldest 114–115
Globe Theatre, London, England 147
Goa, India 123
Goddard, Robert 315–316, **316**
Gold standard 260
Golden Temple, Amritsar, India **112–113**
Goldmark, Peter 349–350
Goodall, Jane 360, **360**
Google (search engine) 398
Gorbachev, Mikhail 386, 389
Grand Canyon, Ariz. 236; see also Havasu Falls
Great Depression 310, 311
Great Pyramid of Khufu, Giza, Egypt 28–29
Great Wall of China, building of 107, 110
Greco-Persian Wars 47–48, 50, **50–51**
Greece: democracy 376; independence 199; see also Athens; Crete
Greek epics 43–44
Green Revolution 370–371
Greenland, settlement of 86
Gregorian calendar 128
Gregory XIII, Pope 138, **138**
Grimm's Fairy Tales 196–197
Guernica, Spain: German air raid 323
Gulliver's Travels (Swift) 175, 180, **180–181**
Gunpowder, discovery of 72, 83, 86
Gupta dynasty 66–67, 76
Gutenberg, Johannes 111, 112

H

Hagia Sophia, Istanbul, Turkey 77–78, **78**, 111
Haiti: independence 194
Hajj 103
Halley, Edmund 162, 172

Halley's comet 172
Hammurabi, Code of 34
Hammurabi medallion **34**
Han dynasty: clay heads **57**; establishment of 57; news sheets 81
Handel, George Frideric 176
Hanseatic League 99
Harappan civilization 29, 40
Hargreaves, James 183
Harrison, John 179
Harvey, William 149
Hastings, Battle of **90**
Havasu Falls, Grand Canyon NP, Ariz. **202**
Hawaii: annexation by U.S. 258; arrival of settlers 74; creation myths 17; introduced species 147; observatory 74; surfing 74; volcanoes 367; see also Pearl Harbor
Hawking, Stephen 348
Heart: circulation explained 149; first artificial heart 385; first pacemaker 350; first transplant 367; heart-lung machine 352
Hemingway, Ernest 309, **309**
Hench, Philip 348–349
Henry IV, King (England) 139–140
Henry the Navigator 110
Henry VIII, King (England) 140
Henson, Matthew 271
Heredity, laws of 392
Hillary, Edmund 351–352
Hindenburg (airship), explosion of 262, 322, **322**
Hinduism 42, 67, 72, 112; sacred texts 38, 65–66
Hippocrates 49, **49**
Hirohito, Emperor (Japan) 304, **304**
Hiroshima, Japan: bombing of 336
Hitler, Adolf 285, 289, 304, 310, 319, 336, 346; appeased by Allies 323; beginning of

WWII 326; failed putsch 299; invasion of Soviet Union 328–329; Mussolini and 324–325; rise to power 314
Ho Chi Minh 337, 352
Holocaust 329–330, 346
Holy Roman Empire, birth of 82
Homer 43–44, 53, 238, 298
Hominid remains, earliest known 374
Hominins, dispersal of 17–18
Homo habilis 17
Homo sapiens: emergence of 18; remains **18**
Hooke, Robert 155, 158, 161
Hormones: mechanism identified 265
Horses 24, **24**; domestication of 25; horse-collar harness 92
Horyuji, Japan: temple complex 79, **79**
Hospitals, first 49, 52
Hoyle, Fred 347–348, 349
Hubble, Edwin 177, 308, **309,** 348
Hubble Space Telescope 390–391
Hudson Bay, and region, Canada 145–146
Hull House, Chicago, Ill. 248
Human Genome Project 399
Hungary, kingdom of 127
Hussein, Saddam 383, 391, 394, 400; statue **401**
Huygens, Christiaan 154, 161
Hyatt, John Wesley 237
Hydrodynamics, theories of 175
Hydrogen bomb, first 350, **350**
Hydropower plant, first 255
Hydrothermal vents. see Deep-sea vents
Hypodermic syringe, use of 213

I

I Ching, compilation of 42
Ice ages, cause of 256
Icemaker, invention of 204
Iguazú Falls, Brazil 131
The Iliad (Homer) 38, 43, 44, 238
Inca 73, 113, 128
India: Britain's colonization 183; caste system 40–41; epics 65–66; independence 346–347; nonviolent resistance movement 294; rebellion 227; see also Ellora Caves; Goa; Taj Mahal
Indonesia: arrival of Islam 102–103; see also Bali; Krakatau
Inheritance, principles of 226
Interferon, discovery of 355, 358
Internal combustion engine 179, **179,** 239
International Space Station **398,** 398–399
Internet: dial-up access 332, 391; protocol 385–386; search engine 398; video-sharing format 400; word coined 332; see also World Wide Web
Introduced species 147
Iran: Muslim clerics 382
Iran-Iraq war 383; Iraqi troops **382**
Iraq: gained by Ottoman Empire 132–133; invasion of Kuwait 391–392, 394; nationhood achieved 313; U.S.-led invasion 400, 401; see also Baghdad
Ireland: famine 213–214; rebellion 289–290
Iron lung, invention of 306–307
Iron metallurgy: development of 13–14, 38; fishing implements **38**
Irrigation systems, development of 22–23, 24
Isabella, Queen (Spain) 112
Islam: saved by slave sul-

tans 98–99; spread halted 81; spread of 71, 102–104; Sunnis and Shiites 80; Wahabbi 176; see also Crusades; Muhammad
Israel: nationhood 345
Israel, kingdom of 40
Itaipú Dam, Brazil-Paraguay 382
Italy: entrance into WWII 327; fascism 297–298; invasion by Allies 332; unification 237–238; see also Rome; Rubicon River
Ivan IV, Tsar (Russia) 128–129
Iwo Jima, Japan 335–336

J

Jackson, Andrew 208
Jacobs, George 164, **164**
Jacquard, Joseph Marie 189–190
Jainism 45
Jamaica: peace concert 378
Jamestown, Virginia: founding of 144; tobacco 146, 147
Japan: annexation of Korea 274; attack on Pearl Harbor 329; Chinese cultural influence 79; invasion of Korea 139; Manchuria seized 312; Meiji emperor 233, 236; militarization 310; new empire 304; opening of 220–221, 224, **224**; Russo-Japanese War 267; unification of 67; U.S. oil embargo 328; war with China 322; see also World War II
Japanese Americans, internment of 330
Jazz 298–299, 301–302
Jenner, Edward 188
Jenson, Nicolas 112–113
Jerusalem 72; retaken by Saladin 95; see also Dome of the Rock
Jesus Christ: beginning of

ministry 59; depictions of **59, 60**

Jet age, dawning of 325

Jews: homeland gained 291; *see also* Holocaust

Joan of Arc **110,** 110–111

John Paul II, Pope 379, **379**

Jolson, Al 305–306

Judaism: Talmud 94; Zionist movement 257

Jung, Carl Gustav 296–297

Jupiter (planet) 160, 386, 391; moons 138, 160, **378**

K

Kaaba, Mecca, Saudi Arabia **103**

Kabuki theater **142,** 143

Kangxi, Emperor (China) 155, 163

Kant, Immanuel 177

Kennedy, John F.: assassination of 364; funeral **364**; space program 316, 361; speech by 362; visit to Berlin 362–363

Kennedy, John F., Jr. **364**

Kenya: tea plantation **145**

Kepler, Johannes 145, 163

Keynes, John Maynard 322

Khoi hunter-gatherers 153, 154

Khomeini, Ruhollah (Ayatollah) 382

Kimber, John **194**

Kinetoscope, invention of 252, 255

King, Martin Luther, Jr. 342, 347, **363,** 363–364, 366

Kingsley, Charles 196

Kirchoff, Gustav 228

Kitty Hawk, N. C.: first flight 266, **266**

Koch, Robert 239

Korea: annexation by Japan 274; invasion by Japan 139; partitioned 336–337

Korea, North: nuclear weapons program 400–401

Korean War 341, 349

Krakatau (island volcano), Indonesia 244, 245

Krishna 66, **66**

Kublai Khan 99, **99,** 102

Kuwait: invasion by Iraq 391–392, 394

L

La Fontaine, Jean de 158

La Scala Opera House, Milan, Italy 185

Labor unions, organization of 208, 257

Laissez-faire economics 178

Landsteiner, Karl 264–265

Lascaux Cave, France: paintings 20, 328

Lasers 359

Lavoisier, Antoine 184

Lawrence, T. E. 290

League of Nations 293, 304, 337

Leakey, Louis S. B. 360, 374

Leakey, Mary 374, **374**

Leaning Tower, Pisa, Italy 95

Leeuwenhoek, Antonievan 160, **160**

Lenin, Vladimir 291, 300, 308

Leonardo da Vinci 113, 118

Lewis, Meriwether 190–191, 192

Liebniz, Gottfried Wilhelm 160

Life: beginning of 16; clues to origins of 351

Light: analysis of white light 158; lasers 359; photoelectric effect 266–267; spectrum 197, 228; speed calculated 160–161; waves suggested 160

Light bulb, development of 242

Lincoln, Abraham 229, 230, 270

Lind, James 177–178

Lindbergh, Charles 305, 305

Lindenmann, Jean 355, 358

Linear B writing **44**

Linnaeus, Carolus 177, **177**

Lister, Joseph 232–233

Little Bighorn, Mont.: battle 208

Liverpool and Manchester railway 203, 206

Locke, John **163,** 163–164

Logic: linked with math 224

London, England: bubonic plague 154; rebuilt after fire 158; riot by suffragists 274; stock exchange 165; WWII bombing raids 326, 332; *see also* Crystal Palace; Westminster Abbey

London Workingmen's Organization 208

Long, Huey 316–317

Longbows 106

Loom, automated 189–190

Louis XIV, King (France) 142, 151, 172

Lovett, William 208

"Lucy" (australopithecene) 376

Lumiere, Antoine 255

Luther, Martin 119, 124–125

Lyell, Charles 202

M

Macchu Pichu, Peru 275–276

Machiavelli, Niccolò 123

MacIntosh, Charles 199–200

Mad cow disease 391

Magellan, Ferdinand 125, **125**

Magendie, François 200

Magna Carta, signing of 97

Magnetic resonance imaging (MRI) machines, first 385

Magyars, defeat of 86, **87**

Mahler, Gustav 248–249

Mail: regulation of international 239

Maine (battleship): explosion of 258–259

Malaria 257

Mali, kingdom of 103–104

Malthus, Thomas 188–189

Manchuria, China: seized by Japan 312

Mandan **208**

Mandela, Nelson 320, 347, 364, 396

Manhattan, New York, N.Y.: purchase of 149

Manhattan Project 325

Mao Zedong 293, 315, 322, 337, 341, 348

Marathon, Battle of **50–51**

Marconi, Guglielmo 247, 264, **264**

Mark I computer **368–369**

Marley, Bob 378

Marne, Battle of the 286–287

Marshall, George C. 345

Martel, Charles 81, **81,** 82

Marx, Karl 170, 215

Mary II, Queen (England) **163**

Mass extinction 16

Massachusetts Colony 149–150

Mathematics: advances in 34; linked with logic 224; symbols used 113

Mauryan Empire 53–54, 66

Maya civilization 15, 47, 65, 87, 88; scribes **64**

McCormick, Cyrus 206, **206**

McNaughton, Daniel 211–212

Mead, Margaret 307, **307**

Mecca, Saudi Arabia 78, **103,** 105

Medical documents, earliest 35–36

Medical research, quantification of 147

Medical techniques, development of 52

Medical text, earliest 54

Medina, Saudi Arabia 79–80, **80**

Mendel, Gregor 226, 393

Mercator, Gerardus 135, **135,** 136

Mesa Verde, Colorado **63,** 96, 102

Mesabi Range, Minn.: iron mine 252–253

Mesopotamia: development of writing 12; irrigation systems 22–23

Messiah (Handel) 176

Metallurgy, development of 22, 38

Mexico: independence 171, 196; Mexican-American War 171, 213; Mexican Revolution 274, 324; oil nationalization 324; victory at Puebla 229–230; *see also* Chichén Itzá; Tenochtitlan; Teotihuacan

Michelangelo 122, 130–131; frescoes **130**

Microscopes: electron microscope 314–315; homemade lenses 160

Mid-Ocean Ridge 363

Middle East: oil reserves 312

Migration, beginning of 20–21

Mill, John Stuart 211

Milvian Bridge, Battle of the 66

Ming dynasty: end of 153; founding of 107

Minoan civilization 13, 31, 32, 37–38; fresco **32–33**

Moche culture 64–65, 78

Modern humans: appearance of 18; remains of *H. sapiens sapiens* **18**

Mogollon culture 63

Mogul Empire 121, 126, 133

Mongol Empire 73, 96–97

Monroe, Marilyn 354, **355**

Montgomery, Ala.: bus boycott 354, 356, 366

Moore, Gordon 365

Moore, Thomas 201

Moran, John 260
More, Thomas 124
Morgan, Jason 367
Mormon religion 203
Morphine, isolation of 194
Morse, Samuel F. B. 212, 226
Morton, William Thomas Green **214,** 214–215
Moses 39
Mother Teresa 346, **346**
Motion of bodies, explanation of 161
Mound builders 45
Mozart, Wolfgang Amadeus 186
Muhammad (prophet) 71, 78–81, 84, 102–103
Munch, Edward: painting by **254**
Murrow, Edward R. 326
Music conservatories 129–130
Musical instruments: development of 19; first pianolas 256–257; *see also* Stringed instruments
Musical nationalism 231
Musical notation 76
Mussolini, Benito **297,** 297–298, 317, 324; Hitler and 324–325

N

Nagasaki, Japan: bombing of 336, **336**
Nansen, Fridtjof 254–255
Naples, Italy 129–130
Nasca culture 20, 57, 78–79; geoglyphs 20, 57, 79; piece of pottery **78**
National Association for the Advancement of Colored People (NAACP) 270
Native Americans: peace treaty 192, **192–193;** reservations 236; resettlement 208; smallpox 179; *see also* Cherokee Indians; Plains Indians
Navajo Indians 208
Neandertals, extinction of 19–20

Negro Baseball League 344, 345
Nerchinsk, Treaty of 163
Nerves, understanding of 200
Neutron, discovery of 314
New York Sun (newspaper) 207
New Zealand: made a British colony 211; women's voting rights 254, 295
Newcomen engine 173, **173**
Newspapers: appearance of printed newspaper 81; penny newspapers 207; publication of first newspaper 143–144; *see also Daily Telegraph*
Newton, Isaac 119, **162,** 162–163
Nicaragua: Sandanistas 382; U.S. intervention 306
Nicholas, Tsar (Russia) **201,** 201–202
Nicholas II, Tsar (Russia) 221, 267, 283, 291
Nietzsche, Friedrich Wilhelm 246
Nigeria: Fulani empire 194
Nobel, Alfred 233
Norgay, Tenzing 351
North America: early communities 83; first known urban center 37; first permanent English colony 144; introduced species 147; reached by Vikings 87
North America Free Trade Agreement (NAFTA) 392
North Atlantic Treaty Organization (NATO) 348
North Pole: reached by Peary 270
Nuclear fission 313–314, 324
Nuclear power plants: opening of 350; partial meltdown 387
Nuclear weapons: bomb tested 336, **336;** nonproliferation treaty 367,

370; production of 325; *see also* Hydrogen bomb
Number system, spread of 82
Numerals, introduction of 96
Nylon, synthesis of 324

O

Oceanographic research 379, 382
The Odyssey (Homer) 38, 43, 44, 298
Oil drilling 227
Olduvai Gorge, Tanzania 374
Olmec society 39–40
Olympic Games: 1936 Summer Olympics: 319, 322; first 43
Onnes, Heike Kamerlingh 274–275
Operation Desert Storm 391, 394, **394–395**
Operation Iraqi Freedom 400, 401
Oppenheimer, Robert 371
Organ transplants 351
Ørsted, Hans Christian 199, **199**
Ortelius, Abraham 135–136
Ottoman Empire: Balkan Wars 277–278; constitution 240; decline 288; defeat 162, 170; extent 121; Greek rebellion 199; Iraq gained by 132–133; sultan 126, 127; victory over Hungary 127
Overpopulation, idea of 188–189
Owens, Jesse 319, 322
Oxygen, studies of 184
Ozone hole 386–387

P

Pacific Islands, colonization of 36
Pagoda, world's oldest 76
Paine, Thomas 187
Panama Canal, opening of

286
Pantheon, Rome, Italy 62
Paper, development of 28
Paper money, rise of 155
Papermaking: advances in 207; modernization of 61–62
Paris, France: death of Princess Diana 397; exposition 323; first balloon flight **185,** 185–186; meeting of "Big Four" 293; *see also* Eiffel Tower
Paris, Treaty of 182
Parks, Rosa 354, 356, **356**
Parthian Empire 57–58
Particle accelerators 353
Pascal, Blaise 152, **152,** 160
Passenger pigeons 286, **286**
Pasteur, Louis 226, **227,** 230, 245–246
Patent law 149
Paul, Saint 60, **60**
Pauling, Linus 348
Pavlov, Ivan 265–266
Pea plants: flower **226;** study of 226
Peace of Utrecht 173
Pearl Harbor, Hawaii: Japanese attack 329
Peary, Robert 270, **271**
Pendulum physics 137–138
Penicillin, invention of 307
Perkins, Jacob 207
Perry, Matthew C. 220–221, 224
Pershing, John 289, **289,** 291
Persia: book of kings 89; rise of 122; Safavid dynasty 173–174; *see also* Achaemenid Empire
Persian Gulf wars 383, 391, 394, **394–395,** 400
Peru: Chavín complex 41–42; Chimu people 113; Moche culture 64–65, 78; Nasca people 20, 57, 78–79; *see also* Macchu Pichu
Peter the Great, Tsar (Rus-

sia) 164–165, **165,** 173
Philippines: reforms 387–388; retaken by U.S. 220, 335; self-government 318
Phoenicians 14, 39, 40, 44, 93
Phonograph, invention of 241
Photography: daguerrotypes 202, **203;** first photograph 202; first war photographer 225; wildlife photography 268; *see also* Cameras
Piaget, Jean 373
Picasso, Pablo 268–269, 298; paintings by **269, 323**
Pickering, Edward 276, **276**
Pilkington, Alastair 361
Pirates and privateers 93
Pizarro, Francisco 128, **129**
Plague 73, 105–106; victims **105**
Plains Indians 249, 250, **250–251,** 252
Plancke, Max 258
Planets: new planet found 401; planetary motion described 145
Plants: classification of 160, 177
Plastic: invention of 237; invention of synthetic 269
Plate tectonics, theory of 277, 367
Plato 46, 52–53, 75, 76, 124, 143
Plow, development of 25, 83, 92, 208
Pluto (dwarf planet) 312, 386
Plutonium, isolation of 326
Pneumatic tire, invention of 248
Polio: iron lung **306,** 306–307; vaccine 306, 350–351
Polo, Marco 102, **102,** 103
Polynesians, dispersal of 88

Pony Express **227,** 227–228, 234, **234–235**

Port Jacobson, Australia: penal colony 186, **187**

Portugal: Battle of Diu 122; capture of Goa 123; colonization of African coast 115; defeat by Moroccans 137; military coup 376; trading port 133–134

Postage stamps: first adhesive stamp 211

Potatoes: introduction to Europe 128; potato blight 213–214

Pottery, first known 21–22

Powell, John Wesley 236, **236**

Prairie du Chien treaty 192, **192–193**

Prairie Style architecture 272, **273**

Presley, Elvis 353, **353**

Priestley, Joseph 184

Printing: advances in 207; blocks used for 90; creation of "Roman" type 112–113; first high-speed printing press 213

Prohibition 294–295

Proudhorn, Pierre-Joseph 210–211

Prussia 175–176

Psychiatry: drug treatments 352–353

Psychoactive drugs 195, **195**

Ptolemy 151

Puebla, Mexico 229–230

Pulmonary circulation 132, 134

Pulsars, discovery of 371

Punch-card machines 249

Pyrometer, invention of 185

Pythagoras 46, 55

Q

Qin dynasty 56, 57, 104

Qin Shihuangdi 56

Qing dynasty 153, 155, 159, 163, 165, 174, 276

Quangzhou (Canton), China 165

Quantum theory 258, 267, 276

Quarks 393, 396

Quebec, Canada: establishment of 144–145

Quesnay, François 178

R

Rabin, Yitzhak 392

Radar: development of 300; refinement of 316

Radio: commercial broadcasting launched 296; wireless age 264–265

Radio waves: development of radar 300; discovery of 247; transatlantic signal sent 264

Radioactivity, measurement of 258

Railroads: development of 252; diesel engine locomotive **253**; expansion 212, 236; first intercity steam railway 202, 206; steam locomotive **252**

Ray, John 161

Rayon fabric, invention of 253

Red Cross, founding of 242

Reflexes: discovery of conditioned 265–266

Relativity, theory of 267, 347–348

Rembrandt 152, 156; painting by **156–157**

Rhineland, Germany 319

Rhodes, Cecil 218, 244, **244**

Rice, domestication of 24

Richter scale 318–319

Richthofen, Manfred von 292

Riefenstahl, Leni 319

RNA (ribonucleic acid) 355, 358

Robie House, Chicago, Ill. 274, **275**

Robinson, Jack Roosevelt **344,** 345

Roman Empire: Battle of the Milvian Bridge 66; dedication of Colosseum 60–61; Dioclet-

ian's reforms 65; expansion by Trajan 62; fall of 70, 75–76; Jewish revolt 62–63

Roman Republic, founding of 46–47

Romanov dynasty 292

Rome, Italy: founding of 43; march on 297, **297;** *see also* Colosseum; Pantheon; St. Peter's Basilica; Trajan's Column

Römer, Ole Christopher 160–161

Rommel, Erwin **328–329,** 330

Röntgen, Wilhelm Conrad 255, 258

Roosevelt, Franklin D. 285, 314, **314, 327;** address to Congress 329; Japanese Americans interned 330; meeting at Yalta 335, **335;** New Deal 314; oil embargo imposed on Japan 328; Social Security Act 317

Roosevelt, Theodore 268, **268**

Rosetta Stone 199

Rousseau, Jean-Jacques 179

Rubicon River, Italy: crossed by Caesar 58

Ruska, Ernst 314–315

Russia: Croat laborers **225;** Decembrist revolt 200–201; demise of the Romanovs 292; emancipation of the serfs 228–229; first ruler crowned tsar 128–129; pogroms 266; revolution 291, 304; Russo-Japanese War 267; victory at Poltava 173; *see also* Chernobyl; Sevastapol; Soviet Union

Rutherford, Ernest 276, 313, 314

S

Safavid dynasty 121, 122, 173–174

Sagan, Carl 378

Saladin 72, 94–95, 98

Salem, Mass.: witchcraft trials 164

Salk, Jonas 350–351

San Francisco, Calif.: earthquake 268

Sanger, Margaret 291

Saratoga, Battle of 184–185

Sargon **29,** 29–30

Sartre, Jean-Paul 333

Schliemann, Heinrich 238

Science fiction 231

Scopes, John 301

Scott, Robert Falcon 276

Scottsboro, Ala. 312

"The Scream" (Munch) **254**

Scurvy 177–178, 275

Seafarers, early 19

Seasat satellite 379, 382

Selassie, Haile 311, 317, 320–321, **321**

Seminole Indians 208

September 11 terrorist attacks 343, 394, 399, **399**

Sertümer, F.W.A. 194

Sevastopol, Russia 224

Seward, William 233

Sewing machine, invention of 214

Shakespeare, William 142–143, 147

Sheep: cloned **396,** 396–397

Shelley, Mary Wollstonecraft 198

Sherman Antitrust Act 252

Shiras, George, III 268

Sickle-cell anemia 348

Sight: understanding of 88–89

Sikhism 112

Silent Spring (Carson) 362

Silk cloth: manufacture of 27–28

Silk Road 15, 79, 100

Singer, Isaac 226

Sioux Indians 208, 249, **250–251,** 252

Sistine Chapel, Vatican City **130,** 130–131

Skinner, B. F. 324, **324**

Skyscrapers: history of 311

Slave trade: abolished 194–195; colonization movement 198; denounced 134–135; transatlantic, beginning of 125

Slide rule: invention of 148–149

Smallpox 179, 188

Smith, Adam 184

Smith, William 188

Smoking: linked with cancer 365

Snow, John 215, 224

Snure, Dan 257

Social Security Act 317

Sociobiology 376–377

Socrates 52–53, **53**

Solar system: heliocentric 131; space probes 377–378, 386; *see also* Planets

Somme, First Battle of the 290, **290**

Song dynasty, ascension of 86

Songhai Empire 139, 153

Songyue Temple, Hunan Province, China 76

Sound barrier broken 345

Sound recording technology 347

South Africa: AIDS victim **383;** Anglo-Boer War 265; apartheid 364; first black president 364; gold rush 247; *see also* Cape Town

South America: Darwin's travels 207, 229; emergence of Andean cultures 64–65; formation of states 34; reforms 382

South Pole: reached by Amundsen 276

Soviet Union: arms race 341, 342; cosmonaut 316, 361; death of Lenin 300; dissolution of 340, 389; first satellite 358, **358;** German invasion 285, 328–329; policy of glasnost 386; space race 315–316, 361

Space shuttle launch, first

TEXT CREDITS

Most "First Person" features use material in the public domain; for others, all efforts were made to find the copyright owners. P. 150, John Winthrop: translated by Janice Farnsworth; p. 159, Basho: from Sam Hamill, trans., *Narrow Road to the Interior* (Shambhala, 1998); p. 165, Mather: from http://jefferson.village.virginia.edu/salem/17docs.html; p. 176, Kitaab at-Tawheed: from *The Book of Tawheed,* Sameh Strauch, trans., International Islamic Publishing House, http://www.islamicweb. com/beliefs/creed/abdulwahab/; p. 211, Burnett: from www.electricscotland.com; p. 268, John Moran: from http://yellowfever.lib.virginia.edu/reed/collection.html; p. 268, San Francisco Earthquake: from www.EyewitnessToHistory. com; p. 290, Lawrence: from *7 Pillars of Wisdom,* eBooks@Adelaide 2006; p. 297, Mussolini: from The Doctrine of Fascism,www.WorldFutureFund.org; p. 334, Marie-Louise Osmont: from www.Eye witnessToHistory.com; p. 354, Rosa Parks: from *My Soul Is Rested: Movement Days in the South Remembered,* by Howell Raines; p. 378, Sagan: from *Murmurs of Earth,* Ballantine, 1984; p. 385, Barney Clark: by George Raine, *New York Times,* 2 December 1982; p. 389, Dalai Lama, from www.nobel.org; p. 396, Diana: from the Eulogy for Diana, Princess of Wales, by Earl Charles Spencer, 6 September 1997, courtesy of Althorp Charitable Trust; p. 399, Red Cross volunteer: from 911digitalarchive.org/. If we have used copyrighted material in error, please contact the Book Division, National Geographic Society, Washington, D.C. 20036.

1000 EVENTS THAT SHAPED THE WORLD
Foreword by Jared Diamond

Published by the National Geographic Society

John M. Fahey, Jr., *President and Chief Executive Officer*

Gilbert M. Grosvenor, *Chairman of the Board*

Nina D. Hoffman, *Executive Vice President;
    President, Book Publishing Group*

Prepared by the Book Division

Kevin Mulroy, *Senior Vice President and Publisher*

Leah Bendavid-Val, *Director of Photography Publishing
    and Illustrations*

Marianne R. Koszorus, *Director of Design*

Barbara Brownell Grogan, *Executive Editor*

Elizabeth Newhouse, *Director of Travel Publishing*

Carl Mehler, *Director of Maps*

Staff for This Book

Susan Tyler Hitchcock, Judith Klein, *Project Editors*

Erica Rose, *Text Editor*

Carol Farrar Norton, *Art Director*

Sanaa Akkach, *Designer*

Teresa Barry, Julie Cederborg, Patricia Daniels,
Michelle R. Harris, Steven G. Hyslop, Dan O'Toole,
Elizabeth Towner, *Contributing Authors*

Meredith Wilcox, *Administrative Director of Illustrations*

Chris Anderson, *Illustrations Editor*

Rob Waymouth, *Illustrations Assistant*

Susan Straight, *Researcher*

Lewis Bassford, *Production Project Manager*

Jennifer Thornton, *Managing Editor*

Gary Colbert, *Production Director*

Manufacturing and Quality Management

Christopher A. Liedel, *Chief Financial Officer*

Phillip L. Schlosser, *Vice President*

John T. Dunn, *Technical Director*

Chris Brown, *Director*

Maryclare Tracy, *Manager*

Nicole Elliott, *Manager*

Founded in 1888, the National Geographic Society is one of the largest nonprofit scientific and educational organizations in the world. It reaches more than 285 million people worldwide each month through its official journal, NATIONAL GEOGRAPHIC, and its four other magazines; the National Geographic Channel; television documentaries; radio programs; films; books; videos and DVDs; maps; and interactive media. National Geographic has funded more than 8,000 scientific research projects and supports an education program combating geographic illiteracy.

For more information, please call
1-800-NGS LINE (647-5463)
or write to the following address:

National Geographic Society
1145 17th Street N.W.
Washington, D.C. 20036-4688 U.S.A.

Visit us online at www.nationalgeographic.com/books

For information about special discounts
for bulk purchases, please contact
National Geographic Books Special Sales:
ngspecsales@ngs.org

For rights or permissions inquiries,
please contact National Geographic Books Subsidiary Rights:
ngbookrights@ngs.org

This 2013 edition printed for Barnes & Noble, Inc. by the National Geographic Society.

ISBN: 978-1-4351-4808-6 (B&N ed.)
ISBN: 978-1-4262-0314-5 (trade)

Library of Congress Cataloging-in-Publication Data
1000 events that shaped the world.
    p. cm.
  Includes bibliographical references and index.
ISBN 978-1-4262-0192-9 (regular)
ISBN 978-1-4262-0193-6 (deluxe)
  1. History—Outlines, syllabi, etc. I. National
Geographic Society (U.S.) II. Title: One thousand events that shaped the world.
D21.A113 2007
909—dc22   2007037358

Printed in Hong Kong

13/THK/1